DOCUMENTARY HISTORY OF THE
FIRST FEDERAL CONGRESS OF THE
UNITED STATES OF AMERICA

4 March 1789–3 March 1791

SPONSORED BY
THE NATIONAL HISTORICAL PUBLICATIONS AND RECORDS COMMISSION
AND
THE GEORGE WASHINGTON UNIVERSITY

This book has been brought to publication with the generous assistance of the National Historical Publications and Records Commission.

This volume has been supported by grants from the National Endowment for the Humanities, an independent federal agency.

PROJECT STAFF

       CHARLENE BANGS BICKFORD, *Co-Editor*
       KENNETH R. BOWLING, *Co-Editor*
       HELEN E. VEIT, *Associate Editor*
       WILLIAM CHARLES diGIACOMANTONIO, *Associate Editor*

ADMINISTRATIVE ADVISORY COMMITTEE

       ROBERT C. BYRD
       LINDA GRANT DePAUW, *Chair*
       ELIZABETH FENN
       RICHARD H. KOHN
       CHARLES McC. MATHIAS
       GEORGE S. WILLS

VOLUME XVII

CORRESPONDENCE

FIRST SESSION:
SEPTEMBER – NOVEMBER 1789

CHARLENE BANGS BICKFORD

KENNETH R. BOWLING

HELEN E. VEIT

WILLIAM CHARLES DIGIACOMANTONIO

Editors

The Johns Hopkins University Press, Baltimore and London

Printed in the United States of America on acid-free paper

The Johns Hopkins University Press
2715 North Charles Street
Baltimore, Maryland 21218-4363
www.press.jhu.edu

ISBN 0-8018-7162-X

Library of Congress Catalog Card Number 73155164

A catalog record for this book is available from the British Library.

To
Mary M. Wolfskill
gracious and knowledgeable
facilitator of scholarship

CONTENTS

ILLUSTRATIONS

CORRESPONDENCE: FIRST SESSION

September 1789

Abigail Adams to Cotton Tufts

With regard to politicks the Debates of the House will give you an Idea of them, as yet there has been but little Heat upon any Subject. but there is a questions comeing on with regard to the permanant residence of congress which I fear will create parties, & much vexation. I should think that in the present State of their Treasury, an expence so unnecessary ought to be avoided as even removeing to philadelphia, every person here who have not sufficient funds of their own has been obliged to Borrow of the Bank for to supply their Daily necessities and I do not Imagine that the publick could derive any essential Benifit from a Removal, for my own part I dread this continual Roling.

*** Mr. Adams is well and will write to you soon. The Senate are so close to Buisness & he frequently has so much reading to do & such constant attention to the debates, that he comes home quite exhausted & unable to take his pen our Situation is a very Beautifull one and I feel in that respect quite happy, but I find myself much more exposed to company than in any situation which I have ever before been in, the morning is a time when strangers who come to N. york expect to find mr. Adams at home. this brings us Breakfast company besides it is a sweet morning retreat for fresh air & a cool Breize, I should like to visit my friends during the adjournment but our Finnances will not admit of much travelling.

Mr. King makes a very respectable figure as a Senator, and mr. Ames does credit to our State, mr. Madison is a very amiable character a man of virtue & probity, mr. G[erry].   what can I say. you see him always in the minority, you see him very frequently wrong and the poor man looks gastly. I believe he is wasted ~~fortified~~ mortified and quite in the Horrors a constant correspondent of W—n [*James Warren*] & his wife [*Mercy Otis Warren*] all of whom see nothing but ruin & destruction before them, & who will again Set our State by the ears if possible. watch them closely.

ALS, Miscellaneous Manuscripts, NHi. The first part of the letter is missing.

John Adams to James Lovell

I have not yet answered your letter of the 26 of July. You guess well—I find that I shall have all the unpopular questions to determine: and shall soon be pronounced Hostis Republicam generis[1]—What they will do with me I know not, but must trust to providence. You insinuate that I am accused "of deciding in favor of the power of the prince because I look up to that goal." That I look up to that goal sometimes is very probable because it is not far above me, only one step, and it is directly before my eyes: so that I must be blind not to see it—I am forced to look up to it and bound by duty to do so, because there is only the breath of one mortal between me and it. There was lately cause enough to look up to it, as I did with horror, when that breath was in some danger of expiring. But deciding for the supreme, was not certainly the way to render that goal more desirable or less terrible nor was it the way to obtain votes for continuing in it, or an advancement to it. The way to have ensured votes would have been to have given up that power—There is not however to be serious, the smallest prospect that I shall ever reach that goal. our beloved Chief is very little older than his second, has recovered his health and is a much stronger man than I am—a new Vice President must be chosen before a new President—This reflection give me no pain but on the contrary great pleasure: for I know very well that I am not possesed of the confidence and affection of my fellow Citizens, to the degree that he is. I am not of Cæsar's mind. The second place in Rome is high enough for me. Although I have a spirit that will not give up its right or relinquish its place whatever the world or even my friends, or even you who knew me so well may think of me, I am not an ambitious man. Submission to insult and disgrace is one thing: but aspiring to higher situations is another I am quite contented in my present condition and should not be discontented to leave it. Having said too much of myself let me say something of you. The place of Collector would undoubtedly have been yours if the President could have found any other situation for your friend [Benjamin] Lincoln. it was from no lukewarmness to you I am certain. But the public cause demanded that Lincoln should be supported, and this could not be done any other way—If after some time any other permanent place should be found for him, you, I presume, will come in collector. He sailed yesterday in good health for Georgia and may heaven prosper him with all happiness honour and success—It is a very honorable embassy: and will produce great and happy effects to these states.

FC:lbk, Adams Family Manuscript Trust, MHi.

[1] An enemy to the Republic.

William Pickman to Benjamin Goodhue

*** When will Congress adjourn by your Motion, I perceive this month it is still in your mind, you must Inform me that I may clap a stopper on my Letters after the time appointed for rising—several Persons are daily enquiring if you have yet got a quarter gallon Wig—what Answer must be given—I assure you many Persons wish it, & think some parade & dress are necessary among the southern Members, some of whom Judge more from appearances, than Intrinsick Merit—I expect to hear from you soon very soon, as there are Clouds of doubt on our minds—Can A Vessell from N. Carolina—or R. Island. be entered—(being the property of those States) without being subjected to Foreign Tonage &c.—are they coming into the Union—is Vermont likely to make A Link in the grand Chain—will the Frontier Posts be demanded of the British this season—what Troops will be raised for the Western posts—will Congress take charge of Our Castle[1]— when will your board of Treasury be appointed & will there be A Comptroller in each state & when. ***

ALS, Letters to Goodhue, NNS. Place from which written not specified. The beginning of the letter was written on 31 August and is printed under that date.

[1] Castle William, a fortress on Castle Island in Boston harbor.

Anthony Wayne to Pierce Butler and Ralph Izard

I did myself the honor of addressing you on the 4th of July on the subject of Indian affairs & the Southwestern territory, since which I find that the first part the business has been taken up by the Prest. & Congress. The Indian agency & the command in the Southern District are appointements, to which I flatter myself I have some claim. I believe that my military services & professional knowledge will not be questioned, and I have much depending upon a speedy & permanent peace with the Creek Nation. . . . Thus circumstanced & being known to those Indians, with whom I have alternately fought & treated. I have ground to believe that my name, when clothed with proper authority, will have a tendency to convince them, that it wou'd be their true interest & best policy, to enter into an immediate & inviolable peace, for seeing a WARRIOR, by whom they have been more than once defeated . . . I can only promise not to disgrace the appointment & to use my best endeavours to promote the honor, interest & peace of the Union.

Excerpt of ALS, *Parke-Bernet Catalog* 1744(1957):item 230. Written from Richmond County, Georgia. The ellipses are in the source.

OTHER DOCUMENTS

Abigail Adams to Mary Cranch. ALS, Abigail Adams Letters, MWA. Written from "Richmond Hill," outside New York City; addressed to Braintree, Massachusetts. For the full text, see *Abigail Adams*, pp. 22–26.

"I have reason to think that congress will take up the matter and Fund the debt"; "I fear they will Remove from this place I am too happy in the situation of it, I fear to have it lasting I am every day more & more pleased with it; Should they go to Philadelphia I do not know how I could possibly live through the voilent Heats"; "I have now nearly got through all the company that we propose to dine this Session"; comments on "malice" of Edward Church, author of *The Dangerous Vice*; the Vice President "ten times to one goes to Senate in a one Horse chaise."

Richard Bassett to John Adams. Reply card, Hull Collection, DSI.

Accepts dinner invitation for the next Friday.

William Bradford, Jr. to Elias Boudinot. ALS, Wallace Papers, PHi. Written from Philadelphia. Part of the letter was written on 2 September and is printed under that date.

Newspapers report that yesterday the House was to take up the New Jersey disputed election; "We are anxious to *know* the event, tho' one cannot doubt what it will be."

Andrew Craigie to Daniel Parker. FC:dft, Craigie Papers, MWA. Written from Boston.

Congress will wait until second session to take up the national debt; it wants the revenue system and the treasury department established first, and "there are many who are interested in delaying the Busines either because they have borrowed large sums of the Debt which they ~~wish~~ have to purchase or because their private arrangements are not in readiness for speculation."

William Edmond, John Chandler, Nehemiah Strong, and Philo Perry to William Samuel Johnson. LS, Johnson Papers, CtHi. Written from New-town, Connecticut.
  Office seeking: Pierpont Edwards for district judge of Connecticut.

Samuel Henshaw to Theodore Sedgwick. ALS, Sedgwick Family Papers, MHi. Written from Northampton, Massachusetts.
  Office seeking: Charles Jarvis seeks a state excise office; Henshaw cannot account for this "unless He has heard, that the members of Congress have it in contemplation to divide the Union into Districts, as we talked of; or perhaps, (and this may be as probable as the other) He expects Congress will soon take the excise to themselves, *and have a distinct officer to collect it*; and therefore He, (if State collector) will be the immediate object of Presidential Notice."

John McKinly to George Read. ALS, Rodney Collection of Read Papers, DeHi. Written from Wilmington, Delaware.
  Respects to Bassett and to Vining, whose brother and sister are well.

William Maclay to John Adams. Reply card, Hull Collection, DSI.
  Declines dinner for the next Friday because of ill health.

William Paterson to John Adams. Reply card, Hull Collection, DSI.
  Accepts dinner invitation for the next Friday.

George Thatcher to William Taylor. ALS, Taylor Papers, Historical Society of Washington, D.C. Addressed to Baltimore.
  Plans to leave for Massachusetts on the Monday after next; offers to carry any letters to Massachusetts friends; the House will take up the seat of government question on Thursday or Friday; still uncertain whether the site will be in Virginia, Maryland, Pennsylvania, or New Jersey.

Paine Wingate to John Adams. Reply card, Hull Collection, DSI.
  Declines dinner for the next Friday because of a prior engagement.

Daniel Hiester, Account Book. PRHi.
  Trip to Kingsbridge with Beckley.

WEDNESDAY, 2 SEPTEMBER 1789

Cool (Johnson); *cool & pleasant* (J. B. Johnson)

John Adams to Thomas B. Adams

I have this morning received your manly letter of 25th. Ult. I had long intended to write you but as you observe avocations have always intervened. Public business my son, must always be done by somebody—it will be done by some body or other. If wise men decline it others will not: if honest men refuse it, others will not. A young man should well weigh his plans. Integrity should be preserved in all events, as essential to his happiness, through every stage of his existence. His first maxim then, should be to place his honor out of the reach of all men: In order to this he must make it a rule never to become dependant on public employments for subsistence. Let him have a trade a profession a farm a Shop, Something where by he can honestly live, and then he may engage in public affairs, if invited, upon independant principles. My advice to my children, is to maintain an independant character, though in poverty and obscurity: neither riches nor illustration will console a man under the reflection that he has acted a mean a mercenary part, much less a dishonest one. Your handwriting and your style are in my eye and judgment, beautiful; go on my son pursue your mathematics and your morals.

Come with your brother [*John Quincy*], and be here at the meeting of Congress on the first of December. There we will Converse upon these and other subjects, mean time write me, if it is but a line every week.

FC:lbk, Adams Family Manuscript Trust, MHi. Written from "Richmond Hill," outside New York City; addressed to "Student Harvard Colledge."

Thomas Hartley to Tench Coxe

Tho most of our Delegation have engaged with the Gentlemen of the South to vote with them for Potomack and they say they will adjourn to Philadelphia. I fear both will not be effected.

The New Yorkers and Eastern People Yesterday Evening offered Trenton and to have a Law passed immediately—but our Gentlemen had gone too far with the Southern Men. How this Business will end I know not—but hasty Promises some Times embarrass—I mean to do what is right but I have no Engagements—I do not know whether I am any Thing the wiser for not having them.

The New-Yorkers Made a push at the Jersey Election Yesterday—it will

be determind to Day—On to Morrow the Motion for a permanent Residence comes on—I wish we may be able to give a good Account of it.
***

ALS, Coxe Papers, PHi.

Robert Morris to Tench Coxe

Your Letter of the 28th. ulto. I have received and must beg leave to refer you to the Letter which Mr. McClay and myself have written to the Committee of Merchants[1] this day, which will shew you the present State of the Restriction business,[2] on which I long since pronounced that it would be attended with Dangers, and difficulties, that would require much deliberation to enable us to avert, and surmount. As to the Public Debt I think that no man who will read with attention the Journals and Acts of the present Congress can doubt of a fixed intention of Government to provide fully for the Regular and Punctual discharge of the Interest, this and a very little more by way of a sinking Fund is all that can be asked or expected. But in the mean time the Creditors seem to wish for an explicit Declaration that the Government will do this; and my endeavors shall not be wanting to obtain it for them.

You will probably see Mr. Clymer in Philadelphia and I will speak to Mr. Fitzsimons about the Potash Law.[3] I expect to see you in Philadelphia before long.

LS, Coxe Papers, PHi. Addressed to Philadelphia.

[1] The subcommittee appointed in mid July by the "Committee of Merchants of Philadelphia" to correspond with the delegation about the Lighthouses and Collection bills consisted of: John Nixon, William Bingham, Magnas Miller, Tench Coxe, and Miers Fisher.
[2] This is probably a reference to section 2 of the Collection Act [HR-11] restricting imports from the Pacific and Indian oceans to specified American ports.
[3] On 22 February 1790, the Pennsylvania legislature passed "An Act to Regulate the Exportation of Potash and Pearl ash."

Robert Morris to James Lovell

Your favor of the 20th Inst. came too late to enable me to introduce into the Coasting Bill such a Clause as you wish for empowering the naval officers to appoint Deputies, had I been ever so much disposed to do it—But this matter had not escaped the attention of the Senate—They introduced the clause authorizing the Collector to deputize because it was judged there might be cases of absolute necessity to require it, at the same time it was moved that the naval officers and Surveyors might be so authorized to which

many objections were made (and I confess to you that I was one of the objectors) amongst other things it was very forcibly urged that the appearance of authorizing so many Principal Officers in the first instance to act by Deputies would give the appearance of Sine-cure places in the Eyes of the People than which nothing could have a worse tendancy, and after all if upon Experience it should be found necessary, the Remedy could be then applied. ***
P. S. I was out of Town when Gen. [*Benjamin*] Lincoln arrived and did not know of his being here untill a short time before his departure so that when I called to see him it was just after his departure and I am sorry for it.

LS, Joseph Rubinfine, West Palm Beach, Florida (1999). Addressed to Boston.

Edmund Pendleton to James Madison

Besides several Packets of papers I am indebted for your two favrs. of July 15th. & Augt. 21st. received since my last—I congratulate you upon having got through the Amendments to the Constitution, As I was very Anxious that it should be done before yr. Adjournment, since it will have a good effect in quieting the minds of many well meaning Citizens, tho' I am of Opinion that nothing was further from the wish of some, who covered their Opposition to the Government under the masque of uncommon zeal for amendments, & to whom a rejection or a delay as a new ground of Clamour, would have been more agreable. I own also that I feel some degree of pleasure, in discovering Obviously from the whole progress, that the public are Indebted For the measure to the Friends of Government, whose Elections were opposed under pretence of their being ~~opposed~~ Averse to Amendmts.

My anxiety is now directed to the event of the Judiciary System, If that ends in a tolerable one, I think yr. proceedings will meet Genl. Approbation and the Government commence under Fair Auspices. You must expect to hear some Clamor about expence, as in all Governments, but I think it will be less than might be expected.

If you should Adjourn at the time appointed this will be the last time I shall pay you my respects before that event, so I will wish you a good journey to yr. Friends & pleased constituents.
[*P. S.*] Pray present my best respects to the President.

ALS, Gilder Lehrman Collection, NHi. Written from Virginia.

Samuel Phillips, Jr. to Benjamin Goodhue

Your favor of the 11th. Ulto. I received and am much obliged to you for the communication—I believe you will find very few people in Massachu-

setts entertaining different sentiments from those you express respecting
the exorbitancy of the compensations made by Congress or proposed to be
made, for I yet entertain a hope that an amendment will take place in Senate—The Southern people obtain property at a much easier rate than we can,
or their Representatives are greatly wanting in attention to and concern for
the burthens of their Constituents: The old opposers of the Constitution are
now exulting on the verification of one part of their predictions—it's friends
are chagrined & confounded—the public Creditors are still farther disheartened, apprehending there is little ground of hope for them, if Congress and
their officers are to be thus largely Recompenced, and a very deep concern
is visible in the countenances of the best people among us; if the bill should
not receive any alteration before it is perfected—I should not be surprised
if the measures prescribed by the Constitution should be taken to obtain
an alteration of that ~~clause~~ Article which authorizes Congress to establish
their own pay—according to present appearances, this will be attempted,
or something still more disagreable contemplated—As to Mr. Gerry, I
should have supposed his policy, if not his principles would have guarded
him against such extraordinary conduct—I think it ought to be published
in every town of his district, I hope before another election he will be better
known.

Mr. Otis appears to have lost all sense of decency & modesty—if he complains of starving on his present Salary, let him return to Massachusetts &
make half that money if he can—it is possible some other person may be
found equal in capacity & merit—I am sure there are hundreds of very worthy men, who have had the advantages of education, & can plead as great
sacrifices in the public cause, as some who make a great bustle about it, have
really made, that would think themselves happy with ⅔ the sum he has, or
at most with ¾ of it. The Massachusetts members in general have done
themselves honor—you in particular are entitled to many thanks for calling for the yeas & nays—The temper excited by it, shew the occasion for it,
& that very measure may be the means of working a remedy—if the eyes of
the people are open, it will do it. A Recess no doubt will be very pleasing to
you & some others—it may be productive of advantage, and if the expences
of a Session are so great, it ought to be as short as possible.

By forwarding the enclosed per first post unless a direct conveyance offers, you will much oblige me any expence that arises I will chearfully repay.

ALS, Letters to Goodhue, NNS. Written from Andover, Massachusetts. Signed "your real
Friend."

Letter from George Gilpin to [Richard Bland Lee?]

As your countrymen have committed to your care a very important trust, any information which can throw the smallest light upon their interest, I trust will be acceptable to you. Under this impression, I take the liberty of sending you some observations which I made in an excursion up Potowmac river, and across the Alleghaney mountain, to some branches of the Western Waters. By the desire of the Potowmac company, Mr. [*James*] Smith (the conductor of the Potowmac works) and myself, proceeded from the Great Falls[1] up the river in a boat, which, if moderately loaded, would have taken from thirty to forty barrels, till we got twelve miles above Fort Cumberland [*Cumberland, Maryland*], and could with convenience have continued our rout in the same boat to the mouth of New Creek, which is thirteen miles higher up the North Branch [*of the Potomac*], than the place at which we stopped; but being strangers to that part of the river, and being informed by the inhabitants of the country, that the river was then lower than it had been for some years past, we were fearful that in case the dry weather should continue during our progress over the mountain, the river might be rendered so shallow as to prevent our geting the boat down again; we therefore proceeded from this place (Capt. Daniel Cresap's[2]) on foot along the side of the river to the mouth of Savage River. To this place the navigation may be extended, and not much higher without incurring too great an expence for the present times. The mouth of Savage is two hundred and ten miles from tide water at the bottom of the Little Falls, where large vessels may come. After passing the Falls at the mouth of the Shannandoah River,[3] we found no fall which would prevent a boat passing up or down with ease and safety, except in those seasons when the river is very low, then in the broad parts, the water is shallow, and requires to be collected or deepened in those parts which does not appear to be either difficult or expensive to accomplish. From the mouth of Savage, we went along the State Road to the top of the Alleghaney mountain, and from thence to the waters of deep creep [*Deep Creek*] (which take their rise in the green glades) thirteen miles from the mouth of Savage, four miles below the place where the road crosses this water; it is large enough for boats, is gentle and deep, and will afford a good navigation down to the falls in the Yohogany [*Youghiogheny River*] (of which this creek is a branch) called Ohio Phyle Fall, near the ___;[4] so that seventeen miles will join the waters of Potowmac and Yohogany. From the mouth of Savage to Little Yohogany, one mile above the Forks, is twenty-two miles, to Big Yohogany, twenty-four miles, to Salt Lick Creek, a branch of Cheat River, thirty miles, to Cheat River at the Ford at Dunkard Bottom,[5] thirty-seven miles and a quarter, to Morgan Town, fifty miles, to Clerksburg, eighty miles, to the mouth of Muskingum, one hundred and forty miles. These distances, except the last, are from actual measurement. Cheat River at Dunkard Bottom, is nearly or quite as large as Shanandoah at Snicker's[6] or Keyes's Ferry, and is a fine gentle river, except two falls which are now passed frequently, and may at a small expence, be rendered safe and easy. The course of the road from the mouth of the Savage to Cheat River, is nearly due west. About the mouth of Savage River and George's Creek, are inexhaustable bands of coal; some of which the river has laid bare—we found them easy to dig, and the coal of good quality. This range or bed of coal extends along the first ridge of the Alleghaney mountain to Will's creek, above Cumberland; from which place we saw them carrying coal for the nail manufactory at Hager's Town. Upon our return from the other side of the Alleghaney mountain, one or two days moderate rain had raised the river, and we found the navigation in that state much better than we expected. Two boats came down from Old Town [*Green Spring, West Virginia*] with tobacco, two or three from Opeckon with flour; and we went in company with two from Shepherd's Town; one of which was more than seventy feet long, and when fully loaded, would carry from 120 to 130 barrels of flour, these boats went quite down to the Great Falls; and I was informed by Captain Shepherd, that one thousand barrels of flour had been sent down the river this spring from Shepherd's Town only. If we allow ten miles from the head of the Tide to the Big Falls, and seventeen from the mouth of the Savage to Deep Creek—Potowmac has but twenty-seven miles land carriage at this day to the Western Waters, and in two or three years at the farthest—ten of these miles will be taken away. From Fort-Cumberland to the settlements on Yohogany is twenty-one miles, to the Ohiophyle Falls   miles, below which there is a good navigation to Pittsburg. From Fort Cumberland to Fort-Pitt or Pittsburg, is one hundred and fourteen miles. From Fort-Cumberland to Bedford [*Pennsylvania*] is thirty miles, and a good road. I am fully satisfied there can be no navigation found between the eastern and western waters which approaches so near, which will have so good and short a portage, and which can be effected at so small an expence. I am acquainted with the Susquehannah, let there be an actual survey made of that river and its branches, which can be rendered navigable the farthest towards the western waters, as there has been of Potowmac, and I am certain that the difference in favor of Potowmac will be found greater than any person can believe who has not examined them both with an eye of observation. The following branches of Potowmac, when improved, will afford a very extensive navigation, and chiefly through a very fertile country. Monocasy [*River*] about thirty miles, Shannandoah [*River*] one hundred and eighty miles, Conogocheague [*Creek*] about twenty-five miles, Cape Capon the same distance or perhaps further, the

South Branch from seventy to eighty miles, and Patterson's Creek about twenty miles; the country through which these waters flow is remarked for the richness of the land, and is in general thick settled. After giving you this sketch of the Potowmac, its Branches and the Allegany Mountains, permit me to mention to you that fine extensive valley [*Shenandoah Valley*] lying upon the south-east side of what is called the North Mountain, and which extends from the river Susquehannah to James river: I believe I may be bold to say that no quarter of America, or perhaps of the world, can produce a body of land of such extent, equal to this in quality and blessed with so salubrious an air; the necessaries of life are here produced in the greatest abundance, add to this that iron ore, with every convenience for refining it is found here in large quantities and of excellent quality, and coal discovers itself in such quantities upon the margin of the river (from whence it may with ease be conveyed to any part of the continent) as to pronounce it inexhaustible. Should the seat of our empire move westwardly, which sound policy now requires, and which it must do sooner or later from the increasing weight on that side, there is a most beautiful and healthy situation for a large city at the place where Fort-Frederick[7] stands, upon the north banks of Potowmac. The state of Maryland holds two hundred acres of land at this place, and the state in this part is only five miles wide, so that Maryland, Pennsylvania and Virginia, might each be gratified in contributing to the formation of the federal city by fixing it at that place. From the luxuriance of the soil all around, from the many branches of Potowmac which penetrate the country in different directions to a great distance, the most abundant supply of every kind of provision will at all times be commanded, and by the river Potowmac every foreign article, whether of luxury or convenience, may be procured in the same abundance and with the same ease as on the sea coast. Within the limits of your city might be a cannon foundery, an ore bank, forge and other manufactures. From the Great Falls to George-Town sixteen miles, to Alexandria eighteen miles and a half. Should you incline to approach nearer to tide water, William's Port, and Shepherd's Town in the same valley, and Frederick-Town near Monocasy and below the blue Ridge, afford most desirable situations.

NYDA, 10 September; reprinted in Richmond, Virginia. The identification of the writer is based on Gilpin's similar letter to George Washington of the same date (*PGW* 3:593–94).

---

[1] At Great Falls—the greatest obstacle to Potomac navigation, located six miles above its farthest tidewater access—the river falls seventy-six feet in a mile and a quarter. Three miles down river, Little Falls drops the Potomac another thirty-six feet towards tidewater.

[2] Daniel Crespan (d. 1784) served in Hugh Stephenson's Maryland and Virginia Rifle Regiment, 1776–78 (*Heitman*, p. 177).

[3] At Harper's Ferry, West Virginia.

[4] At this point, Gilpin's letter to Washington of the same date contained "Turkey Foot,"

the place near Confluence, Pennsylvania, where the Youghiogheny, Laurel Hill, and Cassel-
man rivers join.
    ⁵ Near present day Kingwood, West Virginia.
    ⁶ Where present day route 50 crosses the Shenandoah River.
    ⁷ On the Potomac, half way between Williamsport and Hancock, Maryland.

OTHER DOCUMENTS

Elias Boudinot to Elisha Boudinot. ALS, Law Library, New York State
Library, Albany. Addressed to Trenton, New Jersey. For the full text, see
DHFFC 8:567–68.
    Resolution of New Jersey disputed election in favor of the sitting members.

Elias Boudinot to Governor William Livingston. ALS, Livingston Papers, MHi. Addressed to Elizabethtown, New Jersey. For the full text, see
DHFFC 8:568.
    Resolution of New Jersey disputed election.

William Bradford, Jr. to Elias Boudinot. ALS, Wallace Papers, PHi. Written from Philadelphia. The part of this letter written on 1 September is calendared under that date.
    Wonders why no action was taken on the Judiciary Bill [S-1] when it was
    taken up; "The general opinion this way is in favor of *commencing* all suits
    in the state Courts: but if that cannot be affected the plan you & I talked
    about of enlarging the jurisdiction of the district Judge seems to be ac-
    ceptable"; "an influx of specie will at this juncture be a very favorable
    event, towards the establishment of good government"; asks Boudinot to
    enquire of the Virginia members how to obtain copies of their state's rat-
    ification debates.

Arthur Campbell to Archibald Stuart. ALS, Stuart Baldwin Papers, ViU.
Written from Washington, Kentucky.
    Tell Madison the importance of transmitting to the states the proposed
    Amendments to the Constitution by early November; "It will do more
    than any thing that can be thought of, to overturn the projects of a junto
    in this State as well as N. Carolina. The wish is to keep out of the union
    several years, from sinister motives of a few. The Amendments will grat-
    ify the great body of the People, and may cause the real motives of the
    junto to be discovered."

William Maclay and Robert Morris to a Committee of Philadelphia Merchants. No copy known; mentioned in Morris to Coxe, 2 September.

Jeremiah Wadsworth to Oliver Wolcott, Jr. ALS, Wolcott Papers, CtHi.
Addressed to Hartford, Connecticut; carried by Mr. Phelps.

Office seeking: auditor of the treasury is the only post to which Wolcott
can be appointed; requests a prompt answer.

THURSDAY, 3 SEPTEMBER 1789

Cool (Johnson); *cool & pleasant* (J. B. Johnson)

Fisher Ames to John Lowell

I saw Gen. [*Benjamin*] Lincoln with the truest satisfaction He was in fine
Spirits, and seemed to manifest the change in his situation & prospects, tho'
his firmness in adverse circumstances has been painfully tried. I had another
reason for rejoicing on his arrival—I knew that his weight would be far
greater on a personal application than by any letters. I conversed with him
very fully on your subject. Indeed, we sate up almost all Saturday night—
Unfortunately, his constant attention to the friends whom he had to see, &
the business which was pressing—He sa prevented my enquiring the result
of his conversation. He sailed on Monday Afternoon—I am obliged to calculate upon the natural effect of his agency. and I think the prospect of an
agreable event much more promising in consequence—For no man would
manage a matter of this nature with more discretion—I am confirmed by
this reflection in the decision I formerly inclined to make against [*lined out*][1]
mode of reasoning has led me to think that it will be hazardous to go in a
body, or individually to recommend any candidate—It might weaken or con-
fuse the impression of Gen. Lincoln's interview—It might do hurt—and I
think could do no good—For the wishes of our members have been indus-
triously, & repeatedly communicated—as the result of ripe reflection—and
in such a way that I doubt not the full effect of them. Now, sir, I submit it
to you whether prudence will dictate any other mode of conduct—You have
been pleased to honour me with your confidence—Let me assure you that I
shall be guided by your opinion of what is expedient to be done.

The Judicial Bill has so far passed the Ordeal as it relates to the number
of judges—supreme & district—The motion to strike out the district courts
failed—11 voting for it—My Argument is published in Fenno's Gazette[2]—
I calculate upon it's being termed heresy by some who will understand it, &
worse names by many who cannot or will not take the pains to understand
it—My ideas will not admit of so clear an explication as I perceive them myself. What is jurisdiction? A power Authority Authority to judge, derived

from a superior power—The law of the U.S. is the law of the land, but not the law of a state—An offence or action created by statute seems to me a new subject of jurisdiction to be disposed of by the Supreme power—It does not fall of course into the state tribunals—For if the servants of the states are of course, or can be made by law, the servants of the U.S. it will produce a strange confusion of offices & ideas—We may as properly assume the services & claim the duties of the state treasurer to keep & pay out our money—or the sheriff to keep our rogues, & declare their bonds valid to secure their doing it—If Judicial officers are not bound to execute our laws, as our servants, we cannot trust them—and if they are, why are ministerial officers less our servants? It seems to me that the Argumentum, ex absurdo,[3] will be found to have some force. Many tell me, the state judges must decide according to law, & the offences &c. are defined by law. I will not trouble you by a further exposition of the arguments which influence my opinion—If we ascend to the first principles of the Judicial power, I think we shall find them analogous to my doctrine.

We have been all day debating the question of the permanent residence of Congress—The Susquehanna is supported by a clear majority—The temporary residence to be in ~~Philadelphia~~ New York An intrigue between the Pennsylvanians & Virginians has been formed & defeated when almost concluded—Now the former say to the Eastern People—fix it *in our state* to your own liking & we will vote with you—& for N. York as the temporary residence—It is now near three o'clock & the Minority are talking to gain time If we should decide to day, as the majority will if possible, I will try to let you know it by this post—Now, I must send this, or run the risk of a failure—as I shall be engaged all the Afternoon—I saw Gen. Lincoln after his seeing the President—but found it impossible to question him, tho I attempted it. I will give you seasonable & frequent intimations of the state of things, if I learn any thing new.

ALS, Diedrich Collection, MiU-C.

---

[1] The editors believe the words were lined out some time after the letter was sent.
[2] For Ames's speech of 29 August, published in *GUS*, 2 September, see *DHFFC* 11:1356–59.
[3] The argument, from the absurdity of it.

Fisher Ames to George R. Minot

You interest me by your account of the school politics of Boston. I will not give an opinion as to what ought to be done. The subject is important, and merits a more manly independency of conduct than you have described.

These sneaking fellows are their own commentators. Art springs from fear, and that fear from weighing their own talents against other men's, and finding them wanting. I mean where the purpose is honest. For art is sometimes practised by able men. Then it is used to conceal the turpitude of the motive. I am sick of art. It requires too severe attention to keep it always guarded. And then the art of one is so overmatched by the art, and indeed by the simplicity of many, that it eternally miscarries. An honest, sincere conduct has to sustain an ordeal. The proudly mean are offended that a man dares to think and act in opposition to the *vox populi*.[1] He appeals to the reasons for his conduct, and never acts without reasons. The same mean censurers will applaud his sense and firmness, and ever after leave him at liberty to act as he sees fit. Public clamor is employed as a means of effecting the removal of that resistance which the unpopular man makes to their will. When it is found that this end cannot be accomplished by such means, they will forbear. I would preach to the *pride* of these hunters after popularity, and show how they degrade themselves, to their love of ease, and make manifest their needless painstaking; and to their cowardice, and evince the peril they incur. You will ask, And why do you preach to me? Forgive me. This is stuff, for a letter.

I believe that the New England people are better taught than any other, and Boston better than any other city. Since I have been here, I have thought of the advantage of our town corporations and town schools. I do not believe that any country has such judicious expedients for repelling barbarism, supporting government, and extending felicity. Boston might be an Athens, and I would wish to make it a London. *Apropos*, we are caballing about the permanent residence of Congress. The Pennsylvanians have made, or are about making, a compact with the southern people to fix it on the Potomac. They can carry this in the House if they think fit, and all unite from Pennsylvania southward. The Pennsylvanians abhor this in their hearts, but the terms are to remove the temporary residence of Congress to Philadelphia; and as the members east of the head of the Chesapeake outnumber the others, they are pretty sure of preventing the future removal to the Potomac. Mr. Morris, who wishes to fix at Trenton, disclaims and abhors the bargain. It is some proof of the nationality of his views. Possibly, however, it is the result of a more discerning selfishness. His opposition in the Senate will be weighty, and perhaps we may effect something in the House. The business is *in nubibus*,[2] and in such dark intrigues, the real designs of members are nearly impenetrable. Reasoning will do no good. You will see, by the papers, what pace we move in the discussion of the judiciary bill. The question whether we shall have inferior tribunals, (except Admiralty Courts, which were not denied to be necessary,) was very formidably contested. Judge Livermore, and ten others, voted against them. You will see, in Fenno's Gazette, my speechicle on the subject.[3] The lawyers will consider my idea of the exclusive nature of certain parts of the national judicial power (offences against statutes, and actions on statutes) in various points of light. If my distinction between *jurisdiction* and the *rule of decision* in causes properly cognizable in a State Court should be clearly understood, they will have the means of judging on the merits of my argument. The idea is not easy to make clear, and I feel embarrassed to choose terms which will make my ideas as clear as I perceive them myself. However, the public has them, and I will not comment on them.

The Jersey election is decided in favor of the sitting member[s], by a large majority. The case, though confined to the construction of their State law, was very complex. I have seldom kept my mind in suspense till the vote was called. In this case, I remain still in suspense, inclining sometimes *pro*, sometimes *con*.

The recess will probably obtain at the time proposed, or very near it. You politicians in Massachusetts say that we are running away from duty. I think that some good will ensue, and considerable inconvenience be prevented by it. There is an interval between the organization of the government and the ordinary business, in which nothing should be done. We shall return in better humor than we should maintain together. We shall find business prepared by our great officers, and a weight given to national plans, which they have not at present.

It is now three o'clock, and we are debating about the permanent residence of Congress. The Pennsylvanians and southern people forced us, loath and supplicating delay, to take it up this day. Now, it turns out that the Pennsylvanians will not pursue the intended treaty with their intended allies, but actual and natural rivals. The former offer to fix it in Pennsylvania where the eastern people may choose, and to stay in New York, till the proposed place is prepared to receive the government. The minority, infinitely disappointed and chagrined, are begging delay, though they denied us, and to get one day, are talking the time out. Whose stomachs will conquer, I know not. I must seal this, because I expect to go out of town, to dine with the Vice. If so, I shall have no time to tell the event.

I think Judge [*Francis*] Dana will be District Judge. It is only guess work.

Ames 1:68–70.

---

[1] The voice of the people.

[2] In the clouds; obscured.

[3] For Ames's speech of 29 August, published in *GUS*, 2 September, see *DHFFC* 11:1356–59.

Richard Bassett to William Tilghman

*** Since I returned hear, the business of Congress has engrossed every hour. ***

As the Judiciary Bill is Still before the House & will Continue there some time, If time permited should be Glad of your Sentiments on those parts of the Bill as Amended by the Senate, which are Still Most objectionable, apprehending when it returns from the House, an oppertunity will be had of offering Amendments to their Amendments if Necessary.

I never presumed that sending a Message to Mr. B.[1] was taking Sufficient Notice of you—It was all I could then do—& such is my regard for some people, that I would wish to prevent them from evil even by a Message—I dont claim privilege yet, tho' cant say how long that May be the case—I mean from arrests—I am ready & willing to see you in Dover, or else where—I hope to be at Cecil [*County, Maryland*] Octr. Court—Congress has resolved to adjourn the 22. of this Month, if that should be the case we shall certainly meet in october, if not before—a dreadful [*lined out*] heat, & Difference of opinion took place yesterday in the House of Representatives Respecting the Permanent Seat of Congress—& from President [*present?*] Appearances believe it will be fixed by that House some where on the East side of the Susquehanna, The Patowmack is in opposition and the Virginians & a part of Maryland in a flame—this day it is said will end the business on that Subject in their House—I expect it will be a warm day with them.

If time permited wish to say more, but it does not.

ALS, Gratz Collection, PHi. Addressed to Chestertown, Maryland.

[1] Possibly Benjamin Bravard (d. 1793), a Cecil County member of the Maryland House of Delegates, 1781–84 and 1786–88 (*DHFFE* 2:194).

Thomas Dwight to Theodore Sedgwick

Yesterday I had the pleasure to receive your's of the 30th. Augt. the judicial bill which you mention as being well supported and by a respectable majority I had supposed would meet with a more formidable opposition than almost any thing else, & that all Kinds of fears & jealousies would be excited on the subject—it is a pleasing consideration, that so indispensible a part of the system is like to be established without difficulty.

I am extremely sorry that any motion has been made in regard to the sitting of Congress as to place, and fear, that it will issue in that odious distinction between Northern & Southern interest which the present Congress have hitherto had the credit of *concealing at least*. however their feelings might be—will it not create a party spirit which will be carried into all other measures as well as that which excites it? if so, we cannot too sincerely deprecate the taking up of the business at the present time. it is risquing too much—the people are naturally disposed to restlessness, and complaints agt. rulers—& are far from having acquired an habitual & settled quiet of mind as to the new Govt.—parties at Court, will extend their poison to every part of the confederacy—the opposers of the Govt. will have their hopes strengthened, and loudly boast of their former prophesies, while its friends who have supported and sought it, as their only political saviour, will be seized with despondency and give up all hopes of future happiness and security. There is no subject from ~~which~~ the discussion of which I fear and expect more pernicious consequences. I hope these expectations will prove groundless.

***

I should not ~~trouble you~~ write to you on these small subjects, while you are constantly agitated with matters of infinitely greater importance, but that I know the *trifling occurences* in a mans own neighborhood and among his friends are not always disagreeable to be told—they derive (altho real trifles) some value from that circumstance.

***

ALS, Sedgwick Family Papers, MHi. Written from Springfield, Massachusetts. Portions of the omitted text relate to local court matters.

Jonathan Sturges to Benjamin Goodhue

In these Days of Improvement, we[*lined out*] are bro't to discard the Notions of an immediate Revelation from Heaven, otherwise you might perhaps be inclined to think, I had ~~been~~ (like some of the wicked Men in old Times) been favoured with a sure Word of Prophesy, when I tell you that precisely in Eight Hours, from the Time I left the Wharf in New York I arrived safe at the happyfying Place we often mentioned in our Hours of pleasant & chearfull Converse ~~and~~ had Mrs. [*Deborah Lewis*] Sturges by the Hand, and was surrounded by my Family all in good Health. but Sir not withstanding the agreable Reception I have met with from my Family & Friends I still remember the worthy Friends and agreable Companions I parted with in New York, and still feel myself so much interested in the Important Business you are there engaged in, that I wish to be informed how it proceeds and what will be the probable Issue of the present Deliberations of Congress. On this Day I conclude you have taken up the Subject of a permanent Residence. The People here express some Surprize that so wise a Body should neglect Business of Importance especially the Judicial System (without which Government cannot be exercised with any Degree of Energy or Decision) for the purpose of discussing Subjects of less Importance, particularly at the present Time, when nothing can be carried into Effect, altho the Question where the Place shall be, may be decided.

I am fully persuaded from my own Reflections on the Subject & find it is the Sense of our People so far as I have opportunity to collect their Sentiments that the Wisdom of Congress would appear much more conspicous should they lay aside the Question of Residence untill their next Session, and pay particular & steady Attention to the other Subject. great Confidence however is placed by my Constituents in their Wisdom and Patriotism and I shall make it my Care as I think it is my Duty to strengthen this Confidence, untill I have better Reason to distrust them myself.

I am resolved to execute the Purpose for which I left you. expect to set off on my Journey the next Week. shall nevertheless be here untill after Monday, so that I shall be in a Situation to enjoy the Pleasure of reading a Letter from you before my Departure. should you have Time & Inclination to do me the Favour. I find we all have our Prattles and like the Children when we are tired with one exchange for another. in this I have the advantage of you. I have made the Exchange and the variety will please for a while when it gets to be an old Story I can exchange for another. you I suppose are still fretted with the old ones I pitty you for that and hope you may soon have a furlough at least if not a Discharge from such a pittyfull Warfare. be that however as it may, I sincerely wish you Patience, and Perseverance to the End of the Siege, which will soon arrive, and as I despair of enjoying the Pleasure of meeting you again before Decemr. wish you and the other Gentlemen of our agreable Family[1] a pleasant Journey And happy Sight of your respective Families & Friends.

ALS, Letters to Goodhue, NNS. Written from Fairfield, Connecticut.

[1] Sturges shared lodgings with Goodhue, Grout, Thatcher, and Wingate at 47 Broad Street during the first session.

George Thatcher to William Taylor

***

I write in the House of Representatives while the Question of fixing upon a permanent Seat of the Government of the United States is under discussion—It is proposed that some place on the Susquehannah be adopted for that purpose—And I am rather inclined to think that a place some where not far from Wrights Ferry will be the Seat of permanent residence—Should this be the case—Will it not be of singular advantage to the State of Maryland? by the silence of your Representatives I presume they are in favour of the place—none of them have yet made any opposition to thats being the Seat of Government.

I am only acquainted with that part of the Union by maps & reports—These join in forming my opinion—And should I live, perhaps, before many years I shall visit those places & have the pleasure of taking my friend once more by the Hand.

ALS, Smith Collection, NjMoHP. A portion of the omitted text states that Thatcher has forwarded the letters inclosed in Taylor's last, as instructed.

Joseph Nourse, Diary

*** This day being indisposed from taking Physic yesterday I attended the debates in the House of Representatives upon this very important Question of Where shall the permanent Seat of the foederal Government be fixed? After some considerable debate it appear'd to be the sense of a majority of that House that the East side of the River Susquehannah some where in the Neighbourhood of Wrights ferry wou'd be most central to population, wealth & Territory—but the decision of this Question is postponed. ***

Ms, hand of Nourse, Nourse Family Papers, ViU.

OTHER DOCUMENTS

Benjamin Goodhue to Frederick Phile. No copy known; acknowledged in Phile to Goodhue, 8 September.

Benjamin Goodhue to Mrs. Hastings. No copy known; mentioned in Frederick Phile to Goodhue, 8 September.

From New York—Last Night. [Boston] *Massachusetts Centinel*, 9 September; reprinted at Exeter and Portsmouth, New Hampshire.
    The majority of the House is against leaving New York until a permanent residence is chosen; sat "until near four o'clock" without deciding; "Much heat was engendered in the discussion."

NYDA, 10 September.
    The Pennsylvania Assembly received a letter from F. A. Muhlenberg resigning as register and recorder of Montgomery County.

Friday, 4 September 1789

Cool (Johnson); *cool & evening some rain* (J. B. Johnson)

William Smith (Md.) to Otho H. Williams

I have only time to tell you that I have yours of the 27th Ulto. & that yesterday the question came on for fixing the residence of Congress, When it appeared, that the Eastern Members were United for the banks of Susquehannah, a great deal of warm debate ensued, which continued till 4 oClock when an adjournment took place—from what passed I have no doubt a majority in our house will Vote in favor of Susquehannah; what the Senate will do I know not. it is proposed that commissioners, Shall be Named by the President to fix the Spot—I will interest myself for the West side of the river, which I think will be material for Baltimore, I apprehend the Spot will be limited from Wrights ferry to Peach bottom.[1] I expect the question will be decided today although there will Still be great opposition.

ALS, Williams Papers, MdHi. Addressed to Baltimore.

[1] Site of the southernmost Susquehannah River ferry in Pennsylvania.

Henry Wynkoop to Reading Beatty

The permanent Seat of Government is at length likely to be fixed & by a much greater Majority than could have been expected. A Situation hath been selected by the Eastern Gentlemen on the east bank of the Susquehannah, which Adds to their Strength three Votes from Maryland & probably some more from the Southward, the Debates of yesterday will afford You Information respecting this interesting ~~debate~~ Subject, since my last to You, when the probabillity was in favour of the Falls [*of the Delaware*], this Business has been continually wavering & uncertain one day the Conclusion might have been in favour of the Delaware & the next the Potowmack, am well aware this will be a Disappointment to the people about You, it is so to me, but as Friends to the general Interests of our Country, we may derive satisfaction from the probability as things stood yesterday, that a place is fixed upon more generally agreable to the various Parts of the Union than could have been expected; Virginia [*lined out*] indeed appear's mortified & chagraind & afforded every Opposition in her Power yesterday which probably will be brought forward with renewed Vigour this morning the House was ripe for the Decision, but sitting until 4 oClock yesterday, at length yeilded to the Solicitations of the Southern Gentlemen & rose without Determining on the Question.

For my own part considering the very disagreable Situation this Subject hath been in for some time past, am happy in the Prospect of its terminating so much to the general Interest of Pensylvania & Acquiescence of the Union.

ALS, Wynkoop Papers, PDoBHi. Addressed to "Falsington," Bucks County, Pennsylvania.

Letter from Rhode Island

The federalists, in this State form a class of citizens more important in a national view than is generally imagined. They are principally merchants, and the circumstances of our commerce require the greatest enterprize and the closest calculation. As our staple is inconsiderable we must have recourse to a circuitous kind of traffic. It is evident we must find employment for we cannot submit to perish, which objects of any kind present themselves which can afford subsistence. Now it is evident if Congress shut us out from a participation of the advantages resulting from the new government, we shall be compeled into a line of business that will injure the interests of the United States. Nothing of this kind is at present dreamed of. But I will not be answerable what turn the imagination of people will take. It is well known that our merchants were formerly celebrated for their skill in smuggling. They have not totally forgot the sweets of their former practice. We lie between two States of an extensive sea coast, inhabitted by people who are not enemies to illicit gains. Should we be deprived of lawful admission into those States on equal terms with the other citizens of the Union, our necessities will drive us to expedients which we now reprobate. Necessity breaks through all rules of justice and patriotism. When once we have got our hand in, we shall not readily relinquish the plan. We know that Connecticut is not unaccustomed to connive at practices that will throw advantages into the hand of their citizens, and as for Massachusetts they are not free from persons who have an inordinate love of money.

GUS, 12 September; reprinted at Philadelphia.

OTHER DOCUMENTS

Thomas Fitzsimons to Benjamin Rush. Summary and excerpt of ALS, *Parke-Bernet Catalog* 468(1943):item 96. The ellipses are in the source.

"refers to Morris; . . . Mr. Clymer appears to be satisfied that the business of [*the state constitutional*] convention will go on with the necessity of our attendance if as you apprehend the Minority should have an intention of breaking up the house [*the Pennsylvania Assembly*]. . . ."

George Read to James Read. No copy known; acknowledged in James to George Read, 9 September.

[Winchester] *Virginia Gazette*, 9 September.
White left "Woodville" in a "sudden return" to New York.

SATURDAY, 5 SEPTEMBER 1789

Cold (Johnson); *cool & pleasant* (J. B. Johnson)

Ebenezer Hazard to Jeremy Belknap

***

Congress have fixed on the Eastern Bank of the Susquehanna for the Seat of their permanent Residence: the Southern Members brought on the Business, & the rest wished to postpone it; but when they f this was not allowed. When they found they were like to be outvoted, & should not be able to carry Congress to the *Potowmack*, the Southern Gentn. wished to postpone the Business, but the Tables were turned upon them, & the others insisted upon finishing it now, which was done. Congress are to remain here til the Federal City is prepared for their Reception.

***

ALS, Belknap Papers, MHi.

Joseph Hiller to Benjamin Goodhue

I feel myself very much indebted for the obligeing communications you make me in your letter of the 27th. ult. which, with the blanks you was so kind as to procure, came to hand the 2d. instant.

The mode of conduct we had adopted was very similar to that practiced at New York, and the forms we use are but very little differant from theirs which are circumstances that afford satisfaction.

The observations you have made yourself and those of others that have been communicated to you respecting the operation of the revenue laws render any of mine superfluous.

There are few imperfections in this new Work which will not be discovered by those who are interested in its opperation.

A vessel arrives, enters, and secures the duties, the owner chuses to sacrifice his interest to the gratification of his spleen & neglects to "begin to unload"[1] till he has cost the government as much for inspection as his duties will amount to, or rather as much as he can. This is not idle fancy. I have reason to suppose such a collusion as this [is] in contemplation, but I hope the folly will subside without coercion. I was going to mention some other instances but I recur to the observation above and desist.

I have had, with Mr. [William] Pickman the pleasure of conversing with Mr. [Epes] Sargent & making repeeted communications to him, the satisfaction is inhanced by knowing it is agreable to you, we will not fail to continue the correspondence.

Your congratulations on my appointment give me a very sensible pleasure and increase the impressions made on my mind by your kind attention to my welfare.

***

ALS, Letters to Goodhue, NNS. Written from Salem, Massachusetts.

[1] At this point, Hiller added a "t" and wrote at the bottom of the letter, "Collection Act Page 12 paragh. 2," which is section 15 of the Collection Act [HR-11].

Samuel Livermore to John Langdon

Since you left us the house (of Poluck[1]) has been ocupied by 2 birds & 2 or 3 Vaughn's.

They all leave us tomorrow morning to go up north river. We have been pretty much agitated in the house (of representatives) abt. the permanent residence of Congress.

The news paper will tell you what is done. I hope you & Mrs. [Elizabeth] Langdon have had an agreable journy & happy sight of your family.

ALS, Langdon Papers, NhPoA.

[1] During the first session, Livermore and Langdon, joined by Dalton, resided at the boarding house of Isaac Polluck at 37 Broad Street.

Hugh Williamson to Governor Samuel Johnston

You have been informed that a Peace with the southern Indians is taken up by Congress as a serious Object and the Business seems now to be in a fair Train. Twenty thousand Dollars are appropriated to discharge the Expences and the Commissioners Genl. [Benjamin] Lincoln, Cyrus Griffin & Col. [David] Humphries sailed on Monday last for Georgia to attend at a Treaty to be held on this Month; They have with them a Guard of fifty

Continental Soldiers.[1] it appears to me that the Safety and Peace of our Citizens in the Western Country [*Tennessee*] is more or less affected by every Treaty that is held with southern Indians. Two Cherokees[2] who lately arrived here by Land with their Complaints are gone in Company with the Commissioners. I wished to take an early Opportunity of impressing the Commissioners with the absolute Necessity of prevailing on the Indians to relinquish all Claim to the Lands on which our People have settled With this View I threw a few Sentiments on that Subject into the Form of a Letter which I handed the Commissioners.[3] Inclosed you have a Copy. It is a Subject to which I never have adverted but with Pain, for though I never knew a Man of more humanity or more Integrity than the Gentleman who was at the Head of the Commissioners who made the Hopewell Treaty [*Benjamin Hawkins*] yet I cannot admit ~~cannot admit~~ of a Doubt but the Settlers must be quieted even though it becomes necessary to make another Purchase of those Lands from the Indians.

You have also inclosed the Copy of a Memorial I thought it my Duty to present to Congress in behalf of our Commerce.[4] I hope the Paper does not require other Explanation. The Subject is under Commitment & you shall be informed whether Congress think fit to alter their Law. I am aware that our Wishes may not be a little thwarted by numerous Petitions come or coming from Rhode Island. Those People seem to be asking things that are not safely to be granted.

ALS, Garrett Historical Manuscripts, The John Work Garrett Library of The Johns Hopkins University, Baltimore.

---

[1] The commissioners met the Creek leader, Alexander McGillivray, at Rock Landing, near present day Lake Sinclair on Georgia's Oconee River, just beyond the eastern boundary of the Creek Nation. In a letter describing the ensuing negotiations, McGillivray estimated that the commissioners had 400 soldiers with them, compared to his own 900 chosen Creeks. Humphries emerged as the chief American negotiator. "Having no communication with Lincoln & Griffin," McGillivray wrote, "I concluded that they pitted that Gentleman against me, being fluent in Speech, and a great boaster of his political knowledge, and his assisting at the former Treaty with the Courts of Versailles, Berlin, &ca. He shifted his ground, modes of attack in various shapes. The arts of flattery, ambition and intimidation were exhausted in vain. I at last told him by G— I would not have such a Treaty cram'd down my throat." McGillivray's sudden rupturing of the treaty negotiations, which Few later tried unsuccessfully to heal, was encouraged by recently renewed promises of Spanish support (John Walton Caughey, *McGillivray of the Creeks* [Norman, Okla., 1939], pp. 39, 251–54).

[2] The two Cherokee chiefs arrived in New York City on 22 August, accompanied by Bennet Ballew. One may have been Keenettetch, who had attempted an earlier embassy in the spring and promised to try again the next time Ballew went to New York (*PGW* 3:388n).

[3] The letter is in the Jenkins Autograph Collection, PHi.

[4] Williamson, in New York as North Carolina's commissioner to settle its accounts with the federal government, petitioned Congress on 31 August; see *DHFFC* 8:387–89.

From New York—Last Mail

I informed you in my last letter, that I should continue here until the question respecting the permanent residence of Congress was determined—and indeed the debate on the subject was well worthy attention—as it was animated, ingenious, and in many instances decently warm. On this subject, the House sat yesterday[1]—and in committee, agreed upon the east bank of Susquehanna, and upon continuing at New-York until the accommodations are provided: The House then took up the report of the committee, and acceded to the same. As also, to Mr. FITZSIMONS' Resolutions *** so far as to fill the *blank* before Commissioners with *Three*—The blank for the sum was filled with 100,000 dollars—the *time* to be repaid in 20 years—interest 5 per cent. or less. They could not agree on the time to be allowed for erecting the buildings. *Five, four, three, two* and *one* years were negatived—So it was agreed to pass over this blank for the present. After all, I have no idea that any thing serious will be attempted at present. It must be considered as an unlucky business at this moment, as it absorbs the time that might be infinitely better employed. The history of this business you will learn from the papers—But there is yet a doubt, to use the words of a member, in the debate of Thursday, whether "Congress shall tickle the trout in the stream of the *Codorus*—build their sumptuous palaces on the banks of the *Patowmack*—or admire commerce, with her expanded wings, on the waters of the *Delaware*."[2]

[Boston] *Massachusetts Centinel*, 12 September; reprinted at Portland, Maine; Portsmouth, New Hampshire; and Salem and Worcester, Massachusetts.

---

[1] An undated draft of a speech on the subject of the COWH debate of this date in the hand of Robert R. Livingston, possibly composed as a reply to Tucker's speech of 4 September on the definition of centrality during the seat of government debate, was apparently never delivered (Ms, hand of Livingston, Livingston Papers, NHi).

[2] Vining made these remarks; Codorus Creek flows through York, Pennsylvania.

OTHER DOCUMENTS

Pierce Butler to Don Diego "James" de Gardoqui. No copy known; acknowledged in Gardoqui to Butler, 5 September; contains "reiterated assurances of friendship."

Don Diego "James" de Gardoqui to Pierce Butler. ALS, Butler Papers, PHi. Promises to take care of Butler's land in East Florida; professes the "high sense with which I esteem our acquaintance, wishing still that it may in a future period promote further advantages to our two Countries."

Stephen Goodhue to Benjamin Goodhue. FC:lbk, Goodhue Family Papers, MSaE. Written from Salem, Massachusetts.

> Fanny has delivered a son and is in good spirits; still of the "oppinion that the impost will not rise the price of imported goods as the Supposed duty hath not raised them in my Judgement any"; hopes Congress will adjourn "at the time fixed that you may have an opportunity of Conversing with your Constituants."

Jonathan Trumbull to Ephraim Kirby. ALS, Kirby Papers, NcD. Addressed to Litchfield, Connecticut.

> Office seeking: promises help in procuring a clerkship in the federal courts, as soon as appointments under the Judiciary Act are announced.

Henry Wynkoop to John Adams. Reply card, Hull Collection, DSI.

> Accepts dinner invitation for next Friday.

SUNDAY, 6 SEPTEMBER 1789

Fine (Johnson); *a pleasant day* (J. B. Johnson)

Fisher Ames to George R. Minot

This has been a week of incessant exertion, and this is not a day of repose. The world will wonder what inflames and busies Congress so much. Hear it. The eastern members had agreed that it was best to postpone the question of the permanent seat of government, and we had no doubt of being able to do it. We were decieved. All south of the Delaware had agreed to make Philadelphia the temporary residence, and the Potomac the permanent seat. To break this intrigue was then our and New York's object. We decided for the Susquehannah. The Pennsylvanians, though really divided, had agreed to act together, and in fact held the balance. After a day's deliberation, they complied with the proposition for the Susquehannah, and New York in the mean time. How they got clear of their allies is none of my business. Then the southerns, finding a majority against them, begged delay, though they had denied us. This was impossible, for Pennsylvania held the balance, and would have us fix in her limits. The minority, with great purity of virtue, exclaimed against the *bargain*, though observe, they had made one themselves, which failed; and now, failing in the committee of the whole, where our propositions for the Susquehannah passed, they make every exertion to embarrass and delay the business. To-morrow we resume the subject in the

House, and as a minority is commonly well united, and this is violent, active, and persevering, and our majority is not perfectly agreed as to the place, I think there is some danger of our final defeat. The recess is less certain on account of this vile, unreasonable business. But a majority are resolutely bent on having one punctually on the 22d. The Judicial slumbers, and, when it shall be resumed, will probably pass, as an experimental law, without much debate or amendment, in the confidence that a short experience will make manifest the proper alterations.

I must close.

Ames 1:71.

William Bradford, Jr. to Elias Boudinot

I am much obliged to you for you[r] late communications, and am rejoiced that the Election business terminated without a division. I could not doubt of the final issue of the question, but there is a mode which some people have of starting difficulties that might have rendered the determination less satisfactory. In your case to make the triumph complete, the decision should have been (as it turned out to be) nearly unanimous.

The question respecting the permanent residence has received an unexpected determination, & one that will not be very satisfactory to this City [*Philadelphia*]. Besides, I have a suspicion that N. York is not sincire & that an after game is to be played. The deleware which washes four States, & is nearer to N. England seems in every point of view preferable; & must present to those States & N. York a more engaging aspect than Susquehanna. Why then should they go over it? Is it from a narrow jealously of Philada., & a desire of prevent[*ing*] her growing importance? or is it, that by fixing on this distant spot, they may hereafter get the question reconsidered, embarrass the business, & keep the Congress stationary at N. York; suspended, like Mahomet's ~~attract~~ coffin,[1] by the equal attraction of the different states? I am not yet sufficiently apprized of the reasons of the measure ~~of~~ to approve of its policy. I have had an account of the debates from the Chief Justice [*Thomas McKean*] who got home last night. But he does not seem to understand the manœuvre.

***

ALS, Wallace Papers, PHi. Place from which written not specified. Part of the omitted text relates to the Pennsylvania constitutional convention.

---

[1] According to legend, Mohammed's coffin at Medina is upheld without any support.

George Clymer to Richard Peters

Seeing from the publick papers you are reciving the petitions for a [*state constitutional*] convention, I suppose an early day will be appointed for taking them up—however anxious I am on this subject I am afraid it may not be in my power to attend it. When I last saw you I had no great expectation from the business which now employs us here, and which will be in a situation of real danger in all its stages until it shall be fairly compleated. This is owing to the violence of the southern people whose pride is the Potowmack, and to the policy of the Jersey members who lie by to mar every project alike that is not to carry Congress to the Delaware. As to Pennsylvania, to answer for its representatives in our house, the point of honour as well as policy will be to accept the gift of N. England and N. York just as it was intended. We are sensible of the variety of local interests in Penna. but the state has but one interest, the common good—and this I should suppose may be as well consulted by admitting the Susquehanna for the federal residence as the Delaware. The latter would have an obvious good effect upon the commerce of Philada., the former I should hope would not prejudice it, for should Maryland persist in opening the Susquehanna to devirt the course of trade, Pennsylvania must counteract her by artificial navigations—this I have a ~~full~~ confidence in which I will trust to, and in the strife of interests both parties may be great gainers. This besides may lead to our favourite scheme of a canal across the istmhus of Delaware[1]—but certainly great will be the benefit should this be a means of accelerating the settlement of that immeasurable region waterd by the Susquehanna and its branches. Really considering this business as of the last importance to the State and that the loss of a single vote might be fatal, which I trust from the aspect of things when at home may not be the case in that of the Convention, my strongest obligation seems to be to stay here and watch. I also suppose that success in the one may influence the other, for the people of the state being flattered and gratified in a federal residence will be brought into good humour ~~not only~~ with themselves and be ~~disposed~~ better disposed, I mean the western, to the measure of a convention. If such should be your opinion it would [*fu*]lly confirm mine.

[*Andrew*] Ellicot is at liberty to begin his work and will proceed immediately to it—He will this year measure along the shore of the lake [*Erie*], and ascertain the point where the meridian will fall on the northern line—but must defer 'till the next the running of the meridian—the quantity however of lands to be paid for by the state will be known without this latter operation.

This letter is to the members not the house.[2]

ALS, Peters Papers, PHi.

[1] The idea of connecting the Chesapeake and Delaware bays by a waterway dated back to at least 1680. See James W. Livingood, *The Philadelphia-Baltimore Trade Rivalry, 1780–1800* (Harrisburg, Pa., 1947), chap. 4, and Hartley to Tench Coxe, 21 September, below.

[2] Clymer meant that his letter was not sent to Peters in his official capacity as Speaker of the Pennsylvania Assembly.

Thomas Fitzsimons to Tench Coxe

As our friends at Philada. will be anxious to Know how the business of Removal may terminate and many Reports may be circulated. While it is under consideration I will give you as brief a Statement of the Rise & progress as I can consistent with the information I wish to convey.

It has allways, between [been?] the intention of our delegation to Obtain, a decision as to the permanent seat of the Governmt. in the present Session—and for this Very Obvious Reason that their weight at present either in the house of Representatives or senate is greater now than it Can be when No. Ca[rolina]. & Rhode Island are Represented besides that the longer Congress sit here the Greater will be the difficulty of Removal whenever. forbore th to mention the subject while Great Objects were proceeded on and the first intimation came to us from the Eastern people—after several delays however we insisted on takeing it up: hopeing the N. E. representatives would be brot. to join us—but When the day came we found they were determined to delay it till beyond the present Session & as we Knew great pains had been taken by the Yorkers to bring them to that determination. We Concluded that the same influence or an Encreased one would allways be made use of And as we considered it absolutely proper that there should be a Removal from this place we declared that we would Join the southern interest this however was not believed by one side, and an attempt was Made to put off the business to Jany. but the Southn. people willing to Catch at our assistance and perceiveing that we were incensed against their opponents, Voted with us & Made it the order of the day for thursday last—this Vote Changed the Complection of the business extreamly we had offered— if any part of Pensylva. was fixed on to [lined out] support it & to Remain here till Accomodation should be provided those who slighted that offer were seriously alarmed as by Joining the Southern interest we might obtain an Adjournment to Philada. provided the permanent seat was fixed on Potomack, and this was Actually the determination of the Pensylvanians—offers from both sides was the Conseq[uenc]e. A Member of the Senate & one of the house of Representatives were appointed to make proposals to us from the Eastern Members[1] but we refused to hear them being determined to adhere to the Southern Interest this determination however could not be adhered to eventu[*ally*] because it was Very doubtfull whether if we Carryd the first point of fixing on Potomack. we could Carry the second, of adjourning to Philada. the So. Carolina people in Senate would be Against the latter, as well as two of the Members of our house,[2] and there Were two of the Marylanders against Potomack[3]—as every mans Opinion was Known the New Yorkers obtained an Agreement of all the Eastern Members—to Vote for Susquehana—and after shewing the probability of being disappointed in the Adjournmt. to Philada. they desired us to consider how we should Acct. to our Constituents if when a place in ~~the~~ our own state was proposed we should Vote Against it—and afterwards—Vote for Potomack—the Conseqe. was too Obvious and as some of our Members were very much attached at all times to that part of the state—a division—of the representation was inevitable if we did not determine to Join in the Vote for Susq[*uehann*]a.— this determination however Necessary on our part—is very Much resented by the Southern people who in one point of View have really reason to Complain, because by Joining ~~with th~~ on the 1st. day with the Eastern Members, the decision would have been put off at least for this Session—I Confess freely I felt more reluctance in this than in any other public business I ever was Engaged in—and if there had been no other consideration than the fixing the seat of Congress, I would have taken the hazard of Voting against it but When I considered the Effect it might have upon our State politicks, I ~~thot~~ could not Justify myself in giveing so great an Advantage to the Antifederalists & Constitutional party.[4]

The New England people would have been outrageous & in Endeavoring to Justify ~~ag~~ themselves would have Criminated us Who for the possibility of a short temporary residence had Sacrificed the Solid Advantages of the permanent one—these Reasons & others which Might be added were all under our Consideration & Obliged us the[*n*] without any premise or Engagement to ~~act~~ Vote as we have done—if the Southern people blame us— they themselves are not without blame—they have ever since our being here been Concerting among themselves the mode of Accomplishing their favorite Object without ever Consulting or trusting us and even at the Moment When every thing was at hazard they meant to bind us to an Absolute engagement for Potomack by Law—While the Removal to Philadelphia Must be left to the uncertain Contingency of a Vote at the end of the session—we Knew too that if the Act was passed for Potomack that great exertions would be made to press [*torn*] [*for acco*]modation & possibly in two year[*s*] [*torn*] Must have gone there tho. there [*seems no?*] doubt but the Governmt. would be [*torn*] injured by such a position at [*torn*].

In the debates on the subject in the [*torn*] good deal of heat and some Ma[*torn*] Very Respectable to the partys—were [*torn*] the Pensylvs. took no part in either [*torn*] the Resolution for Susqa. was Ag[*ain?*] proposed some others for Carrying [*torn*] Effect—Which it was Necessary [*torn*] because I believe both partys w[*torn*] dispense with them—This produced a[*illegible*] diversity of Conduct—and prevented the decision on [*lined out*] my propositions—I expect they will be [*denyd*] tomorrow by a Majority of *two* only as one of the Eastern Members is gone home one from the Southard Returnd and the Jersey people taken off Under the expectation that if we lose Susqa. a Vote May be Obtained for the falls of Delaware but if we Succeed in our house the battle will be to fight thro the senate and it is at least [*torn*] Whether [*our*] bill will be Agreed to [*torn*] it is not—Another project must be [*torn*] at any rate we are but Where we were [*torn*] Southern people were Capable of abber[*torn*] & Really believe what they Assert [*torn*] Agree to the temporary residence [*torn*] Philada. and When the Circumstances [*torn*] Rendered a Removal to Potomack [*torn*] they would Carry it there their best Arg[*ument for?*] that position is that population [*torn*] so Rapidly in that quarter: that [*torn*] Wealth & Convenience will call it [*sh*]ould that turn out to be the case this [*torn*] will inevitably have that affect & till those take place—we ought not upon National principles be Carryd there.

Your friend Madison is so sore & offended upon this Subject that I expect he will Complain to you I acknowledge some fault but the transgression was inevitable & the Effect of it might be prevented if his Idea upon the Subject was more Enlarged—[*lined out*] in no one instance has he lost so much reputation as on this business which has transported him far beyond his Usual Caution & proves that on some points Men are Vulnerable.

I have Applyd for [*torn*] the law for importing pot & pearl [*ash?*] [*torn*] for such Observations of the Officer [*torn*] to Remedy any defects he has found [*torn*] Execution—this other business has [*so much?*] Engrossed me for some days past [*that I do?*] not attend to any other but I will [*trans*]mit all the Information that can [*torn*] upon the subject—I will thank [*you to com?*]municate the purport of this letter [*to our?*] friends.

ALS, Coxe Papers, PHi. Addressed to Philadelphia. The mutilated condition of this letter—including sections of three pages which are missing—may be due to the fact that it was circulated among many Philadelphians at the time of its receipt and at the end of the session when the role of the Pennsylvania delegation during the seat of government fight was much criticized.

[1] King and Goodhue.

[2] Probably Burke and Sumter who voted against a motion on 7 September to make Philadelphia the temporary residence of Congress.

[3] Seney and Smith.

[4] The Constitutional Party, strongest in central and western Pennsylvania, supported the state constitution of 1776. Its opponents, of whom Fitzsimons was one, were working actively for a new constitution.

Benjamin Goodhue to Michael Hodge

I dare say the public will much wonder at our spending our precious time in altercating a place for our permanent residence when much of the business necessary for carrying the Government into compleat operation remains as yet unfinished, but Sir I hope this blame will not be imputed to the Eastern members who have ever been anxiously solicitous to avoid it, but their endeavours for a postponement of this business proving ineffectual they were compelled to consult togather and combine in such a manner as should render abortive a preconcerted plan of carrying us to the Patowmack, We therefore including N. York eastward agreed to propose the East bank of the Susquehanna for a permanent residence and this City as a temporary one till the buildings should be compleated; this proposition founded as We conceived upon principles of national interest and of accommodation to our Southern brethren has detached the Pensylvanians from an understanding which seemed to have existed between them, by giving Philadelphia the temporary residence in order to favour their views for a permanent one on the Patomack—but the Pensylvanians are so circumstanced that they stand ready to profit themselves by the best bargain which may offer for their acceptance—We have a majority including the Pensylvanians for our proposition but the question is not yet ultimately determined—it would still be our ardent wish to postpone the subject if it can be done without throwing the Pensylvanians again into the scale of the Southern interest—its a great pity we are compelled to be tormented with this contentious and as yet quite unnecessary business to the neglect of that for which the public are suffering for want of its being accomplished—but I hope it may terminate soon in such a manner as We may never again be in fear of being carryed to the antient dominion [*Virginia*], and pursue the objects which are expected from our appointment.

The Coasting bill has passed into a law.

[*P. S.*] Yours of the 29th. Ulto. was duely receivd for which I thank you—I do not see any impropriety in your discharging the office of Inspector if you see proper it is no more as I conceive then a principals performing the duty of his deputy.

ALS, Ebenezer Stone Papers, MSaE.

Thomas Hartley to Jasper Yeates

We have just passed over three remarkable Days—such Intrigue such striking Changes I have never been witness to before. Instead of going to the

Potomac a Committee of the whole house voted for the Banks of Susquehanna as the permanent Seat—and New York for the temporary one.

I claim no merit—but as I knew that my Friends in the Center of the
State would expect I would attempt to do them Justice—I have done my
utmost in this Business—almost all our Members are now unanimous in
our Measures—but I assure you I shall have no Confidence in any Thing until a Law does pass.

Yesterday—the Ground was hardly contended for—The Passions of our
Whole Body seem to be up—and the best of Friends are at variance.

Madison is angry and the Southern Gentlemen call us disingeneous.

I am ~~pretty~~ tollerable safe as to Engagements—upon that account I shall
escape pretty well—let Things go as they will.

The New Yorkers and Eastern Gentlemen—with Pennsylvania Cooper-
ate in Measures—but every Inch is disputed—If ~~the~~ our New England
Brethren fly the way we go to pot—and America will become much dis-
united upon the Subject of the permanent Seat.

The Eastern Men have with Reluctance gone to the Susquehanna—not a
Step further will they go—and the Virginians say you must advance to Potomack or the Empire will be divided—New York is with us at this Moment but if the East and South should draw of their Troops—we shall be
obliged to set down contented where we are.

Mr. [*William*] Hamilton has been here—he says he thinks he can be of
no use—I wished him rather to s[*t*]ay for so many strange Things have
happened—that I thought it possible that somewhat might turn up which
might require his Presence—he has gone to Jersey—perhaps he will be here
again.

We are as I have intimated all in Confusion—I hope no bad Consequences will follow.

ALS, Yeates Papers, PHi.

Thomas Jefferson to James Madison

*** I set out on this ground, which I suppose to be self evident, *"that the
earth belongs in usufruct to the living."* that the dead have neither powers nor
rights over it. The portion occupied by any individual ceases to be his when
himself ceases to be, & reverts to the society. ***

The interest of the national debt of France being in fact but a two thou-
sandth part of it's rent roll, the paiment of it is practicable enough: & so becomes a question merely of honor, or of expediency. but with respect to
future debts, would it not be wise & just for that nation to declare, in the
constitution they are forming, that neither the legislature, nor the nation it-

self, can validly contract more debt than they may pay within their own age, or within the term of 19. years? and that all future contracts will be deemed void as to what shall remain unpaid at the end of 19. years from their date? this would put the lenders, & the borrowers also, on their guard. by reducing too the faculty of borrowing within it's natural limits, it would bridle the spirit of war to which too free a course has been procured by the inattention of money-lenders to this law of nature, that succeeding generations are not responsible for the preceding.

On similar ground it may be proved that no society can make a perpetual constitution, or even a perpetual law. the earth belongs always to the living generation. they may manage it then, & what proceeds from it, as they please, during their usufruct. they are masters too of their own persons, & consequently may govern them as they please. but persons & property make the sum of the objects of government. the constitution and the laws of their predecessors extinguished then in their natural course with those who gave them being. this could preserve that being till it ceased to be itself, & no longer. every constitution then, & every law, naturally expires at the end of 19 years. if it be enforced longer, it is an act of force, & not of right. It may be said that the succeeding generation exercising in fact the power of repeal, this leaves them as free as if the constitution or law had been expressly limited to 19 years only. in the first place, this objection admits the right, in proposing an equivalent. but the power of repeal is not an equivalent. it might be indeed if every form of government were so perfectly contrived that the will of the majority could always be obtained fairly & without impediment. but this is true of no form. the people cannot assemble themselves. their representation is unequal & vicious. various checks are opposed to every legislative proposition. factions get possession of the public councils. bribery corrupts them. personal interests lead them astray from the general interests of their constituents: and other impediments arise so as to prove to every practical man that a law of limited duration is much more manageable than one which needs a repeal.

***

Turn this subject in your mind, my dear Sir, & particularly as to the power of contracting debts; & develope it with that perspicuity & cogent logic so peculiarly yours. your station [*lined out*] in the councils of our country gives you an opportunity of producing it to public consideration, of forcing it into discussion. at first blush it may be rallied, as a theoretical speculation: but examination will prove it to be solid & salutary. it would furnish matter for a fine preamble to our first law for appropriating the public revenue; & it will exclude at the threshold of our new government the contagious & ruinous errors of this quarter of the globe, which have armed despots with means, not sanctioned by nature, for binding in chains their fellow men. We have

already given in example one effectual check to the Dog of war, by transferring the power of letting him loose from the Executive to the Legislative body, from those who are to spend to those who are to pay. I should be pleased to see this second obstacle held out by us also in the first instance. no nation can make a declaration against the validity of long-contracted debts so disinterestedly as we, since we do not owe a shilling which may not be paid with ease, principal & interest, within the time of our own lives. establish the principle also in the new law to be passed for protecting copyrights & new inventions, by securing the exclusive right for 19 instead of 14 years. besides familiarising us to this term, it will be an instance the more of our taking reason for our guide, instead of English precedent, the habit of which fetters us with all the political heresies of a nation equally remarkeable for it's early excitement from some errors, and long slumbering under others.
***

ALS, Madison Papers, DLC. Written from Paris; mailed from Monticello on 9 January 1790. For the full text, see *PJM* 12:382–88.

Robert Morris to Mary Morris

I have this moment left my bed, but I did not leave there my thoughts of you. it is now a little after 5 oClock on Sunday Morning and I can but barely see to Scribble, therefore you have proof positive that my first devotions are paid to that Goddess whom I most adore on this earth & who is most justly entitled to them. I hope it will not be long before I may have the happiness to demonstrate in Person the fervency of them—Mr. & Mrs. [*William*] Constable with some of their Friends are gone to the Passaick Falls [*New Jersey*]. they Crossed the North [*Hudson*] River on Friday afternoon and I suppose will Return this Evening, I was invited to be of the party, but the bustle about the permanent Residence of Congress had determined me not to go for Philada. or Trentown this Week and consequently prevented the acceptance of that invitation. *** This Town has been much agitated for a Week past upon the Question's of permanent & Temporary Residence, I have not been a meer Spectator as you may easily suppose, indeed so much the Contrary that it has engaged the greater part of my time & attention You will perhaps be surprized when you find that the House of Representatives have determined to fix the Federal City on the Banks of the Susquehannah; Mr. McClay, is delighted with this fixture and so are some of our Pensylvania Delegates in the other House, but I think differently and have had other places in view, places that in my opinion are much better Suited to the general interest of the Union as well as to the Local advantage of the State of

Pensylvania and altho I do not tell you that I have sanguine expectations of succeeding, yet I am very far from despairing of success. have patience therefore untill I tell you more of this matter. ***

We dine to day at Mr. [*William*] Duers, that is Tom & I am to dine there, Duer dont like the thoughts of Susquehannah and he is at Work to get a better fixture He and some others agree with me exactly in this business and I will set every engine to Work, but this to yourself. I have not been at Court for a fortnight I believe or thereabouts. Major [*William*] Jackson is received into the Family[1] and is as happy as Mortal Man can be. Colo. Hamilton will be Secy. of the Treasury & this appointment will soon be announced. ***

ALS, Morris Papers, CSmH. Addressed to Philadelphia. A portion of the omitted text refers to a recent cold Morris had suffered for a day or two.

[1] Jackson was chosen as an aide to the President, which made him part of Washington's official "family."

Letter from New York

The perplexing and unseasonable subject of a permanent residence for Congress, has engrossed our attention for three days past, and we have not as yet come to an issue on the question. Some time since, when an assignment for taking up this business was in contemplation, the whole of the eastern members pressed a postponement in order to accomplish the necessary business for puting the government into complete operation; but this was rejected by our southern brethren, from a fond persuasion that there existed between them and the Pennsylvania members so good an understanding; as by giving to Philadelphia the temporary residence of Congress, they should in concert be able to effect its permanent residence on the Patowmack. Being thus circumstanced; we were compelled to consult together, and be prepared to meet what was our ardent wish to avoid, and came forward with a proposition for fixing the temporary residence in the city, and the permanent residence on the east bank of the Susquehanna: This proposition, founded as we conceived upon national and accommodating principles, has broken up the plan which first gave rise to this business, and left the advocates for the paradise of the Patowmack chagrined and disappointed, and who in turn have become the suppliants for a postponement, to prevent the doors being ever shut against them for again renewing the attempt of their favourite object. For my own part I believe it would have been happy if the Constitution had never held up the idea of a permanent residence, but had left it to have lighted upon the spot which time and experience should have directed: But in as much as a permanent residential fever prevails in those States where there is any probability that Congress may finally rest, I think we shall be ever tormented with this contentious question, until it is ultimately decided on, and taking things as they are, perhaps the sooner the better—at least after the government is in full operation.

[Boston] *Massachusetts Centinel*, 12 September; reprinted at Portland, Maine; Portsmouth, New Hampshire; and Salem and Worcester, Massachusetts. Goodhue is probably the author of this letter. It was reprinted in the *Salem Mercury* on 15 September and certain of its phrases are similar to those of Goodhue's letter of this date to Michael Hodge. If so, by process of elimination, the likely recipient was Samuel Phillips, Jr.

OTHER DOCUMENTS

Benjamin Goodhue to Frances Goodhue. ALS, Goodhue Papers, NNS. Addressed to Salem, Massachusetts.

Offers congratulations to "both you and myself" on the birth of their son; has not decided on a name, "let it alone till I come home"; hopes to be home by the end of the month, "tho, it is possible the adjournment may not take place quite so soon as was expected."

Benjamin Goodhue to Stephen Goodhue. ALS, Goodhue Family Papers, MSaE. Addressed to Salem, Massachusetts.

"You must make allowances for my mind being for so long a time wholy diverted from [*the family*] bussines and therefore not so fully rely upon my judgement"; Congress may not adjourn when agreed upon; asks Stephen's advice whether he should come home early "and by that means loose perhaps several days pay"; "we have been draged into the consideration of a permanent residence, by those vain Virginians in hopes of carrying us to the Patowmack, their paradise of America—but We shall defeat them."

Christopher Gore to Rufus King. ALS, King Papers, NHi. Written from Boston; carried by Mr. Johnson.

Asks King to intervene with Hamilton in a legal case; show him "my petition to Congress."

William Samuel Johnson to Samuel W. Johnson. ALS, Johnson Papers, CtHi.

The House has decided on Wrights Ferry on the Susquehanna for the permanent seat of government and to remain at New York until the "Federal Buildings" are ready, to which the Senate will probably concur; "there was a warm struggle for the Potomack, & in the mean time to remove to Philadelphia."

George Thatcher to Sarah Thatcher. ALS, Thatcher Family Papers, MHi.
Continues to think he will leave New York City on 14 September, "unless there shall be a prospect that, by tarrying another week, I can recieve some money here—which would be a thing so desirable as to induce me to postpone my seting out a week or ten days"; family news; a letter from Jeremiah Hill says that all is well since Sarah left Biddeford for Weston, Massachusetts; anxious to see the children; "it is eight months to day since I left home."

Daniel Hiester, Account Book. PRHi.
Trip to Flatbush with Mr. (Representative?) Brown.

MONDAY, 7 SEPTEMBER 1789

Fine (Johnson)

Thomas Fitzsimons to Samuel Meredith

My mind has been so much Occupyd for some days past by the Subject of permanent residence and I have had such a difficult Card to play—that I was Obliged to defer Answering your two last letters—you Who have Seen how a business of this Kind was Managed on a former Occasion[1] can form an Opinion of what has Occurr'd in the present the detail would be lengthy— and not very entertaining—at present it stands thus—it is Agreed by resolution that the Seat of the permanent Residence be on the East ~~side~~ bank of the River Susq[*uehann*]a. in the state of Pensylva.—and the Committee have Reported Resolutions for appointing Com[*missione*]rs. with Authority to borrow 100,000 dollars & to purche. the land & Erect buildings Within __ Years—these Resolutions are at prest. under Consideration & as the 1st. is of no avail without them every art is Used to Embarrass and disappoint them. I hope however they will be Agreed to this day and a Committee appointed to bring in a bill in Conseq[*uenc*]e.—after that the Success in the Senate is at best doubtfull—yet I have hopes it will there be Agreed to— the Coasting bill as amended by the senate had passed our house before your information respecting Measurement was received. if it had not—I do not think the alteration would have been Necessary to conform it to the British ~~Measurement~~. we have Simplifyd the Mode ~~of Measurement but~~ & I only wish some allowance had been made for the Rake of the Stern—I am afraid some of the other provisions in that bill will be found inconvenient & Very troublesome to all partys & I suppose it will be Necessary in the Next ses-

sion to make alterations—in both that and the Impost Law—in the Mean
time I am sure it would be advantageous if the officers of the Customs gave
on every proper Occasion a Liberal Construction to the words of the Law—
it is now *certain* that Hamilton will be Nominated by the Presidt.—as Secy.
of treasury and I suppose the appointment may take place in the Next
week—you will soon after receive instructions—and will have a person to
apply to in all cases of difficulty—Since my first advice to You to have the
books of the Inspectors Guagers & Weighers transcribed I have considered
further on that Subject—and have satisfyd. myself that it would be proper—
if the Secy. & Comptr. of the Treasury do not require it You will of Course
discontinue it. but it would be an evidence of your attention for the present.
Which [*lined out*] Might on a future Occasion be taken Notice of.

Ɫ I am not yet informed What mode is pursued by your Weighers &
Guagers in England. the Weighing is attended by some person on the part
of the owner Who Keeps an Acct. and Compares with the Officer the same
is the Case with the Guager. a Cooper attends and takes the dimensions
which is afterwards Worked. I believe the Guagers calculation is allways
ex[*ami*]ned at the Office. there are people at [*torn*] place from Whence information on these poin[*ts?*] [*torn*] be Obtained—as the time of our Adjournment draws Near—I Anticipate the pleasure I shall have in Converseing
upon this Subject.

ALS, Dreer Collection, PHi. Addressed to Philadelphia.

---

[1] Meredith had been a member of the Pennsylvania delegation when the Confederation
Congress debated the controversial issue of where the First Federal Congress would meet.

William Smith (Md.) to Otho H. Williams

The Present serves to Send you the Law for Registering Vessells & regulating the Coasting trade.

Three days of the last week were Spent on the question for fixing the seat
of government & finally the banks of Susquehannah was Agreed to in a committee of the whole house, about 33 for Susqa. & 21 for Potomac, the question will be again agitated to day in the house. Pennsylvania N. York, Jersey
& all the eastern Members, seem determined not to [*go?*] further than the
eastern bank of Susquehannah, & I fear we will with great deficulty be able
to obtain Striking out East bank, & leaving it at large for commissioners to
View & determine, which in the plan proposed, they to be appointed by the
President—I however have some doubts whether any thing will be finally
done, many Obstacles will be thrown in the way, & every deficulty raised to

Obstruct, if Susquehanna is the place, it will be from Wrights ferry downwards. The post Just going I have not time to add.

ALS, Williams Papers, MdHi. Addressed to Baltimore.

Henry Wynkoop to Reading Beatty

Having missed the Post on fryday morning was obliged to put my letters in the care of Mr. McCan [?] who may have forgot leaving them at Morton's. The Resolutions for fixing the federal Town at the Susquehannah have been carried in Committee of the whole by a small Majority & are now before the House where it meets with violent Opposition from the Southern Delegation, Consider it now as entirely lost to the falls of the Delaware, tho Mr. Morris is not yet wholly disheartened; this Measure has taken A most unaccountable turn, ten Days ago should scarcely have considered it as any Risk for A Man to have staked his life in favour of the Delaware, & at present it would be imprudent to risk A shilling. Should the Susquehannah fail, it goes either to Germantown or the Potowmack most probably to the Latter.
***
See no probabillity of being able to attend our Court at Newtown the week ensuing.

ALS, Wynkoop Papers, PDoBHi. The omitted text relates to problems and instructions for posting mail.

Letter from New York

Last week the great question respecting the permanent seat of Congress was brought forward, and, after two days hot and close debate, carried in the House of Representatives, who were resolved into a committee, to be fixed on the East-bank of the river Susquehannah. Dreadful for the Union were the prognostications of the Virginia Members, because the Potowmack was not the place. I was sorry to hear such threats and menaces uttered in our Grand Council. We had better build *thirteen* federal towns, and let Congress go in rotation, as we all have the same right and claim. However, would they but pay the poor and suffering, who lent their money, and spilt their blood, before they build *one* federal town, it would be doing *some* good. I fear many days will be spent in vain on account of this business, as they seem disposed to tread the same ground over again in the House; and when finished there, must go to the Senate, and, finally, as I expect, will fall to the ground.

[Philadelphia] *Independent Gazetteer*, 14 September; reprinted at Baltimore; Fredericksburg, Virginia; and Edenton, North Carolina.

OTHER DOCUMENTS

Richard Curson to Horatio Gates. ALS, Gates Papers, NHi. Written from Baltimore; addressed to "Travelers Rest," Berkeley County, West Virginia.
"Mr. [*Charles*] Carroll gives it as his Opinion" that the seat of government question "will not be Settled this or the Next Session from the Discussions Amongst themselves—and the part they Adjourn to will take Some Considerable Debate—notwithstanding they are So Well fixed for the Present."

George Read to James Read. No copy known; acknowledged in James to George Read, 9 September.

[Portsmouth] *New Hampshire Spy*, 8 September.
Langdon arrived at his house on Pleasant Street in the morning.

TUESDAY, 8 SEPTEMBER 1789

Cool (Johnson)

John Adams to William Cushing

I have not yet acknowledged any obligation to you for your favor of Augt. 22. if my hasty scrawls written in gloomy times and desperate circumstances, have furnished you an amusement for a vacant hour I am glad of it.

My present office is as agreable to me as any public office ever can be: and my situation as pleasing as any on this earth, excepting Braintree. My compensation will be straightened to such a degree, that to live among foreign ministers, travelling Americans, Govenors, Chancellors, Judges, Senators and Repre. in a style which my unmerciful Countrymen exact of all their public men, will require the consumption of the whole of it with the whole in come of my private fortune added to it: and after all I shall be but poorly accommodated. But I have often been obliged to apply to myself what one of my predecessors in the Corps diplomatique in Holland, wrote to his master. The President Jeannin, Ambassador from Henry 4th of France, wrote him from Holland "Sire I have been so long used to labour a great deal, and profit little, that the habit is familiar, and I am contented." Jeannin however profited more and labored less, and never ran the gauntlet among halters, axes, libels, Daggers, cannon balls, and pistol bullets as I have done, nor performed one half of the immense journeys and voyages that have fallen to my lot.

Every unpopular point is invariably left to me to determine so that I must be the scape goat, to bear all their sins, without a possibility of acquiring any share in the honor of any of their popular deeds. If legislative, my friend, and judicial work their way, and the executive has not weight to ballance the former, what will be the consequence? an unballanced Legislative is a tyranny, whether in one few or many. A more important question, than yours concerning treason, never was proposed upon any part of the constitution: and upon the right decision of it will, in my opinion, depend the existence of government. Two sovereignties against which treason can be committed can never exist in one nation or in one system of laws. We should soon see officers of the national government indicted convicted and executed for treason against the separate states, for acts none [*done?*] by virtue of their offices and in discharge of their duty. The clause you refer to in ss. 2 Art. 4 [*of the Constitution*] is this "A person charged in any state with treason, felony or other crime who shall flee from justice, and be found in another state, shall, on demand of the executive authority of the state from which he fled, be delivered up, to be removed to the State having jurisdiction of the crime" But this in the case of treason can mean only that the traitor may be tried, by the national judicial in the State where the crime was committed according to those words in ss. 2 Art. 3 "The trial of all crimes, except in cases of impeachment shall be by Jury: and such trial shall be held in the state where the said crimes shall have been committed." I am not enough acquainted with the subject of Pyracy to form any opinion.

The character biography and merits of our friend N. C. [*Nathan Cushing*] has been long since laid before the President, in as handsome terms as I was master of, and if he is passed by it will be from public motives only, I presume. I hope he will bear it with magnanimity: but I know not the Presidents intentions. Mrs. A. joins with me in kind compts. to Mrs. Cushing & yourself. Your letters sir are not like hundred I receive. They contain profound and careful enquiries, a continuance of them will be a favor.

FC:lbk, Adams Family Manuscript Trust, MHi.

Fisher Ames to Theodore Sedgwick

A doubt whether your attendance would be absolutely necessary prevented the sending the letter which accompanies this—Yesterday the battle was so hard, and success so much endangered by the perseverance of the other side, & the indecision and queerness of some of our own,[1] that it is resolved, *That your return is requisite* and I am desired to state to you—

That a Committee of 3 is appointed to bring in a Bill—This will be reported tomorrow—taken up the next day in committee of the whole, & will be open to your vote on Tuesday or Wednesday next. Mr. Madison has started a new point agt. the temporary Residence—that no bill controuling the adjournment of the two houses can pass constitutionally—The Answer is, that the seat of the Govt. is a different thing from the place where the two houses may meet. The *seat* of Govt. is the place where the public offices are kept—where the Sup[*rem*]e. Court is directed to be held—and Where the executive magistrate resides and acts—and it is further answered, That the objection concludes equally agt. establishing the permanent residence—&c. This objection, and some others, are answerable—but they perplex and delay—and we shall see you return, with exultation.

We are acting on the compensation bills from the Senate—They *adhere* to the discriminating principle—of course, the bill will be lost. We shall go on part of this day & all tomorrow with the Judicial.

P. S. We had the Yeas & Nays 8 times yesterday—Lee made speeches—spoke highly of our candour—and prayed indulgence and concession—We fasted till half past four—and prevailed.

ALS, Sedgwick Family Papers, MHi. Addressed to Stockbridge, Massachusetts.

[1] Ames noted "Vining & Gerry voted agt. us" in the margin.

Silvanus Bourn to John Adams

***

I suppose the poem[1] you allude to to be the infamous production of a disappointed expectant by the name of *Edward Church*, who tainted by his Brother's [*Benjamin Church*] treacherous blood, would hope to poison the public mind—but a Character like yours Sir built on the broad basis of tried Integrity, superior Ability and an ardent love of your Country manifested by a series of painful services, is not to be shaken by the envenomed shafts of Envy—or the rancourous ebulitions of a corroded mind—but shall remain unsullied in the grateful sentiments of the virtuous part of your Countrymen, till time shall be no more, and after that curtain shall drop, which will open to your view, the more peaceful scenes of a future existence.

ALS, Adams Family Manuscript Trust, MHi. The omitted portion of the letter relates to office seeking.

[1] *The Dangerous Vice* ———. *A Fragment* (Boston, 1789).

Pierce Butler and Ralph Izard to Anthony Wayne

We had the honor to receive Your polite letter of [4] July some time ago—We have to appologise for not answering to it sooner—We thought it better to defer it 'till We coud give You some satisfactory information on the Subject matter—this We intended doing very fully by the Commissioners, but were prevented by an Accident—You will, before this can reach You, have seen, And no doubt Conversed with, Your Old Brother Officer General [*Benjamin*] Lincoln; from Him You will learn that the Commissioners are Cloath'd with Ample powers to bring about Peace with the Creeks; and to take such measures as to Secure the Citizens of Georgia in future, from the hostile Incursions of the Savages.

We sounded Congress on the Subject of a New Government West of Georgia; they were not disposed to take up the business at present—they have so much ~~business~~ pressing on them that must be done before the New Government can get into opperation that We coud not Urge[1] any new business on them That woud admit of delay—At a future day Your plan can be taken up—the Esteem & respect We bear to You will induce every attention to it from Us.

We have not succeeded in the business of the Protection afforded by the Spaniards to the fugitive Negroes We must hope that time will bring it about It is an untoward Circumstance—rest assured We exerted Ourselves to place it on a juster footing, but coud not prevail on Mr. [*Don Diego de*] Gardoqui to treat on that business seperately.

ALS, Butler Papers, ScU. Identification of the recipient is based on the acknowledged letter.

_____

[1] "Urge" is written over "press."

Tristram Dalton to Caleb Strong

You will be informed, by the Gazettees, of the zeal with which the House are agitating the old captious Question, on the place for a permanent Seat of the federal Government.

It must surprize our Constituents to find this subject now taken up, before the Government is completely organized—operative—or able to bear the expence.

The members from the eastern States were forced into the business by a full conviction, that the Pennsylvanians, who certainly hold the balance weight, were determined to fix on the Banks of the Potowmack, which they could effect by the voice of the Gentlemen South of them; or, by the assistance of those to the North, on the banks of the Susquehannah.

The last mentioned being the choice of the Gentlemen from ~~Phila~~ Pennsylvania—it is pushed with earnestness—and, hitherto, with success. Some difficulties must arise in the course of the business—and it may be postponed by the house to the next session—Should it come up to the Senate, the fate is uncertain.

The Senate are nearly thro' the consideration of the amendments proposed by the House—having made some alterations.

The Compensation Bill for the Members of the two houses & their officers, is *almost* dead—as they disagree on the discrimination proposed by the
Senate to take place after 1795. It will expire—what substitute will or can
be made, I do not conjecture.

The Members look to the 22nd Inst. as a day of release—agreeably to the
resolution of the two houses that a recess shall then take place.

I thank you for your favors of the 29 Ult. and shall be happy to hear from
you as convenience may permit.

The enclosed Letter I took at the Office.

ALS, Strong Collection, MNF. Addressed to Northampton, Massachusetts. Samuel Davis
noted in his diary on this date that Dalton's family stopped at Fairfield, Connecticut, for
breakfast at 9 A.M., en route home in a coach and phaeton (MHi).

William Ellery to Benjamin Huntington

I am glad that I did not hear of your having been ill until I heard of your
convalescency. For although you are blessed with a good constitution; yet as
you are rather of a gross habit I might have been apprehensive that your life
was in danger, and that would have filled me with concern. The reduction
of your bulk is a matter of moon-shine; and if you should chuse to swell
yourself out to your former rotundity the fat beef ~~of~~ and pork of your State
will furnish you with the needful. If one might with propriety form a judgment of the disorders to which a man's[1] body was subject from the temper
of his mind, I should never have dreamt that you would have been attacked
by a bilious disorder; for from the softness of your disposition I should then
judge that you had scarcely a drop of bile in your composition.

I wrote you two letters by Mr. [*Henry*] Marchant, who left this town last
monday in the afternoon: but had not as Capt. [*Edward?*] Peterson informs
arrived at New york last friday morning. He was accompanied by Mr. [*Benjamin*] Bourn, and they were both charged with petitions for ~~relief against~~
exemptions from foreign tonnage and port charges, which I still conceive
~~were~~ the Collector of New York [*John Lamb*] had not right to exact.

I hope they will arrive before the special Committee shall have reported
on the petitions of Dr. [*Hugh*] Williamson and Capt. Peterson, and that the
petitions will be granted.[2]

***

I don't think the amendments will do any hurt, and they may do some
good, and therefore I don't consider them as of much importance. I am glad
that the gentleman who talks so much from his stick [*Gerry*], was disap-

pointed in all his efforts to procure amendments. He is a restless creature, and if he don't take care, he will ~~injure~~ weaken the reputation for honesty to which I used to think he was justly entitled.

I find by the United States Gazette [*Gazette of the United States*] of the 4th instant which Peterson brought with him, that your house had determined that the federal town should be erected somewhere on the eastern bank of the Susquahanna, and that until suitable buildings should be erected on the spot agreed upon Congress were to continue at New york. This was carrying a great point; for if Congress should remain where they are until they can *afford* money to erect such buildings, they will not probably ~~remove~~ from New york under twenty years.

***

If upon the accession of this State to the Union, we should be treated as a member of the U.S., and that happy event should take place during the recess of Congress, might it not be proper that the President (if the Senate should not be in session) should appoint the proper officers to collect duties &c. Our impost officers and intendants of trade are distinct establishments. The former are the miserable creatures of a vile adminstration, and the latter are the creatures of a silly, whiffling governor.

I think Congress before they rise ought to make some provision for the discharge of the outstanding warrants issued by the Treasury Board. There was one issued in my favour more than seven months ago, and is not yet paid, as I wrote you.

***

P. S. Please to inform me whether the Senate will continue in Session after the adjournment of your House.

ALS, Ellery Letters, R-Ar. Written from Newport, Rhode Island. The omitted text includes news of local election returns, the state legislature's upcoming agenda, and Ellery's request for Huntington's support in procuring him and his son the offices of district court judge and collector, or collector and loan officer, respectively; asks to enlist also the support of Johnson, Ellsworth, and Sherman.

[1] Ellery originally wrote "the humans" and scratched out "the hu."

[2] Williamson petitioned on behalf of North Carolina's merchants and shipowners. Peterson petitioned on behalf of the commanders of packet boats sailing between Newport and Providence, Rhode Island, and New York City who sought to have foreign tonnage duties on their boats suspended until December 1789. See *DHFFC* 8:386–89.

Henry Lee to James Madison

The last le[*tte*]r. I got from you shewed the little leisure you possessed, & together with other considerations induced me to decline for a time writing to you.

***

The views of thousands are pointed to establishments over the mountains for the support of numerous familys—The great objection to characters of reflexion & weight, to the execution of these views has been hitherto, the apprehension, that the country of their choice was by nature severed from the country of their birth—The discovery recently & universally received that the east & the west may & ought to continue members of the same govt. has done away this bar to emigration, & men respectable in character family & fortune begin to leave us in every quarter—they go now with the persuasion that we shall continue long to be one people & that the potomack river will [lined out] strengthen our connexion by the easy exchange it affords of those things mutually wanted.

But I beleive their reasoning on this subject presumes that the national policy will lend its aid to the accomplishment of this happy event. They consider the fixture of the imperial city on the northern banks of the potomac indubitable—Suggestions to the contrary fill every mind with passions indicative of disagreeable consequence to our peace unity & harmony. What the event might do I cannot say, perhaps the moderation peculiar to american character ~~might~~ would soon get the better of early disgust—But in the present unsettled state of the fœderal govt. danger is to be apprehended from a decision of the question concerning the permanent seat. Better would it be in my mind to wait a little longer, let the influence & good of the new constitution be felt among the people & let the edge of opposition be blunted—No injury can result from delay, & much mischeif may be done by precipitation—Indeed the public mind ought to be gradually prepared for the event & if possible should go hand in hand with the measure, otherwise discontent & great discontent will ensue, decide as you may.

It is not conceivable to you at a distance, how the inhabitants of the So. potomac country feel on this subject.

I am told their brethren on the north side are if possible more impressed with hopes & fears—Together they form a most respectable body & I really beleive are the most wealthy [lined out] set of husbandmen in proportion to the extent of country within these States. They inhabi~~tant~~t a region as delightful & as fertile as bounteous heaven ever gave to man—They enjoy the highest health and are hardy in war & industrous in peace. My thoughts have taken this turn on hearing yesterday that Mr. White was summond by Congress from a presumption the seat of govt. would be fixed—If precip[i]tation or evident trick should be connected with the decision, clamor & mischeif will proportionately encrease—Carlisle is the most suitable spot in Pensylvania for the interest of potomac, if hard necessity should force you to fix in that state.

How happens it that your house should determine to rise on the 22—

much important business, essential indeed, not done & yet this question so full of thorns, so inopportunely introduced—Many gentlemen from the south too absent, & the union not completed. What will No. Carolina say, the very moment she is about to unite, a matter of the highest consequence is unseasonably determined, for if you rise agreable to your vote, the decision must be not only unseasonable but hasty & puerile—Already has the hopes of some of the best friends to govt. abated, pray be careful how you add to the causes of disgust.

***

ALS, Madison Papers, DLC. Written from Berkeley, West Virginia. For the full text, see *PJM* 12:388–90. The omitted portion concerns the progress of Potomac River navigation.

George Mason to Samuel Griffin

***

I have received much Satisfaction from the Amendments to the federal Constitution, which have lately passed the House of Representatives; I hope they will also pass the Senate. With two or three further Amendments— Such as confining the federal Judiciary to Admiralty & Maritime Jurisdiction, and to Subjects merely federal—fixing the Mode of Elections either in the Constitution itself (which I think wou'd be preferable) or securing the Regulation of them to the respective States—Requiring more than a bare Majority to make Navigation & Commercial Laws, and appointing a constitutional amenable Council to the President, & lodging with them most of the Executive Powers now vested in the Senate—I cou'd chearfully put my Hand & Heart to the new Government.

If you can make it convenient to spare a Day or two, on your Return from New York, I shall be very happy to See you at Gunston-Hall.

ALS, Mason Papers, DLC. Written from "Gunston Hall," Fairfax County, Virginia. The omitted text relates news of France from Mason's son John and asks Griffin to have one of the Georgia Congressmen carry a letter for Mason regarding escaped slaves to William Pierce in Georgia and also to represent Mason during some depositions on 21 September by Richard Henry Lee and Izard, among others, concerning Mason's lawsuit against William Lee.

Comte de Moustier to Comte de Montmorin

***

It has been generally anticipated that these operations [*of the new government*] would be very slow in view of the diversity of sentiments and interests of the Members who make up the two Houses of Congress, but the reality surpasses all expectations in this regard and it must be conceded that the task of organizing the whole government anew is beyond the capacity of most of the men employed on it. They have managed nonetheless to establish duties on imported goods and on trade, to regulate coasting trade and to organize three executive departments, specifically those of Finance, foreign affairs and war. Some Members did their best to add a fourth Department under the name of *interior* [*Home, Domestic*], but they did not succeed, either because they feared an increase in unnecessary expenses, or because of the goal they had in view, something that has since been accomplished, to extend the Department of Foreign Affairs to those of the interior. Today that Department is known as the Department of State and Mr. Jay is fulfilling the functions while awaiting the nomination that will be made by the President. This Secretary has not suppressed anything of his repulsive manners, his unpleasant character or his extreme bias against France. Born into a refugee [*Huguenot*] family, he retained the feelings of a religious persecutee and he is the only man from the State of New York, who is opposed to tolerance of the Catholic religion, saying that the lands cleared by his ancestors would never serve to nourish those who chased them from their homeland. Although Mr. Jay never ceases to demand generosity from those who negotiate with him, he gives none in return. Attached to the New England party, he is easily tempted by the smallest gains and he neither can nor will see the big picture. His reserve, taciturnity, and grave demeanor give him greater regard than he seems to merit; he is neither an Orator, nor a good writer, nor assiduous in his office and the Department of State will not make him more approachable or more hard-working. I believe that, in spite of the arrogance of this Secretary, it would be possible to win him over if as much account is taken of his personal interest, as he seems to take himself.

The two other departments have just been organized, but their Heads have not yet been appointed. It is generally believed that that of Finance will be Mr. Hamilton, a lawyer who distinguished himself as aide-de-camp to General Washington.

It appears, Sir, that Congress's work should be limited at first to two indispensable objectives, *the creation of a permanent revenue* and *the establishment of Courts of Justice.* These two items forming the basis of all Governments, it would have been easy to move on to the different branches after having opened these principal sources. As for finances they have restrained themselves to placing duties on imports and a tonnage that is very moderate, especially for nationals who make up four fifths of Commercial Transport. In casting a glance, Sir, at the attached Statement of the Sums required for the current year's operations, You will find that the total amounts to more than 43 Million [*livres*] tournois, a sum that the import duties of a great Kingdom like France can hardly equal. The whole commerce of the United States amounts at the most to 73 Million, it is utterly impossible that the impost and tonnage alone could rise to the Sum of 43 millions. An internal method of taxation would have to be found to make up the deficit, but it is so dangerous to touch this chord that Congress did not dare get into it. It is not, Sir, as if direct taxes on land were absolutely unknown in America; this is so only relative to the general Government: the excise, or consumption duties, are quite considerable in many places and make up a substantial portion of the revenue of towns. Each individual State establishes more or less heavy internal taxes, but the immediate destination of the yield of these taxes being known and determined ahead of time and their utility being felt by each Citizen, whether by the opening of new roads, or by the construction of a quay, or by some other improvement, the Citizen submits to them usually without reluctance. It is not the same with those of the General Government, whose operations appear foreign to their interests; debts to be paid, troops to be maintained on the borders, public Ministers and Officials enjoying a good stipend, etc. all these matters are of no personal use to him and he has not the least desire to provide for them. It is a consequence of this mindset that all of the amendments proposed for the new Constitution contain an article by which Congress is not allowed to levy any land tax without having *previously requisitioned the state Legislatures*. Thus it is not surprising that at a time when this structure is still unsteady, Congress has not dared to burden it with additional weight, but the result of this is that the public revenue for this year will hardly suffice to cover the administration's current expenses and that the Creditors of the United States can no longer hope for repayment of the Sums due to them. You notice, Sir, in the attached Statement that the arrearages [*on the public debt*] alone amount to more than 26 millions for this year and that it would be useless to present our claim even though His Majesty may wish to speed up repayment. ***

Meanwhile Congress has nobly spent the revenue that it hopes to raise to the end of this year. It has given the President 25,000 piastres, 5,000 to the Vice President, and six piastres per day to each Member of the Senate and the House of Representatives as well as proportional salaries to the Heads of the departments. This arrangement is not yet ratified by the Senate, but one can believe that it will be adopted with some slight modifications.

As for the establishment of a Supreme Court of Appeals and of lower Federal Courts, the Federalists who find themselves in the Government have done their best to extend the jurisdiction of Congress at the expense of the individual States. Their Antagonists on the other hand are endeavoring to make only Admiralty Courts with the right to arbitrate between the different States. Only with great difficulty has the majority in the Senate managed to create a Bill that establishes the center of justice near Congress, whose effects will be extended to the ends of the union by means of six Justices, charged with traveling periodically in the various states as the Justices of England or our old *Missi Dominici*.[1] This Bill is currently before the House of Representatives, where there are violent but apparently fruitless efforts being made to keep intact the jurisdiction of the individual States.

The President has deferred the nomination of the Heads of Executive Departments up to now and it will not be until then that the Government will be *afloat*, as they say here. It will sail slowly as long as the sounding line touches the bottom of the Treasury's Coffers. One hopes nonetheless that all goes well when these two matters, finance and justice, will be put in order, at least on paper, and it is in Confidence of this that the two Houses of Congress have already set the day for their adjournment, which should take place toward the end of this month.

DHFFC translation of a Copy in Correspondance Politique, Etats-Unis, 34:245–49, Fr. The omitted text mentions Moustier's report of 25 December 1788 and explains that he had not written since 7 July because he was waiting for a dispatch from Montmorin.

[1] Established by Charlemagne to travel around his empire to investigate local conditions, hold court, redress grievances, and enforce royal decrees, the Missi usually traveled in pairs, one ecclesiastic and a lay nobleman.

Josiah Parker to Tench Coxe

I am favored with yours of the 3rd. instant and Should have answered it by our friend [*John*] Dawson; but wishd to protract it untill the Issue of the future & present residence of Congress was determined on.

Yesterday the report of the House was finishd, Susquehanah & New York triumphant; the combination formd by your Members. New York & the Eastern States could not be shaken. even Philadelphia for the residence of Congress pro. tem. had no influence with Clymer & Fitzsimmons. it is presumeable that a Solemn Oath had been taken but I conceived if there had— it was only to be compared to Lord Mansfields to the late Pretender[1] whether it will hold out the last tryal is uncertain—as a Bill is to be reported in conformity to the Resolutions we shall know if there is no evasion for their decree. if they Vote to have the Bill ingrossd & read a third time without committing it to a Committee of the Whole House—a great part of the Community will be convinced they have no occasion for representatives in the United Councils of America—as this matter has afforded much food for the press, as well as been the Subject of all parties you will think it unnecessary to say much to you on the occasion.
***

Poor Dawson as well as myself will be much hurt that our next Session cannot be with you.

ALS, Coxe Papers, PHi. Addressed to Philadelphia.

[1] William Murray Mansfield (1705–93), chief justice of England from 1756–88, prosecuted the Scottish rebels after the 1745 uprising in support of "Bonnie Prince Charlie," Charles Edward Stuart (1720–88), the Young Pretender. James II's son, James Francis Edward Stuart (1688–1766), was known as the Old Pretender.

Josiah Parker to Tobias Lear

I do myself the Honor of inclosing a letter from the Surveryor of the Customs at Suffolk.

If the President of the United states Should find any employment for an active young man, acquainted with writing and being well acquainted with the business of a Custom House—Possessing a good Share of Honor and integrity. you will oblige me by naming my Brother Mr. Copland Parker to him who wishes to be in a situation that will make him Serviceable to his Country. and afford only a common means of a genteel subsistence.

ALS, Washington Papers, DLC.

Frederick Phile to Benjamin Goodhue

I receiv'd your Friendly letter of the 3d instt. with one inclosed for Mrs. Hastings which I delivered to her immediately. I was sorry I was I was obliged to leave N. York so hastily without being able to take leave of my good Friends, and to make my acknowledgments to them for their kindness in my behalf, I shall always consider you, as one, first on the list of my best freinds, and whose Friendship to me shall never be errased from my Memory. I am also much obliged to you for the kind Wishes expressed in your letter to me concerning my Office. Mr. [Sharp] Delany & self are going on very clever together in transacting the Business of the Office, I shall endeavour all in my power to conduct my self in Office, so, as to merit the Confidence Our worthy President and my good Friends were pleased to honor me with. It gave me great Satisfaction when I return'd to Philada. to find that almost all my fellow Citizens were so much pleas'd with my Appointment, that as I walk the Streets almost every body heartily wish'd me Joy, and warmly expressed their resentment against the Persons who spread those malicious reports against me, however I told them I had the Satisfaction of their (my Enemies) being disapointed, and I have got my Wish. My I have at present one of my Youngest Daughters in N. York at Mrs. Morton's in Broadway, I should be happy you would honor her to call to see her and drink Tea with her some leizure afternoon.

[*P. S.*] May I trouble you to present my best respects to the honorable Mr. Wyngate [*lined out*] & the other Gentlemen who lodge with you. Messrs. Grout, Thatcher & Sturges.

ALS, Letters to Goodhue, NNS. Written from Philadelphia.

George Washington to James Madison

Confidential

The points which at present occur to me, and on which I wish your aid, are brought to view in the enclosed statement—I give you the trouble of receiving this evening that you may (if other matter do not interfere) suffer them to run through your Mind between this and tomorrow afternoon when I shall expect to see you at the appointed time.

Besides the enclosed

Would it do *now* that Mr. [*William*] Barton has declined the Judges Seat (western Territory) to nominate Col. [*Edward*] Carrington for that Office? If not, do can you think of any other that would suit him, of new creation—by this I mean, which has not an actual occupant or one who from similarity of Office may have better pretensions to it.

Can you bring to mind any fit character for the vacancy just mentioned (west of New Jersey)—As Virga. has given & may furnish characters, for important Offices probably it would be better to exclude her also on this occasion.

What sort of a character in point of respectability and fitness for this office has Majr. [*George*] Turner late of So. Carolina now of Philadelphia.

Have you any knowledge of the character of Mr. Laurence [*John Lawrence*]—a practising attorney and Son in law to General [*Arthur*] St. Clair.

What can I do with A__ L__ [*Arthur Lee*] he has applied to be nominated one of the Associate Judges—but I cannot bring my mind to adopt the request—The opinion entertained of him by those with whom I am most conversant is unpropitious and yet few men have received more marks of public favor & confidence than he has. These contradictions are embarrassing.

Should the sense of the Senate be taken on the propriety of sending public characters abroad—say, to England, Holland & Portugal—and of a day for thanksgiving.

Would it be well to advise with them before the adjournment, on the expediency and justice of demanding a surrender of our Posts?

Being clearly of opinion that there ought to be a difference in the wages

of the Members of the two branches of the Legislature would it be politic or
prudent in the President when the Bill comes to him to send it back with
his reasons for non-concurring.

ANS, Rosenbach Foundation, Philadelphia. The editors are using the date supplied in
PGW 4:4–5.

OTHER DOCUMENTS

Thomas Fitzsimons to Benjamin Rush. Summary of ALS, *Parke-Bernet Catalog* 499(1944):item 117.
"On political and civic affairs. Relates to establishment of the seat of government at Philadelphia, government finances, activities in Congress; etc."

NYDG, 11 September.
At the first public levee at the President's house since the death of his
mother (Mary, on 25 August), several members of Congress attended
dressed "in American mourning," a "silent mark of respect."

WEDNESDAY, 9 SEPTEMBER 1789

Cool (Johnson)

Edward Carrington to James Madison

I am just honored with your several favors of the 12th. 26th. & 28th. Ult.
a trip of business through several of our southern Counties as far as that of
Halifax on the borders of North Carolina took me out of the way of getting
them sooner. in my route ~~was taken in~~ the principal Antifederal parts of the
Country were comprehended and I can assure you that the people appear to
be perfectly quiet & reconciled to the Govt. I have not heard of a refusal to
take the oath ~~of~~ by any Majestrates except two old Gentlemen in Prince Edward. being actually present at the Court of Halifax, a County distinguished
for its violence in opposition, I can speak from my own observation as to
it—the oath was taken by every Majestrate & officer present, nor did I hear
of any one in the County who intended to decline it. the people enquire with
composure what Congress is doing, and discover no apparent apprehension
for the fate of the proposed amendments—I mention these things to you,
because reports may reach you of a different [*lined out*] nature. Stories have
been brought to this City by a few weak, as well as wicked, men that the Majestrates in the southern Counties would generally refuse the Oath. a very
considerable change has taken place amongst the Anti's as to yourself, they

consider you as the patron of amendments, and it is no uncommon thing to hear confessions that they had been formerly imposed on, by representations that you were fixed against any alteration whatever. the subject of direct taxation is veiwed in its proper light by many who were clamorous aginst it sometime ago, but the generality of the people seldom appear to think of it at all. indeed I see no appearance of any thing but acquiescence in whatever may be agreed on by those whome they have deputed to take care of their affairs.

I have observed with some little attention the amendments which have been agreed on in the Hs. of Rs. One of them which seems at present to be much approved of & was indeed made a considerable object of by all the States, will not, I apprehend, be found [lined out] good [lined out] in practice—I mean the excessive enlargement of the representation; and what is still worse it will produce its inconveniences very unequally by their falling principally on the distant States: the greater the Representation, the more difficult will it be to find proper characters whose convenience will admit of a punctual attendance, and this difficulty will be encreased in proportion to the distance from the Seat of Government—small as the Representation now is, compared with ~~with~~ what is proposed, disadvantages of this kind would be felt by the distant States as soon as the novelty of the service might have in some degree worn off. but independently of these considerations, I would prefer a small representation. Numerous Assemblies deliberate but badly even when composed, and it is almost impossible to keep them so. I am satisfied that had the Assembly of Virginia amounted to but one fourth of the present number we should not have been so frequently disgraced by wicked & puerile Acts, nor would our sessions have been so long as we have generally seen them.

I expect nothing from the motions for taking a permanent position for the Govt. this will ~~never~~ not be effected from N. York but by an union of Pensylvania & the southern states—Pensylva. will not join them unless they will fix it where she pleases, which must be within her own limits, and this is not the object of the southern States, hence there can be no agreement amongst them as to a permanent position. ~~She~~ Pensylva. might perhaps agree to take a temporary position—if the southern States would ~~agree to~~ unite with her for this object, several considerations of a commercial kind might some short day hence induce the Eastern States to join the southern in coming further. I find however a temporary position has not been hinted, & therefore ~~I~~ expect nothing will be done on the subject this session.

Upon the compensations to the members a variety of observations are made mostly in disapprobation, but those who reason at all ~~about~~ soon relinquish their objections when put in mind of former allowances to the old Congress, and the other considerations which are mentioned in vindica-

tion—I can however with safety declare that it occasions but little or no uneasiness amongst the people. I think the Representatives ought to have had
five, & the Senators Eight dollars.

***

P. S. The collection Bill will prove I fear, ruinous to the Commerce of Virga.
Diffused as it will be, there will be no object here to attract great foreign adventurers: Phila. N. York & Boston, will receive [*lined out*] their ships & the
their coasting vessels for our valuable staples of these Cities will be employed
in carrying our valuable staples to them. was our Port Bill[1] forgotten?

ALS, Madison Papers, DLC. Written from Richmond, Virginia. For the full text, see *PJM*
12:392–94.

---

[1] See Madison to Wilson Cary Nicholas, 18 July, n. 1, volume 16.

George Clymer to Richard Peters

I wrote you on Sunday on the affair of the federal residence which has
since progressed and a bill will be brough[t] on this morning. To take a subject depending on this house, especially of the present kind, is painting from
the chameleon, so quickly may appearances change—I shall only say that
every strategem has been devised by its opponents to defeat it, and will be
continued to the end of the chapter—our integrity has been tempted and
may be tried again. Their best dependence now seems to be on the conditional clause respecting the lower navigation of the Susquehanna, which
'tho once rejected will doubtless be brought forward again with all the other
impediments and molestations.[1] So specious a proposition may gain ever so
many many auxilliaries as they force us either to comply with it or to renounce every thing. They have been told it is not in the present power of
Penna., as the law tends, to prevent any undertakers from clearing the away
the obstructions to the navigation, and that it would be as little in its disposition—this will have no effect on those whose intent is nothing more
than mischief—for my own part I should be mortified by the necessity of
any public act on the part of Penna. to promote that navigation without connecting with it that of the istmhus of the Delaware—this will may however
be a matter for our consideration in the coming stages of the business as I
throw it out for yours and our other friends—I wish you would write me by
the next post.

ALS, Society Collection, PHi.

---

[1] The Maryland Condition, also known as the Proviso Clause, was inserted into the Seat
of Government Bill by the House in the committee of the whole. First proposed on 7 Sep-

tember, it declared that land could not be purchased at the site on the Susquehanna River selected for the seat of government until Maryland and Pennsylvania had satisfied the President of the United States that they had made provision for the removal of all obstacles to navigation between the mouth of the river and the seat of government.

Tench Coxe to James Madison

From the manner in which you have been pleased to communicate with me both verbally & otherwise I have been led to write to you without reserve and with less ceremony perhaps than could be justified but that I generally had in view the public good. I trusted you would believe that such was my end, and therefore hesitated not to trouble you. on No occasion perhaps has such an apology been more necessary than on the present, as it is a case of infinite delicacy and importance.

I have been made extremely unhappy, Sir, by the debates of last week on the subject of Congressional residence. You will do me the justice to say that I have never pressed that matter upon you. I believe I have not even mention'd it. I have sometimes blamed myself for too scrupulous a delicacy with you about it, for the subject is of very great importance. Tis not however the loss of the temporary seat to Philada., nor the permanent seat to Delaware [*River*], nor the fixture of it, if it shall so issue, on the Susquehannah that could interest me in the degree I now feel myself affected. My anxiety and Apprehensions arise from an appearance of dissention and loss of confidence among the best and ablest friends of our Constitution. I have received partial, that is limited information from gentlemen of the middle and of the Southern states, that has created some fears; but I confess my dear Sir I read with considerable alarm a statement of one of your Speeches in which you first observe upon the deportment of Congress to the day on which you were speaking, and then upon the measures of that day and upon the qualities or characters of some of the members as those measures on that day had discovered them.[1] From these and other circumstances I too plainly see, that some things seriously to be regretted, and most probably very much to be censured have taken place. I fear too that a phalanx, that has been forming for two years by the states east of Jersey, has manifested itself in such a way as to make us tremble upon all great Subjects—the seat of government— the judicial officers—the Treasury and other great departments may be affected in the first appointments & those appointments maintained by such extensive & powerful Combinations. This unconstitutional power will be held as it is obtained. The middle & Southern states will murmur—but may not be able to obtain redress. They will become impatient and the Union itself may be in danger. Perhaps my apprehensions are too quick & strong.

At present however they do not appear so to me. But the proceedings have another effect almost as much to be deplored. The Divisions of our friends revive the expiring hopes of the opposition. What use will be made of it I cannot say, but if their troops will rally their officers are encouraged to think of it. Such wide dissentions, such strong censures and such appearances of absolute breaches before the Government is organized would animate a less anxious enemy to every exertion. I wish not to make improper Enquiries, but, Sir, when I consider your Attachment to the Union, and, permit me to say, when I remember my long continued & fixed opinions of your heart & head I feel most sensibly the language of the Speech refered to. I dread the unknown causes of such high disapprobation. You will relieve me exceedingly by such communications on this Subject as you shall see fit to make & they shall be as confidential as you may desire. It may be of service should any thing grow out of the matter in this quarter that may affect the Constitution. It may be of service too perhaps as [*lined out*] it may afford me an op-[*portuni*]ty. without disclosing any thing to lend my little aid to restore that confidence, which is indispensible among the friends of the Constitution.

Since my Journey to Annapolis, where I hazarded a vote *unsupported*, and unauthorized by my powers,[2] I have deemed capital Alterations in our general government indispensibly necessary. I have thought success to the plan of the last Convention or ruin the Alternatives before us. The first thing I ever committed to paper was the little enquiry into our Commerce, wch. was printed at the meeting of the Convention.[3] Occupied by a profession that is very disagreeable to me and unused to any kind of composition—especially upon subjects of so much Moment you may judge of my anxiety upon the subject of the Constitution when I assure you that I got thro near thirty lengthy publications before the expiration of a year from its formation. My profession was too often postponed—and I am now suffering very seriously for it—and my health was nearly sacrificed by the sedentary habits I was led into. I mention these things, Sir, to evince my anxiety on this great Subject [*deem*]ing it the best apology I can make for the preceding part of this letter.

ALS, Madison Papers, DLC. Written from Philadelphia.

[1] The paragraph originally appeared in the coverage of *NYDA*, 7 September, of the debates of 3 September, and was quoted in the [Philadelphia] *Pennsylvania Packet*, 9 September. For the remarks and *NYDA*'s elaboration of 10 September, see *DHFFC* 11:1412–13.

[2] Coxe was Pennsylvania's sole delegate to attend the Annapolis Convention in September 1786, where he signed the "Address" to the states recommending another convention with a broader mandate, which met in Philadelphia in May 1787.

[3] *An Enquiry into the Principles on Which a Commercial System for the United States of America Should Be Founded* (Philadelphia, 1787).

John Dawson to James Madison

On my arrival at this place [*Philadelphia*] I found as I expected the attention of every person fix'd on the subject which I left before you—different are the opinions of different persons—some, who are interested are much pleased with the Susq[*uehanna*]h others reprobate the conduct of their representatives—while some consider the fixing on the Susqh. as a thing which can never take place—and the vote only a New-England threat—in a letter from Mr. Fitzsimons to his friend[1] he declares his discontent with the business as it now stands—his uneasiness at the means by which it has been brought about—and says, he woud have voted agt. the Susqh. had the Seat of Goverment been the only consequence—but he dreaded the Effect it woud have on the politicks of this state, by giving the party to which he is opposed great advantages, whereby they woud be enabled to remove [*the state capital*] from this place.

Mr. Morris, in a letter to his lady, gives it as his opinion that the bill will never pass the Senate; shoud it your house, and still entertains hopes of Trenton.

I will thank you for the papers by the return of the Stage, and your opinion as to [*t*]he event of this important business. Will you direct your servant to inquire, if there are any letters in the office for me, and if there are return them to this place.

ALS, Madison Papers, DLC. Place from which written not specified, but clearly Philadelphia. Written in the morning. The date of this letter is supplied from internal evidence; it is placed at the end of 1789 on the Madison Presidential Papers microfilm.

[1] See Fitzsimons to Tench Coxe, 6 September, above.

Richard Bland Lee to George Washington

At the request of Mr. Roger West I take the Liberty of forwarding the inclosed letter: at the same time I beg leave to present to you the most respectful regards of Mr. Francis Corbin; who requests me to inform you that Mr. John Segar, would be happy to be appointed Surveyor [*at Urbanna, Virginia*] in the place of Mr. Stage Davis, who has or will resign and to assure you that he is well fitted to execute the duties of the office.

AN, Washington Papers, DLC.

James Manning to Nicholas Brown

*** Immediately after my arrival, I went to Congress & saw Messrs. Bourne & Mercht. [*Henry Marchant*] who had arrived only the day before, being 7 Days on their Passage. They had been very industrious amongst the Members to whom letters were addressed, of both Houses, after waiting on the ~~Senate~~, President; They had presented ~~their~~ Petitions, & they were referred to a Commtee. of three, the Same to whom the Petition of the Coasters[1] had been referred, who are to meet on that business this Morng. at 9 OClock, & have desired us to meet with them—Mr. Goodhue, one of the Comee. tells us they shall, undoubtedly report to day: Every one with whom they & I have conversed, (& since my arrival I have seen & conversed with several of both houses) encourage us that we shall certainly obtain redress respecting the Tonage; & most probably, from the foreign Impost, by Water; but both the Gentlemen of Connecticut & Massachusetts, are warm against opening the communication by land; So that we do not expect to get that included in the report to day—Indeed prudence may dictate not to urge it too for lest we loose the whole, but when the bill comes before the Senate, we have made considerable Interest, already, to have that added as an Amendment by the Senate, which, should it be rejected by the House of representatives may not endanger the whole bill. Should the Senate do this it will give us time to try to raise an influence in the house in favour of such an Amendmt. by the Senate—Indeed the utmost we shall attempt will be to obtain the establishmt. of a Port of Entry & delivery in Rehoboth [*Massachusetts*]—It is easy to see that what is not brought to Providence & Newport to Market must go to Boston, New London, &ca. I do not say that Gentln. will be influenced by the compe[*ti*]tion between us & others, but you well know that is human Nature. I see that I must have a long & laborious piece of business of this as the other Gentlemen, most probably, must have the business unfinished, if they attend the call of the Assembly—And to do all this, after hurrying from home, &ca. &ca. without any compensation, or advances from the Town, is doing what I cannot afford, if it be doing according to the Tenor of my former practice. I wish to serve the Town & State, but I think myself intitled to a just compensation as well as others who do their business—I mention this that the Commee. may take up this business and make me a Grant now, if they cannot get the money to send on which would be very grateful, as my stay here will very considerably swell my expenses, having several of my family with me—But I urge no further. Mr. Bourne can tell you more, if you wish to hear from me.
***

ALS, Brown Papers, RPJCB. Erroneously dated 16 September. The date supplied by the editors is based on the date the petitions were presented.

[1] For the several Rhode Island petitions relating to the revenue laws, see *DHFFC* 6:1957–64, 8:386–98.

Robert Morris to Mary Morris

***

The Grand question for permanent Residence seems to the Public Eye as if it were fixed on the Susquehannah, but it has yet to go through much Agitation and I still think as before, altho not sanguine yet I do not despair, I had a long talk with a Great Personage [*Washington*] last Night on this Subject, He was very Cautious in expressing himself, but I perceived that He is much dissatisfied with what is doing in this business and I think not a little Angry at my Agency in it, which I suppose has been represented to him as proceeding from interested motives but as I know my motives to be pure, and as I believe that I am promoting the Public interest, and faithfully discharging my Duty. I shall go on let who will dislike or like it.

I will See you Soon either at Home or at Colo. [*Matthias?*] Ogdens, unless this same question of Residence comes into the Senate at a time to stop me of which I shall tell you more by next Post I cannot spare you another moment.

ALS, Morris Papers, CSmH.

Peter Muhlenberg to Benjamin Rush

As I had no doubt you were anxious to hear what progress was made in the attempt to fix the Permanent Seat of The Government of the United States, I should ere this have wrote you on the subject, had I not daily expected the matter would be brought to a final decision—The Report of the Committee of the whole House, which fixes the Permanent Seat, on the Susquehanna, & the temporary one, in New York, has been carried thro' The House, after much debate, & Altercation.

We have been charg'd in the House, with having made Bargains—forming an impenetrable Phalanx, with being a silent Majority, and a number of other things; and tho' I deny the truth of those charges—yet I acknowledge matters were understood, & I believe The Delegation of Pensylvania are Justifiable in every respect, so far as relates to this transaction—I do not mean however, to be so explicit to anyone else on this occasion, as it might not be alltogether prudent to make these facts too public—The intention of The Southern Members clearly was, to remain in New York until the prospect of a removal to Potowmac should become more than probable—The Eastern Members had no inclination to move, at least for the present Session in this business it was therefore necessary to express favorable Sentiments with regard to Potowmac, to induce the Southern Members to assist in bringing the business on this Session—when this was carried, and the Eastern Members found matters becoming serious, They began to exert themselves; and it was then found, as I allways expected; that Pensylvania would be able to turn the scale either way—The offers (I will not say direct—but understood:) from the South, were Potowmac the Permanent, & Philada. the temporary—To this I absolutely refusd to accede; I know the Activity of The President, and that if He was Authorisd, & requested, to take the necessary steps, for fixing the permanent Seat of Congress on Potowmac, That then the continuance in Philada. would be of short duration—The Eastern Members were then sounded with regard to the Falls of Delaware but it would not do—The last recourse therefore was the Susquehanna, which was generally agreed to, provided the Motion to be brought in for that purpose should contain two Propositions—the permanent Seat on Susquehanna the temporary in New York—This Motion obtaind, tho' every act was usd to penetrate, & divide the Phalanx In the last stage of the Business, an effort was made to divide us, and from which They promis'd themselves certain success—a Motion was made to strike out New York and insert Philada. but as we knew the Motive which led to this Measure; we (except Genl. Hiester:) thought it our duty to vote agt. it. Their Plan was to carry Philadelphia if possible, in order to induce the New York and Eastern Members, to vote agt. the Susquehanna when the Bill should be brought in, and then if the Susquehanna was negativd, a Motion should be made to reconsider & rescind the vote for Philada. The Bill will probably be brought in this day. I expect the debates will be renewd, but I have no conception any alteration will take place—The enclosd Paper will tend to throw more light on the matter—The discrimination The Senate have proposd in the Compensation Bill[1] will probably occasion the loss of it.

P. S. just as I had finishd my Letter my Brother [*F. A. Muhlenberg*] communicated to me your Letter of the 6th. I am very happy to find from that That the termination of the business in fixing the Seat of Government is likely to prove satisfactory to our Constituents.

ALS, Society Collection, PHi. Addressed to Philadelphia.

[1] The Salaries-Legislative Bill [HR-19].

James Read to George Read

*** I observe by the paper, the Virginia Gentlemen are much displeased with what has been done, but I apprehend neither their perswasions or threatnings will effect a change in the conduct or opinions of their opponents in that business. Many people here admit, that the Spot proposed on the Susquehanna for the permanent Residence, is Judiciously chosen on the principles of Mr. Scott's original Motion;[1] but, that its being so much nearer to Baltimore than this place, will be the means of securing to the former all the advantages of Trade upon which the Seat of Congress can have an Influence, they also say that if the Seat of Government was fixed on the Delaware or at Some favorable distance from this place, the loan proposed to be negotiated might be executed for a far greater Sum and upon terms much more favorable to the United States than those held out in Mr. Fitzsimons's proposition.[2]

ALS, Rodney Collection of Read Papers, DeHi. Written from Philadelphia.

[1] For Scott's resolution, see *DHFFC* 6:1862–63.
[2] For Fitzsimons' resolution, which included authorization for a loan to buy land and erect buildings at the seat of government, see *DHFFC* 6:1864–65.

OTHER DOCUMENTS

Peter Bonnetheau to Pierce Butler. ALS, Butler Papers, PHi. Written from Charleston, South Carolina.
Office seeking: "any appointment for this State."

Edward Carrington to James Madison. ALS, Madison Papers, DLC. Written from Richmond, Virginia. For the full text, see *PJM* 12:391–92.
Office seeking: federal marshal for Virginia.

Theodorick Bland Randolph to St. George Tucker. ALS, Brock Collection, CSmH. Addressed to Williamsburg, Virginia.
Senate is engaged on Amendments to the Constitution: Richard Henry Lee "told me that he proposed to strike out the Standing army in time of peace but could not carry it. He also sais that it has been proposed, and warmly favoured that, liberty of Speach and of the press may be stricken out, as they only tend to promote licenciousness. If this takes place God knows what will follow."

Jeremiah Wadsworth to Oliver Wolcott, Jr. ALS, Wolcott Papers, CtHi. Addressed to Hartford, Connecticut. For the full text, see *Wolcott* 1:20.

Office seeking: asks again if Wolcott would accept the post of auditor; "I pray you to answer me imidiately."

THURSDAY, 10 SEPTEMBER 1789

Warm (Johnson)

Letter from New York

That moderate salaries and compensations should be agreed upon, is of the last importance to the manners and habits of the citizens of America, as well as to the credit of the nation. Had I time it would not be a very difficult task to demonstrate that a million of vices, and those vices pregnant each with millions more, must flow from profuse salaries and compensations.

Equality of property ought to be preferred in a free government; and this equality kept alive more by the activity and labour of individuals than grants and compensations from the publick. Every deviation from this is a stride towards luxury—and this luxury will be pernicious in proportion as it is supported from the publick funds—The man who labours for the publick has a claim on the publick for his support, in the same manner as if he had laboured for himself on his farm, at his trade or profession, or had laboured for another man, and no otherwise. Why should a man because he labours for the publick one or two years, live in idleness the remainder of his life? or why should he as soon as he enters the publick service, live in riot and luxury. Idleness and dissipation of men employed in publick service is an example of extensive influence; and ought to be guarded against even by laws.

[Portland, Maine] *Cumberland Gazette*, 18 September. This is probably from a letter written by Thatcher to the newspaper's editor, Thomas B. Wait.

OTHER DOCUMENTS

John Langdon to Paine Wingate. No copy known; acknowledged in Wingate to Langdon, 17 September.

Thomas Lloyd to Governor Thomas Mifflin. ALS, Supreme Executive Council Records, PHarH.

Solicits Pennsylvania's Supreme Executive Council to subscribe to the *Congressional Register*, "in which as I flatter myself are united both information and entertainment."

Robert Morris to Gouverneur Morris. No copy known; acknowledged in Gouverneur Morris, 3 February 1790.

Gerald Walton to Peter Van Schaack. ALS, Van Schaack Papers, NNC.
   Ames and Sedgwick are much admired for their role in the seat of government debate; Sedgwick is your neighbor and "it would be worth yr. while to pay him a Visit that you may hear from him more on this Subject."

Oliver Wolcott, Jr. to Jeremiah Wadsworth. FC:lbk, Ford Collection, NNPM.
Written from Hartford, Connecticut. For the full text, see *Wolcott* 1:21.
   Office seeking: declines the office of auditor, with "gratitude for your friendly Offices."

[Worcester] *Massachusetts Spy*, 10 September.
   Langdon passed through town last week on his way to Portsmouth, New Hampshire.

FRIDAY, 11 SEPTEMBER 1789

Warm (Johnson)

Robert Morris to Mary Morris

I am just got up and set down in my Chamber to tell you my Dear Molly that the Fates are not propitious. I cannot leave New York this Week, the delay of a day or two in the proceedings respecting permanent residence obliges me to remain here, altho I had made up my mind for the jaunt to Trenton if not to Philada. but I have had & continue to have too much agency in this affair to leave it at risque; but Beside this, our assembly have Sent an Address to the President and desired the Senators to deliver it,[1] Mr. McClay is sick therefore this matter falls entirely on me. I waited on the Presidt. last Night and he has appointed. Monday Morning 10 Clock to receive it, and were I to go even to Princetown I could not be back in time, and between this & Monday I must summon all the Pensylvanians I can muster to attend the delivery. Thus you see my dear that our meeting is inevitably delayed. which to me is no small mortification and I dare say it will be a disapointment & a disagreable one to you. *** I expect Major [*William*] Jackson to Breakfast this morning he is in *high Glory* The parties & intrigues about the place of Residence run deep. Mr. Madison I believe, repents most sorely that He did not come into my Views last March,[2] it is now too late. I have played a bolder stake & will see it out—Keep this to yourself untill I tell you all.

ALS, Morris Papers, CSmH. Addressed to Philadelphia. Dated "Friday Morning, 6 oClock."

---

[1] See *PGW* 4:24–25n.
[2] Madison had refused to support the Pennsylvania delegation's proposal in March 1789 to adjourn Congress to Philadelphia as soon as a quorum formed.

John Randolph to St. George Tucker

*** Uncle [*Thomas Tudor*] Tucker has behaved like a Father to us & I shall always feel myself under the greatest Obligations to him. But the Sphere in which he acts renders it impossible for him to be master of scarcely any of his Time. I have dined with him three Times & Uncle [*Theodorick*] Bland twice since my arrival—He (Uncle T.) takes every possible notice of both of us.

The Congress will rise without deciding their Salary or that of their officers. A majority of the Senate were for not allowing the militia arms & if two thirds had agreed it would have been an amendment to the Constitution. They are afraid that the Citizens will stop their full Career to Tyranny & Oppression—They have given the President the power of deposing Officers & they now talk of giving him the sole power of appointing them. Mr. Vice President says no man can be a sensible man with out understanding Latin or French & a Gentleman ask'd him what he thought of Genl. Washington. ***

ALS, Tucker Papers, DLC. Addressed to Williamsburg, Virginia; franked by Tucker.

Henry Wynkoop to Reading Beatty

Have the pleasure to acknowledge the Receipt of Yours the 6h. & 9h. I feel very sensibly for the People of the Falls, to have been so very nigh gaining A great Object & missing it at last, ever tends to encrease the Disapointment, You will readily perceive by the Votes that had the eastern Members fixed on the Delaware, it had would have been carried by at least three Votes more than Susquehanah, for you would have gained Jersey & Delaware 5 & lost two in Maryland which would have left a Ballance of three.

The place on the Susquehanah will be selected by the Commissioners, who on viewing the Ground will be enabeld to decide with propriety.

The Bill for allowing Compensation to the Members & Officers of Congress, was lost yesterday, owing to A Principal of Discrimination in favour of the Senate, the establishment of which was refused by the Representatives, this was introduced by proposing 7 Dollars ℔ day to the Senators & 6 to the Representatives; so that, as matters now stand, we shall have to find our Way home with Purses pretty well emptied.

Am this day for the first time, to dine with the Vice President.

The establishment of the Judiciary is yet undetermined, together with so many other Matters of great Importance, that the adjournment will with great difficulty be acomplished by the time proposed.

ALS, Wynkoop Papers, PDoBHi. Addressed to "Falsington," Bucks County, Pennsylvania.

OTHER DOCUMENTS

Pierce Butler to George Washington. ALS, Item 78, 4:601, PCC, DNA. Written at 3 o'clock.
> Office seeking (possibly Nicholas Eveleigh as comptroller): "I feel in all it's force the attention that You honord my recommendation with—I am not an Ungrateful Man."

George Clymer to Samuel Meredith. ALS, Read Family Papers, PPL at PHi; dating based on content.
> Meredith's nomination as treasurer "this morning" was "a real surprise"; "you must determine how far it will be worth while to follow Congress with Mrs. [*Margaret*] M. and the girls—I could have wished no alternative of the kind had been put to you."

George Clymer to an Unknown Recipient. Listing for ALS, *M. Thomas and Sons Catalog*, 1 November 1878:item 69.
> Content unknown.

John Langdon to Samuel Livermore. No copy known; acknowledged in Livermore to Langdon, 20 September.

George Read to James Read. No copy known; acknowledged in James to George Read, 14 September.

Letter from a Member of Congress. [Philadelphia] *Federal Gazette*, 14 September; reprinted at Baltimore; Winchester, Virginia; and Edenton, North Carolina.
> Announces the nominations of Samuel Meredith as treasurer of the United States, William McPherson as surveyor of the port of Philadelphia, and George Turner as judge of the Northwest Territory.

SATURDAY, 12 SEPTEMBER 1789

Hot (Johnson)

George Clymer to Samuel Meredith

I am told by the bearer a Mr. Mifflin that your nomination is confirmed by the Senate & that of course you are superceded by [*William*] McPherson in the surveyorship and no choice is left to you. On a comparison of advantages I found myself great disturbed by the change in your situation but on talking with Major [*William*] Jackson this morning who is in the Presidents family,[1] he tells me the possible disadvantage to you was represented to him but in reply the President said he had long known you and was determined on the appointment as he thought you a proper person for it, and had more regard to that than your own conveniency—The moment you get official notice you must come here—and enter upon the employment leaving Mrs. [*Margaret*] M. to shift for herself for sometime—Morris has great hopes that Congress some how or other will not be far from Philada. and in that case he says the Office will be much more agreeable to you—There are vast discontents here among the old officers on being omitted in the new appointments—I write this while the bearer waits—he is a Mr. Mifflin who wants to [*be*] a clerk under you.

In more than usual haste.

[*P. S.*] Make no promise to any body for an Officer of Clerk till you get here. this may or may not be a proper man for anything I know—It will be of great consequence to get a fit person.

ALS, Clymer-Meredith-Read Collection, NN. Addressed to Philadelphia. Headed "Saturday Evening"; dating based on content.

---

[1] Washington's official "family" included his aides.

Oliver Ellsworth to Oliver Wolcott, Sr.

Before I had an Idea that you could have been prevailed on to accept the appointment of a district Judge for Connecticut, I had named Mr. [*Richard*] Law as a candidate for that office. In a late conversation with the President I took the liberty also of naming you. I found he was not a stranger to your character & abilities, nor indisposed to give any testimonial of his esteem for them that he might reconcile with his ideas of expediency. It was not delicate, nor would it have been of use for me to endeavour to influence his choice further than by a just statement of facts. In the course of the conver-

sation he remarked the circumstance of Mr. Law's being in the professional line, & specially designated by the State to the highest judicial trust; but was not very explicit, nor perhaps fully settled in his own mind.
***

I think your Son's [*Oliver Wolcott, Jr.*] merit ~~would have~~ entitled him to the comptrollership, but he is young enough to rise, & I think it will be best for him to accept his appointment.

ALS, Wolcott Papers, CtHi. The omitted text lists the appointments and salaries of the treasury department.

John T. Gilman to John Langdon

As I am probably Expected in New York by this time I have wrote a Letter to the President of the United States of this date in which I have Informed him that the State of my health is such that I cannot well Return at this time, that I am in Hope to be able to be there in few weeks and no Circumstance but that of my Health would detain me for a Day—That I should be glad to Hold my Appointment as One of the Board if I may without Injury to the public service, but not otherwise.

Whether either of the Commissioners [*for settling accounts among the states*] are there I know not, but if they are waiting for me, or any other Circumstances in the Presidents Judgment should make it Necessary that another person be now Appointed in my place, I have desired that he would Consider that Letter as my Resignation, although by this I put myself out of all public Employment.

Whether the President will Conclude to accept of my Resignation Immediately I cannot Say, yet if he should, I should think it of Importance to have some person appointed from New Hamp. if possible—not knowing but you would wish to write to New York on this Subject Occasions my troubling you with this.

ALS, Langdon-Elwyn Family Papers, NhHi. Written from Exeter, New Hampshire.

Richard Bland Lee to Theodorick Lee

***

The inclosed papers will give you a slight Sketch of the proceedings of the house of Representatives on the Subject of a permanent seat of government. A combination between Pensilvania and the states East of the Hudson has I fear given a fatal Stab to the pretensions of the Potomack: and it's only resource for Justice is the President: Who I hope, will put his veto on a measure formed in injustice, and partial interests. The Bill for fixing the seat of government on the Susquehannah has not yet passed either house; and it may be possible tho' improbable that we may arrest it in its progress: In which case Potomack may yet lift it's head. The establishment of the Judiciary—is the only capital business which detains us at present: and I hope that we shall have it [in] our power to adjourn at all events in the course of a fort night. In which case I shall endeavor to be at the Loudoun October court.

I am astonished that you have not received my letters as I have regularly answered your's. ***

ALS, Custis-Lee Family Papers, DLC.

James Manning to Nicholas Brown

I have just written to Govr. Bowen[1] a full Acct. of our progress in the business with which we were charged; and we have the most flattering prospect that we shall succeed to our utmost wishes, except the opening an intercourse wt. the Country—The only point we are likely to carry relative to this is, the establishmt. of a Port of entry & delivery in Rehoboth [*Massachusetts*]; this with placing our Citizens precisely on the same footing with respect to Tonage & Impost, we expect will be reported by a Comee. of the Senate this day. A bill for exempting us from foreign Tonage past the House Yesterday: and a Comee. of the Senate consisting of Messrs. Robt. Morris, Elsworth & Dalton appointed, to take up our business & report on it. The Senate immediately adjourned, & they called us to attend the Committee, who agreed to report exactly agreeably to our wishes. Though they, & members of the house before our arrival were obstinately bent on taking off the Exemption from the Produce & Manufactures of the country, & had a bill ready drawn for this purpose; & it was with the utmost difficulty that we could persuade them to lay a side this design. The 15th. of January was the utmost limit we could prevail on Congress to extend this indulgence to. After that, if still out of the Union, both Towns & Country will to all intents be considered & treated as foreigners—This has been a most fatiguing business, for every exertion has been necessary; and we have lost no moment, & seized every handle which could be graspd.

I am really astonished at the Attention with which we have been treated from the President down through the House of Representatives, all of whom wishd to stretch forth their arms for our relief, but the close of the session being at hand, & their business so crouding, which must be finished before they rise, rendered them reluctant to enter on a business, which breaks in upon their whole commercial Siysystem. For a time, therefore, the Die spun doubtful, but I hope we have weathered the [*present?*]—If the success answers our expectations, the Country Interest,[2] & indeed North Carolina will be as much indebted to ~~this success of~~ this application, as the Trade of Rhode Island.

Except the presenting the Petitions, which was done the day I arrived, I have taken my full share of the fatigue & attention to this business, as my Colleagues arrived but a day before me—Mr. Bourne returned two days ago, & Mr. [*Henry*] Marchant returns to Morrow, to attend the Assembly and leave me alone to attend on this business and guard every avenue against a failure. This will probably detain me here near a week longer, which will greatly add to the unexpected Expences I have already incurred by having my family, Horse, &ca. on Expence; and if I go to Jersey this afternoon must return to Morrow Evg. or monday Morng. You will judge therefore whether some provision is not necessary for my services, & to defray my Expences. If it is not judged by my Colleagues that my Exertions and influence in this business has not had their weight to accomplish this object, I will relinquish every claim. But if I serve in my own departmt. at home for next to Nothing, it is no reason I should [*be*] abroad in a cause where the community are so much interested, & if we succed, benefitted—I need not hint to you that if this business is not attended to in time, that it is generally over looked; And, if the money, cannot be raised now, the allowance for Town pay should be made by the Committee of the Town, in their grant to me.

ALS, Brown Papers, RPJCB. Addressed to Providence, Rhode Island.

[1] Probably Jabez Bowen, deputy governor of Rhode Island, 1781–86.
[2] The Rhode Island political party which represented the interests of the farmers and the small towns.

Comte de Moustier to Comte de Montmorin

The plan for an adjournment of Congress that I have just had the honor of reporting to You appears all the more necessary because the emergence of several parties whose animosity needs to be calmed by mutual absence has been visible for some time. Two important questions that the wisdom of the Majority would willingly postpone for another time, but which restless minds have not grown tired of proposing, have divided Congress into several factions, which a large gathering of citizens at the public debates has increasingly incited. These questions are the *amendments to the Constitution* and *the determination of the Permanent Residence of Congress.*

The Federalists, or the majority of this Assembly, were not in any way disposed to take up any amendments before the Government was completely organized, but perceiving that their rivals were preparing a long list of amendments suited to weaken or entirely upset the new system, they are taking the position of proposing on their own what they know they cannot prevent in order to steer the debates and render them less unfavorable. This manoeuver has had the desired success. The Antifederalists did not dare oppose themselves publicly to amendments on which they insisted so strongly. These amendments are conceived by the dominant party in such a way as to not cast any blow at the spirit of the Constitution, but only to calm the exaggerated anxiety over the possible despotism of Congress. *** All these points conform generally to the spirit of the Constitution and to the individual [*state*] Governments of the United States, but they leave undecided the delicate question of the power of Congress to levy direct taxes, to form and organize an army, and to control the resolutions and acts of the individual States and extend its jurisdiction to them. These essential points were indeed brought up by the Antifederalists but rejected by a large majority. It remains to be seen if the public will be satisfied with the amendments I have mentioned. Discussion of these has produced great ferment in the House and the minority appears very displeased by the ruse employed [*by the majority*] to look as though they were acting, in order to avoid acting with impunity. In any case the consent of two thirds of the Senate and of the [*state*] Legislative Assemblies is necessary to insert these amendments into the Constitution.

The other question, which is that of the Permanent Residence was discussed much more spiritedly because a large number of Delegates were personally interested in having the Seat of Government in their vicinity and others have given their word to support one or another party. The principle of equality among all Members of the union leaves no other expedient in resolving this question than to find a point that is central in terms of population, wealth and territory, which would have at once the advantages of easy access to the ocean, the South and North of the union and the western territories. The impossibility of combining all these advantages in a single place is readily apparent; therefore, an attempt is being made to get as close as possible. The Potomac and the Susquehanna seem to deserve equal preference; the one for its easy communication with the West, the other for its fertility and the population of its surrounding areas. After long debates that entertained the public for four days, the majority finally decided for the Susquehannah and authorized the President to appoint Commissioners to choose land there and construct a city by means of a loan of around 500,000 dollars for the first year. It has been resolved to remain in New York in the meantime. Despite this resolution there are some informed individuals who think that Congress will end up going to Philadelphia next year. If it is true, as the fomenters of this dispute claim, that the Southerners would sooner break away from the confederation than allow the Congress to sit any longer in the North, then the necessity that this Assembly finds itself in, of deciding a question relatively indifferent in itself but dangerous in its consequences, can only be lamented. As Congress should be adjourning toward the end of the month, the establishment of the Temporary Residence will still be cause for new debates. Moreover the Senate has not yet had its vote and given how little its opinion differs from that of the House of Representatives, the Government will remain in New York.

None of these discussions, Sir, affect either the peace or the attention of the President of the United States; he seems to embrace no party and limits himself to the exercise of the functions prescribed to him by the Constitution. Up to now he has approved all the laws proposed by the two Houses without any amendment. He has appointed the various posts under the General Government with the exception of the Heads of departments and the Judges, whose existence and appointments are not yet definitively determined. The Senate, which must confirm the nominations made by the President, has adopted the ballot system, which could eventually be very inappropriate. It would seem suitable that a Senator in rejecting a candidate proposed by the President make his reasons known; this is why for several days now the Senate has approved the method of voting by word of mouth and justifying their votes. Although the nominations have been numerous, only one customs Officer from Georgia displeased the Senate [*Benjamin Fishbourn*], all the others were unanimously confirmed.

***

Another measure also recommended by the President, not taken up with the same urgency, is the organization of the militia in the whole extent of the United States. Congress postponed this task until the next session, but the President seems to put great stock in it, because a large number of Officers trained during the war and capable of training the militia are dying or quietly dispersing without the public benefitting from their experience.

***

DHFFC translation of a Copy in Correspondance Politique, Etats-Unis, 34:256–61. The omitted text is a paraphrase of the proposed Amendments to the Constitution, comment on the commission to the Creek Nation, and discussion of the popularity of George Washington and the possibility of a party forming against him.

Adam Stephen to James Madison

In the reading the debates of your House, there appears some heat of parties; and it is no more than may be naturally expected, after so long a Session, and the discussion of so many and Various subjects. Mr. Scots Motion for bringing the Attention of the House to the permanent Seat of Government for the United States, is in my Opinion Premature—I wish the Temper of the House may Suit it.

The Western Country is daily moving into greater importance, and many Members of Congress are not sensible of its Consequence to the United States, perhaps untill they now met, they never had occasion to bestow a thought upon it. Proper Attention to that Country is Absolutly Necessary, in time it will give Law to America.

***

The Middle States could do better without the Territory to the East of Hudson River, than without the friendship and intimate Coalition with the Inhabitants of the Transappalacian Country.

With great Judgement, and Propriety did the President Recommend Attention to the Militia; but it appear[s] to me that the Martial Spirit is extinct.

In the Cities, and on Tidewater; Commerce, Agriculture, Speculation, pleasure and dissipation Seem to engross the minds of the People. The Strength and Vigour of the United States, ly in the Mountains and to the Westward. Our Coasts are as liable to be insulted and Ravaged, as those of the Spaniards were less than a Century ago, when the celebrated Buccaneer Morgan[1] took possession of Panama and Maracaybo with other Rich places, on their Coasts.

For that Reason the Seat of Government, and the treasury is not Safe on Tide water. Where the Seat of Government is; the monied Interest will reside. What dreadful Consequences would a Squadron of Algerine Corsairs produce in our Cities and on our Coasts, Navigated by American Renegadoes, and the Rhode islanders are exellent Navigators, and by their behaviour to one another, Seem Calculated for Such Service.

If a place that is nearly Central, and convenient as can be Expected to the Back country is hatched upon: The people have reason to be pleased. In the discussion of this Affair we shall discover whether our Confederacy is well or ill Combined. It is my Wish that the Matter may be postponed to a future day, perhaps till after the next Election, when men will be better acquainted in the General Interests of the rising empire.

ALS, Madison Papers, DLC. Written from Berkeley County, West Virginia. For the full text, see *PJM* 12:398–99.

---

[1] Sir Henry Morgan (1635?–88), a notorious British privateer of the West Indies, captured Maracaibo, Venezuela (1669), and Panama (1671), before becoming lieutenant governor of Jamaica.

David Stuart to George Washington

*** The success of amendments will leave but a fiew scattering opponents—Mr. Maddison will be a very popular character hereafter, on the South side of James river, for his conduct in this business, as Colo. [*Edward*] Carrington informs me—The same Gentleman informs me, that there has been scarce an instance where the oaths have been refused—It is perhaps somewhat singular, but the Opponents to the Government, appear more generally pleased with the constru[c]tion of the Constitution, which vests the power of removal in the President, than the friends to it—Their satisfaction however, entirely reconciles the latter to it—Mr. [*Patrick*] Henry is the only one of the party, I have heard of, who disapproves of it—He still thinks too that the single amendment purposed in our Convention restricting direct taxes worth all the rest.

*** The people here say, that their expectation of it's being on the Potowmac, were allways centered in you, and hope that as your opinion has been long known on the subject, it [*Seat of Government Bill HR-25*] will never pass with your concurrence—For my part, I fear from the majority which has prevailed on the question, that even that will not avail—I am unacquainted with the various steps which have preceded the decision, but it appears to me that some advantage has been taken of the absence of many members from the Southward. A question which involves all the passions and interests of the different parts of the Union, ought not to have been decided on without much previous notice. Perhaps, it ought not to have been decided on at all, in the absence of two States, who will probably soon join the Union. I have no doubt, but the Opponents to the Constitution in those States, and North Carolina particularly, will consider it, as a striking instance of disrespect— A member of that State, tho' a friend to the government, will I think be justifyed in refusing to accede to it, ~~government~~ when, a question which is to affect them to the latest ages, has been decided on, without their voice—No possible injury could have arisen, from a suspension of the question for a fiew months—As the arguments of population & wealth seem to have been considered as frivolous, and therefore disregarded, I cannot concieve on what principle the question could have met with such a fate—But, it is too probable, tho' they were not insisted on, that they have had their influence— Upon the whole, it is considered as unfortunate, that a matter of such magnitude should have been agitated at this time, and much more so, that it should be generally considered, that any other circumstances, than that of extent of territory should be supposed to have operated.
***

ALS, Washington Papers, DLC. Written from Alexandria, Virginia. For the full text, see *PGW* 4:25–29.

James Sullivan to John Langdon

***

Before I was so very happily connected with your family I had the highest regard for you. and shall be very happy in opportunities to express its great encrease. I thank you and all my friends Who have honored me with a mention of my name to the president. I have been frequently informed of my being mentioned at N. York as a Candidate for the office of a District Judge, or Judge of admiralty. Should my Country call me to any further Duties I shall endeavour to Execute them with integrity. and Shall be happy in doing my utmost to Support the General Government. the two houses have proposed more amendments than I wished to see because some of them I think are rather alterations than amendments.

I am rather of opinion that Judge Livermore is wrong in his ideas of a Judicial System. but do not know what your opinion is.

***

ALS, Langdon-Elwyn Family Papers, NhHi. Written from Boston. The content of this letter suggests it may have been written after the date.

Marston Watson to Benjamin Goodhue

Several of the Principal Inhabitants of this and the neighbouring Fishing Towns have together express'd the very great Anxiety & apprehensions that they suffer from the Unexpected Operation of a part of the Revenue System, which they had flatter'd themselves was intended to Compensate in some degree for the heavy burdens which the Revenue imposes on the Fishery, & by duties tantamount to a prohibition on the Foreign Fisheries to give Countenance and Encouragement to Ours.

These suggestions have been propos'd to be Communicated to you in a regular manner & form, as a Circumstance of serious Consideration; but the short time between the present, & the recess of Congress will Scarcely allow an application to you in the most hasty manner; on that account therefore I am requested to say, That whatever was the Intention of Congress in laying those duties on foreign Fish We find our Expectations of benefit therefrom totally disappointed; as the Nova-Scotians can obtain for their Fish at our own ports the same prices that we can for ours within the Interests of the duty to be drawn back upon Exportation: and it is very Notorious that our Fishery is so Clog'd by foreign Regulation, and so over-abundant by the admission of foreign fish that our Stocks remain in hand without a Market a large part of the year; and thereby it becomes extremely difficult to carry on the business, without great risque & loss of property, which has already produc'd a Considerable declension of the business. the Concern'd in the business reflecting on this appearance, are immediately led, to look for relief through the medium of their own particular friends & Representatives; & therefore hope it not improper to request your voice for them, That if Congress did intend the duty on foreign fish to Operate as a prohibition of it within the United States, that you will be Pleas'd to endeavour to Procure such a further regulation as will produce that Effect. And if otherways that it is their Intention to allow a drawback of the duties paid on foreign Fish that you will so far Espouse our Interest as to Exert all your influence to have it otherways regulated, so that the duty as we have been taught to expect, may operate as a Prohibition. as otherways the business under its numerous foreign, & domestic embarrassments must very shortly become totally Extinct.

ALS, Letters to Goodhue, NNS. Written from Marblehead, Massachusetts.

OTHER DOCUMENTS

Oliver Ellsworth to Oliver Wolcott, Jr. ALS, Wolcott Papers, CtHi. For the full text, see *Wolcott* 1:20.
    Office seeking: lists appointments and salaries of the treasury department; advises Wolcott to accept appointment as auditor.

Thomas Fitzsimons to Benjamin Rush. Summary of ALS, *Parke-Bernet Catalog* 499(1944):item 117.
    "On political and civic affairs. Relates to establishment of the seat of government at Philadelphia, government finances, activities in Congress; etc."

Stephen Goodhue to Benjamin Goodhue. FC:lbk, Goodhue Family Papers, MSaE. Written from Salem, Massachusetts.
    Advises Benjamin to stay in New York City if there is a prospect of adjourning in mid-October, otherwise he should be home by the tenth of October; there seems to be general uneasiness about high federal salaries.

John Langdon to Samuel Livermore. No copy known; acknowledged in Livermore to Langdon, 20 September.

John Parker, Jr. to George Washington. ALS, Washington Papers, DLC. Written from Charleston, South Carolina. For the full text, see *PGW* 4:22–23.
    Office seeking: something in South Carolina; mentions Grayson, Johnson, Wingate, King, and Few as references.

George Thatcher to Henry Sewall. No copy known; mentioned in Sewall Diary, 2 October.

Benjamin Thompson to George Washington. ALS, Washington Papers, DLC. Written from Morristown, New Jersey. For the full text, see *PGW* 4:30–31.
    Office seeking: consulate at a French port; mentions Paterson, Boudinot, and Cadwalader as references.

SUNDAY, 13 SEPTEMBER 1789

Hot (Johnson)

Fisher Ames to John Lowell

I am happy to find that you approve my opinion that a direct application is improper and inexpedient—I am so certain that every accessible path has been explored, & every thing attempted that ought to be, that I should have some uneasiness, if more was now to be attempted ~~that~~ lest it should do hurt—Gen. [*Benjamin*] L[*incoln*].'s personal interview was a fortunate thing and tho' he did not have opportunity to mention the success of it, some hope, tho' not a sanguine one, naturally springs from it. I think so highly of Col. Hamilton's moral & intellectual qualities that I consider his appointment to the head of the Treasury as an auspicious event—Mr. [*Samuel*] Osgood is not nominated to any office.
    Mr. [*Jonathan*] J[*ackso*]n. has been mentioned to the P[*residen*]t. by his closet friends in very warm terms of esteem. He will stand well for any future appt. and I hope the Marshal's place may be had now—Tho' it is in fact inadequate to his merits & wishes—I am afraid it is all that can be expected at present—The post office will not probably be taken from Mr. [*Ebenezer*] Hazard—The Vice appears to be friendly to Mr. J[*ackson*]. Let me inform you of the secret of the poetical attack on that respectable gentleman[1]—Mr. [*Edward*] Church was at the Prest.'s levee—seeing the vice pt. in discourse with the prest. he took that opportunity to make him a low bow—Mr. Adams had not seen him before—but, mindful of the etiquette of Europe, which forbids attention to any other while in conversation with the Sovereign, he did not return the bow. As Church, & most Americans, know nothing of this rule of Etiquette, perhaps he had better have bowed in return—Still, Mr. As. hoped he should see him almost instantly & pay him proper attention—It happened that he did not see him again—Behold the poetical fruit—Indeed it is poetical license—Mr. Adams has acted with a noble decision, and

has repeatedly given the casting voice on great questions—I thank you for your kind sentiments and sensible advice in regard to newspaper censures on my conduct—I am not clearly impressed with the nature of the observations in my last which you seem to allude to. I think, however, that I endeavoured to explain the leading idea or principle of my Speech in Fenno's paper[2]—not because I was under concern about it's reception with the people—for on a legal question, I never supposed they would have either curiosity or understanding. But I was afraid that the *lawyers* wd. either hurry over or misconceive my doctrine, and deny it's orthodoxy—I tried to state it a little more clearly than the Gazette [*of the United States*], in order that I might not be misunderstood by you—and indeed I was afraid of having expressed my ideas rather obscurely in the printed Speech—for, in fact, the house did not appear to understand my doctrine—As to the paragraphs in Edes' & Adams & Nourse[3] I assure you, with great sincerity, that I am only discomposed by the fear that some zealous friend will attempt my vindication—Newspaper praise may lower & bring into question any new character—It provokes the envious, disappoints the malignant—puts the suspicious on their guard—If people think good or evil of a man they chuse to say it themselves—and they are disgusted when it is said *for* them, & tho' they may approve they will not feel *bound* to maintain it as they do with regard to what they say themselves—Add to all this 9/10ths are careless & indifferent & only know that a man's character is contested—To think well of him, they know it should be incontestible Malignant paragraphs, if unanswered, excite the pity, & appeal to the sense of justice of the public with these sentiments, I was chagrined to see the [*Massachusetts*] Centinel puffing me off,[4] as if it was necessary—The question of the permanent residence has been delayed, partly because it was desired to hasten the Judiciary, & principally because the return of Mr. Sedgwick, Mr. Sturgis & Mr. Leonard was desired and expected—They have not returned—and the Bill will be reported tomorrow notwithstanding—Maryland claims a proviso to make the whole depend on the passage of a law by Pen[n]s[*ylvani*]a. to permit the Susquehannah to be opened—Phila. is jealous that Baltimore wd. have the river produce in that event—Whether without such proviso the Maryd. people, or any of them, will vote for the Bill, or, with it, whether the Pen[n]-s[*ylvania*]ns. will vote for it, is the hazardous contingency upon which it depends—In case of failure of the bill, we shall be in confusion, and perhaps a majority will be for meeting next at Phila.—It is a vexatious business of intrigue, in which some act agt. their judgments & many more agt. their wishes—Prudence seemed to direct that the business should be delayed— probably the federal town is made a matter of artificial importance—But as we must decide, I think the decision should be made as useful as possible to the preservation of the union—I have considered the Patowmak & the Delaware as two extremes.

ALS, Diedrich Collection, MiU-C.

¹ *The Dangerous Vice* ——— (New York, 1789), by Edward Church.
² *GUS*, 2 September, printed Ames's speech of 29 August against a motion opposing the creation of federal district courts. See *DHFFC* 11:1356–59.
³ The article, which appeared in Benjamin Edes's *Boston Gazette*, is printed above under 7 September. The attack on Ames in Boston's *Independent Chronicle*, edited by Thomas Adams and John Nourse, is printed under 27 August, volume 16.
⁴ Printed under 29 August, volume 16.

John Brown to Harry Innes

The Western Post sets out in half an Hour therefore have only time to write you a short Letter acknowledging your favor of the 31st of July which reached me last night. From my knowledge of the Characters which composed a Majority of the Convention¹ I had expected that the result of their deliberations would be such as you have represented I think every exertion should be used to obtain a change in the Representation—'tis unsafe tis dishonorable for the District to trust a Business of the last importance to the determination of such men as compose that Body a few excepted—If the District were now to apply for admission into the union I believe there would be no opposition made as Vermont is expected shortly to come forward with the consent of N. York—My present Opinion is that both the Interest of the Union & of Kentucke require that she should become an independent Member—my reasons I will give you at another time.

The Governour of the Westn. Territory [*Arthur St. Clair*] sets out from this place in a few days & expects to pass through your Country the last of Octr. on his way to the Wabash & Illinois, to adjust the Claims of the French Settlers & to treat with the Indians in that quarter—I expect a new Disposition of the Troops more favorable for the protection of Kentucke will shortly take place with perhaps the addition of some Companies of Rifle Men—of this I shall be able to inform you more fully in my next.

***

In answer to your questions—I arrived safe at New York & found the Dutch Ambassador [*Pieter Johan van Berckel*] & his Daughter in perfect Health—but I can with truth assure you that I had no such Views as you seem to imagine I esteem her much as a friend—But she could not be happy in Kentucke & there I am determined to live.

The inclosed Journal together with the News papers sent my Brother [*James*] will inform you of every thing worth notice in this quarter. I expect

Congress will adjn. in 10 Days to meet 1st. of Decr. I shall Visit my friends in Virga.

Shall write you next Post I fear this will not reach the office in time.

ALS, Emmet Collection, NN. Addressed to Danville, Kentucky.

[1] Held in July 1789, Kentucky's eighth convention to consider separation from Virginia decided against applying to Congress for statehood on the grounds that some of the conditions proposed by Virginia were unacceptable. It did petition the Virginia legislature for repeal of the most objectionable condition, permanently restricting Kentucky's jurisdiction over certain lands without Virginia's consent; see George Nicholas to Madison, 8 May, n. 2, volume 15; (James Rood Robertson, ed., *Petitions of the Early Inhabitants of Kentucky to the General Assembly of Virginia, 1769–1792* [Louisville, Ky., 1914; reprint, Baltimore, Md., 1998], p. 140).

John Dawson to James Madison

You'll be pleased to accept my thanks for your two letters with the enclosures, which I received on thursday & saturday—by the papers I discover that the bill for fixing the Seat of Government &c. was not reported on Friday morning, and I have been assurd by a Gentleman *in this place*, that the committee appointd woud not bring it in untill they had collected, and *sworn in* all their forces—the same Gentleman inform'd that the bill was drawn ten days ago—if this is the fact, and their Design as stated, you'll be able to judge whether it will be expedient to hurry or procrastinate the business. Altho the policy of the delegates from this State is not relishd generally in this city, yet I believe they are encouraged by some few with whom they correspond—it is approvd off by the back [*country?*] members, now attending the assembly—& from thence an argument is drawn, that it will not only have a tendency to destroy all opposition to the fœderal goverment, but will enable those who are friendly to the measure to call a convention for the purpose of altering their state constitution—the last post brought no letters from New York, to those with whom I am in the habits of intimacy, I therefore am not able to collect what is the plan, and what the expectations of the members from this State.

On going into several circles in this place I found that an observation, which fell from you was the subject of general conversation—that it had excited the apprehensions of many, and the displeasure of some—being present at the time, and apprehending that what you said alluded to measures & not to particular persons, (in which I thought you were justified by the occasion) I had it in my power to contradict, as far as I recollectd, what was inserted in the paper, and am happy to find by Friday's paper, that my memory had not faild me.[1]

Actions must be right which proceed from friendly motives therefore there can be no impropriety in my making this communication to you; and in farther observing that I have it from good authority that there are some characters in New York, who have enterd into a combination, and will with avidity catch at any possible triffle to injure you, if possible in the public estimation—that they have asserted that all was peace or quiet on the subject of amendments untill the business was stir'd up by you; and however distant, have endeavourd to connect your conduct on *that*, with what you have said on the late occasion.

ALS, Madison Papers, DLC. Written from Philadelphia. Dated only "Sunday." Date supplied by internal evidence. The remainder of this letter was written on 14 September and is printed under that date. On the Madison Presidential Papers microfilm the letter is placed at 21 March 1790.

¹ Probably a reference to the *NYDG*, 11 September, reprint of *NYDA*'s 10 September elaboration of its 7 September coverage of the speech in question. See *DHFFC* 11:1413n.

Thomas Fitzsimons to Tench Coxe

Since the recet. your favor of the 8th. the business of residence has been suspended. as we expect every Kind of Opposition: it was thot. prudent to obtain from our legislature a Cession of the district which has accordingly been Applyd for. I hope proper pains is taking to get it Speedily. the want of it will certainly be made an Argument against us, tho I am not sure that the Obtaining it will insure our Success. there are three of the N. E. Members¹ absent While two of the Southern² have been called back. and as the New Yorkers have all the disposition that could be expected to disappoint every thing—We may yet fail in our Attempt. I believe however we shall get it thro our house and that they rely upon disappointing us in the Senate. the Opinions there are Various. So. Carolina wishes to remain here some others are averse from going to any distance from the Sea, and Jersey has in View the falls of Delaware. out of those Contrary Opinions it will be difficult to obtain a Concurrence in any one place. but I hope it is not impossible, and no pains is spared by us to bring that about.

The arrangement of the treasury department was Compleated Yesterday. Hamilton Secy. [*Nicholas*] Eveleigh of So. Carolina Compt[*rolle*]r. [*Samuel*] Meredith Treasurer. [*Oliver*] Wolcot [*Jr.*] of Connecticut. Auditor. . . the Policy seems to have been to divide them Among the States. I suspect too the President was not without difficulty in finding proper Characters. he wished to have men of such Characters and Abilitys as would have given dignity to the Offices and ensured a due execution of them At the same time, that the

States from whence they were taken Might be gratifyd but the Salarys are too Small to induce such men to leave their homes & to execute high Responsible offices for a Sum inadequate to their expences. this is the Consequence of too rigid an Oeconomy. if it prevails in the Same degree in the Judiciary, it may have the most injurious consequences— *** With Such Reforms Pennsylvania will grow into wealth and Importance even tho the seat of the Governmt. of the U.S. should not be placed in it but with that her progress will be Rapid. ***

As the business of this week will be very important you will probably hear Again from me if not I shall have the pleasure of seeing you in a [few?] days—our Session being very Near its end.

ALS, Coxe Papers, PHi. Addressed to Philadelphia. The omitted text discusses a new constitution for Pennsylvania and the new Assembly.

---

[1] Leonard, who did return, and Sedgwick and Sturges, who did not.
[2] White, who did return, and Huger, whose periodic absences continued.

Thomas Fitzsimons to Samuel Meredith

I have Just time before this person goes to mention that in Conseqe. of a Conversation with Cadwalader Mr. Clymer he & I are of Opinion you ought to come on Imm[editel]y. particularly if you mean to decline the last appointment Mr. Reade of Delaware Very wisely & as a friend got [*William*] McPhersons appointment put off in the senate, till you had made Your Election between the two—I am not sure that this will be in your power—~~if~~ but if you have any doubts As to the Acceptance the matter can be much better Negotiated by yourself than by a third person—Cadwr. tells me he has written you fully—yours with Mrs. [*Margaret*] M. good sense will better determine than any friend can for you—but you must guard Against giving offence to the Presidt. Whose friendship ought not to be hazarded. if you have made up your mind to Accept the Necessity of coming on will not be so urgent—in the other case you should set out in a few hours after the receit of this leav'g with [*Sharp*] Delanys consent—your business to the Care of some trusty person—in any event Make no *promise* or Engagement for the offices under you—in this appointment you will Need a very able Assistant. & you should look round before any is Engaged—I am sure you will forgive me the freedom of this Advice. I desired Mr. Clymer to mention the same thing to a person Who Called for a letter & intended to engage some preference—We have a bed at our Lodgings which may be more Convt. for you than going to any other place—because you can here consult yr.

friends without interruption—believ'g McPherson was appointed yesterday I wrote him to that Effect if you see him tell him I was Mistaken in haste.

ALS, Dreer Collection, PHi. The letter is dated "Sunday." Internal evidence indicates it was written on this date.

Benjamin Goodhue to Stephen Goodhue

I receiv'd yours of the 5th. and join with you in sentiments in thinking it is time the members should go home and see their Constituents, and when they come together again they would not be likely to be so wild as they now are, but I have my doubts whether the Southern members can ever be reclaimed—I am afraid the bussines which is intended to be finish'd before a recess will postpone our adjournt. beyond the 22d, but I hope not but if it should I hope not much longer—I suppose We shall be paid off either in Cash or partly in cash and partly in orders on the Collectors for our travel and attendance, I shall be able therefore doubtless to supply you pretty soon with a considerable sum if you should have occasion for it, its not worth while for you to write me after you receive this, for I may be on my return.

ALS, Goodhue Family Papers, MSaE. Addressed to Salem, Massachusetts.

Benjamin Goodhue to Samuel Phillips, Jr.

The session is drawing towards a close, tho' I think from the slowness of our doing bussines, and the quantum yet remaining to be finish'd, the time of adjournment may be prolonged ~~before~~ beyond the 22d instant, I veryly believe we shall have advanced quite as far in our public measures as will be found beneficial untill We have had an opportunity of seeing the effects likely to be produced and the sentiments of our constituents by an adjournment, indeed if We could have stop'd the progress of the compensation bills, untill the next session and in the mean time have passed a short resolution giving us a temporary supply of money (which I tryed to effect) there can be no doubt but on the return of the members, a bill for those purposes would have been perfected infinitely better suited to the circumstances and sentiments of our Country—I was in hopes by reason of a disagreement between the two Houses touching the discrimination which the Senate insisted should be made in their favour by giving them 7 dollrs. pr. day a while hence would have proved the death of the bill, but the perseverance of the Senate and the wants of the members, after several tryals bro't at length a majority of our house to an acquiescence—I was yesterday one of a Committee of conference with Morris & others from the Senate upon the pay of the V. Pre't the House had voted him 5000 and the Senate insisted upon 6,000, soon after We met, the members from the Senate observed this Officer was the second in rank in the United States, and consequently ought to be also the 2d in rank of pay &c. that it would be necessary to give our chief Justice 4 or 5000 dollars, and therefore it became necessary to raise the one in question, I observed to them I trusted it was by no means the sense of the House to give our Judges such salaries, and then detailed the sums given by the several States to such Officers, that even in Virginia the Judges had but 1000 dollars, and if We gave them double I conceived it would be quite sufficient that We must cut our coats according to our cloth &c. but such arguments have but a little avail with such Kind of characters who are ever talking of respectibility public tables parade &c. I told them the quantum which ought to govern us as necessary to give any person for performing the duties of any Office, never ought to exceed the sum which would purchase abilities and respectibility adequate thereto, and to give more would be as absurd as to give more for a commodity then the seller even asked or had any expectation of obtaining and no one could possibly doubt who had the least Knowledge of America but a choice might be had any where for half the sums which Congress have been in the practise of giving—but many of our members think or say that large salaries are necessary for supporting the dignity of government, tho' persons might be procured to perform the service for half the money, in short it has appear'd to me that a majority of Congress have ever since We met gone upon this idea that the Governm't was so firmly established, and their feet stood so secure that any indulgences however extravagant could never shake them, and its a great pity that the former Congresses gave such salaries, as too much to favour such an opinion, for they often say, the old Congress gave such and such sums, and why complain now—the truth is the old Congress were extravagant but the body of the people were ignorant of it—when I told Morris We must cut our coat according to our cloth and if We did not We should as certainly be ruined by such practises as an individual would, (which perhaps he took to himself) he answer'd me by saying that We had but just put our thumb upon the latch of revenue and the next session We should open the door which would supply easily all our wants, I asked him how, by a stamp duty of papers, Excises and if necessary a land tax—I told him he would find himself mistaken if he supposed the people of America would submit to such impositions for the purpose of feasting a few favourites in luxury and profusion, thus you see what the ideas of the greater part of Congress are with regard to salaries and I see no probability of correcting such conduct but their seeing such conduct reprobated by the general voice of their constituents, King was one of the conferees, We broke up as We came together—the Judicial bill after so many delays and interruptions is almost through a second reading without any material alteration as it came from the Senate—the Amendments have come from the Senate with amendments, such as striking out the word *vicinage* as applied to Jurors, and have struck out the limitation of sums for an appeal to the federal Court &c. those two have been the darling objects with the Virginians who have been the great movers in amendments, and I am suspicious, it may mar the whole bussines, at least so far as to refer it to the next session—the subject of permanent residence has lain a sleep for the week past and I should be happy if it were possible it could continue so for a great while to come, and I suspect it will terminate this session without a decission—all the Eastern members ever had in view in this bussines was to defeat a combination which had previously taken place with the pensylvanians to carry us to the Patowmack by some means or other, and if this can be effected by leaving the bussines unsettled or rather leaving it so disagreable to them as to make them intirely sick of the subject, our purposes and wishes will be compleatly answer'd We try'd all in our power to postpone it, but they were so sure of attaining their object with the aid of the Pensylvanians, that all arguments for that purpose were unavailing—I would not wish you to write me after the receipt of this letter, for before one from you could reach me I expect to leave this City for Salem where I should be extreamly happy to have you take a ride to visit him who is with unfeigned sentiments of regard.

[*P. S.*] I cannot excuse the absence of Strong and Sedgwick at this important period of our session, how they can justify it I don't know.

ALS, Phillips Family Papers, MHi. On this date Goodhue wrote an abbreviated version of this letter to the Insurance Offices of Salem (ALS, Goodhue Papers, NNS).

Christopher Gore to Rufus King

I am much obliged by your kind attention to the business with Colo. Hamilton—I shoud suffer great distress if I suppos'd he had any just cause to think as he did. the friends of the federal government, regret that so much time has been devoted to the subject of a permanent residence—before the government was organiz'd—what causes the delay of appointing the executive officers? We have been in the expectation of hearing the appointments every post the week past—and such is the celebrity of Colo. Hamilton's name in this part of the country that if he is appointed to the office of Secretary of the treasury, it will afford great joy to all—C[*harles*]. Jarvis—the Honesti[1]—& John [*James*] Winthrop are the only cavillers at the doings of Congress among us—and their influence is not so great as to cause any apprehensions.

ALS, King Papers, NHi. Written from Boston.

---

[1] The "Honesti" refers to those in agreement with a series of essays written, probably by Benjamin Austin, Jr., under the pseudonym "Honestus" and published in Boston's *Independent Chronicle* in 1786. They argued for legal reform and later became identified with Antifederalism (*DHROC* 4:392).

Thomas Hartley to Tench Coxe

I receved your Favor of the 9th. inst. and I could have wished the Gentlemen had been a little more guarded in the Arguments about the permanent Seat of Congress—but in Matters of this Kind & where Passions and Interests are so highly engaged an allowance must be made, and tho' some Gentlemen may be disappointed in their Views as to the Spots which should be selected for the permanent Seat and be irritated for the Moment yet if a judicious Position is taken, the Minds of the Union will be soon reconciled—and if the Banks of Susquehanna should be ~~chosen~~ preferred: the Inhabitants of the antient Dominion will in a few Months be fully sensible that they have suffered no great Injustice in the Choice.

The Members are getting in a better Humor with each other—but I immagine this will not last long—as soon as the Bill for fixing the permanent Seat is reported which will be to Morrow Morning—The Fire will rekindle.

We have suspended the Business for a few Days past waiting for some Act or Acts of your Assembly which have been wrote for—if we are obligd to go on without them, we run the greater Risque.

We have in a Committee of the whole gone through the judiciary Bill to the 29th. Sect. and to Morrow shall finished it in Committee. The Reporting will take a few Days longer—very few Alterations are made [*lined out*] from the Bill sent by the Senate & none that are essential—So that you may safely take it for granted, that the last Printed Bill for regulating the Judicial Courts of the United States, will in Substance be the Law. we expect to rise on the 22d. and it will perhaps be difficult to agree on a future Day for adjournment—but this is uncertain.

ALS, Coxe Papers, PHi. Addressed to Philadelphia.

Thomas Hartley to Jasper Yeates

I received your Favor of the 25th. ult. and am much obliged to you for the Trouble and Interest you take in my Concerns.

We have been engaged on the Business of fixing a Seat for the permanent ~~Seat~~ Residence of Congress. I have before hinted to you the immense Difficulties we had to encounter—we take the Field to Morrow on the same Subject and if our Troops stand firm we shall chuse a Spot not far from you. I must however again tell you that all is still uncertainty—so much Shifting—such Changing and so many various Interests jarring with each other puts every Thing a float I have been reconnoitring to Day and I really think our Affairs do not look bad All South of Potomack—4 from Maryland and 4 from Jersey are agst. us—and would you think it the Delaware State has also joined the Virginians—Vining is likely to play off another Carney[1] agst. Pennsylvania—3 of our New England Bretheren are away[2] we have sent for them I wish they would arrive in Time. The Southern Forces expect to defeat us by a Provisionary Clause about Clearing the Susquehanna and by saying the States of Pennsylvania and Maryland are to make Laws on the Subject and they immagine Maryland will not—upon that Question the two Marylanders[3] will probably leave us—If our three Eastern Men come on we shall be safe at all Points—otherwise there is Risque—The Judiciary Bill will pass nearly as I sent it to you—and we shall adjourn some Time this Month—I shall then set off Home and see you and my Friends as soon as possible—if we carry the Federal Seat for Pennsylvania we shall be in a good Humor—but if we are blown up we must sing small.[4]

ALS, Yeates Papers, PHi.

[1] An allusion to Dyre Kearney (d. ca. November 1791), a lawyer of Dover, Delaware, who represented that state in Congress in 1788 when he split the delegation's vote and lost Philadelphia its bid for the site of the meeting place of the First Congress (*Creation of D.C.*, p. 88).

[2] Leonard, Sedgwick, and Sturges.

[3] Smith and Seney.

[4] Cease boasting and assume a more withdrawn demeanor.

Richard Henry Lee to Francis Lightfoot Lee

Your letter of the 8th Ulto. has lain long unanswered because I have been absorbed about the Amendments to the Constitution. They have at length passed the Senate, with difficulty, after being much mutilated and enfeebled—It is too much the fashion now to look at the Rights of the People, as a Miser inspects a Security, to find out a flaw—What with design in some, and fear of Anarchy in others, it is very clear, I think, that a government very different from a free one will take place e'er many years are passed. It is very far from want of Knowledge that confines our Revenue to Impost—A little reflection will point you to other causes—The House of Rep. after much debate. have ordered in a Bill for fixing the permanent Seat of Government on the Susquehanna in Pennsylvania, and the temporary residence at this place. Evans,[1] after Nature, pointed out Potomac for the Seat of Empire—But Evans & Nature are nothing to the purpose N.H. to Pen. inclusive can, & will give law. The Treasury System is finished & all New Officers appointed— every one of the Old Commissioners are returned into private life—The Judiciary bill not yet thro the H. of R. *** A Resolve to adjourn on the 22d instant passed both Houses of our Congress some time ago, but 'tis plain now that it was premature—It will probably be early in October.

ALS, Park Collection, NjMoHP. For the full text, see *Lee* 2:500–501. The identification of the "Dear Brother" to whom this is written is from a nineteenth century transcription in the Lee Family Papers, ViHi. R. H. Lee included a list of the proposed salaries for federal officials. Part of the omitted text discusses the French Revolution; Lee observes that "The love of liberty has fled from hence to France."

[1] "A general Map of the Middle Colonies in America," published by the cartographer Lewis Evans (ca. 1700–1756) in 1755 and frequently pirated thereafter (*PGW: Confederation* 1:200n; E. M. Sanchez-Saavedra, *A Description of the Country: Virginia's Cartographers and Their Maps, 1607–1881* [Richmond, Virginia, 1975], p. 49).

Samuel Livermore to John Langdon

I recd. yours from Worcester & rejoycd to find you got on safe to that place. Mrs. [*Ruth*] Dalton & family arrived on Wednesday evening.

Gilman & [*Abiel*] Foster in spight of all my endeavours got the district courts divided between Portsmo. [*Portsmouth*] & Exeter. And afterwards attempted to carry the Circuit court from Portsmo. to Exeter altogether—in that they faild—We are in comtee. abt. two thirds through the bill & no great alteration. compensation bill for senate & house & their officers is past 6 dols. each—and the senate to have 7 dols. after 4th March 1795. Col. Hamilton is first L—d of the treasury.

ALS, Langdon Papers, NhPoA.

Robert Morris to Samuel Meredith

The President has given you unequivocal proof of his respect for your Character by this last nomination of you, which flowed spontaneously from his own mind without the instruction or even Suggestion of any of your Friends, and altho I have not had an opportunity to converse with him since Yet I am convinced that one of his motives for this measure was to Remove you from an Office which He considered as rather inconsistent with the Rank you have always held in Society. Mr. Clymer has supposed that you will not accept this Office of Treasurer and entertains doubts whether you ought to Accept it. for my part I think differently. my Opinion is that you ought to Accept it, if you wish to hold an office, it is highly honorable, the Duties easily performed, and the Salary altho not high, yet very respectable in Comparison with those which are generally allowed to other officers of this Government. The only objection is the Residence of Congress, should this be fixed on the Susquehannah you know how to live there from former experience if they go to the Banks of Potowmac it cannot make much difference: but should the Governmt. fix itself in the Northern Liberties your own House will probably be in the Heart of the Federal City, and if it fixes near the Falls of Delaware you can remove your Family there with as little inconvenience as any body, and notwithstanding all you see in the Newspapers about Susquehannah & Potomac, my own opinion is, that the Northern Liberties, or Falls of Delaware at this Moment Stand the best Chance, and that if one or other of those last mentioned places is not fixed for the permanent Residence, the chance in that case is that Philadelphia will be the place to which they will next adjourn. These however are mear matter of opinion, it is necessary that you determine immediately for in the Senate we have hung up Major [*William*] McPhersons Nomination in Suspence untill Your Acceptance or refusal shall be known, otherwise if we had approved him and you had declined the Treasury you would have been Superceded. I believe the President expects your acquiescence but I am sure he would not wish to force your inclination. at all events I should think it very adviseable for you to come here immediately where upon the best information you can judge and determine for yourself. ***

ALS, Read Family Papers, PPL at PHi. In the omitted text Morris says he hopes to be in Philadelphia in ten or twelve days.

Robert Morris to Richard Peters

If Mr. Clymer had acquainted me at the time He wrote you to get a Law passed immediately for the purpose of making a Cession of ten Miles Square in any part of the State, that Congress might be disposed to accept for the place of permanent Residence, I should have added a letter on the Same Subject; not that I should expect more attention to my letter than to his but as He & I have entertained different Ideas, as to the place to be fixed on, the Contents of both letters holding forth different objects would unite in shewing the propriety and necessity of such a Law.

I have constantly had it in my intention to get the General Government Seated as near to the City of Philadelphia as possible and if the State Convention had not made a reserve of the City,[1] I should have tried for that in preference to any other Position. My Aim now is to fix them in the district adjoining the Northern Liberties on the line described by the Convention and altho I shall Vote in the Senate in the first instance for Susquehannah (the reasons for this Vote I will explain when we meet) yet I expect that Vote. will not carry it, and that a second will settle the matter in the Neighbourhood of our City or at Germantown or failing of this that a third Vote will fix it on the Banks of the Delaware near the Falls, this last decision if effected will be by the Jersey delegation's refusing to Vote for the Northern Liberties, but I have already got assurances from Some of them that they will Consent, to go to Germantown or some where in that district.

Pensylvania holds the balance at this Moment between the Southern & Eastern interests and if she delays, she will loose the power of fixing the Government within her own boundaries, an early Adoption of the Constitution by North Carolina inevitably Carries us to the Potomac, a Speedier Adoption of Rhode Island & Vermont, fixes us forever where we now are, therefore the present is our time & the only danger to which we are now opened is a Coalition of the Southern & Eastern Members to pass off the matter without doing any thing, each may be induced to this in the expectation of being the first that will by the Accession of their Neighbours be strengthened in the Two Houses so as to decide according to their own Will. At present they are jealous of, and Angry at each other; their passions are engaged; delay is therefore dangerous to our Views; and the present delay is occasioned by the want of the Law for which Mr. Clymer has applied. Urged it along therefore as fast as you can, those Members of Assembly who favour the Banks of Susquehannah will be for pushing the Law and those who wish it nearer to Philada. must believe in me, altho I do not profess to be Sanguine in my expectations yet I do not despair, and I will leave nothing undone on my part to carry my point. I think you will do well to communicate the Contents of this letter only to such Members as would wish the Federal Governmt. near the City or at the Falls of Delaware.
***

The Judicial Bill is Working its way Slowly through the House of Representatives They have a Number of Lawyers that keep Snarling at it, but I fancy they are too Lazy or too Weak to make a bold Attack on it, they must propose a better or pass this previous to the adjournment which will take place on the 22d of this Month.

The Amendments to the Constitution are done with in the Senate but altered from those passed by the House they are what Centinel calls them, "a Tub for the whale."[2]

In spite of Doctor [*George*] Logan, Centinel,[3] & all other discontents I have voted for the highest Salaries well knowing that the Public is best served when they pay well.

ALS, Peters Papers, PHi.

---

[1] The same day it ratified the Constitution (15 December 1787), the Pennsylvania convention passed a resolution offering to cede to the new federal government for its seat any jurisdiction in the state not exceeding ten miles square, excepting the city of Philadelphia, the district of Southwark, and most of the "Northern Liberties," present day Kensington (*DHROC* 2:612).

[2] See Clymer to Peters, 8 June, n. 1, volume 16.

[3] Samuel Bryan, writing as "Centinel Revived No. XXIX," [Philadelphia] *Independent Gazetteer*, 9 September, attacked high Congressional salaries.

OTHER DOCUMENTS

Abraham Baldwin to Joel Barlow. AL, Baldwin Family Collection, CtY.
   Appointments; John Rutledge or John Jay will probably be chief justice; "The Senate has concurred in the greater part of our proposed amendments of constitution, they have struck out three or four of the worst. The old subject of permanent seat of government has bewitched us again for several weeks"; provisions of the pending Seat of Government Bill; "We shall probably adjourn for two months on or about the 22d."

Erkuries Beatty to Josiah Harmar. ALS, Harmar Papers, MiU-C.
   Knox expects Congress to appropriate money for the army this week; appointments.

Lambert Cadwalader to Samuel Meredith. ALS, Berol Collection, NNC. Dated "Sunday Noon," and further dated from internal and external evidence.
   Had just written a long letter to Meredith, "but this Instant Fitzsimons came in and it is his Opinion and mine that you come here without Delay"; "Make no Promises to any Person to be employed under you—it is necessary you have the best Person you can get if you should be the Treasr. of the U. States."

Thomas Fitzsimons to Benjamin Rush. Summary of ALS, *Parke-Bernet Catalog* 499(1944):item 117.
   "On political and civic affairs. Relates to establishment of the seat of government at Philadelphia, government finances, activities in Congress; etc."

Richard Henry Lee to Mann Page, Jr. No copy known; dated from the endorsement on Page to Lee, 23 July.

Edmund Randolph to James Madison. ALS, Madison Papers, DLC. Written from Williamsburg, Virginia. For the full text, see *PJM* 12:401.
> Promising to "enter upon and complete the statement of my introductory ideas" at the Federal Convention.

Theodore Sedgwick to Peter Van Schaack. ALS, Van Schaack Papers, NNC. Written from Stockbridge, Massachusetts; addressed to Kinderhook, New York.
> Friends wished him to be present for the seat of government question; is too unwell to go without risking his health, but has not decided yet; may leave in the morning.

Jeremiah Wadsworth to Oliver Wolcott, Jr. ALS, Wolcott Papers, CtHi. Addressed to Hartford, Connecticut. For the full text, see *Wolcott* 1:21.
> Wishes Wolcott had been nominated comptroller rather than auditor, as does Hamilton; refrain from hiring clerks until arriving in New York City; in a postscript, "I shall say nothing about your refusal, but let your appointment go forward. Mr. Trumbull & my selfe both gave our Opinions before that you would not accept."

Daniel Hiester, Account Book. PRHi.
> Trip to Flatbush with P. Muhlenberg.

From New York. [Boston] *Massachusetts Centinel*, 19 September; reprinted in Portsmouth, New Hampshire, and Worcester, Massachusetts.
> Of the permanent seat of government, "it is said, that the spot which will probably be chosen, is like the *Garden of Eden*"; if an officer, under the Salaries-Executive Act, "should have six or seven hundred pounds, it would be thought moderate; but two thousand dollars *sound* loud and alarming."

Letter from New York. [Portland, Maine] *Cumberland Gazette*, 25 September. This is probably from a letter written by Thatcher to the newspaper's editor, Thomas B. Wait.
> Congress has raised the compensation of Senators to seven dollars per day.

MONDAY, 14 SEPTEMBER 1789

Cool (Johnson)

John Adams to John Lowell

I received your Letter of the 7th. in due Season and have delayed my Answer, in hopes it might be more determinate. I have received also Letters from Governor [*James*] Bowdoin and Mr. [*Stephen*] Higginson on the Same Subject. The Contents of these Letters appeared to me of Such Importance, that I thought it my Duty to lay them before the President, as [*in*]formation that he ought to be possessed of; since which I have had more than one personal Conference with him on the Subject. What his decision will be I am not able to say. Applications and Recommendations and Representations are made to him from all Parties. Mr. H. [*John Hancock*] & Mr. A. [*Samuel Adams*] are not Silent, any more than others who are more zealous for the new Govt. The President examines and weighs with great Attention and Care, and determines according to Principles which he has laid down for himself, which in general are good & wholesome. For my Part, I am So clearly convinced, of the Necessity of an *Unity* in the Executive Authority of Government, and of the Propriety of having all Appointments vested in one Breast, that I wish my Friends would excuse me from interferring on any Occasion. The Daily Labour, of my Attendance in Senate, is fatiguing, the delicacy of finding proper times to converse with the President, on appointments, renders it difficult, and after all, my information can be but partial, when his is compleat. Especially as I am to be made the Scape Goat, on whom all the sins of Unpopularity are to be laid. My Exertions for [*Benjamin*] Lincoln, have torn open an hornets Nest at Boston, and my Vote for the Presidents Power of Removal, according to the Constitution, has raised from Hell an host of political and poetical Devils.

I have waited on the President expressely in behalf of our Friend [*Jonathan*] Jackson: He listenened Attentively to all my Representations: but I found that other Characters were in contemplation, meritorious Officers in the late Army and amiable Men, it must be confessed.

***

ALS, Pequot Deposit, The Beineke Rare Book and Manuscript Library, CtY. Recipient identified from the letterbook copy, Adams Family Manuscript Trust, MHi.

George Clymer to Tench Coxe

When I left home the affair of a [*state constitutional*] Convention appeared in tolerably good train, and I rejoice to hear that appearances still mend— Our fellow citizens mendicate on the subject of the Susquehanna—I never imagined they ought to have been displeased. If the position of a federal town is to have effect upon industry population and the value of property, it cannot admit of a doubt in the mind of any man but that the waters of the Susquehanna are a much nobler and promising subject than those of the Delaware—And so much more would the state at large benefit by the one position than the other—I doubt whether the City would not also be more benefited, for as a defensive measure the navigation between Schuylkill and the Suitara [*Swatara*] must be immediately attempted, and that once compleated would not every article from the river above and all the vast branches of the Susquehanna be secured to Philada.—Were the natural bed of the river below ~~be~~ improved to tolerable navigation which perhaps is impracticable I should suppose it would always be deserted for the other. A permanent residence whenever determined on will be a subject of great discontent, but I do not suppose of disunion—The Virginia pride is at present much hurt and heaven and earth will be moved, but they will never be able to bring us to the Potowmack—The post just going.

[*P. S.*] A bill will be reported this morning for the Susquehanna.

ALS, Coxe Papers, PHi. Addressed to Philadelphia. Endorsed as written on 13 September but Clymer dated it "Monday." This and the postscript suggests it was written on 14 September.

John Dawson to James Madison

On yesterday I din'd at Mr. [*William*] Hamilton's in company with ten or twelve gentlemen most of them persons of some political chara[c]ter—the subject of fixing the Seat of government was brought on the carpet, and the policy of the members from this State highly reprobated; indeed they had but one advocate Mr. C——e [*Tench Coxe*]—it was considerd that they had given up an immediate certain advantage for a distant and very doubtful one—I took the liberty to mention, in private to three or four that if there Sentiments were as they had declar'd it woud be well to communicate them to their representatives for they might be mistaken as to the wishes of the city—They all assur'd me that they woud by this mornings post—This circumstance may perhaps render Fitzsimons & Company less anxious.

I took the liberty of hinting to you some time since that an appointment under the goverment woud not be disagreeable to me—since then I had re-linquishd the Idea, and therefore have mention'd it to no person—but some circumstances have revivd the wish—We are told that Mr. Hamilton is nom-inated a Scy. to the Treasury—Mr. Evely [*Nicholas Eveleigh*] Compr. and Mr. [*Samuel*] Meredith Treasr. but have not heard the the Auditor or Regis-ter is appointd—if this is the case, and there is a probability of succeeding I will thank you to name [*me*] to the President for one of the offices, and I woud prefer the latter—Shoud the appointments be made it will be unnec-essary to make known my wish on the subject.

ALS, Madison Papers, DLC. Written from Philadelphia. Dated "Monday." Date supplied by internal evidence. The beginning of this letter was written on 13 September and is printed under that date. On the Madison Presidential Papers microfilm the letter appears at 21 March 1790.

Elbridge Gerry to John Wendell

The conduct of Vermont as stated in your letter of the 23d of July is ex-traordinary: but I think no disadvantage can finally accrue to citizens of other States holding lands in that State: or to citizens thereof holding under grants of different States, for they State must become part of the Union & in that event the illegal proceedings of their courts will be reversed & damages decreed by a federal court on the cases mentioned.

Whether the present constitution will preserve its theoretical ballance, for I consider it altogether as a political experiment, & if should, what will be the effect, or if it should not, to what system it will verge, are secrets that can only be unfolded by time: as to the amendments proposed by Congress, they will not affect those questions or serve any other purposes than to rec-oncile those who had no adequate idea of the essential defects of the Consti-tution. I shall however console myself with the reflection, that should the consequences be injurious or ruinous, nothing has been wanting on my part in [*the Federal*] Convention or Congress to prevent them.

The State laws for electing representatives must be altered so as to pre-serve some uniformity & more punctuality in forming a Congress, the failure of which in march last has been very much felt by the Union. the estimate for the current year of 8 million will be increased by an equal sum arising from the arrearages of interest due to the 31 Decr. 1787. but 16 millions dol-lars cannot be paid by the revenue of this year, for the impost & tonnage to the 31st of Decr. next will not exceed 800,000 dollars & we shall be obliged next year to make principal of the greatest part of the Interest now due; which will enhance the annual estimate to upwards of four million dollars which is double the sum that will be realized by the impost & tonnage. Congress have established a Financier & I expect at the next session he will offer his plans for supplying the deficiencies—whether this will be effected by loans excises or direct taxes time must determine—What will be done with the old or new emission of Congress, the expences of the penobscot expedition &c. &c., I know not, for other concerns which have required a more immediate attention have absorbed the time of Congress, during the present Session.

The judicial bill is now under consideration of Congress. this department I dread as an awful tribunal. by its institution the Judges are compleatly independent, being secure of their salaries & removeable only by impeachment, not being subject to discharge on the address of both Houses as is the case in G. Britain—the courts have cognizance of common law equity & exchequer causes & also those of maritime & admiralty jurisdiction: their power also extends to criminal cases, & notwithstanding the supreme Court has original cognizance of causes that will affect the lives liberty & property of the citizens & there is no appeal from this tribunal; they are not only a court of law but also of equity.

Congress have agreed, alias the House to fix the federal city on the Susquehannah & to borrow 100,000 dollars to begin the work: this will cost at least half a million dollars, & for this reason & because if the city must be built new, it can be raised without expence to the people by placing it on the Delaware, I voted against it—indeed at all events I am against such idle modes of spending money previously to the establishment of publick credit.

ALS, Fogg Collection, MeHi.

Richard Henry Lee to Patrick Henry

I have written two letters to you since my receipt of <yours> dated March the 23d., both which I enclosed to our friend <Mr. George> Fleming at Richmond, and he has informed me of <their safe> arrival, and that he had forwarded them to you. <I have> since waited to see the issue of the proposed amend<men>ts to the Constitution, that I might give you the most <exact> account of that business.[1] As they came from the <H. of> R. they were very far short of the wishes of our Convention, but as they are returned by the Senate they are certainly much weakened. You may be assured that nothing on my part was left undone to prevent this, and every possible effort was used to give success to all the Amendments proposed by our Country—We might as well have attempted to move Mount Atlas upon our shoulders— In fact, the idea of Subsequent Amendments was delusion altogether, and so intended by the greater part of those who arrogated to themselves the name of Federalists. I am grieved to see that too many look at the Rights of the people as a Miser examines a Security to find a flaw in it! The great points of free election, Jury trial in criminal cases much loosened, the unlimited right of Taxation, and Standing Armies in peace, remain as they were. Some valuable Rights are indeed *declared*, but the powers that remain are very sufficient to render them nugatory at pleasure.

<The> most essential danger from the present System arises, <in my> opinion, from its tendency to a Consolidated government, instead of a Union of Confederated States—The history of the world and reason concurs in proving that so extensive a Territory <as the> U. States comprehend never was, or can be governed in freed<om> under the former idea—Under the latter it is abundantly m<ore> practicable, because extended representation, knowledge <of> characters, and confidence in consequence, <secure that good> opinion of Rulers, without which, *fear* the offspri<ng of force> can alone answer. Hence Standing Armies, and des<potism> follows. I take this reasoning to be unrefutable, a<nd> therefore it becomes the friends of liberty to guard <with> perfect vigilance every right that belongs to the Sta<tes> and to protest against every invasion of them—taking ca<re> always to procure as many protesting States as possible—This kind of vigilance will create caution and probably establish such a mode of conduct as will create a system of precedent that will prevent a Consolidating effect from taking place by slow, but sure degrees. And also not to cease in renewing their efforts for so amending the federal Constitution as to prevent a Consolidation by securing the due Authority of the States. At present perhaps a sufficient number of Legislatures cannot be got to agree in demanding a Convention—But I shall be much mistaken if a great sufficiency will not, e'er long concur in this measure. The preamble to the Amendments is realy curious—A careless reader would be apt to suppose that the amendments desired by the States had been graciously granted. But when the thing done is compared with that desired, nothing can be more unlike. The Southern Indians having repeatedly declared the little confidence they had in the justic<e of the bor>dering States, it was thought that sending Commissioners <from> hence to treat with them, who were totally unconnec<ted> with the parties and their disputes, would be the most <likel>y way to gain the Indian confidence, and thereby <obtain a> secure and lasting peace—Upon this idea, three <gentleme>n have been sent from hence to treat with the <Creek>s, where probably some measures may be taken with <the> Cherokees also— In this mode of doing business, there <was> no opportunity for suggesting Gen. [*Joseph*] Martin—And those <gen>tlemen who have gone, are only appointed pro hac vice,[2] to return here when the treaty is over. It is probable that this Treaty will end in a large cession of Territory to Georgia, which may cause a cession of some part to the U. States. In either case, those who

choose, may have an opportunity of obtaining grants in that country, said to be a very fine one. As the laws that have passed Congress this Session will all be sent to Richmond, where I am happy to hear that you will be on the Assembly, it is unnecessary for me to say any thing of them in this letter, already I fear too long. I have endeavored successfully in the Judiciary bill to remedy, so far a<s> law can remedy, the defects of the Constitution in that line. It is now proposed to adjourn on the 22d. instant, but I think it will be the last of the month at least before this event takes place—And when it does, I shall return to Virga. and lay up for the Winter Season which is pretty uniformly my Gouty <Seas>on—I am sure that nothing I write politically <to yo>u will be improperly communicated.

[*P. S.*] By comparing the Senate Amendments, with <those> from below by, carefully attending to the m<atter> the former will appear well calculated to enfeeble <and> produce ambiguity—for ~~Rights~~ instance—Rights rese<rved> to the States or the *People*—The people here is evidently designed fo<r the> People of the *United States*, not of the Individual states [*torn*] the former is the Constitutional idea of people—*We the People* &c. It was affirmed the Rights reserved by the States bills of Rights did not belong to the States—I observed that then they belonged to the people of the States, but that this mode of expressing was evidently *calculated* to give the Residuum to the people of the U. States, which was the Constitutional language, and to deny it to the people of the Indiv. State—At least that it left room for cavil & false construction—They would not insert after people thereof—altho it was moved.

ALS, Henry Papers, DLC. Unitalicized words in angle brackets are taken from historian Charles Campbell's pre-Civil War transcript in the Hugh Blair Grigsby Papers, ViHi. The bracketed words in the first two sentences are taken from *Lee* 2:501–4.

---

[1] Immediately after Lee's election to the Senate, Henry wrote him regarding this issue, "I firmly believe—the *American Union depends on the Sucess* of Amendments" (ALS, 15 Nov. 1788, Henry Papers, DLC; for the full text, see *DHFFE* 2:374–75).

[2] For this occasion only.

James Madison to Edmund Pendleton

I was favd. on saturday with yours of the 2d instant. The Judiciary is now under consideration. I view it as you do, as defective both in its general structure, and many of its particular regulations. The attachment of the Eastern members, the difficulty of substituting another plan, with the consent of those who agree in disliking the bill, the defect of time &c. will however prevent any radical alterations. The most I hope is that some offensive violations of Southern jurisprudence may be corrected, and that the system may speedily undergo a reconsideration under the auspices of the Judges who alone will be able perhaps to set it to rights.

The Senate have sent back the plan of amendments with some alterations which strike in my opinion at the most salutary articles. In many of the States juries even in criminal cases, are taken from the State at large—in others from districts of consider[*able*] extent—in very few from the County alone—~~The~~ Hence a [*dis*]like to the restraint with respect to *vicinage*, which has produced a negative on that clause. A fear of inconvenience from a constitutional bar to appeals below a certain value, and a confidence that such a limitation is not *necessary*, have had the same effect on another article. Several others have had a similar fate. The difficulty of uniting the minds of men accustomed to think and act differently can only be conceived by those who have witnessed it.

A very important [*lined out*] question is depending on the subject of a permanent seat for the fedl. Govt. Early in the Session secret negociations were set on foot among the Northern States from Penna. inclusively. The parties finally disagreeing in their arrangements, both made advances to the Southern members. On the side of N.Y. & N. Engd. we were led to expect the Susquehannah within a reasonable time, if we wd. sit still in N. York, otherwise we were threatened with Trenton. These terms were inadmissible to the friends of Potowmac: On the side of Penna. who was full of distrust and animosity agst. N. Engd. & N. York, the Potowmac was presented as the reward for the temporary advantages if given by the S. States. Some progress was made on this ground, and the prospect became flattering, when a reunion was produced among the original parties by circumstances which it wd. be tedious to explain. The Susquehanah has in consequence been voted. The bill is not yet brought in and many things may yet happen. We shall parry any decision if we can, tho' I see little hope of attaining our own object, the Eastern States being inflexibly opposed to the Potowmac & for some reasons which are more likely to grow stronger than weaker—and if we are to be placed on the Susquehannah, the sooner the better.

ALS, Madison Papers, DLC.

James Read to George Read

***

There is a clause in the coasting Bill (Sect. 27) which gives great uneasiness to the Merchants and traders here; its operation will be very injurious to the Commerce of this city, without affording any benefit (that I can perceive) to the United States. I cannot discover the policy of oblidging vessels of 20 tons or upwards to make an entry at the Custom house every time they arrive, before they can unlade their Cargo, when Vessels under that burthen carrying on the same traffic may trade for a year under one licence or permit. I can account for the Clause on no other principle, than that the Legislature supposed, the River trade was wholly carried on in Vessels under twenty tons, but the fact is otherwise, I believe I am safe in saying that more than two thirds of the Vessels alluded to are above that burthen, Some will measure more than 30 tons, particularly what we call the Flour shallops, the restriction will injure that business in a very great degree; it is very frequent that five, six or more such Vessels arrive in one tide in the Night, and when trade is brisk they will all be unloaded and gone for another Cargo before eight oClock the next morning, whereas under the operation of the Clause in question, at least one half of the day will be spent before they all can be entered at the Custom House, especially if other Vessels had arrived in evening before them, who would claim the right of prior entry; wherefore all those Shallops as well as the vessels which are to receive their Cargo's on Board, with the people employed in them, must remain idle until manifests can be received at the Custom House, and permits granted to unload. I flatter myself that upon receiving proper information, Congress will not hesitate to repeal a any Clause which should appear to impose unnecessary restraints upon the trade and industry of their fellow Citizens; I understand the Merchants and traders have had a meeting and agreed to address a Memorial to Congress on this subject.

ALS, Rodney Collection of Read Papers, DeHi. Written from Philadelphia, with an unidentified enclosed letter.

William Smith (Md.) to Otho H. Williams

Yours by Mr. [*John*] White I duly recd. which gave me the pleasure of hearing you were all well.

The inclosed papers will give you the news of this place. Much has been said respecting the seat of government, and I am not sure but it will end in wind for the present Session. The N. Yorkers & Eastern members I believe repent, that they consented to go as far south as susquehannah, & the Pennsila. or rather the Phila. members, are much alarmed at an amendment offerd to the Motion. To Wit, that they Should be obliged, or at least consent to the Navigation of the Susquehannah being opened to Chesopeake. one of those gentlemen declared in the house, that he would rather loose the bill that than consent thereto. The committee appointed to report a bill will probably bring it in to day. Should any difference arise on this occasion, the

consequence will either be a postponement this Session or a Coalition for Some place on the Delaware (for Potomack has no chance). The Philadelphians are not quite Satisfied with Susquehana. the Virginians much opposed to it. & the eastern men luke warm, thinkg. they have consented to go too far.
***

The Judiciary plan is now under consideration & will probably, take up the greatest part of the time of the house till an adjournment takes place, which I expect will be about the last of this month, & I hope to See my friends in Baltimore early in October.

P. S. Should your brother [*Elie Williams*] & Mr. [*Robert*] Elliot offer for the Victualling contract I have no doubt, the payments will be tollerably punctual perhaps drafts on the collectors, will be given.

ALS, Williams Papers, MdHi. Addressed to Baltimore. The omitted text lists the officers nominated to the treasury department.

George Thatcher to George Washington

I take the liberty of handing to you the names of two Gentlemen either of whom, in my opinion will make [*a*] respectable District Judge for the District of Maine—viz. the Honourable David Sewal—& William Lithgow Junr. The former was appointed one of the Judges of the Supreme Judicial Court; for the Commonwealth of Massachusetts, about the year 1776—which office he has sustained to the present time—He lives at York in the District of Maine.

The latter is a respectable Attorney at Law of about thirteen years standing he lives at Hollowel on Kennebeck River He served four or five years in the Army—where he lost the use of his right arm by a ball he recieved in an engagement with the enemy—He is now Major General of the Militia in the eastern Division of Massachusetts.

Should the former be appointed Judge in Maine District—the latter appears to me the most suitable person in that District for the Attorney to the United States in the said District—But if the latter be appointed Judge, I wish to mention Daniel Davis of Portland as a suitable person for the Attorney in that District.

I further take the liberty of recommending Joshua Bailey Osgood as a proper person for the Marshall in Maine District. His situation at Portland or Biddeford will accommodate the District—His property education & ~~reputation~~ general Character, where they are known, I believe, will fully justify this recommendation.

ALS, Washington Papers, DLC.

Paine Wingate to Samuel Hodgdon

I will trouble you with ~~one of~~ another letter for Mr. [*Timothy*] Picker-ing—I hope to leave this city about the middle of next week—The com-pensations granted by Congress are agreeable to the wishes of the southern gentlemen generally, but much against my opinion. The sentiments of the public, and the consequences of our excessive liberality remain yet to be known—You have heard no doubt of our late appointments to offices. Mr. [*Michael*] Hillegas is extremely disappointed & troubled. If Mr. [*Samuel*] Meredith shall accept of his office Mr. [*William*] McPherson will be Surveyor at Philadelphia. I doubt whether the bill for a permanent residence of Con-gress will be compleated this session. I wish that Congress was fixed at Phila-delphia and an end put to that disagreeable dispute.

ALS, Timothy Pickering Papers, MHi. Addressed to Philadelphia.

Paine Wingate to Timothy Pickering

*** I have not had any letters from Salem lately, but hear from there every week by Mr. Goodhue that our friends are all well. I hope next week to leave this place for home. I do not know what political news to tell you & suppose that you see in the newspapers the chief of what we have here. There has been a mighty struggle, & not a little heat in the house of Representatives re-specting the permanent residence of Congress. They have by a bare major-ity ordered a bill to be brought in for fixing it on the Susquehannah & to appropriate one hundred thousand dollars to provide the accommodations. After all I think it doubtful whether it will pass that house, and it is more doubtful in the Senate. I begin to be of opinion that it will not be expedient to attempt a federal town until the states are more united upon that subject, as well as upon some others, and unless the accommodations can be provided without considerable expence to the union. We seem disposed to contrive other ways enough for the public money without applying any of it to that, or to paying the national debt. I now believe that if we should remove Con-gress to Philadelphia, which I am ready to give my vote for, that all parties will be tollerably satisfyed, except the citizens of New York and that we should be likely to remain quietly there for some time until circumstances should turn up more favorable to a general harmony as to residence. That we shall adjourn there at the close of the present session is possible but not probable. We could compass it if the southern Gentle men were united & I think we shall never be quiet until that takes place.

*** You will observe the old officers in the treasury are drop'd except [*Joseph*] Nourse. How they are affected by those appointments I have not heard, excepting Mr. [*Michael*] Hilligas who is exceedingly disappointed. The Secretary of State is not yet nominated. The reason of that I conclude is that Mr. Jay is designed for chief Justice when the birth is provided, if the emoluments should be better than the place he now holds. It is suspected that Mr. Morris has the ear of the President as much or more than any man. How it is or where the influence lies I can not say, nor do I care if that influence is not abused. It was the ardent wish of many that you should have been in some of those important departments. But I cannot say further. I have thought the place of district Judge might be very proper for you, as it will properly fall to one of your profession & be simular to that office you held in Massachusetts in the maritime court. It will be respectable with a permanent & liberal Salary in the road to the other court. Who are destined for the favorites of the court I know not. Kissing goes by favour and it is very possible that sedulous courtiers or their friends may get in; to the exclusion of more deserving men I have no other wish than to see the best men for ability & integrity promoted. It is yet uncertain whether the judi[*ci*]al officers will be appointed in this session or what will be their Salaries. It is generally expected they will be appointed and that their salaries will be large. For my part I may be too œconomical perhaps; but the salaries to ourselves & to the officers in general are in my opinion much larger than would purchase the best abilities & larger than the circumstances of the Country will afford, & such as I expect will give great disgust in New England. I will not trouble you on this subject, time will decide the question & who have been the promoters & aiders the journals of Congress will shew. The Amendments are not yet done with. I believe amendments in Congress are as much wanted as in the constitutions. But it is dangerous to grumble so long as all our doings are popular. & I have not room to add any more if I wished. I shall not have time to hear from you after you receive this before the recess. I probably may return here the beginning of Decr. & shall be happy to receive your communications as often as maybe.

ALS, Pickering Papers, MHi. Part of the omitted text is a list of the officers nominated to the treasury department. For the full text, see *Wingate* 2:332–34.

Henry Wynkoop to Reading Beatty

***
You see the Officers of the Treasury Department except Mr. [*Joseph*] Nourse are all new Men; This is the Machine that must give life & Vigour to every thing & no Doubt the President is posessed with good Reasons to satisfy himself in making this Revolution in the management of our money Affairs; I pitty poor [*Michael*] Hillegas.

Am just going to the Presidents, in Company with the Pensylvanians in Town, to present the Adress of the Legislature of our State.

The Judiciary is the present Subject of Discussion, the Bill respecting the permanent Seat is not yet reported, tho' probably will be this day, it's fate not perfectly certain, the probabillity is in favour of it's Success.

ALS, Wynkoop Papers, PDoBHi.

OTHER DOCUMENTS

John Adams to John Warren. FC:lbk, Adams Family Manuscript Trust, MHi.
   Office seeking: hospital department of the army; promises support, but advises he write to Knox.

Nicholas Van Staphorst & Hubbard to John Adams. LS, Adams Family Manuscript Trust, MHi. Written from Amsterdam.
   A European war would benefit greatly American commerce and credit in Europe; as Adams is "the Parent of the American Credit in this Country," forwarding a copy of a letter by the Dutch commissioners of the American loan to the secretary of the treasury "more early perhaps than you wod. know thro' your official Channel"; future loans will be easily raised.

Hugh Williamson to William Samuel Johnson. *NYDA*, 29 October; reprinted at New Haven, Connecticut; Philadelphia; and Edenton, North Carolina; see [Philadelphia] *Federal Gazette*, 10 November and 30 December for comment on the letter.
   On the role of Latin and Greek in American education.

TUESDAY, 15 SEPTEMBER 1789

Cool. Rain (Johnson)

Fisher Ames to Caleb Strong

A man so much a patriot as you are must feel some pain that your aid is withdrawn from the transaction of the very important business which has occupied us since your departure from N. York.

The discrimination in the pay of the Senate was a question which your house considered as summoning all their Spirit to contend pro aris & focis[1]—The importance of it seemed to me strangely overrated by both houses—and yet the principle has always satisfied my mind as a proper one, and is analogous to our State practice. The Amendments too have been amended by the Senate, & many in our house, Mr. Madison, in particular, thinks, that they have lost much of their Sedative Virtue by the alteration A contest on this subject between the two houses would be very disagreeable. I thought so in regard to the pay, & therefore I am glad that the point was compromised by a limitation of the Bill—The Bill is a bad one, & one part of it exposes the other—and yet our house was so divided between the discrimination which many eastern people were for, & the high rate of pay which they were agt. that I do not see how the affair could have been ended so well. Had the two houses contended, the public would not have maintained a philosophic neutrality and the newspapers wd. be the Beacons to alarm & set the world on fire—whether in case of voting no pay, the non attendance of members at the next session wd. not delay business & cost more money than the odds in controversy you will judge—On the whole, I wish a speedy repeal of the Bill, as in some respects it is totally wrong, & in all respects imprudent at this time.

The permanent residence has been as fruitful of speeches parties & delays as that vile subject has formerly been. But as fate decrees that we must decide upon it, we prefer'd the Susquehannah Here again, danger occurs, For the river is now obstructed by Bars, & Philadelphia is not fond of having them removed—Whether a proviso in the Bill, that Acts shall pass allowing this to be done, will not ruin the Bill by setting the supporters of it by the ears is very doubtful. It is probable the whole business will be thrown into confusion & whether, in the scuffle, Philadelphia will not be voted as the place to meet in next, cannot be foretold. Mr. Sedgwick has run away— *you* will pass a light censure on his desertion. But we think it an heinous thing—for we need his manly sense.

The Judicial is passing rapidly We are yet in the dark whether our friend, L. [*John Lowell*] will be promoted to the Bench. The prest. is profoundly secret in his Movements.

You see I write as fast as I can.

P. S. You left me in your debt. I wd. have given twice the sum inclosed to have seen you—We fully expect the Adjournment will take place next Tuesday—tho a good deal of business remains in our house. The Senate is nearly at leisure.

ALS, Thompson Collection, Hartford Seminary Foundation, Hartford, Connecticut. Addressed to Northampton, Massachusetts; marked by Ames, "To be left at Post Office in Springfield."

---

[1] For God and country.

George Clymer to Richard Peters

Your express with the law of cession arrived about noon.[1] This we consider as a good event and will give us the more spirits to go on with the bill which was reported yesterday—and Thursday, this morning, appointed for going into a Committee upon it—We hope to have by that time a small reenforcement of New-England which will throw the odds more on our side—These we shall want to fend off the Maryland clause, which if to be renewed in any thing like its first form we must reject at all hazards. We hope however the attempt will not be renewed as we can shew it not to be necessary from a copy of the Act of some years standing appointing Commrs. to receive contributions for opening the river downwards.[2] If this should satisfy Smith of Baltimore and Senie of the Eastern Shore who are earnest in the bill with us—and who would be sorry to risque the loss of it we shall be able to throw out such a clause.

Your express waiting below for a few lines certifying that he had performed his service I have only to add my satisfaction at the present fair prospect of the State [*constitutional*] Convention.

ALS, Peters Papers, PHi. Addressed to Philadelphia; written at 3 P.M.

[1] See Morris to Peters, 13 September, above. This bill passed on 14 September.
[2] In 1771 the Pennsylvania Assembly declared the Susquehanna a public highway above Wright's Ferry, and in 1785 extended the designation to the Maryland line. This meant that both the Susquehanna and its tributaries could be cleared of all obstructions to navigation.

Oliver Ellsworth to Oliver Wolcott, Jr.

You may wish to know what would be the probable expence of your living in this place.

House & Stable would be about 200 dollrs.

Wood ₩ Cord	best	4
	Oak	2½
Hay ₩ Ton		8

Marketing higher than at Hartford 25 ₩ Ct.

It would not be expected that your Office should Subject you to more expence of Company or a different Stile of living than you would chuse—It is my opinion that you would live within 1000 dolls. as your family now is, & that you might expect on some future occasion such further advancement as your talents & Services will entitle you to—I wish to see you transplanted into the National Government for its sake & your own.

ALS, Wolcott Papers, CtHi. Addressed to Hartford, Connecticut.

Samuel Livermore to Tobias Lear

Since you left me I thought of Major [*Jonathan*] Cass of Exeter whose Character merit & capacity would point him out for the office of marshall preferable to any other I can thin[*k*] of in Exeter or in any part near the place of holding the Court. I need not enlarge as I presume you know the gent.

ALS, Washington Papers, DLC.

Samuel A. Otis to Jonathan Dayton

It[1] has fallen out as I expected—The impressions natural from daily intercourse, the opportunity to hedge & form plans & connexions, gave them every advantage—I can only say as it respects you I am mortified; as it respects the public I regret the circumstances.

Well Congress have nearly compleated their first session—"What think you of them now?" What says the world about them? Cooped up in my office I shall be the last to hear the thunders roar—as I have but little time to make enquiry—If a man derives advantage from hearing what the people say of him, good or ill—~~And~~ why not a body of men? It must be said I think they are industrious—It would be mortifying indeed to find they have laboured in vain.

I have made no permanent domestic arrangements. ***

ALS, Gratz Collection, PHi. Addressed to Elizabethtown, New Jersey; franked by Paterson.

[1] The reference is to the disputed Congressional election in New Jersey.

James Sullivan to Elbridge Gerry

Our people are making calculations of the expences of their Government and appear to be very uneasy. I have never heard any one complain of the Establishment of the Vice Presidents Salary. it may be a question where the money will be found to pay the Interest of the public and Private states Debts. and to build a federal town & pay the salaries granted.

The principles adopted now are very wide from what we talked of in the Revolution. but I begin to think all public felicity chimerical & am making up my mind to bear all things with patience and fortitude the measures pursuing when felt may give us Calamity. the high Sticklers for what they call federalism are more open in their murmers than those whom they once abused.

ALS, Gerry Papers, MHi.

Thomas Tudor Tucker to St. George Tucker

*** I shou'd be very glad to see a Copy of your Farce whenever you have finish'd it.[1] But I am perswaded that it is too unpopular a Subject to meet with Success in the Representation either here or in any other commercial Town. Indeed I know not how far it may be good Policy to make a direct Attack on Individuals unless a Baseness of Intention can be made very evident. And certainly there are very many who are ready to applaud as Marks of a manly & independent Mind disdaining to court popular Approbation at the Expence of national Happiness, those Sentiments & Measures which we deem hostile to Liberty. Evil loses its Effect where a Majority are not disposed to receive it, & Ridicule, which has been said to be the Test of Truth, is very apt, if not powerfully supported, to recoil instead of fixing on the intended Object. I am much inclined to think that you have Talents adequate to the Execution of the Work you propose, & I shou'd like to see it tried; but I wou'd suggest that it wou'd be best to render the Subject as ridiculous as possible without marking with too much precision particular Characters. Men are more generally free to laugh at Absurdities not particularly applied, & the persons satirized, if not too plainly distinguish'd, may sometimes, to screen themselves, join in the Laugh & strengthen the Party against themselves. If they are absolutely stigmatized they are put necessarily on their Defence & carry with them all their Adherents. Mr. L.[2] has been said to be a Man of republican Principles. Whether this be true or not I am intirely ignorant. If it be true in any degree it wou'd be imprudent to drive him over to the aristocratical Party, already too powerful. Were we to make every Man our Enemy who is not *wholly* in Sentiment with us, we shou'd have very little Support left. These Observations I submit to your Consideration, without relying much on them myself. A Poem (which I have by some means fail'd yet to get sight of) has lately appear'd on this Subject,[3] & I am told it has considerable Merit. I will get a Copy & send you. Whilst writing, I receiv'd your Favor of the 6th. September, for which I am much obliged to you. I have never heard any thing of the Circumstance you mention of Theodorick [*Randolph*], nor had I any Reason to suspect it. Shou'd any thing of the kind come under my Observation or Knowledge, I shall certainly mention it to him. Colo. Bland seems to be apprehensive that they [*Theodorick and John Randolph*] are wasting Time & Money here. I have been always uneasy lest my own Indulgence to them shou'd be injurious. But I know not how to treat them with Authority. I have a very sincere Regard for them & think them both very promising Youths. ***

ALS, Tucker-Coleman Papers, ViW.

[1] St. George Tucker's "Up and Ride: Or the Borough of Brooklyne." See St. George Tucker to Tucker, 3 June, volume 16.

[2] R. H. Lee. Tucker's satire features a character named "Leashore," who is allied with the character "Goosequill" (Adams) in supporting aristocratic titles.

[3] A reference to Edward Church's *The Dangerous Vice* ——.

Cotton Tufts to Abigail Adams

***

The Author of the scurrilous Poem referred to in yours is well known here and it is generally refuted and considered as the Work of a malicious & disappointed Seeker—it appears to me to be a Stab upon the President through the Side of the Vice President and as paving the Way for an Attack upon Him, whenever a favorable oppertunity shall present—Too many there are to our Sorrow, that can never be contented but in Broils & Contests, wishing to embroil Government, and to throw our publick Affairs into Confusion, they are seeking every Occasion to gratify their restless Spirits and to wriggle themselves into Places favourable to their Desig[ns] But as they are generally devoid of Principle, they sooner or later fall into the Pit which they have diggd for others.

***

ALS, Adams Family Manuscript Trust, MHi. Written from Weymouth, Massachusetts.

Letter from a Member of Congress to a Gentleman in This State

We are all very sanguine in our Hopes, that you will send us Members of both Houses, before the 15th of January, indeed on the First Monday of December. All unkind Questions will then be done away. But if unhappily Rhode-Island should not call a Convention, or calling one, not adopt the Constitution, something much more serious than has ever yet been done or talked of, will most probably be undertaken.

We have very often been irritated with Rumours of Correspondences between the Anti's in your State and those in Massachusetts, New-York, Virginia, North-Carolina, &c. and even with Insinuations of Intrigues with

British Emissaries. These are very serious Reports: Such Intercourses are extremely criminal in the Citizens of the Union, and hostile at least in those who are not. If the Citizens of Rhode-Island place themselves in the light of Correspondents with criminal Citizens of the Union, or in that of Enemies to the United States, their good Sense will suggest to them, that the Consequences will be very speedy and very bitter. I rely upon it, therefore, unless your State is devoted and abandoned to the judicial Dispensations of Heaven, that your People will open their Eyes before it be too late. This is the very serious Advice of one who has ever been and still is their hearty Friend, but who must cease to be so when they become the Enemies of the United States. There can be no Medium: Enemies they must be, or Fellow-Citizens, and that in a very short Time.

[Providence, R. I.] *United States Chronicle*, 1 October; reprinted at Newport, Rhode Island; Boston; Hartford and Norwich, Connecticut; New York; and Carlisle and Philadelphia, Pennsylvania. This is a letter from John Adams to John Brown; for the full text of the FC:lbk in Adams Family Manuscript Trust, MHi, see *DHFFE* 4:391.

OTHER DOCUMENTS

Nicholas Gilman to George Turner. No copy known; acknowledged in Turner to Gilman, 23 September.

Walter Jones to James Madison. ALS, Madison Papers, DLC. Place from which written not indicated. For the full text, see *PJM* 12:403–4.
"Liberty was never placed in a less hazardous Situation, than in our States, and our inattention to her protection would therefore be the more criminal—I think the general Conduct of your House is calculated to Secure her, but their is a wide & secret inlet of mischief in our manners, that if not controlled, will make legislative Forms of no avail"; fears "ruinous adoption of European Fashions"; threat is greatest in states northeast of the Susquehanna, while Virginia is the "great Repository of Republican principles"; "A Separate Confederacy, which I have hitherto abhorred, may one day ~~day~~ *possibly*, be a means of preserving our Liberty by an union of parts more homogeneous in their Nature, than the present may eventually be."

Arthur Lee to Tench Coxe. ALS, Coxe Papers, PHi. Addressed to Philadelphia.
Office seeking: encourages Coxe to apply for postmaster general; "If you can gain Mr. Madisons interest with the President, I think you will suceed; & that Mr. Morris will not be able to prevent the approbation of the Senate"; Morris "is endeavoring to re-instate" Richard Bache; prom-

ises to "immediately engage my friends in the Senate"; please reply under cover to Richard Bland Lee; progress of Post Office Act [S-3].

George Logan to Pierce Butler. ALS, Butler Papers, PHi. Written from Charleston, South Carolina.

Office seeking: appointment as marine hospital physician in Charleston.

Thomas Russell to John Langdon. ALS, Langdon-Elwyn Family Papers, NhHi. Written from Boston; addressed to Portsmouth, New Hampshire.

Disappointed Langdon did not visit during his journey home; encloses copy of an order on Russell dated 15 August, for $300 for Langdon, charged to Willing, Morris, and Swanwick, for which Russell requests a receipt.

Jeremiah Wadsworth to Catherine Wadsworth. ALS, Wadsworth Papers, CtHi. Addressed to Hartford, Connecticut.

Family health; "I have had a bad cold and my old Eyes are lame or lazy they will not see very well. I am otherwise very well and think I shall see you in a little time at Hartford."

Samuel Davis, Diary. MHi.

"Visit the Federal Hall where I meet *Mr. Partridge*—member of Congress from Massa. who told me I was the first person he had ever seen from his district—engage to breakfast with him to morrow."

WEDNESDAY, 16 SEPTEMBER 1789

Cold (Johnson)

John Adams to John Bondfield

I have received the letter you did me the honor to write me on the 15 of May. and take this opportunity to return you my thanks for your polite congratulations. It is now five months within a few days since I entered on the execution of my office: and although I had many apprehensions from the novelty of It, and from my own long habits formed to different scenes of life, in the course of a ten years residence abroad in Paris, London and the Hague; yet I have not found much injury to my health or depresion of spirits. The greatest pleasure I enjoy is in the reflection that I am now employed in doing every thing in my power to form a system of policy and Finance that may enable us to pay those debts both at home and abroad which I had so great a hand in contractting. You will always oblige me Sir by transmitting me

any information concerning the public affairs of France in whose happiness and prosperity I am not a little interested.
***

FC:lbk, Adams Family Manuscript Trust, MHi.

John Adams to Comte de Sarsfield

Your friendly letter of the 23 of April, has laid me under obligations to you which it shall be my endeavour to discharge. It will ever be a pleasure to me to hear of your health and happiness: and perhaps you may have a curiosity to hear of mine. I have been here about five months, and without missing a single day, (excepting one when my own salary was under consideration, and delicacy induced me to absent myself) have constantly attended the Senate. Such constancy in attending to the deliberations of such an assembly on such a variety of buisiness, and the continual exercise of speaking, are laborious service, and will endanger my health. Hitherto, however, by good air at home, and regular daily exercise at vacant hours, I have preserved a good share of health and spirits. ***

FC:lbk, Adams Family Manuscript Trust, MHi.

Thomas Fitzsimons to Tench Coxe

I thank you for the cautions communicated in yours of the 14th. and am perfectly aware of the difficultys we shall have to encounter in the business alluded to—there is this ground for hope however our friends are all aware of the design and will Neither be Misled nor diverted from their Object— the Eastern Delegates are Impressed with a sense of their situation—and that by the Accession of No. Ca. the southern interests would outweigh them they are convinced Pensylva. would Agree to a more Southern position, as permanent—and an Imm[ediat]e. Removal to Remaining here— Without Limittation and as they [are] utterly averse from going beyon[d] Pensylva. their interest is Materially concerned in Carrying thro the present Measure: What may be done in senate is not very certain unfortunately two N. E. Members Who would undoubtedly be in favor of Susq[uehann]a. are absent and will not return this session[1]——the how the Delaware senators will Vote is not quite certain—we are not without hopes from them—if it was not for the expectation that disappointing us in that we must of Necessity come to the falls of Delaware—the thing would be certain—but that hope will divide Jersey, from us—tomorrow the bill will be taken up—I suppose the Next day will determine its fate with us—the interim is a period of Anxiety & suspence.

ALS, Coxe Papers, PHi. Addressed to Philadelphia.

---

[1] Langdon and Strong.

Richard Bland Lee to Charles Lee

Yesterday I had the pleasure of receiving your favor of the 8th. and have the satisfaction to inform you that so much of the Collection Act as is complained of by the merchants on the Potomack has been suspended until may next. In the mean time I expect a revision of our Commercial regulations, will take place, and that they will be more accomodated to the interests and wishes of the Various parts of the United States.

By this time you must have seen the debates and dicision of the Representatives on the subject of a permanent seat of Government. The Bill on this subject is under Commitment for tomorrow. We have a faint hope of frustrating the project for the present—but even if this should be the case I very much doubt the practicability for a long time to come of prevailing on the Eastern & middle states to remove to Potomack.

It seems to be yet the determination of Congress to adjourn on the 22d. instant, to which I hope they will adhere. The Judiciary System will be completed in a few days—this subject and the amendments to the Constitution seem to be the only things which press for a decision this session. I am sorry to hear that Mr. Madison's influence is decreasing, as his conduct has in my opinion been governed by the best motives and in most instances by an enlightened policy. And I hope when he becomes more acquainted with the interest of the Potomack that he will be as popular there as he deserves to be Every where.

***

ALS, Roberts Collection, PHC. Addressed to Alexandria, Virginia.

OTHER DOCUMENTS

John Adams to Cotton Tufts. ALS, Miscellaneous Manuscripts, NHi. Addressed to Boston.

"The Heat has been excessive and my daily Toil Somewhat exhausting besides a very extensive Correspondence, without a Clerk."

James Madison to John Dawson. No copy known; acknowledged in Dawson to Madison, 18 September.

John Adams, Diary. Adams Family Manuscript Trust, MHi.
Relates what Ellsworth told him about the Federal Convention.

Samuel Davis, Diary. MHi. Davis recorded this account of his visit to the House under 17 September, although it clearly corresponds to the business of 16 September.

"Breakfast with Mr. Partridge, at Mrs. Lorings. *** Mr. [*Tobias*] Lear the Secretary called on Mr. P. respecting appointment at Rehoboth (Massa.)"; "Visit the Gallery—prayers performing—the members sit in semicircles—covered—uncovered when speaking—Mr. Lear is announced— and delivers a message—the debates appear to be desultory this morning—and unimportant—meet Mr. Jno. Fenno in the gallery— who ~~informs~~ designates all the members as they sit—he is taking their debates for publication—and is glad to see me, tho' unknown, because I came from Massachusetts."

THURSDAY, 17 SEPTEMBER 1789

Cool. Rain (Johnson)

John Adams to Henry Marchant

Your kind letter of August 29th gave me much pleasure There is more confinement, in my present situation, than in any I have ever been in these thirty years: and another evil is come upon me, under which I suffered formerly, but from which I have been wholly releived during my absence from America. Public speaking ever gave me a pain in my breast, which was not only troublesome for the time, but dangerous for the future. My present office not only obliges me to a constant and close attention of mind, but to continual reading and speaking, which has again affected La poitrine,[1] as it used to do, and raises many doubts how long I shall be able to go on.

*** Congress have passed a law [*the Collection Act HR-23*], as you solicited but a clause has been introduced relative to rum & which perhaps your people may not relish so well. It is now the universal expectation that your State will come in, before winter—but if the public should be disappointed, something very unpleasant will undoubtedly be the consequence. It would not be difficult for Congress to make the Unsocial Rhode Islanders see and feel, that the Union is of some importance to their interest and happiness Winning however by mildness and condescention is much more agreable. ***

FC:lbk, Adams Family Manuscript Trust, MHi. Parts of the omitted text mention John Quincy Adams's arrival the day before, and advice for persuading Rhode Island to ratify the Constitution. The excerpted text and part of the omitted text were printed in newspapers at Newport, Rhode Island, and Boston.

¹ The breast.

John Adams to James Sullivan

In your letter of the 18th of August, you ask why we may not have as much paper in circulation in proportion to our circulating silver and gold, as Great Britain has in proportion to hers? Give me leave to answer you without hesitation. We may as soon as we shall have any credit. We have none. No man of common sense will trust us. As long as an unlimited democracy tyrannized over the rich, no man of property was safe. If ever an unlimited Aristocracy shall tyrannize over the poor, and the moderately rich at once, the greater portion of society will not dare to trust the less. But if a government well ordered mixed and counterpoised should take place, and inconsequence of it the commandment *Thou shalt not steal*, be observed, then and not till then you may circulate what paper you may find necessary—But I doubt very much whether our circumstances will require any paper at all. The cash paid in imposts, will immediately be paid to creditors and by them circulated in society.

FC:lbk, Adams Family Manuscript Trust, MHi.

Tench Coxe to James Madison

***

By yesterdays post I recd. a letter from New York that has placed me in a situation of considerable delicacy and embarrassment. It is from a single gentleman, who appears to move in behalf of friends who think and wish on the Subject as he does. He informs me that they consider it as certain that the Postmaster general [*Ebenezer Hazard*] will be removed from the Report of the Board of Treasury¹—and [*lined out*] advise me to an Application to the president. I am averse to any application of so delicate a Nature both as it concerns the present incumbent, and as it regards the amiable and excellent Character that Presides in our government. Yet I am told by the Communicant that there are public Reasons, which induce the advice. It comes from a quarter that convinces me some of the Senators know of the letter—and I think there is no doubt that it would be supported by that part of them which is least fond of the federal Constitution. I believe there is an apprehension that Mr. [*Richard*] Bache may be nominated, for the letter speaks of him & goes into the grounds & reasons of his Removal from the office, and it seems to be thought that those Reasons continue in force.[2]

How the matter stands I really do not know, Sir, for I am unused to sollicitations and intrigues. But I am entirely at a loss how to proceed. If I were ever so anxious for the office I could not I think bring myself to make a formal Application in my own name directly to the President. And so far as there may really exist public reasons that influence the minds of any to wish me to apply, I am loth absolutely to decline. While I am mentioning the matter to you I feel that I am imposing a matter upon you which I have very little right to do. Yet, if the state of this matter leaves an openening & the mention of my name might involve any public advantage or convenience— I would submit it [*to*] your Judgment and discretion entirely either to [*lined out*] do what you might think perfectly right and proper or let the matter rest in total Silence.

***

In the Senate for Pennsa. I believe Mr. McClay is my partial friend. Mr. Morris by requesting me to correspond with him at New York, and his gentlemanly stile of treating that correspondence has shewn his confidence and his good dispositions, but He has an old Acquaintance in the convivial way with Mr. Bache. Mr. Clymer has shewn his good Opinion by nominating me to the more important duty of Congress as have both he & Mr. Fitzsimons by giving me their unsollicited influence & votes in my election on that Occasion.[3] But they also have some social Acquaintance with Mr. Bache—tho they do not go much into those Scenes. The Speaker, Mr. Wyncoop, & Col. Hartly I consider as men who would be pleased to serve me— also Genl. Muhlenberg & Gen. Hiester. Tho I have not any pretensions to a claim upon the friendship of the latter, yet [*he*] has always acted towards me with the greatest Kindness & respect. I believe therefore that my name would be treated with Candor by our delegation by most of them with partiality. Mr. Scott I should except for I am entirely unknown to him. He has been little in Philada. & I have never been in our Western Country. I respect his Character, & am pleased with his so well justifying the choice of Pennsa. I am satisfied therefore that my name would meet no unfavorable observations from any of the delegation tho probably some of the three first Gentn. are more or less engaged in the support of Mr. Bache. They would not however do me the smallest Injustice in their most secret conversations. Any of the others I believe, but Mr. Scott, would go lengths to serve me—particularly the Speaker, Mr. McClay & Mr. Wyncoop: and if it was thought any public Convenience would arise from it, I feel a confidence that ~~the~~ either of them would mention or join in mentioning me to the President. I have not said any thing to one of the whole Number upon the subject; but I am satisfied that if it should be thought of any use one of them would move alone or with you upon the least communication. The speaker would be perhaps the most weighty from his station. They may have been applied to by Mr. Bache but I presume they would make no engagements—& I am sure several of them would shew more partiality to me than to Mr. Bache.

In regard to the office I do not consider it as a mere regulation of mails, & distribution of letters. But it is intimately ~~connected~~ blended with the connexion of the Members of the Union & particularly of the Atlantic & western territory. It may be made to aid considerably the advancement of internal commerce and territorial improvement, and to expedite the sudden operations of the Executive department.

***

[*P. S.*] I have concluded to write on this matter to the Speaker only.

ALS, Madison Papers, DLC. For the full text, see *PJM* 12:404–8. In the omitted text, Coxe discusses his previous public offices, including being twice elected to the standing "Committee of Merchants of Philadelphia." Also, Madison is requested to retrieve papers Coxe had sent Thomas Jefferson in 1787 relative to procuring confidential information about British textile manufacturing methods.

---

[1] On 21 August the board of treasury replied to Washington's request for a statement of the post office accounts, indicating that no final adjustment had been made in Postmaster General Ebenezer Hazard's accounts for the previous two years (*PGW* 3:503–7).

[2] Richard Bache was replaced as postmaster general in 1782 and Hazard assumed the position.

[3] Coxe's election on 14 November 1788 to serve on the Pennsylvania delegation during the remaining months of the Confederation Congress.

Andrew Moore to George Washington

The Judicial Bill now before us Requires that a Martial should be appointed ~~be appointed~~ in each district It is with Reluctance I mention A person Who I consider as qualified to discharge the duties of that office and would not have presumd to have thus held up to your view—Had I not been informd that you wisht to be informd of such Characters as might have Pretensions—Colo. Jno. Steel [*John Steele*] of Virginia I consider as well qualified to fill such an office He has been some time engagd in Studying the Law. And has for some Years been Employd in a Clerks office—I expect he has acquird a sufficient legal knowledge for the Discharge of the Duties—Colo. Steel early in the War was appointed an Ensign in the Ninth Virginia Regiment and servd to the End ~~of the War~~ He has been high in the Estimation of his Acquaintances not only in the Army But in private life. Should you consider Colo. Steel as worthy your Attention in this Business—I beg leave to refer you to Colo. Grayson—General Matthews and Genl. Muhlenburgh for his Character His present situation is not so Comfortable as I think his Merits Entitle him to—This Sir Was one Reason with me for thus Presenting him to View. And I hope will plead my Excuse.

ALS, Washington Papers, DLC.

Comte de Moustier to Comte de Montmorin

On the 13th of this month, Mr. Hamilton, to whom the previous day I had paid my compliments on his nomination to the post of Secretary of the Department of the Treasury, came to see me and discussed his project to propose that Congress take out a loan in Holland in order to liquidate all arrearages on the domestic and foreign debt. He seemed to expect that this Affair would succeed and he already foresees that the customs revenue added to that of several other sources that could be created will suffice to provide for Government expenses and for paying the annual public obligations. Thus according to him who affirms that Congress should not avoid or retreat from the payment of public debts, the King would be reimbursed purely and simply according to the terms of the Contract by means of sums borrowed in Holland and which could be deposited into the Royal Treasury. It is desirable that the fine hopes of Mr. Hamilton be realized. In spite of the dispatch that he brings to bear on this operation, it cannot be finished in less than a year. It can only be at the return of Congress, after the adjournment that will take place at the end of the month, that the first legal opening of this issue could be made. It seems that all Congress will do before adjourning will be to assign the Secretary of Treasury to prepare a report on the state of the public debt and on the means to provide for it. This resolution will be accompanied by a declaration to make known the intention of Congress to faithfully fulfill public obligations. It is not fine words that the creditors of the United States have lacked to this point. The question is to know what are the means more than the intentions of Congress. If new lenders are persuaded by the pretty pictures that will be presented to them of the current and future resources of the United States, this would be very well for their old creditors. Moreover I have no doubt that Mr. Hamilton genuinely wishes to fulfill the responsibilities of the United States toward His Majesty. He was born English and I do not believe him very well disposed toward France; he would like nothing better than to completely disengage this Republic [from France] and to put it in closer relations with the Estates General of the Low Countries, current Allies of England.

Mr. Hamilton asked me in our Conversation on the King's loan if a proposition had not been made by a company in France to acquire the King's loan to the United States. I told him that I had heard this mentioned as an unofficial rumor and that I had also heard it spoken of here, but that I had nothing in my instructions that would have anything to do with this plan; that these were limited to prescribing me to mention the loan of the King, who does not doubt that the United States will fulfill their obligations toward His Majesty; that I had however, given the singular situation in which I found the United States, taken it upon myself not to take any actions on this subject and that I was limited to examining the means by which one could facilitate paying off this debt. Mr. Hamilton did not pay great attention to this idea and he confined himself to the one he had of paying within the terms of the Contract. I think that he would not be sorry if the project of selling the King's loan took place, to judge him by his association with well-known and brazen speculators and stock-jobbers. But I have always thought and I have the honor of remarking to You, Sir, that we have no place being anxious over the repayment of the Sums His Majesty advanced to the United States; that they have more than sufficient means to honor their obligations; that meanwhile we can consider the delay of this repayment as a political advantage because His Majesty's loan is, in the current torpor of our Commerce, the only link that ties us to the United States; that the dignity of the King and the regard due to his Allies excludes any arrangement with a Company of Capitalists who would like to take on this loan; that the needs of our fleet and the advantage of multiplying our ties with the United States seem to demand the conclusion of an arrangement by which naval munitions, masts and rations for our Fleet would be purchased in America with Letters of exchange drawn on Congress from the accumulation of the lapsed yearly interest. I developed this plan in my Report #3 which accompanied my Dispatch of 25 December. I can only trust in this, because I believe that Mr. Hamilton does not himself have the confidence in these measures that he endeavors to inspire in others.

***

DHFFC translation of a Copy in Correspondance Politique, Etats-unis, 34:272–75, Fr. The omitted text concerns Brissot de Warville and French speculation in the American debt.

Roger Sherman to Governor Samuel Huntington

Your Excellency has doubtless Seen the amendments proposed to be made to the Constitution as passed by the House of Representatives, enclosed is a copy of them as amended by the Senate, wherein they are considerably abridged & I think altered for the better.

The present session draws near to a close, the 22d Inst. being the time fixed by both Houses for adjournment Some Bills for laws and other business begun will be continued to next session; but the arrangements that will

Roger Sherman, by Ralph Earl, 1751–1801, oil on canvas. (Courtesy of the Yale University Art Gallery.)

Roger Sherman to Samuel Huntington, 17 September 1789, p. 1.
(Courtesy of the Yale University Library.)

be compleated will enable the Executive to administer the Government in the recess of Congress.

It was impossible to make any Special appropriation for paying the Interest of the public debt without further information than can be obtained at present, the Secretary of the Treasury will be directed to make proper Statements and report to the Next session.

The Salaries of Some of the Officers are higher than I thought was necessary or proper considering the State of the finances and the just and meritorious demands of the creditors who have long been kept out of their dues, especially Such of them as originally loaned their money, or rendered Services or Specific Supplies. & Still hold their Securities. I dont know whether any discrimination will or ought to be made between them & others, but if there Should I think it ought not to be made for the benefit of the public, but of the original creditors who were necessitated to Sell their Securities at a discount.

I was absent when the Bill for fixing the compensation of the members & officers of Congress was brought in and passed the House, the Senate concurred with an alteration that in the year 1795 the pay of a Senator Should be augmented one dollar a day. on this principle that a Senator ought to have higher pay than a Representative, though they were willing to dispense with it during their continuance in office, a great majority of the House of Representatives thought the principle not admissible, but on conference rather than lose the Bill it was agreed by way of accommodation to limit the continuance of the law to Seven years, so that the extra pay of a Senator will continue but one year.

The pay is fixed at one dollar a day more than was last Stated by the Legislature of the State of Connecticut which is perhaps as Oeconomical a State as any in the union, and I suppose the members from that State would have been content with that allowance, if they had to provide only for themselves, but the members from those States who had formerly *been* allowed Eight dollars a day thought it hard to be reduced to Six. but mutual concession was necessary. It's is important that a full representation be kept up, and it is well known that in Connecticut as well as in other States, it was difficult out of Seven Members to keep up a representation by two. and Some could not be induced to attend at all.

The judiciary Bill which had passed the Senate was this day concurred with by the House of Representatives with Some Small alterations—The Salaries of the Judges have been this day reported but not considered by the House. The Enclosed papers contain the news of the day.

ALS, Lane Collection, CtY. The contents of this letter became an issue in the second Congressional election in Connecticut.

James Wilkinson to Governor Esteban Miró

***

Since the plan of assigning lands to immigrants meets my approval, in order to justify the apparent unsteadiness of my conduct I must explain to you the motives that led me to ask Mr. [*Don Diego de*] Gardoqui for 6,000 acres. You are well aware that I have always been opposed to the plan of Colonel [*George*] Morgan:[1] to frustrate this project, by preventing emigration to his settlement, which I regarded as dangerous to Louisiana and unbefitting the crown under the conditions of which he boasted, was one of the objects of my solicitude; to assure a refuge and a settlement for myself and friends, in case of misfortune, was the second motive; but the most important consideration that drove me to it was that of engaging my political associates in Kentucky in some interesting affair likely to show up their principles and opinions, which would serve as a guaranty of their faithfulness whenever tested or jeopardized, this being at the same time a recompense for the aid they had afforded me. This was the more necessary because I knew very well that one of these gentlemen, Mr. John Brown, would be our representative in the new Congress, in which it was indispensable that I should have a confidant, and as he had full knowledge of our ideas, prudence demanded that I should make clear on my part the obligation which held him to silence and fidelity. When the position in Congress was offered me by the people, I declined it because my presence in Kentucky was very necessary for our purposes, and consequently it was given to Mr. John Brown. This gentleman immediately after his election to the Congress intended to withdraw from the connection he had formed with us, in his argument with me making use of the strong reason of the incompatibility of keeping a seat in the Congress while he was negotiating with the Spanish minister for a settlement in Louisiana. This step clearly proved how excellent my precautions had been, because if he had not been previously pledged along with us to submit the request to Mr. Gardoqui, he would have deserted our cause and divulged our confidences without fear of misapprehension or of public censure. I protested vigorously against his proposition, and appealing to the critical situation of our section of country, to the duties with which we were bound toward it, and to the solemn obligation that held us together, I drew a lively picture of the consequences that would necessarily attend union, fidelity, and perseverance, depicting in contrast the terrible spectacle that would accompany disunion, treachery, and dejection of mind. After some difficulty he resolved to adhere firmly to our plan, and agreed to send me regularly all the proceedings of the Congress which might affect our cause.

***

Translation of a Copy in Archivo-Nacional, Madrid, Estado, Legajo 3898B. Written from New Orleans. For the full text, see *AHR* 9(1903–4):751–64. Wilkinson claimed later in the letter that "from motives of policy I turned the election in favor of Mr. John Brown." For further information on Brown's involvement with Wilkinson, see Patricia Watlington, "John Brown and the Spanish Conspiracy," *Virginia Magazine of History and Biography* 75(1967):52–68.

[1] See Madison to Washington, 26 March, above.

Paine Wingate to John Langdon

I received your favour of the 8th. instant and am happy to hear that you had an agreeable journey and arrived home safe with Mrs. [*Elizabeth*] Langdon. I doubt not but that with the most pleasing emotions you met your numerous friends and acquaintance again at Portsmouth, especially your amiable daughter [*Elizabeth*]. You need not wonder that I think of her for I know, & have often felt the heart of a fond parent long absent. You may easily conceive how different is my situation here, where I am repeatedly mortifyed in seeing things go contrary to my opinion, especially in matters of salary. You inculcate the doctrine of contentment but I shall not be able to practice it. The Judicial bill was this day sent to the Senate with a number of amendments, but they none of them materially alter the plan. One alteration I will mention which will not be agreeable to your sentiments, and that is that half the courts in New Hampshire should be at Exeter. I wish you had thought with me to have had one circuit court only at Exeter and all the rest at Portsmouth. In that case I suspect there would have been no alteration in the other house. The whole bill I dislike as much as you do & hope that it soon will be made better or good for nothing. The compensation bill to the members of Congress has passed as it was reported by the committee of the Senate excepting that it is limitted to seven years & the Chaplins to be paid only during the sessions. The pay of the Serjeant at Arms was turned by the President & that to the Secretary & clerk was carried by a bare majority, which shews that we wanted your assistance and Mr. Strong's. You and he must not find fault if we do ever so wrong. The house of Representatives do adhere to the 5000 dollars for the vice president and I suppose the Senate will receed. We still hope to adjourn on next tuesday but I fear we shall not get away until the last of next week, as many things must yet be done. Mrs. [*Ruth*] Dalton arrived here well in seven days from Newbury-Port. I will enclose to you two Newspapers which will give to you the news we have here this day especially the important news from France. The house of Representatives have this day been on the subject of permanent residence of Congress. They have yet compleated nothing & I hope will not this session. As to amendments to the Constitution Madison says he had rather have none than those agread to by the Senate. You will excuse the rapidity of this letter as I am in a mighty hurry this moment.

ALS, Dreer Collection, PHi.

[William Maclay] to "Messrs. Printers"

IT seems generally agreed, that the Susquehannah is the nearest to the center of wealth, territory, and population, taking our view of the United States on the Atlantic side. So far, no doubt is raised against it. The objection most strongly urged against this river, is the connection with the western waters. The western country is a large field—some point must be taken as a center. Fort Pitt has been called the Key of this country—let then our arguments point to this object.

From the tide water on the Potowmack to Fort Pitt, following the usual calculation, the distance is 304 miles. From the tide water on Potowmac to Fort Cumberland 200, portage to the three Forks of Turkey Foot 30, water carriage 8, portage at the Falls of Yohiogena 1, down the Yohiogena to Monongahela 50, to Fort Pitt 15—in all 304 miles. The rout by the way of Cheat River, between the same places is 360 miles.

From the tide water on the Susquehannah to Fort Pitt, following also the usual calculation, which is certainly best in both cases, as all new calculations may be more liable to suspicion. The distance is 276 miles, viz. from Havre de Grace at the head of Chesapeake Bay, to Wright's Ferry [*Columbia, Pennsylvania*] 40, to Harris's Ferry [*Harrisburg, Pennsylvania*] 26, to the mouth of Juniata 15, up Juniata River to Standing Stone, now called Huntington, 75, from thence to Cohnimaugh, Old Town 36, down the Kiskemenetas to the Ohio [*Allegheny*] 60, down the Ohio [*Allegheny*] to Fort Pitt 30—in all 276.

It is allowed by all competent judges, that there are not two rivers which approach nearer to each other in circumstances of size, than the Potowmac and Juniata, with this difference, that Juniata having a more northern situation, is known to retain its water better. The Potowmac, it is well known, is made serviceable only by great expence and labor. The Juniata in its natural state, is navigated, from Huntington downwards, by boats of the burthen of from 1000 to 600 bushels of wheat; from Huntington up to Poplar run, by boats of about the burthen of 400 bushels. The present portage from Poplar Run to the Connemaugh is 23 miles, where a good road is now made. This pass over the Allegany Mountains used to be the most frequented of any by the old Indian traders, and is still declared to be the easiest that can be found any where over these ridges. The latest observations however assure us, that the waters of Poplar run, and Connemaugh approach within 40 perches of each other, are of sufficient size for supplying canals; and that they may be connected by a lock navigation. The navigation down the Connimaugh to the Kiskemenetas, is equal in goodness to the part of Juniata between Poplar Run and Huntington. That of the Kiskemetas and the Allegany, down to Fort Pitt, is unexceptionable. The navigation of the Juniata is no matter of speculation—it is a thing of daily practice. A second communication between the Susquehannah and the Allegany, is by the heads of the West Branch and Toby's Creek [*Clarion River*]—This is not so direct to Fort Pitt, nor has it been so well examined, but by the Indian accounts it may in some respects be considered as preferable, the different waters approaching very near each other in the low grounds, called the Buffaloe swamp; a well attested fact will place this in a clear point of view. John Hart, an Indian trader, was taken dangerously ill on the Allegany; he was brought by two Indians in a canoe up Toby's Creek, and down the Susquehannah to Harris's Ferry—the Indians carrying him, and dragging the canoe over the necessary portage in half a day. This communication may be serviceable to the parts of the Allegany in the neighborhood of French creek.

The Sinnemononing, or north fork of the West Branch, has but a portage of 11 miles to good navigation on the head of the Allegany River; from here by the way of the Chittockyay [*Chatauqua*] Lake there is a portage of 7 miles only to Lake Erie. This communication is almost direct, and has been lately well explored. The east branch of the Susquehannah affords a still more enlarged navigation extending upwards of 300 miles from the Forks at Sunbury. Boats have been repeatedly hauled into it, from the Mohawk River in the State of New York. It was thus that General Clinton transported his whole army in the year 1779, descending the Susquehannah to the forks of the river at the Tioga Point, and then ascending the Tioga [*Chemung River*] on his way to the Genisee country.

From the main branch of the Tioga, a portage of 18 miles connects the navigation with the Cannodasago [*Seneca*] lake. This is in fact connecting it with lake Ontario. Thus taking the connections of the Susquehannah, we find a double one with the Allegany or Western Waters, that by the Juniata superior to the Potowmac connections, both in distance and convenience. The one by the west branch and Toby's creek, more circuitous to Fort Pitt, but better adapted to the upper parts of the Allegany. The connections with lake Erie is unrivalled in point of convenience; and the northern communications with the waters of Ontario, and all the western waters of New-York, so far as respects the Potowmac are exclusively connected with the Susquehannah. In those quarters, it seems highly probable, that new regions will one day be opened to commerce. The lands watered by the Susquehannah have been estimated at forty thousand square miles. This whole extent of country, the small parts hitherto cultivated excepted, is cloathed with the finest timber. Iron ore, limestone and stone coal are found in abundance, the soil in every place where it has been essayed, has not disappointed the husbandman. It is found adapted to the winter grains, as well as the summer crops. And the new settlements are at this time proceeding with great rapidity.

It may however, be worth while to pause a moment, and ask, for what purposes the federal town is to be seated on a river? the answer is plain and obvious. For the more easy supplying the inhabitants with provisions, materials of building, fewel, &c.

Has there during all the time of the high price of wheat, flour, &c. in the Atlantic states, a single boat been loaded with these articles at Fort Pitt, and ascended the Monongohela or any other stream, so that these same articles reached the mouth of Potowmack? The answer must be, no. Have not boats without number, been loaded at Fort Pitt, with provisions, &c. to take their chance of the Mississippi market at 2000 miles distance? the answer must be yes. This precludes all speculation on the subject. The commerce of the western waters, so far as respects the carrying out of country produce has made, its elegit, and the reason is obvious. Boats with country produce, to neat any thing worth while, must be heavily loaded, such cannot ascend streams with ease if the water is high; oars will not do, and the bottom cannot be purchased with setting poles. If shallow, they cannot proceed for want of water; critical times only will suit, and even then the labor of the boatmen is extreme. Hence country produce will always descend the full stream, be the prospect of the market ever so distant. Thus it is plain, that the Atlantic rivers never can supply any town on their banks with provisions or any heavy articles, but those which are produced on their own lands.

Let applications of these principles be made to the Potowmac and the Susquehannah. State the whole produce of the Potowmac, be it what it may, as 1. The Juniata is allowed by men of candor who know both rivers, to be quite equal to the Potowmac, with, perhaps, generally speaking, a more productive country in grain, on its banks. It will therefore stand as 1. But the Juniata is not equal to one fifth part of the whole waters of the Susquehannah; it is not half so large as the west branch, and bears a still less proportion to the east branch. As to what respects air, climate, soil, &c. the difference is trifling; the 2 branches then being rated as 4. the clear result is, that the advantages to a city situated on the Susquehannah with respect to the navigation will be as 5 to 1, compared with the Potowmac.

But if connections with the Western Waters, must still be attended to, and considered as a fundamental principle, it is plain that the Susquehannah possesses them, in a greater degree than the Potowmac, and is besides intimately connected with the northern waters, and great lakes; advantages which the Potowmac cannot pretend to.

NYDA, 17 September. The editors identified Maclay as the author based upon *DHFFC* 9:150–51.

OTHER DOCUMENTS

Pierce Butler to Luke Breen. FC:lbk, Butler Papers, PHi. Addressed to Charleston, South Carolina.
Office seeking: will try to get Breen the appointment he requested in his letter of 28 July if it is in Butler's power, but Butler thinks the collectors are empowered to hire their own gaugers.

Elbridge Gerry to James Sullivan. No copy known; acknowledged in Sullivan to Gerry, 27 September.

Benjamin Goodhue to Stephen Goodhue. ALS, Goodhue Family Papers, MSaE. Addressed to Salem, Massachusetts.
"I expect We may adjourn some time next week tho' perhaps not the day agreed upon."

Thomas Jefferson to James Madison. ALS, Madison Papers, DLC. Written from Paris. For the full text, see *PJM* 12:408–9.
Sending plaster busts of John Paul Jones for Madison and Wadsworth among others.

Rufus King to Christopher Gore. No copy known; acknowledged in Gore to King, 27 September.

Josiah Parker to Tench Coxe. ALS, Coxe Papers, PHi. Addressed to Philadelphia.
Asks Coxe to deliver the enclosed to John Dawson; "It is probable I shall have the pleasure of seeing you in a few days on my way to Virginia—as you dayly have the proceedings of our body by the papers. you will excuse me from illustrateing on that Subject—It is in the power of the Pennsilvania Delegation to have the next session of Congress in Philadelphia."

John Quincy Adams, Diary. Adams Family Manuscript Trust, MHi.
"Attended this morning in the gallery of the house of representatives, to hear the debates. They were upon the judiciary bill. Mr. Gerry, Mr. Jackson, Mr. Burke, Mr. Stone, Mr. Lee, Mr. Maddison, & Mr. Benson all took a part in this debate. But I confess, I did not perceive any extraordinary

powers of oratory displayd by any of these gentlemen. The subject had been already so much discussed, that little could be said of further importance. The eloquence had all been exhausted, but the spirit of contention still remained."

Samuel Davis, Diary. MHi. Davis combined several days in his account of September 18, including this portion which corresponds to events of September 17.
"Repair to the Gallery of Congress this morning—prayers offered by *Dr. Prevost* [*Samuel Provoost*]—only 13 members present the House were engaged by private petitions—the question of Permanent Residence was taken up—and it was proposed to fix the future seat of Government on the Susquehanna—in Pennsylvania—on the amendments—"*or in Maryland*"—an animated debate ensued—Messrs. Stone—Lee—Jackson—Page—Madison—Gale—for the Amendment—Hartley—Clymer—Ames—Sherman—against it—on a division there was a tie 27 & 27—the Speaker (Muhlenberg of Pennsyla.) was against the Amendment."

William Samuel Johnson, Diary. Johnson Papers, CtHi.
Dined at the President's.

NYDA, 19 September.
At the funeral for Job Sumner, who died on 16 September, the Vice President, the Massachusetts delegation, and other members of Congress were in attendance.

Letter from New York. [Portland, Maine] *Cumberland Gazette*, 25 September. This is probably from a letter written by Thatcher to the newspaper's editor, Thomas B. Wait.
Proposed salaries of Supreme Court judges, district judges, and attorney general; Judiciary Bill passed; Congress will probably adjourn on 22 September.

FRIDAY, 18 SEPTEMBER 1789

John Adams to William Tudor

Yours of July 9 & 27 are unanswered.
I cannot reconcile myself to the Idea of a Division of this Continent, even fifty years hence. great Sacrifices ought to be made to Union, and an habit of Obedience to a well ordered, and judiciously limited Government, formed

at this early Period. a Dissolution of the Union involves Consequences of so terrible a kind, that I think We ought to consent to an Unity of Executive Authority at least, if not even to a Consolidation of all Power in one national Government rather than Seperate. We must first, however make a fair Tryal of the present system.

The Compensation to the Vice President, is, to be Sure, a Curiosity. But the fault is entirely in the Massachusetts. There is not a State in the Union so weak in its Policy as that. There is not and never was these 15 years any Union or Harmony among her Delegates They never had a head—those whose Vanity pretended to be foremost had no heads on their shoulders. The Consequence has been, that altho the first Men have been produced by that state tho their military Power has been equal to almost all the rest: tho their commercial Advantages are superiour to any other; Yet they have the Reputation of nothing: their Commerce has been half ruined, and their Liberties nearly overwhelmed. I Seriously think that their whole State Policy has been weaker than any in the Union.

The opposition to the V. P. salary originated in Massachusetts. Massachusetts moved to cutt off 500£ of my salary in Europe immediately after I had made them a Peace. If that State is not made a signal Example of Vengeance against Injustice and Ingratitude, it will not be because it has not deserved to be.

Other States reward their Benefactors. King, only for manœuvring Congress out of their design to go to Philadelphia has been nobly rewarded.[1] But a Man may drudge forever for Massachusetts and die a beggar; nay what is worse die in disgrace. God forgive them.

How the President will decide, on the judiciary Appointments I know not. There is no system nor Harmony among the Men from Massachusetts— one recommends one, and another another. Dont you be chagrin'd, mortified humiliated nor vexed but let it go as it will.

ALS, Tudor Papers, MHi. Addressed to Boston.

---

[1] King, as a Massachusetts delegate to the Confederation Congress, played a key role in the summer of 1788 in the successful effort to convene the First Federal Congress at New York.

John Dawson to James Madison

By yesterday's post of receiv'd your two letters dated on Monday and Wednesday—The legislature of this State have pass'd an act granting to Congress the *Jurisdiction* of ten miles square on any part they shall please, not have said nothing relative to the Susqh.[1]

I lament with you the decisions of the Senate on the subject of amendments—this circumstance added to the combination formd to fix the seat of goverment will make an unfavourable impression on the Southern States— agreeably to your request I spoke to Mr. [*Tench*] Coxe—he has just be[*en*] appli'd to be a *friend* in New York to know whether he will accept of the office of Postmaster General, as the present incumbent [*Ebenezer Hazard*] will probably be discontinu'd—he has determin'd he will, and at his request I mention the subject to you, who are fully acquainted with his pretentions, and will, if they are better than any other persons who shall be brought forward, I am sure mention him to the President.

I am anxious for the arrival of tomorrow's post as I expect the Susqh. is by this time "done over."

ALS, Madison Papers, DLC. Written from Philadelphia, on "Friday morning." The editors have supplied the date based on the content.

1 This act passed on 14 September.

Thomas Hartley to Jasper Yeates

I am afraid we are blown up—we shall probably divide to day—and then I fear all will go to ruin—the Jealousy of the Susquehanna—will probably lose Pennyslvania the federal Seat I can say [*little?*] more at present I wish to prepare your Minds for the Worst a stronger Representation from the Center of the State would have done no Injury upon the present Occasion—I have much to tell you when I see you—and am in great Haste.

ALS, Yeates Papers, PHi.

James Madison to Tench Coxe

Your favor of the 9th. was not received till it was too late to be answered by the last mail. I now beg you to accept my acknowledgments for it. The Newspaper paragraph to which it alludes discoloured much the remarks which it puts in my mouth.1 It not only omits the occasion which produced them, but interpolates a personal reflections which I never meant, wch. could not properly be expressed, and which I am assured by a number of gentlemen attending at the time, was not countenanced by any thing that fell from me. In reply to Mr. Laurence who reminded me of a former declaration that if the Convention of Virga. had foreseen the moderate and liberal exercise of the power over trade which was taking place, her objections to the Constitution would have been lessened; I was led by his manner and other circumstances of the moment, to declare my beleif that if the contrast of proceedings on the subject under debate, could have been prophetically brought to the view of that Convention, the State of Virginia might not now be a party to the Union: of the truth of this declaration, I have not the smallest doubt, every conciliating picture of [*lined out*] the probable justice and liberality of the New Government, having been found necessary in the Convention to abate the fears of an overbearing Majority at this end of the Union. How far it was warranted by the occasion, The impartial bystanders, if such there were, can best decide: My own judgment does not disapprove it; nor can my feelings regret it in any other view than as it ~~may~~ is a feature in a transaction, the whole face of which is inauspicious to the public repose. The origin progress and incidents of this transaction can not be explained in a letter. If they should ever become subjects of conversation between us, the freedom of my communications will evince the confidence I place in the motives which dictated the enquiry to which I am sorry to be obliged to give so brief an answer.

ALS, Madison Papers, DLC. Madison misdated this letter "1787," probably because during September and October 1789 he was transcribing a copy of the journal of the Federal Convention and often writing "1787."

[1] See *DHFFC* 11:1412–13 for Madison's speech of 3 September.

William Smith (Md.) to Otho H. Williams

I Recd. yours of the 13th last evening. Govr. [*Arthur*] St. Clair is not yet gone but will I expect in a few days. I believe he only waits for the passage of a bill [*Troops Bill HR-27*] read twice yesterday enabling him if necessary to call out the Virginia & Penna. Militia to defend the frontiers in the Western Country. Capt. [*Erkuries*] Beatty I know nothing of but will enquire, & inform you in my next.

***

Yesterday a bill was reported in our house, for fixing the permanent Seat on the banks of Susquehanna. it was debated with more temper than I expected, On Motion a Clause was introduced, obliging the States of Pennsilva. & Maryland, to make Such provision as may be Satisfactory to the President of the U.S. for the removal of the obstructions in the river below the federal Town, not that those States should be at the expence of clearing the Navigation, but permit it to be done.[1] This clause so alarmed the Philadelphians, that they declared the bill should not pass. if they Vote against it, it will be lost; perhaps this day will determine the question in the house of Representatives. how it will go in the Senate I know not. Our house is very Nearly divided.

The inclosed papers will Shew you the alarming Situation, of our good friends & allies in france, if those accots. are Authentic it must end in civil War, the most dreadfull of all evils.

I hope to See you all soon When I will convince you, that it is not only the interest of Maryland in Genl. but Balt[*imor*]e. in Particular, & equally so for the U.S. that the permanent Seat Shall be on Susquehannah, but what opperates Strongly on my mind, is a full persuasion, that if Susquehaa. fail, Deleware, will be the place, & in confirmation of this opinion a Gentleman has this moment called in to tell me, that if we do not give up the clause respecting the Navigation of Susquehannah, they will Vote out the bill. to this condition I will never consent, *be it as it may*—the opening the river & the Seat on the Western Side ~~which~~ which I hope will be the case, were two Objects I always had in View & had great weight ~~in my mind~~ with me— Perhaps my obstinacy on this head m[*a*]y leave open a Chan~~g~~ce for your expectations on Potomack. that was always my Second Object, as the prevailing opinion is against a Seaport or commercial Town, I however think that opinion will be found, one day to be inconsistent with the interest of the U.S.

I Informed you in my last, who were the officers of the treasury. none of those appointments have given more Surprise than that of the treasurer [*Samuel Meredith*], & the removal of the Old [*Michael Hillegas*]. I have not heard any reason assigned.

ALS, Williams Papers, MdHi. The omitted text includes directions for the sale of a property in order to invest in certificates.

[1] See *DHFFC* 6:1866, n. 5, for the proposed text of and actions on this proviso and section 2 of the Seat of Government Bill [HR-25].

Henry Wynkoop to Reading Beatty

I thank You for Your Communications of Monday last, the Compensation Bill [*Salaries-Legislative Act HR-19*] which stood lost, when I wrote You on fryday last, was revived again next morning by the Majority moving for a reconsideration & an adoption of the Report of the Conferees, which limits the Bill to seven Years, the last of which, the Senators are to receive 7 Dollrs. thus fixing the Discrimination in such way as to have a future Operation & in the mean time to afford an opertunity for the Decision of the State Legislatures on the Subject.

***

People are mistaken in supposing the permanent Seat on the Susquehanah would injure the Trade of Philadelphia, for whatever Improvements might be made, in consequence thereof, in the navigation of that River, it can never be rendered equal to the Communication, with Philadelphia, by A Junction of the Susquehanah to the Schuylkill, thro' the Swatarra & the Tolpohoken [*Tulpehocken*].

With respect to our Voting against the temporary Residence in Philadelphia & the permanent one on the Delaware, You have only to look at the Debates & You will readily perceive the whole of those kind of Propositions introduced for the purpose of embarrasment & to carry us to the Potowmack, in Opposition to which we were obliged to stand firm & Vote thro' thick & thin against every Measure which would lead to the attainment of that Object.

At present conceive the Susquehanah as good as lost, by the introduction of the Clause[1] You will see in the Debates of yesterday, by way of proviso to the Bill for establishing the permanent Seat, do not see at present how we can assent to it's passing under those embarrasments, & without them the thing is impossible, so ~~that~~ that at present, provided my Colleagues can again be induced to vote with us, & fall in with the Proposition of Mr. Gerrey, it may yet come back to the Falls [*of the Delaware*]; What turn this day will produce is utterly uncertain & depends upon the Negotiations of this morning, possibly we may think half the Egg better than an empty Shell.

ALS, Wynkoop Papers, PDoBHi. For the full text, see *PMHB* 38(1914):184–85.

---

[1] See Smith to Williams, 18 September, n. 1, above.

Samuel Davis, Diary

The *Salary of the Judges* was taken up this day—Mr. Goodhue moved that 4500$ for the Chief Justice be struck out and 3000$ inserted—supported by Judge Livermore (N. Hamp.)—Mr. Ames—Mr. White—Gerry—and S—n [*Sherman?*]—Opposed by Smith (So. Car.)—Lawrence N. York—Benson Ditto—Vining (Dela.) *** District Judges—under consideration—Judge Livermore moved that 800 be struck out & 500 be inserted for *Maine*—Mr. Madison proposed to equalise them—overruled—a reduction made in every instance—In the course of these debates Mr. Ames observed on the subject of the *Chief Justice* salary—that he thot 1500 $ would command the first legal abilities in New England—he therefore thot 3000 an ample compensation—that the integrity of the Judge was not secured by the quantum of compensation—but by a habit of right action—that it was often the case, that men politically bad—made very good judges—&c. &c.

Some other business of less moment occured this day Mr. Goodhue called for the report of the committee on the value of the rouble of Russia.

A petition of Mr. [*James*] Rumsey on improvements in hydrostatics was—read—and of the Revd. Mr. [*William*] Stoy of Pennsyla. on a nostrum for the cure of the hydrophobia—a general smile.

*** Take tea at Mrs. Loring's—with Mr. Partridge—Ames—& Col. Leonard—who arrived this morning—to increase the vote on the question of *permanent residence*—I suppose.

MHi. Portions of the account, which Davis erroneously recorded under this date, have been printed under their correct dates, as determined by the legislative business they describe.

OTHER DOCUMENTS

John Adams to Jabez Bowen. FC:lbk, Adams Family Manuscript Trust, MHi. For a partial text, see *DHFFE* 4:392.

Passage of the Collection Act [HR-23] "was done in full confidence, that you will adopt the constitution and send us senators and Representatives before next session. If we should be disappointed I presume that serious measures will be suggested, to let your Anti's know their interests are connected with ours"; "out of the union there is no hope for your people but misery to themse[*l*]ves and mischief to others."

Elias Boudinot to William Bradford, Jr. No copy known; acknowledged in Bradford to Boudinot, 20 September.

Thomas Hartley to Tench Coxe. ALS, Coxe Papers, PHi. Addressed to Philadelphia.

Personal financial transactions; encloses a fiscal note endorsed by "Mr. [F. A.?] Muhlenberg"; newspaper piece, apparently transmitted and probably written by Coxe, on maple sugar has been republished in New York (*NYDG*, 12 September), "and I dare [*say*] will have useful Effects."

Jonathan Jackson to Elbridge Gerry. ALS, Gerry Papers, MHi. Written from Newburyport, Massachusetts.

St. Paul's Church in Newburyport hopes Gerry can attend the Protestant Episcopal Convention at Philadelphia at the end of September; expects Dalton will attend; refers Gerry to Dalton for copies of the correspondence between the church and other Episcopal congregations "in this quarter."

Thomas Jefferson to Ralph Izard. FC, Jefferson Papers, DLC. Written from Paris. For the full text, see *PTJ* 15:443–45.

Encloses information on the quantity of rice imports to France, and prices at Marseilles and Constantinople; "but we must get rid of the Algerines.

I think this practicable by means honorable and within our power"; will converse on this when Jefferson arrives in New York, probably in February.

John Hoskins Stone to Walter Stone. ALS, Miscellaneous Vertical File, MdHi. Written from Annapolis, Maryland; addressed to Port Tobacco, Maryland.
"I expected Michael [*Jenifer Stone*] before this, but the great question respecting the permanent residence of Congress has detained him."

James Wilkinson to Governor Esteban Miró. Written from New Orleans. Translation of a Copy in Archivo-Nacional, Madrid, Estado, Legajo 3898B, from *American Historical Review* 9(1903–4):764–66.
Asks that Miró's "loan" to Wilkinson be kept secret so that it is not brought to the attention of Congress, "and by arousing the jealous fears of that body, expose me to great embarrassment"; encloses list of "notables" with payments judged necessary to pledge them to the interests of Spain; John Brown is listed for $1,000, among those who are "my confidential friends and support my plan."

John Quincy Adams, Diary. Adams Family Manuscript Trust, MHi.
"I attended again this day in the galleries of the house. The principal debate was upon the salaries of the Judges. The subject was not very interesting; but like almost every other subject exhibited the difficulty of adjusting the opposing sentiments which direct the conduct of men living in different climates and used to very different modes of living."

SATURDAY, 19 SEPTEMBER 1789

John Adams to John Laurance

My second son [*Charles*] the bearer of this letter as soon as he was out of College was entered as a student at Law in the office of Colo. Hamilton upon certain conditions, one that if I should remove from New York, he should be at liberty to remove with me, and another was that if Hamilton should be made a minister of State his pupil should look out another patron. The latter condition being now realized, I send my son to you sir in order to know upon what conditions you will take him into your office.
If it should not be inconvenient to you to receive him I should be obliged to you for your answer. I must still make a condition that I may be at liberty to take him with me wherever I may go. He will board with me, and at-

tend your office as he did Col. Hamiltons, from ten in the morning till three in the afternoon.

FC:lbk, Adams Family Manuscript Trust, MHi.

John Carnes to Benjamin Goodhue

Your Motion was well timed, and had a happy issue, relative to the future residence of Congress. ~~and~~ It is thought so by every Gentleman that is a friend to his Country; and I hope that the permanent residence for ten or fifteen Years, will be the City of New-York. I was sorry that it was taken up, but am glad that it ended as it did. I give You Joy upon Mrs. [*Frances*] Goodhues account, who was very comfortable upon Monday last, and will be below again before your return.[1] I call'd with Mrs. [*Mary*] Carnes, but it was so late that we didn't stop.

The chief of the News this way is the News from France, & what we hear from Congress; and I am glad that our eastern Members are allow'd to be equal to the Southern, and that Mr. Goodhue from the respectable County of Essex, has done Himself, and County so much Honour. Your Motion was, I repeat it, much to the purpose as the matter was taken up, and must be decided. And Now You will have a little quiet. I expect our General Court will come together this Fall if the proposed Amendments shou'd be sent out, and by this time I suppose You know, whether they will, or not.

Upon the whole, I think Congress have done well; but I wish that the importation of many Articles manufactured among Us had been prohibited. *I think it must be done sooner, or later.*

In our County, nothing very remarkable has lately turn'd up, and the uneasiness among the Merchants that I acquainted you with relative to the Impost, I hear but little about; so conclude that they didn't understand the matter. They were very high at first.

We have fine Weather, fine Crops, and our Fishery have done very well, and I hope you will find every thing agreeable when You return. In Boston the Officers of the French Ships, with our Governour [*John Hancock*], & Others, go round with their Visits, & Entertainments, and endeavour to make one another jovial and happy. And perhaps it is right. Your return is so near that this will be my last Epistle, unless You shou'd set longer than You expect, or something remarkable shou'd turn up here.

P. S. I hope my Sons call'd upon You to pay their Compliments.

ALS, Letters to Goodhue, NNS. Written from Lynn, Massachusetts.

[1] The reference is to the birth of Goodhue's seventh child, Stephen, on 27 August.

OTHER DOCUMENTS

Elbridge Gerry to James Sullivan. No copy known; acknowledged in Sullivan to Gerry, 27 September.

Elbridge Gerry to James Warren. No copy known; noted in the endorsement, Warren to Gerry, 27 August.

Hugh Williamson to George Washington. ALS, Washington Papers, DLC.
For the full text, see *PGW* 4:58.
    Office seeking: judgeship for James Iredell; mentions Johnston as his
    brother-in-law and notes that Iredell is "well known" to Major Butler.

SUNDAY, 20 SEPTEMBER 1789

Fine (Johnson)

William Bradford, Jr. to Elias Boudinot

I am glad to find by your letter of the 18th. that Congress will certainly
adjourn in the Course of the present week: & we hope that Elizabeth Town
will detain you but a few days from us. The question of permanent residence
I presume will lie over; a rumor prevailed last night, that the compact had
been broken thro' & Susquehanna rejected. As a citizen of Philada. & indeed
of the union, I should not be sorry of if this proves true. There is something
so Utopian in going into the woods, so far distant from the sea or navigable
water that I have been uniformly of opinion, that it was a mere device to perplex the question & finally postpone the decission.
    ***
What is the fate of the resolution propo[*sed by*] the Committee on the
petition of the public creditors?[1] Was it approved of by both houses or
by either? and may one venture to invest money in this hitherto precarious
property? I wish your advice on this point as some propositions are made to
me & I cannot tell how to decide.
    ***

ALS, Wallace Papers, PHi. Written from "Rosehill," Bradford's estate outside Philadelphia. The omitted text includes a request for assistance with subscriptions to Alexander Dal-
las's reports of Pennsylvania judicial cases.

[1] For the petition of the public creditors of Pennsylvania (1789), see *DHFFC* 8:260–90.

Tench Coxe to James Madison

I am favored with your letter of the 18th. from wch. I find the ground of apprehension, particularly refer'd to by me, entirely removed. In regard to the probable effects of a position on Delaware or Susquehannah upon the Convention of Virginia could they have foreseen it, I am convinced they would have been fatal. *** In regard to the merits of the Question upon the two Rivers I have endeavoured to view it as impartially as in my power. I think the future state of population has not been well conjectured by either side. I am satisfied that the balance of Agricultural population will preponderate in favor of the Potowmack, but I really doubt whether Susquehannah where it intersects our County of Lancaster will be as near to the centre of agricultural, manufacturing & commercial population as some part of the Delaware. You are not to understand however that I am decided for placing the permanent Seat upon any part of this last River. The agricultural centre, and the facility of Western communication, and the Union of the Southern and N. Eastern States furnish stronger arguments in favor of Susquehannah than my interest & attachments to Delaware are able to answer. I have always considered [*lined out*] it as a great argument in favor of the Scheme of American Manufactures, that it would, in a manner not obnoxious, gently counteract that scattering of our population which too rapidly went on from the moment of peace; a principal Objection to which was that it too much co-operated with the vices of our general government. A weak—and relaxed civil Authority and a very sparse and extending population presented to my mind no prospect of the ~~Contin~~ restoration of order among ourselves—or of confidence among our foreign friends. This and other weighty reasons to which your attention need not be drawn will convince you that the progress of Manufactures will be very great & that the Southern states which from the nature of things will be almost entirely agricultural will not be populated in proportion to territory when considered relatively with the Country North of Potowmack where the commercial hives already exist, and where manufacturing Scenes must yearly open and encrease. It is a little remarkable that when the seat of the general Government was formerly under consideration two positions were taken at the same. Trenton to meet occasionally the wishes of the North—George Town with the same view to the South.[1] It should seem that it was then the Opinion that neither place would accommodate both parties. So far as the argument goes it is against each place—and forces us into a middle position. Tis a certain truth of no small weight that ~~Trenton~~ Delaware, & Potowmack are the extremest stations ever proposed by the contending interests. I am deeply impressed with the dangerous situation of our Union with the South-Western people. I would be just & liberal towards them. But I consider Vermont—and even the

Northern Country of the New England states in the Union as having severally manifested very unfavorable dispositions. We are in a situation where
small deviations from distributive Justice may put much hazard. I trust however very confidently in the impartiality—virtue—and wisdom of the most
influential Members of our government for as good a decision as circumstances will admit—and an early correction of any error which they may
discover.

***

ALS, Madison Papers, DLC. For the full text, see *PJM* 12:412–15. The omitted text reports on Coxe's conversation with Marbois on French trade regulations in St. Domingo and
political events in France, the Pennsylvania constitutional convention, and the constitution
of the Protestant Episcopal church.

---

[1] In the October 1783 "dual residence" compromise proposed by Gerry, the Confederation Congress decided to build two permanent residences and alternate between them.

Tristram Dalton to Michael Hodge

The permanent residence Bill will not be completed this session—great
difficulties must present themselves in the prosecution of this affair, and for
years to come real disadvantages accrue, if the Plan succeeds of fixing on any
Country Place, distant from a large Town.

After spending a little more time on this business and vibrating from
one *proposed* place to another, it is probable they will by and bye sit down in
the neighborhood of Philadelphia. The Eastern Gentlemen were obliged to
press the scheme for the Susquehannah, to prevent going to the Potowmak.
The Virginians & those who were violent for the latter are now much chagrined at their insisting on the Question's being brought on at this time.

EIHC 25(1888):24. This source omitted the beginning and the end of the letter.

Benjamin Goodhue to Michael Hodge

Yours of 15th came to hand last evening. We are now finishing off the
bussines of the present session which will doubtless close in the course of this
week—the Judicial bill will probably be sent tomorrow or next day to the
President for his approbation, its materialy the same as reported at first in
the Senate—the Amendments made by the Senate to our amendments are
now before us, in which they have struck out the word Vicinage as applied to
juries, and the sum limiting an appeal to the Supream Court, these are great
objects to the Virginians, who have been the great Agents in this bussines,
and what the effect will be is quite uncertain whether We may finaly agree

with the Senate or whether it may occasion a postponement of the whole subject to next session—the place of permanent residence is so cloged, that I think We shall hardly get there this session which will answer our purposes quite as well as tho' it was decided on, if it does but make them willing not again to disturb our quiet with the alurements of the Patowmack.

[*P. S.*] An estimate has been made of the probable amount of our present revenue, agreably to the best accounts We can get of the whole imports for 1788 and We make it to be about 1,500,000 Dollrs. ℔ annum—Philada. has already secured and receiv'd I am informed near 60,000 Dollrs. and this City abt. 40,000 Dollrs.

ALS, Ebenezer Stone Papers, MSaE.

Thomas Hartley to Jasper Yeates

I wrote you on Friday and told you that I believed we were blown up or in a bad way—our Circumstances are very little better at present—The inclosed proviso[1] gave so much Disgust to the City Member[s] that they stoped Short at once—whether this was Finess or not I will not undertake to say—We shall at a future Day be able to be more decided.

For my own Part I cannot say that I like the Proviso very well I would have rather had the Bill without it, but to abandon the Principle because we cannot obtain all—To relinquish the general Interest of Pennsylvania—because a Measure might do a partial Injury to the City—tho' otherwise of general good, is what I cannot subscribe to. There was a possibility that the Proviso would be corrected in the Senate.

The President was put in a critical Situation—It is true—but he has a strong Biass for the Potomac but the Rules of Candor and Honor which have ever governed him in Life would not have been deviated from upon this Occasion—and even a Mistake would have been exposed.

A great Body of the People of Pennsylvania are interested in the Navigation of the Susquehanna—They have a right to improve the *Navigation* of it—and in Future (let Matters turn out as they will in the present Business), the Object will certainly be obtained.

We mean to try to get the Clause reconsidered to Morrow—and if possible strike it out—but if we cannot succeed in that still we ought to pass the Law and leave it to the Discretion of the State Legislature to adopt the Terms or not.

Maryland has already done what is necessary, or at least little more will be wanting.[2]

We are now confined to so short a Time before adjournment and the Impatience of the Senate as well as our own Body to get away may tend to frustrate the Bill—on Friday we might have carried the Bill with the Proviso but I fear the Suspension will totally defeat us—I do not know with Certainty if even the City Members will vote to Morrow—but I shall not be surprized to hear Trentown named again.

The Game was in our Hands in my opinion but my Confidence was never firm—I have now little hopes of Succeeding.

*** I shall probably see you at the Close of next Week or the beginning of the Week after that.

***

ALS, Yeates Papers, PHi. The omitted text discusses a Pennsylvania constitutional convention.

---

¹ See Smith to Williams, 18 September, n. 1, above.

² Maryland incorporated the Susquehanna Canal Company in 1783 to clear the river of obstructions and to provide short canals around major obstacles between the Pennsylvania line and Chesapeake Bay.

Rufus King to Caleb Strong

Mr. Sedgwick will explain to you the mazy business of a permanent residence, the bill is yet in the house of representatives, and we are told that it is yet uncertain whether they will pass it in favor of the Susquehannah or the Delaware—the judiciary bill is nearly finished, it went through the house without material alterations—the Bill concerning Crimes & punishments is referred by the house to the next Session—the bill fixing the judiciary Salaries came up yesterday from the house—the senate raised the Salary of the Chief Justice from 3500 to 4000 Dollars, and will go through the bill Tomorrow.

I subjoin a schedule of the salaries as fixed in the house.
***

You are quite as able to guess [*blot*] the judiciary appointments as I am; the Mass. Gentlemen say that the probability stands thus—Ch[*ief*]. J[*ustice*]. [*William*] Cushing, or Mr. [*John*] Lowell associate Judge—Mr. [*Francis*] Dana District Judge, Mr. [*Christopher*] Gore or Mr. [*William*] Tudor Attorney for the District—Judge [*David*] Sewall District Judge of main, & Genl. [*William*] Lithgow Attorney.

I hope that Mr. Jay will be ch. Justice, and the probability in that case is that Mr. Jefferson will be secretary of State.

[*P. S.*] Tuesday next is proposed for the adjournment, whether we shall get through with our business I am uncertain; but the adjournment will be very soon.

ALS, Thompson Collection, CtHC.

Samuel Livermore to John Langdon

I recd. your favours of the 11th & 12th instant. I have nominated to Mr. [*Tobias*] Lear, who waited on me for the purpose, Mr. [*John*] Sulivan & Mr. [*John*] Pickering one of which for district Judge. The salary is 1000 dols. per ann. Major [*Jonathan*] Cass of Exeter for marshal no salary. My son Ned [*Edward*] for Atto. genl. for the district no salary. I don't know who will be appointed.
[*P. S.*] In hopes to set out the middle of the week.

ALS, Langdon Papers, NhPoA.

Samuel A. Otis to John Langdon

Altho Mr. Wingate and the other Gentlemen will detail to you all the news, I cannot omit so good an opp[*ortunit*]y. to pay my respects to you & Mrs. [*Elizabeth*] Langdon, & to hope you got home well & found all friends so—There were many knotty points to discuss when you was here, & there were some agitated with great celerity since. The Compensation bill [*Salaries-Legislative Act HR-19*] was so tossed & tumbled from House to House, that I thot the poor thing would have died with convulsions; and had you heard the zealous attack upon your Secretarys two dollars pr. diem allowance, you would have supposed I was going to lay my sacrilegious hand upon the whole Treasury of the United States—After all its squeesings I dont know but it will be strangled by the President, for it has been with him several days, & never a word has been heard of the poor thing—All I can say is, if it dies, I hope its Ghost will haunt some people who shall be nameless.

Vice Precis [*President*] too cannot get a farthing above £1500, altho' the Committee reported £1800, this I think is confounded hard as they wont give him *a Title*, they should have comforted him with 'tother thousand.

I hear [*Benjamin*] Fishbourn is come to fight himself into character—Now I do not think a Senator obliged to fight in doors & out too, At least not, unless he has double pay, as the Speaker has, or at least more than six Dollars.

If however *our Gun* [*Gunn*] should go off, it appears to me it will be a two & forty[1]—So Mr. F[*ishbourn*]. may as well take care of his head at the same time he is defending his reputation—There is a most outrageous attack on the Georgia Senators in their papers.[2]

Enclosed is a list of the Laws & Resolves which are perfected—Also of some appointments since Your departure.

The Journals & Laws are printed, but not knowing how to convey them to you, those you may still want, must be reserved until your return.

By the way had you not better bring a few spare dollars to purchase a farm on the East Bank of the Susquehannah?

[*P. S.*] The *Keeper of the Tower* [*Jay*] is waiting to see which Salary is best, that of Lord Chief Justice or Secretary of State.

ALS, Langdon Papers, NhPoS.

<hr>

[1] The largest guns carried on the lower deck of a first rate ship of the line in the British Royal Navy, named for the forty-two pound balls they fired.

[2] See Letter from New York to [*Benjamin Fishbourn*], 10 August, volume 16.

Samuel A. Otis to Caleb Strong

Altho I can furnish you with little news, I cannot refrain my remembrances to you & your friends, whom I hope you found all well—There were many knotty points to discuss before you left the Senate, but you had not the unravelling of all of them—Compensation [*Salaries-Legislative Act HR-19*] was a bone indeed—Bless me how the man of Connecticut [*Ellsworth*] did gnaw, & pick, & growl at it, & after all he could not bite it—You would have thot however that your poor inoffensive Secy., was going to lay his avaricious paw upon Excise & impost, if not the whole property of the Union—What says Oliver! two dollars ₩ day "to a very *subordinate* officer indeed"? "It will never do; Your Goverment is gone"—I am glad by the way your honor was with your dear wife, Otherwise, rolling down Hill, I fear you too would have given me a kick—The poor bill had like to have died of Convulsions between the two Houses, but I dont know but its reserved to be smothered to death by the Prest. for it has been with him a number of days—*Vice* [*Adams*] too cannot get a Cent beyond 5000 [*dollars*], altho a Committee reported 6000, and confered "about it and about it"—As they give him *no title* they *should* have comforted him with the other thousand.

Lord high Treasury, and many other appointments have taken place since your departure. Mr. Jay is to be chief Justice, or Secy. of State, at option—Suppose he will take that which gives the *best Salary*. Mr. Few you heard went with Commissioners to Georgia.

Enclosing you a list of the laws & resolves.

ALS, Strong Collection, MNF. Addressed to Northampton, Massachusetts. The date has been supplied based on its references to the Salaries-Legislative Act [HR-19] and its similarity to Otis's letter of this date to Langdon.

From New York

The report of the Committee on the Salaries of the Judiciary, was taken up yesterday, in the House, and the salaries further curtailed—Chief Justice to 3500—and reduced the Attorney-General to 1500 Dollars. The Bill was then sent to the Senate, who raised the Chief Justice to 4000–but the rest were not acted upon. The Bill for *confirming the acts of the late Congress for establishing troops in the Western Frontiers* [*Troops Act HR-27*] was ordered to be engrossed. Further accounts of hostilities by the Indians have been recently received. The AMENDMENTS, as amended by the Senate were yesterday brought on the carpet, and *again* amended. What the Senate has done, does not suit—I believe it will be extremely difficult to obtain a coincidence of sentiment on this subject. PERMANENT RESIDENCE business comes on tomorrow—this business does not appear to be in a train for a speedy settlement—still they talk of an adjournment, by the last of next week. The JUDICIAL BILL as amended by the House, has been returned from the Senate, with a concurrence in all the amendments but *four*, which it is supposed will be given up by the House. I think the adjournment will take place next Friday. There is such a confidence in the Government, that the *needful*, I am told, for the present occasion, has been very easily raised. From a computation of the amount of the Impost for two or three years last past—and from the proceeds in some of the Custom-Houses, it is estimated that the Impost will net 2,500,000 dollars per annum. The Civil List expenses, including Executive, Legislative and Judicial, is estimated at 350,000 dollars per ann. In Philadelphia, I am told, the Collection has been in the first month after the Impost Law took effect, 55,000 dollars—In this city upwards of 40,000. And the second month will be much greater.

[Boston] *Massachusetts Centinel*, 26 September; reprinted at Portsmouth, New Hampshire, and Worcester, Massachusetts.

OTHER DOCUMENTS

Elias Boudinot to William Bradford, Jr. No copy known; acknowledged in Bradford to Boudinot, 22 September.

Benjamin Goodhue to Stephen Goodhue. ALS, Goodhue Family Papers, MSaE.
　　Has heard that he will receive all his pay in cash at New York, if he chooses; "I think it is universaly understood and expected We shall be up in all this week tho' I don't suppose We shall on Tuesday."

Rufus King to Christopher Gore. No copy known; acknowledged in Gore to King, 27 September.

Tobias Lear to John Langdon. ALS, Langdon-Elwyn Family Papers, NhHi.
    Office seeking: intended judicial nominees for New Hampshire; "P. S. As these nominations are not made, and there is a *possibility* that something may occur to make an alteration of them proper—You will not consider this information as *public*."

Robert Morris to James Milligan. ALS, Morris-Milligan Papers, PPL. Addressed to Philadelphia.
    Office seeking: the President has received Milligan's letter.

James Sullivan to Elbridge Gerry. ALS, Gerry Papers, MHi. Written from Boston.
    Regrets the "uneasiness prevailing" respecting the treasury appointments; "what will be the political Consequences of raising an Army at this Time to gain possession of the forts [*occupied by the British in the Northwest Territory*]?"

George Thatcher to Sarah Thatcher. ALS, Thatcher Family Papers, MHi.
    "I begin to fear the adjournment will be postponed till Thursday or Saturday"; is detained "only to get money to bring me home"; will not have time to tarry more than a day or two after he meets her in Weston, Massachusetts; on their way home he must stop in Boston two or three days, and another two or three in Newburyport.

Daniel Hiester, Account Book. PRHi.
    Traveled to Harlem with F. A. Muhlenberg and Beckley.

MONDAY, 21 SEPTEMBER 1789

Fine (Johnson)

John Adams to Stephen Higginson

*** Your "Ideas of revenue and commerce" I should be glad to receive, as well as any other information relative to the affairs of this nation, whose welfare is near my heart tho' it is not probable it will ever be in my power to do it much service. My own opinions of what is necessary to be done, to secure the liberty, and promote the prosperity of this Country if not singular, have too small a number of supporters to be of much use. May heaven grant that tradgedies and calamities may not in time convince Americans, when it is too late, that they have missed the tide in the affairs of men.[1] Democratical powers equally with Aristocratical powers pushed to extremities, necessarily produce a feudal system. this Country has already been very near the brink: within a short space of seeing hostile armies commanded by factious leaders, encamped on every great mountain and defended by a Baron's castle. And if more pains and care than any disposition for has yet appeared are not taken to limit and adjust our national government, to raise it decidedly above the state government, and to prevent collisions of sovereignties, we may yet be not so far removed from a scene of feudal anarchy as we imagine. Thus you see I begin to be a *croaker*. Tho' the character is not natural to me.

FC:lbk, Adams Family Manuscript Trust, MHi. Addressed to Boston. The omitted text, printed in *DHSCUS* 1:663, concerns federal appointments and the role of the Supreme Court.

---

[1] "Tide in the affairs of men," from Shakespeare's *Julius Caesar,* act 4, scene 3.

John Adams to James Sullivan

Your letter of the 23 of July remains unanswered. There is in the United States and the regions to the southward of it a body of people, possesed of too much of the public confidence who are desperately in debt, and therefore determined [*against?*] all or any government, which shall have power to compel them to pay. Untill the property possesed by some of these men shall change hands, no government will be consistent in this Country. Trial by jury by the judicial bill and by the amendments to the constitution, already passed I imagine is secured to the utmost of your wishes.

The exorbitance of the power of the crown as it was exercised in this Country before the revolution was not generally complained of—it was the authority claimed by Parliament, and the attempt to increase the power of the crown and to diminish and annihilate the power of our legislatures which gave the alarm. The legal prerogatives of the crown were asserted and contended for by Mr. [*James, Jr.*] Otis Mr. [*Oxenbridge*] Thatcher and Mr. S[*amuel*]. Adams in speeches and writings constantly, as essential to the protection of the rights of the people, and the liberties of the subject.

What ever there is of danger in England at present from the power of the crown, arises not from its having an over ballance, but it arises from the Aristocracy's having an over ballance. The truth of fact is, that the people on one side and the crown on the other are each of them singly weaker than the Aristocracy; and as power increases like a snow ball, by rolling, if the influence of that Aristocracy should increase much farther so strong an union will be formed between the people and the crown in opposition to it, that the King will be absolute. If a few leading characters among the great land-holder's were united as they were by the late Coalition administration,[1] the Constitution would be overturned. King and people both would be prison-ers to an oligarchic Junto. King and people would then unite to pull it down, as they did. You hope that our limbs will gain strength by time. Indeed they will. But what limbs? Will the weak ones gain, and the strong ones loose? This would be contrary to nature and experience. The strong arm by con-stant exercise grows stronger, and draws the juices and nutrition from the weaker. If at our first setting out the executive power is not a counterpoise to the legislative; and if in the legislature, there be not a mediating power, sufficient at all times to decide the disputes between the poor and the rich, we shall not have law, nor consequently liberty nor property. The older we grow the more those ideas of equilibrium to which we were born and bred will wear out of the minds of the people, and Barons wars of a thousand years may be the miserable fate of America as it has been of Europe—a little longer delay might have exibited the feudal scene in America—[*John*] Hancock encamped upon Bacon [*Beacon*] hill, and [*Benjamin*] Lincoln on Pens hill the one entitled Duke of Tremontain and the other duke of the blue hills[2]—Washington encamped on mount Vernon and [*Patrick*] Henry on some other hillock—[*George*] Clinton on one side of Hudsons river and [*Robert*] Yates or a Livingston on the other. Pushing to extremities either Democratical or Aristocratical powers without attending to a ballance, pro-duces a feudal system as naturally and necessarily, as the collision of flint and steel produces fire. I may expose myself to abuse and misrepresentations by such sentiments as these: but I have uniformly entertained them, and time will discover who is in the right. I have run the gauntlet too long among li-bels, halters, axes, daggers, cannon balls and pistol bullet, in the service of this people, to be at this age afraid of their injustice. Those who wish for an-archy and civil war will not easily gain me over to their party.

FC:lbk, Adams Family Manuscript Trust, MHi.

---

[1] The name given to the ministry headed by the former enemies Lord North and Charles James Fox between February and December 1783, when it was succeeded by George III's popular ally, William Pitt "the Younger."

[2] Beacon Hill, the highest point in Boston, was the site of Hancock's mansion and one of the three hills that gave the city its earliest English name, "Tremont." Penn's Hill and the Blue Hills are prominent landmarks in Massachusetts' South Shore, in the neighborhood of Lincoln's hometown of Hingham.

John Quincy Adams to James Bridge

***

Since my arrival here, I have been very constant in my attendance in the galleries of the house of representatives and have heard almost all the speakers, upon the various topics of the permanent seat of residence, the amendments, the judiciary system, judges salaries &c. &c. The greatest speakers in the house, as to *quantity* are, *Gerry, Jackson* of Georgia, and *Burke* of S. Carolina; and as to quality, *Ames, Maddison* and *Vining.* Yet you might search in vain throughout the house, for the flashes of Demosthenes, or for the splendid illumination of Cicero. Nay I frankly acknowledge, that I have as yet heard no speaking equal to what I have heard from Dr. [*Charles*] Jarvis in our State legislature.

ALS, Gilder Lehrman Collection, NHi. The remainder of the letter was written on 27 September.

Gaetano Drago di Domenico to Pierce Butler

I did myself the honour to write you on the 7th. Inst. in order to forward you the duplicate of my Petition to the most Honorable Congress and also to Solicit your powerful interference in behalf of my project, which I flatter myself with hoping you will kindly deign to grant to it: I likewise made bold to give you Sir, a few Current prices of your Articles on our Market, and shall hear with pleasure if you would desire the Continuance of them either for yourself or your friends.

Although as yet in suspense with respect to the reception my project may meet with before the Most Honorable Congress, yet as I would not wish to fail in any instance that may prove by the most unremitting attention my earnest desire to Communicate an Account of whatever transactions may happen to occur in this place worthy of note, in hopes that it may be agreeable to it, and will pardon the boldness of my attempt. The purport of this present serves to inform you that in Consequence of a project that has been formed here to make a Truce with the Barbary Regencies in order to Obtain a free Navigation for the flag of this Republic, provided the payment of a fixed sum for a year, I have therefore taken the liberty to enclose here a Copy of the Said project together with a letter to the Most Honorable Congress, which Sir if you will graciously Condescend to present to It, you will add a very great weight to the many obligations I already owe you, and which will be greatly impressed with gratitude in my heart.[1]

***

ALS, Butler Papers, PHi. Written from Genoa, Italy; addressed to "Peter Buttler." The enclosed letter and proposal are printed in *DHFFC* 1:227–28.

[1] For background on Domenico's proposal, see *DHFFC* 8:1–2.

Thomas Hartley to Tench Coxe

I received your Favor of the 16th inst. with the News paper enclosed and with pleasure take Notice of the Honorable Resolution your Merchants[1] have entered into respecting the Collecting of the Duties.

We a few Days ago had a fair Prospect of fixing the permanent Seat of Congress in Pennsylvania, but that Business has now become very problematical if not totally lost for this Session.

A Proviso[2] which was intended by our Adversaries as an embarrassment and their last Stake was offered—two of the Maryland Gentlemen[3] who generally went with us left us upon that Question by which it was carried— and your two City Members said that as the Proviso was delusive and might tend to the Injury of the City they could not vote for the Bill with such a Clause—a Suspension happened—and I fear it will be difficult to get Things in so good a Train again.

I enclose you the Mighty Proviso—I can assure you it does not alarm me very much.

We had a ~~very~~ good Chance to get it corrected or rejected in the Senate— but if it had remained, was it not proper to have left it to the Discretion of the State of Pennsylvania to determine whether she would have accepted the Conditions? nay would she not have renewed her ~~former~~ Negotiations with Delaware and Maryland before she came to a Conclusion.[4]

I presume some Attempt will be made to Day to forward the Bill—its Fate will be uncertain.

In this Important [*lined out*] Consideration So many various Interests have occasionally operated that it is almost impossible to determine how the final Issue will be—If there has been a Mistake I presume it will be detected— No Doubt but the Blame will fall some where, perhaps I may not escape myself. As I shall see you soon, I shall now conclude.

P. S. Your Name will be mentioned this Morning respecting a certain Matter.[5]

ALS, Coxe Papers, PHi. Addressed to Philadelphia.

[1] Presumably the same committee of merchants that had written the Pennsylvania delegation on 16 July. The resolution proposed a change in the Coasting Act [HR-16]. See Read to Read, 14 September, above, Meade to Coxe, 25 September, below, and *DHFFC* 4:277–80.

[2] See Smith to Williams, 18 September, n. 2, above.

[3] Seney and Smith.

[4] At a conference in Wilmington, Delaware, in November 1786, delegates from Pennsylvania, Maryland, and Delaware failed to agree on a plan for constructing a canal across the fourteen mile wide isthmus between the Delaware and Chesapeake bays (Ralph D. Gray, *The National Waterway: A History of the Chesapeake and Delaware Canal, 1769–1985* [Urbana, Ill., 1983], p. 8]).

[5] Coxe sought to be appointed postmaster general.

Frederick A. Muhlenberg to Tench Coxe

Your favour was delivered to me on Saturday Evening, when it was too late to wait on the president, but I shall this Morning together with My Brother wait on him and urge the Matter in Question[1] to the utmost of my Power. I have also seen Mr. A[rthur]. Lee, Col. Hartley Genl. Hiester & Wynkoop who think with me on the Subject. I have not yet had a good Opportunity to converse with Mr. Maddison, but shall have it to Day. Mr. Lee is indefatigable &, I think saw Maddison last Evening after he left me. Poor McClay is still confined to his Room, but hope a few Days more will enable him to be out.

Business has crouded upon us so fast that we shall probably not adjourn before friday or Saturday, and the Maryland Gentlemen have carried a Clause[2] in the Bill for establishing the Seat of Congress by one Vote only, which probably will defeat the Bill this Session. We shall try it this Day or tomorrow.

ALS, Coxe Papers, PHi. Addressed to Philadelphia.

[1] The question of appointing Coxe postmaster general.
[2] See Smith to Williams, 18 September, n. 1, above.

William Smith (Md.) to Otho H. Williams

The Govr. of the Western territory [*Arthur St. Clair*] went from hence on Saturday last. Capt. [*Erkuries*] Beatty the paymaster, not yet gone, he waits for Cash, And as Congress will, I expect rise the last of this week, the members will probably Sweep away all the money in the Treasury to enable them, to pay their debts & go home, therefore, Beatty must probably wait a little longer. I expect to leave N. York About ~~this day week~~ Next Monday or Tuesday, tell Peggy [*Margaret Smith*] She must prepare to go to house keeping by the latter end of *Next week*, when I hope to reach home, I thank you for your kind invitation to yr. house, but as my business is much deranged by my long absence, I must apply ~~to business~~ for sometime, & for that purpose it will be necessary that I am in my own house where I may probably remain during the Winter.

The bill for the permanent seat, has not yet been brought forward, perhaps both parties are afraid to try their Strength, & it may Still remain undecided this Session. The friends to Delaware [*River*] are not without their hopes & great interest is Still making for that place.

ALS, Williams Papers, MdHi. Addressed to Baltimore.

OTHER DOCUMENTS

Elias Boudinot to William Bradford, Jr. No copy known; acknowledged in Bradford to Boudinot, 22 September.

William Hunt to John Adams. ALS, Adams Family Manuscript Trust, MHi. Written from Watertown, Massachusetts.
    Office seeking: federal marshal for Massachusetts; Hunt is known to the entire state delegation.

George Read, Jr. to George Read. ALS, Rodney Collection of Read Papers, DeHi. Written from New Castle, Delaware. For a partial text, see *DHSCUS* 4:520.
    Acknowledges newspapers with seat of government debate; seeks information about how to proceed in Adam Caldwell revenue case (see *DHFFC* 8:429–30).

William Smith to George Washington. ALS, Item 78, 21:541, PCC, DNA. Written from the College of Philadelphia. For the full text, see *PGW* 4:63–64.
    Solicits the Washingtons as subscribers to his "Proposals for Printing a Body of Sermons" before application is made to members of Congress; has asked Morris to solicit the Washingtons before he presents it to any Senators.

Charles Thomson to William Samuel Johnson. Written from "Harriton," Thomson's home outside Philadelphia. Copy, Miscellaneous Letters, RG 59, DNA.
    Laments that Roger Alden has not been provided with an office; encloses a letter to be forwarded to Alden.

John Quincy Adams, Almanac Diary. Adams Family Manuscript Trust, MHi.
    Attends House debates: "Amendments. Burke, Gerry, Bland &c."

Ezra Stiles, Diary. Stiles Papers, CtY.
Paid his respects to Washington, in company with Sherman.

TUESDAY, 22 SEPTEMBER 1789

Fine (Johnson)

Benjamin Goodhue to Samuel Phillips, Jr.

The inclosed came to me under cover. We have passed the bill establishing the salaries of the Judicial department, and after much labour reduced
them from the sums reported to what youl see in the inclosed news paper,
they are now before the Senate, and yesterday they took it up and raised the
chief Justice up to 4000 by a vote of 8 to 7 and I am sorry to find a Massachusetts Gentleman [*Dalton*] in the majority as I am afraid it will be give a
direction simular to the subsequent ones and cause us trouble to bring it and
others back again, don't by any means lisp what I have above hinted at—if
I had had a suspicion of his voting so I would have made it my bussines to
have talked with him previously on the subject, I still will do it—the subject of permanent residence will probably end without any issue, as I have
all along hope'd and expected, the amendments to the Amendments as come
from the Senate are before us, some of them are not relished by the Virginians and I have some doubts whether after all thats been done, We shall be
able to agree upon them this session—I expect We shall rise in the course of
this Week, and be at home the next week—I have no doubt but the opinions of the House are so much changed relative to compensations, that was
the bussines to do over again We should be likely to do it in such a manner
as would not be liable to great objections—I am determined to try a repeal
the next session of those we have passed at least of the most exceptionable
ones and I think I shall be supported.

ALS, Phillips Family Collection, MHi. Goodhue misdated this letter 20 September; the
correction is based on internal evidence.

William Grayson to George Washington

I do myself the honor to inform you that the Honble. John Tyler & Mr.
[*James*] Henry Judges of the late Court of Admy. in Virga. have signified
their desire of serving in the capacity of district Judge of that State.
Mr. [*James*] Innis Atto[*rney*]. Genl. of the State of Virga. has also expressed
his inclination of serving as Atto. general of the district Court; I should also

presume that the Office of Atto. general of the supreme Court would not be disagreeable.

ALS, Washington Papers, DLC.

George Thatcher to Sarah Thatcher

The time of adjournment is this day post-poned to saturday—which will also delay my arrival at Weston till the next week on Thursday; & I verily think I shall be there by that time if I am well—at lest I know of nothing that can prevent—For all the business, now before Congress, will be dispached by saturday; and almost all the members have set their minds upon going home.

It is in contemplation that when Congress adjourn they do not meet again till the first of January—should this be the case it will give me one month more to tarry at home, and be some compensation for the disappointments I have several times met, in not returning at the times appointed.
***

I assure you I am not a little solicitous to get home—I fear Phillips will wholly forget me—as for Sally, it is impossible she should have any knowledge of her papa—And it is quite uncertain whether I should at first recognize her countenance, were I to see her unexpectedly, at a place, where I did not expect to meet her.

You will have no more last words from me at this place—that is—it is so highly probable I shall leave this place on Monday, that I ~~think~~ promise myself the wished pleasure of being with you on the thursday after this comes to hand.

ALS, Thatcher Family Papers, MHi. Addressed to Weston, Massachusetts. In the omitted text Thatcher complains about the lack of letters from home.

Other Documents

John Adams to Cotton Tufts. FC:lbk, Adams Family Manuscript Trust, MHi.
Forwarded Tufts' letters to the President regarding federal appointments in Newburyport, Massachusetts, but the final choices were influenced by the recommendations of Governor John Hancock.

William Bradford, Jr. to Elias Boudinot. ALS, Wallace Papers, PHi. Place from which written not specified, but presumably Philadelphia. For the full text, see *Boudinot* 2:53–55.
Office seeking: "the Gentlemen of the law at this place" unanimously favored Edward Shippen as federal district judge for Pennsylvania, but

questioned the propriety of making a recommendation; if Shippen is dropped, recommends William Barton.

William Samuel Johnson to Pierpont Edwards. ALS, American Manuscripts, CSmH. Addressed to New Haven, Connecticut.
Edwards will be appointed federal attorney, not a federal judge; Wadsworth and Johnson did everything in their power to obtain the latter for him; "will tell you all when I have the pleasure to see you next Month in Connecticut"; adjournment is postponed until Saturday.

Arthur Lee to Tench Coxe. ALS, Coxe Papers, PHi. Addressed to Philadelphia; franked by Richard Henry Lee.
Has spoken with the Speaker, who promised to speak with the President in favor of nominating Coxe as postmaster general, "which joined with Mr. Madison I think will form a more powerful interest than any one else can have."

Richard Bland Lee to Sir John Temple. Copy, Foreign Office 4/7 p. 207, PRO.
Refers to Lee's delivery of documents "some time ago," relating to efforts to locate Matthew Whiting, Jr., son of a constituent; acknowledges Temple's offer to send the documents to "British residents on the Coast of Barbary"; has been informed by Arthur Lee that Temple has mislaid the documents; describes Whiting; "If you should be instrumental in recovering this valuable young gentleman, you will render a most grateful service."

Moses Levy to George Read. ALS, Read Manuscripts, PHi. Written from Philadelphia. For the full text, see *Read*, pp. 487–88.
Office seeking: has not corresponded since Read went to New York; "the greater part of the Lawyers here" hope Edward Shippen will be appointed Pennsylvania district judge instead of Francis Hopkinson.

George W. Smith to James Madison. ALS, Madison Papers, DLC. Written from Tappahannock, Virginia. For the full text, see *PJM* 12:418.
Office seeking: concurs with Madison's advice about the slim prospects for appointment to federal office; "as it is possible that *** an *equitable principle of defusive* Appointments may prevail; I shall endeavour to qualify myself *generally*" for some future office.

Edward Tilghman to George Read. ALS, Rodney Collection of Read Papers, DeHi. Written from Philadelphia. For the full text, see *Read*, p. 488.
Office seeking: Edward Shippen for Pennsylvania federal district judge; "I am not upon such a Footing with any of the Delegates from Pennsyl-

vania as to justify an Application to them. This you will consider as made also to Mr. Bassett."

John Quincy Adams, Almanac Diary. Adams Family Manuscript Trust, MHi.
"Went to see Mr. Ames."

[Winchester] *Virginia Gazette*, 23 September.
Eleanor (Mrs. William) Grayson died in Frederick County, Virginia.

Letter from New York. [Worcester] *Massachusetts Spy*, 1 October; reprinted at Portsmouth and Exeter, New Hampshire.
Congress has resolved to adjourn on 26 September: "by that time the business before Congress will be completed"; some contemplate a law "for altering the time fixed in the constitution for the meeting of Congress from the first Monday in December, to some time in January or February."

Letter from New York. [Portland, Maine] *Cumberland Gazette*, 2 October. The editors believe that the writer was probably Thatcher and the recipient Thomas B. Wait, the newspaper's editor.
"The business of the Session is nearly compleated, and it is probable that Congress will adjourn on Saturday next.
The President this day returned the Bill for establishing the Court of Justice, having approved and signed the same. He also made the following nominations to the Senate of persons for Judges, Attornies and Marshals: *** "

WEDNESDAY, 23 SEPTEMBER 1789

Hot (Johnson)

Agreement between the Pennsylvania and New York Delegations

The citizens of new york having been at considerable expence in preparing buildings for the accomodation of Congress—we the subscribers severally engage upon our honor that we will not consent to the removal of congress from the City of new york to any other place prior to the month of January 1793—that we will use our influence to prevent such removal; and we do hereby enjoin upon our Successors the observance of this Engagement—Provided that this engagement is to be void unless a law passes during the present session to establish the permanent ~~Residence~~ seat of congress within a district in Pennsylvania including the Town of Germantown.

Copy, King Papers, NHi; hand of King. This agreement was signed by every member of the Pennsylvania delegation except Maclay, Hartley, and Hiester. The New Yorkers did not sign the document.

Abiel Foster to Oliver Peabody

I find the judicial Bill now before Congress has given some uneasiness in New Hampshire: I wish those polititions who are opposed to it, will be pleased to propose a substitute; & I call on them to suggest a plan for administring Justice, in those instances in which the general Goverment is invested with it by the Constitution, which will be less objectionable than the general principals contained in the present one. It will perhaps be said, that the State Courts might well enough have been entrusted with the matter in the first instance, and the expense of the district Courts thereby saved to the public. I wish those who have adopted this Idea, to examine the Constitution in those parts of it which relate to this subject. They will there find, that the Judicial powers of the Union, are to be vested in one Supreme Court, & such other inferior Courts as Congress shall think proper—that the Judges of those Courts, are to have fixed & permanent Salaries, and to hold their places during good behavior—This you must be sensible, cannot apply to the State Courts, whose Salaries depend only on the Legislatures of the respective States, and who hold their places by the precarious tenure—The arraingment therefore contained in the Bill, is such an one, as I conceive every member of the general Goverment is bound by the Constitution to adopt who has taken an Oath to maintain the same. I would further observe, that no confidence can be placed in the State Courts to decide properly, while they are not amenable to the general Goverment, but wholly dependent o[n *the State*] Goverment. In those cases where the interests of the general Goverment & a particular State may happen to interfere, to which side is it to be supposed the State judges will feel a biass? I concieve to the interest of that Goverment on which they are imediately dependent for their support & their places, and may not this biass take place in instances, that relate to the very existance of the general Goverment? This I believe may be expected. I should consider the general Goverment as of very little consequence without its having a judicial coextensive ~~without~~ with its legislative power, & of equal energy; for of what avail are the wisest & most salutary Laws, without a firm & unbiassed judicial, to carry those Laws into effect? In some of the States the Judges have no fixed tenure in their Offices, but are Elective at certain fixed periods; can those Judges, so appointed, be sufficiently permanent in their Offices to ensure an impartial administration of Justice? It will not be pretended—Why then should they be entrusted with it? I further observe, that I believe no individual State would permit Congress to appoint, pay & controul Judges, who were to decide on the Laws of that State; and if this would endanger the rights & liberties retained to each individual State—if this would be considered as a measure distructive ~~distructive~~ of particular Goverments; will not the like regulation have the same effect to abolish those rights & liberties which the particular State Goverments have consented to forego for the general good? This to my apprehension is quite evident. It must prove a worm at the Root of the general Goverment which must soon destroy its existance. I have given my hearty concurrence to the judicial Bill, and for the reasons before Stated—I am however, very willing to be convinced that I have done rong, & that a less exceptionable plan might have been hit upon, but untill this is done I must adhere to my opinion. The Salaries of those Judges are fixed much too high; this would not have taken place but from the absence of some of the eastern Senators[1]— [*lined out*] It is the more unhappy, as the Saleries are not liable to future reduction. If the general Goverment acquires, by [*lined out*] means of these Courts, a stability which will fully secure life, liberty & property; it may be an object worth the expense; and untill it is found to have a different effect, I hope, will be acquiessed in.

ALS, Chamberlain Collection, MB.

---

[1] Langdon and Strong.

James Madison to Edmund Pendleton

The pressure of unfinished business has suspended the adjournment of Congs. till saturday next. Among other articles which required it was the plan of amendments, on which the two Houses so far disagreed as to require conferences. It will be impossible I find to prevail on the Senate to concur in the limitation on the *value* of appeals to the Supreme Court, which they say is unnecessary, and might be embarrassing in questions of national or constitutional importance in their principle, tho' of small pecuniary amount. They are equally inflexible in opposing a definition of the *locality* of Juries. The vicinage they contend is either too vague or too strict a term, too vague if depending on limits to be fixed by the pleasure of the law, too strict if limited to the County. It was proposed to insert after the word juries—"with the accustomed requisites"—leaving the definition to be construed according to the judgment of professional men. Even this could not be obtained. The truth is that in most of the States the practice is different, and hence the irreconcilable difference of ideas on the subject. In some States, jurors are drawn from the whole body of the community indiscrim[*in*]ately; In others, from large districts comprehending a number of Counties; and in a few only from a single County. The Senate suppose also that the provision for vicinage in the Judiciary bill, will sufficiently quiet the fears which called for an amendment on this point. On a few other points in the plan the Senate refuse to join the House of Reps.

The bill establishing the permanent Seat of Govt. has passd. the H. of Reps. in favr. of the Susquehannah. Some of the Southern Members, despaired so much of ever getting any thing better, that they fell into the majority. Even some of the Virginians leaned that way. My own judgment was opposed to any compromise, on the supposition that we had nothing worse to fear than the Susquehannah and could obtain that at any time, either by uniting with the Eastern States, or Pennsylva. The bill however is by none means sure of passing the Senate in its present form. It is even possible that it may fall altogether. Those who wish to do nothing at this time, added to those who disapprove of the Susquehannah, either as too far South, or too far North, or not susceptible of early conveniences for the fiscal administration, may form a majority who will directly or indirectly frustrate the measure. In case of an indirect mode, some other place, will be substituted for Susquehannah, as Trenton or Germantown, neither of which can I conceive be effectively established, and either of which might get a majority, composed of sincere and insidious votes.

***

ALS, Madison Papers, DLC. For the full text, see *PJM* 12:418–20. The omitted text summarizes the news from France reported in enclosed newspapers.

John Page to George Washington

That I may not obtrude on you & to the Interruption of other Applicants, I again have Recourse to this Mode of Application in behalf of Gentlemen who wish to be recommended to you for Appointments. The inclosed Letter was left by Mr. [*Robert*] Andrews with a Friend the Day he set out on his Return to Virginia. I hope you will excuse my troubling you with it as I shall only add respecting him that I think his Knowledge of the Law, as a Justice of James City for several Years & as high Sheriff two Years added to his Study of Law, & his extensive [*gen*]ius leave no doubt with me that he is qualified for the office he solicits. In Justice however to Mr. St. G[*eorge*]. Tucker one of our Judges & to the Gentn. whom he recommends I must add that Mr. Wm. Nelson a Pratitioner of the Law in the General Court for some Years past is warmly recommended by him, & I am requested by Mr. Tucker to nominate that Gentleman to you as a proper Person for the same Office. I am very sorry to be so troublesome, but your Goodness will pardon me.

ALS, Washington Papers, DLC.

Richard Peters to Robert Morris

***

I see all your Residence Bussiness is likely to go off in Smoke. If so it will be unfortunate as our Chance will [be] the less & the Federalists will be embittered against othe each other on this local Point which will be carried into others to the no small Gratification of the Antis.

I received yesterday a Letter from Fitzsimmons who mentions what I wrote to you respecting myself. After what I wrote to you I thought it was over & not wishing to give you any Trouble or revive the Subject I have never turned my Thoughts further to it but determined to be passive & am averse to any Competition. I have therefore never stirred in the Business nor do I mean to do it. I am however extremely obliged by your kind Attention of which I am not without a grateful Recollection of repeated Instances. Some Employment to be executed at Home would have been agreeable to me but any one that would have induced a Removal out of the State would injure my Affairs & be unpleasant to so domesticated an Animal as I am.

FC, Peters Papers, PHi. Written from Philadelphia. The omitted text relates to state politics and prospects for a state constitutional convention.

Theodore Sedgwick to John Jay

Convinced that you will do honor to the supreme national court by presiding in it, you will pardon the freedom of suggesting to you the interest of a freind of mine—Mr. John Tucker of Boston one of the Clerks of the supreme court of this state, possesses equal to any man I have ever known, all the requisite abilities & qualifications of such an officer. It would afford me the most sincere pleasure that he may find employment for those talents in the national government. Sensible how very disagreable applications of this kind must be to men who have the power to confer offices, I should not have addressed you on the subject, had I not the most perfect reliance on your candor, and the vanity to beleive that you will not suppose me influenced by any improper motives—Mr. King knows I beleive Mr. Tucker and all who know him have the same opinion of his honor—of his capacity for business and of his fidelity in the execution of it.

[*John*] Fenno the Printer hath done something, and hath a disposition to do much for the honor & interest of the government. Cannot he be employed as Printer to the executive?

I am happy to have it in my power to inform you that the popularity of the government is daily gaining ground against all the efforts of antifederalism.

ALS, Sedgwick Family Papers, MHi. Written from Springfield, Massachusetts.

George Washington to James Madison

My solicitude for drawing the first characters of the Union into the Judiciary, is such that, my cogitations on this subject last night (after I parted with you) have almost determined me (as well for the reason just mentioned, as to silence the clamours, or more properly, *soften* the disappointment of smaller characters) to nominate Mr. [*John*] Blair and Colo. [*Edmund*] Pendleton as Associate & District Judges. And Mr. E[*dmund*]. Randolph for the Attorney General trusting to their acceptance.*

Mr. Pendleton could not I fear discharge, and in that case I am sure would not undertake, to execute the duties of an Associate under the present form of the Act. But he may be able to fulfil those of the District—The Salary I believe is greater than what he now has; and he would *see* or it might be *explained* to him, the reason of his being prefered to the District Court rather than to the Supreme Bench; though I have no objection to nominating him to the latter, if it is conceived that his health is competent, and his mental faculties unimpaired, by age.

His acceptance of the first would depend in a great measure, I presume, upon the light in which the District Judges are considered—that is, whether superior in Rank to any State Judges.

I am very troublesome, but you must excuse me. Ascribe it to friendship and confidence, and you will do justice to my motives. Remember the Attorney and Marshall for Kentucky, and forget not to give their Christian names.

*Mr. Randolph, in this character, I would prefer to any person I am acquainted of not superior abilities, from habits of intimacy with him.

ALS, Madison Papers, DLC.

OTHER DOCUMENTS

Elias Boudinot to George Washington. ALS, Washington Papers, DLC.
Office seeking: encloses David Brearly's letter of recommendation for John N. Cumming for U.S. marshal.

Pierce Butler to Weedon Butler. ALS, Butler Letters, Uk.
Provides instructions for son Thomas's education; "I have exceedingly at heart His distinguishing himself early in life as a public Speaker. *** I have my self experienced and do daily, ~~the~~ the inconvenience of entering late into Publick life, I mean so far as relates to Speaking in publick, I wish Him not to have such difficulties to Encounter."

Sir John Temple to the Duke of Leeds. ALS, de Coppett Collection, NjP.
Congress will discourage emigration and settlements in Spanish territory; encloses letter from Richard B. Lee requesting intervention in the recovery of Matthew Whiting, Jr., an Algerine captive.

Edward Tilghman to George Read, written from Philadelphia. *Read*, pp. 488–89n.
"if the sense of the bar should be requested, it would certainly be warmly in favor of Mr. [*Edward*] Shippen, and would have been sent to the President, but for doubts of the propriety of so doing."

George Turner to Nicholas Gilman. ALS, Rice Collection, Ohio Historical Society, Columbus. Written from Philadelphia.
Will soon send additional blank diplomas for Society of Cincinnati certificates, the stationer's supply being exhausted by recent demands of the Pennsylvania Line; predicts that "The Judiciary bill may and possibly will yet prove a tough business in Congress" and will keep it in session longer than planned; "some friends in Congress" had suggested him for judge in the Western Territory early in July; presents compliments to Langdon.

THURSDAY, 24 SEPTEMBER 1789

Hot (Johnson)

Pierce Butler to George Washington

Tho no Member of Senate wishes more than I do to avoid intruding on Your time, yet I fear I am doing so. It is not for myself, or any Relative of mine. It is merely to discharge those offices that the Citizens of the State I represent, conceive They have a Claim to. The inclosed letter Sir is from a Mr. [*John*] Parker of So. Carolina, an Old, Respectable Citizen, of good Family, who, by the devastation of the late War is reduced from a good future to a very moderate One. He is a Strict honest Man and I doubt not woud prove grateful for any mark of kindness.

[*P. S.*] Mr. Parker was a Member of the late Congress and is known to Colo. Hamilton.

ALS, Washington Papers, DLC.

Tobias Lear to John Langdon

I did myself the honor to write to you on the 20th inst. acknowledging the receipt of your favor—and informing you that Mr. [*John*] Pickering, Mr. [*Samuel*] Sherburne & Mr. [*Jonathan*] Cass were in contemplation to be nominated to the Offices in the Judicial department for the District of New Hampshire unless some circumstance, or a further consideration of the matter, should render an alteration proper. This has been the case—I have just returned from the Senate where I have been to give in the President's nominations—a list of which you have enclosed—The Gentlemen from New Hampshire were of opinion that Genl. [*John*] Sullivan would accept the office of District Judge if he should be appointed thereto—as the sallary annexed to it was larger than that of President of the State—that it would leave him a very considerable portion of time to attend to his private ~~matters~~ affairs—and that it was a permanent provision not depending on the popular voice, & a dignified office—Upon these considerations—the idea of his not being willing to accept the appointmt. was removed, & the President conceived that he would be a proper man for that office, & accordingly put him in nomination—Mr. [*John*] Parker was thought the proper person for the office of Marshall and is accordingly in nomination for that office—Mr. Sherburne was brot. forward by me & is nominated—several others were mentioned to the President for attorney; but I undertook to speak very decidedly in favor of Sherburne.

We have company to dine here to day—& of course I must quit my pen— Your Old friend Major [*William*] Jackson is in the family[1] as an assistant Secry.—and I find him a very agreeable man.

The Senate are to day upon the business of permanent residence—& it is thought they will finish it.

***

P. S. I [*recd.*] by the Last Post a letter from my Mother franked by you—for which I am much obliged to you.[2]

ALS, Langdon-Elwyn Family Papers, NhHi.

---

[1] Washington's official family included his aides.

[2] Langdon may have sent the letter under the frank of his brother Woodbury, the revenue collector of Portsmouth. Members of Congress were not normally accorded franking privileges after leaving the seat of government.

Paine Wingate to John Langdon

***

I suppose there is not a doubt but the nominations will be approved of. I will defer saying any thing about the candidates who were mentioned to the President until I shall see you which I hope to have the pleasure of shortly. The Senate have been this day on the subject of the permanent residence of Congress & were equally divided between Germantown [*Pennsylvania*] and the Susquehannah. The Vice president turnd the vote in favour of the former. The dispute however is not yet at an end. I hope that an adjournment will end this disagreea[*ble*] struggle in a day or two. I think we have run mad with high salaries. Have suffered extremely for want of you & Mr. Strong, as the votes have been carried by a bare majority several times & sometimes turnd by the vice president.

But I will not trouble you further with finding fault.

ALS, Dreer Collection, PHi. For the full text, see *Wingate* 2:337. The omitted text lists the judicial nominations.

Other Documents

Fisher Ames to John Lowell. ALS, Diedrich Collection, MiU-C.
    Judicial nominations for Supreme Court and Massachusetts, Maine, and New Hampshire districts; "Every effort was made to the last. Causes not disrespectful to you operated ag[*ains*]t. your gaining the seat where your friends wished you. I cannot explain them."

David Brearly to Jonathan Dayton. ALS, Ely Autograph Collection, NjHi. Written from New Brunswick, New Jersey, in the morning; addressed to Elizabethtown, New Jersey.
    Office seeking: Boudinot "is taking very great pains" on behalf of James Kinsey's nomination for New Jersey district court judge; believes his influence will be decisive as Paterson is neutral; Elisha Boudinot told Brearly that a "bargain was made so long ago as last June," that in exchange for Kinsey's appointment, Elisha would be appointed district court clerk.

Tristram Dalton to John Langdon. ALS, Langdon-Elwyn Family Papers, NhHi.
    Judicial nominations for Supreme Court and Massachusetts, Maine, and New Hampshire districts; the newspapers render accounts of Congressional proceedings by letter "needless"; Congress expects to rise Saturday; the Senate has not acted on the Time of Meeting Bill, "being now very

busily engaged" with the Seat of Government Bill, "the Event of which is as yet very problematical"; Mrs. Ruth Dalton arrived safe with their daughters in seven days from Newburyport and sends regards to Mrs. Elizabeth Langdon.

Elbridge Gerry to John Lowell. ALS, Gerry Papers, DLC.
Announces Lowell's nomination as Massachusetts district judge, "after all our efforts"; "the history of this matter perhaps I may hereafter communicate to you"; advises acceptance; "it is proposed to annex fees of office but this is at present uncertain"; lists other judicial nominations.

John Lloyd to Henry Lloyd. FC:lbk, Lloyd Family Papers, NHi. For the full text, see New-York Historical Society *Collections* 40(1927):811.
Has turned to Wadsworth who believes he will be able "to effect my Wish"; he will tend to it when he returns to Hartford on Saturday; he "Assures me You will be perfectly safe in takeing Security in this Country. And that the New Constitution to all intents and purposes sets Aside the proscription [*anti-Loyalist*] Law of this State [*New York*] and every State."

A Member of Congress to His Friend. [Philadelphia] *Federal Gazette*, 28 September; reprinted at Baltimore; Alexandria, Virginia; and Edenton, North Carolina.
"This morning the residence of Congress came on before the Senate, and Susquehannah was struck out by a majority of 12 to 6. The blank has since been filled up with 'Germantown' by the casting vote of the Vice-President. This, I expect, will occasion warm debates in the house of representatives. I hope it will be fixed at Trenton at last. Congress will certainly adjourn on Saturday if this new manœuvre about Germantown does not prevent it. The adjournment will be to the first Monday in January."

From New York. [Boston] *Massachusetts Centinel*, 30 September; reprinted at Exeter, New Hampshire.
"The amendments by compromise between the two Houses, will, I expect get through. The Senate have this day struck out 'Susquehannah' in the Residence Bill, and inserted 'Germantown, near Philadelphia', with this condition, that the buildings be erected free of expense to the Union. This, I think is making a more eligible situation and a better bargain. I somewhat expect that Congress will not be up until the middle of next week."

FRIDAY, 25 SEPTEMBER 1789

Hot (Johnson)

John Adams to Governor George Walton

***

Union peace and liberty to North America, are the objects to which I have devoted my life and I beleive them to be as dear to you as to me. I reckon among my friends all who are in the communion of such sentiments: tho' they may differ in their opinion of the means of obtaining those ends. I will not say that an energetic government is the only means: but I will hazard an opinion that a well ordered, a well ballanced, a judiciously limited government, is indespinsably necessary to the preservation of all or either of those blessings. If the poor are to domineer over the rich, or the rich over the poor, we shall never enjoy the happiness of good government: and without an intermediate power sufficiently elevated and independant, to controul each of the contending parties in its excesses, one or the other will for ever tyrannize. Gentlemen who had some experience before the revolution and recollect the general fabric of the government under which they were born and educated and who are not too much carried away by temporary popular politicks, are generally of this opinion. But whether prejudice will not prevail over reason passion over judgment and declamation over sober enquiry is yet to be determined.

FC:lbk, Adams Family Manuscript Trust, MHi. Addressed to Augusta, Georgia.

Thomas Fitzsimons to Benjamin Rush

It is not Necessary for me to answer your last favors as I shall soon have the pleasure of takeing you by the hand—our Adjournmt. is fixed for tomorrow & the bill for fixing the permanent Residence can only detain us—in ~~Sen~~ a Commitee of the Senate yesterday—Susq[*uehann*]a. was Struck out and a district includeing Germantown [*Pennsylvania*] inserted—McClay Voted Agst. it. the V. P. casting vote, carryd it—every effort will be used to disappt. it. delay is most Relyd upon—but we are takeing Measures to prevent it—our situation is & has been a Critical one—but you may rest satisfyd that our Conduct will bear the test of examination throughout Pensylva.—if the bill comes to us with this Amendment, I believe we are on good ground & will Carry it but between insidious friends & Avowed Enemys there is much to be feared. [*James*] Wilson is Nominated one of the

Judges of the Supr. Court [*Francis*] Hopkinson's for the district Court [*William*] Lewis atty. Genl. for the Later.

ALS, Sang Collection of Signers of the Constitution, NjR.

Robert Morris to Mary Morris

*** My Trunk of Papers [*water stains*] strong indica[*tion*] that I shall soon follow, this however may not happen quite so soon as you & I wish, for I begin to doubt whether we can adjourn sooner than Tuesday.

I am exceedingly plagued & harrassed, fretted Vexed, & pleased, alternately on the progress of this business of the permanent Residence.

So far as we have gone I have carried my points but I doubt a good deal whether I shall be able to hold what I have got I will however continue to pursue the object with Ardour & Zeal, another day or [*water stains*] good thing certain and the prospect of [*water stains*]—dont think of sending Peaches. or any thing for me: I will be with you as soon as possible.

Mr. Jay is Nominated by the President as Chief Justice, Mr. [*James*] Wilson as one of the Puisne[1] Judges. Mr. [*Francis*] Hopkinson District Judge Mr. Wm. Lewis Attorney for the District & Clement Biddle Marshall— send for Mr. Wilson & Mr. Hopkinson the Moment you Receive this & tell them, altho it is probable they may hear of ~~it befo~~ their Nominations before you see them. I am too much engaged in pursuit of permanent Residence to write to either of them.

***

ALS, Morris Papers, CSmH. Addressed to Philadelphia; carried by "Mr. Richard." The date, salutation, and possibly the last name of the person who carried the letter are obliterated by water stains.

---

[1] Junior or associate, as distinguished from the chief judge.

William Smith (Md.) to Otho H. Williams

As I expect to leave this on monday Next I should not have troubled you with any more of my communications; but to hand you the inclosed list of Nominations, which the President made to the Senate yesterday, & which will probably be all confirm'd on this day—I have not seen yr. Brother [*Elisha Otho Williams*] this morning, he will probably write you by the Post, a State of his business. I presume he will not get his old accots. settled, the Comptroller [*Nicholas Eveleigh*] not being yet arrived at N. York.

On Tuesday a bill passed in our house for establishing the permanent seat

on the Banks of Susqueha. 31 for it 17 Against. The Bill was warmly debated yesterday in the senate, & on a motion made to Strike out Susquehana.
& insert Germantown [*Pennsylvania*], that house was equally divided, when
the Vice President decided in favor of Germantown. The consequence, I expect will ~~the~~ be the loss of the Bill in our house, Although, on this head I
am not certain, for there is such Jobing & bargaining on this Subject, that
it is impossible to say what will be the Vote of tomorrow, If the N. Yorkers
Join in the last Manuvre, they will carry the question in favor Germantown,
& of this I have a very Strong Suspicion, because I am told Schuyler & King,
who Advocated the Susquehanna warmly *at first*, yesterday voted for G[er-
man]. Town in the Senate, I therefore conclude that the Philadelphians, who
were greatly mortified & alarmed at the Prospects of Susquehannah, have
found means to reconcile themselves to the New Yorkers with whom they
were at the greatest enmity, & that a new bargain has been Struck, which
may probably decide this business.

I hope to See you in Baltimore by the latter end of Next week.

ALS, Williams Papers, MdHi.

Henry Wynkoop to Reading Beatty

Have the pleasure to acknowledge the Receipt of Your's the 21st. am sorrey to hear Miss Nancey is so unwel, hope I shall hear of her Restoration
when I return home which will be the begining of the ensuing Week; The
Bill respecting the permanent Seat passed I think on Wednesday for Susquehanah [*lined out*] 31 to 17. it was taken up in Senate yesterday & this day
stands amended with Germantown, likewise with a Proviso[1] anexed against
Pensylvania, for her paying the 100,000 Dollars, what will be its fate at last
is yet uncertain, the Maneuvering of this Affair has been so various & also so
interesting, that I confess myself heartily tired of it, yet feel myself anctious
for a Termination favourable to the State. Germantown is certainly the first
place in the National Scale & the Falls [*of the Delaware*] with me is the next.
***

ALS, Wynkoop Papers, PDoBHi. For the full text, see *PMHB* 38(1914):186.

[1] See Smith to Williams, 18 September, n. 1, above.

"One of your Constituents"

SIR, you make me think of an old story "A citizen of antient Rome of no
very pleasing flavor, having by mere good luck raised himself to a post above

his merit, happened on a certain time to be guilty of a misdemeanour for which he was obliged suddenly to decamp in the night from the city. A body of the city guards being immediately dispatched after him—'Tis unfortunate, says the officer who headed them, that this fellow has the advantage of the night in his retreat—we shall do well to find him. Not at all replies an arch soldier; for so long as he carries that confounded stanch with him, we shall need no other guide in our pursuit, but our noses.'"

No. 1. Was your letter written to a person in New York, or one in this town? If the latter, are you not a Representative from this State? In truth your importance is so characteristically striking, that it requires no adept in the Connecticut art of guessing to tell who you are. Permit me to hazard a conjecture upon you, and leave it to yourself to determine whether it be a just one.

Some time since, a Gentleman of this State who has resided about six months in New-York falling into a circle who were mentionning the profits which a Citizen of that place was making in an honest, but inferior branch of business, the subject immediately caught his attention and drew from him this reply. "If, says he, so insignificant a man can make so much money, what think you, ought to be given to us members of Congress?" Whoever you are, you will doubtless give me the liberty to ask you a few questions.

Was it not a reasonable expectation, that when the members of Congress accepted their seats they should consult the feelings and circumstances of their constituents? Is not the public voice opposed to the high wages which the present members of Congress have voted to themselves and their dependants?

And is not cruelly sporting with the public happiness to risque the existence of government for the sake of a few additional pence? Tis true the late Congress had five dollars per day; but, are not two things obvious to all, 1st, that at the time when that sum was voted, specie had not half the value when compared with the articles of living that it has at present; and 2d, that the members of Congress were not nearly so numerous as they now are? The wages and mileage of the seven members from this State will, upon the most moderate calculation amount to about FIVE THOUSAND POUNDS in cash. Is not this a far greater sum than men of equal respectability can make at home? and is not clear, notwithstanding your delusory statement, that the concerns of so extended a government will make it necessary for the Legislature to set by far the greatest part of their time? They will probably have a recess in the heat of summer and no other time; and the mileage and wages will make up to each member salary of about SEVEN HUNDRED POUNDS a year.

Have you Sir, the confidence to assert that this sum is necessary in order to induce what you call respectable men to go into Congress, when you see that all the northern States of the Union and even the English government have always been supplied in their Legislatures with their best citizens at an incomparably lower rate than that which Congress have affixed? Is not your proposition nonsensical in which you say that salaries ought to be large because there will be fewer Candidates and those more respectable men—as if a man void of honesty must necessarily be so modest that he would not seek an office, because it would furnish him with a fat living? High salaries have ever been thought dangerous in republican governments—there is no assignable reason why they should be higher than to give a decent support to the persons who are and while they are in the service of the public—if they do this the government may always command the services of its best Citizens. Real virtue is the first quality in a Citizen—but he may be serviceable to his country from motives of ambition or a desire to be esteemed and respected—perhaps this is the most common motive—but baneful are the consequences when he is called into public life by his avarice. It is a monster at whose shrine every fairer principle expires.

Your observation about the door keeper is truly laughable, you say "the door keeper is, out of his three dollars a day, to pay a herd of satellites, with brooms, brushes, and wheel barrows, and so on." If the House of Representatives were a kennel of hogs, I grant you, some curious Virtues might possibly think it worth their while to keep them clean, as it is they will not probably thank you for your compliment. However Sir, if you are a Representative from this State, your fate is decided; and it is with real pleasure I anticipate the time when I shall "wish you a safe return to your family."

[Connecticut] *Norwich Packet*, 25 September. The letter was printed in italics. It was addressed to the author of the "Extract of a letter from a member of Congress" to his friend in Philadelphia, written on 17 August and printed under that date, volume 16.

OTHER DOCUMENTS

John Chaloner to Jeremiah Wadsworth. ALS, Wadsworth Papers, CtHi. Written from Philadelphia.

Office seeking: seeks recommendation to Hamilton for any work he needs done in Philadelphia.

Tench Coxe to William Samuel Johnson. ALS, Johnson Papers, CtHi. Written from Philadelphia.

Questions the method of removal of judges under a new state constitution; has discussed it with Madison; "as you have many respectable law

Characters in your body," asks Johnson to discuss it with other members "at some leisure season for private Conversation."

Pierpont Edwards to William Samuel Johnson. ALS, Johnson Papers, CtHi. Written from New Haven, Connecticut.
    Office seeking: thanks Johnson for efforts on his behalf.

John Hall to George Washington. ALS, Washington Papers, DLC. For the full text, see *PGW* 4:83. The author was probably John Hall (d. 1792) of Burke County, Georgia, son of Dr. Lyman Hall (1724–90), one of Georgia's signers of the Declaration of Independence.
    Office seeking: federal marshal for Georgia district court; mentions state delegation as references.

William Jackson to Benjamin Fishbourn. FC:lbk, Washington Papers, DLC. "I am directed by him [*the President*] to inform you that when he nominated you for Naval Officer of the Port of Savannah he was ignorant of any charge existing against you—and, not having, since that time, had any other exibit of the facts which were alledged in the Senate than what is stated in the certificates which have been published by you, he does not consider himself competent to give any opinion on the subject."

James Madison to John Dawson. No copy known; acknowledged in Dawson to Madison, 27 September.

George Meade to Tench Coxe. ALS, Coxe Papers, PHi.
    Has not heard Coxe's or anyone else's name mentioned for postmaster general by any member of Congress, in or out of doors; Clymer says a Senate "Committee [*on the Coasting Bill HR-33*] has the Representation of the Merchants of Philada. before them"; doubts Congress will adjourn tomorrow.

Robert Morris to Richard Peters. ALS, Peters Papers, PHi. Addressed to Philadelphia.
    Lists judicial nominees; "before I leave this place I shall Converse with the Presidt. on your Subject [*a federal office?*], and by the middle of next Week I hope to converse with you."

George Turner to Nicholas Gilman. No copy known; listed at NHi as part of the now dispersed H. C. Van Schaack "Autographic History of the American Revolution."

William Samuel Johnson, Diary. Johnson Papers, CtHi.
Visited the President.

SATURDAY, 26 SEPTEMBER 1789

Hot (Johnson)

John Adams to Jeremy Belknap

***

Unhappy am I, to be destined to spend two thirds of my life in defending this people against an host of ennemies, I might have said against an host of nations, and the remaining third in feebleness and infirmity against their own ignorance, folly and __ I will not say more. I have not been assaulted by malice. Ned Church has been actuated by the purest motives of patriotism for any thing that I know. I never [*lined out*] injured or offended him. I know nothing of him. There has not been a word exchanged between him and me these dozen years that I know—If it was not patriotism it was mere caprice or the lust of fame. Let him have it, tho' he who burnt the temple could not obtain it.[1]

FC:lbk, Adams Family Manuscript Trust, MHi. Addressed to Boston.

[1] Probably a reference to the destruction of Jerusalem's Temple of Herod by Titus in 70 A.D., when the Romans' fire attack went out of control and consumed the sanctuary Titus had hoped to capture.

Tristram Dalton to Caleb Strong

There remaining business before the Senate unfinished—a resolve is this moment sent from them to the House, proposing to continue in session untill next Tuesday—a resolution passed the two houses yesterday, *determining* their next meeting to be on the ~~secon~~ first Monday in January.

You must have been informed of the nominations of Mr. [*William*] Cushing as an associate Justice—Mr. [*John*] Lowell as a District Judge for Massa. C[*hristopher*]. Gore Attorney & Jona. Jackson Marshal—Judge [*David*] Sewall for Main.

Yesterday E[*dmund*]. Randolph was nominated for Attorney General.

Time will not permit me at this Moment to add—You know the hurry of a last day.

ALS, Strong Papers, MNF.

Governor John Eager Howard to the Maryland Delegation

It is with concern that we inform you that the Justices of the Peace for the County of Prince George in this State have neglected to take the Oath for the Support of the Constitution of the United States by the time required by the Law—It is the practice in this State for the Judges of the several Courts to take the Oaths required of them by Law in Court, and as the Court in this County stood adjourned until after the first Day of September the Judges could not take the Oath for the support of the Constitution of the United States in the usual manner before that time.

A Doubt arises whether any Proceedings of the Court under these Circumstances will be legal, we therefore wish a law may pass to aid the Proceedings of this Court and to remove any disabilities or Penalties the Justices may have incurred—The same difficulties may have occurred in some of the other Counties in this State, we therefore wish that if a Law should be passed it may be general.

FC:lbk, State Papers, MdAA.

Ralph Izard to Edward Rutledge

I am just returned from the Senate where the following Officers have been approved of—Mr. [*John*] Jay Chief Justice: Judges of the Supreme Court J[*ohn*]. Rutledge, [*William*] Cushing, [*James*] Wilson, [*Robert H.*] Harrison, and [*John*] Blair. Edmund Randolph Attorney General, Major [*Thomas*] Pinckney is appointed District Judge for South Carolina. The Judges both of the Supreme Court and the District Courts are chosen from among the most eminent and distinguished characters in America, and I do not believe that any Judiciary in the world is better filled. The President asked me before the nominations were made, whether I thought your Brother John, Gen. [*Charles Cotesworth*] Pinckney, or yourself would accept of a Judge in the Supreme Court. I told him that I was not authorized to say you would not, but intimated that the office of Chief Justice would be most suitable to either of you: That however was engaged. Mr. Jay's Office has this day been filled by Mr. Jefferson, who is expected here soon from France. The home Department is added to it, and the name of the office changed. Mr. Jefferson is called Secretary of State. I hope it may suit your Brother to accept, if it should be only for two or three years; as it is of the first importance that the Judiciary should be highly respectable. The Office of District Judge I hope will be agreeable to Major Pinckney. If either of them should refuse to accept, let me know of it by the first opportunity, and tell me whom you wish to be appointed that will accept. The President will not nominate any but the most eminent: and if none in South Carolina of that description will accept, he will be obliged to have recourse to some other state. I write this letter in a hurry *** Your son [*Henry Middleton Rutledge*] is above stairs drinking tea with the Ladies. I never saw him look so well. He is not absolutely fat; but as near it as you would wish him to be.

AHR 14(1908–9):777.

Rufus King, Summary of the Political Background to the Seat of Government Bill

A Treaty being on foot between the Delegates of Penn. and those of the Southern States to fix the permanent residence of congress on the Potomoc and to make philadelphia the temporary residence; the Delegates of the States east of N. York met Mr. King & Mr. Laurance on behalf of the those of N. Yk.—and after considerable discussion whether the permanent residence ought to be on the Susquehannah or the Delaware, they agreed that Mr. King & Mr. Goodhue shd. offer to the Delegates of Penn. that they wd. vote the permanent residence on the east bank of the Susquehannah with in the state of pensylvania provided the Delegates of Penn. wd. agree to fix the temporary residence at N. York until the buildings for the permanent shd. be ready—Mr. K. & Mr. G. met the pen. Delegates soon after the meeting and before the subject was mentioned. Mr. Madison came in and after conversing with the Delegates of Penn. by themselves for some time, the Delegates informed Mr. K. & Mr. G. that they were so embarrassed with a connection with the Southern Delegates, that they cd. not confer with us concerning the subject of our meeting them—Mr. K. observed to them that he & Mr. G. shd. not offer any proposition until they were ascertained from the Delegates of Pen. that they were not under any engagements upon the subject of the future Residence of congress—Mr. K. further observed that he & Mr. Goodhue were authorised to speak on behalf of all the Reps. & Senators except two east of N. Jersey—the two gentleman's opinion—whom they excepted, they had not had opportunity to confer with (Elsworth & Wingate) & that they could not therefore speak positively of their opinion, but that they expected their concurrence with their Colleagues—Mr. K. added that the eastern states were now united, but that whether they ever wd. be so combined in future he could not say—Mr. Morris being present at this Meeting after conferring with the Delegates of pen. requested Mr. K. & Mr. G. to suspend their business until he shd. confer with them in future.
On the next day Mr. Morris informed Mr. K. that the Delegates & Sena-

tors of Penn. agreed to the proposition wh. Mr. K. & Mr. G. were authorised to offer them.

In consequence of this agreement the house of reps. passed a bill which was carried by the votes of the Eastern States, carrying into Effect the foregoing arrangement—they also agreed to a clause in the bill mortgaging 100,000 Dollars of the impost to defray a like sum which the secretary of the Treasury was directed to borrow for the purchase of the Land & the erection of the buildings—The bill came to the Senate with a proviso suspending the powers thereof until the President of the U.S. shd. be satisfied that all legal impediments in the states of *Maryland* & Penn. were removed touching the opening of the navigation of the Susquehannah—the senators of N. YK. requested of the Delegates of penn. to inform them. 1st. whether they considered the proviso as operating against the engagement to fix the permanent seat in maryland [*Pennsylvania*], And that of consequence the senators of N. YK. shd. vote to expunge it? 2d. whether if it was not expunged they held them bound to vote for the Delaware River? 3d. if that could not be carried whether they held them bound finally to vote against the Bill? to the first the Reps. of penn. answered unanimously in the affirmative—to the second they answered seven ay. and one no—to the third four answered Ay and four no. and seven out of Eight were in favor of the Germantown District if the proviso could not be expunged—in this stage of the business Mr. Morris a Senator from penn. offered the Senators of N. YK. that provided they wd. vote for the Germantown District, for the permanent seat of Cong.: the Delegates of Pensylvania, himself, Mr. Read and Mr. Basset Senators from Delaware would engage on honor to vote against the removal of Congress from N. York prior to Jany. 1793—Mr. Read & Mr. Basset both entered into this engagement with Mr. K. Mr. Morris, & Messrs. Fitzsimons, Clymer, Scot the two Muhlenburghs & Wynkoop signed such an engagement on the 26 sep. 1789[1] & Mr. Morris engaged verbally to Mr. K. to unite Mr. Patterson & Mr. Elmer Senators of New Jersey, & Mr. Langdon Senator of New Hampshire in the same engagement—connected with the Germantown plan was this proviso "that Penn. shd. advance the 100,000 Dols. for purchasing, building &c." this arrangement was laid before the Reps. of N. YK. by the Senators of that State, who told the Reps *they* were not engaged, that they asked their advice; if they advised for or against it, they wd. vote accordingly—that they must take an equal portion of the merit or Demerit of the measure which ever way they decided and advised—the reps. unanimously with the excepn. of Genl. Floyd advised the Senators to vote for the Germantown District, provided that the Susquehannah shd. be struck out by the Senate and the senators of New York voted accordingly and the bill passed the senate.

King Papers, NHi, hand of King. This document was written after this date, perhaps as late as the summer of 1790, when the New York Senators had to defend themselves in the wake of the removal of Congress from New York City. It covers events from as early as 28 August through 26 September.

¹ See 23 September, above.

OTHER DOCUMENTS

John Barnes to John Langdon. ALS, Langdon-Elwyn Family Papers, NhHi. Carried to New Hampshire by Livermore.
  Office seeking: a clerkship in one of the executive departments.

Robert Craddock to John Brown. ALS, Brown Collection, CtY. Written from Danville, Kentucky.
  "In consequence of the information given in your letter that enclosed a paper containing the Current prices of Publick securities," has contracted for lands northwest of the Ohio River; "Upon being certainly that an [land] Office is opened I shall trouble you again on this subject."

William Few to Georgia Executive Council. No copy known; receipt acknowledged in council's minutes of 19 October, misdated 19 September.

Edmund Randolph to James Madison. ALS, Madison Papers, DLC. Written from Williamsburg, Virginia. For the full text, see *PJM* 12:421.
  Sends his papers from the Federal Convention; "The president is supposed to have written to Mr. Adams, while titles were in debate, that if any were given, he would resign. Whether it be true or not, it is a popular report."

John Quincy Adams, Almanac Diary. Adams Family Manuscript Trust, MHi.
  Dined with Dalton.

NYDG, 26 September.
  "One of the members [*Gerry*] yesterday, in the house of Representatives, with pleasantry observed that the Federalists and Anti-federalists were different only in sentiments respecting the adoption of the New Constitution in one simple point, viz. The Federalists were set on unconditional ratification; the Anti-federalists for a conditional one: It therefore followed, that the most expressive epithet which could be hereafter applied to the parties, was Ratifiers and Anti-ratifiers; or, better yet, *Rats* and *Anti-rats.*"

SUNDAY, 27 SEPTEMBER 1789

Rain Storms (Johnson); *Violent storm* (J. Q. Adams)

Elias Boudinot to William Bradford, Jr.

***

The permanent Residence of Congress, will oblige us to continue our Sessions till Tuesday Evening when I believe there will be no keeping the House together longer—The Senate has sent the Bill to us with an Amendment, striking out "Susquehanna" and inserting German Town, with Lines so as to take in all the Northern Liberties left out by your Act of Assembly—This takes in Rose Hill[1]—I am by no means pleased with this amendment, altho' I can not be reconciled to the Susquehanna—I foresee great Evils arising from being in so large a City, and greater from the Clashing of Jurisdictions between the exclusive Jurisdiction of Congress and so large a Commercial City—I am confident it will give great dissatisfaction to the Union, ~~and~~ who will have a very jealous Eye over, so great an addition of Power & Influence to so large a State—I am cleer that the amendment is injudicious & productive of great Jealousy & heart burning—There appears to be a dead Majority for concurring with the Senate, but on what Principles it is hard to guess, as New York and the Eastern People have always been so terrified with the influence of Philadelphia—If some other unexpected Maneuvre, does not take place, I believe the amendm. will be concurred in—It is on Condition that Pennsylvania or its Citizens will provide the 100,000 Dollars to erect the federal Buildings.

I suppose our friend [*Ezekiel*] Forman, has heard of his Fate—There have been many dissappointments and of Course many long Faces with us—Do give my Compliments to him and assure him that every thing was done for him, as if he had been present—The unanimous application of the Delegation of Jersey on another account shared the same fate.

***

AL (incomplete), Wallace Papers, PHi. Written from Elizabethtown, New Jersey. Part of the omitted text reports on his wife's health at Elizabethtown, where he had arrived the evening before, and mentions that he has begun wearing mourning for the death of his brother Lewis (b. 1753), a merchant mariner thought lost at sea.

---

[1] Located two miles above Philadelphia on the road to Frankford, "Rose Hill" was a seventy acre farm which Boudinot purchased in September 1784, and was frequently used by Bradford and his wife Susan, Boudinot's daughter. The Northern Liberties was a Philadelphia County township on the Delaware River adjacent to the northern border of the city.

John Dawson to James Madison

By yesterday's post of receivd your favour of Friday. Shou'd Trenton be substituted by the Senate I apprehend that your house will not agree to the amendments, and consequently the bill will be lost, and the question as to the permanent Seat left open—this I have expected for some time woud be the fate of the business, and upon the whole I do not know but it is the best course it can take—the prospect of acquiring strength by N. Carolina, and the manner in which Potomac has been brought forward and treated, will I think ensure its success at a day not far distant—whether it will be politic to remain at N. York or to remove to a more Southern position as the temporary seat is doubtful in my mind. I shoud however prefer the latter—The Susq[uehanna]h. appears to be relinquish'd in this place [Philadelphia], Mr. Elmer, who pass'd through a few days since having declard that it woud be rejected by the Senate.
***

ALS, Madison Papers, DLC. For the full text, see PJM 12:423. The letter is undated; on the Madison Presidential Papers microfilm it is placed at 13 September.

Benjamin Goodhue to Stephen Goodhue

I expected to have set out for home before now, but We could not get through the bussines, so as to adjourn yesterday and have therefore postponed it till the day after tomorrow, at which time I think we shall rise tho' it is possible we may be detained a day or two longer, the only bussines which now keeps us together is the bill which yesterday came down from the Senate respecting the permanent residence, in which they have inserted Germantown and the neighbourhood of Philadelphia instead of Susquehana, and with this condition that the buildings shall be erected free of expence to the continent, the only question is whether We concur with the Senate, and from appearances there is little doubt but We shall, tho' the Southern men I suppose will throw every thing in the way they can to embarrass and plague us, it is thought best to finish this ugly bussines since it has taken up so much time or else We shall have probably to go over the whole ground again the next session—please to tell Mr. [John] Norris that the bill for altering the value of the Russian Ruble [Coasting Bill HR-33] is yet before the Senate, and that no endeavours on my part shall be wanting to get it through before We rise. ***
[P. S.] You may expect to see me in about 10 days from this.
The Amendments are finished—a Thanksgiving is to be recommended by the President.

S[*amuel*]. Osgood, is appointed Postmaster, and I wish you would tell Mr. [*William*] Vans, in confidence that I have spoke to him, that he might have that office in Salem, and I think he will give it [*to*] him.

ALS, Goodhue Family Papers, MSaE. Addressed to Salem, Massachusetts.

Thomas Hartley to Tench Coxe

I received your Favor of the 25th. inst.—The Carrying the Banks of the Susquehannah for the federal Seat was a great Point for pennsylvania—By the Sentiments of a *great* Majority [*lined out*] they were held to be the Center of the Union—The unfortunate Proviso[1] was the ostensible Cause for abandoning them in the Senate.

German Town is named by them as the Spot—If the Troops remain steady it may carry—every attempt will be made to postpone the Question until next Session—a Motion was made Yesterday to that purpose—we carried it against it by a Majority of 4.

I shall have no Confidence in one place or other until the Moment I see the Law pass.

Some of the Maryland Delegates say they will never come back—nay that they will strive to break the Union if German Town should be fixed upon—strong words have also been used by others.

For my own part I shall trust to Consequences, if we can get Congress to any Part of our State.

The Banks of the Susquehannah were it is true my object, but I must submit.

We shall not break up until Tuesday—I *mean* to set off on wednesday and hope for the Pleasure of Seeing you upon my way Home.

ALS, Coxe Papers, PHi. Addressed to Philadelphia.

[1] See Smith to Williams, 18 September, n. 1, above.

Ebenezer Hazard to John Langdon

My Enquiries for Lodgings for you proved fruitless: I could find none that would be suitable, & Mrs. [*Abigail*] Hazard & I concluded to try to accommodate you ourselves; provided nevertheless that you could suit yourself elsewhere for a little while first. You must know that we expect an Increase of our Family in December, & when that Business is over we shall have Room which we can spare. Congress will not meet til January.

The Senate did not approve of the Mode of continuing the Post Office

Business by Resolve, & passed a Bill for the Purpose, which made the Appointment of a Postmaster General necessary. Last Friday the President nominated Mr. [*Samuel*] Osgood (late of the Treasury) for that Office, & I suppose he has been approved by the Senate; so that this is probably the last Post by which I can write to you without putting you to Expence.[1]

ALS, Dreer Collection, PHi.

---

[1] I.e., by the loss of Hazard's franking privileges.

Richard Henry Lee to Patrick Henry

*** My third letter to you on the 14th. inst. will satisfy you how little is to be expected from Congress that shall be any ways satisfactory on the subject of Amendments. Your observation is perfectly ~~right~~ just, that right without power to protect it, is of little avail. Yet small as it is, how wonderfully scrupulous have they been in stating Rights? The english language has been carefully culled to find words feeble in their Nature or doubtful in their meaning! The power of displacing Officers was contested with a zeal and constancy that the nature of it deserved. In the Senate we were divided, so that the V. P. determined the question, as you will see in the Journal. This is one of the ill consequences derived from giving a person the Right of voting in the Senate who is not a Member of it, and who has so probable a prospect (as he may think) of coming to the possession of that power which he agrees to magnify!

The contenders for this measure insisted that the Constitution gave the power. this was at once to make it both absurd and arbitrary. because it expressly gives the P[*resident*]. a right to call upon the officers for information in writing concerning their departments—how ridiculous this if it intended him the power to remove them from Office at pleasure? What vest a right to give political death, and say that the person so vested may demand a paper from him over whom he can exercise destruction! The next attempt, and which will probably succeed, is to send forth all process in the name of the P. instead of the U.S. only—Here is another absurdity. In England, they say the King can do no wrong. But here the P. may be impeached. There, process in name of the Culprit is not to issue for bringing Witnesses to try him at the Bar where he is put upon his defence, but here it may. But, where Consolidation is the plan, the States authority must be kept out of view as much as possible, and the head of the Empire shewn as much as may be. These things demonstrate the Vigilance necessary to guard against encroachments, as was suggested in my last letter. The appointments to Offices in the great and influential departments, are pretty universally among the most zealous federalists, the Salaries are vast, and the State departments and supports weakened by the drafts in this way made from them. Consolidation must therefore inevitably take place in process of time, without great care and much wisdom on the part of the States. The cause of public liberty and the success and strength of the Union depending essentially, in my opinion, upon the System of Confederated Republics, every wise and proper measure should be invariably pursued by the friends of freedom both in the State and federal governments to secure from invasion the just rights of the former. Let us take counsel from what we see, and fill our State Offices with Men of known attachments to radical amendments, and whose firmness and abilities may serve as a counterpoise to any attempts that may be made against Statistical rights. ***

By an Address,[1] received two days ago from the Assembly of R. Island, copy of which I will send you by my brother [*Arthur Lee*], to the federal government; it appears to me as if they intended to keep out of this Union until effectual Amendments were made—We ought in common prudence to have done the same—Does N.C. design to act in the same manner.

[*P. S.*] I refer you to my last letter for further observations on Gen. [*Joseph*] Martin—You will see by that how the manner of treating with the Indians necessarily prevented his appointment, if other difficulties had been removed—But at present, no such officer as a standing Indian Agent is appointed—The Governor of the Western Territory is charged with such affairs.

ALS, Custis-Lee Family Papers, DLC. For the full text, see *Lee* 2:504–7. Part of the omitted text makes reference to an unlocated "general letter" to the Virginia delegation, probably also written by Henry, on the subject of the Prince Edward Academy, and discusses the delegation's efforts to procure an instructor for it.

––––––––

[1] The letter from Rhode Island Governor John Collins on behalf of the legislature of that state to the President, Senate, and House of Representatives was forwarded by Washington to the Senate and House on 26 September. It is printed in *DHFFC* 8:396–98.

Robert Morris to Gouverneur Morris

It is now late on Sunday evening. I am just come from a Committee of the Senate, which has been sitting the greatest part of this day, in order to make a report tomorrow morning, so as to forward the business, that we may adjourn on Tuesday evening.

Ever since the receipt of your letters, I have been so much engaged with the public business, that it has been impossible to attempt answering them, and I must do it after my return to Philadelphia, where I hope to be on Thursday or Friday next.

Congress is to meet again on the first Monday in January, and I expect we shall then turn our attention to an excise, a stamp tax, or rather a tax on law proceedings, &c. so as to provide sufficient funds for paying the interest of our *whole debt*, which, from all my observation I am led to believe, that every one concerned in the government is seriously bent upon doing. I have not a doubt but Rhode Island and North Carolina will come into the union this winter, and you will readily perceive, from the progress which the government has made, and is making, that the price of public securities will rise. Nothing but the very great scarcity of money keeps them down at present, but this is a scarcity very likely to continue; and, as the same cause will, while it exists, continue to produce the same effect, you will naturally conclude, that the value of these papers depends much upon the speculations therein, which are formed in Europe.

The President conducts himself with so much propriety and good sense, that he rises, if possible, in the general esteem. I am on the best terms with him, but observing that jealousies were beginning to take root, I have absented myself very much from his house, taking care to let him know the cause. God knows he cannot render me any service; I want nothing of him, either for myself or any of my connexions.

I have, however, by giving him useful, faithful, and just information, had opportunities of serving several worthy, deserving men amongst my friends and acquaintances. But if the doing of this is to create heart-burnings, and set the whole pack of envious hounds in full cry against me, I must beg to be excused, and rather choose to retreat a little from the public view, although I will never shrink from the service of a *deserving* friend.

I have been exceedingly plagued with the question of "Permanent Residence." You were very right in the opinions, given in one of your former letters on this matter. We have been playing hide and seek on the banks of Potomac, Susquehannah, Conegocheague, &c. &c. It has constantly been my view to bring the ramblers back to the banks of the Delaware, but the obstinacy of one or two, and the schemes of some others, prevented my getting them so high up as the Falls [*at Trenton*]. The Bill for fixing the seat of government went down from the Senate yesterday to the House of Representatives amended, by striking out "the banks of the Susquehannah," and inserting "The Germantown District [*near Philadelphia*]." It would have passed in that House, as it had done in the Senate, but the southern people prevented the vote being taken, by calling for, and carrying, an adjournment until Monday. Tomorrow, therefore, it will be carried, unless this day's intrigues may produce some change. However, I have put my hand to the plough, and must go on.

I have been the prime mover in this affair, and shall continue so, until it is decided one way or the other. Madison, Grayson, and Company are very warm, but that I do not mind; they will cool again. I have worked in concert with the New Yorkers, and we are to remain here until the buildings are erected, which will, under all circumstances, require three years. Therefore, I shall probably reside with you at Morrisania some part of that time, provided you build a bridge across Hærlem River; and this you must do, not so much for the convenience of your friends, as for the promotion of your own interest.

Jared Sparks, *Life of Gouverneur Morris* (3 vols., Boston, 1832) 3:4–6.

George Thatcher to Sarah Thatcher

Dont you begin to say, you believe I never mean to come home? And that you are tired of looking out & expecting me? I declare I am almost weary of appointing times when I propose to return. I have so often been disappointed And I hardly dare assure you I shall be at Weston on saturday coming; because 'tis possible I may not set out on Tuesday.

Congress could not get thro the business before them yesterday, as was expected; consequently, the adjournment was again put off till Tuesday—should we rise on Tuesday I hope to be with you saturday—but should we be obliged to put off the adjournment till Thursday or saturday. you must not look for me till the middle of next week.

You must content yourself till I come to you—& not think of going home before I come—You are anxious to see & be with our dear children I have no doubt; but this anxiety is much greater in my mind; & in conjunction with many other reasons, will induce me to set out for home as soon as I can without subjecting myself to blame for leaving my duty here.

I shall send this to the care of Mr. [*Isaiah*] Thomas at Worcester, & desire him to give it to the Stage-driver; by this means I hope you will receive it on Thursday.

Yesterday it was uncommonly hot for the season—The mercury stood at 78—in Fereignheights Thermomiter—And this day we have a north east storm.

ALS, Thatcher Family Papers, MHi. Addressed to Weston, Massachusetts; forwarded to Biddeford, Maine.

Letter from New York to Portland, Maine

Yesterday the President laid before the two Houses a letter signed by the Governour of Rhodeisland, in the name and behalf of the Legislature of that State.[1] It recapitulated the dangers in which they had embarked in common with the present eleven united States—their affection for them, and their great attachment to the rights and liberties of the people, which they with their sister States had undertaken to defend. They had examined the constitution, and thought it an insufficient security to the great principles of liberty for which they had fought, and thousands had sacrificed their lives. They had viewed with pleasure the Amendments proposed by the Congress, and apprehended that they might in part remove the difficulties from the minds of the people: But they did not even hint any direct encouragement of their coming into the union: On the contrary, rather held up an idea that they would pass laws & regulations whereby that State would be enabled to discharge her part of the debt of the confederation, both principal and interest, as it became due. They prayed, however, that peace and harmony might be continued between that State and the Union.

[Portland, Maine] *Cumberland Gazette*, 9 October. This letter may have been excerpted from one written by Thatcher to the newspaper's editor, Thomas B. Wait.

1 For the letter, see *DHFFC* 8:396–98.

OTHER DOCUMENTS

Abigail Adams to Elizabeth Shaw. ALS, Shaw Family Papers, DLC. Written from "Richmond Hill," outside New York City; addressed to Haverhill, Massachusetts. For the full text, see Charles F. Adams, ed., *Letters of Mrs. Adams* [Boston, 1848], pp. 200–203.

Description of Richmond Hill; "tho I am not the only person who question there making a congress again till April, but the punctuality of Mr. Adams to all publick Buisness would oblige him Strickly to adhere to the day of adjournment, however inconvenient it might prove to him, he has never been absent from his daily duty in Senate a single hour from their first meeting, and the last months buisness has pressed so hard that his Health appears to require a recess."

John Quincy Adams to James Bridge. ALS, Gilder Lehrman Collection, NHi. Concludes a letter begun 21 September.

"I have met several times Mr. Dalton, who has been extremely civil to me; and yesterday I had the honour of ~~his~~ dining at his house in company with grave Senators and ministers of State. He talks of going this week to Philadelphia, and intends to spend some part of the recess in Massachusetts."

Erkuries Beatty to Josiah Harmar. ALS, Harmar Papers, MiU-C.

Military pay issues; the Appropriations Bill is in the Senate; the Senate has overturned the whole Seat of Government Bill and sent it back;

Germantown to be the place and Pennsylvania to "build the town, for the Honor (I suppose) of its being in that State"; some think it will pass, others think it will be held over; judicial appointments.

Christopher Gore to Rufus King. ALS, King Papers, NHi. Written from Boston. For a partial text, see *King* 1:368–69.
Potential federal judicial appointments in Massachusetts.

Ebenezer Hazard to Jeremy Belknap. ALS, Belknap Papers, MHi. For the full text, see *MHSC*, ser. 5, 3:190–94.
"Was busy *electioneering*; a friend in Congress intimated that I was in danger of losing my office [*as postmaster general*], & advised me to bestir myself: my friends were to be informed, & urged to Exertions"; Morris supported Richard Bache.

William Irvine to Governor Arthur St. Clair. ALS, St. Clair Papers, Ohio State Library on deposit at Ohio Historical Society, Columbus.
Introduces Hannibal Dobbyn whom Madison has asked Irvine to assist.

Robert Morris to James Wilson. Summary and excerpt of ALS, *Parke-Bernet Catalog* 939(1948):item 339 and *Carnegie Book Shop Catalog* 134:item 158. The ellipses are in the sources.
Informs Wilson of his appointment as an associate justice; mentions other appointees for the Supreme Court and the appointment of Francis Hopkinson as a Pennsylvania district judge; urges Wilson to accept, as "the station is Honorable, and the Salary . . . not contemptible altho neither comes up to my wishes for you"; *"I have laboured hard to bring Congress into the neighbourhood of our City. . ."*

James Sullivan to Elbridge Gerry. ALS, Gerry Papers, MHi. Written from Boston.
Reaction to not being appointed to office: "the Time will come when the president of the united States will see who are the true & real friends of the union and in whom the people place their confidence. men, are by the ferment of the new Constitution brought into public life upon a very short acquaintance with the people. and without Either a moral or habitual regard to their Interest."

Governor John Sullivan to John Adams. ALS, Adams Family Manuscript Trust, MHi. Written from Durham, New Hampshire.
Livermore informed him that Sullivan was a candidate for federal district judge in New Hampshire; seeks Adams's support.

MONDAY, 28 SEPTEMBER 1789

Rain Storms (Johnson)

John Brown to Harry Innes

The Act establishing the Judicial Courts of the United States passed a few days ago & has recd. the approbation of the President. I[*t u*]nderwent several Alterations & amendmen[*ts*] [*torn*] passed the Senate & state it is acknowledg[*torn*] In my opinion the System is [*torn*] for the present time & I fear in the administration of it great difficulties will arise from the concurrent Jurisdiction of the Federal with the State Courts which will unavoidab[*ly o*]ccasion great embarrassment & clashing—But it [*is?*] absolutely n[*e*]cess[*ary*] to pass a Judiciary Law at this Session & the one which passed is as good I believe as we at present could make it, experience may point out its defects—The Officers of this as well as of the other Departments of the Government are already appointed. *** & it is with pleasure I add you are appointed Judge for the District of Kentucke. I was induced to take the liberty to recommend you to the President for this office from a confidence that the appointment would meet with the unanimous approbation of the District & from a conviction that you were better qualified to fill it than any other we could hope to obtain. The Salary is 1000 Dollars a year payable quarterly I could not at present get it raised beyond that Sum as an opinion prevailed that the Business in that Court would be inconsiderable—should it prove otherwise I have not a doubt but the Salary will be augmented at a future day. I flatter myself with [*torn*] that you will consent to accept the app[*ointment*] e[*speci*]ally as the Law does not prohibit you f[*rom*] [*torn*] [*y*]our present Docket. *** Congress I expect will adjourn tomorrow or next day to meet again the 1st of Jany. Many of the Acts passed this Session e[*spe*]cially those relating to Revenue are experimental [*torn*] the proposed adjournment the more necessary that the members may mix with their Constituents & have an opp[*ortunit*]y. of marking how the Laws operate upon the different parts of the Union—A Bill fixing on the place for the permanent residence of Congress is now under consideration A majority of Our House after a long but unsuccessful Struggle for the Potomack decided in favor of the Banks of the Susquehannah But the Senate have stricken out that River & inserted German Town—that amendment is under consideration & the event is yet doubtful—Excepting upon this question which has occasioned great warmth greater harmony has prevailed in Congress than I expected to find! Indeed our public affairs in every department go on so smoothly & with such propriety that I entertain sanguine hopes that the present Government will answer all the reasonable expectations of its friends—Judgement impartiality & decision are conspicuous in every transaction of the President & from the Appointments which he has made there is every reason to expect that the different Departments will be conducted with Justice & Ability—I consider the appointment of Mr. Jefferson (Vice Jay) as a measure favorable to the Interests of the Western Country & calculated [*to*] remove those fears which exist respecting the Navigati[*on of*] the River Mississipi—I am now fully convinced that we ha[*ve*] nothing to fear on that score from the present Go[*ve*]rnment at least during the administration of the present President—This I speak from a knowledge of his Sentiments The public papers I forward to the District will inform you of every thing new in this quarter worth Notice—France has lately been in a Situation truly [*torn*] alarming—exposed to all the horrors of Anarchy Insurrection & Famine—a Revolution in favor of Liberty—a consequence of American Independence the beneficial effects of which to mankind are daily disseminating & extending throughout the World.

I do not expect to write to you again untill after Congress shall meet on the first of Jany. as I intend to set out for my Fathers[1] in a few days—were I to continue here I should not have the priviled[*ge*] of franking & my letters would not be worth postage your letters if directed to me at Staunton would probably reach me. I shall write to you from that place. ***

[*P. S.*] N.B. Fees in federal Courts are to be the same for the present as in Supreme Courts of each State. The Bill regulating process is under consideration.

ALS, Innes Papers, DLC. Part of the omitted text lists other recent appointments to office.

[1] John Brown, Sr., a Presbyterian minister, resided in Rockbridge County, Virginia.

Tench Coxe to James Madison

I received information of the nomination of Mr. O[*sgood*]. yesterday. He is certainly a very suitable character, and well entitled to this place from his former employments.[1] I have to make you my Apologies for the trouble I have given you, and my acknowlegements for such good offices as you have rendered, the extent of which I am sure was as great as your Ideas of public good would admit—I am well pleased that the Case has occur'd, as it proves to me that in my exertions in the fedl. cause I have gained friendship & confidence among its opponents. I have only to add that I would not have permitted my name to appear had I known of a competitor who was unexceptionable—and *that it is totally unknown here Who were my friends*.[2] Indeed Application for me was quite unknown, till it was brought by some of the letters in Saturday's mail.

The Seat of Government I see is varied. You know my opinions on that point. My more immediate interests being promoted by the depending proposition do not diminish the decision with which I prefer the other position. I presume the new Change will not be accepted by your house. If the bill for a permanent seat falls thro entirely, it will certainly be sound policy in the friends of a proper position to adjourn to Philada. *if* they can effect it.

I hope we shall have the pleasure of seeing you here soon in your way to Virginia, or on a visit, if you do not return thither immediately.

ALS, Madison Papers, DLC. Written from Philadelphia.

[1] Samuel Osgood was appointed postmaster general after serving on the board of treasury from 1785 to 1789.

[2] The editors cannot determine when the emphasis was added.

Thomas Fitzsimons to Benjamin Rush

When the winds blow worship the Echo, was the advice of some of the Antient Philosophers. Apply it to present circumstances & suspend your opinion of present measures until you are informed of the reasons on which they are founded. I venture to assure you if any blame is to be, the consequences will not fall where you seem to apprehend. the bill for Establishing the Seat of the Government came down about 2 o'clock on Saturday totally changed. [A] district of 10 miles square including Germantown and Northern Liberties has taken place of the banks of the Susq[*uehanna*]. and a proviso that 100,000 dollars be supplied by the State of Penna. and/or its citizens made a condition . . . all I apprehend from the delay is further intrigue. it is scarcely possible for you to conceive the motives which could influence the New Yorkers.

Excerpt of ALS, Philadelphia Autograph Company, *Unique Collection of Autograph Items of and Associated with the Bench and Bar* [ca. 1950]. The ellipses are in the source.

Daniel Hiester to James Hamilton

Agreeable to the wish expressed in your last Letter, I moved that the district Court for Pennsylva. might be held alternately at Philada. and Carlisle. Colo. Hartley had moved to the same purpose in favour of York. I stated, the greater distance of Carlisle from Philada. its proximity to the Western Country, its more central situation in the State, easy access to & from the Counties on the Susquehanna & its waters, &c. It was objected that it did not Adjoin an other State, consequently not much business wod. arise in the County. upon the whole York prevailed. ***

The Senate have amended the Seat of Govermt. Bill with striking out

Susquehanna and inserting Germantown N. Liberties &c. on Saturday a Motion was made to put off the bill till next session this was Negatived 29 to 25. the question was then put off to this day. I believe it will carry for the latter place.

ALS, Cumberland County Historical Society, Carlisle, Pennsylvania. Addressed to Carlisle, Pennsylvania. The omitted portion lists appointments to office.

Richard Henry Lee and William Grayson to Thomas Mathews, Speaker of the Virginia House of Delegates

We have now the honor of enclosing the proposition of amendments to the Constitution of the United States that has been finally agreed upon by Congress. We can assure you Sir that nothing on our part has been omitted to procure the success of those radical amendments proposed by the Convention, and approved by the Legislature of our country [*Virginia*], which as our Constituent, we shall always deem it our duty, with respect and reverence to obey. The journal of the Senate herewith transmitted, will at once shew how exact and how unfortunate we have been in this business. It is impossible for us not to see the necessary tendency to consolidated Empire in the natural operation of the Constitution, if no further amended than as now proposed. And it is equally impossible for us not to be apprehensive for Civil Liberty, when we know of no instance in the records of history, that shew a people ruled in freedom when subject to one undivided government, and inhabiting a territory so extensive as that of the United States: And when, as it seems to us, the nature of Man and of things join to prevent it. The impracticability in such case of carrying Representation sufficiently near to the people for procuring their confidence and consequent obedience, compels a resort to fear resulting from great force, and excessive power in government. Confederated Republics, where the federal hand is not possessed of absorbing power, may permit the existence of freedom, whilst it preserves union, strength, and safety. Such amendments therefore, as may secure against the annihilation of the State governments we devoutly wish to see adopted.

If a persevering application to Congress from the States that have desired such amendments should fail of its object, we are disposed to think, reasoning from causes to Effects, that unless a dangerous Apathy should invade the public mind, it will not be many years before a constitutional number of Legislatures will be found to *demand* a Convention for the purpose.

***

ALS, Custis-Lee Family Papers, DLC. Written by the only Antifederalists in the Senate, this, and the following letter to the governor, sparked widespread commentary. The House of Delegates read it on 19 October, but the legislature officially refused to publish it. The letters appeared in Richmond as a broadside on or before 26 November, when Edmund Randolph sent Washington a copy. One or both of the letters were reprinted at least twenty-five times between 10 December 1789 and 17 March 1790 at Bennington, Vermont; Newburyport, Boston, Northampton, and Springfield, Massachusetts; Hartford, Litchfield, and Middletown, Connecticut; New York; Philadelphia; Baltimore; and Alexandria, Fredericksburg, and Richmond, Virginia. For public reaction to the Lee and Grayson letters, see *DHFFC* 18, especially David Stuart to George Washington, 3 December, and "A Familiar Epistle," 14 January 1790.

Richard Henry Lee and William Grayson to Governor Beverley Randolph

We have long waited in anxious expectation of having it in our power to transmit effectual amendments to the Constitution of the United States, and it is with grief that we now send forward propositions so inadequate to the purpose of real and substantial amendment, and so far short of the wishes of our Country [*Virginia*]. By perusing the Journal of the Senate, your Excellency will see that we did in vain bring to view the amendments proposed by our Convention, and approved by the Legislature. We shall transmit a complete set of the Journals of both houses of Congress to your Address, which, with a letter accompanying them, we entreat that your Excellency will have the goodness to lay before the honorable Legislature at the ensuing meeting.

ALS, Custis-Lee Family Papers, DLC. See location note to the previous document.

Roger Sherman to Simeon Baldwin

I received yours 25th instant—I have not wrote to you for some time having nothing Special to acquaint you with. I have from time to time transmitted the Gazette [*of the United States*] to you which contains the proceedings of Congress. I now enclose the last. *** Mr. Ellsworth told me he had talked with the President on your behalf. Majr. [*William*] Judd had previously applied and I was informed that Mr. [*Pierpont*] Edwards had made interest to be appointed District Judge and if that could not be obtained to be attorney which last I hear he is nominated for—I dont know that the Senate have passed on any of them—The Subject of Salaries is a difficult one, Some of them are much higher than I thought necessary, some were augmented by the Senate after they had passed the house Some of the additions were concurred with & others not. The Bill for compensation of the members & officers of Congress was brought in and passed, while I was at home,

so that it would ill become me to find fault with it—Congress have length-
ened the session to Tuesday the 29th instant, when I believe they will adjourn. The house had Scarce any business on Friday & Saturday but the
Senate had Several Bills not Closed—please to let Mrs. [*Rebecca*] Sherman
know that I am well & expect to come home this week—John [*Sherman*] is
here & expects to Sail for Georgia this monday.

ALS, Sherman Collection, CtY. Addressed to New Haven, Connecticut. Sherman mis-
takenly wrote "New Haven" in his dateline. The omitted text lists appointments to federal
office.

Paine Wingate to Timothy Pickering

I have received your favor of 15 instant and forwarded your enclosure to
Capn. [*George*] Williams. I am happy to hear of your welfare and that of your
family, and am much mortifyed that it has not been in the power of your
friends to bring you from your retirement into public life. I had flattered
myself with the hope that in the long list of the late nominations I should
have found your name. I did not think it proper in my connection with you,
personally to solicit the President, but I know that in conversation you was
mentioned by many & most earnestly wished for to be placed in some department of the Treasury & the President could not be unacquainted with
the Idea. But there is such a crowd of candidates that he must be puzled
to know which to select, & not unlikely is some times prevailed upon by
importunities when his own Inclination would have lead him otherwise. I
know that it will be no great disappointment to you, nor do I suppose that
your private interest will be affected; but your friends (& such you have
many at Philadelphia as well as at the Eastward) have faild being gratifyed.
*** You will observe that in the nominations very few old officers fill the
places they before had. I suppose that Mr. [*Samuel*] Meredith was made treasurer principal[*ly*] to make an opening for Capn. [*William*] McPherson who
was very anxious for a place. It is thot by some that Mr. [*Nicholas*] Eveleigh is not the best man for a comptroller & I do not know what induced his
appointment.
   Much time & heat has been expended upon the question of the permanent residence of Congress. The house of Representatives passed a bill for
fixing it on the Susquehannah; But the Senate have proposed an amendment
by putting in Germantown in the place of Susquehannah, with a proviso
that Pennsyla. or individuals shall engage to pay towards the expence one
hund. thousand dollars, which I am told will be no obstruction to the bill—

I expect the house will agree to the amendment this day & if the President shall approve, the dispute will be at an end—It is said the president is strongly in favor of Potomac, but it is expected he will not reject the bill. I hope yet that in a year or two we shall be quietly fixed in Pennsyla. & that you will be at the seat of government in some department ~~of government~~ or other. I do not think it a visionary wish. The doings of Congress I conclude you will see in the news papers & need not my recital. I think we have been profuse in the fixing of salaries & expect it will excite disgust at the East-ward especially. I have not heard very lately from home—To morrow is the day fixed for our adjournment & I hope soon to be on my return to N.H. It is probable I shall be here again the beginning of Jany. and shall be very glad to hear from you.

P. S. Since I wrote this letter I was told by one who had it directly from Mr. Clymer, that he & Mr. Fitzsimons both mentioned you to the President as a very suitable person for comptroller. The President discovered an approba-tion of the opinion; but observed that he thought it expedient to disperse the officers among the several states, & he did not know whether the Penn-sylvanians would consider you as one of them. Mr. Clymer replyed that he was confident the most respectable citizens of that state would not ~~not~~ only be satisfyed with your appointment but heartily wished it. What recom-mendation Mr. Eveleigh had I do not know, but I am told that he is rather an inactive man & supposd not very well fitted for the place. He was last spring very unwell here, & appeared to me to have but a broken constitu-tion. & I suspect that he will not be likely to fill the place long. I still please myself that your numerous friends will not be easy until they see you in some office in which you may be useful to the public, & which shall be hon-orable and agreeable to you. I am very glad that you have let me know your sentiments so freely in your last & trust you will not let your sentiment be known respecting the President's, not nominat[ing] you as has been ex-pected by many.

ALS, Pickering Papers, MHi. The omitted text lists appointments to office. For the full text, see *Wingate* 2:340–42.

Other Documents

Abraham Baldwin to [Joseph Clay?]. ALS, NNPM.
Regarding some matter that was to be laid before the board of treasury; Secretary Hamilton "has promised to write you as soon as he can get time to look into the matter"; "We shall probably adjourn tomorrow"; "I shall set out immediately by land for Augusta; the story of our proceedings you learn from Genl. Jackson by whom I send this."

Pierce Butler to Thomas Butler. ALS, Butler Letters, Uk. Addressed to Chelsea.

Letters from England "relieved Your Mother from great distress of mind, and myself from as much anxiety as a Man ought to shew"; a report on Thomas's progress in Latin "alarms me. If You are not among the foremost of Your Age and standing, there is an end to all my peace of mind Now then my Son, if You realy love me You will forego play, in order to improve Your mind."

Extract of a Letter from New York, written at 3 P.M. [Philadelphia] *Pennsylvania Packet*, 30 September; reprinted at York and Carlisle, Pennsylvania; Baltimore; Winchester and Fredericksburg, Virginia; and Edenton, North Carolina.

"The house have this moment" returned the residence bill to the Senate.

TUESDAY, 29 SEPTEMBER 1789

William Grayson to Patrick Henry

I have recieved your favor for which I am exceedingly thankful; indeed I was very uneasy at not hearing from you apprehending some indisposition might have prevented you: I remain still in a low state of health; but hope to get better from a cessation of business and from exercise.

The session is this moment closed, and the members would have parted [*in*] tolerable good temper if the disagreable altercations on the score of the seat of government had not left very strong impressions on the minds of the Southern gentlemen; they suppose with too much reason that the same kind of bargaining which took effect with respect to the Susquehannah may also take effect in other great National matters which may be very oppressive to a defenceless naked Minority—the bill has been ultimately defeated in the Senate & the point remains open, but gentlemen now begin to feel the observations of the Antis, when they informed them of the different interests in the Union & the probable consequences that would result therefrom [*to?*] the Southern States, who would be the milch cow out of whom the substance would be extracted; If I am not mistaken, they will e'er long have abundant cause to conclude that the idea of a difference between carrying States & productive States & manufacturing States & slave States is not a mere phantom of the imagination—If they reflect at all on the meaning of protecting duties—by way of encouragement to manufactures & apply the consequences to their own constituents, I think they would now agree that we were not totally beside ourselves in the [*Virginia ratifying*] Convention—In my opin-

William Grayson miniature, artist unknown. (Courtesy of the Library of Congress with the permission of Camilla Hoes Pope.)

milch cow out of whom the substance would
be extracted; If I am not mistaken, they
will 'eer long have abundant cause to
conclude that the idea of a difference be:
tween carrying States & productive States, or
manufacturing States & slave States is not
a mere phantom of the imagination. If
they reflect at all on the meaning of protecting
duties—by way of encouragement to manufactures & apply the consequences to their
own constituents, I think they would now agree
that we were not totally beside ourselves in
the Convention — In my opinion whenever
the Impost bill comes into action the federals
of the South will be let into some secrets that
they do not or will not at present apprehend.
You would be astonished at the progress of
manufactures in the seven Easternmost States
if they go on in the same proportion for seven
years they will pay very little on imports:
while the South will continue to labor under
the pressure: This added to the advantage
of carrying for the productive States, will place
them in the most desirable situation whatever.
‡   with respect to amendments matters
have turned out exactly as I apprehended
from the upward? doctrine of playing the
after game: the lower house sent up amend:
ments which held out a safeguard to per:
sonal liberty in a great many instances, but
this disgusted the Senate, and though it

William Grayson to Patrick Henry, 29 September 1789, p. 2. (Courtesy of the
Library of Congress.)

ion whenever the impost bill comes into action the fœderals of the South will be let into some secrets that they do not or will not at present apprehend. You would be astonished at the progress of manufactures in the seven Eastermost States if they go on in the same proportion for seven years they will pay very little on imports: while the South will continue to labor under the pressure: This added to the advantage of carrying for the productive States will place them in the most desirable situation whatever.

With respect to amendments matters have turned out exactly as I apprehended from the extraord[inar]y. doctrine of playing the after game: the lower house sent up amendments which held out a safeguard to pers[on]al liberty in a great many instances, but this disgusted the Senate, and though we made every exertion to save them, they are so mutilated ~~scarified~~ & gutted that in fact they are good for nothing, & I believe as many others do, that they will do more harm than benefit: The Virginia amendments were all brought into view, and regularly rejected Perhaps they may think differently on the subject the next session, as Rhode Island has refused for the present acceeding to the constitution; her reasons you will see in the printed papers—There are a set of gentlemen in both houses who during this session have been for pushing matters to an extraordy. length; this has appeared in their attachment to titles, in their desire of investing the Presidt. with the power of removal from Office & lately by their exertion to make the writs run in his name; their maxim seems to have been to make up by construction what the constitution wants in energy.

The Judicial bill has passed but wears so monstrous an appearance that I think it will be felo de se[1] in the execution; the amendment of Virginia respecting this matter has more friends in both houses than any other, & I still think it probable that this alteration may be ultimately procured: Whenever the federal Jud[iciar]y. comes into operation I think the pride of the States will take the alarm, which added to the difficulty of attendance from the extent of the district in many cases, the ridiculous situation of the Venue, & a thousand other circumstances, will in the end procure it's distruction.

The salaries I think are rather high & for the temper or circumstances of the Union, & furnish another cause of discontent to those who are dissatisfied with the government.

I have made every exertion in favor of Mr. [*Joseph*] Martin, but there have been such representations agt. him, that I fear he will derive no benefit from any thing in my power to effect.

With respect to the lands at the Natches,[2] they are unquestionably according to prevailing ideas the property of Georgia, but the Spaniards are in the actual possession and hold it by force: Georgia some time ~~since ordered~~ ago offered to cede a great part of their state including this territory to Congress, but the cession was so loaded as they conceived with unreasonable conditions that they rejected it:[3] it is highly probable that the present treaty will produce peace with the Creeks, & that excellent lands may be procured reasonably on the Altimaha. if I can be of any service to you in this or any other matter your commands will be a pleasure.

ALS, Henry Papers, DLC.

[1] Suicide.
[2] Spain did not relinquish its claim to these lands in present day Mississippi until 1795.
[3] The Georgia cession act of 1 February 1788 was rejected by the Confederation Congress on 15 July (*JCC* 34:323–26).

OTHER DOCUMENTS

Fisher Ames to an Unknown Recipient. Summary of ALS, *John Heise Catalog* 91(1913):item 29; ibid 101(1914):item 33.
Letter of introduction.

Abraham Baldwin to Joel Barlow. ALS, Baldwin Family Collection, CtY. Addressed to London; forwarded to Paris.
Appointments; "We have agreed in recommending some conciliatory amendments, about trial by jury, liberty of press, all power not given reserved &c. which will do no hurt and may give ground to antifeds to wheel about with a salve to their pride. There was much scramble about seat of government, it is a draw battle, all as we were."

William Samuel Johnson to Tench Coxe. ALS, Coxe Papers, PHi.
Prevented from writing earlier by "The hurry unavoidably attending the closing of the session of Congress"; opinions on Great Britain's removal of judges.

Henry Knox to George Clymer. FC:dft, Knox Papers, Gilder Lehrman Collection, NHi.
Since talking to Clymer that morning, learned that a copy of the map of the Susquehanna River was being made, precluding "the necessity of your taking the map with you."

Hezekiah Welch to John Adams. ALS, Adams Family Manuscript Trust, MHi. Written from Boston.
Office seeking: writing a second time; asks Adams to recommend him to Benjamin Lincoln.

NYDG, 30 September.

Chief Justice Jay delivered two messages relating to foreign affairs from the President to the House of Representatives.

WEDNESDAY, 30 SEPTEMBER 1789

Fine (Johnson)

Tristram Dalton to Governor John Hancock

Inclosed your Excellency will receive a copy of a Treaty formed at Fort Harmar in January last,[1] between Arthur St. Clair Esqr. Governor of the Western Territory on the part of the United States, and the Sachems and Warriors of the six nations (the Mohawks excepted)—this treaty proposes the establishment of a line of property between the United States and the six nations different from the line of division between the United States and the States of Massachusetts and New York—A reference to the deed of Cession of Massachusetts entered upon the printed Journals of Congress upon the 19th day of April 1785: and to that of New York entered upon the printed Journals of Congress upon the 1st day of March 1781, will shew the Western Boundary of those States[2]—The Line proposed by the inclosed Treaty is far to the Eastward of that boundary, and, if established, would deprive Massachusetts, or Messrs. [*Nathaniel*] Gorham & [*Oliver*] Phelps, of her, or their property, in an extensive tract of Territory, and would also divest New York of her Jurisdiction over the same.

Your Excellency is apprised that several of the States have reluctantly submitted to the Claims of those States which are, by Charter, interested in vacant or western Territory: this Treaty draws this Question into Discussion, and will not be without its friends and advocates.

The Senators from New York united with me in opposing the Ratification of this Treaty, when it was laid before the Senate for their advise and consent; and upon our joint representation the consideration thereof was postponed untill the next session. The Treaty is liable to objection not only, as it affects the boundary line aforesaid, but if by ratification it becomes the supreme Law of the Land, the Article confirming to the *six Nations* all the Lands which they inhabit east and south of the proposed line of property will materially prejudice the Indian Purchases made by Messrs. Gorham & Phelps during the last year, as well as those made under the Authority of New York.

I have considered it as my duty to transmit this information to your Excellency.

ALS, Miscellaneous Legislative Papers, M-Ar.

---

[1] For the treaty, see *DHFFC* 2:160–63.
[2] *JCC* 28:281–83, 19:208–13, respectively.

Richard Bland Lee to James Madison

I called on you to day, but was unfortunate enough not to see you, as well to take leave of one of my most esteemed friends, and dearest patriots to his country, as to communicate a wish, in the success of which I feel myself very much interested that, you would be good enough to mention to the President, in case American affairs should require Ministers, at the courts of London or Versailes, that I should be happy, if he deemed me a proper person to go as Secretary to one of the Legations. This communication is made ~~with~~ in the confidence of the warmest friendship.
N. B. I hope to see you in Virginia.

ALS, Custis-Lee Family Papers, DLC. The editors have identified the recipient by his endorsement on the letter.

William Tudor to John Adams

Your Letter of 18th. I received last Evening & it was particularly acceptable as I had experienced much Uneasiness from the Time which had intervened since your last Favour. Notwithstanding your kind Hint at the Close of it, I was chagrined, greatly so, by reading the Paper of this Morning, not because I was not named as a Judge, for I think the Judges from this State are well selected & I know their Pretensions in various Respects better founded than any I could lay claim to—But the appointment of the attorney for the District of Massachusetts, has disappointed me. The Man who has obtained that Place [*Christopher Gore*] has ~~been~~ built up a very handsome Estate in Consequence of his agency for most of the Refugees who had Debts due to them in this Country, & which most lucrative Employment he got by the Sollicitations of his Father [*John Gore*] while, he continued in England as a Refugee. I never heard of any Attachment or Services shewn by his Family to *this* Country, but something very different the public Acts of this Commonwealth attest to.

But my Humiliation is forgot in the Assurance of the Continuance of your Friendship, & I have now only to regret the occasioning you Trouble in my behalf; & that I ever wrote a Line on the Subject to the President. Blessed is the Man who never expecteth for he shall never be disappointed. This Beatitude in future I will make my own, & thus I bid adieu to the Subject forever.

It is singular that Massachusetts should continue "nothing" from a Want of System & Union in her Delegates. And what is still more disgraceful that Her paltry Policy, & debasing Œconomy should withhold a Compensation for the noblest Services of her ablest Citizens. Had the Vice President been born on the other side the Potomac, how greatly would his Foreign services & American Merits have been estimated! As he belongs to New England, it is to be left to Posterity to do Justice to his Character, his Talents & his un-parralleld negotiations. And with such a glorious future Prospect, a Man ought to be content to be a Beggar—say the ungrateful, the Envious & the Miserly.

ALS, Adams Family Manuscript Trust, MHi. Written from Boston. Addressed on the inside to "President Adams."

OTHER DOCUMENTS

Joze da Silva Loureiro to Daniel Carroll. ALS, Washington Papers, DLC.
Office seeking: Joze Eleuterio Barboza de Lima for American consul at Oporto, Portugal.

SEPTEMBER 1789 UNDATED

Samuel Adams to [Elbridge Gerry?]

The Congress say the Light houses now erected shall be supported at the Expence of the U.S. one year, but no longer unless they shoud then be ceded by the respective states in which they stand.[1] The Means of supporting these Buildings in this State are taken from its Legislature—It is presumed not to be intended that this Legislature shall be told at the End of the Year, you must cede your Lighthouse to Congress & the Territory on which it stands together with the exclusive Power of Legislation, or it shall be of no Use to your state. Congress is confessedly empowered by the Constitution to exercise this [*lined out*] exclusive Legislation; but it was said to be very wholesome Advice given by the Bishop of St. Asaph[2] to the British Government "not to govern too much." This he held to be the true Art of governing. The British Ministry by refusing to hearken to his sage Advice lost the Government of the Nation over thirteen of her Colonies. The Earl of Dartmouth, when he was in Administration, *condescended* to bring himself down to a Level with a Speaker ~~with~~ of our House of Representatives, and wrote him a *private* ~~Lett~~ & *confidential* Letter; wherein he informed the Speaker that in his opinion the Parliament had a Right to make Laws binding on the Colonies in all Cases whatsoever.[3] His Lordship was indeed, or he affected to be as cautious & wise as the good Bishop; for he added, that though the Parliamt. had the Right, they ought never to exercise it but in Cases of extreme Necessity. Thus he endeavoured to coax the Speaker & through him the House to acknowledge the Right & believe it would be thus sparingly & prudently exercised. But the House had too often discovered a Disposition in the British Parliament & King to ruin their Country by governing too much, to comply with the Ministers wish ~~to admit to such a~~ by yielding to them the Right ~~in them~~, [*lined out*] & trusting them to hit on the Cases of extreme Necessity. Lord Chatham [*William Pitt "the Elder"*] & other great Patriots & Friends of America brought in & carried that Declaratory Act;[4] but those were not the Men who afterwards violently drove the Parliament to exercise a Right to make Laws binding on us in all Cases whatever. The prudent Members, altho they judgd that the Right was in Parliament did not think it proper to exercise it lest it should be thought governing too much. And is there not Danger that such will be the Common Opinion if Congress after having taken from a State the Means of supporting its Lights shall lay it under a kind of Necessity of ceding the Jurisdiction with the Property or lose the Benefit of them—If the Buildings which we have erected at great Expence are of general Utility to the U.S. why should not they maintain them while they remain so, without the exclusive ~~Right~~ Power of Legislation? For although Congress will ~~be~~ be vested with this Power according to the Constitution if the Property shall be ceded to them, yet they will not be obligd to exercise the Power. ~~But what And~~ It may be asked What is the mighty ~~Jure~~ Power of Jurisdiction over a Light house & a single Family on a barren Island? But will not a Crime which may happen to be committed on that Barren Island by a Citizen ~~of~~ of [*this?*] this Com[*mon*]. W[*ea*]lth. & not living on the Island & therefore not within the exclusive Jurisdiction of Congress, be triable in a fœderal Court. And should "other publick Buildings" be multiplied we know not how many parts and parcels of the Territory of the Common Wealth may become subject to the exclusive Legislation of Congress. Perhaps so many and so scatterd as to marr and ruin its Sovereignty.

FC:dft, Adams Originals, NN. Written from Boston. The manuscript does not indicate the recipient, but Adams had written Gerry on the subject twice before, on 20 and 22 August.

---

[1] Section 1 of the Lighthouses Act [HR-12]; see *DHFFC* 5:1245.

[2] Jonathan Shipley (1714–88), bishop of St. Asaph, was a close friend of Benjamin Franklin and an outspoken defender of colonial rights. His *Speech Intended to Have Been Spoken*, summarizing his views on imperial government, saw at least twelve printings in America in 1774.

[3] William Legge (1731–1801), the second earl of Dartmouth, served as Britain's secretary of state for the American Department, 1772–75. It was ostensibly in a private capacity, however, that he addressed his unprecedented and controversial letter to Thomas Cushing, speaker of the Massachusetts House of Representatives, on 19 June 1773 (B. D. Bargar, *Lord Dartmouth and the American Revolution* [Columbia, S.C., 1965], p. 89).

[4] The Parliamentary act of 1766 asserting authority to make laws for America "in all cases whatsoever."

October 1789

THURSDAY, 1 OCTOBER 1789

Pierce Butler and Ralph Izard to Anthony Wayne

We had the honor of answering your Letter of 4th. July, & have since been favoured with that of 1st. September. The distressed situation of Georgia required the immediate attention of Government; & the President took the earlyest opportunity of recommending such measures to Congress, as we hope will afford her effectual relief. The rank, & abilities of the Commissioners can not fail making a proper impression on the minds of the Indians. The great Warrior [*Benjamin Lincoln*] at the head of them, & the late President of Congress [*Cyrus Griffin*], are characters well known to the Indians; and when they are informed of the poetical, & biographical abilities of the other Gentleman [*David Humphreys*] in the Commission; when they know, which no doubt they will, that he is tam Marte, quam Mercurio,[1] there is every reason to hope that we shall have a solid, and lasting Peace. What you say respecting "the Indian Agency in the Southern District, & the Military Command in that quarter," is perfectly conformable to our opinions, & wishes. It is yet uncertain whether any farther military establishment will be made: & if there should be any, the power of nominating to Offices is by the Constitution vested in the President. To him it will be proper that you should write on the subject: Stony Point[2] is certainly not forgotten at Head Quarters. Whenever an opportunity shall be afforded us of rendering you service in the Senate, we shall embrace it with the greatest pleasure.

ALS, Wayne Papers, PHi; hand of Izard.

[1] As much like Mars as Mercury; as warlike as he is artistic.
[2] Wayne received the thanks of Congress and a gold medal for his morale building victory over the British at Stony Point, New York, on 16 July 1779.

Elbridge Gerry to John Clark

I am favored with yours of the 7th and 22d of September and for reasons which I have not time to enumerate, I have thought that there will be a bet-

New York Octr. 1.st 1789. —

Dear Sir

We had the honor of answering your Letter of 4.th July, & have since been favoured with that of 1.st September. The distressed situation of Georgia required the immediate attention of government; & the President took the earliest opportunity of recommending such measures to Congress, as we hope will afford her effectual relief. The rank, & abilities of the Commissioners can not fail making a proper impression on the minds of the Indians. The great Warrior at the head of them, & the late President of Congress, are characters well known to the Indians; and

Pierce Butler and Ralph Izard to Major General Anthony Wayne, 1 October 1789, p. 1.
(Courtesy of the Historical Society of Pennsylvania.)

Ralph Izard and his wife Alice Delancey, by John Singleton Copley, 1738–1815,
oil on canvas, 1775. (Courtesy of the Museum of Fine Arts, Boston,
Edward Ingersoll Browne Fund.)

ter prospect of giving general satisfaction, by placing the permanent residence on the Delaware than on the Susquehanna. But not wishing to oppose the prevailing opinion of Pennsylvania and the states east of it, excepting New Jersey, I voted with them for Susquehanna. The senate however, Nonconcurred in the bill, and this being agreed to by the House, with one amendment, is referred by the Senate to the next session. I took no share in the debates, but thought too many of the speakers influenced by local views, held forth principles which must make unfavorable impression: I hope, however, liberality will be generally diffused in the next discussion.

PMHB 20(1895):82–83.

From a Correspondent

The motion in the last Journal, respecting the partial publication of the debates of the House of Representatives of the United States,[1] underwent some discussion on Saturday last, and was afterwards withdrawn by Judge Burke, who declared he should renew it next session, when there would be more time to consider the subject. The practice adopted during the present session of *passing* some members by a full and correct publication of their speeches, and of *misrepresenting* other members, by mutilating, altering, partially stating, or suppressing theirs, was reprobated by several members; and whilst these expressed the warmest desire of giving full information to the public, of the debates of the House, they were at the same time very severe on all cringing, servile Printers, who, not having independence of spirit sufficient to preserve a free press, were disposed to prostitute it to the mean and corrupt purposes of faction, and of deceiving the public. Those opposed to it, did not deny the facts stated in the motion, but hoped the subjects of it would be more careful in future, and remove the cause of the complaint.

NYJ, 1 October; reprinted at Philadelphia.

---

[1] For Burke's motion and the debate, see *DHFFC* 11:1503–6.

OTHER DOCUMENTS

William Grayson to Alexander Hamilton. Promissory Note, Hamilton Papers, DLC.
   Promises to pay on order $200 specie value.

George Washington, Diary. Washington Papers, DLC. For the full text, see *DGW* 5:448.
   Dined with Read, Bland, and Madison.

[Rhode Island] *Providence Gazette*, 3 October.

Goodhue, Leonard, Partridge, and Wingate arrived in the evening from New York on the *Hancock*; Trumbull had traveled with them as far as New London, Connecticut.

FRIDAY, 2 OCTOBER 1789

James Sullivan to John Adams

I have to acknowledge the honor of receiving yours of the 17th & 21st instant [*ultimo*].

In my Letter of the 18th of agust, I suggested to your consideration, the idea of encreasing the circulating medium of the united states, by some kind of paper Credit. I hinted that I beleived, the duties, and Impost, established, would call for more cash than is in circulation within the union, and that there was no Instance in any Country where one half of their medium passes through the public treasury annually. in your obliging answer you reply, that the money, as soon as received into the treasury, will be a gain paid to the creditors of government, and so be passed immediately into circulation. and that the States are destitute of that Credit which is necessary to the support of a paper Currency. these positions may be both true, but I am by no means convinced of the certainty of the one last mentioned, provideded the government is administred with firmness moderation and prudunce.

I have been in the Country upon business where money would have appeared if there had been any, and do assure you, that since my first introduction into the world, I never new so much complaint, or saw so much foundation for complaining. Our Common people have more money than the Peasants of other Countries, but you know Sir, that their Leaders in the revolution engaged that they should have more. their habits of expenditures cannot be suddenly changed without great convulsions, and perhaps civil wars. it is no easy task to learn ~~the habit~~ to bear poverty with patience, but I only mean this as an apology for having troubled you on the subject and urge the matter no further. Time decides upon all things.

I have read with great pleasure yours of the 21st, wherein you mention with great strength of expression, your determination to urge with integrity, those political principles which tend to give Government a proper balance, and consequently to secure to the people, those rights, for which all good governments are instituted. I beleive the people are too sensible of your services to treat you ill, and that your fellow Citizens are too much enlightned to persecute a Real friend. if you are ever injured it will be by those, who from a real regard to the principles of Despotism abhor every one who took an active part in the late revolution, or by them who have no idea of Government, but as it affords them wealth and Emolument. these will Court you while you are in power to serve them, but the moment your old friends, and the People at large shall be induced to neglect you, these men will fatten on the triumph.

I might complain of being used not so well as I think I had aught to Expect; I engaged early in defence of my Countrys freedom, God knows it was on the purest, and most disinterested Principles. I spent the prime of my life in Legislative, and Judicial, Capacities with no Emolument but paper money. I have, while there, been threatned with Halters, Gaols, &c., by men who are now in the warm embraces of Government. when the People by an unhappy combination of circumstances were exceedingly oppressed, and a number of them run mad, I took those healing Measures on our small scale, which [*Jacques*] Necker is taking in the great world. and Established without shedding blood by the civil arm, peace and Tranquility. for I beleive, that in all civil commotions, the less blood there is shed by the civil authority, the more lasting the succeeding peace will be. when the Constitution of the united states was submitted to the Consideration of the people, notwithstanding the Enthusiastic fervour which then reigned, I was honest enough to express my wishes for such amendments as I considered Essentially necessary to guard those rights which my countrymen have bled to preserve, and for no other amendments than what congress have agreed to, but for this, I find myself neglected by the national Government. as I do not want an office for the Emolument of it, so I can make myself very happy with the Esteem and Love of the People in private life.

Your ideas of an equipoise of powers in civil Government are always entertaining, and Instructive to me: and I am generally cautious of expressing opinions to one, on whom the Learned world looks with so much respect as they do on you, but out of respect to you, I will venture to offer a few observations.

All writers upon civil Government agree, that there naturally exists three powers, which in a free Government can never be united in one man, or in one body of men: that such a Constitution as these writers speak of ever existed, compleat in all its parts I have yet to learn. the Europeans pretend that their orders of nobility are an aristocratic bodys forming one balance, of the three powers, but it appears to me, that the nobility in every Kingdom in Europe are an artificial, and not a Natural branch of Government, and that the People at at Large, while they suffer much by them, derive no other benefit from them, than what arises from the wars between them and the sovereign power; without any regard in Either for the rights of the people.

When the united states declared themselves Independent, they became Seperate sovereignties: and according to Montesqui, and other writers, the people were both Sovereign, and subjects. their Magistratrates were ~~their~~ their ministers to Execute the Laws, while the body of the People were the Supreme Legislatures.

Upon the adoption of the General Government, a part of this sovereignity was yeilded, but the several States yet possess a great Share of that Sovereignty, over ~~the the greater parts of~~ the Subjects, and property they held before In the departments of the General Government I cannot find any provision *expressly made* for the three great powers so much talked of. The President under certain advisory checks, holds the Executive Power; the Senate, and House, under the Check of the Presidents negative holds the Legislative Authority, the Senate is said to be a substitute for an aristocratic body, but while the two Houses of the Legislature, in the several states choose the Senators, they are still but the representatives of the People though introduced by a sort of double refinement in election.

An aristocracy, as I conceive of it, must be independent both of sovereign and People & hence it follows that a Democracy cannot admit the appearance of an Aristocratic body. when I say an Aristocracy is independent of the Sovereign and the People, I mean that they are so, as to their future Existance and duration.

The Supreme Judicial holds that office during Good behaviour, which is a Tenure quite incompatible with the Ideas of an Aristocracy, but this tenure however pompous it may sound, when coolly examined will be found to be no more than a tenancy at will. and what is worse ~~he~~ it depends upon the Legislative branch for ~~their~~ existance. though they Judges are appointed by the Supreme Executive, during good behaviour, and their salaries irrevocably fixed by the Legislature, yet they may be impeached by the House, and tryed and removed by the Senate. therefore should there ever be a Time, when the President, House and Senate, shall agree upon a Law for changing the Constitution, and the Judges shall refuse to carry it into Execution; they may be removed by one branch of the Legislative power, and their Seats filled with men who will Act in consort with the other powers of State. then where is the Conterpoise which is so much talked of? it may be answered that the Judges will have integrity and firmness Enough to do right. that no doubt is the case with the Present Bench, nor is their Danger of a violation of the Constitution in the Present age. but these observations if they have any weight, may be used to prove all Constitutional checks, and balances to be un necessary.

The Method taken by all the Governments that I know any thing about to support themselves, and counterpoise their ~~Governments~~ Systems, is to rob the People of their wealth, their Liberty, and their understanding, and to press them down with Standing Armies, and all this under pretence of defending them from a foreign power, which could not make them more unhappy, even by a Conquest. but this can never be the case in America; because the People have got a habit of understanding their own Interest, and cannot loose the use of Arms.

But I am by no means aware, that the insufficiency of the the Judicial, to counterpoise the other powers of Government in the plan adopted by the People of the united States, can ever become dangerous. the constitution has made as I conceive full provision in this case. the Existance of the States with uncontroulable, and Sovereign powers as to in some things, is preserved and guarantied by the General Government, and are necessary to the Election of Presidt. vice President, and Senators, the Legislative of each hath certain honors, rights, and priviledges which they will Jealously defend, and their very Existance as Soveriegn States depends upon the preservation of the balance of the New general Government. to these I look as the most powerful checks and contemplate them as possessing all the powers necessary both to Counterpoise the Union, and to defend the people against the Encroachments which may in future ages be attempted upon their Liberty.

This Species of balance may no doubt be attended with all the evils which you mention as flowing from the Encampment of great men, in the various parts of the Continent, but there can be no way to prevent it, unless by the mode of European Governments, that is to rob the people of the power of acting at all. for nature has irrevocably established it, that where man has the power of doing good, he has the power of doing evil, you must therefore rob the people of the power of free agency, or they may do wrong.

In a Government where the People have any Share of freedom, and possess any quantity of property, the beam of balance will be always Vibrating, and will Turn more, or less according to the agitation of the Surrounding Atmosphere, or other accidents. this flows forever from the imperfection of man, and must for the sake of the rights of human nature, be born in the political, as we bear Storms, and Tempests, in the Natural world.

The dependance I have for Peace and good order, is in the wise administration of all our Governments, and in the intelligence and goodness of my Country men. they possess property, and hope for more, and have given full Evidence of their wishing for a Government to protect them in the enjoyment of it. they have indeed unhappily fallen into such mistakes and irregularities, as will Essentially injure them, but I beleive their habits are quite averse to the frequent repetition of them.

Should the americans ever become ignorant, poor, and undisciplined, a Strong State may be erected on the ruins of freedom, but I beleive they never will. should such a government succeed, it will wax voluptious, arrogant, arbitrary, and cruel, and finally like the Roman, & other Empires will die of wounds received from its own hands.

Should there ever be an unhappy Controversy between the General

Government, and the particular states, a division of the whole into two or more states will be the probable Consequence, when the Northern States will contend still for freedom but how Long they will hold a free Constitution, the Century in which the Controversy shall take place may determine.

At present we can be in no danger while the General Government is administred with Impartiality, Moderation, and Prudence. an attempt to alter the Constitution or to infringe the Rights of the particular states, would undoubtedly kindle a fire to be quenched only with blood.

I do not give you the trouble of reading this, supposing you would be instructed by it. or that any thing I can write will be ent[ert]aining to you: but I wish you to beleive that I am fully convinced, that the happiness of a people, depends much upon the principles of the Government under which they Live, and that I am firmly of opinion, that the *United Independence* of America must be preserved by Moderation, Prudence, & Virtue, as certainly as it was acquired by Wisdom, Valour and firmness.

ALS, Adams Family Manuscript Trust, MHi.

A Citizen

Who would have thought it? I am sure the aspect of the question respecting the permanent residence of Congress at the beginning, during its progress, and almost to its determination, would have led any one to conclude that the Susquehanna was to have been the favoured place, for there was a very large majority for it, in the House of Representatives of Congress, and a like majority would have voted for the same place in the Senate, if Mr. M—s [*Morris*] had not opposed it, nay, if he had not have gone further, in promising in behalf of this state and its citizens, that provided Congress agreed to change the place of permanent residence from the Susquehanna to Germantown, the state of Pennsylvania, or its citizens, should grant to Congress as a free gift, the sum of 100,000 Dollars—Whereupon the Senate by the Chairman's [*Vice President Adams*] casting vote, substituted the word "Germantown" in the place of the "Susquehanna," and then the bill being sent down to the House of Representatives, the same proposition was made there, which induced a majority of that body to rescind their former resolution in favor of the Susquehanna, and to concur with the Senate for Germantown.

Now, altho' I am highly pleased with Germantown being fixed on as the place of permanent residence of Congress, yet I do not approve of the mode by which it was obtained, as I think it reflects great dishonour on Congress, that they should be influenced in so important and durable a point by the promise of a present of money, which besides may not be so easily procured as promised, for is it at all probable, that the inhabitants of Lancaster, York, Northumberland and the western counties, will consent to a tax for raising 100,000 dollars for the purpose of inducing Congress to change their residence from the Susquehanna to Germantown? No. They will say, it is too much to wrest Congress from us by our own Representatives, and oblige us also to defray the expence of it.

[Philadelphia] *Independent Gazetteer*, 2 October.

OTHER DOCUMENTS

Tobias Lear to John Brown. FC:dft, Miscellaneous Letters, RG 59, DNA.
The President asks Brown to deliver the commissions for Kentucky's federal judicial officers; "The reason of giving you this trouble is ~~the~~ a want of a regular & certain communication with that Country and your situation ~~will probably~~ as an inhabitant of Kentuckey offering modes of conveyance to you that would not be known to others."

John Moriarty to George Washington. ALS, Washington Papers, DLC.
Written from Salem, Massachusetts. For the full text, see *PGW* 4:127–28.
Office seeking: unspecified; "I applied to Some of the members of the Honorable house, who I had earnestly Intreated to Solicit in my behalf, but in this, was disapointed as prior Engagemts. & motives of Consanguinity Superceded my Claims to their Intercessions"; mentions Morris as a reference.

Thomas Tudor Tucker to St. George Tucker. ALS, Roberts Collection, PHC.
Addressed to "Matoax," St. George's estate outside Petersburg, in Chesterfield County, Virginia.
Is just about to depart for Charleston, and is fatigued with preparations; has spoken with William Constable about St. George's stepsons (Theodorick B. and John Randolph "of Roanoke") "& he promises to attend to them in my Absence, which I expect will be little more than 2 months"; makes arrangements for the payment of his rent balance to Michael Huck; "Our Friend Mr. Page will inform you how we have conducted ourselves in our late Session. You will find our Amendments to the Constitution calculated merely to amuse, or rather to deceive."

[Boston] *Massachusetts Centinel*, 3 October.
Wingate, A. Foster, and Goodhue arrived in the evening.

[Worcester] *American Herald, Massachusetts Spy*, 8 October.
Thatcher passed through Worcester.

SATURDAY, 3 OCTOBER 1789

William Few to Governor George Walton

Agreeable to the request of the Honourable The Executive Council I accompanyed the Commissioners of the United States (for treating with all the Indian tribes lying on the South side of ~~Sout~~ the River Ohio) to the Rock Landing and there recieved of Henry Osborn Esqure the papers which I herewith deliver.

With respect to the Indian Negociation I beg leave to refer you to the Commissioners who I presume will give you full and Official information on that Subject.

ALS, Edward Telfair Papers, NcD. Written from Augusta, Georgia.

Comte de Moustier to Comte de Montmorin

***

Finding myself bedridden I sent the King's letter to Mr. Jay, then interim head of the department of foreign affairs, asking him to submit it to the President of the United States. He in turn communicated it to the Senate and simply announced its subject to the House of Representatives in a message whose expression was quite acceptable, showing, I believe, the true sentiments of the head of the American Federal Republic as well as those of a large part of his people. If I could have submitted the King's letter on this subject myself I would have had a special audience with the President like those the Sovereigns of Europe grant as circumstances dictate to foreign ministers, the President considering himself with regard to them as the Representative of the entire union. It also follows from this principle that this first Magistrate will probably write in his own name to the King in response to His Majesty's letter.

The idea that You have, Sir, of Gen. Washington and his disposition toward France, seems very well founded and if the proofs are often limited or restrained one can still be consoled that it is as a result of his great circumspection, which leads him to want never to appear to be guided in his public conduct by personal feelings, though he is as susceptible to them as other men generally. There still exist even among members of the Government many people in America, whose feelings with regard to France are not very favorable and Gen. Washington takes great care not to expose himself to their malicious interpretations. Thus on that account one must limit oneself to enjoying useful results without imagining that you will have the pleasure born of a free expression of feelings. I am in general well received by the President, but the importance he attaches to his dignity and his natural reserve render his communication infinitely cold. Nevertheless in an informal visit that I paid him yesterday and at which I was tête à tête with him for an hour he was much more open than usual and on the subject of recently arrived accounts of events in France he expressed a concern for His Majesty and the nation which I believe is firmly in his heart.

The Vice President is nowhere near as important a personage as Mr. Adams would like to make him; all the efforts he has made in this regard have only served to render him ridiculous and expose him to many unpleasantnesses. They almost came to the point of expressing in front of him in the Senate the absolute uselessness of a dignity such as his. Thus his position affording him but little consideration, while his personal pedantry renders him odious or ridiculous it must be hoped that his influence will have very little effect. The little success that he had in England has greatly tempered his exaltations in favor of that former Mother Country. As for the rancor which he always has at the bottom of his heart against France, for not having known to appreciate his merit and great talents (as a political compiler and speculative thinker) I hope that this will produce few noticeable effects.

Mr. Jay whose spite is more active and whose conduct is more cautious, would have been more dangerous if he had held on to the department of Foreign Affairs. Fortunately, he was just replaced by the man whom we could most hope to see at the head of this department. Mr. Jefferson whose return we expect at any moment is named Secretary of State and it is presumed that he will accept this post to which Interior Affairs other than Finance and War are attached as well as foreign relations. Mr. Jay is named Chief Justice, a permanent position and third in dignity. He is well known for his Jurisprudence and well suited to the important position he is going to fill. His personal qualities, the dryness of his manner, his irascible character and his tendency to put himself first render him inappropriate for the position that he formerly occupied, rather than filled well. He has shown me greater regard recently than he was accustomed to, and I think Gen. Washington must have insinuated to him not to give the King's Minister reason to believe that Mr. Jay harbored prejudices against France, because my personal conduct toward him, which never varied, could not induce him to treat me either better or worse. It will always be of interest to maintain a good outward relationship with Mr. Jay, while waiting for an inner change, because of the great influence his position gives him on the decision of many questions that must be decided by the federal courts of which he is the first Judge and where he will try to raise himself up as an Oracle.

I have not been fortunate in having the occasion for any discussion of etiquette since the establishment of the new Government. That which You did the honor of telling me, Sir, about Holland's ceremonial could very well serve as a guide in this country. I raised the difficulty that existed under the old form of government with regard to polite visits paid to Members of Congress in declaring that I believed that in that regard those who wished to entertain relations with the French Minister could indicate it to him so that if he were eager to make the particular acquaintance of one of the members he would seek out the means of doing so. A few of them who resented the bother, and others who still have the old pretension, in general disapproved of *owing* the French Minister the first visit and have abstained from coming to see me, but I have received the majority and the leadership of both Houses. That should suffice as precedent. If circumstances ever dictate sending an Ambassador I doubt if the President would do as much on his part, as the Stadtholder in Holland, because the President of the United States regards himself as much superior to the first Magistrate of the United Provinces. It is certain that in heredity and wealth almost all the advantage is on the side of the President.

Congress finished its first Session which lasted nearly seven months on the 29 of the month. With the exception of some idle discussions occasioned or prolonged either by ignorance or by the spirit of locality which affect the Americans more and which misleads most from the path of public good, one should applaud the transactions and the conduct of Congress and the Head of the Federal Republic. The coolness of the Americans and the limitation of the number of people who compose the two Houses of the legislative body appear to be the two principal reasons for the success of its deliberations. I am attaching here the summary of that first Session during which the American Government organized itself following the principles of the new Constitution adopted by the eleven States which compose the current confederation, forming a great consolidated Republic which leaves only a weak portion of absolute independent sovereignty to its Members. Congress will adjourn until the first Monday of the month of January next. In this interval it will be up to the Heads of the executive departments to prepare materials for the deliberations and discussions of the legislative body. The most important objective without question will be the Financial system. I think they wish to obtain a loan of an appropriate Sum to cover all the back interest and part of the payment due for several years past. It is to be presumed but not proven, that the revenue of the Republic will suffice for its annual obligations, but it would be better if it could also create a fund for repayment of debts, above all without being forced to have recourse to direct taxes.

***

[Enclosure]

Summary of the First Session of the New Government of the United States, from 4 March to 29 September 1789

The operations of the new government can be reduced to four Principal Heads, namely:

1. *The consolidation of the new confederation of the United States.*
2. *The establishment of a permanent revenue.*
3. *The administration of both interior and external affairs.*
4. *Justice in relation to private property of Citizens, foreigners and Individual States.*

In order to decide on such important points and to make the majority of Delegates accept them despite their coming from all parts of the Continent and being generally disposed to assert their zeal for local interests in the service of their Constituents, it was necessary to use alternately argumentation, ruse, insinuation and threats, in short all the methods known and used in England, with the exception of those of corruption and injury, of which the one is prohibited by the equality of fortunes and the other by the mildness of character of these Americans. I am going to give in a few words the substance of the debates and the acts of Congress that form the basis of this new edifice.

I. *Consolidation of the New Confederation of the United States.*

This goal could only be attained in two ways, in binding all the members of this body by a solemn oath and in giving some satisfaction to those who appeared upset by the use that Congress appeared to make of the powers accorded to it.

Thus not only was the oath prescribed by the Constitution offered to all the Members of both Houses of Congress the first week, but it was ordered by the first act emanating from this Government to make all Officials and employees whatever of the 11 States that compose the new Confederation take the same oath, so that in less than two months all men of influence were bound to uphold the Constitution, whatever may be their individual disposition toward that Constitution. The amendments that Congress proposed do not change any essential part; they serve rather as explication and corollary to this instrument, which is already considered with a kind of respect and which is no longer allowed to be touched without raising a clamor from patriots. These explications and corollaries will be part of the Constitution as soon as three fourths of the Legislatures consent to them.

II. *Establishment of a Permanent Revenue.*

This matter, which is without question the principal motive for the change in Government, incited long and interesting debates. Each Delegate strove to have the main burden of the impositions fall on districts other than his own, or at least to have the imported articles particularly charged that might be furnished advantageously by his district, the result is that the repugnance of each Member to contribute to public livelihood has especially burdened foreigners with it.

In the current state of things it was impossible to take up direct and property taxation. One is thus limited to opening two forms of revenue, namely

1. *Duties on imported merchandise* and

2. *Tonnage duties on navigation.*

As to imported merchandise the Congress took care especially to burden those that could be provided advantageously by locals; but in order to encourage domestic industry for objects of primary necessity they placed extraordinary duties on articles which in truth are manufactured in the country, but which are still too expensive to be widely consumed. The double goal of this measure, to procure a considerable revenue and at the same time to encourage domestic manufactures, was perhaps incompatible with the situation of the Americans, but the Congress saw itself obliged to concede on this occasion to the impetus it received from all sides. As a result of this there are large imperfections in the act concerning the impost. There were placed, among others, duties on several imported raw materials such as Hemp and Cotton, only because the planters wish to receive incentives. The greatest advantage that could result from this system of imposts is that all the parties of the Continent find themselves tied by a uniform law and that a large number of customs officers and collectors have the same base of operations and are so many Links that strengthen the general body.

The tonnage act is equally a result of the private interest of a certain class of Citizens, those who engage in navigation. The duties on *foreign* vessels amount to 50 cents per ton, while *domestic* ships pay only six. The Southern States, who have almost no vessels, find themselves almost entirely at the mercy of Northern navigators; foreigners being discouraged by the tonnage duties. Rhode Island and North Carolina which have not yet adopted the new Constitution are considered foreigners and charged the duty of 50 cents per ton, but Congress, in hopes of drawing them into the confederation, has given them a reprieve that will expire next January. At that time their vessels will be treated as foreign.

By an act regulating the accounts of the Individual States with the

United States, Congress aims to draw still more of the sums due to it, but it is doubtful that this branch will render much and it is possible that reciprocal claims are absorbing the product.

III. *Administration of both interior and exterior affairs.*

This part had greater success, not having undergone, as that of which I just spoke, an inevitable conflict of passions and interests. The large executive departments were formed successively. By the Constitution the nomination of the Heads of these departments belongs to the President and the Senate conjointly, but as it does not define how to dismiss them some feel it is dangerous to give this important right to the President alone; in spite of that opposition the majority of the two Houses implicitly gave to the President the power to discharge the principal Officers of State with the exception of judges.

This base being established Congress proceeded to the formation of the departments of finance, foreign affairs and war.

Finance is no longer in the form of a commission as under the former Congress. It has only one voice as opposed to the three men who were in charge of it. In order to give this department more cohesion, vitality and responsibility, it is being given to a single man.

The department of foreign affairs has taken on the name of the Department of State; it comprises not only foreign affairs, but those of the interior and in general all that is not immediately concerned with finance and war. This will be at all times the most extensive department and the one whose head will be closest to the President of the United States and will have more in his favor in terms of becoming President himself.

The department of war has not undergone any fundamental changes, Congress simply adapted the regulations made by the former Government to the new Constitution and by another act confirmed the troops levied under the old confederation.

As for the Indian Department, Congress reserved a considerable Sum for it in order through Federal Commissioners to end amicably the differences that have arisen on the frontier.

The encouragement of the national coasting trade interested Congress particularly. It took care to prescribe all the necessary precautions to verify the goods of a vessel to the point where the vessel of an American, residing in a foreign land is not even considered domestic. The biggest advantage of this rule will be without doubt for the Northern States though it must be stated that these States have few competitors to fear because their Citizens trade cheaper than any other nation, but the certainty they will now have to control all the coasting will give them renewed vigor.

Congress also took up means of facilitating landfalls through lighthouses and beacons.

A provisional regulation of the post made by Congress will suffice as far as the first Session.

This assembly has set the salary not only of the President and all Executive Officers, but of all Members of the Legislature and all employees of the Government generally and it voted a Sum of 639,000 Dollars not only for the current year's expenses, but to pay the obligations of the former Office of Finance.

IV. *Justice in relation to private property either of Americans or of foreigners and of the Individual States.*

Congress considered this matter the most important of all, and it underwent a long and laborious examination. It is a matter of tying together all the various parties of the Confederation and making them a whole able to resist encroachments of the particular jurisdictions of the States.

By the act of this Assembly all the States belonging to the new Confederation are divided into 13 districts, in each of which the President names a Judge, who holds a Court four times a year.

These districts are divided in three large circuits; that of the *East*, of the *Middle*, and of the *South*. Two of the six Supreme Court Justices travel there alternately to judge cases that are within their purview or to entertain appeals. These two Justices and the District Judge form the Circuit Court and the most important matters go in the last resort before the Supreme Court of Congress, composed of six Justices, of whom the principal has the title of *Chief Justice*. In order to be more independent they are irremovable except by decree of the House of Representatives. What is most interesting to us in this establishment, is that Consular Affairs and all discussions between foreigners are constitutionally within its jurisdiction. It is certain that Judges nominated and confirmed by Congress could more uniformly observe a Treaty made by this Assembly, an advantage that it would have been difficult to expect under the old form of Government where the Judges of each State followed different practices and sometimes different whims. The jurisdiction of these Federal Judges is already extended considerably by the act of Congress and it will be still more so in practice, so that if the new Constitution endures, as there is every reason to hope, the entire Continent will find itself in a few years subjugated to Congress, not only politically, but for civil laws and procedures. It is a very desirable revolution from the point of view of the union of the 13 American Sovereignties under a Congress adorned by them with the most extensive powers and under a President strong enough to execute the collective will of the States and limited enough to never abuse his authority.

In recapitulating these various points we find that in the first Session Congress consolidated the Government by making all military and civilian Officers of the United States take an oath and in proposing to the States under the name of amendments some explications of the Constitution appropriate to reassure the incensed partisans of liberty; that it cast the foundations of a permanent revenue in placing duties on imports and a tonnage on navigation, two matters desired in vain by the former Congress for more than 8 years; that it organized the political administration of the United States by the creation of the departments of treasury, State, foreign affairs, war, Indians and western territory—that it regulated the coasting trade in such a way as to render it particularly advantageous to its Citizens—that it took measures to establish lighthouses, beacons &c. on the coasts—that it provisionally organized the direction of the postal service, finally that it strengthened the chief bond of the United States by establishing Federal Judges whose jurisdiction and purview extend gradually to the point of making the laws, customs and privileges of the Individual States obsolete, all by skill and insinuation rather than by force.

To these measures, generally dictated by prudence and a spirit of conciliation, the President of the United States has added the finishing touches by his approval and by an excellent choice of Citizens from the eleven States to fill the principal posts as well as the subordinate places of the administration.

DHFFC translation of a Copy in Correspondance Politique, Etats-Unis, 34:277–89, Fr.

Newspaper Article

A correspondent observes, that the *Susquehannah* interest have baulked the *Morrisites* in their attempt to change the permanent residence of Congress to *Germantown*, for this session at least, by a piece of management, which was as follows, viz. The Senate having struck out the word Susquehannah, and inserted Germantown, by the Chairman's [*Vice President Adams*] vote only, the members being equally divided, the bill was thereupon sent down to the House of Representatives, where the promise of the 100,000 dollars prevailed with a majority of this House likewise to rescind their vote in favor of the Susquehannah, and concur with Germantown. However, whilst this was passing, and when every body considered the business as determined, one of the members of the Senate [*Schuyler*] was prevailed upon, by the private solicitation of the Susquehannah advocates, to agree, that if the bill could, by any means, be sent back to the Senate, he would change his vote so far as to vote for postponing the question of permanent residence, until next session. As soon as this was understood, Mr. *Madison* was induced to move so immaterial an amendment to the bill in the House of Representatives, which should be so unexceptionable as to meet with no opposition; and he accordingly got that House to agree to a frivolous alteration; whereupon, it became necessary to send the bill back again to the Senate, that they also might concur in this amendment. Accordingly, when the Senate had got possession of the bill again, a motion was made, and carried, by one vote, to postpone the further consideration of the bill till next sessions; so that there is a further chance given by this means, in favor of the Susquehannah, although the Morrisites insist, that Germantown will be the place as sure as fate, as three Members of Senate, who are in favour of this place, were absent when the vote was taken; and in the other House there is a large majority for Germantown, viz. 31 against 24; and that they will have this business fixed as soon as Congress meet again in January.

[Philadelphia] *Independent Gazetteer*, 3 October. This letter is a reply to "A Citizen," printed in the same paper the day before, and printed above under that date.

OTHER DOCUMENTS

Tristram Dalton to Gilbert Deblois, Sr. ALS, Miscellaneous Manuscripts, NHi.
    The business of Congress has so engrossed his attention that he could not previously acknowledge Deblois's letter of 10 September; expects to be in Boston shortly.

Alexander Hamilton to Jeremiah Wadsworth. ALS, Wadsworth Papers, CtHi. Addressed to Hartford, Connecticut; marked "Private." For the full text, see *PAH* 5:422–23.
    To combat smuggling that may have begun in "our eastern extremity," is considering the establishment of revenue cutters and would appreciate Wadsworth's ideas on the subject: usefulness, type of boats, plans, and cost.

Roger Sherman to Richard Law. ALS, Unbound Manuscripts, Connecticut State Library, Hartford. Written from New Haven, Connecticut; addressed to New London, Connecticut. For the full text, see *Sherman*, pp. 225–26.
    Congress adjourned, "having made such Arrangements as will enable the Executive to administer the Government"; Congress could not obtain enough information to make appropriations for interest on the public debt but have directed the secretary of the treasury to report; "The judiciary Act passed with but little alteration from the original draft"; recommends that Law appoint Simeon Baldwin as clerk to the Connecticut federal district court.

[Worcester] *American Herald, Massachusetts Spy*, 8 October.
    Grout arrived at Petersham, Massachusetts.

SUNDAY, 4 OCTOBER 1789

Daniel Carroll to James Madison

It is more to comply with my promise, than to give you any information that I take up my pen—Col. Grayson will probably in form you what has pass'd between him & Morriss, who has given him notice that on the meeting of Congress he shall immediately take up the Bill *only postpond*—this Idea may possibly be thrown out here to brake his fall in this business—it appears to Col. Grayson & myself that it wou'd be prudent during the recess to have some papers publishd on the question respecting the permanent Seat of Congress—it is probable the adverse party will be at work—think of this. Let me hear from you.

ALS, Madison Papers, DLC. Written from Philadelphia.

James Madison to Henry Lee

I meant to have acknowledged your favor of the 8th Ult. by your brother [*Richard B. Lee*], but in the hurry of the occasion missed even the pleasure of seeing him after the adjournment—He will give you the details of our proceedings, particularly on the subject of the seat of Government.

I am extremely afraid that the hopes of the Potomac do not rest on so good a foundation as we wish. Every circumstance which has marked the late altercations betrays the antipathy of the Eastern people to a south-western position—It can no longer be doubted in my opinion that they view the country beyond the mountains with an eye that will every day see fresh objections against carrying the Government into its neighborhood—I am not able to suppress my apprehensions that some begin already to speculate on the event of a seperation of that part of the Union—and if Measures be taken on that supposition, they will soon and of themselves Realize it—add to these unfavorable ideas that the presumptive successor [*Vice President Adams*] to the presiding Magistrate has been brought to a vote and explanation which will Render his administration an ominous period for the Potomac— If a proper decision of the question be attainable, it must be under the auspices of the present Chief Magistrate & by some arrangement with Pennsylvania. From the views which apparently govern this state it does not seem very probable that she will easily & sincerely accede to the idea of placing Congress South of her own limits—If any thing can reconcile her to it, it must be her animosity to the Eastern States—a despair of Germantown & Trenton & the opposition of the City interest to the Susquehanah—A division of the States into districts for the election of Representatives would be very favorable to the Potomac by unfettering the votes which incline to that position, as well as others which are opposed to the Susquehanah—there is however little prospect of such a change in her election law[1] and even with that advantage a very faint prospect of an effectual change in her politics.

The susquehanah has always appeared to me, as it still does, the only formidable rival to the Potomac—Trenton & still more Germantown will be rejected by many of the eastern and N. York members from a variety of motives—the partiality wd. be too glaring to be concealed from their own eyes—it is not probable that Germantown will ever be tolerated by the feelings of N. York or that it has been the real object with many of the other states which lately voted for it. In proportion to the degree of danger however, to be apprehended from either of these two places as well as of the improbability or Remoteness of the success of the Potomac are we pressed with the question whether it may not be our duty to acquiesce in the susquehanah, as the least of the evils from which a choice must be made. Hitherto I have resisted every idea of compromise, and shall continue to do so, untill every remaining effort of prudence shall be exhausted—But in this *confidential* communication I cannot deny that some limits as to time must be set to the struggle for what is *perfectly* right.

I am extremely alarmed for the Western Country. I have within a few days seen fresh and striking proofs of its ticklish situation—Mr. Brown thinks that the susquehanah would for the present satisfy them on the subject of the seat of Government—and in his own judgement, prefers it to delay— There are others even from Virginia who could with difficulty be prevailed on to contend for the Potomac, with so little chance of success—and against the danger of plans which would be fatal to the harmony, if not to the existence of the Union—Several of the more Southern Members tho attached to the object of Virginia, do not view the rival of it, precisely with her eyes— I make these remarks for yourself alone, and to prepare you for a disappointment which I hold to be very possible, but which I shall certainly be among the last to concur in.

***

Contemporary manuscript copy, Madison Papers, DLC. For the full text, see *PJM* 12:425–28. Misdated "1787." Part of the omitted paragraph describes Madison's plan to wait for Jefferson's arrival before returning with him to Virginia.

---

[1] Pennsylvania's first Congressional election law did not provide for Congressional districts; consequently, most of the men elected resided in the more heavily populated counties at the eastern extreme of the state. Many believed a new law creating districts would result in the election of members more sympathetic to the West and the Potomac.

Richard Peters to William Lewis

I send you Mr. Clymer's Letters to me on the Subject of the federal Residence to make such prudent Use of as you think proper if the ground less Jealousy about local Views in this Quarter continues. If there is a Disposition to drop the Matter I think it best on all Sides that it should not be kept alive. Why it should be thought censurable that those in this Quarter should not only wish but be of Opinion as to the general Interest that this should be the federal Residence I cannot concieve. Others will surely allow us the Right they give themselves in this Business. Mr. Clymer authorized me to shew to some Friends his Letters but I am not in that Situation with Respect to other Gentlemen. I can however truly say that among all of our Delegation who did me the Honner to correspond with me there appeared an Elevation of Sentiment on this Subject very incompatible with the narrow Views of those who held local Opinions to which they would sacrifice general Interests. There was most assuredly a Disposition & this not confined to our Representatives to give up every local Wish so as to combine the Weight of the State in Congress at all Events to secure the Seat of Government in some Part of Pennsilvania.

FC:dft, Peters Papers, PHi. Written on "Sunday" from "Belmont," Peters's home across the Schuylkill River from Philadelphia. This is the most likely Sunday on which such a letter could have been written, because it was in the midst of the period of general clamor against the Pennsylvania delegation after the postponement of the Seat of Government Bill [HR-25].

OTHER DOCUMENTS

Abigail Adams to Mary Cranch. ALS, Abigail Adams Letters, MWA. Written from "Richmond Hill," outside New York City. For the full text, see *Abigail Adams*, pp. 26–29.

"If the united States had chosen to the vice p.s Chair a man wavering in his opinions, or one who Sought the popular applause of the multitude, this very constitution would have had its death wound during this first Six months of its existance, on Several of the most trying occasions it has fallen to this dangerous *vice*, to give the casting vote for its Life—there are Several Members of the House & Some of the S[*enat*]e. who are to Say no worse wild as—Bedlammites but hush—I am speaking treason. do not you betray me."

John Armstrong, Jr. to Frederick William Steuben. ALS, Miscellaneous Manuscripts, NHi. Written from Carlisle, Pennsylvania; addressed to New York.

"The Western & middle parts of the State are also quite outrageous at the turn which the subject of residence has taken—They View Morris as the

Cause of the alteration—& execrate him with as little reserve as they did Lord [*Prime Minister Frederick*] North during the [*Revolutionary*] War."

Elbridge Gerry to James Sullivan. No copy known; acknowledged in Sullivan to Gerry, 11 October.

Samuel Phillips Savage, Diary. MHi.
    Thatcher arrived in Weston, Massachusetts, last night, very ill.

MONDAY, 5 OCTOBER 1789

Abigail Adams to Cotton Tufts

*** We have been very near determining to come home & spend the winter, & nothing prevents us but the foolish adjournment of congress to a period when they know the Southern members will not come. so that a part of the Body ~~will~~ only will be here a useless expence to the states, had they Set one month more & then adjournd to April, it would have been much more convenient, by the way I See the Boston newspapers report that congress agreed to Borrow 50 thousand dollars of the Banks of Newyork & phyladelphia as the Bill past the Senate the united States were to be at no expence at all. pensilvania was to erect the Buildings & make every accommodation at their own expence, but the whole is happily posponed. it was unwise to bring on a Subject which must necessaryly involve them in dispute, before any ~~thing~~ means was devised for the payment of publick creditors, or any ~~means~~ way marked out for discharging the publick debt.
    ***

    ALS, Miscellaneous Manuscripts, NHi. Place from which written not indicated, probably "Richmond Hill," N.Y.; addressed to Boston.

OTHER DOCUMENTS

John Brown to Harry Innes. ALS, Innes Papers, DLC. Written from Philadelphia. Badly damaged document.
    Left New York on 1 October.

Pierce Butler to Weeden Butler. ALS, Butler Letters, Uk. Written from Philadelphia; addressed to Chelsea near London.
    Has made an excursion as far as Philadelphia "to Shake off the effects of a long session. I return to New York the latter end of the week."

James Madison to Alexander Hamilton. ALS, Hamilton Papers, DLC. For the full text, see *PJM* 12:428–29, where the editors postulate the date as ca. 5 October.

Returns two books; sends a pamphlet received from France; asks Hamilton to forward a letter to Schuyler; mentions Reuben Burnley for a clerkship in the auditor's office.

James Madison to Philip Schuyler. No copy known; acknowledged in Schuyler to Madison, 1 November.

Paine Wingate, Memo of Attendance in Congress. Typescript, Wingate Papers, MH.

"Left home again Feb. 16, 1789, and returned Oct. 5, 1789; being 234 days, received 1449 dollars at 6 doll. per day."

TUESDAY, 6 OCTOBER 1789

Fisher Ames to Theodore Sedgwick

I am in Mr. [*John*] Hooker's office, and am to thank you for your esteemed favour dated at Springfield. I have not had breath or spirits to hold a pen since my arrival till this Morning—Riding three hours before sun rise three mornings successively, shivering, starving & nodding for want of sleep, had brought me, by the third, in view of another heaven than that which you allude to in your's, & which, I assure you, I was not half so impatient for. A severe cold, little short of a fever, succeeded—and I just begin to respire. I thought, when [*I*] reached this place, that it would have cured me to have found you & Strong here It was an aggravation of my disappointment that I arrived only half an hour after you left it. I should have seen you with infinite pleasure to recount the bloody battles that closed the campaign—The printers are such anticipating fellows that I can not relate facts—The permanent residence was the principal subject of intrigue within doors & of expectation without—It has blown up however. After you left us, we delayed reporting the Bill in the hope of your, Leonard's, & Sturgis' return. Leonard did return. whether the Pensylvanians would vote for the Bill if the Maryland proviso[1] was inserted, as it was known it would be, if they should persist in requiring it, was a very doubtful point—If they should vote agt. the Bill, it would be lost, and we should be in the clouds—perhaps light at Philadela. Persuasion was used & reiterated upon Smith [*Md.*] & Seney to vote agt. the proviso—in vain—it was inserted—Then we had to deal with

Clymer & Fitzimons—who protested they never would vote for the Bill—
Finally they *did* vote for it in the hope of what took place in the Senate—
which was thrown out to them seasonably to prevent their forming any new
compact with the Patowmacs—Many of the latter voted for it Either despairing of success, or dreading the Delaware. In truth, they were more convinced of the hollowness of the argument in favour of the Patowmac than
they would own in public So that you may infer from all this detail, that
your mere vote could be spared. Many a fervent wish, & perhaps prayer, was
uttered for your return—tho' I do not know any praying folks that took part
in the business It was lamented as much as the sudden departure of D'Estaing from Newport,[2] and dismal auguries of a disastrous event were drawn.
You will be obliged to make it appear that your head aked very perversely
indeed—perhaps it would be a piece of prudence to break your leg, or to go
to bed a few weeks with a fever, to make your excuse current next winter in
New York. I will conceal your following the courts. By concealing facts, we
shall frequently serve each other—especially with regard to voting against
the instructions of the Convention.[3]

To go on—as [*Samuel*] Nasson used to say—The Bill, as was expected,
came down amended with Germantown—Our people were so weary of the
business, it was difficult to urge them on to further efforts—It was moved
to postpone it to the next session—negatived—Then I moved to concur—
Madison moved that it should lie on the table—I insisted on my motion as
prior—Then an adjournment was moved & Trumbull (who is not hearty for
Germantown) and Vining voted with them for an Adj[*ournmen*]t. It was a
hair breadth business—for a vote in five minutes would probably have made
it a law—except the *king's* signature. The next day, a new scene opened—
The N. Yorkers had voted in Senate for Germn. The citizens were seized
with a panic—The buildings would be finished, they said, next summer,
and Congs. removed after next session—Some supposed that proper engagements had been made to stay in New York three years. The security,
however, was doubtful, the danger plain. The members were loth to stand
responsible for the event—especially as they were thought to have been out-
witted in the Affair. They wished, several others, to postpone—Madison
moved an Amendment, providing that the laws of Pensa. should remain in
force in the district till the further pleasure of Congress. This passed without debate. It was supposed that if the Bill should get into the Senate again,
they would postpone it, and he seemed to think it a piece of address to send
it back. Many of the gallery folks tho't that he had taken us in—You will
see that it was not so, by the detail I have made of the situation of the
Yorkers. The Bill was sent back & postponed as was expected—and thus the
house that Jack built[4] is vanished in smoke—for the Lord knows what next
session will produce in regard to the subject.

The debate about the style of writs was ridiculous beyond conception. Madison cannot recover my confidence speedily in that regard. He was silent—but voted with the champions of liberty who are not willing to do anything but talk for it—who foretell events that never happen, and who see invisible things. Such are the southern blusterers They spouted, because the president was about to get the sword in his hands, in virtue of the Senate's amendment to the Bill establishing the troops—They authorised his calling out such parts of the militia as might be necessary to repel the savages. This set the geese of the capitol a cackling[5]—on the yeas & nays it was non-[con]cur'd—The Senate insisted—& the next day, we concur'd—Gerry figured as usual. My stupid head will not furnish ideas to proceed—and if I had them, the action of writing has set it aking too severely to permit it. You will think I have written too much already—I wish they may furnish some gratification to your curiosity—Only note this letter is strictly confidential. I esteem it an acquisition to the felicity of my life that I am to spend an interesting part of it with you as your associate. I think with great pleasure of the marks of your confidence & friendship towards me—and with no small pride that those sentiments are reciprocal. For I esteem it so[me] proof of my own merit, and raise my opinion of myself, when I look into my own heart and discern with what respect and cordial affection I am, dear Sir, your friend and very humble servant.

ALS, Sedgwick Family Papers, MHi. Written from Springfield, Massachusetts.

[1] See Clymer to Peters, 9 September, above.
[2] The unexpected withdrawal from Narragansett Bay by the French fleet commanded by Admiral Charles Hector, Comte d'Estaing, on 21 August 1778, precipitated widespread desertion from the allied American forces and contributed to their defeat at the battle of Rhode Island one week later.
[3] The Massachusetts Ratification Convention instructed the state's delegation to the FFC to support its proposed Amendments to the Constitution.
[4] An old nursery rhyme, referring to a convoluted chain of events.
[5] In 390 B.C. a party of attacking Gauls secretly advanced as far as Rome's Capitoline Hill before disturbing a gaggle of geese. The resulting alarm saved Rome, where a golden goose was carried in an annual procession to commemorate the event.

William Smith (S.C.) to Edward Rutledge

Congress adjourned on the 29th. last month & two days after Mrs. [Charlotte] Smith & myself set off for this place. We came from New York to Elizabeth Town by water & the rest of the way we travelled leisurely with our own horses & got here in two days—on our passage to Elizab. Town we met with a great alarm owing to a violent head-wind which, in a sudden squall, had very nearly overset the Boat; however, no other mischief was done than frightening us all very much, except the loss of a hat to one of our fellow passengers, who bemoaned his misfortune in the most deplorable terms; he assured us that it was a brand new hat which he had just paid 30/ for & moreover that it was a *fur* hat—"yes," said I to him, "it is *fur* enough by this time, for you'll never see it again—& if it is any consolation to you, I lost just such a one crossing from Dover to Calais some years ago." Vining, (who was with us & relishes a *bad pun* mightily,) broke out in a loud horse laugh & put an end to our bare headed passenger's lamentations.

***

ALS, Smith Papers, ScHi. Written from Philadelphia; addressed to South Carolina. For the full text, see *South Carolina Historical Magazine* 69(1968):24.

OTHER DOCUMENTS

John Brown to George Washington. ALS, item 78, 4:621, PCC, DNA. Written from Philadelphia.

Has received and forwarded the judicial commissions to Kentucky.

Elbridge Gerry to James Sullivan. No copy known; acknowledged in Sullivan to Gerry, 11 October.

Ralph Izard to John Lowell. Summary and excerpt of ALS, *Henkels Catalog* 1347(1924):item 145.

Congratulates Lowell on his appointment; complains about date for opening the second session: "If Congress were to sit at any time between April and November, the Southern members could go home, and pay some attention to their private affairs; &c."

James Maury to James Madison. ALS, Madison Papers, DLC. Written from Liverpool, England. For the full text, see *PJM* 12:429–30.

Office seeking: American consul at Liverpool; encloses a letter to the President on that subject which he asks Madison to read and, if he approves, forward to President Washington.

[York] *Pennsylvania Herald*, 7 October.

Hartley arrived in town in the afternoon.

[Portsmouth] *New Hampshire Spy*, 10 October.

Wingate arrived in Portsmouth.

WEDNESDAY, 7 OCTOBER 1789

John Brown to Harry Innes

Colo. Grayson called upon me to Day & we spent an hour or two in conversation relative to the Interests of the Western Country & the Navigation of the Mississipi. Though apprehensive that the free & unconditional Navigation of that River cannot immediately be obtained yet we were of opinion that such Concessions on the part of Spain might be had as for the present would answer the purposes of the Western People & would lay the foundation for the full possession of that Right at a future day. The President has expressed himself in terms favorable to our Claim—We also Know Jeffersons Sentiments & I think a Majority of the Senate may be had—The Senators of this State would now be in our favor & I believe the Merchants of this City wi[*ll un*]ite their influence in our behalf They expect [*to ex*]port our Goods & want our Produce in return especially Hemp which now sells at £70. ℔ Tonn—The Manufacturing Interest would probably oppose—The Policy of Spain I believe is not well know. I believe at present she does not well know what to be at Colo. Grayson thinks with me that it might probably bring on the Business at an earlier Day & perhaps to better effect if the [*statehood*] Convention or people of Kentucke would address the President & Senate upon the Subject & State what would satisfy the People. If such an address was inclosed to me I would present it & use every exertion in its behalf. The inclosed is the outlines of a plan which Gray[*son thin*]ks might probably be carried into [*effec*]t.

In a letter I w[*ro*]te you two days ago I informed of my indisposition. I am still confined to my Room but am on the recovery.

ALS, Innes Papers, DLC. Written from Philadelphia. The enclosure is missing. On this date Barthelemi Tardiveau wrote from Danville, Kentucky, to St. John de Crèvecoeur in New York, "Scarcely a fortnight goes by but that Mr. Brown's friends hear from him, and are informed by him of public happenings" (Howard Rice, ed., *Barthelemi Tardiveau* [Baltimore, 1938], p. 34).

William Grayson to James Madison

I was so much fatigued with the trip in the stage, as to be rendered utterly unqualified to proceed on my journey before the day before yesterday, when I got something better; I should have been more unhappy than my state of health would have made me, if I had not been informed here that Mrs. [*Eleanor*] Grayson was greatly recovered.[1]

The visits which I have recieved & the Company I have kept have served to convince me that the conduct of the Pa. delegation is much reprobated in this City: Judge McKaine [*Thomas McKean*] Doctr. [*Benjamin*] Rush, Judge [*Jacob*] Rush, Blair McClanaghan cum multis aliis² ([*William*] Bingham excepted) think the Potowmack a marvelous proper place, & that the good of the Union requires it to be noticed—they are not unacquainted with the breach of faith, but I find they execrate their folly more than their perfidy. These gentlemen all agree that the idea of bringing the same bill before the Senate again is the desperate effort of a dying man is by way of apology to their constituents: perhaps in all this business there may be something of constitutional & Anti Constitutional.³

I have had a tete a tete with Morriss in the Streat & afterwards dined with him, though very unwell; I found him very much irritated with his dissapointment; in the course of the conversation, he gave me notice that he should call up the bill the first week of the session but said I, how if the bill won't come, on wch. he went into an unmeaning elaborate discourse on the subject; he drew from me however no other reply than that there were certain things in this world that were so monstrously absurd as to require no argument: I thought it would be rather improper to touch too eagerly while he remained under this delusion; of course I left him with this impression that if we could do nothing they could do nothing, for that if any place in Pensylva. was proposed except Susquehannah, that N. York would be agt. them, & that if Susquehannah was made the happy spot we should have the assistance of Jersey; that I even doubted N. York & the Eastern people of possessing any other *real* sentiments than those that were *frustratory* that we should be cautious about stirring the subject again unless upon sure grounds & thereby bring on them to form combinations against us.

Yesterday evening I had full information of the real sentiments of Morriss & Co. from Scott who dined with him in compy. with Hartley, & which is as favorable as we could wish; After bewailing their misfortunes in as pathetic strains as ever Don Quixote & Sancho⁴ did Hartley said, But Sir it is in *our power* to *move* them, & says M[*orris*].—damn him that won't agree to it—I asked Scott what this mean't & he ~~who~~ went fully into detail with very little agency on my part: I urged the impracticability of a reciprocal confidance, on which he proposed pen & ink as the only expedient—I found that the conduct of Bland & White & Brown has made a deep impression on Scott, & I believe [*lined out*] on the other Pensylvanians of the delegation: they fear the want of force: they calculate on the loss of Tucker Smith [*S.C.*] & Huger with certainty, & are very doubtful of the others: I told him there was no danger in our delegation except as to Bland, & that nothing could be done with him unless he was groun'd over again Upon the whole I have no doubt but the conspirators have already formed their plan, to be carried into execution at the next session if No. Carola. is upon the floor; I am of opinion we should play the Precieux,[5] & hold out the idea of nolo episcopari[6]—but in such a manner as not to discourage advances. Our great danger is ~~of~~ in stirring the subject, & frightning the Yankees into measures (which if left to themselves) they abhor: When we strike [*lined out*] it should be on full conviction of success. Morriss with all his prudence I find has a great deal of resentment, & Scott thinks that a majority of the delegation are so irrietated as to go unconditionally to the Potowmack by way of spiting N. York—It is clear to me that our contest about the Potowmack has been of infinite consequence; she is gaining friends daily, by being brought into view; & I agree with you that we played a great game & staked nothing—I would now (though never sanguine before) bett her agt. the field; since Peachum & Lockett[7] have falln out it is possible honest people may come by their own. [*P. S.*] Please make my compls. to Mr. Jefferson.

ALS, Madison Papers, DLC. Written from Philadelphia.

[1] Eleanor Smallwood Grayson died on 22 September after being in ill health throughout the first session.

[2] Among many others.

[3] A reference to Pennsylvania's political parties.

[4] The famous characters of Cervantes's *Don Quixote*.

[5] An aloof man.

[6] "I do not wish to be made a bishop," an expression conveying false modesty or naivete.

[7] Characters from John Gay's *The Beggar's Opera*.

Newspaper Article

From Mr. Greenleaf's Weekly Register of Sept. 24.
The following motion[1] made by Mr. Burke, on Monday, in the House of Representatives of the United States, which is supposed to respect Francis Childs, Printer of the Daily Advertiser, John Fenno, Printer of the Gazette of the United States, and Thomas Lloyd, Editor of the Congressional Register, was laid on the table for the Consideration of the members.
***

As the foregoing motion of Mr. Burke respecting the supposed misrepresentations of the debates of the house of representatives, has been officiously printed, and an application of its censure made by THOMAS GREENLEAF, we think proper to acquaint the public that the intended resolution was published without the countenance or knowlege of the honorable mover, and as the motion itself, extravagant as it is, and which was withdrawn after being faintly supported, may leave an unjust impression on the minds of the

Public, we think proper to subjoin the following remarks, which we flatter ourselves will have a circulation and impression, at least co-extensive with the other.

It is extremely difficult to conceive how any person possessing common sense, could so far mistake the plain, full and positive meaning of the debates in the hon. house [of] Representatives, as to "mispresent them in the most glaring deviations from the truth;" but to "distort the arguments from their true meaning," requires some degree of ingenuity—it is extremely difficult however to suggest any plausible reason, which should induce the editors of the debates to do this—The whole world would resent the insult, so far as it was known; and the publishers would risk the countenance and patronage of the public. It is still more difficult to account for the long silence of those who would be more immediately concerned had this been the case—it can be imputed only to a conviction in the minds of the majority, that this has never *intentionally* taken place: It may have happened that *one* gentleman's name *may* have been placed before the speech of *another*; this *may* have happened without any *design* of "imputing to some gentlemen arguments contradictory or foreign to the subject, and which were never advanced," or to others, remarks and observations which never were made for *humanum est errare*[2]—Mutilations of speeches are sometimes made with advantage; they seem to be the necessary consequence of a very rapid enunciation, or when the speaker's voice is small and low.

It would so completely establish the reputation of a public register of the debates to have them *perfectly accurate*, that is more difficult than all the preceding difficulties, to account for a Printer's *wilfully* making them imperfect, when it is in his power to do otherwise—it is a sort of *felo de se*[3] against his own interest. To attempt to "throw a thick viel of misrepresentation and error over the whole proceedings" of the house of representatives, would be an undertaking so complicate in its nature, and so impracticable in its execution, that the person who should conceive the idea of making the effort in this land of freedom, and where the public proceedings are open as the day, would be a fit subject for a *strait waistcoat*; and this to be done too "at the very foot of the speaker's chair," is so ridiculous and absurd, that it carries its own refutation with it.

From whence it follows, that for a printer in his publications to misrepresent the debates of the house, "whether it arises from incapacity, inattention or partiality," can have no "tendency to infringe the freedom of speech:" for it is impossible that any person can suppose that the house could sanction such publications, nor can any system of corruption for deceiving the people be predicated of such publications, as they would certainly appear to be without object or design.

The appeal is made to the candid and impartial. The original publishers of the debates in the newspapers, never proposed to give those debates so as to comprise the whole of the speeches at full length—Sketches only of the proceedings were their object, they have aimed to be impartial; their labors have met a favorable reception; their own sentiments have never influenced them in stating a single question; and it is not in the power of *any person whatever*, to point out an instance of their being *controuled* or *influenced* either directly or indirectly, by any man, or body of men, to alter, curtail, mutilate or suppress an individual speech, that has ever been heard by them, or published in their papers.

NYDA, 7 October.

---

[1] Burke's resolutions of 21 September are printed in *DHFFC* 11:1503; Greenleaf printed them in *NYJ* on 1 October.

[2] "To err is human."

[3] Suicide.

OTHER DOCUMENTS

Thomas Hartley to Jasper Yeates. ALS, Yeates Papers, PHi. Written from York, Pennsylvania; addressed to Lancaster; carried by Ferdinand Schroub.
"The Yorkers were glad to see me but I presume they would have still been better satisfied had the permanent Residence been fixed upon the Banks of the Susquehanna."

Samuel Phillips Savage, Diary. MHi.
Thatcher left for Maine.

[Boston] *Herald of Freedom*, 9 October.
Thatcher arrived from New York.

[Massachusetts] *Salem Mercury*, 13 October.
Wingate's house robbed, including the bedroom where he and his wife were asleep; silver, an overcoat, and a hat were stolen.

THURSDAY, 8 OCTOBER 1789

James Madison, Memorandum for George Washington

On the supposition that the business can be more properly conducted by a private agent at London, than a public Minister at a third Court, the letter and instructions for the former character appear to be well adapted to the purpose. If any remark were to be made, it would relate merely to the form, which it is conceived would be made rather better by transposing the order of the two main subjects. The fulfillment of the Treaty already made seems to be primary to the enquiries requisite to a subsequent Treaty.

The reasoning assigned to those who opposed a commercial discrimination, states the views of a part only of that side of the question. A considerable number, both in the Senate & H. of Reps. objected to the measure as defective in energy, rather than as wrong in its principle. In the former, a Committee was [*lined out*] appointed, who reported a more energetic plan.[1] And in the latter, leave to bring in a bill, was given to a member who explained his views to be similar.[2] Both of these instances were posterior to the miscarriage of the discrimination first proposed.

As Mr. Jefferson may be daily expected, as it is possible he may bring informations throwing light on the subject under deliberation, and as it is probable [*lined out*] use may be made of his own ideas with regard to it, A quere suggests itself, [*lined out*] whether the advantage of consulting with him might not justify such a delay, unless there be special reasons for expedition.

FC:dft, Madison Papers, DLC. The date of this memo, which is approximate, was supplied by the editors of *PJM*. See also *DGW* 5:456. Madison is commenting on a draft of the President's letter to Gouverneur Morris of 13 October (*DHFFC* 2:451–52).

[1] On 17 June, after rejecting a tonnage discrimination, the Senate appointed a committee "to arrange and bring forward a system, for the regulation of the trade and intercourse between the United States and the territory of other powers in North-America, and the West-Indies, so as to place the same on a more beneficial and permanent footing" (*DHFFC* 1:69). Its report of 5 August is printed in *DHFFC* 1:109–10.

[2] On 7 August, on a motion by Gerry, the House appointed a committee to bring in a bill "for the further encouragement of the commerce and navigation of the United States" (*DHFFC* 3:137).

OTHER DOCUMENTS

Richard Curson to Horatio Gates. ALS, Gates Papers, NHi. Written from Baltimore; addressed to Hagerstown, Maryland.

"The Members of the New Congress are all Returned from New York, Mr. [*Charles*] Carroll of Carrollton dined with me On Monday last, and gives most pleasing Accounts of the Harmony Subsisting in the Several Branches."

James Madison to Thomas Jefferson. ALS, Madison Papers, DLC. Misdated "1787." For the full text, see *PJM* 12:433.

Urges him to accept the office of secretary of state: "The Southern and Western Country have it particularly at heart. To every other part of the Union, it will be sincerely acceptable."

George Washington, Diary. Washington Papers, DLC. For the full text, see *DGW* 5:456.

> Dined with the Daltons; Madison took his leave, and saw no "impropriety" in the proposed presidential tour of the Eastern states.

"Electioneering," [Philadelphia] *Independent Gazetteer*, 8 October.

> Clymer and Fitzsimons are not recommended as candidates for the state constitutional convention "for we ought not to risk the loosing a single vote in Congress by their absence, when perhaps the question of removing to Germantown may be decided."

FRIDAY, 9 OCTOBER 1789

Theodore Sedgwick to Peter Van Schaack

***

P. S. There is now in this town a young man of the name of [*Loring*] Andrews, recommended to me as a sober, sensible & ingenious man & a federalist, who is about to commence the business of a printer here. could not a post be established from Kinderhook to this place? Such an event would tend as well to the general information of the people here in the affairs of the national government as to cement more closely the neighbourhood of the two states. I will be greatly disappointed if the editor of the paper should defeat the public expectation. Pray let me know what you think of such a project?

ALS, Sedgwick Family Papers, MHi. Written from Stockbridge, Massachusetts; addressed to Kinderhook, New York. The letter also mentions "our friend Benson" and sends Sedgwick's regards to Silvester.

OTHER DOCUMENTS

John Fenno to Joseph Ward. ALS, Ward Papers, ICHi. For the full text, see *AASP* 90(1980):340.

> "The adjournment of Congress has taken off 100 Subscribers—and tho' the paper [*GUS*] during the session appeared to be of consequence to them—there is not quite a dozen who have entered their names as Subscribers during the recess."

[Massachusetts] *Salem Mercury*, 13 October.

> The burglar of Wingate's house, Marcus Plantain, captured by mail stage driver, a friend of Wingate's, who recognized his "senatorial habit."

SATURDAY, 10 OCTOBER 1789

John Berry to Henry Hudson. ALS, Hudson Family Papers, MSaE. Addressed to Newburyport, Massachusetts.
"Congress [*h*]as left us for sometime as such this place, dont look quite so brisk, however doe Suppose it will revive much on their return, as am inform most of them will bring their Family's."

James Bowdoin to Sir John Temple. ALS, Bowdoin-Temple Papers in the Winthrop Family Papers, MHi. Written from Boston; addressed to New York.
Temple's letter of 28 September was received per Thatcher yesterday.

Aedanus Burke to Elbridge Gerry. Summary of ALS, *Robert K. Black Catalog* 47(1956):item 242. Written from Philadelphia.
Part of letter describes the delight with which Philadelphians have greeted the suggestion that their city become the seat of government.

Royal Flint to Jeremiah Wadsworth. ALS, Wadsworth Papers, CtHi. Addressed to Hartford, Connecticut. (For more on the subject of Glaubeck, see *DHFFC* 7:198–99.)
Has not been able to find Baron de Glaubeck "since you put the papers respecting him into my hands."

Edmund Randolph to James Madison. ALS, Madison Papers, DLC. Written from Williamsburg, Virginia. For the full text, see *PJM* 12:434–35.
Will accept the office of attorney general of the United States despite the "curse of expatriation" (from Virginia).

SUNDAY, 11 OCTOBER 1789

James Sullivan to Elbridge Gerry

*** We have nothing here worth communicating. our People appear to be generally nearly universally uneasy at the administration of the new Government the compensation act is very disgusting indeed the people say they can never pay such salaries. on a computation they say there are not ten ~~men~~ men in the U. States who have an income from Estates equal to what is given the Judges. the part or clause in the Judicial bill which gives writs of Error to the Court of the united states upon Judgments given in the State Courts will be a Source of Contention it is said to be a violation of the Constitution the Conversation among our ~~political~~ Politicians is to Encounter the views of the administration of the union by strengthening and rendering respectable the particular Government of the states, to prevent the necessity of a Standing Army, or at least to avoid the danger of it by haveing an armed and well disciplined militia how long this fervour will hold I know not. but there may be serious Times yet amongst the politicians I have no share in it Thatcher has been with me today. from all your speeches writings &c. we conclude here that your idea of the people at large is that they are venial and Corrupt and can all be bought because the Love of money is the predominant passion of the age. but I beleive there is yet in New England a great share of Lacedemonian[1] & Spartan virtue.

I notice that in your Resolves you leave out the word *Supreme* before the word *Executives* when you speak of the States.

[*P. S.*] our papers have nothing in them.

The high feds or Rats[2] appear most uneasy at the administration.

ALS, Gerry Papers, MHi. Written from Boston; addressed to New York.

[1] The part of Greece surrounding Sparta.

[2] In a 15 August speech, reported in the *Congressional Register*, Gerry had opined that the two sides in the ratification struggle "ought not to have been distinguished by federalists and antifederalists, but rats and antirats" (*DHFFC* 11:1262).

OTHER DOCUMENTS

Abigail Adams to Mary Cranch. ALS, Abigail Adams Letters, MWA. Written from "Richmond Hill," outside New York City; addressed to Braintree, Massachusetts. For the full text, see *Abigail Adams*, pp. 29–31.

"I think it not unlikely that there will be a summer recess next year."

[Charleston, South Carolina] *City Gazette*, 12 October.

Tucker arrived after a six day voyage from New York.

[Savannah] *Georgia Gazette*, 15 October.

Gunn, his wife, and Jackson arrived on ship from New York.

MONDAY, 12 OCTOBER 1789

Alexander Hamilton to James Madison. Printed in *DHFFC* 18.

Second session subject matter.

TUESDAY, 13 OCTOBER 1789

John Beckley to Governor Beverley Randolph. LS, Executive Papers, Vi. A similar letter was sent to each of the state governors.

Transmits "three setts of the Journal of the House of Representatives for the late Session, one for the Supreme Executive, and one for each branch of the Legislature of your State."

Jonathan Sayward, Diary. MWA.

Thatcher, "with a Number of other Gentlemen Spent the evening at my house and he Entertained the Company with the State of the Continent, and of the revenue he Saith the port of N. york hath received one thousand Dollars a day ever since the impost took place. he doth not seem to doubt, but that it will answer the purpose for which it is intended."

WEDNESDAY, 14 OCTOBER 1789

Alexander Hamilton to Comte de Moustier

Mr. Hamilton presents his compliments to the Count de Moustier and has the honor to inclose, agreeably to his intimation a memorandum of the idea suggested in conversation yesterday. Mr. Hamilton begs leave to remark that if the Count should feel himself at liberty and see it expedient to make, previous to his departure an offer of the suspension intimated it would add to the value of the favour as the knowlege of it would facilitate the arrangements of Congress when the subject may be intered upon at the next session and which will of course be sooner than any communication from Europe can be had.

[Enclosure]

Memorandum for his Excellency the Count de Moustier

The   session of Congress, beside some of immediate urgency respecting navigation and commercial imposts was wholly occupied in organising the Government. Time was requisite afterwards for the proper departement to prepare a plan for the consideration of the legislature with regard to the public debt. And accordingly Congress, after giving directions for that purpose to the Secretary of the Treasury, concluded upon a short adjournment. It is expected, that a provision for the public debt will be a premary object of discussion at the ensuing session. and it is presumeable, that the part of it wich is due to france will engage particular attention. It would be a valuable accommodation to the United States, if his Most Christian Majesty should see fit, as a new instance of his good will, to suspend the payment of the installments of the principal now due and to become due, for the term of five or six years; on the idea that effectual arrangements should be made to pay, speedily the arrears of interest, which have already accrued, and, punctually the future interest as it shall arise. There being no person authorised to speak this language; this is of course intended as a mere private intimation. Indeed it will be on every account desireable, that the measure should proceed from his Most Christian majesty as an effusion of his friendship to the United States.

Copies, Correspondance Politique, Supplement, 19:110–14, Fr. We are printing these documents because they are not available elsewhere. Moustier replied on this date that while he must maintain official reserve on the matter of the debt, should he receive an official request from the Americans, on putting it to the king, the result would most likely be that his majesty would agree to push back payment on the principal of the U.S. debt. His majesty would only demand the payment of back interest. Hamilton acknowledged receipt of Moustier's "confidential communication" on 15 October.

OTHER DOCUMENTS

John Adams to Abigail Adams. ALS, Adams Family Manuscript Trust, MHi. Written from Fairfield, Connecticut; addressed to "Richmond Hill," outside New York City. Addressed to "My dearest Friend."
    Is in good health and spirits en route home; will accompany Dalton to Boston, or at least Cambridge; plans to spend the Sabbath at Springfield, Massachusetts.

[Boston] *Massachusetts Centinel*, 14 October.
    Thatcher and Ames arrived in Boston after 10 October.

THURSDAY, 15 OCTOBER 1789

Pierce Butler to Charles Cotesworth Pinckney. FC:lbk, Butler Papers, PHi. Addressed to Charleston, South Carolina.
    Family members have been sick throughout the summer; his wife still confined to her bed; no political news except developments in France; for Congressional news, refers Pinckney to members of the state delegation who returned home.

Letter from Stratford, Connecticut, dated 19 October. [Philadelphia] *Pennsylvania Packet*, 24 October.
    Adams was given full military honors while passing through on the way home from New York City.

FRIDAY, 16 OCTOBER 1789

Nathaniel Barrett to John Langdon. ALS, Langdon-Elwyn Family Papers, NhHi.

"You complaind when here of the dullness of this City—It is a thousand Times more so at this Time—the absence of Congress is much felt by Idlers like myself—as the Social Intercourse of the eastern states has not an existance here"; hopes an office can be found for former postmaster general Ebenezer Hazard, "an honester Man I think never lived."

SATURDAY, 17 OCTOBER 1789

William Cumming to Elbridge Gerry. Excerpt of ALS, *Paul Richards Catalogue*, 150 (n.d.): item 94. Written from Edenton, North Carolina. The ellipses and brackets are in the source.

"From a Recollection of our former friendship while in Congress, I use the freedom of solliciting your Interest with the President of the United States in behalf of my nephew Mr. John Hamilton. This little town has chosen him as its Representative in Assembly and as there is a moral Certainty of our adopting the Constitution at the Convention in November next, I hope my application at this present period will not be either premature or impertinent. . . . I am hopeful of your . . . support to him in the appointment [as Judge or Marshall] by the President. . . ."

George Washington, Diary. Washington Papers, DLC. For the full text, see *DGW* 5:464.

Visited in Stratford, Connecticut, by Senator and Mrs. Johnson; in New Haven, Connecticut, by Sherman, its mayor.

[Springfield, Massachusetts] *Hampshire Chronicle*, 21 October.

Adams and Dalton arrived.

SUNDAY, 18 OCTOBER 1789

Benjamin Goodhue to Alexander Hamilton. No copy known; acknowledged in Hamilton to Goodhue, 29 October.

Richard Henry Lee to Charles Lee. ALS, Personal Papers, Vi. Written from "Chantilly," Westmoreland County, Virginia. Addressed to Alexandria, Virginia; carried by Joe.

Shipped his goods from New York to Richmond; purchased some goods as he passed through Baltimore; arrived home one day after leaving Alexandria.

William Maclay to Tench Coxe. ALS, Coxe Papers, PHi. Written from Sunbury, Pennsylvania; addressed to Philadelphia. Maclay also wrote Benjamin Rush on this date on the same subject (ALS, Rush Papers, PPL at PHi).

Seeks office of Pennsylvania surveyor general: "My ill health at New York I confess has had considerable weight with me in this business. For altho' I now feel perfectly recovered, I really dread returning to that place, as I expect a return of all my Ailments; this may however turn out contrary to my expectations. I cannot pretend to Judge in my own Case, but I really think I could be more Useful to the State, in the appointment ~~now~~ alluded to, than in that which I now hold."

John Story to John Langdon. ALS, Langdon-Elwyn Family Papers, NhHi. Addressed to Portsmouth, New Hampshire.

Office seeking: wants to be mentioned to the President for appointment to the board of commissioners for settling the accounts of the states with the United States if John Taylor Gilman resigns; John Kean, commissioner from South Carolina, has arrived and the commissioners need a third in order to meet; "should not have thus troubled you, had it not been for the Presidents intention of being at Portsmouth"; had previously given a copy of his application to Langdon, along with a letter from Gunn.

George Washington, Diary. Washington Papers, DLC. For the full text, see *DGW* 5:465.

Accompanied to New Haven Congregational Church by Sherman and then had tea at his home.

MONDAY, 19 OCTOBER 1789

William Irvine to James Madison. ALS, Madison Papers, DLC. For the full text, see *PJM* 12:436–37.

Thomas Lloyd "said he had sent the paper you wished"; reports from the negotiations with the Southern Indians say that Alexander McGillivray "went off in wrath," that Few was sent to convince him to return, and that David Humphreys had personally insulted McGillivray.

Ralph Izard to John Langdon. Excerpt of ALS, *Remember When Auctions Catalog* 44(1998):item 289. The ellipses are in the source.
". . . The plan at the Treasury is to employ all the clerks that have served in that Office, which is very proper . . . New York is almost entirely abandoned. The President, & Vice President are gratifying New England with their company. The Ministers of France [*Moustier*] & Spain [*Gardoqui*] are on their passage to Europe; & most of the members of Congress are gone home. I most heartily wish that I could have done so likewise . . . The future sessions of Congress ought not to be in the Winter. Let us have an opportunity of paying some little attention to our private affairs. . . The convulsions in France appear to be abated. I most sincerely wish that tranquillity may be entirely restored, & that their new government may be carried into operation without more bloodshed. But the revolution has been so extraordinary, that I fear it will not be the case . . ."

Robert Morris to Thomas Sim Lee. ALS, Lee Papers, MdHi. Written from Philadelphia; addressed to Frederick County, Maryland.
Had wanted to write "by our mutual Friend Colo. Grayson"; "your Susquehannah expectations are frustrated, in Fact that place never was Seriously thought of by those who agitated the Question, but whether it was or was not, would not in my present circumstances, have influenced My Conduct, I cannot take back the Lands which you bought of me there."

George Washington, Diary. Washington Papers, DLC. For the full text, see *DGW* 5:468.
Escorted to Hartford from Wethersfield, Connecticut, by a delegation headed by Wadsworth.

[Springfield, Massachusetts] *Hampshire Chronicle*, 21 October.
Adams and Dalton left for eastern Massachusetts.

TUESDAY, 20 OCTOBER 1789

Abigail Adams to John Adams. ALS, Adams Family Manuscript Trust, MHi. Written from "Richmond Hill," outside New York City. Addressed to "My dearest Friend."
On Sunday, the President told Tobias Lear he was anxious that he had not been urgent enough with Adams to have him join the President's tour of

New England; he will probably invite Adams to accompany the presidential party to Portsmouth, New Hampshire; Butler, Laurance, and others have gone grousing on Long Island.

Henry Knox to William Eustis. FC:dft, Knox Papers, Gilder Lehrman Collection, NHi. The date has been provided from a later acknowledgment by Eustis.

The Invalid Pensioners Act provides for no further inspection of claims at present, as Congress "were of opinion that it would have a very improper Aspect to subject the invalids to any further investigations."

Samuel A. Otis to John Langdon. Excerpt of ALS, *Remember When Auctions Catalog* 44(1998):item 307. Written from Boston. The ellipses are in the source.

". . . Thinking it might be agreeable to you to have a Sett of Journals Laws &c. I have forwarded you one of each—The others you will please to give orders about on your return. We are all in pleasing expectation of seeing the President in a short time in this Metropolis—I am not able to learn whether he proceeds farther East or not. . ."

Otho H. Williams to Nathaniel Pendleton. ALS, Pendleton Papers, NHi. Written from Baltimore; addressed to Georgia; carried by Capt. Riley.

"Do not, however, infer that I was indifferent to your request, or the merits of Mr. [*James*] Seagrove—The measures of Congress were precarious, in the begining, respecting appointments, and applicants were at a Loss where, or how, to apply; Many looked to the Senate, and as I had opportunity I mentioned to such of the Members as I was acquainted with, The Characters whose interest I wished to promote."

George Washington, Diary. Washington Papers, DLC. For the full text, see *DGW* 5:468.

Visited the Hartford Woolen Factory with Ellsworth and Wadsworth; dined and drank tea at Wadsworth's.

[Worcester] *Massachusetts Spy*, 22 October.

Dalton and Adams passed through town in the morning.

WEDNESDAY, 21 OCTOBER 1789

Newspaper Article

On Saturday last arrived in town [*Springfield, Massachusetts*] from New-York, his Excellency JOHN ADAMS, Vice-President of the United States of America, accompanied by the most hon. TRISTRAM DALTON, one of the Senators of this state to the National Congress: On the Monday following they proceeded on their journey to the eastward. How pleasing the idea, that the most venerable and respectable characters of our Federal Legislature, pay such strict attention to the Sabbath. That time, which is by many gentlemen too often appropriated to serve their temporal interests, in journeying, &c. is spent by our national rulers in such a manner, as, while it reflects the highest honor on our holy religion, must be considered as a gentle rebuke to those whose conduct on such days, is truly reprehensible.

[Philadelphia] *Federal Gazette*, 2 November.

OTHER DOCUMENTS

Fisher Ames to Benjamin Goodhue. ALS, Letters to Goodhue, NNS. Written from Boston; addressed to Salem, Massachusetts.
> Some of our mutual friends think we should go to Watertown to meet President Washington; Dalton is here; "I know you will wish to pay every suitable mark of respect to the President of the U.S."

John Barnes to John Langdon. ALS, Langdon-Elwyn Family Papers, NhHi. Addressed to Portsmouth, New Hampshire.
> Office seeking: delivered Langdon's letter of recommendation to Izard who received him politely but feared it was not in his power to help; it seems Hamilton wrote Nicholas Eveleigh "not to engage any Clerk previous to his Arrival" at New York; "your Other Letter addressed to Mr. [*Tobias*] Lear, I shall preserve till his return."

John Langdon to Alexander Hamilton. No copy known; acknowledged in Hamilton to Langdon, 1 November.

Alexander White to Horatio Gates. ALS, Gates Papers, NN. Written from "Woodville," near Winchester, Virginia.
> Sends as much of the Journals of the Senate as he has.

George Washington, Diary. Washington Papers, DLC. For the full text, see *DGW* 5:470.

Spent about an hour at Ellsworth's in Windsor, Connecticut.

THURSDAY, 22 OCTOBER 1789

A Citizen

THE paragraph in *Childs'* Advertiser of the 7th instant, republished in *Fenno's* Gazette[1] of the   has had the opposite effect to what they intended, and rendered them *more,* instead of *less* culpable. The motion for correcting their *misrepresentations* of the debates of the federal representatives, was made on the 21st, published on the 24th, and debated on the 26th of September; and no vindication of their conduct has appeared until the 7th of Oct. which was several days after Mr. *Burke* left this city; they then say "the intended resolution was published without the countenance or knowledge of the honorable mover"—but what evidence is there of *this,* except the assertion of the *parties charged?* If the resolution was published "*without* his countenance," there is not the least probability that he has given them the information, for it is a fact that he would not suffer *one* of them to *speak* to him on the subject—and the use of this gentleman's name, in *his absence,* is unjustifiable— If, indeed, their assertion is just, does it exculpate them? Does it follow, that the charges in the motion are not well founded, because the mover did not send it to the press? This is flimsy reasoning, and can never justify them— They say, "the motion itself was *withdrawn* after being *faintly* supported." This is but *part* of the *fact,* for the mover declared, "he should renew it early in the next session when there would be more time to discuss it." Such a mode of *withdrawing* is but a *suspension* of a motion; and by concealing this circumstance, they have *mistated* the fact. How the motion could be "*faintly* supported," is inconceivable, for the charges in it were generally admitted, even by those who opposed its passing in its present form. The "remarks" of the editor, of its being "difficult to conceive" how they should "misrepresent" or "distort" the debates, can have little weight when opposed to *facts. These,* as stated in the motion, were so notorious, as to induce the culpable parties to attempt to *vindicate,* which they never could have done without a full conviction that they could not *disprove* the facts alluded to—They therefore say "*mutilations* of speeches are sometimes made with *advantage;* they seem to be the necessary consequence of a very rapid enunciation, or when the speaker's voice is small and low." These assertions are unfounded, and if not, they would not, as intended, justify the parties charged, because the speeches of some speakers of this description, have been published at *full length*, and of others of the same description in a *mutilated manner*, during the session. This has been a matter of common observation to those in general who have attended the debates. And although it is undoubtedly true that "mutilations are made with advantage" *to a faction*, it is equally true, that they are to the *disadvantage* of the respective speakers, and of the public; the former of which will by these means be *abused*, and the latter *insulted* and *deceived*—The remark, that "because it would establish the reputation of a register of the debates to have them *perfectly accurate*," it is therefore extremely difficult to account for a printer's *willfully* making them imperfect, can have no more weight than the other remark when opposed to the facts mentioned. *Misrepresentations* are often made from a vain expectation that they will *not* be detected; but if the *reputation* of their newspapers is always attended to by printers, how happens it that some of them so frequently prostitute their presses to the basest purposes of party, and to the perversion of truth and justice? The assertion of these printers that "sketches only of the proceedings were their object" is invalidated by their papers, in which we have frequently seen several columns appropriated to the speeches of particular members, on one side of a question, and not more lines perhaps to other members who have entered as fully into the discussion on the other side. True it is, the instances "of *their being controuled* or influenced" may not be pointed out, however *numerous* they may be, but the best and only satisfactory evidence to the public of *uninfluenced* and *independent* presses, will be the *impartiality* of the conduct of the editors.

NYJ, 22 October.

---

[1] Francis Childs edited *NYDA*; John Fenno, *GUS*.

FRIDAY, 23 OCTOBER 1789

John Langdon to George Washington. ALS, Washington Papers, DLC. Written from Portsmouth, New Hampshire. An ALS of this date to Tobias Lear on the same subject is in the Gilder Lehrman Collection, NHi.

Invites Washington to reside in Langdon's home when he is in Portsmouth.

Robert Morris to Anthony Wayne. ALS, Wayne Papers, PHi. Written from Philadelphia; addressed to Georgia.

Will support him for Indian agent in the "Southern District"; Gunn spoke highly of him "so much so as to convince me that he is ~~and~~ & wishes to remain your Friend. As to Major [*Benjamin*] Fishbourne. I am extreamly sorry for what happened it is past & irrevocable now, He must never look again for a Nomination by the President, for having been once Rejected by the Senate, He would not if it were his nearest and best Friend on Earth Name him a second time for appointment to Office by those that had once Refused."

SUNDAY, 25 OCTOBER 1789

Frederick William Steuben to William North. ALS (in French), Steuben Papers, Oneida Historical Society, Utica, New York.
All the members of Congress have left except Izard, Smith (S.C.), Butler, Huger, and Griffin.

MONDAY, 26 OCTOBER 1789

Frederick A. Muhlenberg, George Clymer, Thomas Fitzsimons, and Robert Morris to Governor Thomas Mifflin. Copy, Timothy Pickering Papers, MHi.
In support of Timothy Pickering's request to be appointed surveyor general of Pennsylvania.

George Washington, Diary. Washington Papers, DLC. For the full text, see *DGW* 5:477.
Dined with Dalton and others at Boston.

WEDNESDAY, 28 OCTOBER 1789

George Mason to Rufus King. ALS, King Papers, NHi. Written from "Gunston Hall," Fairfax County, Virginia; addressed to New York; carried by Joseph Fenwick. For the full text, see *PGM* 3:1177–78.
Office seeking: Joseph Fenwick for American consul at Bordeaux, France.

John Page to St. George Tucker. ALS, Tucker-Coleman Papers, ViW. Written from "Rosewell," Gloucester County, Virginia.
"Your Brother [*Rep. Tucker*] who resembles you too much in many Respects not to attract my Esteem, & with whom, after some Time, for you know he is more reserved than you I contracted a perfect Intimacy, & reposed my utmost Confidence in, as I do in you," sailed for Charleston the same day Page sailed for Norfolk; he promised to visit Virginia on his next trip home.

[Newburyport, Massachusetts] *Essex Journal*, 28 October.
Dalton expected to arrive in Newburyport today.

THURSDAY, 29 OCTOBER 1789

Alexander Hamilton to Benjamin Goodhue

I am duly favoured with your letter of the Eighteenth instant, and receive the observations you have been so obliging as to make, not only with candor but with thanks as—a mark of your friendship and confidence.

I am far from relying so much upon my own judgment, as not to think it very possible, I may have been mistaken in both the constructions on which you remark. Indeed I see abundant room for adopting opposite ones, and did not, 'till after mature reflection, conclude on those which have been announced, and not then, intirely, without hesitation.

The reasoning which prevailed in my mind in each case was of this nature. First as to the Bounty.[1]

The original and express object of the allowance was by way of *compensation* for the *duties* on salt. The declared motive of the suspension was, that there was salt within the United States, on which no *such duties* had been paid: The *Equity* of the suspending clause, which is, that there ought to be no *compensation* where there is no *consideration*; [*lined out*], and the *general intent* of the Legislature, which was, that there should be no *compensation* where there had been no such *consideration*, were therefore both, manifestly, against the allowance of the bounty on the articles shipped between the passing of the first Act and the passing of the second. And though the *letter* of the suspending clause is *future*, yet its reason being retrospective and as the *actual making* of the allowance for articles already shipped being *future* also, I thought it admissible so to construe the law as to *arrest* this allowance, in that sense future; in conformity to the real justice of the case and the main design of the legislature. In a circumstance in which the equity was palpable, and the law doubtful, I thought it my duty as an *executive servant* of the government, not to let the public money be parted with, on a *mere point* of construction, till that construction should be judicially established. This resource will be open to any individual who will choose to pursue it; by an action against the collector of the Port, from which the articles were shipped.

Secondly As to the Discount for Prompt Payment.[2]

The words "prompt payment" are in my apprehension synonimous with *immediate* payment or payment *down*. The most obvious import of the clause in question seems therefore to be this. Where the amount of the duties exceeds fifty dollars, time shall be given for payment upon proper bond security; but if the party prefers making immediate payment, or paying the money down, he shall have an allowance of ten per Cent, *on all above fifty dollars*, for doing it. The confining the discount to the *excess* illustrates the meaning of the provision and shews that payment in the first instance was contemplated; for if it had been intended, that the discount might be made at any time before the bonds became due, it would be difficult to imagine why it should not extend to *the fifty dollars* as well as to the *excess*.

I was the more inclined to this construction because I supposed the contrary one was of a nature to be rendered more beneficial to any Collector, who might choose to avail himself of it, than to the Public. And in general I doubt much that it is the interest of the public to make such a discount; (as they now borrow at less *in its operation* than 6 ⅌ Cent) On which account I felt no inclination to extend the discount.

Thus have I, My Dear Sir, freely explained to you the motives by which I have been governed in the instances in question. And I shall be happy that they may appear to you satisfactory. I am sure at least that you will view the intention favourably.

ALS, Letters to Goodhue, NNS. Addressed to Salem, Massachusetts.

---

[1] Section 4 of the Impost Act authorized an allowance to be paid on exported salted provisions in lieu of a drawback on imported salt. This allowance was suspended until 31 May 1790 by section 36 of the Coasting Act.

[2] The discount was authorized by section 19 of the Collection Act [HR-11].

OTHER DOCUMENTS

William Bentley, Diary. MWA.
The Salem address to President Washington was read by Goodhue.

Thomas Fitzsimons to Alexander Hamilton. No copy known; acknowledged in Hamilton to Fitzsimons, 27 November.

Inhabitants of Salem, Massachusetts, to George Washington. FC, Goodhue Letters, NNS. Goodhue signed this address. For the full text, see *PGW* 4:255n.
Welcomes the President.

[Boston] *Massachusetts Centinel*, 31 October.
Goodhue, chairman of the Salem committee to welcome Washington, conducted the President to a balcony where Goodhue read the town's address to the President and received Washington's reply.

FRIDAY, 30 OCTOBER 1789

Fisher Ames to Thomas Dwight. *Ames* 1:74–75. Written from Boston.
Has "dangled" after the President; the President "has (I think) seen that the zeal for supporting government, and the strength, too, are principally on this side the Hudson."

Edward Rutledge to Jeremiah Wadsworth. ALS, American Manuscripts, CSmH. Place from which written not specified.
Discusses Nathanael Greene's estate; "pray tell me what are your Prospects respecting Relief from Congress [*for Catharine Greene*]—That Business must be taken up & executed with Dispatch."

John Sullivan to George Washington. ALS, Washington Papers, DLC. Written from Durham, New Hampshire. For the full text, see *PGW* 4:262–63.
Understands Langdon means to entertain Washington at dinner on Monday, 2 November.

George Washington, Diary. Washington Papers, DLC. For the full text, see *DGW* 5:486.
Met at Ipswich and escorted to Newburyport, Massachusetts, by a committee that included Dalton.

NYDG, 16 November.
Madison passed through Georgetown, Maryland, en route to Richmond.

SATURDAY, 31 OCTOBER 1789

George Washington, Diary. Washington Papers, DLC. For the full text, see *DGW* 5:486–87.
Breakfasted at Newburyport, Massachusetts, with Dalton, who then accompanied him to the New Hampshire border; met there by Langdon and Wingate; dined with them, Gilman, and others in Portsmouth; drank tea with the Langdons after dinner. (*GUS*, 18 November, reported that Gilman was among those who met Washington at the border and Langdon was among the delegation that conducted Washington to his lodging.)

OCTOBER 1789 UNDATED

Alexander Hamilton to Jeremiah Wadsworth. ALS, Wadsworth Papers, CtHi. For the full text, see *PAH* 26:486. Written between 9 and 15 October.
Asks Wadsworth to collect data for him on foreign ships and seamen for the purpose of formulating a general idea of the comparative advantages for navigation between the United States and other countries.

Amariah Jocelin to Jeremiah Wadsworth. ALS, Wadsworth Papers, CtHi. Written from Wilmington, North Carolina; addressed to "Either at New York or Hartford," Connecticut; arrived in New York on 10 November and forwarded to Hartford.
Office seeking: felt under great obligation for Wadsworth's "proffers of service in my favour" in his letter of 18 June; comments on Burke's observations on the Society of the Cincinnati; reports on the North Carolina ratification convention.

November 1789

SUNDAY, 1 NOVEMBER 1789

Alexander Hamilton to John Langdon. LS, Langdon-Elwyn Family Papers, NhHi.
Regarding payment of the sum mentioned in his letter of 21 October.

James Madison to Thomas Jefferson. ALS, Madison Papers, DLC. Written from Fredericksburg, Virginia. For the full text, see *PJM* 12:439.
Office seeking: George William Smith, Benjamin Grayson Orr, and John Fisher for clerkships in the state department.

Philip Schuyler to James Madison. ALS, American Manuscripts, RPJCB. Written from Albany, New York; addressed to Fredericksburg, Virginia. For the full text, see *PJM* 12:439–40.
In response to Madison's letter of 5 October, regarding the 900 Mohawk Valley acres that Madison and Monroe were to purchase: about the time Madison will return to New York, John Taylor "will send down the [*lined out*] lease & release and advise you to whom."

George Washington, Diary. Washington Papers, DLC. For the full text, see *DGW* 5:488.
Attended Episcopal and Congregational services at Portsmouth, New Hampshire, with Langdon.

Letter from a London Merchant to Boston. *Massachusetts Centinel*, 2 January 1790.
Other nations are pressing our government to admit their lumber and pot and pearl ashes duty free as we do yours.

GUS, 4 November.
Gerry's son Thomas died in the morning.

MONDAY, 2 NOVEMBER 1789

Pierce Butler to Messrs. Simpson and Davisson

***

Our Fœderal Legislature adjourned last month to meet in January. The Creek Indians thro' McGuilvery [*Alexander McGillivray*] having lately declined to treat with the Commissioners of the United States on the difference between the State of Georgia and the Creek the Union will be obliged to take the business on themselves and give the Creeks a brush in their own Country—If the Spaniards should be imprudent enough to interfere they will possibly have cause to repent it.

I am much obliged to You for Your kind enquiries respecting my overset. My leg was much wounded but is now quite healed Mr. Huger who was with me, is still on His back.[1] ***

FC:lbk, Butler Papers, PHi.

[1] On 24 June, their horse took fright and both men were thrown from the chaise in which they were riding.

Henry Glen to Philip Schuyler

*** I like wise wrote you that I was dayly thretned to be seued for the money of the Indian department which is still the Case I wish to no How I am to Get this money Part of the Accounts I left in the hands of the then Controlar [*James Milligan*] Which was for Certificate to be Given But he would not finish my Accounts till the Old Commisiners had Settled all their Accts. the Rest of the Accts. I have with me which was meant to be paid in Specie according to a Resolusition of the old Congress.

And as their is General Change in Adminstration meaning that the Controler & Board Treasury are no more I now wish to no what I am to do to Get these Account Settled as to depending on Mr. Dow [*Volckert P. Douw*] Settling them I dont Exspect will Ever be the Case for I have Exsperiend for Several years I think its a heardShip for me to Serve my Country So long & not Reciving any Reward & the war So long to An End & these Accounts Still Remaining unsettled and Every thing is Complyd with that was directed by the Board people all Swore to their Accounts which was Requestd. & does not necesary to be Sworn too were Certifyd by me as your agent & by your directions. As You are Goeing Down to N. York I wish you to take my Voucher &c. &c. I Shall furnish you with an abstract of those lists in the hands of Mr. Mullagen the then Controler.

As Mr. Hamilton is now at the head of this Business he will be able to direct in what manner I am to Get pay for these Accounts.

Their is Numbers at Schonectady means to Seue me I have all alonge Keept them of[f] with Some Storry or other But thats Got so far they dont belive a word more about it they Say I Imployd. them & must pay them by the Same principle I have to Look to the Commisiners who undoubtly Imployd. me. I am Very Schure if you will take the matter in hand with Mr. Hamilton their will Soon be an End to the matter I wish you would Trop alien [drop a line] for me at Louies when it will be Convenient for me to Call [on] you & bring with me the Voucher &c. &c.

ALS, Schuyler Papers, NN. Written from Albany, New York; addressed to near Albany, New York.

George Nicholas to John Brown

***

The district affords very little worth communicating at present. You have no doubt before this been informed of the proceedings of the [statehood] convention; nothing has happened since in the political line. The parties seem to rest upon their arms; perhaps the proceedings of the next session of the Virga. assembly may set them in motion. The continental troops so far from affording the district any aid appear to consider it's inhabitants as enemies. The inclosed paper will give you a state of their proceedings in a late instance.[1] You know [Henry] Lee's character and that his information may be relied on. From Judge Simmes [John Cleves Symmes] down to Mr. [Winthrop] Sergeant their conduct has been mighty reprehensible. If we can see any of them in the district a jury may make them repent their conduct. Such conduct if continued may make an irreparable breach between us and the people on that side of the [Ohio] river.

The business of the court is carried on much as usual; very rapidly in common matters and very heavily in land disputes. I think all land causes that can will for that reason be instituted in the federal court. We are impatient to see your regulations on that subject and to know who is to judge for us. Much will depend on his prudence as well as knowledge, as to making the business palatable here. Do you draw together or do you pull in different directions as much as was foretold by the enemies to the new government? The subjects of impost and the seat of government would be as likely as any that could happen to put parties into motion. Do all sides still look up to the President with reverence and has his conduct given general content: Does not the Vice President attempt to form a party and to throw obstructions in the way of his superior? The public acts of Congress we are informed of by the papers, but the secret movement can only be known by the spectators and from their information. What situation is the Vermont business now in and what the probability of it's becoming a member of the union. Will that remove all difficulties as to accepting Kentucky if she and Virga. agree on the terms.

I never intend to have any hand in the game of government but wish to know how the *hands* are managed.

This will be sent by one of my neighbours with directions to leave it in Staunton if you should not returned to Virginia. Have you not discovered too much of the school boy's impatience in adjourning before you have set the government in motion for until it is organized in all it's parts we must consider it's movements as very uncertain and precarious.

Tell Isaac Coles I thought him a little out of his head when he joined Cousin Patrick [*Henry*] in his opposition to the government, but that if he marries a young wife I will apply for a statute of lunacy against him. It would divert me—to see him take up the lady's fan before a large room full of company, or follow her carrying her muff. If he is not yet married I will answer for it if he will sleep with one of the willing fair ones of the city a few nights that he never will engage a young woman. I intend this friendly advice for his private information but have not time to write to him at present but will have to consider this paragraph as an introduction to a correspondence which I ~~shall~~ am desirous of carrying on with him married or single. If married ask his wife if he had not better have taken my advice.

[*Harry*] Innes and I propose joining in taking three or four of the most approved periodical publications. Do you think we could get them out regularly and at what price.

ALS, Nicholas Collection, Kentucky Historical Society, Frankfort.

[1] The [Lexington] *Kentucky Gazette*, 24 October, published an article signed by Henry Lee describing how a U.S. Army regiment abused the residents of Limestone (now Maysville), Kentucky, on 24 August by stealing food, money, and farm equipment as well as arresting one man without a warrant.

George Nicholas to James Madison

***

In our late convention the most important characters of that party which has always been in favor of a seperation opposed the agreeing to it at this time upon a supposition that the terms had been changed by Virginia so as to make them inadmissible in their present form.[1] Their enemies say that this could not have been their true reason for although they do not deny that alterations have been made yet they assert that they were of such a nature that a politician really a friend to a seperation upon constitutional principles ought to have accepted of them. Let their motives have been what they may their joining the party opposed to a seperation on any terms made a majority against accepting the present propositions from Virga. I believe no late attempts have been made by either Spain or England to detach the district from the union; but Spain is playing a game which if not counteracted will depopulate this country and carry most of the future emigrants to her territory. They have established a new government independent of the government at New-Orleans at the Natchez and have sent there as governor [*Manuel Gayoso de Lemos*] a man who from his character and abilities would never have accepted the appointment if their only object had been the government of the subjects they now have in that country. For two years past they have received all the tob[*acc*]o. carried to New-Orleans f[*ro*]m. this district into the king's stores at a very high price. The new governor has put a stop to this and declares that in future these stores shall only be open to Spanish subjects and that they shall have ten dollars a hundred for their tobo. when private adventurers from this country have been obliged to take three dollars a hundred at New-Orleans this summer. He also holds out great advantages to settlers such as a donation of land and a certain sum in money for each family. I leave you to judge what will be the consequence if they are permitted to exclude us from the navigation of the [*Mississippi*] river and give such advantages [*to*] their own subjects. The difference of religion and of government are the only things that could prevent any man from giving the preference to the Spanish government under these circumstances; and this governor gives the most positive assurances that the settlers shall enjoy what they have been accustomed to in both ways. I think they will not only in future get a great part of the emigrants to the western country but that a large proportion of the present inhabitants of the district who are not tied down to this country by owning valuable lands will leave it to go to a country where they have such encouragement given them. If Spain perseveres steadily in this conduct for only two years no man can say how far the emigration to that country may be carried. And if those who shall go there from this country should really enjoy those advantages I doubt no obstacles will be sufficient to prevent the people who continue here from putting themselves into a situation which will enable them to avail themselves of those advantages. This consideration I should suppose should make the new governt. take the most decisive steps as to our right of navigation and also induce her to pay particular attention to the gaining the affections of the people. So far have the steps that have been taken hitherto in the western country been from having a tendency that way that they must necessarily have produced a contrary effect. No support has been given us by the general government and the regulation of Indian matters has been placed in hands who were interested in a continuance of their depredations on us. It is known to every person that if a trade is not established with them on such a footing as to supply their real wants that they will supply themselves by plunder. The management of Indian affairs being placed in the hands of persons living on, and interested in the welfare of, the other side of the Ohio, and no adequate provision being made to supply the Indians with those articles they cannot subsist without it became their policy to hold out to the Indians that we were a seperate and distinct people from them and that they might be at peace with them and at war with us. By this means giving them security at our expence. Besides as long as this difference subsists between the different sides of the river in the opinion of the Indians it gives their settlement a much better chance of being inhabited. Thus our interests are placed in the hands of men who have a contrary one to pursue and who have already given sufficient proofs that they will follow their own interests when they clash with our's. Having the commissioners always named from persons living on that side of the river and having the treaties always held there contribute greatly to establish this difference in the minds of the Indians as to the people on the different sides of the river. Surely this district the inhabitants of which are twenty times as numerous as the people on the other side of the river ought to have as great a share in the management of Indian affairs as the people on the other side. I am well convinced the bulk of the people here are strongly attached to the union and that characters might be found in the district better qualified to manage this business than those in whose hands it is now placed. If it is not the desire of the new government to lose *all* its' freinds in this quarter a change must be made in this business. Let them take such steps as will convince the Indians that the Americans are all one people, that they shall never attack any of them with [*lined out*] impunity, and that in future their real wants will be supplied in time of peace: this is all we ask. We do deny in the most positive manner what we are told is asserted to government by the officers on the other side of the river that hostilities are always commenced by the people of the district: on the contrary our people never cross the river but in revenge for the depredations committed within the district. Several expeditions of this kind have been and will be carried on until government take up the matter effectually. To convince you in what light we are considered by the officers & on the other side of the river I refer you to Mr. Brown to whom I write by this opportunity. I know that the want of money prevents the government from doing many things which would otherwise be undertaken; but that need not stop the necessary steps in this business for if they will only give their sanction to it we can raise any number of men and any quantity of provisions that may be wanting to carry it into execution and will wait until their finances will enable them to make us satisfaction. I fear they have taken up the idea that this country may be defended by a few posts on the river. If so it is a most erroneous one for it wd. take such a chain of posts to cover this country as could only be occupied by a large army. I say this upon a supposition that the post opposite the mouth of Licking[2] is erected as a guard to us; if indeed as is more generally thought it is intended as a check upon us I can only say if we are treated as fellow citizens any check will be unnecessary, but that if it is intended to withhold from us all the benefits of good government, a little time will shew that as heretofore we have found the troops useless and faithless as [lined out] friends, hereafter, we shall despise them as enemies. Upon the whole I shall close this subject with assuring you that government has been deceived in the accounts they have had from this country; and that it is my opinion that the most serious consequences will follow from their persisting in the measures which have been pursued for some time past.

***

ALS, Madison Papers, DLC. Written from Kentucky. For the full text, see *PJM* 12:442–46.

---

[1] Kentucky's eighth statehood convention, which met on 20 July, remonstrated against the conditions for separation as set forth by a Virginia act of December 1788; see Nicholas to Madison, 8 May, n. 2, volume 15.

[2] Fort Washington (Cincinnati, Ohio).

Letter from London

I thank you for the news-papers you sent me, containing the debates of Congress. Your legislature in their first session, made good progress. The most interesting subjects are however yet to be brought forward. The present complexion of your public affairs appears favourable, and if Congress in their *second* session pursue their determinations expressed in the *first*, your system will be complete; your friends in this country have strong expectations that the American government will soon assume the most respectable character on earth. There are now no difficulties in the way. If your legislature make the most of their situation, your country will rise into honor and prosperity.

I have perused the debates of Congress, with most critical attention. They do honor to your representatives, who generally have given indications of abilities and integrity; but I must confess I am in some respect a little disappointed. The debates discover less independence of spirit than I expected from men so favourably situated for giving scope to their talents: I will explain to you my ideas on the subject.

In the first place it may be remarked, that the speakers in Congress have not yet acquired confidence in themselves; they speak as if they thought themselves unequal to the talk they had to accomplish. In many instances, we find good arguments lose their weight from not being more confidently urged; and the members appear to want resolution more than sense or honesty. They view their situation in a light so new and untried, as to create a distrust of their own abilities to act in it with propriety. This diffidence may be commendable from the motive that gave rise to it, but it will retard public measures and beget unreasonable precautions. Your legislators have good ground for confidence in themselves. The world think favourably of them, and believe them competent to the part they have assumed.

Another circumstance observable in the debates is, that your representatives appear not to have confidence in their constituents. The speakers often express fears how a measure will affect the feelings of the people. There is more evil to be apprehended from this kind of diffidence than from any other source; and yet there is little foundation for cherishing such a diffidence. The people of your country will submit to any thing that promotes the public good. There is no formidable opposition against the government; and your legislators have no reason to doubt that such measures, as are intrinsically the best, will be the most universally approved. Whatever is just and useful will not among so enlightened a people, for any length of time, be unpopular. The disposition of your citizens is as favourable as can be wished, and they will chearfully acquiesce in all the honest measures of government. The resources of your country are immense, and no part of the globe has such inherent advantages for revenue. Where is the mighty difficulty in establishing public credit, and in that way, acquiring an honorable character and realizing all the benefits that your situation affords? The legislators of the United States have nothing to fear from their constituents while the plans of the government are founded in wisdom and honesty. The public opinion is scarcely formed on the most important subjects, and it is the business of the legislature to impress the public mind with virtuous principles, before vicious ones have gained a prevalence.

The objects that rise into view, in reading the debates of Congress impress a most favorable idea of the situation of America. Your citizens seem to be contemplating useful points in the science of morality and government. Every subject is discussed on rational grounds, and decided upon the real merits of the question. The important truth seems to be acquiesced in, that public honesty is the only basis of public happiness. What improvements may not be expected from a people who are so fast progressing into habits of order, economy and justice! This is the more pleasing to the philosophic mind, as this reformation in your affairs is effected by the free consent of the people at large. There is no force or deception in the matter. The citizens of the United States, having experienced most bitterly the effects of a want of public credit, and of deranged finances, come forward voluntarily and enter into arrangements to find themselves to be honest and virtuous. It is a noble triumph of reason over error. It reflects the highest honor on your country, and if this spirit of reformation can be kept alive till your public credit is effectually established, your nation will be held up as a model to all the world. The name of America will sound gratefully in the ears of every philosopher on earth.

The approaching session of your Legislature will be an interesting one. From the measures then to be adopted, your government must take its character. The executive officers will no doubt faithfully collect information relative to their different departments; and I presume the Legislature will weigh with candor, the plans that may be suggested. The greatest danger to be apprehended in your public affairs, is a jealousy between the different branches of government. I could perceive by the debates that the representatives were not free from a suspicion, that the executive officers would establish too powerful an influence. It is very certain that men of abilities and rectitude will have influence in whatever department they are placed. This circumstance should not create so much jealousy as to prevent men of talents from acquiring confidence, and promoting the public good by their exertions. All men in office should be controuled by certain checks that are interwoven in the institutions, under which they act, but it will always be found that a temper of suspicion indulged by individuals against public characters, or by one branch of the government against the other, will impede public business and be attended with no useful consequences.

[Philadelphia] *Federal Gazette*, 15 February 1790; reprinted at Lansingburgh, New York.

OTHER DOCUMENTS

William Lambert to James Madison. ALS, Madison Papers, DLC. For the full text, see *PJM* 12:442.
    Office seeking: solicits a letter of recommendation and assistance for Reuben Burnley as clerk in the state department.

George Washington, Diary. Washington Papers, DLC. For the full text, see *DGW* 5:488–89.
    Toured Portsmouth, New Hampshire, harbor with Langdon and others; dined at the Langdons with others.

WEDNESDAY, 4 NOVEMBER 1789

Philip Schuyler to Henry Glen. FC:dft, Schuyler Papers, NN.
    Acknowledges Glen's letter of 2 November; cannot recommend him for a federal office as there are none in the state outside New York City; will

deliver Glen's accounts to the comptroller of the treasury and recommend a speedy examination and settlement.

Jeremiah Wadsworth to Alexander Hamilton. No copy known; acknowledged in Hamilton to Wadsworth, 8 November.

FRIDAY, 6 NOVEMBER 1789

Alexander Hamilton to Robert Morris. No copy known; acknowledged in Morris to Hamilton, 13 November.

Jeremiah Wadsworth to Alexander Hamilton. No copy known; acknowledged in Hamilton to Wadsworth, 12–14 November.

SATURDAY, 7 NOVEMBER 1789

Governor George Walton to John Adams. ALS, Adams Family Manuscript Trust, MHi.
　　Office seeking: associate justice of the United States Supreme Court; Gunn, who is with him, sends his respects.

SUNDAY, 8 NOVEMBER 1789

Alexander Hamilton to Jeremiah Wadsworth. ALS, Sol Feinstone Collection, PPAmP. Addressed to Hartford, Connecticut. For the full text, see *PAH* 5:503.
　　Seeks his assistance in apprehending Francis Crane and his gang who were counterfeiting notes of the Bank of New York.

MONDAY, 9 NOVEMBER 1789

Henry Knox to Winthrop Sargent

Although personally I cannot have the least objection to an application for more troops being posted near Marietta [*Ohio*], yet I believe it will not be politic and might defeat the intention—The arrangement directed is with the entire concurrence of the President of the United States and embraces a variety of views—It seems to be a pretty prevalent opinion among

the Members of the Eastern States that the expences for the Western territory should be rather lessened than encreased—An application might be
attended with the effect of calling this opinion or disposition into activity—The establishment of the troops is only to be in force—untill the end
of the next session This temporary arrangement "may have been dictated
more with a view of retrenching than enlarging the establishment."

FC:excerpt of ALS, Knox Papers, Gilder Lehrman Collection, NHi.

OTHER DOCUMENTS

William Constable to Robert Morris. FC:lbk, Constable-Pierrepont Collection, NN.
   Dined with Hamilton on Saturday; "I tried him on the subject of In-
   dents—'they must no doubt be funded tho it cannot be done immediately' was his Remark—'they must be all put upon a footing'—meaning
   these as well as the funded Debt—In short, I am more & more of opinion that they are the best object at present."

NYJ, 12 November.
   Gerry left for Boston.

TUESDAY, 10 NOVEMBER 1789

Fisher Ames to John Jay

I presume the office of clerk of the Supreme Court of the United States
will be sollicited by many candidates of merit and capacity for the trust. For,
I think, pretenders of a different description will not delude themselves
with any hopes of success. With this impression on my mind, I should not
venture to recommend even common merit to your favour and patronage.
John Tucker Esq., Clerk of the Supreme Court of Massachusetts, possesses
so much worth, and is so eminently qualified for the office, that I feel myself authorised to recommend him to your notice. Being a gentleman in his
manners as well as principles, and bred to the law, it was natural to expect
from him fidelity assiduity and accuracy in the performance of his duty.
And, accordingly, he has given uncommon satisfaction to the court, to the
bar, and to the suitors. Mr. [*William*] Cushing, your honorable associate, is
well acquainted with Mr. Tucker's character and pretensions, and will furnish any further necessary information.
   Please to accept my apology for the trouble of this application.

ALS, Jay Papers, NNC. Written from Boston; addressed to New York.

OTHER DOCUMENTS

George Washington, Diary. Washington Papers, DLC. For the full text, see *DGW* 5:496.

Met Gerry at New Haven, Connecticut, traveling to Massachusetts by the stagecoach.

[Philadelphia] *Pennsylvania Packet*, 21 November.

Members of Congress who were in Philadelphia attended the opening of the Pennsylvania federal district court.

WEDNESDAY, 11 NOVEMBER 1789

Tristram Dalton to John Langdon

I fully intended to have paid my respects to Mrs. [*Elizabeth*] Langdon & your good Self at Portsmouth, before my return, to New York, not only because you had my promise to, but that I knew one of the greatest pleasures I could enjoy in N. England would be the result of a visit to your hospitable & friendly Mansion.

Your known Candor, and Mrs. Langdon's usual Goodness, will plead an excuse for me—especially on again pledging myself, that, in the course of the next Summer, I will not be at Portsmouth myself only, but accompany Mrs. [*Ruth*] Dalton. She charged me with the *personal* delivery of sincere regards—and I pray that mine may be made agreeable to your Lady.

The time taken up on account of the President's Visit—and other circumstances, since occurring—have detained me longer than I expected—and I find myself under the necessity of leaving this place for New York on Saturday Morning.

If you have any commands I shall be very happy to receive and execute them. Mrs. D. will rely on the happiness of seeing Mrs. L. at N. York during the coming session of Congress.

ALS, Langdon Papers, NhPoA. Written from Newburyport, Massachusetts; addressed to Portsmouth, New Hampshire.

OTHER DOCUMENTS

Frederick William Steuben to William North. ALS, Steuben Papers, Hamilton College, Clinton, New York. Written from New York City. *DHFFC* translation of a copy in French.

Describes the negotiations between the Creeks and the American commissioners at Rock Landing, Georgia; when Alexander McGillivray abruptly quit the talks, Senator Few and another were sent after him; McGillivray made them wait an hour and a half outside his tent before giving them an audience and then sent them back without any hope of another meeting.

THURSDAY, 12 NOVEMBER 1789

Tristram Dalton to George Thatcher. ALS, Foster Autograph Collection, MHi. Written from Newburyport, Massachusetts; addressed to Biddeford, Maine.

Planning "to proceed this day on my return to New York"; mentions accomplishing the private business "agreeably to the memorandum you were so kind as to take from me at New York."

FRIDAY, 13 NOVEMBER 1789

Robert Morris to Alexander Hamilton. LS, Hamilton Papers, DLC. Written from Philadelphia. For the full text, see *PAH* 5:513–15.

Regarding the sale of stock in the Bank of North America held by Hamilton's brother-in-law, John B. Church.

SATURDAY, 14 NOVEMBER 1789

Tobias Lear to John Langdon

***

We arrived in this City yesterday about 3 o'clock without meeting any accident on the Journey—and, what is still more extraordinary, without having had an hour of bad weather since we left Portsmouth. The President expresses himself highly gratified by his tour, and I think it will have a happy political effect; he declares that he never experienced so much real satisfaction in his life as he has felt on this journey—the general state of the Country—the good crops—the industry of the people—and the affectionate attachment which they discoverd towards him have all conspired to make favourable impressions.

We brought the first news of our approach here and consequently came upon the city by surprize.

We met the Commissioners here from Georgia—they have not been successful in their mission as to forming a permanent treaty with the Creeks, but they have concluded a truce for some months—in which time it is to be hoped some steps may be taken to form a lasting peace—Mr. [*Alexander*]

McGillivery & the Indians did not go off in disgust as was reported. They parted with the commissioners in a freindly manner—but they would not acceed to the terms of concluding a treaty which the Commissioners were authorized to hold out, being, as it was imagined, under the influence of the Spaniards. If these nations should be mad enough to persist in their hostile attempts on our frontiers—and again refuse to treat on the liberal terms held out by these States, they will draw the vengence of United America upon their heads—and I think if the Union should once seriously determine to oppose them, they would feel a weight which all the assistance that might be derived from their spanish connexions could not enable them to avoid— they would be driven from their lands, & if the Southern Spaniards should join them—our ~~northern~~ hardy sons of the north wou'd soon strip them of their mexican Wealth—and this I dare say would be no difficult task—for the inhabitants of New Spain would readily join any power that might enter their dominions against the Spanish Government.

ALS, Langdon-Elwyn Family Papers, NhHi. The report of the commissioners is printed in *DHFFC* 2:210–41.

OTHER DOCUMENTS

William Constable to Jeremiah Wadsworth. FC:lbk, Constable-Pierrepont Collection, NN.

Hopes Wadsworth will bring his family to New York for the winter; offers to find a comfortable house.

Alexander Hamilton to Jeremiah Wadsworth. ALS, Wadsworth Papers, CtHi. For the full text, see *PAH* 5:512–13. Written between 12–14 November.

Sends a copy of his letter of 8 November; further suggestions for apprehending Francis Crane and his gang.

SUNDAY, 15 NOVEMBER 1789

Thomas Thompson to John Langdon

I am extremly disapointed not arriving [*in*] time enough to have the pleasure of seeing you in Portsm. which port I enterd 8th Instant after an absense of three months & 16 Days. I left London 25th Sept. doubtless you have news after that date—every preperation was Stil going on for war by (Sea)—but the Genl. opinion was no war—I wish to convey to you the great abuse we meet with in that Country respecting the ~~abuse of~~ Impressing our Seamen and distressing our Ships contrary to the Laws of nations—the greatest Evil is and which wants the most Imeadiate attention of Congress is to fix the Period when and at what time a mand became an American Subject—The Admiralty (make Laws of their own) they do not admitt any man an American but such as were born within the Limits of the united States to which the man and the Capt. must make Oath—any person Born in England &c. and moved into america at two years of ages—they claim him as a British Subject—and take him accordingly. You well know a large proportion of our Seamen are natives of England &c. altho maried and Seteld here for many years yet cannot Claim the priviledge of an American Subject if caught in a British port—tis an intolarable hardship and a very great abuse whch Congress ought imeadially to look into and redress those unhappy Set of People now Suffering wrongfully the loss of liberty in a British man of war and the united States deprived of two or three thousand Seamen—these are facts—as to myself I was treated very well—but people that are unaquainted have had their whole Crews taken—and hurryd down to the Nore[1] &c. before they knew where to look for them. I told them if they persisted in this vilianous practis we would Strip every British ship that came into our ports and put the Crews in Prison until they releasd every american Subject, Joyne the french and Spaniards against them (which they are afeard of) Stop our present Trade, turn all into Privateers, and sweep the Seas of all there merchant Ships—this is a game we can play at a great odds with the British whenever forced to the expedient all tho I have not any desire of Seeing it tryd—You have doubtless better information on this Subject then I can give and I hope decisive measures are taken previous to this Period you have my good wishes for its sucess and my earnest solicitations to proceed in the matter which Justice and Policie loudly call for. tis an Imeadiate object worthy the attention of Congress—taken in a national only—tis probable that the produce of the southern will be carried to England in American bottoms this season—and under the present circumstances seamen will not ship for these voiages except their persons can be secure from being Impress on board a British ship of war—Some Ship which lost their Crews have been obliged to give three pounds Sterlg. pr. month (the common wages) for very ordinary hands to bring the Ships Home to America—half the mercht. ships in the River Theams [*Thames*] are laid up for want of men and the cause of such extravagant wages and freights continuing on the Peace Establishment—In short England is in the very Stranges Situation with respect to navigation that she ever before expereanced.

P. S. I expect to spend the winter by the fire side.

ALS, Langdon Papers, NhPoA. Written from Portsmouth, New Hampshire.

---

[1] A famous anchorage in the Thames estuary.

Joseph Bloomfield to Jonathan Dayton. ALS, Dayton Collection, NjHi. Written from Burlington, New Jersey.

"Paterson has lately said at Trenton—that He intends in the Spring to resign his seat in Senate & return to his practice &c."; suggests Dayton as replacement.

Elbridge Gerry to Ann Gerry. ALS, Gerry Papers, MHi. Written from Cambridge, Massachusetts; addressed to New York.

Arrived last night after a "disagreable & unfortunate" journey; his trunk was stolen; it contained private accounts, all the letters he received "on private concerns," copies of all those he wrote while in New York City, and "a number of Interrogatories from Judge Burke which I had never read respecting political information he wanted"; two letters he was carrying from Richard H. Lee to Samuel Adams and James Sullivan were also lost; "my eyes were so bad the first & second day that I expected to lie by *** the inflammation was so great, as to raise apprehensions that the ride would endanger the loss of my sight, but they are much better altho too bad to write so long a letter"; slept in the house with the President at New Haven.

William Irvine to James Madison. ALS, Madison Papers, DLC. Addressed to Fredericksburg, Virginia. For the full text, see *PJM* 12:446.

"The absence of Congress makes a surprising alteration in the face of affairs, Men & Women, at New york, it can be observed even in the streets— no wonder they do not like to let them go."

George Washington, Diary. Washington Papers, DLC. For the full text, see *DGW* 5:497.

Visited by Butler and Smith (S.C.).

MONDAY, 16 NOVEMBER 1789

Pierce Butler to George Washington

My situation as a senator from Carolina obliges me to trouble You with the perusal of the inclosed letters—As they will speak for themselves I will not intrude further on Your time.

ALS, Item 78, 4:645, PCC, DNA. The enclosures have not been identified but were probably related to foreign or Indian affairs.

TUESDAY, 17 NOVEMBER 1789

William Short to James Madison. ALS, Madison Papers, DLC. Written from Paris. For the full text, see *PJM* 12:447–49.

Has been approached by several members of the French national assembly about First Congress precedents on titles; for a reply, he showed them Madison's recorded speeches, which were well received.

WEDNESDAY, 18 NOVEMBER 1789

Nathaniel Rochester to an Unknown Recipient

The Inhabitants of Hagers Town, Martinsburg & this place have petitioned Congress for an alteration in line of Continental Posts.

At present a post from Phila. to ~~fort~~ Pittsburg & takes in Lancaster, York, Carlisle Shippensburg & Chambersburg, another goes from Alexandria to Pittsburg & takes in Winchester. Our Petition prays that these two posts may meet at Hagers Town in which case Martinsburg & Sheppards Town will be taken in the line by the Alexandria post & Green-Castle by the Philadelphia post, We further petition that another post may be established from Baltimore to Hagers Town and make it appear that thirty one Miles riding is saved to the United States after taking into the line of inland Communication Frederick Town, Hagers Town, Sheppar Town Martinsburg & Green-Castle. I woud have call'd on you on my way from Martinsburg to this place, but immagine your assent or approbation to such a measure signified in a Letter to Colo. [*Thomas*] Hart to accompany the Petition will have more weight than your barely signing a Petition, We think of forwarding our Petition by Genl. [*Joseph*] Heister who will leave Hagers Town the last of next week, shall therefore be happy to hear from you on the subject before he goes.

ALS, Stauffer Collection, NN. Written from Shepherdstown, West Virginia. Horatio Gates may have been the recipient.

OTHER DOCUMENTS

Thomas Fitzsimons to Alexander Hamilton. ALS, Hamilton Papers, DLC. Written from Philadelphia. For the full text, see *PAH* 5:520–21.

Problems with implementing the revenue system at Philadelphia.

Thomas Fitzsimons to Samuel Meredith. ALS, Dreer Collection, PHi. Written from Philadelphia.

Office seeking: "I shall apply to you with freedom when I have Occasion for your Service: it is for you to Judge whether what I Require be proper & to Act Accordingly"; asks him to apply to Nicholas Eveleigh on behalf of a job for Clement Buren in the comptroller's office.

THURSDAY, 19 NOVEMBER 1789

James Madison to Alexander Hamilton. Printed in *DHFFC* 18.
Second session subject matter.

George Washington, Diary. Washington Papers, DLC. For the full text, see *DGW* 5:499.
Dined with the Butlers, among others.

FRIDAY, 20 NOVEMBER 1789

James Madison to George Washington

***

You will recollect the contents of a letter shewn you from Mr. [*Harry*] Innis to Mr. Brown. Whilst I was in Philada. I was informed by the latter who was detained there, as well as myself by indisposition, that he had recd. later accounts though not from the same correspondent, that the Spaniards have finally put an entire stop to the trade of our Citizens down the [*Mississippi*] river. The encouragements to such as settle under their own Government are continued.

A day or two after I got to Philada. I fell in with Mr. Morris. He broke the subject of the residence of Congs., and made observations which betrayed his dislike of the upshot of the business at N. York, and his desire to keep alive the Southern project of an arrangement with Pennsylvania. I reminded him of the conduct of his State, and intimated that the question would probably sleep for some time in consequence of it. His answer implied that Congress must not continue at New York, and that if he should be freed from his Engagements with the E[*astern*]. States by their refusal to take up the bill and pass it as it went to the [*lined out*] Senate, he should renounce all confidence in that quarter, and speak ~~in earnest~~ seriously to the S[*outhern*]. States. I told him they must be spoken to very seriously, after what had passed, if Penna. expected them to listen to her, that indeed there was probably an end to further intercourse on the subject. He signified that if he should speak it would be in earnest, and he believed no ~~would~~ one would pretend that his conduct would justify the least distrust of his going throug[h] with his undertakings; adding however that he was determined & accordingly gave me as he had given others notice that he should call up the postponed bill as soon as Congs. should be re-assembled. I observed to him that if it were desirable to have the matter revived we could not wish to have it in a form more likely to defeat itself. It was unparliamentary and highly inconvenient; and would therefore be opposed by all candid friends to his object as an improper precedent, as well as by those who were opposed to the object itself. And if he should succeed in the Senate, the irregularity of the proceeding would justify the other House in withholding the signature of its Speaker, so that the bill could never go up to the President. He acknowledged that the bill could not be got thro' unless it had a majority in both houses on its merits. Why then, I asked, not take it up anew? He said he meant to bring the gentlemen who had postponed the bill to the point, acknowledged that he distrusted them, but held his engagements binding on him, until this final experiment should be made on the respect they meant to pay to theirs. I do not think it difficult to augur from this conversation the views which will govern Penna. at the next Session. Conversations held by Grayson both with Morris & others in Philada. and left by him in a letter to me,[1] coincide with what I have stated. An attempt will first be made to alarm N. York and the Eastern States into the plan postponed, by holding out the Potowmac & Philada. as the alternative, and if the attempt should not succeed, the alternative will then be held out to the Southern members. On the other hand N.Y. & the E. States, will enforce their policy of delay, by threatening the S. States ~~with~~ as heretofore, with German Town or Trenton or at least Susquehannah, ~~I presume of an~~ [*lined out*] ~~with Pennsylvania~~ and will no doubt carry the threat into execution if they can, rather than suffer an arrangement to take place between Pena. & the S. States.

***

ALS, Washington Papers, DLC. Written from Orange, Virginia. Some blotted out text is supplied from a FC in Madison's hand (Madison Papers, DLC). For the full text, see *PJM* 12:451–53. Most of the omitted text relates to the Virginia legislature's ratification of the proposed Amendments to the Constitution.

[1] See 7 October, above.

SUNDAY, 22 NOVEMBER 1789

Phineas Bond to the Duke of Leeds. ALS, Foreign Office, 4/7 pp. 339, PRO. Written from Philadelphia. For the full text, see *AHA*, pp. 656–58.

"Being seldom at the Seat of Goverment, my Lord, I have no Opportunity of making fit Inquiries from the Deputies of the different States, which a frequent Intercourse with them, would afford."

John Chaloner to Jeremiah Wadsworth. ALS, Wadsworth Papers, CtHi. Written from Philadelphia; addressed to Hartford, Connecticut.

Informs Wadsworth that his carriage would not be ready until January and would be sent to New York by the time Congress sits.

Elbridge Gerry to Ann Gerry. ALS, Gerry Papers, MHi. Written from Cambridge, Massachusetts; addressed to New York.

Has not yet found his trunk; "so many unhappy events in so short a period produced a depression of spirits which I was apprehensive would destroy my health *** but God be praised I retain my health & have recovered in a great degree from the distresses of my mind"; Dalton called on his way back to New York; the Vice President also stopped by but they missed each other.

Alexander Hamilton to Silvanus Bourn. ALS, Miscellaneous Manuscripts, NHi. For the full text, see *PAH* 5:536.

Office seeking: "I did however, as Mr. Ames communicated to you, inform him, that nothing then was in my power" to appoint Bourn to an office.

MONDAY, 23 NOVEMBER 1789

Abraham Baldwin to the Speaker of the Georgia House of Representatives. FC, Baldwin Papers, NHi.

If he does not get paid for his service as a delegate to the Confederation Congress at New York, "I cannot think of returning to that place, without being enabled in some measure to meet the expectations of those [*his creditors*] who have so long reposed confidence in my own promises."

Thomas Fitzsimons to Pierce Butler. No copy known; acknowledged in Butler to Fitzsimons, 30 November.

Mercy Otis Warren to [Elbridge Gerry]. ALS, Fogg Collection, MeHi. Written from Plymouth, Massachusetts.

"Mr. [*James*] Warren bids me thank you for your friendly interposition in a late instance where Justice has long been denied him"; expresses sympathy on the death of Gerry's child.

TUESDAY, 24 NOVEMBER 1789

David Sewall to George Washington. ALS, Miscellaneous Letters, RG 59, DNA. Written from York, Maine. For the full text, see *PGW* 4:322–23.

"But from the laws of the United States hitherto Enacted, it strikes me, that some other provision is necessary to be made, before a Trial of this nature [*for piracy*] can with propriety be had: And more specially, in case of Conviction, to have the Judgement carried into Execution. These difficulties I shall take the liberty of stating to some Gentlemen in the legislature, to the end they may be there considered and obviated; rather than arrest your attention from the many other important businesses of the Union."

George Washington, Diary. Washington Papers, DLC. For the full text, see *DGW* 5:500.

Took the Schuylers, the Kings, and Butler (Mrs. Butler was ill) to the theater.

WEDNESDAY, 25 NOVEMBER 1789

Henry Lee to James Madison

*** The enmity to govt. is I beleive as strong as ever in this state. Indeed I have no doubt of this fact if the assembly be considered as a just Index of the feelings of the people. Never adventure direct taxation for years—This event now would be attended with serious consequences. Can you not make your W[*estern*]. lands equal to the support of your domestic debt & its redemption. This being done will the revenue arising from commerce be sufficient for the support of govt. & the payment of the interest on the foreign debt. I hope so, for indeed if it is not I am at a loss to see what you will or can do.

I have not heard of Mr. Jefferson's arrival yet nor have I heard from him in reply to our proposition.[1] Soon we shall know I suppose & then I hope we shall be enabled to use the property at the [*Great*] falls.

***

ALS, Madison Papers, DLC. Written from Richmond, Virginia. For the full text, see *PJM* 12:454–55.

¹ The proposal was to generate European interest in land speculation at Great Falls, Virginia, on the Potomac River.

George Washington to Robert Hanson Harrison

***

I find that one of the Reasons, which induced you to decline the appointment,¹ rests on an idea that the Judicial Act will remain unaltered. But in respect to that circumstance, I may suggest to you, that such a change in the system is contemplated, and deemed expedient by many in, as well as out of Congress, as would permit you to pay as much attention to your private affairs as your present station does.

As the first Court will not sit until the first Monday in Febry., I have thought proper to return your Commission, not for the sake of urging you to accept it contrary to your interest or convenience, but with a view of giving you a farther opportunity of informing yourself of the nature & probability of the change alluded to. This you would be able to do with the less risque of mistake, if you should find it convenient to pass sometime here, when a considerable number of Members of both houses of Congress shall have assembled; and this might be done before it would become indispensable to fill the place offered to you. If, on the other hand, your determination is absolutely fixed, you can, without much trouble, send back the Commission, under cover.

***

ALS, House Records, 22nd Congress, DNA. This letter was submitted with other documentation in support of a petition to the 22nd Congress from Harrison's daughters Sarah Easton and Dorothy Storer, seeking his unpaid benefits as a Continental Army officer.

¹ Washington had informed Harrison on 28 September of his appointment as a Supreme Court justice. Harrison declined on the grounds that the duties were extremely difficult and burdensome (*PGW* 4:98–102).

OTHER DOCUMENTS

George Washington, Diary. Washington Papers, DLC. For the full text, see *DGW* 5:501.

Visited Izard, Schuyler, and Mrs. Dalton; dined with the Smiths (S.C.), the Izards, and the Johnsons.

THURSDAY, 26 NOVEMBER 1789

Daniel Cony to George Thatcher. ALS, Thomas G. Thornton Papers, MeHi.
Written from Hallowell, Maine; addressed to Biddeford, Maine; carried by
Henry Sewall.

> Wants to know when Thatcher will return to Congress, when there will
> be "a new arrangment" of the post office, if it will "be necessary for the
> Citizens in this quarter to take any further measures to have a post office
> established in this Town"; argues that the "Court of justice" (federal dis-
> trict court) should be held there as well, rather than at Pownalsborough;
> road from Portland to "utmost limits of the United States" runs through
> Hallowell which will "undoubtedly be the most considerable Merchan-
> tile Power and place of business, Portland excepted, in the District."

FRIDAY, 27 NOVEMBER 1789

John Wendell to Elbridge Gerry

Your esteemed favour of 14th. Septr. I have had the Honour to receive but
not to acknowledge before Now I hope your Indulgence of a Pardon when I
assure you it was not from the want of a due Sense I have of the Obligation
I am under to you for your Judicious Remarks on the operation of the experimental political Constitution of the Union—the more I consider it, the
more distressing it appears to me, and should direct Taxation take Place, I
pronounce without Hesitation its Subversion—but that horrid Engine of
Perdition, the federal Court, which has never been yet thought on by the
People, will prove to be an Instrument equal to the Inquisition of Spain or
the Bastile of France[1] which must & will be eradicated, For Heavens Sake,
my Friend what is to become of our fellow Citizens who happen to be in debt
to a Citizen of other States or foreigner Upon a Judgment a Writ of facias
ad satisfaciendum[2] issues and his Property is taken from him for perhaps a
20th. Part of its Value without Redemption there being no alternative left
but a Prison or a Bankruptcy, the former will be more Eligible to a Person
of a large family who would prefer Imprisonment rather than the Distruction of his rising family—add to this the fatal Effects of the Power of this
Court without Controul, and even so absolute as to border on Despotism—
Here my Friend opens a Field for your inquisitive Mind to be exercising itself to check its Jurisdiction, One Amendment should be, by the Right of
Redemption for three years—This would check an inexorable Creditor who

in this dreadfull State of Poverty w[oul]d. monopolize the Estate of his Debtor, in the interior Parts of this State I dont believe Ten Dollars could be found in whole Township, Then what fatal Distruction w[oul]d. Executions make in such Towns—The summary Mode of Trial as Mr. Livermore observed,[3] would render Property too precarious, and our Prisons will soon be fill'd and even before the Debtor will be sensible of his Danger.
***

ALS, Gerry Papers, MHi. Written from Portsmouth, New Hampshire. Part of the omitted portion consoles Gerry on the death of his son.

[1] Since 1478, the Spanish Inquisition had been charged with rooting out heresy by censorship, torture, and its notorious autos-da-fé (burning at the stake). The Bastille, Paris's infamous prison from the fourteenth century until its demolition in the French Revolution, was a symbol of absolutism, arbitrary punishment, and terror.
[2] A writ authorizing seizure to satisfy a plaintiff's claim.
[3] This is probably a reference to Samuel Livermore's speech of 31 August as reported by GUS (see DHFFC 11:1375–76).

OTHER DOCUMENTS

Alexander Hamilton to Thomas Fitzsimons. Printed in DHFFC 18.
    Second session subject matter.

John Jay to Fisher Ames. William Jay, The Life of John Jay: With Selections from His Correspondence and Miscellaneous Papers (2 vols., New York, 1833), 2:201.
    Sedgwick gave Jay the same character of John Tucker as Ames had given.

SATURDAY, 28 NOVEMBER 1789

Henry Knox to Anthony Wayne

***

~~At present nothg.~~ During the recess of Congress nothg. can be decided upon as the two Houses possess the Constitutional right of makg. War. They will With difficulty be brought in to the measure—unless the necessity shall be apparent—If the Creeks make ~~war on Georgia~~ inroads into Georgia it must be presumed the government will act with decision and vigor.
***

FC:dft, Knox Papers, Gilder Lehrman Collection, NHi.

MONDAY, 30 NOVEMBER 1789

Pierce Butler to Thomas Fitzsimons. ALS, Gratz Collection, PHi. Addressed to Philadelphia.

Regarding payment of the money Butler owes Fitzsimons which was the subject of Fitzsimons' letter of 23 November.

Tench Coxe to Alexander Hamilton. FC, Coxe Papers, PHi. Written from Philadelphia. For the full text, see *PAH* 5:569–70.

Encloses his *"present State of the Navigation of Pennsylvania"*; "As the Gentlemen in the Senate for Pennsylvania, & Some of those in the House of Representatives have been pleased to request my Communications on the Subjects, that from time arises in the Legislature, I have taken the liberty to show this Paper to one or two of them; & indeed it seems to be a matter both of propreity & prudence, as I [am] a Citizen of Pennsylvania, & they are the Guardians of her interests."

Thomas Fitzsimons to Samuel Meredith. Printed in *DHFFC* 18.

Second session subject matter.

George Washington, Diary. Washington Papers, DLC. For the full text, see *DGW* 5:502.

Took the Daltons and the Johnsons to the theater.

Undated 1789

George Beckwith: *Conversations with Different Persons*

[*With William Samuel Johnson*]

[*Beckwith*] You have passed a Revenue bill, I have not seen it, but am informed it has been greatly modified in Your house; there are times, in which candour appears to me to be the best policy, and I am authorized to acquaint You, and the gentlemen in public office here, that had the Bill in question passed, as sent up from Your House of Representatives, with those discriminating clauses, which appeared in Your public papers, we were prepared to meet it; a discretionary power is by an annual Act of Parliament, vested in the King in Council for such purposes, and the continuance of the indulgencies shewn to Your shipping in our ports in Europe, depends upon Your own conduct.

[*Johnson*] We greatly modified the Bill in question in the Senate. In both Houses, but particularly in the House of Representatives, there is a very warm party; in the latter, Mr. Maddison, a Delegate from Virginia took a very active and leading part, he is an Eleve[1] of Mr. Jefferson's, who is still our Minister at Paris, and may be esteemed as not exempt from a French bias; this gentleman pushed the discriminating clauses with great warmth and spirit, and being a man of genius and talents, his exertions had a considerable influence in that house; their object doubtless was unfriendly to Great Britain, and favourable to France, but when the Bill came before us, the majority were too enlightened and too moderate, to approve such measures; they viewed the Act as a declaration of Commercial War, which it was neither just nor wise to commence against a powerful nation, and they took infinite pains to collect from the best materials, within their reach (which indeed were very indifferent ones) the real condition of our shipping in Your ports in Europe, and indifferent as these sources of information were, they furnished proofs of Your indulgencies, to which the advocates for discrimination could not oppose any solid reply. From these exertions the Bill has been reduced into its present form; all the powers of Europe, without exception, stand upon a similar footing, and it appears to me, that notwithstanding the operation of the Impost and Tonnage Acts You will possess many great advantages from our consumption, and from the import of our raw materials.

It was an argument used by the party, who passed the Impost bill, in the House of Representatives, as well as of those, who approved that measure in the Senate, that Great Britain would not be disposed to check the importation of raw materials, which She wanted, nor to impede so considerable a vent, as that which She found in our consumption, which is a great and an encreasing object, for a trifling consideration, and that they might depend on it, She would not risk such objects for a moderate encrease of duties; but, if she did, it was better for the States to suffer a temporary inconvenience, to look out for such articles from abroad, as were absolutely essential, and to use every exertion to create manufactures at home, than to persevere in a ruinous system; these arguments are at least plausible.

An other object of great importance to You is now in agitation; a Committee has some time since been appointed to consider the situation of our shipping in *the American Islands*, and in *the Continent of North America, not within the dominions of the States*; that is in other words in Your Provinces and in the West India Islands. This is doubtless pointed at You, and the majority of this committee being composed of Gentlemen, who were the advocates for a discrimination of duties, they made a speedy report, and wished to act on it; it had for its object; *the not permitting Your shipping to clear out from our ports, either for Your West India Islands, or for Your provinces upon this continent, but the senate thought it prudent to let the matter lay over until next session.*

With respect to General Washington I cannot pretend to determine from the conversations I have held with him, whether his mind is perfectly free from a French bias or not, but the moderate and thinking party wish greatly for a Commercial Treaty with Great Britain, and nothing would facilitate this more than the admission of small vessels into Your Islands under certain regulations. With respect to the Senate I think I can assure You, that the majority of this body are in a disposition to enter upon the consideration of such a subject dispassionately; with regard to the House of Representatives, and to the public, I should still pause in deciding.

I am upon the point of making a tour through a part of New England, in the course of which I shall meet with several members of the Legislature. Will You give me leave to mention Your communication to them?

[*Beckwith*] By all means.

[*Johnson*] For my own part I think the matter is in a narrow compass. Great Britain may think it an object to pass over the effects of the Impost and Tonnage Acts, for the sake of our consumption; we are considerable and encreasing customers, but to be sure, if she can command a market for her manufactures else where on better terms, she may be expected to resent it.

The Sessions on the whole has passed smoothly, and a foundation has been laid, from which much future good will arise. I think the Legislature will meet in January, with an improving spirit of moderation.

In the adjustment of late pecuniary arrangements, previous to our adjournment of yesterday, it was proposed to empower the President to apply certain sums of money towards the payment of ministers abroad, should *He* judge it necessary to send any to Europe, prior to our next meeting in January, but the Senate objected, and the clauses for this purpose, which formed a part of a general appropriation bill for the year, were struck out. No Minister will therefore be sent, and indeed, if one had gone to London, he would not have been a person of a disposition to promote those views of harmony and friendship between the two Countries, which I have at heart; it would have been a second edition of Mr. Adams.[2]

There has been a late application to Lord Dorchester, for the purpose of ascertaining the Longitude of a certain part of one of the Great Lakes, in order to determine a matter in contest between two of the States, to effect which it is necessary to come upon Your territories.[3] As to the idea of any application at this time, relative to the western Forts, it is not founded.

I am naturally well disposed to the Country, in which I live, and however I may lament and condemn the dismemberment of a great Empire, to the government and principles of which I have ever been strongly attached, in the present posture of affairs I certainly cannot have any views or motives unconnected with the general good, but I do think that, in the hands of able and dispassionate men, a system might be formed to the advantage of both countries. To suppose that Great Britain should in any shape sollicit our Commercial Friendship is idle, and absurd; there are individuals, who profess such opinions, but the more enlighten'd part of the Senate hold them to be ridiculous; were this to be done I should be sorry for it.

I regret Mr. Jay's removal from the Department of Foreign Affairs, as he is a man of a just and firm character; his successor Mr. Jefferson I do not so much approve of.

North Carolina will join the Union during the next Sessions. I think Rhode Island must follow shortly afterwards.

[With Philip Schuyler]

[*Beckwith*] Having upon different occasions had the honor of conversing with You upon very important subjects, I wish to take the present opportunity to speak freely to You upon a point of some consequence, in which You are the more interested from being a member of the Upper House. Amongst other important Acts, that You have passed during the present session, there is a Bill, which underwent a long and spirited discussion, which in consequence found its way into Your News papers, and from thence was reprinted in London. From the complexion of that Bill in some of its early stages, and from the language of many of the gentlemen, who debated it, it has been considered by us, as a mark of the disposition of the New Government, how it has been modified afterwards (for I have lately heard it has undergone a very considerable degree of alteration) I do not know, but if it had passed into a law with those discriminations, which it was originally stated to contain, I am authorized to say that it would have produced, on our part, an immediate abrogation of those indulgencies, which the Shipping of the States enjoy in our ports in Europe. Our Cabinet regret this necessity, and will be guided by the conduct of the States in those respects.

Whilst You were without an efficient Government, and some of the local Legislatures adopted such measures, we did not take any steps whatever, trusting that the formation of a strong government here would lead to their repeal, but if one of the first measures of the present government had such objects in view, the case was materially altered, and certainly if the States chose to mark commercial hostility to us, we were to lose no time in changing our system.[4]

[Schuyler] The discriminating clauses in question were greatly disapproved in our House, where the Bill was modified; and, as it passed into a law, leaves no distinction whatever between the different powers of Europe; and I can further assure You, it was generally regretted by us, that the nature of our treaties with France did not admit of our giving a decided preference to Great Britain; for my own part, my opinion is, that a firm connexion with You, is to be preferred to that of all the powers of Europe besides; the President wishes well to this principle, so does the Vice President, who is the speaker of the Senate, and who, although from thence without a right to debate questions, did request leave to give his opinion during the discussion of this Bill; and I must say his sentiments gave me much satisfaction. The French Minister [Comte de Moustier] did exert all his influence upon this business, and marked no little dissatisfaction upon its failure.

As to our sending a Minister to You the President did apply for a general power to defray the expences necessary for the support of Ministers in Europe, should such a step be requisite before our next meeting in January, but the Senate being of opinion, that the extent of those appointments ought to depend upon the character of the men employed, and the nature of the objects, this command over the public purse was withheld.

Would You send a Minister to Us, if we sent one to You?

Will You permit me to mention this conversation to __ (see seventh [Hamilton])?

[Beckwith] I cannot give You any answer to Your first question; to the last I have not the smallest difficulty in saying "by all means."

***

With Alexander Hamilton

[*Beckwith*] Sir, I have mentioned to ___ (see second [*Schuyler*]), what would have been the effect of Your Revenue Bill, had it passed in the form in which it appeared from Your Prints, with those discriminating clauses, which undoubtedly were levelled at us. . . . He requested my permission to communicate this to You, and I believe I may conclude that this conversation arises from that source.

[*Hamilton*] It does.

[*Beckwith*] I thought it consistent with the spirit of that communication, not to withhold it, notwithstanding the modifications, which afterwards took place, although I can give no opinion whatever, as to the effects, which it may produce, under its present form, nor to the light in which we may view it at home; I speak very freely to You, but you will of course readily comprehend, that now, this is merely private conversation.

[*Hamilton*] Certainly, and in Your situation, mine cannot be esteemed anything more, although I can assure You, that the ideas I have thrown out, may be depended upon, as the sentiments of the most enlightened men in this country, they are those of General Washington, I can confidently assure You, as well as of a great majority in the Senate.

***

[*Beckwith*] As you have done me the honour of mentioning to me the turn of party, during Your late sessions, I cannot avoid saying that I was much surprized to find amongst the gentlemen, who were so decidedly hostile to us in their public conduct, the name of a man, from whose character for good sense, and other qualifications, I should have been led to expect a very different conduct.

[*Hamilton*] You mean Mr. Maddison from Virginia. I confess I was likewise rather surprized at it, as well as that the only opposition to General Washington was from thence. The truth is, that although this gentleman is a clever man, he is very little acquainted with the world. That he is uncorrupted and incorruptible I have not a doubt; he has the same end in view that I have, and so have those gentlemen, who act with him, but their mode of attaining it is very different. You have I take it for granted seen our Debates?

***

[*Hamilton*] If the present favourable occasion shall pass away, and a system of Commercial Warfare shall take place, it may lead to the adoption of an other idea, in the contemplation of gentlemen, who are advocates for discrimination, and which did not respect a Tonnage, or Impost duties, but had in view *a much stronger measure.*

[*Beckwith*] N. B. He did not say what it was, but I understood it to mean the idea of shutting their ports to our shipping, that might wish to clear out either for our possessions in North America, or the West Indies, with lumber, provisions &c.

***

Copy, Colonial Office 42/66, pp. 278–309, PRO. The ellipses are in the source. For the full text, see Douglas Brymner, *Report on Canadian Archives . . . 1790* (Ottawa, 1891), pp. 121–29. These conversations were sent to Lord Dorchester at Quebec who sent them to Lord Grenville in London on 25 October 1789. Those whom Beckwith interviewed were identified by a numbered code; the key to which was provided in a separate document. Johnson was "No. 1," Schuyler was "No. 2," and Hamilton was "No. 7." Other important individuals Beckwith interviewed later in the First Congress included Jay, Knox, R. H. Lee, Paterson, Ames, Scott, and Sherman. For an exhaustive treatment of Beckwith's role in the First Congress, see Julian P. Boyd, *Number 7: Alexander Hamilton's Secret Attempts to Control American Foreign Policy* (Princeton, 1964).

[1] Disciple.
[2] John Adams served as American minister to Great Britain from 1785 to 1788.
[3] On 4 September, acting Secretary of Foreign Affairs John Jay wrote Lord Dorchester requesting permission for Andrew Ellicott to enter Canadian territory in order to determine the longitude of the westernmost point of Lake Ontario. According to New York's 1781 act of cession and a Congressional resolution of 6 June 1788, that line, if greater than twenty miles west of the westernmost bend of the Straits of Niagara, was to be considered New York State's western boundary. Pennsylvania's annexation of the public domain that lay beyond it—the so-called Erie Triangle—had already been confirmed by Congress in September 1788 (*PGW* 3:602; *DHFFC* 8:192–94).
[4] Following this paragraph are several lines of dashes. The number of dashes varies from line to line, suggesting some kind of code.

AEDANUS BURKE'S PROPOSED HISTORY
OF THE CONSTITUTIONAL REVOLUTION OF 1787–88

Probably just after the first session of the First Federal Congress ended,[1] the South Carolina Antifederalist Representative Aedanus Burke drafted a questionnaire for the purpose of gathering information for "a regular History of the late remarkable revolution in Government." Samuel Bryan, author of the influential "Centinel" essays, thought there was "every reason to believe [*the history*] will be highly advantageous to the interests of republicanism."[2] Writing to his wife on 15 November 1789 while traveling home to Cambridge, Massachusetts, from New York City, Gerry described in detail the incidents surrounding the theft of one of his trunks. He listed among the items stolen "a number of Interrogatories from Judge Burke which I had never read respecting political information he wanted."[3]

Bryan and Gerry, both prominent Antifederalists during the ratification campaign, were the only individuals to whom Burke is known to have submitted his questionnaire. Bryan in turn appealed to John Nicholson in late

November for help in framing his response. He was particularly interested in obtaining from Pennsylvania's comptroller general some statistics indicative of "the excessive imports that were made of foreign goods, and thus account for the distresses of the Country, which led to the late change in the federal government."[4] Nicholson kept the questionnaire among his papers and it remains the only version known to exist. The phrasing indicates that it was specifically adapted to the circumstances of Pennsylvania and neighboring states. The questionnaire submitted to Gerry was likely cast in terms appropriate to the New England states. Joined with Burke's own interpretation of the events of 1787–88 in the Southern states, the three sets of answers could have constituted a survey of the entire nation.

Bryan mailed a response to Burke sometime during the middle of December. It arrived at Charleston after Burke's departure for the second session of the FFC, and was forwarded to New York City, where Burke acknowledged its receipt on 3 March 1790. Whether Burke made any use of the response is not known, in part because he ordered his papers burned at his death.

---

[1] This supposition is based on the existence of Burke to Gerry, 10 October, noted above, and the fact that both Gerry and Bryan mentioned the request in November.
[2] To John Nicholson, 21 November 1789, Nicholson Papers, PHarH.
[3] Gerry Papers, MHi.
[4] 5 December 1789, Nicholson Papers, PHarH.

Burke's Questionnaire

General Convention of 1787

1. In what State, and in what year was the measure proposed? What were the causes which led to the measure? by what men, or body of men or party? Or was it for the purpose of investing Congress with any additional and what powers then deemed necessary? Tell particularly.

2. What was the State of navigation, trade, and the General, and particular State police of the Union about the latter end of the year 1786? Or at that time was there in the States in general, and in any, and what particular State, what is commonly called *Anarchy*? or a spirit in the people of Licentiousness? or of enmity to their magistrates, or opposition or dislike to order and Government? Was the embarrassments of the U.S. at that period & since the peace owing to this kind of spirit? or to other & what causes? Tell particularly.

3. To what cause necessity or pretext, was it owing, that after the peace, the commerce and navigation of the U.S. was ruined? Why their credit abroad & confidence at home lost? To what cause is it to be ascribed their

issuing paper money? Or what States did issue such money? The terms of redeeming it in each State, the consequence of such paper emissions—its intrinsic value.

4. Was there in 1786 or at any time before that period any influential men, or any, and what party, and in what States, whose views, interests or sentiments were unfavorable, or otherwise to the popular Govt. or favorable to a regal one? Or if so from what motives? Or was there any party, and who were they inclined to avail themselves of the popularity of a certain *personage* [*Washington*] to bring about any, and what revolution in the Government?

5. When the different States appointed delegates to the Convention, what was the general opinion of the people of Pennsylvania or its neighbouring States concerning the powers & duty which those delegates were about to execute? Or was it in contemplation of the people, or of any and what part, that the republican system of Govt. should be overturned, or materially altered? What was the opinion of the people, their attachment, or dislike to the Confederation? If it was deemed practicable were it amended by conferring more authority in affairs relating to commerce? or what other affairs?

6. What is your opinion, whether confederate Republics can manage the affairs of the Confederacy, in the mode of the old Confederation; or by putting the powers of the Confederacy into high departments, & parcelling it out after the form of a regal Govt. as at present?

7. What are the special words of the act of Pennsylvania & neighbouring States, by which authority is given to their respective delegates for the Convention?

8. At what time did the General Convention meet, & in what part of Philadelphia? And in what manner public or private, was the business or debates conducted? Or if the Convention was split into any and what parties? Or if a certain personage took any and what active part, in framing the system? The history and proceedings of this Convention is particularly requested.

9. Did the Cincinnati [1] meet at the time the Convention sat or not? What part was taken by that Society then or afterwards.

10. What were ~~the Public op~~ the public opinion & expectations of the Convention's proceedings while they sat? Or did the public or any party, expect any system of govt. like that which was offered, or not?

11. When the new system the result of their deliberations, was offered to the Public, what was the effect produced on the minds of the public upon the subject? Or did the people split into any and what faction or party in consequence.

12. What part or side was taken by the following classes of citizens of Pennsylvania & elsewhere vizt.

Cincinnati	Mechanics	
Civil Officers	Seafaring men	
Monied men	Creditors	
Merchants	Debtors	
Lawyers	Middle Country	
Divines	Sea Coast	Inhabitants
Men of Letters	Back Country	
Whigs	Foreigners—	
Tories		
Women		

Which of all these were instrumental, and to what extent, and from what views or motives for or against the system?

13. What was their temper & disposition of the two parties against each other? What party names—or if any beside federalist and Antifedt.? Who invented the latter names? What effect had it?

14. Among those who were in opposition to the new-system, was there any preconcert, correspondence or mutual understanding to act with unanimity? Or if not thro' what cause was it neglected or omitted?

15. Among the federalists was there any such preconcert, or system of mutual aid, in any and what States, and what men or party combined to adopt the New Constitution? And what was the nature of such combination?

16. Was there any attempt and what to prevent an investigation of its merits? Or any was there sufficient given for that purpose? or take the opinion of the people on it? or any attempt made by the antifederalists to gain time & for what purpose, or to prevent publications on the subject?

17. Or did the federalists use any and what means to prevent any such publications from going forth? or to intercept letters or communications [?] What use was made of the Post-Office, and by whose means or agency was it done?

18. What were the principal publications for and against the New-System? Who the reputed authors?

19. How soon after the system was offered to the public that the Legislatures of and States of Pennsylvania, Jersey, Delaware &ca. took it up, and passed it—the history of this business in Pennsylvania.

20. If any arts used to accelerate its adoption? or to elect, or reject for State Convention, such as were friendly, or otherwise to the system? When Convention met, what the temper of the parties? In discussing the system, whether violent, insolent, or otherwise?

21. Who were the leading and influential men in Pennsylvania in favor of it? Their names? Who in Jersey? Who in Delaware and Maryland? Their views and character.

22. In those States who were the Leading and influential Antifederalists? and from what parts of the States?

23. In State Convention of Pennsylvania or Legislature, was there a secession of some of the members? How many and for what cause? Were they not made prisoners and forced back again to form a house? by whom and in what manner—the history of this business.

[24] Was the Constitution adopted in Pennsylvania in consequence of such force put on the seceding members? Was it resented by the public? If not why? How palliated or justified by the federalists? Conduct of minority after adoption? Their protest or address how received by their constituents?

24 [25]. Through this whole business, what was the spirit of the populace of the City, or low Country? or were the Anti's in any fear or danger of writing or speaking against the Constitution? Or was there any Mob to crush or punish opposition or was it practicable to raise a mob—the history of this business.

26. If any and what arts used by the federalists to mislead or deceive the people to adopt it? or to suppress the publications or objections of the other party?

27. If any rumours, or false reports spread to defame, or ascribe any and what improper motives to the opposition of the Anti's—what were the arts used?

28. If any and what impediments in the Printing offices—the conduct and character of the Printers in general in this business? Were there any Printers and who & where, who opposed the Constitution? Or were Printers under any and what fear or restraint to publish against the New-System? Or did the Printers act independently or otherwise?

29. How far was the Press instrumental in bringing about the Revolution in Govt.? Or could this be brought about without availing themselves as they did of the partiality of the Printers?

30. Were any Printers, and who abused, or oppressed or had subscriptions withdrawn for ~~the~~ publishing against the system? The treatment to Coll. [*Eleazer*] Oswald, [*Thomas*] Greenleaf [*lined out*] and what other Printers?

Ms, hand of Samuel Bryan, John Nicholson Papers, PHarH.

[1] Burke was an early and prominent critic of the Society of the Cincinnati, joining many who thought it politically subversive. Burke's influential philippic, *Considerations on the Order of the Cincinnati*, published in 1783 under the pseudonym "Cassius," was reprinted several times in the United States, England, Germany, and France.

Response to Aedanus Burke's Questionnaire
Submitted by Samuel Bryan after 5 December 1789

1. Previous to the Appointment of the Convention there seemed to be in Pennsylvania a general Wish for a more efficient Confederation. The public

Debt was unpaid & unfunded. We were deluged with foreign Goods, which it was evident might have paid large Sums to the Continental Treasury, if Duties could have been generally laid & collected, & at the same Time the levying such Duties would have checked the extravagant Consumption. Whilst Congress could only recommend Measures & the States individually could refuse to execute them it was obvious that we were in Danger of falling to Pieces. The opposition of Rhode Island to the five per Cent had made a deep Impression upon Peoples Minds. A Desire of strengthening the Hands of Congress was very general; but no particular Scheme seemed to be digested, except that most Men seemed to wish Congress possessed of power to levy Duties on imported Goods. At this Time the Convention was proposed & Members were elected for Pennsylvania about the Beginning of the Year 1787; I do not remember the particular Time. Very little Bustle was made & little or no Opposition. What has been called the anti constitutional or Aristocratic Party then governed our Councils and the Representatives in Convention were chosen almost wholly of that Party & I think entirely from the City of Philadelphia. The Convention met without much Expectation of any thing very important being done by them till towards the Close, altho some Intimations were made, before hand, by some foolish Members (as they were thought) of the Society of Cincinnatus that Nothing less than a Monarchy was to be erected & that the People of Massachusetts were driven into Rebellion for the very Purpose of smoothing the Way to this Step by their Suppression. Little Regard however was paid to these Speeches till towards the Close of the Session of the Convention, when Surmises were spread from other Quarters that Something injurious to the Liberties of the People was about to be produced. These Surmises were again contradicted in some Degree; and the Convention rose with favourable Prospects.

2. I am not able to give[1] a particular State of Trade in Pennsylvania in 1786. But in General it was in a very unfavourable Situation. Our Navigation was almost wholly in the Hands of Foreigners, chiefly English; and a great Part of the Negotiation & Sale of Merchandize was in the same hands. The numerous Classes of Tradesmen who depend on Trade Commerce & particularly those who depend on Navigation were distressed. There was no Anarchy nor any considerable Degree of Licentiousness in Pennsylvania. Party Spirit was high; but much more violent on Paper than any where else. The Tories, with the Spirit of Chagrin & Resentment which flowed from their Disappointments & what they called Persecution (chiefly arising from the Test law) had taken Side with the Anticonstitutional or aristocratic Party in Opposition to the Constitutionalists who had before held the Reins of Government. But on the whole we were much more peaceable & orderly than our Neighbours, who read our Newspapers, believed us to be. And

Pennsylvania, all along, besides supporting her own Government, had given the most effectual Aid to the United States, particularly in Money.

3. The Ruin of the Commerce & Navigation of the United States was owing to a Concurrence of Causes. Some of the Northern Fisheries had been long nourished by Bounties from Great Britain before the War; and these Bounties ~~have been~~ were now withdrawn. We had a Deluge of Money at the Close of the War, which raised the Prices of our own Commodities at home and the vast Diminution of Industry ~~helped~~ increased this Mischief. Trade during the War had fallen into the Hands of successful, but ignorant, Adventurers who did not understand Commerce. The English Manufacturers at the End of the War, were vastly overloaded with those kinds of Goods, which were calculated only for the American Markets, and they crowded them upon us by the Hands of their own Clerks & Agents, in such immense Quantities, that it was impossible for us ever to pay for them. These Goods were either sold for small Prices or trusted out without Discretion & never paid for. ~~The paper Money issued since the War in Pennsylvania was~~ But the Exclusion of our Ships from so many of the British & French Ports & the Want of Mediterranean Passes[2] have contributed to the Destruction of our Navigation more than all other Causes.

As to the Paper Money of Pennsylvania which has been issued since the War, it was made in 1785 for the Purpose of establishing Funds for Payment of the Interest to public Creditors & to lend to such as were under the Necessity of borrowing, at a Time when there were very few private Lenders. I am not well acquainted with the Detail of its Funds, Quantities & Times of Redemption. It has too much fluctuated in its Credit & has been as low as 33⅓ ℔ Cent Discount. In Jersey the same Motives for issuing Paper money prevailed & its Fate has been similar. I understand it is now at two thirds of its nominal Value.

4. When the federal Constitution was proposed to the People, the Desire of increasing the Powers of Congress was great & this Object had a mighty Influence in its Favor. The Popularity of Genl. W[ashington]. & Doctor [Benjamin] Franklin had still more. The People in the Towns who depended, in any Measure, on Trade, expected great Relief from it. The Gentlemen of the late Army, & the Tools of Aristocracy were loud in its Support; and as the chief Opposition to it was believed to arise from such as belonged to the Constitutional Party, the whole Body of the old Tories, a numerous & wealthy Sett of Men, joined in its Support. There is too much Reason to believe that some Men among us had deeper Views than they chose to declare & wished a Government even less popular than the one proposed; but in Pennsylvania they have been very reserved on this Head. The Opposition was very powerful & their Language was for adopting the Constitution & procuring Amendments afterwards.

5. I have anticipated this Question.

6. The Writer of this had confined his Views of Alteration to be made in the old Confederation to a mere Enlargement of the Powers of Congress, particularly as to maritime Affairs. He thinks the Experiment ought at least to have been tried, whether we could not have succeeded under a Confederation of independent States, before we proceeded to consolidate all Power in one general Government.

7. A Copies³ of the Acts of Assembly, which are public, will furnish the best Answer to this Question.

8. The Convention sat in the State house & debated in Private. It has nevertheless been said &, I suppose, is beyond a Doubt that they Members were much divided & that the present Form of Constitution was agreed to as a Compromise, when they had almost despaired of agreeing upon any one.

9. The Cincinnati met shortly before the Convention. Some speeches of Individuals in private Companies were reported to the Effect before mentioned.

10. This is anticipated.

11. When the System was published some Writers in the News papers stated many Objections to it. The Party in opposition were the old Constitutional Whiggs for the most part. Numbers of these however &, especially in the Towns, joined in supporting the new federal Constitution.

12. The Cincinnati were in Support of it.

The civil Officers were threatned in News paper Publications, if they should oppose, & were mostly in favor [of] it.

Monied Men & particularly the Stockholders in the Bank were in favor of it.

The Merchants in favor of it.

Lawyers—the greatest part in favor of it.

Divines of all Denominations, with very few Exceptions, in favor of it. They had suffered by Paper Money.

Men of Letters, many of them, were opposed to it.

Whigs—the Majority of them opposed to it.

Tories—almost all for it.

The Women—all admire Genl. W[*ashington*].

Mechanics—such as depend on Commerce & Navigation in favor. The others divided according to their former Attachments to the Revolution & Constitution of Pennsylvania or their Prejudices against them.

Seafaring Men followed the Mercantile Interest & were strenuous in favor of it.

Creditors were influenced in favor of it by their Aversion to Paper money; yet some were opposed to it.

Debtors are often Creditors in their Turn & the Paper money had great

Effect on Men's Minds. The Public Creditors were much divided, according to their ~~other~~ former Predilections & Attachments.

The Counties nearest the Navigation were in favor of it generally; those more remote in Opposition. The Farmers were perhaps more numerous in Opposition than any other Sett of Men. Most Townsmen were for it.

The Foreigners were chiefly connected with the Mercantile People & were in favor of it. Even the foreign Seamen were made *useful* to the Support of it in Philadelphia.[4]

13. The Party Names, before the Convention sat, were Whigs & Tories, which Names were wearing out; and Constitutionalists & those who called themselves Republicans & who were also called Aristocratics & Anticonstitutionalists. In this last Class were included most of the Merchants, most of the monied Men, most of the Gentlemen in the late Army & many of the Mob in the Towns.

The Name of Federalists or Federal Men grew up at New York & in the Eastern States, some Time before the Calling of the Convention, to denominate such as were attached to the general Support of the United States, in Opposition to those who preferred local & particular Advantages, such as those who opposed the five per Cent Duty or who with held their Quotas of Contribution to the general Treasury of the United States. This Name was taken possession of by those who were in favor of the new federal Government as they called it & the opposers were called Antifederalists.

14. Those in Opposition seem to have had no Preconcert, nor any Suspicion of what was coming forward. The same Objections were made in different Parts of the Continent, almost at the same Time, merely as they were obviously dictated by the Subject. Local Ideas seem to have entered very little into the Objections.

15. The Evidence of a preconcerted System, in those who are called Federalists, appears rather from the Effect than from any certain knowledge before hand. The thing however must have been easy to them from their Situation in the great Towns & many of them being wealthy Men & Merchants, who have continual Correspondence with each other.

16. The Printers were certainly most of them more willing to publish for, than against the new Constitution. They depended more upon the People in the Towns than in the Country. The Towns People withdrew their Subscriptions from those who printed Papers against, and violent Threats were thrown out against the Antis & Attempts were made to injure them in their Business.

17. Letters were frequently intercepted, & some of them selected & published by the Federalists. Private Conversation was listened to by Evesdroppers. Pamphlets & Newspapers were stopt & destroyed. This was the

more easily done as most of the Towns, even down to the smallest Villages, were in possession of the Federalists. I can say Nothing about the Post Office.
18. The Writer of this has very imperfect knowledge on this Subject.
19. In Pennsylvania the Business of the Ratification was extremely hurried. The Assembly voted, if I remember right, to call a Convention for its Ratification before they were officially notified of its being recommended by Congress; and the Election was hurried through before it was generally known what was doing. Many even in the Counties not very remote were totally uninformed of any Election being intended before it was finished. I have not Materials to be more particular.
20. In the State Convention the Behavior of the Federalists was highly insolent & contemptuous. Out of Doors, even in Philadelphia, their Behavior was more moderate after the Election for Members of Congress than before. The Election had discovered a Degree of Strength in the Antis which they did not expect & which Nothing but Surprize & the Accident of extreme bad Weather ~~could ha~~ which was unfavorable to the collecting of People scattered thro the Country could have got the better of. There was one Instance of Violence ~~afterward but it~~ a short Time before which was not generally countenanced.
21. I have not Time to enumerate the Persons w[ho] were active in supporting the Measures.
22. Nor of those against.
23. There was a Secession from the Legislature for the Purpose of Preventing Measures from being precipitated. Some of those seceding were made Prisoners insulted & dragged back, by the Sergeant at Arms & a Mob of Assistants.
24. The publications of the Day will be the best Answer to this Question.
25. The Minds of People in Philadelphia were highly inflamed against the Opposers & some of them were unquestionably over awed; some of them injured. Nothing perhaps checked this Spirit of Outrage so much as similar Instances in Cumberland County & Huntingdon County & others & a Discovery of the real Strength of Opposition.
26. The usual Arts of Party were used, besides those which have been enumerated.
27. The Adoption of the Constitution by North Carolina was frequently asserted & published in pretended Letters. Other Letters were fabricated & published; but they have slipt my Memory.
28. In General it may be said that Col. Oswald was almost the only Printer who published in Opposition in Philadelphia & that he has been injured in Consequence. I cannot be more particular.

29. The Printing Presses were notoriously the great Instruments of the American Revolution.

30. I cannot be very particular on this head.

Ms, unknown hand, George Bryan Papers, PHi.

[1] The author originally wrote "general" here, crossed out the last three letters, and converted the remainder to "give."

[2] The United States concluded a treaty in 1786 granting its Mediterranean shipping immunity from Moroccan piracy, but it had not yet negotiated guarantees from the three neighboring Barbary states of Algiers, Tripoli, and Tunis.

[3] The author wrote this over the word "Copy."

[4] The author is probably referring to the exertions of the sea captain John Barry and the merchant Michael Morgan O'Brien, both prominent Irish-born Philadelphia Federalists. On 29 September 1787 they led a mob (Irish sailors presumably numbered among them), that forcefully returned two "seceding" state assemblymen in order to form the quorum that enabled the call for a state ratifying convention (*DHROC* 2:110n).

OTHER DOCUMENTS

William Bradford, Jr. to Elias Boudinot. Summary of ALS, Robert Black Catalog 56 (1957): item 26.

Family news; use of Boudinot's influence to make Philadelphia the seat of federal government.

A Citizen of the United States, *Observations on the Agriculture, Manufactures, and Commerce of the United States. In a Letter to a Member of Congress.* New York, 1789.

A discursive essay, written by a New Englander and not Tench Coxe, according to *Coxe*, p. 150n; includes a section on the importance of titles.

William Samuel Johnson and Oliver Ellsworth to Governor Samuel Huntington. Summary of ALS, *Collector* 51(1937):item 597.

"In regard to bills pending in Congress."

Residences of Members

The addresses listed below are taken from the *New York Directory and Register for the Year* 1789, published on 4 July (Evans #22021). Discrepancies between that source and Otis's earlier list of addresses (see Otis to Adams, 21 April) may be due to members' moving on 1 May, when most leases in the city expired. The residence numbers are keyed to the map at the best approximated locations, as indicated by Smith's *New York*, I. N. Phelps Stokes, *The Iconography of Manhattan Island* (6 vols., New York, 1915), and cross-references within the *Directory*. Antifederalist members appear in *italics*; state names appear in parentheses. Foster (N.H.) was not seated until after the *Directory* was published and there is no known record of his address.

1. Mrs. Dobiney's, 15 Wall Street
   Bassett (Del.)
   Cadwalader (Md.)
   Contee (Md.)
   R. B. Lee (Va.)
   Moore (Va.)
   Read (Del.)
   Stone (Md.)
   Seney (Md.)
2. Vandine Elsworth's, 19 Maiden Lane
   Brown (Va.)
   Hartley (Pa.)
   Hiester (Pa.)
   Madison (Va.)
   Page (Va.)
   White (Va.)
3. Mrs. Dunscomb's, 15 Great Dock Street
   Ames (Mass.)
   Leonard (Mass.)
   Partridge (Mass.)
   Sedgwick (Mass.)
   Strong (Mass.)

4. Philip Mathers's (?), 47 Broad Street
   Goodhue (Mass.)
   Grout (Mass.)
   Sturges (Conn.)
   Thatcher (Mass.)
   Wingate (N.H.)
5. Michael Huck's, 81 Wall Street
   Burke (S.C.)
   Huger (S.C.)
   Scott (Pa.)
   Tucker (S.C.)
6. Mrs. Van Cortlandt's, 52 Smith Street
   C. Carroll (Md.)
   D. Carroll (Md.)
   Gale (Md.)
   Smith (Md.)
7. Mrs. Vandervoort's (?), 57 Maiden Lane
   Bland (Va.)
   Coles (Va.)
   Grayson (Va.)
   Parker (Va.)
8. Isaac Polluck's, 37 Broad Street
   Langdon (N.H.)
   Livermore (N.H.)
   Dalton (Mass.)
9. Greenwich and Partition streets
   Maclay (Pa.)
   Wynkoop (Pa.)
10. Nathan Strong's, 12 Albany Pier
    Hathorn (N.Y.)
    Van Rensselaer (N.Y.)
11. Mrs. Lewis's (?), 59 Water Street
    Huntington (Conn.)
    Sherman (Conn.)
12. Richard Platt, broker, 195 Water Street
    Trumbull (Conn.)
    Wadsworth (Conn.)
13. Mrs. Childs's (?), 193 Water Street
    Baldwin (Ga.)
    Ellsworth (Conn.)

14. Mrs. Seabring's, 63 Broadway
    Jackson (Ga.)
    Mathews (Ga.)
15. Mr. Anderson, Pearl Street
    Clymer (Pa.)
    Fitzsimons (Pa.)
16. Rev. John C. Kunze, 24 Chatham Street
    F. A. Muhlenberg (Pa.)
    Peter Muhlenberg (Pa.)
17. Widow Blau's, 47 Little Dock Street
    Schureman (N.J.)
    Sinnickson (N.J.)
18. Mrs. Greenelly's, 27 Queen Street
    Floyd (N.Y.)
    Henry (Md.)
19. Lower Broadway at the Bowling Green
    Smith (S.C.)
20. 99 Broadway
    Izard (S.C.)
21. Lower Broadway (?)
    Schuyler
22. Mrs. Johannah Ursin's, 5 Wall Street
    Gilman (N.H.)
23. John Marsden Pintard, 12 Wall Street
    Boudinot (N.J.)
24. 14 Wall St.
    Laurance (N.Y.)
25. 19 Wall St.
    Vining (Del.)
26. Mrs. Sheldon's, 40 Wall Street
    Sumter (S.C.)
27. John Alsop, 38 Smith Street
    King (N.Y.)
28. Corner of Thames and Broadway
    Gerry (Mass.)
29. 37 Great Dock St.
    Butler (S.C.)
30. William Constable, 39 Great Dock Street
    Morris (Pa.)
31. 48 Great Dock Street
    Elmer (N.J.)

32. 51 Great Dock Street
    Paterson (N.J.)
33. Mrs. McCullen's, 84 Broadway
    Gunn (Ga.)
34. Corner of Nassau and King (Pine) streets
    Benson (N.Y.)
35. Mrs. Hicks's, 45 Maiden Lane
    Silvester (N.Y.)
36. Columbia College
    Johnson (Conn.)
37. Greenwich Village
    R. H. Lee (Va.)
38. Near the Hospital
    Griffin (Va.)
39. "Richmond Hill," Greenwich Road
    Adams

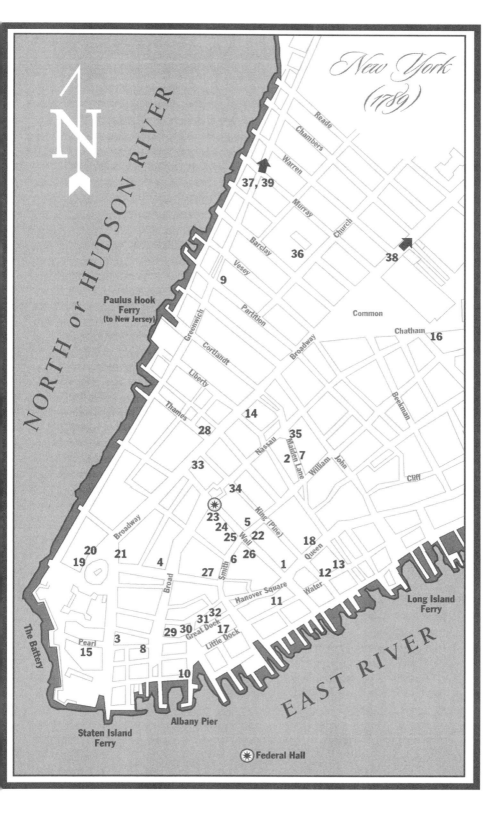

New York City Weather Charts

Archibald McLean published monthly weather charts during the first session of the First Federal Congress, missing only the month of September. He indicated that the thermometer on which the charts were based "is constantly in the open air, though guarded from the influence both of the sun and wind."

Meteorological Observations, March

Day of Mon.	Degrees of Heat. by Farenheit's The. A.M.	P.M.	P.M.	Prevailing Winds.			Change & Full of Moon.	OBSERVATIONS, &c.
	8 o'clo.	1 o'clo.	8 o'clo.	8 o'clo.	1 o'clo.	8 o'clo.		
1	38	46	46	S	SW	SW		Cloudy—cloudy—cloudy.
2	33	38	35	N	N	N		Clear—clear—clear.
3	33	38	45	NE	SE	SE		Cloudy—rain—foggy.
4	28	28	21	NW	NW	NW		Fair—fair—fair.
5	14	25	25	NW	S	S		Ditto—ditto—ditto.
6	27	37	36	S	S	S		Clear—dull—rain.
7	40	36	25	NW	NW	NW		Clear—clear—ditto and strong wind.
8	18	24	28	NW	NW	W		Clear—clear—clear.
9	27	38	35	W	NW	SW		Fair—fair—fair.
10	32	41	39	NW	N	SW		Ditto—ditto—ditto.
11	35	46	39	SW	SW	S	Full	Ditto—ditto—ditto.
12	39	49	47	SW	SW	SW		Ditto—ditto—thick fog.
13	42	46	41	NW	W	NW		Dull—cloudy—clear.
14	37	41	32	NW	NW	NW		Clear—clear—clear.
15	33	39	37	SE	S	S		Clear—clear—clear.
16	42	51	51	S	W	SW		Drizling—clear—clear.
17	45	52	45	NW	NW	NW		Fair—fair—fair.
18	38	45	43	NE	E	E		Clear—dull—rain.
19	38	50	47	NW	NW	W		Dull—clear—clear.

20	40	47	45	W	W	W	Fair—ditto—ditto.
21	39	45	40	N	S	S	Dull—clear—clear.
22	41	55	48	SW	W	NW	Cloudy—ditto—ditto.
23	30	40	35	NW	NW	NW	Clear—ditto—ditto.
24	28	38	38	NW	NW	NW	Ditto—ditto—ditto.
25	28	37	35	NW	NW	NW	Ditto—ditto—ditto.
26	32	45	42	W	N	NW	Ditto—ditto—ditto.
27	40	45	43	W	S	S	Ditto—ditto—ditto.
28	43	45	46	S	S	SE	Dull—rain—storm.
29	40	52	45	SW	NW	W	Fair—fair—fair.
30	42	44	40	NE	NE	NE	Rain—rain—rain.
31	37	46	45	NW	N	S	Fair—fair—fair.

NYDG, 3 April.

Meteorological Observations, April

Day of Mon.	Degrees of Heat. by Farenheit's The.			Prevailing Winds.			Change & Full of Moon.	OBSERVATIONS, &c.
	A.M. 8 o'clo.	P.M. 2 o'clo.	P.M. 8 o'clo.	A.M. 8 o'clo.	P.M. 2 o'clo.	P.M. 8 o'clo.		
1	40	38	37	SE	NW	E		Rain—dew—foggy
2	38	47	47	NW	NW	W		Fair—clear—cloudy
3	44	54	52	S	S	S		Fair—fair—fair
4	50	60	54	NW	SW	SW		Ditto—ditto—ditto
5	46	59	50	NW	NW	S		Ditto—ditto—ditto
6	48	51	51	S	SE	S		Dull—rain—heavy rain and high wind
7	50	44	39	SW	W	W		Rain—cloudy—cloudy—heavy gale
8	35	45	44	W	W	W		Fair—fair—fair
9	39	47	44	W	W	E	Full	Fair—cloudy—cloudy
10	46	52	52	SE	SE	SW		Rain—heavy gale—cloudy
11	45	53	43	SW	W	W		Clear—cloudy—clear
12	45	45	42	SW	NW	NW		Clear—dull—dull
13	36	42	45	W	W	SW		Clear—cloudy—clear
14	42	55	45	SW	S	S		Cloudy—clear—clear
15	62	64	40	SW	W	NW		Clear—clear—clear
16	45	52	46	NE	S	S		Ditto—ditto—ditto
17	43	52	51	SW	NW	NW		Ditto—ditto—ditto

Day	A.M. 6	P.M. 1	P.M. 8	A.M. 6	P.M. 1	P.M. 8	Change	Weather, &c.
18	45	53	52	SW	S	S		Ditto—ditto—ditto
19	49	63	60	SW	W	S		Clear—cloudy—clear
20	55	66	54	S	SE	NW		Cloudy—rain—rain
21	47	47	47	N	NE	S		Rain—drizling—clear
22	44	55	54	W	S	SW		Clear—clear—clear
23	53	54	45	S	S	S		Clear—cloudy—hard wind and rain
24	55	57	55	S	S	N		Cloudy—cloudy—rain and hard wind
25	47	52	49	N	N	NW	New	Clear—clear—clear and high wind
26	42	51	51	W	NW	SW		Clear—clear—clear
27	43	52	48	NW	SE	S		Ditto—ditto—ditto
28	46	50	49	SW	S	S		Dull—dull—dull
29	43	50	47	NW	NW	NW		Clear—clear—clear
30	49	59	50	NW	NW	NW		Ditto—ditto—ditto

NYDG, 6 May.

Meteorological Observations, May

Day of Mon.	Degrees of Heat. by Farenheit's The.			Prevailing Winds.			Change & Full of Moon.	Weather, &c.
	A.M. 6 o'clo.	P.M. 1 o'clo.	P.M. 8 o'clo.	A.M. 6 o'clo.	P.M. 1 o'clo.	P.M. 8 o'clo.		
1	47	56	52	NW	S	SE		Clear—clear—cloudy
2	46	54	50	NE	NE	S		Rain—rain—dull
3	48	65	56	SW	S	S		Cloudy—clear—clear
4	53	59	55	N	E	N		Cloudy—cloudy—cloudy
5	55	62	52	NE	S	NW		Cloudy—clear—clear
6	48	56	59	W	NW	NW		Clear—clear—clear
7	49	56	53	SW	S	N		Cloudy—cloudy—drizzling
8	52	52	51	SE	N	NE		Drizzling—cloudy—cloudy
9	47	58	56	NW	S	S	Full	Clear—fair—clear
10	55	52	49	E	E	NE		Cloudy—rain—rain
11	47	55	55	NW	E	S		Cloudy—cloudy—clear
12	53	59	57	SW	SW	S		Ditto—ditto—ditto
13	55	62	55	N	SW	SE		Clear—clear—cloudy
14	50	46	45	E	E	E		Cloudy—cloudy—rain

15	49	60	51	N	SE	SE		Clear—clear—cloudy
16	52	55	58	NE	N	SW		Rain—cloudy—clear
17	55	65	57	S	S	S		Clear—clear—clear
18	53	66	61	NW	SE	S		Ditto—ditto—ditto
19	57	61	57	S	S	SE		Ditto—cloudy—rain
20	52	57	55	W	SW	W		Cloudy—cloudy—fair
21	57	60	54	NW	S	W		Cloudy—clear—clear
22	49	65	64	W	W	W		Clear—clear—clear
23	55	65	70	W	W	W		Ditto—ditto—ditto
24	60	70	66	N	SW	S	New	Ditto—ditto—ditto
25	58	62	55	NE	SW	NE		Cloudy—rain—rain
26	51	61	51	E	N	NE		Cloudy—clear—clear
27	55	61	55	SW	S	S		Cloudy—clear—cloudy
28	52	57	58	NE	NE	NE		Cloudy—clear—clear
29	51	67	54	S	SW	S		Clear—clear—clear
30	55	72	56	SW	SW	N		Clear—clear—rain
31	54	66	56	N	NE	NE		Clear—clear—clear

NYDG, 4 June.

Meteorological Observations, June

Day of Mon.	Degrees of Heat. by Farenheit's The.			Prevailing Winds.			Change & Full of Moon.	WEATHER, &c.
	A.M. 6 o'clo.	P.M. 2 o'clo.	P.M. 8 o'clo.	A.M. 6 o'clo.	P.M. 2 o'clo.	P.M. 8 o'clo.		
1	57	72	64	NE	SW	S		Clear—clear—clear
2	58	70	68	NE	SW	SW		Ditto—ditto—ditto
3	61	76	68	W	SW	W		Ditto—ditto—ditto
4	58	68	58	NE	E	S		Ditto—ditto—ditto
5	55	62	69	NE	SW	W		Cloudy—clear—clear
6	69	80	75	SW	SW	SW		Clear—clear—clear
7	73	76	72	SW	SW	S	Full	Cloudy—cloudy—rain
8	68	76	75	W	S	S		Cloudy—clear—clear
9	70	79	69	N	S	S		Cloudy—cloudy—cloudy
10	66	76	67	S	S	S		Rain—cloudy—heavy rain and thunder
11	65	74	69	S	S	S		Rain—clear—thunder showers
12	67	72	69	S	S	S		Rain—cloudy—clear
13	67	76	73	NW	SW	N		Cloudy—cloudy—cloudy

14	66	74	72	SW	S	S		Cloudy—clear—clear
15	72	81	74	NW	NW	NW		Clear—clear—clear
16	65	75	73	NW	NW	NW		Ditto—ditto—ditto
17	64	74	68	NE	NW	SW		Cloudy—clear—clear
18	62	72	70	W	S	S		Clear—clear—clear
19	72	78	75	SW	SW	S		Clear—showery—clear
20	73	80	75	SW	S	S		Clear—clear—clear
21	74	82	86	SW	SW	S		Ditto—ditto—ditto
22	76	79	72	NW	SE	S		Cloudy—rain—rain
23	73	79	70	W	NW	W	New	Clear—clear—clear
24	65	75	72	NW	NW	NW		Ditto—ditto—ditto
25	63	72	68	NW	W	W		Clear—cloudy—clear
26	61	75	75	W	W	SW		Clear—clear—clear
27	70	76	73	W	S	S		Ditto—ditto—ditto
28	70	78	73	NW	S	S		Ditto—ditto—ditto
29	72	80	73	SW	SW	S		Ditto—ditto—ditto
30	75	88	82	SW	SW	SW		Ditto—ditto—ditto

NYDG, 4 July.

Meteorological Observations, July

Day of Mon.	Degrees of Heat. by Farenheit's The.			Prevailing Winds.			Change & Full of Moon.	WEATHER, &c.
	A.M. 6 o'clo.	P.M. 2 o'clo.	P.M. 8 o'clo.	A.M. 6 o'clo.	P.M. 2 o'clo.	P.M. 8 o'clo.		
1	77	87	80	SW	SW	SW		Fair—fair—cloudy
2	77	85	78	SW	S	S		Fair—fair—fair
3	75	82	76	SW	S	S		Cloudy—fair—cloudy and rain
4	74	85	75	SW	S	S		Cloudy—fair—rain and thunder
5	74	76	73	SW	S	S		Cloudy—rain—rain
6	68	77	68	SW	S	N		Cloudy—cloudy—clear
7	70	78	76	NW	S	S	Full	Clear—clear—clear
8	70	78	75	SW	SW	SW		Ditto—ditto—ditto
9	76	86	78	SW	SW	SW		Ditto—ditto—ditto
10	74	83	75	NW	NW	NW		Ditto—ditto—ditto
11	65	78	73	NW	NW	NW		Ditto—ditto—ditto
12	73	80	78	SE	S	SW		Rain—clear—clear
13	73	77	75	S	NW	W		Rain—cloudy—cloudy

14	68	76	70	NW	W	W		Clear—clear—cloudy
15	70	71	69	NW	NW	W		Clear—clear—clear
16	66	71	68	N	N	S		Ditto—ditto—ditto
17	65	75	70	W	S	S		Ditto—ditto—ditto
18	67	76	71	SW	S	S		Ditto—ditto—ditto
19	70	76	73	S	S	S		Ditto—ditto—cloudy and rain
20	70	80	74	W	SW	W		Clear—clear—clear
21	67	78	74	W	SW	SW		Ditto—ditto—ditto
22	72	79	71	SW	SW	S	New	Cloudy—clear—clear
23	70	80	75	S	SW	S		Foggy—clear—clear
24	74	85	82	SW	SW	SW		Clear—clear—clear
25	76	75	74	NE	NE	N		Cloudy—rain—cloudy
26	64	78	73	NW	NW	NW		Clear—clear—clear
27	67	75	70	N	SE	S		Cloudy—clear—clear
28	67	78	72	N	SE	SE		Ditto—ditto—ditto
29	66	76	72	N	E	SE		Clear—cloudy—clear
30	68	70	69	E	E	E		Cloudy—rain—rain
31	69	74	70	NE	NE	NE		Rain—cloudy—cloudy

NYDG, 4 August.

Meteorological Observations, August

Day of Mon.	Degrees of Heat. by Farenheit's The.			Prevailing Winds.			Change & Full of Moon.	WEATHER, &c.
	A.M. 6 o'clo.	P.M. 2 o'clo.	P.M. 8 o'clo.	A.M. 6 o'clo.	P.M. 2 o'clo.	P.M. 8 o'clo.		
1	68	73	71	SE	SE	SE		Cloudy—cloudy—rain
2	70	78	75	SE	SE	SE		Clear—clear—clear
3	72	72	72	NE	NE	NE		Cloudy—rain—cloudy
4	70	73	72	NE	NE	SW		Cloudy—rain—rain
5	70	72	72	SW	S	S	Full	Cloudy—heavy rain—rain
6	72	78	75	SW	S	S		Clear—clear—clear
7	71	80	78	SW	S	S		Ditto—ditto—ditto
8	74	80	78	S	S	S		Ditto—ditto—ditto
9	73	82	79	SW	S	S		Ditto—ditto—ditto
10	76	84	82	SW	S	S		Ditto—ditto—ditto
11	76	85	83	S	SW	SW		Ditto—ditto—ditto

12	78	85	81	SW	NW	SW		Clear—cloudy—thunder shower
13	76	83	81	NW	W	SW		Clear—cloudy—clear
14	79	88	82	SW	SE	W		Clear—clear—cloudy
15	78	85	80	S	S	S		Clear—clear—clear
16	77	84	82	N	S	S		Clear—cloudy—rain and thunder
17	65	70	71	NW	NW	NW		Cloudy—clear—clear
18	67	72	71	N	SE	S		Cloudy—cloudy—drizzling
19	69	71	67	NE	E	E		Rain—rain—dull
20	64	75	63	NW	S	S	New	Clear—clear—clear
21	63	75	63	NE	S	S		Ditto—ditto—ditto
22	61	74	63	N	E	S		Ditto—ditto—ditto
23	63	75	69	E	S	S		Ditto—ditto—ditto
24	63	73	70	NE	S	E		Ditto—ditto—ditto
25	66	75	71	NE	NE	NE		Cloudy—dull—dull
26	73	80	75	N	E	S		Cloudy—cloudy—clear
27	74	83	77	S	S	SW		Cloudy—showery—showery
28	68	75	73	N	NW	N		Cloudy—dull—dull
29	67	76	66	N	NW	NW		Dull—rain—dull
30	64	70	50	NW	NW	NW		Cloudy—clear—clear
31	51	63	61	NW	NW	W		Clear—clear—clear

NYDG, 3 September.

BIOGRAPHICAL GAZETTEER

The following directory is intended to provide certain kinds of information about individuals who appear in the first three volumes of the correspondence series either as letter writers, recipients, or persons mentioned with some regularity within the text. The information includes, when available: life dates; residence and occupation during the First Congress; prior significant political, military, economic, or social positions, including family ties to members of Congress and to each other; role in the first federal election; and any formal involvement with the First Congress, primarily as appointees or nominees to federal office, or petitioners. Information for the period after March 1791 is provided only if it directly relates to the First Congress or its members, such as the results of the second federal election. Military records include regimental assignments in the Continental Army as well as membership in the Society of the Cincinnati, in the belief that such affiliations may have contributed to mutual ties that affected correspondents' interactions with each other.

More extensive biographical data available in other volumes of the *DHFFC* is omitted and cross references are provided to those sources. Significant information deemed unreliable or inadequate subsequent to the publication of volume two of the *DHFFC* has been corrected here. Basic information drawn from the *Biographical Directory of the United States Congress*, the *Dictionary of American Biography*, the *Dictionary of National Biography*, or other standard encyclopedia sources is not cited. Lengthy sketches of all members of the First Congress can be found in *DHFFC* 14:487–932.

Much of the information made available here, drawn from sometimes very obscure sources, was brought to light through the notable efforts of Douglas E. Clanin, currently an editor at the Indiana Historical Society. Over the course of several years in the 1970s, Mr. Clanin exhaustively researched and compiled a biographical file for use in editing *The Documentary History of the First Federal Elections* and *The Documentary History of the Ratification of the Constitution*. These files have been very ably maintained and generously shared by the editors of the latter project. We heartily acknowledge the heavy debt owed to them and particularly to Mr. Clanin for his unique contribution to research.

ABBOTT, STEPHEN (1749–1813), a hatter of Salem, Massachusetts, commanded George Washington's military escort during his visit to Salem in October 1789. During the Revolutionary War he rose from ensign in the 8th Regiment to first lieutenant in the 11th Regiment of the Massachusetts Line in 1776 to captain in 1778, before transferring back to the 8th Regiment in 1783. (*EIHC* 75[1939]:54)

ADAMS, ABIGAIL SMITH (1744–1818), of Braintree (now part of Quincy), Massachusetts, married John Adams in 1764. She arrived in New York City on 24 June 1789 with their son Charles and Abigail's niece Louisa Smith (1773?–1857), all of whom resided with the Adamses at "Richmond Hill," north of the city throughout the first and second sessions of Congress. See also *DHFFC* 9:136n.

ADAMS, ANDREW (1736–97), a lawyer of Litchfield, Connecticut, was a member of the state's Council of Assistants in 1789. He graduated from Yale in 1760, served in the state House of Representatives from 1776 to 1781, and signed the Articles of Confederation as a member of Congress in 1778. (*Yale Graduates* 2:640–41)

ADAMS, CHARLES (1770–1800), the second son of Abigail and John Adams, accompanied his father in Europe, 1779–81. After graduating with Harvard's class of 1789, he resided with his parents at "Richmond Hill" while studying law under Secretary of the Treasury Hamilton, July–September 1789, and under Representative Laurance thereafter. (*Adams* 3:54n, 234n, 4:191; *PAH* 5:363–64n)

ADAMS, JOHN (1735–1826), of Braintree (now part of Quincy), Massachusetts, was sworn in as Vice President of the United States on 21 April 1789, after a first federal election in which the front runner for that post was never clear. He returned from Europe the year before, having served almost continuously since 1777 in various diplomatic missions to France, the Netherlands, and Great Britain. He served in Congress, 1774–77, where he signed the Declaration of Independence, and was elected to serve again in 1788–89 but never took his seat. Besides being a noted lawyer and gentleman farmer, Adams authored several books on political theory. See also *DHFFC* 9:4n.

ADAMS, JOHN QUINCY (1767–1848), son of John and Abigail Adams, studied law under Theophilus Parsons in Newburyport, Massachusetts, beginning shortly after his graduation from Harvard in 1787 until his admission to the bar in July 1790, when he opened a practice in Boston. He visited his parents at the seat of government in September 1789 and the spring of 1791. (Robert A. East, *John Quincy Adams: The Critical Years, 1785–1794* [New York, 1962], pp. 88, 121, 122, 133)

ADAMS, SAMUEL (1722–1803), of Boston, an unsuccessful candidate against Representative Ames in the first federal election, served as lieutenant governor of Massachusetts, 1789–93, having previously served as president of the state Senate, 1781–85 and 1787–88. He graduated from Harvard in 1740, became a patriot leader in the colony's House of Representatives where he sat from 1766 to 1774, and signed the Declaration of Independence and the Articles of Confederation as a member of Congress between 1774 and 1781. Despite his well known Antifederalism, he voted to ratify the Constitution at the state convention. (*Harvard Graduates* 10:420–63; *DHROC* 4:432)

ADAMS, THOMAS (ca. 1757–99), printer for the Massachusetts legislature, 1783–95, was editor of Boston's *Independent Chronicle*, 1784–99. (*Boston Printers*, pp. 5–9)

ADAMS, THOMAS BOYLSTON (1772–1832), the youngest son of Abigail and John Adams, graduated from Harvard in 1790 and joined his parents at "Richmond Hill," outside New York City, during the second session. In late 1790 he followed them to Philadelphia where he began his legal studies.

ALDEN, ROGER (1754–1836), served as chief clerk of the domestic division of the state department from 1789 until his resignation in July 1790. In January 1790 he successfully petitioned Congress for his expenses in assuming responsibility for congressional records the previous summer. During the Revolutionary War he served as adjutant to the 5th Regiment of the Connecticut Line from 1777 until transferring to the 2nd Regiment the next year, from which he resigned as captain in 1781. At the close of his military career, for which he was enrolled as a member of the Society of the Cincinnati, he studied law under Senator Johnson and was married to the Senator's daughter from 1783 until her death two years later. See also *DHFFC* 8:132–34, 9:264–65n.

ALL, ISAAC (d. ca. 1789), was a retired sea captain in Philadelphia. (*PGW* 2:251n)

ALLAIRE, PETER (1740–1820), was a New York City merchant secretly employed by the British Foreign Office, whose "Occurences" (reports) were enclosed in letters to Sir George Yonge. His role as secret agent was unknown even to the British foreign service in North America. During the Confederation he was landlord to several members of Congress, including Senator Lee. (Julian Boyd, *Number 7: Alexander Hamilton's Secret Attempts to Control American Foreign Policy* [Princeton, N.J., 1964], pp. 60–61n)

ALLEN, JEREMIAH, was a merchant of Boston and sheriff of Suffolk County, Massachusetts, in 1789. He was a companion to John Adams during the latter's journey to Paris in late 1779–80, and advised him on fisheries during the peace negotiations of 1782. (*Adams* 2:402, 3:83)

ANDREWS, LORING (1769–1805), began publication of the [Stockbridge, Massachusetts] *Western Star* on 1 December 1789. He was formerly co-editor of Boston's semi-weekly *Herald of Freedom*, 1788–89. (*Boston Printers*, p. 19)

ANDREWS, ROBERT (ca. 1747–1804), professor of mathematics at the College of William and Mary, represented James City County, Virginia, at the state convention, where he voted to ratify the Constitution, and in the state House of Delegates, 1790–99. He tutored Representative Page's children briefly in the early 1770s, was ordained an Anglican minister, and served as chaplain of the 2nd Regiment of the Virginia Line in 1777. He was an active promoter of the Dismal Swamp Company in the 1780s. (*PGW* 4:68n)

APPLETON, NATHANIEL (1731–98), a Boston merchant, served as commissioner of loans for Massachusetts from 1775 until his death. He was father to Nathaniel Walker Appleton. See also *DHFFC* 2:500.

APPLETON, NATHANIEL WALKER (1755–95), of Salem, Massachusetts, graduated from Harvard in 1773 and became a physician. He was brother-in-law to Thomas Dawes, Jr., James Greenleaf, and Noah Webster. (*Harvard Graduates* 18:204–9)

ARCHER, ABRAHAM, was appointed collector at York, Virginia, in 1789, having served as collector and naval officer there under the state, 1781–87. He became mayor in 1790. See also *DHFFC* 2:547.

ARMSTRONG, JAMES (ca. 1728–1800), a native of Pennsylvania, by 1786 had settled in Camden County, Georgia, which he represented at the state's ratification convention in 1788 and House of Assembly, 1787–90, simultaneously serving in the Executive Council, 1787–88. He received one of Georgia's electoral votes for President in the first federal election. In 1791 he became justice of the Camden County court. Following his wartime service as quartermaster of the 2nd Pennsylvania Battalion, 1776–77, first lieutenant in Pulaski's Legion, 1777–79, and then captain, 1779–83, he enrolled as a member of the Society of the Cincinnati. (*DHFFE* 4:294–95; *Pennsylvania Cincinnati* 1:242–43)

ARMSTRONG, JOHN, JR. (1758–1843), originally of Carlisle, Pennsylvania, was defeated by Senator Maclay in the first federal election and resettled in New York City upon his marriage to Alida Livingston, younger sister of Chancellor Robert R. Livingston, in January 1789. He was a member of the Society of the Cincinnati. See also *DHFFC* 9:180n. (*Pennsylvania Cincinnati* 1:247–48)

ARNDT, JOHN (d. 1814), was treasurer and recorder of Northampton County, Pennsylvania. He served as captain in the Pennsylvania Battalion of the Flying Camp in 1776, on the council of censors, 1783–84, and at the state convention, where he voted to ratify the Constitution. (*DHROC* 2:262n)

ARNOLD, WELCOME (1745–98), was a West Indies merchant and distiller of Providence, Rhode Island, which he represented in the state House of Deputies almost continuously from 1778 until 1795, including five terms as speaker. In August 1789 he served on the committee that drafted the petition from the inhabitants of Providence to Congress for relief from impost and tonnage legislation, and he moderated the town meeting that voted to accept it. An active Federalist, he voted to ratify the Constitution at the state convention. He served as treasurer of the College of Rhode Island (Brown) from 1783 until his death. See also *DHFFC* 8:389–96.

ATLEE, WILLIAM AUGUSTUS (1735–93), an early leader of the Revolutionary movement in Lancaster, Pennsylvania, was an associate justice of the state supreme court from 1777 until his death. He served simultaneously as deputy commissary of prisoners under Elias Boudinot from 1777 until war's end. (*LDC* 10:33)

AUSTIN, DAVID (1732–1801), father-in-law of Representative Sherman's son John, was a merchant of New Haven, Connecticut, for which he served as alderman in the 1780s. (*PGW* 3:264n; *Sherman's Connecticut*, p. 319)

AVERY, JOHN, SR. (1711–96), a 1731 Harvard graduate, was a colonial rights activist and a former merchant of Boston, like his son John, Jr. (*Harvard Graduates* 9:8–11)

AVERY, JOHN, JR. (1739–1806), a Boston merchant, distiller, and colonial rights activist, served as Massachusetts secretary of state, 1780–1806. He graduated from Harvard in 1759. (*Harvard Graduates* 14:384–89)

BACHE, RICHARD (1737–1811), a Philadelphia merchant, married Benjamin Franklin's daughter Sarah in 1767, two years after emigrating from England, and succeeded him as postmaster general, 1776–82. (*PGW* 2:96–97)

BACKUS, ELIJAH (1759–1811), of Norwich, Connecticut, was appointed by his uncle, Governor Matthew Griswold, to serve as state collector at New London, 1785–89. The 1777 Yale graduate subsequently practiced law. (*Yale Graduates* 3:651–52)

BACON, WILLIAM (ca. 1740–1819), was a farmer of Sheffield, Massachusetts, which he represented in the state House of Representatives in 1777. (*Massachusetts Legislators*, p. 154)

BALDWIN, SIMEON (1761–1851), a lawyer of New Haven, Connecticut, married Representative Sherman's daughter Rebecca in 1787. He graduated from Yale in 1781 and served as city clerk, 1789–1800, and as clerk of Connecticut's federal courts, 1790–1803. (*Yale Graduates* 4:178–80)

BALDWIN, WILLIAM (1760–1818), a 1779 Yale graduate, became principal of the grammar school at Norwich, Connecticut. (*Yale Graduates* 4:97)

BALLARD, ROBERT (d. 1793), served as port surveyor of Baltimore from 1789 until his death. He assumed the additional duties of inspector of the port in 1791. During the Revolutionary War he rose from captain in the 1st Regiment of the Virginia Line in 1775 to lieutenant colonel in 1777, transferring to the 4th Regiment the next year before resigning in 1779. (*PGW* 1:208)

BALLEW, BENNET, a Scottish trader, acted as agent, interpreter, and negotiator for a Cherokee delegation that unofficially visited the federal government in 1789.

BANCKER, GERARD (1740–99), served as New York state treasurer, 1778–98. (*PRM* 3:220n)

BANKSON, BENJAMIN, was employed as clerk to Secretary of the Senate Otis, 1789–90, having served as clerk to the secretary of Congress since at least 1781 and clerk for the commissary of issues prior to that. In September 1790 he worked briefly as an "additional clerk" in the State Department. (*JCC* 19:323; *PTJ* 17:358n)

BANNING, JEREMIAH (1733–98), a merchant and planter of Talbot County, Maryland, served as collector at Oxford, 1789–91. See also *DHFFC* 2:495.

BARBÉ-MARBOIS, FRANÇOIS, MARQUIS DE (1745–1837), served as secretary of the French legation in the United States, 1779–85, performing the additional duties of consul in Philadelphia and consul general from 1781, and chargé des affaires from 1784. Thereafter he served as Intendant of St. Domingue until 1789, when he was recalled to France. (*FRUS* 2:288n)

BARCLAY, THOMAS (1728–93), a Philadelphia merchant, performed diplomatic services for the United States between 1781 and 1787. See also *DHFFC* 8:119, 9:93n.

BARD, SAMUEL (1742–1821), and his father John (1716–99) opened a medical practice together in New York City in 1767. Samuel was also professor of medicine at Columbia College. See also *DHFFC* 9:470n.

BARLOW, JOEL (1754–1812), a teacher and poet known as one of the "Hartford Wits," graduated in 1778 from Yale, where Representative Baldwin had been his roommate, tutor, and close friend. He married Representative Baldwin's sister Ruth in 1781, during his service as chaplain to the 4th Regiment of the Massachusetts Line, 1780–83. He resided in Paris, 1788–90, and London, 1790–92, as European agent for the Scioto Land Company. (*Yale Graduates* 4:3–10)

BARLOW, RUTH BALDWIN (1756–1818), of New Haven, Connecticut, was the younger sister of Representative Baldwin and wife of Joel Barlow. (*Yale Graduates* 4:4, 7)

BARNARD, JOSEPH (1748–1817), of Kennebunk, Maine, was postmaster of neighboring York in 1789. (George Folsom, *History of Saco and Biddeford* [Saco, Me., 1830], p. 310)

BARNES, DAVID LEONARD (d. 1812), studied law under Daniel Leonard after graduating from Harvard in 1780, and opened a practice in Taunton, Massachusetts, three years later. (*Massachusetts Bar* 1:644)

BARNES, JOHN, resided in Bedford, Hillsborough County, New Hampshire, in 1790.

BARNES, JOSEPH, a Philadelphia lawyer, represented his brother-in-law, inventor James Rumsey, and the Rumseians, in efforts to secure a steam engine patent during the First Congress. See also *DHFFC* 8:40.

BARNES, RICHARD (d. 1804), a planter of St. Mary's County, Maryland, served in the state House of Delegates, 1773–74, Senate, 1779–85, and at the state convention, where he voted to ratify the Constitution. (*Maryland Legislators* 1:116)

BARNEY, JOSHUA (1759–1818), a failed Baltimore merchant, was appointed clerk of Maryland's federal courts in March 1790. The defeat of the Barney Bill denied his January 1791 petition for compensation for various expenses as a Continental Navy officer between 1776 and 1784. See also *DHFFC* 7:458–60.

BARNWELL, ROBERT (1761–1814), a planter of Beaufort, South Carolina, sat in the Confederation Congress in New York from 1 January until at least 10 February 1789. Following his distinguished service in the state militia during the Revolutionary War, he was elected to the state House of Representatives in 1787 and to the state convention the next year, where he voted to ratify the Constitution. He was an unsuccessful candidate for Representative in the first federal election, but succeeded when Representative Burke declined to stand for reelection to the Second Congress. (*DHFFE* 1:219; *LDC* 25:469, 496)

BARRELL, ELIZABETH, sister of Senator John Langdon and Woodbury Langdon, was the wife of Colborn Barrell of Newcastle, New Hampshire, and sister-in-law to Joseph and Nathaniel Barrell. (Lawrence Mayo, *John Langdon* [Port Washington, N.Y., 1937], pp. 23–24n)

BARRELL, JOSEPH (1739–1804), brother of Nathaniel, was a prominent federalist Boston merchant and shipowner involved in the Pacific trade. His brother Colborn was married to Senator Langdon's sister Elizabeth, while his brother William's marriage to Langdon's other sister, Martha, ended in divorce in 1766. (*PGW* 5:251n; Mayo, *John Langdon,* pp. 23–24n)

BARRELL, NATHANIEL (1732–1831), a merchant of Portsmouth, New Hampshire, prior to the Revolutionary War, settled on a farm in York, Maine, which he represented at the Massachusetts ratification convention. Unlike his brother Joseph, he was an avowed Antifederalist, although he ultimately voted in favor of the Constitution. His brother Colborn was married to Senator Langdon's sister Elizabeth, while his brother William's marriage to Langdon's other sister, Martha, ended in divorce in 1766. (*DHROC* 5:492n; Mayo, *John Langdon,* pp. 23–24n)

BARRETT, NATHANIEL (1743–93), a Boston merchant, was appointed consul to Rouen, France, in 1790. Continental loan officer for Massachusetts, 1778–81, he was involved in negotiations for trade concessions from France on behalf of the New England whaling industry in the late 1780s. See also *DHFFC* 2:500. (*PGW* 2:265n)

BARRETT, SAMUEL (1738–98), a 1757 Harvard graduate, was a failed merchant of Boston and judge of the court of common pleas of Suffolk County. (*Harvard Graduates* 14:135–42)

BARTON, WILLIAM (1748–1831), was a lawyer and merchant of Providence, Rhode Island, for which he was appointed port surveyor in June 1790. During the Revolutionary War he served as colonel of a state militia regiment under Senator Stanton, carrying the equivalent rank and pay in the Continental Army from 1777 until the close of the war, when he became a member of the Society of the Cincinnati. See also *DHFFC* 2:538.

BARTON, WILLIAM (1754–1817), a Philadelphia lawyer, declined appointment as one of three judges of the Northwest Territory in August 1789. He unsuccessfully solicited the office of assistant secretary of the treasury in April 1790 and Roger Alden's former post as chief clerk of the state department the following August. David Rittenhouse was his mother's brother. (*PGW* 6:142–43; *PTJ* 17:350)

BATCHELDER, JOSIAH (1736–1809), a sea captain and the state's naval officer at Beverley, Massachusetts, served as surveyor of that port and neighboring Salem from 1789 until his death. He sat in the state House of Representatives, 1774–80. See also *DHFFC* 2:500.

BAUMAN, SEBASTIAN (d. 1803), was a New York City grocer who served as lieutenant colonel and commander of the state militia's artillery regiment at the time of George Washington's inauguration, and as the city's postmaster beginning in October 1789. A native of Germany, he was commissioned a captain in the Continental Army's 2nd Regiment of Artillery in 1777 and rose to major before retiring in 1784. (*PGW: Revolution* 5:249)

BAYARD, JOHN (1738–1807), mayor of New Brunswick, New Jersey, in 1790, resided until 1788 in Philadelphia, where he was a leading merchant.

He served in the state's General Assembly, 1776–79 and 1784, and in Congress, 1785–86. From 1777 to 1779 he commanded the 2nd Regiment of Philadelphia Volunteers. His wife Joanna was Senator Paterson's sister-in-law. (John E. O'Connor, *William Paterson, Lawyer and Statesman* [New Brunswick, N.J., 1979], p. 190)

BAYLIES, HODIJAH (1756–1842), was collector at Dighton, Massachusetts, 1789–1810. A 1777 Harvard graduate, he served as a first lieutenant in Henry Jackson's Continental Regiment in 1777 and major and aide-de-camp to General Benjamin Lincoln, 1777–82, transferring to George Washington's staff, 1782–83. He later joined the Society of the Cincinnati. See also *DHFFC* 2:500. (*PGW* 3:301)

BAYNTON, PETER (1754–1821), a merchant of Germantown, Pennsylvania, and son of a prominent Philadelphia mercantile family, read law before his appointment as comptroller of the post office under Richard Bache, 1776–82. (*PGW* 2:220; *PMHB* 48[1924]:282–83)

BEALL, SAMUEL (d. 1792?), was a West Indies merchant of Williamsburg, Virginia, where he had moved from Washington County, Maryland, ca. 1777. (*PGM* 1:xxxiv; *DGW* 5:128)

BEATTY, ERKURIES (1759–1823), brother of Reading, was appointed a captain in the United States infantry regiment in September 1789, commanding Fort Knox (Vincennes, Indiana) until 1790. After rising from second lieutenant of the 4th Regiment of the Pennsylvania Line in 1777 to first lieutenant of the 3rd Regiment by war's end, he was commissioned a lieutenant in the federal army in 1784 and paymaster to the army in the west, 1786–88. He was a member of the Society of the Cincinnati. See also *DHFFC* 2:532. (*Pennsylvania Cincinnati* 1:265–66)

BEATTY, READING (1757–1831), a physician of Falsington, Bucks County, Pennsylvania, brother of Erkuries, married Representative Wynkoop's daughter Christina in 1786. He served as a junior officer with the 5th Battalion and 6th Regiment of the Pennsylvania Line, 1776–78, and as a surgeon and surgeon's mate with the 6th Pennsylvania and the 4th Continental Artillery regiments for the remainder of the war. He was a member of the Society of the Cincinnati. (*PMHB* 38[1919]:43–45, 44[1920]:196–97)

BECKLEY, JOHN (1757–1807), was clerk of the House of Representatives from 1789 until his death, except between 1797 and 1801, when the Federalists kept him out of office. See also *DHFFC* 9:11n.

BECKWITH, GEORGE (1753–1823), a British army major who fought throughout the Revolutionary War, undertook four intelligence missions to the United States on behalf of Great Britain between 1787 and 1790. His most important of several pro-British contacts within the government was Secretary of the Treasury Hamilton, who divulged to President Washington and Secretary of State Jefferson in July 1790 the fact that he was conversing with Beckwith. His fifth mission lasted from then until early 1792, when Great Britain's appointment of its first minister to the United States rendered Beckwith's informal mediation unnecessary. (Julian Boyd, *Number 7: Alexander Hamilton's Secret Attempts to Control American Foreign Policy* [Princeton, N.J., 1964], pp. 5–7)

BEDFORD, GUNNING, JR. (1747–1812), a lawyer of Wilmington, Delaware, was state's attorney general from 1784 until his appointment as federal district judge, 1789–1812. He was an unsuccessful candidate for both Senator and Representative in the first federal election. See also *DHFFC* 2:489. (*Princetonians, 1769–1775*, pp. 131–35; *DHFFE* 2:75, 83)

BEDFORD, NATHANIEL (ca. 1754–1818), came to America as a British Army surgeon and settled in Pittsburgh, Pennsylvania, where he opened its first medical practice. (*Western Pennsylvania Historical Magazine* 38[1955]:101–2)

BEDINGER, DANIEL (1766–1818), was port surveyor at Norfolk and Portsmouth, Virginia, 1789–97, having served as the state's deputy collector and naval officer at Norfolk from 1783. During the Revolutionary War he served as a first lieutenant in the 11th Regiment of the Virginia Line and afterwards enrolled in the Society of the Cincinnati. See also *DHFFC* 2:548. (*PGW* 2:344n)

BELKNAP, JEREMY (1744–98), was a Congregational minister who settled in Boston in 1787 after a twenty year pastorship in New Hampshire. A 1762 Harvard graduate, he published the first volume of his famous *History of New Hampshire* in 1784; the remaining two volumes were published in 1791 and 1792. (*Harvard Graduates* 15:175–95)

BERRIEN, JOHN (1759–1815), was a planter who was appointed port surveyor at Savannah, Georgia, in 1789. During the Revolutionary War he rose from second lieutenant of the 1st Regiment of the Georgia Line in 1776 to captain in 1777 and brigade major of the North Carolina Brigade in 1778, serving as aide-de-camp to General Lachlan McIntosh. See also *DHFFC* 2:491.

BICKER, WALTER (d. 1821), of New York City, served as a captain in the 3rd and 4th regiments of the Pennsylvania Line, 1776–77, and in Colonel John Patton's Additional Continental Regiment, 1777–79. He became a member of the Society of the Cincinnati.

BIDDLE, CLEMENT (1740–1814), a Philadelphia merchant, was federal marshal for Pennsylvania, 1789–93. George Washington entrusted him with preparing the presidential mansion when Congress moved to Philadelphia in 1790. Dr. James Hutchinson was his brother-in-law. See also *DHFFC* 2:533.

BIDDLE, ELIZABETH, widow of Edward Biddle (m. 1761), died on 8 August 1789 near Havre de Grace, Maryland. She was the daughter of John Ross, an older brother of Senator Read's wife, Gertrude. Her daughters Catherine and Abigail married George Lux and Dr. Moore Falls, respectively.

BINGHAM, WILLIAM (1752–1804), of Philadelphia, was a wealthy banker and speculator in land and public securities. His wife Anne was the daughter of Robert Morris's longtime business partner Thomas Willing. As a member of Congress, 1786–88, he led the fight to establish Philadelphia as the seat of the First Federal Congress. He was an unsuccessful candidate for both Senator and Representative in the first federal election. See also *DHFFC* 9:125n. (*DHFFE* 1:365, 413)

BIRD, HENRY M. (1755–1818), of London, was principal partner in the mercantile and banking firm of Bird, Savage & Bird, England's major traders in South Carolina rice. He became a speculator in the South Carolina war debt, and in 1790 offered his firm's services as European agent for servicing and discharging the national debt. He traveled throughout America from at least April 1789 until the summer of 1791. (*PGW* 5:41–42n)

BISCOE, GEORGE, of St. Marys County, Maryland, served as naval officer and deputy collector for the Patuxent River since before the Revolutionary War. In 1789 he was appointed collector at Nottingham (in present day Prince Georges County), Maryland. (*PGW* 2:145–46n)

BISHOP, NATHANIEL (1751–1826), was a lawyer of Richmond, Massachusetts, where he migrated from his native Connecticut in 1778. His previous military service included second lieutenant with the 20th Continental Regiment in 1776 and first lieutenant with the 4th Regiment of the Connecticut Line, 1777–78. He often sat in the state House of Representatives and served on the bench of the court of common pleas. (*Massachusetts Bar* 2:165)

BISHOP, PHANUEL (1739–1812), of Rehoboth, Massachusetts, represented Bristol County in the state Senate, 1788–91. First elected in 1787 but denied his seat because of voting irregularities, he was returned to the state House of Representatives instead and to the state convention, where he voted against ratification of the Constitution. He was an unsuccessful candidate for Representative in the first federal election. (*DHFFE* 1:744)

BLACKBURN, THOMAS (ca. 1740–1807), a former burgess and justice of the peace of Prince William County, Virginia, served as a colonel in the state militia during the Revolutionary War. His daughter married George Washington's nephew, Bushrod Washington. (*PGW* 6:315n; *DGW* 3:108n)

BLACKSTONE, SIR WILLIAM (1723–80), English jurist and Oxford law professor, wrote the famous *Commentaries on the Laws of England* (4 vols., 1765–69).

BLAIR, HUGH (1718–1800), was the author of *Lectures on Rhetoric*.

BLAIR, JOHN (1732–1800), a lawyer and jurist of Williamsburg, Virginia, was a United States Supreme Court justice, 1789–96. He studied law at London's Middle Temple and served as judge of the state's general court, 1778–80, high court of chancery, 1780–88, and supreme court of appeals, 1788–89. A signer of the Constitution, he later voted for it at the state convention as a delegate for York County. See also *DHFFC* 2:548. (*DHROC* 9:626)

BLAND, MARTHA DANGERFIELD (d. 1804), wife of Representative Bland, resided at "Cawsons," their plantation in Prince George County, Virginia. They married sometime between 1765 and 1771.

BLOOMFIELD, JOSEPH (1753–1823), a lawyer of Burlington, New Jersey, served as register of the state's admiralty court, 1779–83, and attorney general thereafter until 1792. Although one of 54 nominees to emerge in the preliminary vote for Representative in the first federal election, he declined to serve and actively supported Jonathan Dayton. During the Revolutionary War he rose from captain to major in the 3rd Regiment of the New Jersey Line in 1776, serving simultaneously as deputy judge advocate general, and resigning from both in 1778. (*DHFFE* 3:25n, 41, 57)

BLOUNT, JOHN GRAY (1752–1833), was a merchant of Washington, Beaufort County, North Carolina, which he represented in the state's House of Commons, 1782–89. He supported the Constitution at both the 1789 and 1790 ratifying conventions. His brother and business partner William

Blount was an unsuccessful candidate for Senator in the first federal election. (*DHFFE* 4:353n)

BOND, PHINEAS (1749–1815), a Pennsylvania Loyalist who fled to Great Britain during the Revolutionary War, served as British consul to New York, New Jersey, Pennsylvania, Delaware, and Maryland, 1787–1812. (*LDC* 24:187–88)

BONDFIELD, JOHN, was a Montreal merchant who was driven from Canada for supporting the American invasion, 1775–76, and settled briefly in Philadelphia before establishing a mercantile firm in Bordeaux, France, in 1777. He served as Congress's commercial agent there from 1778 until at least 1789. (*PGW* 4:283; *Emerging Nation* 3:531n)

BONNETHEAU, PETER (1742–98), of Charleston, South Carolina, served as clerk of the state Senate, 1778–80, and of the city council, ca. 1784–98. (*South Carolina House* 1:160)

BOUDINOT, ELISHA (1749–1819), a lawyer of Newark, New Jersey, was the younger brother of Representative Boudinot. (*DHFFE* 3:36n)

BOUDINOT, HANNAH STOCKTON (1736–1808), of Elizabethtown, New Jersey, married Representative Boudinot in 1762. Their niece Julia Stockton married Dr. Benjamin Rush in 1776. See also *DHFFC* 14:683.

BOURN, SILVANUS (ca. 1756–1817), a merchant of Barnstable, Massachusetts, was consul to Hispaniola, 1789–92. On 6 April 1789 the Senate selected him to inform John Adams of his election as Vice President and he subsequently escorted Adams to New York City. See also *DHFFC* 2:500–501, 8:710.

BOWDOIN, JAMES (1726–90), an important figure in Massachusetts' Revolutionary movement, was a Boston merchant and governor of the state, 1785–87. The 1745 Harvard graduate served in the colonial legislature almost continuously from 1753 to 1774, played a major role in drafting the state constitution of 1780, and voted to ratify the federal Constitution at the state convention. (*Harvard Graduates* 11:514–49; *DHROC* 4:433)

BOWEN, JABEZ (1739–1815), a physician and jurist of Providence, Rhode Island, served as the federal commissioner of loans for the state, 1790–1800. He graduated from Yale in 1757 and was a member of the state's superior court, 1776–78, and House of Delegates, 1777–78 and 1788–90, serving also as deputy governor, 1778–80 and 1781–86. He voted to ratify the Constitution at the state convention in 1790 and was an unsuccessful candidate for Senator in the first federal election. See also *DHFFC* 2:539. (*Yale Graduates* 2:452–54; *DHFFE* 4:447)

BOWEN, OLIVER (1742–1800), of Savannah, Georgia, was the brother of Jabez Bowen. He had moved from Providence, Rhode Island, by the outbreak of the Revolutionary War and commanded the Georgia state navy, 1778–80. (*PGW* 2:177n)

BOWNE, THOMAS, was appointed collector at South Quay, Virginia, in 1789. He served with the 10th, 1st, and 6th regiments of the Virginia Line between 1777 and 1783, when he retired as a captain and joined the Society of the Cincinnati. (*DHFFC* 2:548)

BOYD, JAMES (ca. 1736–98), of Boston, was a native of Scotland who settled on a fifty-thousand acre grant along the Maine-New Brunswick border in 1767. A supporter of the Revolutionary cause, he abandoned his property and subsequently lobbied to obtain an American title to it. See also *DHFFC* 2:383–85. (*PGW* 4:329n)

BOYD, ROBERT (1734–1804), sheriff of New York City, 1787–91, was born in Ireland and settled in New York, where he operated an ironworks south of Newburgh. (William P. Boyd, *History of the Boyd Family and Descendants* [Conesus, N.Y., 1884], pp. 244–46)

BRACKETT, JOSHUA (1733–1802), a physician of Portsmouth, New Hampshire, served as judge of the state admiralty court, 1776–89. The 1752 Harvard graduate married Joseph Whipple's sister Hannah. (*New Hampshire State Papers* 21:784–85; *Harvard Graduates* 13:197–201)

BRADFORD, SUSAN VERGEREAU BOUDINOT (1764–1853), of Philadelphia, was the only daughter of Representative Boudinot. She married William Bradford, Jr., in October 1784. (*Princetonians, 1769–1775,* pp. 187, 190; *Elias Boudinot,* p. 17)

BRADFORD, WILLIAM, JR. (1755–95), of Philadelphia, was attorney general of Pennsylvania from 1780 until his appointment to the state supreme court in August 1791. He served as captain in the Flying Camp and in the 11th Regiment of the Pennsylvania Line from 1776 until his retirement in 1779 with the rank of lieutenant colonel. In October 1784 he married Representative Boudinot's daughter Susan. See also *DHFFC* 9:100n. (*Princetonians, 1769–1775*, pp. 185–91)

BRADLEY, STEPHEN ROW (1754–1830), associate justice of the Vermont superior court from 1788, had practiced law since settling in Westminster, Vermont, in 1779. The 1775 Yale graduate was a native of Connecticut, which he served as a militia officer from 1776 until his retirement as a major in 1779. (*Yale Graduates* 3:549–52)

BRAXTON, CARTER (1736–97), a planter of King William County, Virginia, served in the state House of Delegates, 1776–83, 1785–86, and 1790–94, and Executive Council, 1786–91. He graduated from the College of William and Mary in 1755 and studied for several years at Cambridge. During the Revolution he was a conservative who nevertheless signed the Declaration of Independence as a member of Congress in 1776. His daughter Elizabeth married Representative Griffin in 1778. (*PGW* 2:59)

BRAXTON, CORBIN (ca. 1764–1822), Representative Griffin's brother-in-law and the son of Carter Braxton, served as surveyor for the port of Richmond, Virginia, from August 1789 until his resignation in December 1790. He was the state's port inspector for West Point, Virginia, 1787–89. (*PGW* 2:59n)

BREARLY, DAVID (1745–90), a lawyer of Hunterdon County, New Jersey, served as United States district judge for New Jersey from September 1789 until his death in August 1790, having previously served as chief justice of the state supreme court, 1779–89. During the war, he rose from the rank of captain in the 2nd Regiment in 1775 to lieutenant colonel of the 4th and later the 1st regiments of the New Jersey Line before resigning in 1779, subsequently serving as vice president of the state Society of the Cincinnati. He sat at both the Federal and state conventions, and voted as a Presidential Elector in 1789. See also *DHFFC* 2:518. (*DHFFE* 3:180)

BRECK, SAMUEL (1747–1809), of a prominent mercantile family, represented Boston in the Massachusetts House of Representatives, 1784–91, and was elected a delegate to the Annapolis Convention in 1786. (*Political Parties*, p. 410; *DHROC* 4:xxxvi–xxxvii)

BRICE, JAMES (1746–1801), was a lawyer and planter of Annapolis, Maryland. He served on the state's Executive Council, 1777–83 and 1785–90, and as mayor, 1782–83 and 1788–89. (*PGW* 3:399–400n)

BRIDGE, JAMES (1765–1834), a lawyer of Bucksport, Maine, graduated from Harvard in 1787 and studied law under Theophilus Parsons in Newburyport, Massachusetts, with his friend John Quincy Adams during the First Congress. (*Maine Bar,* pp. 154–59)

BRIGHT, FRANCIS (ca. 1746–ca. 1803), a captain in the Virginia navy since 1776, undertook an active campaign for appointment to command a federal revenue cutter. He stayed with Representative Page in Virginia in September 1790, when he intended to sail to New York to resume his efforts. References on his behalf from Page and others commended him particularly for alerting authorities to the British approach to Philadelphia in 1777. (*PGW* 6:497–98n)

BROCKENBOROUGH, NEWMAN, served as state Representative, 1781–82, and sheriff, 1783–84, for Essex County, Virginia. He lost a bid for delegate to the state ratification convention. (*DHROC* 9:581n)

BROOKS, JOHN (1752–1825), a physician of Medford, Massachusetts, was an unsuccessful candidate against Representative Gerry in the first federal election. During the Revolutionary War he rose from captain of a Minuteman company in 1775 to lieutenant colonel of the 8th and 7th regiments of the Massachusetts Line by war's end, when he enrolled in the Society of the Cincinnati. In 1786 he became an original proprietor of the Ohio Company. The same year, he was commissioned a major general in the state militia raised to suppress Shays's Rebellion. He served in the state House of Representatives, 1786–88, and voted to ratify the Constitution at the state convention. He was elected to the state Senate in 1791, the same year he became United States marshal for the state. (*DHFFE* 1:744; *DHROC* 4:33n; *PGW* 3:133n; *Massachusetts Cincinnati,* pp. 68–69)

BROOM, JACOB (1752–1810), a merchant and manufacturer of Wilmington, Delaware, represented New Castle County in the state House of Assembly, 1784–87 and 1788–89. He attended the Federal Convention and signed the Constitution. From 1790 to 1792 he was postmaster of Wilmington. (*DHROC* 3:52n, 114)

BROUGH, ROBERT, was the state's port inspector for Hampton, Virginia, 1788–89. The 1771 graduate of the College of William and Mary served as an adjutant in the state militia during the Revolutionary War and was appointed a justice of the peace for Elizabeth City County in October 1789. (*PGW* 3:241n)

BROWN, ANDREW (ca. 1744–97), was the printer of Philadelphia's *Federal Gazette* since founding it in 1788 as a pro-Constitution newspaper. His petition during the third session of Congress for a mode of authenticating laws led to the Resolution on the Printing of Federal Laws. See also *DHFFC* 8:743–44, 14:xviii–xix.

BROWN, BENJAMIN (d. 1802), of Wells, Maine, was a store owner, marine insurance officer, and attorney in neighboring Kennebunk since 1782. (Edward Bourne, *The History of Wells and Kennebunk* [Portland, Me., 1875], p. 755)

BROWN, JOHN (1728–1803), father of Representative Brown, was born in Ireland and immigrated to Augusta County, Virginia, in 1738. He graduated from the College of New Jersey (Princeton) in 1749, was ordained a Presbyterian minister in 1753, and settled in Rockbridge County, Virginia. (*Princetonians, 1748–1768*, pp. 15–17)

BROWN, NICHOLAS (1729–91), a Federalist merchant and securities speculator of Providence, Rhode Island, was a partner in the firm of Brown and Benson, 1783–91, and co-owner of a distillery with Welcome Arnold beginning in 1788. (James B. Hedges, *The Browns of Providence Plantations* [Cambridge, Mass., 1952], pp. 311, 318–19)

BROWN, GUSTAVUS RICHARD (1747–1804), was a physician of Port Tobacco, Maryland. (*PGW* 1:120)

BRUCE, ROBERT, was a New York City landlord and grocer at 3 Front Street.

BRYAN, GEORGE (1731–27 January 1791), an Irish born merchant of Philadelphia, was a member of the state's Supreme Executive Council, 1776–79, a state Assemblyman, 1779–80, and associate justice of the state supreme court from 1780 until his death. Although he was not, as many thought, the author of the Antifederalist "Centinel" series, 1787–88, he did oppose ratification of the Constitution as a delegate to the Harrisburg Convention in 1788. See also *DHFFC* 9:372n. (*DHROC* 2:727)

BRYAN, SAMUEL (1759–1821), son of George Bryan and clerk of Pennsylvania's Assembly, 1784–85, authored the famous Antifederalist "Centinel" essays in 1787–88.

BUCKMINSTER, JOSEPH (1751–1812), was pastor of the North Congregational Church of Portsmouth, New Hampshire, from 1779 until his death.

The 1770 Yale graduate was a native of Rutland, Massachusetts. (*Yale Graduates* 3:366–74)

BULLITT, CUTHBERT (ca. 1740–1791), was a lawyer and planter of Prince William County, Virginia, which he represented in the state House of Delegates, 1776–77 and 1785–88, and at the ratification convention where he voted in favor of the Constitution. In 1788 he was appointed a justice on the state's General Court. (*DHROC* 8:310n; Herbert A. Johnson, Charles T. Cullen, and Charles F. Hobson, eds., *The Papers of John Marshall* [9+ vols., Chapel Hill, N.C., 1974–], 1:138n, 5:xxxii)

BURKE, EDMUND (1729–97), an Irish philosopher, political theorist, and member of Parliament since 1765, was a spokesman for liberal imperial policy in America and, after the Revolution, India.

BURNLEY, REUBEN (1766–1808), originally of Orange County, Virginia, resided at the seat of government from September 1789 until 1791 as clerk to the commissioner for settling Virginia's accounts with the United States. By 1793 he became engrossing clerk for the United States House of Representatives. (*PJM* 12:429)

BURNLEY, ZACHARIAH (ca. 1730–1800), of Orange County, Virginia, served as justice of the peace, sheriff, county lieutenant, and member of the state House of Delegates, 1780–81. He was father to Reuben Burnley. (*PJM* 1:148n)

BURR, JOSIAH (1753–95), a merchant of New Haven, Connecticut, was involved with Representative Wadsworth in various industrial and land speculation ventures. (Charles B. Todd, *A General History of the Burr Family* [New York, 1902], p. 188)

BURR, THADDEUS (1735–1801), was a major landowner and public securities holder of Fairfield, Connecticut, which he represented for most of the period 1775–89. The 1759 College of New Jersey (Princeton) graduate voted to ratify the Constitution at the state convention in 1788 and served as a Presidential Elector the next year. (*Princetonians, 1748–1768*, pp. 135–37)

BURR, THEODOSIA PREVOST (d. 1794), who married Aaron Burr in 1782, died of cancer after a long illness. Their only child to survive infancy was a daughter, Theodosia (1783–1812). Burr had been a friend of Theodore Sedgwick since the early years of the Revolutionary War. (*Sedgwick*, p. 16;

Samuel H. Wendell and Meade Minnigerode, *Aaron Burr* [New York, 1925], p. 103; *Princetonians, 1769–1775,* pp. 196, 198, 202)

BURRALL, JONATHAN (1753–1834), of Connecticut served as commissioner for settling the accounts of the quartermaster general and commissary departments from 1786 until 1789, when he was appointed assistant postmaster general. During the Revolutionary War he rose from assistant to the paymaster general of the Continental Army in 1776 to deputy paymaster general, 1781–83. See also *DHFFC* 9:151n. (*PGW* 3:577, 4:139)

BUSH, GEORGE (d. 1796), was a merchant of Wilmington, Delaware, where he served as collector, 1789–96, having held the post under the state collector since 1781. During the Revolutionary War he served as lieutenant in the Delaware Battalion of the Flying Camp, 1776, and as captain in Thomas Hartley's Additional Continental Regiment, 1777–78, before transferring to the 6th Regiment of the Pennsylvania Line, 1778–81, and the 3rd Regiment thereafter until retiring at war's end as a brevet major. See also *DHFFC* 2:489.

BUTLER, SENATOR PIERCE, family during the First Congress: his wife Mary Middleton (m. 1771), who was the daughter of wealthy Charleston planter Thomas Middleton; and four daughters who lived with them during the first and second sessions: Sarah (1772?–1831), Anne Elizabeth (1774–1854), Frances (1774–1836), and Harriot (1775?–1815). Anne and Frances moved to Philadelphia with their father after their mother's death in New York City on 13 November 1790. (Malcolm Bell, Jr., *Major Butler's Legacy: Five Generations of a Slaveholding Family* [Athens, Ga., 1987], pp. 484–87)

BUTLER, RICHARD (1743–91), an Irish born immigrant who became an Indian trader in western Pennsylvania in the 1760s, served as Indian commissioner in 1785–86 and superintendent of Indian affairs for the northern department, 1786–88. During the Revolutionary War he rose from captain of the 2nd Pennsylvania Battalion to major and then lieutenant colonel of the 8th Regiment of the state Line in the single year 1776. Promoted to colonel of the 9th Regiment in 1777, he transferred to the 5th in 1781 and again to the 3rd in 1783, when he was discharged as brevet brigadier general, having participated at the battles of Saratoga, Stony Point, and Yorktown. See also *DHFFC* 9:7n, 126. (*JCC* 29:735–37, 31:517)

BUTLER, THOMAS (1778–1838), the only son of Senator Butler to survive childhood, was sent to England in 1784 to study under Reverend Weeden Butler (no relation). Returning to America briefly in 1795, he later married without his father's blessing and settled permanently in France. Butler eventually disinherited him for not becoming a "Distinguished ornament." (Malcolm Bell, Jr., *Major Butler's Legacy: Five Generations of a Slaveholding Family* [Athens, Ga., 1987], p. 486)

BUTLER, WEEDEN (1742–1823), an Anglican minister of Margate, England, was for more than forty years master of a classical school in the Chelsea section of London, where the son of Senator Butler (no relation) was enrolled as a student during the First Congress.

CABOT, GEORGE (1752–1823), was a merchant of Beverly, Massachusetts, whose extensive business interests included directorship of the Bank of Massachusetts from 1784 and proprietorship of the Beverly Cotton Manufactory from 1787. On behalf of the latter he lobbied Congress in June 1789 against a high cotton duty, and petitioned in April 1790 for other encouragement of the industry. He represented Essex County in the state Senate in 1783, voted to ratify the Constitution at the state convention, ran unsuccessfully for Presidential Elector from Essex County in January 1789, and succeeded Tristram Dalton in the Senate, 1791–96. See also *DHFFC* 8:365–71. (*DHFFE* 1:744–45)

CABOT, FRANCIS (1757–1832), was a merchant of Salem, Massachusetts, who served as a major under General Benjamin Lincoln in the state militia during Shays's Rebellion. (Lloyd V. Briggs, *History and Genealogy of the Cabot Family, 1475–1927* [2 vols., Boston, 1927], 1:195–96)

CALDWELL, SAMUEL (ca. 1738–1798), an Irish born merchant of Philadelphia, was appointed state collector of that port in 1788, and clerk of the United States district court for Pennsylvania in October 1789. (*PGW* 2:51–52n)

CALHOUN, JAMES (1743–1816), had been a merchant of Baltimore since 1771. He served as a deputy quartermaster general for Maryland's Western Shore, 1778–80, and the state's commissary general for the Western Shore in 1781. (*PGW* 3:61–63n)

CAMPBELL, ARTHUR (1742–1811), represented Washington County, Virginia, in the state House of Delegates, 1776–88. Deeply involved in western land speculation, he was a principal supporter of Kentucky statehood and the creation of the state of Franklin, in present day eastern Tennessee. (*PJM* 4:126n)

CAMPBELL, DONALD, became an alderman of Norfolk, Virginia, in 1793.

CARBERRY, HENRY (1757–1822), of Baltimore, rose from lieutenant to captain in Thomas Hartley's Additional Continental Regiment from 1777 until its redesignation as the 11th Regiment of the Pennsylvania Line in 1779. Wounded in action later that year, he had been discharged for two years before his leadership role in the Line's mutinous demonstration before the Pennslyvania State House in June 1783. (*PGW* 3:310–12n)

CARGILL, JAMES (1725–1812), represented Newcastle, Maine, in the Massachusetts House of Representatives, 1788–89. (David Q. Cushman, *The History of Ancient Sheepscot and Newcastle* [Bath, Me., 1882], p. 362)

CARMARTHEN, MARQUIS OF. See Leeds, Francis Osborne, Duke of.

CARNES, JOHN (1723–1802), a former Congregational minister and chaplain of the 18th Continental Regiment in 1776, settled permanently as a merchant in Lynn, Massachusetts, in 1777. The 1742 Harvard graduate served the town as state Representative, 1785–93, delegate to the state convention where he voted to ratify the Constitution, and justice of the peace beginning in 1788. (*Harvard Graduates* 11:137–42)

CARRINGTON, EDWARD (1749–1810), a lawyer of Powhatan County, Virginia, was federal marshal for the state, 1789–90, and supervisor of distilled spirits, 1791–94. He served as lieutenant colonel of the 1st Continental Artillery Regiment, 1776–81, and as deputy quartermaster general of the southern department thereafter until war's end, when he joined the Society of the Cincinnati. He sat in Congress, 1786–88, and was an unsuccessful Federalist candidate for the state convention in 1788. See also *DHFFC* 2:548–49. (*DHROC* 9:606–7)

CARROLL, CATHERINE "KITTY" (1778–1861), was the daughter of Senator Carroll. Like other Maryland Catholic families, the Carrolls enrolled her in the school of the English Canonesses of the Holy Sepulchre in Liège, in present day Belgium, which she attended from the summer of 1789 until 1794. (The Catholic Record Society *Miscellanea* 17[London, 1915])

CASS, JONATHAN (1752–1830), a blacksmith of Exeter, New Hampshire, was appointed a captain in the federal army in March 1791. During the Revolutionary War he rose from private in 1775 to ensign in the 3rd Regiment of the New Hampshire Line in 1776 and first lieutenant in 1778. He transferred to the 2nd Regiment in 1781, was promoted to captain in 1782, and retired at war's end, when he joined the Society of the Cincinnati. See also *DHFFC* 2:514–15.

CHALONER, JOHN (1748–93), a merchant of Philadelphia, signed the memorial of the public creditors of that city in August 1789. From 1778 to 1780 he served as an assistant purchasing commissary for Commissary General Jeremiah Wadsworth, thereafter acting as agent for Wadsworth's partnership with Alexander Hamilton's brother-in-law, John B. Church, to supply the French army in America. (*PRM* 2:28n; *PAH* 3:433n; *DHFFC* 8:264)

CHAMBERS, STEPHEN (ca. 1750–16 May 1789), a lawyer of Lancaster County, Pennsylvania, was an unsuccessful Federalist candidate for Representative in the first federal election. Born in Ireland, he rose from first lieutenant in the 12th Regiment of the Pennsylvania Line in 1776 to captain the following year, retiring in 1778, and later becoming a member of the Society of the Cincinnati. He served a single term in the state's Assembly, 1778–79, and voted to ratify the Constitution at the state convention in 1787. Wounds received in a duel led to his death. (*DHROC* 2:727; *DHFFE* 1:413–14)

CHAMPION, RICHARD (1743–91), was an American sympathizer who left England in 1784 and settled as a planter near Camden, South Carolina. He was naturalized in 1787 and participated in the state constitutional convention in 1790. (*South Carolina House* 3:136–37)

CHANDLER, JOHN (1736–96), of Newtown, Connecticut, sat on the state's Council of Assistants, 1790–95. The 1759 Yale graduate served as colonel of the 8th Regiment of the Connecticut Line, 1777–78, and voted to ratify the Constitution at the state convention. (*Yale Graduates* 2:575–76)

CHANDLER, THOMAS B. (1726–90), was an Anglican minister of Elizabethtown, New Jersey. A 1745 graduate of Yale, he became a Loyalist and fled to England in 1775, but returned to his pastorate ten years later.

CHASE, SAMUEL (1741–1811), a lawyer of Baltimore, represented Annapolis in the colonial and state assemblies, 1764–84, and sat in Congress, 1774–78, where he signed the Declaration of Independence. He represented Baltimore in the state House of Delegates, 1787–88, and voted against the Constitution at the state convention as a delegate from Anne Arundel County. He was appointed Baltimore County court judge in 1788, and chief judge of the state's General Court, 1791–96. (*DHFFE* 2:109n; *DHSCUS* 1:105–10)

CHASE, THOMAS (1739–87), was a Boston merchant who had served as deputy quartermaster general for the eastern department under Thomas

Mifflin and Nathanael Greene. He married Elizabeth Bagnall in 1771. (*PNG* 2:330n)

CHESLEY, ROBERT, JR., was appointed port surveyor of St. Mary's County, Maryland, 1789–92. During the Revolutionary War he rose from first lieutenant in the 2nd Regiment of the Maryland Line in 1776 to captain in 1777, transferring to the 3rd Regiment in 1781 in which he served for the duration of the war. (*PGW* 3:92n)

CHESTER, JOHN (1749–1809), a farmer of Wethersfield, Connecticut, was federal supervisor of distilled spirits for the state, 1791–1801. A 1766 graduate of Yale, he joined the 2nd Regiment of the Connecticut Line as a captain in 1775 and transferred to a state militia regiment, retiring as its colonel in 1776. After the war he became a member of the Society of the Cincinnati. He served in the state House of Representatives almost continuously from 1772 to 1788, as speaker from 1785 to 1788. He did not attend Congress when elected in 1787 and 1788, but did attend the state convention where he voted to ratify the Constitution. An unsuccessful candidate for Representative in the first federal election, he subsequently served on the state's Council of Assistants, 1788–92. See also *DHFFC* 2:483–84. (*DHFFE* 2:52)

CHETWOOD, JOHN (1736–1807), a lawyer of Elizabethtown, New Jersey, represented Essex County at the state's ratification convention and in its upper house, or Legislative Council, in 1788. He served as associate justice of the state supreme court, 1789–97. (*DHFFE* 3:11n)

CHEW, BENJAMIN (1722–1810), was a Philadelphia lawyer and jurist and the father-in-law of Edward Tilghman and of Maryland's Governor John Eager Howard.

CHILDS, FRANCIS (1763–1830), moved to New York City from Philadelphia in 1785 and with the assistance of his patrons, John Jay and Benjamin Franklin, established *The Daily Advertiser*, which he edited until 1796. With John Swaine, who became his partner in July 1789, Childs enjoyed a lucrative printing contract with the House of Representatives. In 1790 he followed Congress to Philadelphia where he and Swaine printed the *National Gazette*, 1791–93. (*DHFFC* 4:xxviii, 8:737–39, 10:xxxviii–xxxix; *American Newspapers* 2:925)

CHILLEAU, MARIE CHARLES, MARQUIS DE, was France's governor of St. Domingue (Haiti) from December 1788 until his recall in mid 1789. During his controversial tenure, he suspended the regulations forbidding the importation of American flour for three months, beginning in March 1789, and decreed the opening of five additional Haitian ports to American shipping the following May. (E. Wilson Lyon, *The Man Who Sold Louisiana: The Career of François Barbé-Marbois* [Norman, Okla., 1942], p. 61)

CHILTON, CHARLES (1741–1824), of St. Mary's City, Maryland, was appointed port surveyor at Town Creek on the Patuxent River in 1790. He served in the state House of Delegates in 1788. See also *DHFFC* 2:496. (*Maryland Legislators* 1:219–20)

CHOATE, JOHN (1737–91), was a shipbuilder and shipowner of Ipswich, Massachusetts, which he served as justice of the peace, 1778–88, and state Representative, 1781, 1783, 1785–86, and 1788. (Main, *Political Parties*, p. 411; Joseph B. Felt, *History of Ipswich, Essex, and Hamilton* [Cambridge, Mass., 1834], p. 184)

CHOATE, STEPHEN (1727–1815), a farmer of Ipswich, Massachusetts, served in the state House of Representatives, 1776–79, and Senate, 1780–83. (*Massachusetts Legislators*, p. 188)

CHRYSTIE, JAMES (1750–1807), one of New York City's leading East Indies merchants, participated in George Washington's first inaugural procession as lieutenant colonel of the city militia. He emigrated from Scotland and had settled in Pennsylvania by 1776, when he was commissioned a first lieutenant in the state's 2nd Battalion. Promoted to captain, he served in the 3rd Regiment of the state Line until transferring to the 2nd Regiment in 1783, when he resigned. (*New York*, p. 67)

CHURCH, EDWARD (1740–1816), was a Boston merchant who by 1787 had settled in Georgia for the purpose of "repairing a ruined fortune" in the cotton business. He was appointed United States consul to Bilboa, Portugal, in 1790 but did not serve. He graduated from Harvard in 1759. See also *DHFFC* 2:501. (*Harvard Graduates* 14:389–93; *PGW* 2:269–70n)

CHURCH, JOHN B. (d. 1818), emigrated from England shortly before the Revolutionary War and, with Jeremiah Wadsworth as a partner and John Chaloner as their Philadelphia agent, made a fortune contracting supplies for the French and American troops, 1780–85. Like Wadsworth, he was a principal investor in the Bank of North America. In 1777 he married Angelica Schuyler, oldest daughter of Senator Schuyler and sister of Secretary of the Treasury Hamilton's wife, Elizabeth; Hamilton had power of attorney over Church's business affairs after the family moved to England in 1783. In 1790 he was elected a member of Parliament. (*PRM* 1:374n; *PAH* 3:433n, 4:280n)

CHURCHMAN, JOHN (1753–1805), a Quaker surveyor and cartographer of East Nottingham, Pennsylvania, took up residence in New York City at the beginning of the first session to petition Congress for copyright protection for his published atlases and a subsidy for his scientific experiments. A second petition in the third session sought changes in the Copyright Act and repeated the request for a subsidy, without success. See also *DHFFC* 8:8–9, 12–13, 16, 29–30.

CILLEY, JOSEPH (1734–99), was justice of the peace of Rockingham County, New Hampshire, and major general of the state militia. During the Revolutionary War he served as major of the 2nd Regiment of the New Hampshire Line in 1775 and of the 8th Continental Regiment from 1776, and lieutenant colonel of the 1st Regiment of the state Line from 1776 until his promotion to its commanding colonel, 1777–81. He was an unsuccessful candidate for Presidential Elector in the first federal election. (*DHFFE* 1:854)

CLARK, ABRAHAM (1726–94), a lawyer of Rahway, New Jersey, served as commissioner to settle the United States' accounts with New Jersey, 1789–90. He represented Essex County periodically in both the General Assembly and Legislative Council throughout the 1770s and 1780s, and was a delegate to Congress, 1776–78, 1780–83, and 1786–88, where he signed the Declaration of Independence. He attended the Annapolis Convention in 1786 but declined his election to the Federal Convention. His defeat for Representative in the first federal election was disputed in an unsuccessful petition campaign in 1789. He was elected two years later and served two terms. (*DHROC* 3:196; *DHFFE* 4:181)

CLARK, GEORGE ROGERS (1752–1818), of Louisville, Kentucky, was a frontier explorer honored for his military conquest of the Old Northwest during the Revolutionary War, a history of which he completed in 1791. He served for a number of years after the war on the Virginia state commission overseeing land grants to veterans in the Virginia Military Reserve, which lay between the Scioto and Little Miami rivers in the Northwest Territory. His reputation as a drunkard, combined with his participation in an aborted plan to attack Spanish Louisiana in 1790–91, discredited him. (*PTJ* 19:xxxiii)

CLARK, JOHN (ca. 1751–1819), was a lawyer of York, Pennsylvania. During the Revolutionary War he served as a first lieutenant in the 1st Continental Regiment and a major in the 2nd Pennsylvania Regiment of the Flying Camp in 1776. (*PMHB* 20[1896]:77–86)

CLARKE, ELIJAH (1733–99), represented Wilkes County, Georgia, in the state's House of Assembly in 1782 and 1784–89. A native of North Carolina, he settled in Georgia in 1774 and became a brigadier general of the state militia during the Revolutionary War. (*DHFFE* 2:445n; *DHROC* 3:207)

CLARKSON, LEVINUS (1740–98), originally of Charleston, South Carolina, settled in New Brunswick, New Jersey, before the Revolutionary War and became a merchant and land speculator. (*PGW* 2:26)

CLAXTON, THOMAS, a former Federalist newspaper publisher from Albany, New York, served as assistant doorkeeper of the House from 4 April 1789 until 1794. A month earlier, he had petitioned the Senate and probably also the House to be appointed messenger. See also *DHFFC* 8:518–19.

CLAY, JOSEPH (1741–1804), a British born merchant and lawyer of Savannah, Georgia, was deputy paymaster general for the southern department of the Continental Army, 1777–78. He declined to attend Congress when elected in 1778, but served as state treasurer in 1782 and represented Chatham County in the state's House of Assembly, 1782–83 and 1787–88. (*DHROC* 3:232n)

CLINTON, GEORGE (1739–1812), of Ulster County, New York, was governor, 1777–95, and unsuccessful Antifederalist candidate for Vice President in the first federal election, in which he received three electoral votes. He led the state's political faction that was opposed to the one led by Senator Schuyler. See also *DHFFC* 9:136n. (*DHFFE* 4:295)

CLOPTON, JOHN (1756–1816), represented New Kent County, Virginia, in the state House of Delegates, 1789–91. The 1776 graduate of the College of Philadelphia (University of Pennsylvania) served as a captain of the state militia during the Revolutionary War and later enrolled in the Society of the Cincinnati.

CLYMER, REPRESENTATIVE GEORGE, family during the First Congress: his wife, Elizabeth Meredith (m. 1765, d. 1815), residing in Philadelphia; and their children Henry (1767–1830), Meredith (1771–1794), Margaret (1772–99), Anne (d. 1810), and George, Jr. (1783–1848). (Jerry Grundfest, *George Clymer, Philadelphia Revolutionary* [New York, 1982], pp. 31–32n)

COBB, DAVID (1748–1830), was a physician of Taunton, Massachusetts. The 1766 Harvard graduate volunteered as a regimental surgeon in 1775 before being commissioned lieutenant colonel in Henry Jackson's Continental Regiment, 1777–80. He also served as aide-de-camp to George Washington while officially assigned to the 9th Massachusetts Regiment (1781–83) and the 5th Regiment in the last year of the war, when he was breveted brigadier general. He was judge of the Bristol County court of common pleas, 1784–96, speaker of the state House of Representatives, 1789–93, and an unsuccessful Federalist candidate for Representative in the first federal election. (*DHFFE* 1:745)

COBB, MATTHEW (1757–1824), a merchant of Biddeford, Maine, was known as "King Cobb" for his fleet of merchant ships. ([Maine] *Portland Advertiser*, 27 March 1824)

COCHRANE, ROBERT (ca. 1735–1824), was employed by Charleston, South Carolina, to measure the tonnage of incoming ships.

COCKLE, JOHN, of New York City, grandson of the noted Loyalist John Cockle of Jamaica, New York, sought federal office in order to support his widowed mother and sisters. (*PAH* 5:343–44)

COFFIN, EDMUND, a sea captain of Portsmouth, New Hampshire, was appointed harbor master of that port in 1792.

COKE, SIR EDWARD (1552–1634), jurist and chief justice of England (1613–16), initiated the Petition of Right (1628) as a champion of the common law and leader of the opposition to the Stuart kings.

COKE, THOMAS (1747–1814), was appointed superintendent of the Methodist Church in America by John Wesley in 1784. "Bishop" Coke attended the Methodist Conference in New York City in May 1789 and departed for England on 5 June. (*New York*, pp. 161–62)

COLEMAN, ROBERT (1741–1825), emigrated from Ireland in 1757 and became a wealthy iron manufacturer in Lancaster County, Pennsylvania, which he represented in the state Assembly, 1783–84, and at the state convention where he voted to ratify the Constitution. (*American Conservatism*, p. 336)

COLLIN, NICHOLAS (1746–1831), was the Swedish born pastor of Philadelphia's Old Swedes Church. His twenty-nine pro-ratification essays written under the pseudonym "Foreign Spectator" were printed in the [Philadelphia] *Independent Gazetteer* in August–October 1787, and parts were widely reprinted and circulated thereafter. Between October 1788 and February 1789 he revived the series to argue against the need for amendments to the Constitution. (*DHROC* 13:290)

COLLINS, CORNELIUS (d. 1791), served as collector at Sunbury, Georgia, 1789–91. A first lieutenant in the 2nd Regiment of the Georgia Line, 1777–82, he joined the Society of the Cincinnati at war's end. See also *DHFFC* 2:491.

COLLINS, ISAAC (1746–1817), was a Quaker printer who settled in Trenton, New Jersey, where he edited and published the *New Jersey Gazette*, 1778–86. From 1770 he was the official provincial and then state printer. (*Philadelphia Families* 2:1410–15)

COLLINS, JOHN (1717–95), a farmer of Newport, Rhode Island, served as governor, 1786–90, in which capacity he cast the deciding vote in the state Senate for calling a ratification convention in 1790. He sat in Congress, 1778–80 and 1782–83.

COLLINS, STEPHEN (1733–94), was a Philadelphia Quaker merchant who was sympathetic to the Revolutionary cause during the war. (*Drinker* 3:2129)

COLLINS, THOMAS (1732–29 March 1789), a planter of "Belmont Hall," near Smyrna, in Kent County, Delaware, was president (governor) of the state from 1786 until his death. During the Revolutionary War he served as an officer of the state militia and frequently as a member of the state's Legislative Council, prior to occupying the bench of the Kent County court of common pleas as chief justice, 1782–86. (*DHROC* 3:114; John A. Munroe, *Federalist Delaware, 1775–1815* [New Brunswick, N.J., 1954], p. 103)

COLT, PETER (1744–1824), a businessman of Hartford, Connecticut, served as state treasurer, 1789–93. The 1764 Yale graduate was deputy commissary general for the eastern department, 1777–80. His close business connections to Representative Wadsworth dated to 1778. (*Yale Graduates* 3:65–66)

CONNOLLY, JOHN (ca. 1743–1813), was an agent of the royal governor of Canada who used Detroit as his base for fomenting separatism in Kentucky in 1788 and 1789. A native Pennsylvanian, the former trader and land speculator became a British pensioner for his services commanding a Loyalist corps during the Revolutionary War. (*PGW* 1:189–90n)

CONSTABLE, WILLIAM (1752–1803), a prominent New York City merchant and speculator in land and public securities, was a business partner of Senator Morris, who resided with the Constables at 39 Great Dock Street during the first and second sessions. In 1782 he married Ann Townsend of Philadelphia. See also *DHFFC* 9:183n.

CONY, DANIEL (1752–1842), a physician of Hallowell, Maine, represented that town in the Massachusetts House of Representatives from 1786 until 1789, when he was an unsuccessful candidate for Presidential Elector. He subsequently served in the state Senate, 1790–91. (*DHFFE* 1:745–46; *DHROC* 4:141n)

COOK, FRANCIS (ca. 1755–1832), a merchant of Pownalborough, Maine, was collector at Wiscasset, 1789–1829. He sat in the Massachusetts House of Representatives, 1787–89. (*DHFFC* 2:502)

COOPER, WILLIAM (1754–1809), originally of Philadelphia, settled in present day Cooperstown, Otsego County, New York, in 1788. Beginning in the late 1780s, he acquired and speculated in lands along the Upper Susquehanna and Delaware rivers in Pennsylvania and New York State, both on his own behalf and as agent for several other prominent land speculators, including Robert Morris, Tench Coxe, and Henry Drinker. (Alan Taylor, *William Cooper's Town: Power and Persuasion on the Frontier of the Early American Republic* [New York, 1995], pp. 74, 119)

CORBIN, FRANCIS (1759–1821), was a London trained lawyer of Middlesex County, Virginia, which he represented in the state House of Delegates, 1785–95, and at the ratification convention where he voted in favor of the Constitution. (*DHROC* 8:525)

COTTRINGER, GARRETT (ca. 1759–1816), was a Philadelphia merchant and associate of Robert Morris. (Morris to Horatio Gates, 19 June 1787, Gates Papers, NHi)

Cox, John (1731–93), was a prominent Philadelphia merchant who retired to his estate, "Bloomsbury Farm," outside Trenton, New Jersey, shortly after the war, having served as an assistant quartermaster general, 1778–80. He signed the petition of the citizens of New Jersey and Pennsylvania regarding the location of the seat of government presented to Congress in August 1789 and the petition of the public creditors of the Trenton area and Burlington County, New Jersey, presented in December 1790. (*PJM* 5:457n; *DHFFC* 8:298, 452)

Coxe, Tench (1755–1824), was a Philadelphia merchant, land speculator, economist, and Federalist essayist who became assistant secretary of the treasury on 10 May 1790. He overcame a wartime record of Loyalism sufficiently to serve as the only Pennsylvanian in attendance at the Annapolis Convention of 1786 and a member of Congress, 1788–89. In 1782 he married his first cousin Rebecca Coxe (1763–1806), a widely respected musician and composer. See also *DHFFC* 9:78n. (*Coxe*, pp. 55, 84, 155)

Craddock, Robert (d. 1837), was a land speculator who settled in Danville, Kentucky, by late 1787.

Craigie, Andrew (1754–1819), was a New York City merchant heavily involved with William Duer in public securities speculation, was Duer's and Royal Flint's partner in the Scioto Company's land speculation ventures in the Northwest Territory. He served as apothecary general of the Continental Army, 1777–83, and became a member of the Society of the Cincinnati. In 1791 he settled permanently in Cambridge, Massachusetts. (*PGW* 6:492; *DHFFC* 9:185n)

Cranch, Mary Smith (1740–1811), of Braintree (now Quincy), Massachusetts, was the elder sister of Abigail Adams and wife of Richard Cranch. (*Adams* 1:122n)

Cranch, Richard (1726–1811), was a glass manufacturer of Braintree (now Quincy), Massachusetts. In 1762 he married Mary Smith, whose younger sister Abigail married his lifelong friend John Adams two years later. A Suffolk County judge, 1779–93, he served simultaneously in the state Senate, 1785–87, and voted to ratify the Constitution at the state convention in 1788. (*Harvard Graduates* 11:370–76; *Adams* 1:16n)

Crèvecoeur, Michel-Guillaume St. John de (1735–1813), was French consul in New York City from 1783 until his return to France in May 1790. His famous *Letters from an American Farmer*, published in 1782, was based on the years he lived in Orange County, New York, 1769–80. His daughter married Louis Guillaume Otto on 13 April 1790. (*PGW* 1:96n; *PTJ* 16:356n, 17:13n)

CROCKER, JOSEPH (1749–97), a Boston shopkeeper and merchant, graduated from Harvard in 1774 and taught school before joining the 3rd Regiment of the Massachusetts Line in 1777. He rose from paymaster to lieutenant in 1778 and became captain in 1780, resigning the next year. He was a member of the Society of the Cincinnati and an active Federalist. (*Harvard Graduates* 18:406–9)

CROSS, RALPH, was a Boston merchant.

CROSS, STEPHEN (1731–1809), a merchant and shipbuilder of Newburyport, Massachusetts, was serving as the state's excise officer there when he was appointed collector for that port in 1789. He was removed for misconduct in 1792. See also *DHFFC* 2:502. (*PGW* 3:84)

CULVER, JONATHAN (ca. 1745–1807), was a sea captain of Norwich, Connecticut.

CUMMING, JOHN NOBLE (1752–1821), a businessman of Newark, New Jersey, was appointed deputy federal marshal for that state in 1789. The 1774 College of New Jersey (Princeton) graduate served in the 1st, 2nd, and 3rd regiments of the New Jersey Line during the Revolutionary War, rising from first lieutenant to lieutenant colonel between 1775 and 1783, when he joined the Society of the Cincinnati. His many business ventures in 1789 included part ownership in the Ohio Company and a major overland stage company that won federal mail contracts during the First Congress. His sister Catherine married Representative Boudinot's brother-in-law Philip Stockton in 1767. (*Princetonians, 1769–1775*, pp. 51, 370–75)

CUMMING, WILLIAM (1724–ca. 1797), uncle of John Hamilton, was a lawyer of Edenton, Chowan County, North Carolina, which he represented in the state's House of Commons, 1783–84 and 1788. He attended Congress in 1785 and in 1790 was nominated for a federal judgeship. (William S. Powell, ed., *Dictionary of North Carolina Biography* [6 vols., Chapel Hill, 1979–96], 1:473)

CURSON, RICHARD (ca. 1725–1805), was a Baltimore merchant and shipowner. In November 1789 he was one of the more than two hundred signers of a letter to Postmaster General Samuel Osgood supporting Mary Katherine Goddard as the city's postmistress. See also *DHFFC* 8:231–33, 237.

CUSHING, NATHAN (1742–1812), a lawyer of Scituate, Massachusetts, sat on the state's admiralty court and Executive Council from 1777, and in the state convention in 1788 where he voted to ratify the Constitution. The 1763 Harvard graduate went on to serve on the state supreme judicial court, 1790–1800. (*Harvard Graduates* 15:376–78)

CUSHING, WILLIAM (1732–1810), of Boston, Massachusetts, was chief justice of the state supreme judicial court from 1777 until his appointment to the United States Supreme Court in 1789, where he served until his death. A 1751 Harvard graduate, he was vice president of the state convention, where he voted to ratify the Constitution, and served as Presidential Elector in the first federal election. He married Hannah Phillips in 1774. (*Harvard Graduates* 13:26–39; *DHSCUS* 1:24–27)

CUSTIS, ELEANOR "NELLY" PARKE (1779–1852), and her brother George Washington Parke Custis (1781–1857), youngest children of Martha Washington's deceased son and stepchildren of David Stuart, resided with the Washingtons throughout the First Congress. (*PGW* 1:4–5n)

CUTLER, MANASSEH (1742–1823), was a Congregational minister as well as a practicing lawyer, physician, and amateur scientist of Ipswich, Massachusetts. After graduating from Yale in 1765 he served as chaplain of the 11th Regiment of the Massachusetts Line in 1776. One of the founders of the Ohio Company in 1786, he helped frame the Northwest Ordinance of 1787 while lobbying Congress for the sale of Ohio lands. He spent 1788–89 in the Ohio Valley and traveled to New York City to lobby for Ohio Company interests from 21 February to 23 April 1790. (*Yale Graduates* 3:112–17)

CUTTING, JOHN BROWN (ca. 1755–1831), an apothecary from Massachusetts who sometimes served as John Adams's secretary while studying law in London in 1787–88, returned to the United States in late 1788 as an agent of a European creditor against the state of South Carolina. Back in Europe by 1790, he joined American diplomats in lobbying for seamen's rights against British impressment. During the Revolutionary War he served as apothecary general of the eastern department, 1777–79, and of the middle department until 1780. (*DHROC* 9:631n, 896n; *PGW* 3:312–13; *DHFFE* 1:214n)

DAGGETT, DAVID (1764–1851), graduated from Yale in 1783 and three years later opened a law practice in New Haven, Connecticut, which he represented in the state House of Representatives, 1791–96. (*Yale Graduates* 4:260–64)

DALLEY, GIFFORD, served as House doorkeeper from 1789 to 1794. See also *DHFFC* 8:529–30, 9:226n.

DALTON, RUTH HOOPER (1739–post-1817), of Newburyport, Massachusetts, married Tristram Dalton in 1758. She resided with her husband during the first and second sessions of the First Congress. See also *DHFFC* 9:60n.

DANA, FRANCIS (1743–1811), a Boston lawyer who was a Presidential Elector and an unsuccessful candidate for Senator in the first federal election, served on the state supreme judicial court, 1785–1806. He graduated from Harvard in 1762, sat in the state's Executive Council, 1776–80, and signed the Articles of Confederation as a delegate to Congress, 1777–78 and 1784. In between he served as secretary to peace commissioner John Adams, 1779–81, before accepting his own assignment as minister to Russia, 1781–83, and voted to ratify the Constitution at the state convention. (*Harvard Graduates* 15:204–17; *DHROC* 4:xxxvi, 434; *DHFFE* 1:747)

DANA, JAMES (1735–1812), a 1753 Harvard graduate, was installed as Congregational minister of the First Church of New Haven, Connecticut, in April 1789. (*Harvard Graduates* 13:305–22)

DANDRIDGE, JOHN (d. 1799), was a lawyer of New Kent County, Virginia, which he represented in the state House of Delegates. (*PGW* 1:76n)

DANE, NATHAN (1752–1835), a lawyer of Beverly, Massachusetts, was an unsuccessful candidate for Senator and for Representative of Representative Goodhue's district in the first federal election. The 1778 Harvard graduate served in the state House of Representatives, 1782–86, and in Congress, 1785–88, where he was the principal author of the Northwest Ordinance of 1787. In 1790 he was elected a state Senator. (*DHFFE* 1:747–48)

DARRELL, EDWARD (1747–97), a Charleston, South Carolina merchant and a major investor in the state debt, represented St. Philip and St. Michael Parish in the state House of Representatives, 1782–90, voted to ratify the Constitution at the state convention, and served on the Privy Council,

1789–90. A former sea captain, he also served as Charleston's pilotage commissioner in 1788. (*South Carolina House* 3:169–70)

DAUBING (DOBINEY), MARY, operated a popular boardinghouse at 15 Wall Street, New York City, where Senators Bassett and Read, and Representatives Cadwalader, Stone, Seney, Contee, Lee, and Moore resided during the first session of Congress.

DAVIDSON, JOHN (1754–1807), a member of Maryland's Executive Council from Anne Arundel County, 1783–1801, was appointed collector of Annapolis in 1789. He served as a captain in the 2nd Regiment of the Maryland Line, 1776–81, and major in the 5th Regiment until the war's end, when he enrolled in the Society of the Cincinnati. (*PGW* 3:106)

DAVIE, WILLIAM R. (1756–1820), was a lawyer and planter of Halifax County, North Carolina, which he represented in the state's House of Commons almost continuously between 1784 and 1798. The 1776 College of New Jersey (Princeton) graduate rose from lieutenant of Pulaski's Legion in 1779 to colonel of a state cavalry corps the next year, serving until war's end. He attended the Federal Convention and later led the fight for ratification at both state conventions. In 1790 he declined appointment as federal district judge. See also *DHFFC* 2:527. (*DHFFE* 4:318n; *Princetonians, 1776–1783,* pp. 25–31)

DAVIES, WILLIAM (1749–1812), of Mecklenburg County, Virginia, had resided in New York City since early 1789 as commissioner for settling the United States accounts with Virginia, to which position he had been appointed the previous September. From 1775 until the close of the Revolutionary War he rose from captain of the 1st Regiment of the Virginia Line, to major of the 7th, lieutenant colonel of the 5th and 14th, and finally colonel of the 20th, 10th, and 1st regiments. (*PJM* 3:32n, 12:12n, 13:190n)

DAVIS, CALEB (1738–97), was a merchant, shipowner, and sugar refiner of Boston, which he represented in the state House of Representatives, 1776–81 and 1783–88, and at the state convention, where he voted to ratify the Constitution. In 1786 he was appointed a delegate to the Annapolis Convention, but joined Dalton, Gerry, and Goodhue in resigning his commission. (*LDC* 11:288; *Political Parties,* p. 411)

DAVIS, DANIEL (1762–1835), a native of Barnstable, Massachusetts, moved to Portland, Maine, in 1782 and became a successful lawyer and leader of the district's separatist movement. He represented Portland in the state House of Representatives, 1789–91. (Ronald F. Banks, *Maine Becomes a State: The Movement to Separate Maine from Massachusetts, 1785–1820* [Middletown, Conn., 1970], p. 27)

DAVIS, GEORGE (d. ca. 1799), had emigrated from Ireland by 1771 and resided briefly in Philadelphia before settling permanently in Trenton, New Jersey, in 1777. (*PGW* 3:367n)

DAVIS, SAMUEL (1765–1829), of Plymouth, Massachusetts.

DAVIS, STAIGE (d. 1815), collector at Urbanna, Virginia, under the state government since late 1788, declined appointment as port surveyor there in 1789. See also *DHFFC* 2:549. (*PGW* 4:7n)

DAVIS, WILLIAM (1727–1812), of Boston, was a mariner, merchant, and longtime town officeholder. He graduated from Harvard in 1745. (*Harvard Graduates* 11:556–57)

DAWES, THOMAS, JR. (1758–1825), was a Boston lawyer and member of the "Wednesday Night Club" who ran unsuccessfully against fellow club member Representative Ames in the first federal election. The 1777 Harvard graduate studied law under John Lowell, served in the state House of Representatives, 1787–89, and in the state convention, where he voted to ratify the Constitution. He was appointed judge of probate for Suffolk County in 1790, the same year he lost his bid to unseat Ames in the second federal election. His wife was the sister of James Greenleaf and sister-in-law of Nathaniel Walker Appleton and Noah Webster. His own sister Ann married Joseph Pierce in 1771. (*DHROC* 4:141n; *DHFFE* 1:748; *Ames*, pp. 104, 159, 161)

DAWSON, JOHN (1762–1814), was a lawyer and planter of Spotsylvania County, Virginia, which he represented in the state House of Delegates, 1786–90, and at the ratification convention, where he voted against the Constitution. The 1782 Harvard graduate served in Congress, 1788–89. (*DHROC* 8:17n, 355n)

DAYTON, ELIAS (1737–1807), a merchant of Elizabethtown, New Jersey, and father of Jonathan Dayton, served as colonel of the 3rd and 2nd regiments of the New Jersey Line between 1776 and 1783, when he retired as a brigadier general. He was president of the state Society of the Cincinnati.

DAYTON, JONATHAN (1760–1824), a lawyer of Elizabethtown, New Jersey, and the son of Elias Dayton, represented Essex County in the state's Legislative Council in 1789 and in the General Assembly the next year. His defeat for Representative in the first federal election was disputed in a First Congress petition campaign in April 1789, spearheaded by his brother-in-law, Matthias Ogden. The 1776 College of New Jersey (Princeton) graduate joined the 3rd Regiment of the New Jersey Line in that year and rose to captain by 1780, retiring at war's end when he enrolled in the Society of the Cincinnati. He sat in Congress, 1787–88, and was the youngest signer of the Constitution. In the 1780s and 1790s he was an agent for John Cleves Symmes' Miami Purchase. In the second federal election Dayton won a House seat which he retained until 1799, serving as Speaker the last four years. (*DHFFE* 3:182; *Princetonians, 1776–1783,* pp. 31–42)

DEARBORN, HENRY (1751–1829), federal marshal for Maine, 1789–93, was a physician of Pittston (now Gardiner), Maine, where he settled shortly after his discharge as lieutenant colonel of the 1st Regiment of the New Hampshire Line, 1781–83. Previous military service included captain of the 1st Regiment, 1775–76, and major, 1776–77, and lieutenant colonel, 1777–81, of the 3rd Regiment. See also *DHFFC* 2:502.

DEBLOIS, GILBERT, SR. (d. 1791), was a Boston merchant.

DELANY, SHARP (ca. 1739–1799), an Irish immigrant who settled as an apothecary in Philadelphia before the Revolutionary War, served as collector, 1789–99, having held that post under the state government since 1784. See also *DHFFC* 9:7n.

DENNIS, FRANCIS (ca. 1747–1812), of Salem, Massachusetts, served as a captain in the state militia during the Revolutionary War.

DENNIS, PATRICK, was a New York City merchant, sea captain, and harbor pilot. See also *DHFFC* 9:49n.

DERBY, ELIAS HASKET (1739–99), a merchant of Salem, Massachusetts, twice petitioned the First Congress for a temporary suspension of the Collection Act relating to the duty on teas. See also *DHFFC* 8:403–4.

DESAUSSURE, DANIEL (1736–98), was born into a Huguenot family in Beaufort, South Carolina, where he became a merchant and early activist in the Revolutionary movement. He sat in the state's House of Representatives, 1776–80, the privy council, 1783–85, and the Senate, 1785–90, where he presided, 1789–90. He voted in favor of the Constitution at the state ratification convention. (N. Louise Bailey, Mary L. Morgan, and Carolyn R. Taylor, *Biographical Directory of the South Carolina Senate, 1776–1985* [3 vols., Columbia, S.C., 1986], 1:384–86)

DEVENS, RICHARD (1721–1807), a merchant of Charlestown, Massachusetts, served in the state House of Representatives, 1775–76, and as commissary general of the state militia, 1776–82. (*LDC* 4:65n; *Massachusetts Legislators*, p. 206)

DEXTER, AARON (1750–1829), was a Boston physician who graduated from Harvard in 1776 and became professor of chemistry there in 1783.

DEXTER, SAMUEL (1761–1816), a 1781 Harvard graduate and member of Boston's Wednesday Night Club, practiced law in Weston, Massachusetts, which he represented in the state House of Representatives in 1789. (*DHFFE* 1:641n)

DICKINSON, JOHN (1732–1808), older brother of Senator Dickinson, a lawyer and planter of Kent County, Delaware, was known as the "Penman of the Revolution" for his many tracts and official documents, most famously *Letters from a Farmer in Pennsylvania* (1768). He represented both Pennsylvania (1774–76) and Delaware (1779) in Congress, where he wrote the first draft of and later signed the Articles of Confederation. He also served as president (governor) of both Delaware, 1782–83, and Pennsylvania, 1783–85. He chaired the Annapolis Convention in 1786, served in the Federal Convention, and became a Federalist essayist during the ratification debate, although he declined to stand as a candidate for the Senate in the first federal election. (Milton E. Flower, *John Dickinson: Conservative Revolutionary* [Charlottesville, Va., 1983], p. 253)

DOBBYN, HANNIBAL WILLIAM, arrived in New York City from Ireland in September 1789 to settle on the western frontier with some former tenants. In January 1790 he unsuccessfully petitioned Congress for "a considerable purchase of the public lands." See *DHFFC* 8:196–98.

DORCHESTER, SIR GUY CARLETON, LORD (1724–1808), commander in chief of British forces in North America during the last year of the Revolutionary War, was governor general of Canada, 1775–78 and 1786–96. In the latter role he employed George Beckwith as the British foreign ministry's agent in New York City.

DORSEY, WILLIAM (1764–ca. 1819), of Georgetown, Maryland (in present day District of Columbia), was a large landowner, lawyer, and ironmaster of Montgomery County, Maryland, which he represented in the state House of Delegates in 1788. (*Maryland Legislators* 1:279)

DOUGHTY, JOHN (ca. 1757–1826), of New Jersey, was a major in the federal army, 1789–91. The 1770 King's College (Columbia) graduate rose from captain in 1776 to General Philip Schuyler's aide-de-camp in 1777, and brevet major of artillery at war's end, when he became a member of the Society of the Cincinnati. He was active in the fortification of the Northwest Territory during the Confederation Period and was selected by Secretary of War Knox to conduct diplomatic negotiations with the Chickasaw and Choctaw nations in March 1790. See also *DHFFC* 2:518. (*DGW* 6:84n)

DOMENICO, GAETANO DRAGO DI, was a Genoese merchant whose letter to Senator Butler, repeating an earlier petition to the Confederation Congress offering to negotiate a treaty with the Barbary Pirates, was presented in the Senate and forwarded to the House in January 1790. See also *DHFFC* 8:xix, 1–2.

DRAYTON, WILLIAM (1732–90), of Charleston, South Carolina, was federal district judge for that state, 1789–90. A graduate of London's Middle Temple and a former chief justice of British East Florida, 1767–76, he spent much of the Revolutionary War in England but became admiralty judge and state supreme court justice after his return in 1780. See also *DHFFC* 2:543.

DRINKER, HENRY (1734–1809), was a prominent Quaker merchant of Philadelphia who was also engaged in iron mining and land speculation in northern Pennsylvania. He was exiled to western Virginia for alleged treason to the Revolutionary cause, 1777–78. An active abolitionist, he served in the eleven member delegation that delivered and lobbied on behalf of the Philadelphia Yearly Meeting's antislavery petition to Congress in February 1790. (*Drinker* 3:2139)

DUANE, JAMES (1733–97), was a New York City lawyer who served as mayor, 1784–89, and state Senator for the southern district, 1782–85 and 1788–90, before being appointed federal district judge for New York State, 1789–94. He sat in Congress for part of every year between 1774 and 1783, and voted to ratify the Constitution at the state convention. Although he was the choice of a Federalist caucus, Duane lost a bitterly contested first federal election to Senator King. By his marriage to Maria Livingston in

1759 he became a cousin of Chancellor Robert R. Livingston and brother-in-law of Senator Schuyler's daughter Cornelia. He was an honorary member of the Society of the Cincinnati. See also *DHFFC* 2:522. (*DHFFE* 3:558)

DUER, WILLIAM (1747–99), a New York City merchant and speculator in public securities and land, particularly the Scioto Land Company, was appointed assistant secretary of the treasury in September 1789, having served as secretary to the board of treasury since 1786. In April 1790 Congress forced his resignation after a secret House committee investigated evidence of his insider trading. Duer served in Congress, 1777–79, and was named an honorary member of the Society of the Cincinnati. See also *DHFFC* 9:185n. (*PAH* 13:222)

DUER, CATHERINE ALEXANDER, who married William Duer in 1779, was the daughter of Revolutionary War General William Alexander and Chancellor Robert R. Livingston's cousin, Sarah. Through her mother she was first cousin to Walter Livingston, who married Senator Schuyler's daughter and Secretary of the Treasury Hamilton's sister-in-law Cornelia in 1767. Her father's claim to the British title Lord Stirling gave her the name by which she was popularly known, "Lady Kitty." (*PAH* 20:455n; Robert F. Jones, *"The King of the Alley": William Duer, Politician, Entrepreneur, and Speculator* [Philadelphia, 1992], p. 65)

DUMAS, CHARLES GUILLAUME FRÉDÉRIC (1725–96), was a Swiss Frenchman residing at The Hague, where he served as Congress's agent and the unofficial chargé d'affaires to the Netherlands from 1775 until his death. (*PGW* 1:137n; *PRM* 5:532)

DUNCAN, ROBERT, was apprenticed to a merchant in his native Boston before moving to Philadelphia, where he operated a boardinghouse for members of Congress in 1776–77. He had returned to Boston by 1789. (*LDC* 6:448)

DUNSCOMB, ANDREW (ca. 1758–1802), resided in New York City as Virginia's agent for settling its accounts with the federal government. In February 1790 he unsuccessfully petitioned Congress for services he claimed to have performed as commissioner for settling federal accounts with Virginia in 1784–85. See also *DHFFC* 8:96–97.

DUPONCEAU, PETER STEPHEN (1760–1844), arrived from France in 1777 to serve as Baron von Steuben's military aide. In October 1781 he took the oath of allegiance and applied his command of languages as a clerk in the department of foreign affairs, serving as under-secretary, 1782–84. After the war he settled in Philadelphia and practiced international commercial law.

DUVALL, GABRIEL (1752–1844), was a lawyer of Annapolis, Maryland, which he represented in the state's House of Delegates, 1787–93, having earlier served on the Executive Council, 1782–86. (*Maryland Legislators* 1:290)

DWIGHT, THOMAS (1758–1819), a lawyer of Springfield, Massachusetts, represented that town in the state House of Representatives, 1784–86. He graduated from Harvard in 1778. His cousin Pamela married Representative Sedgwick in 1774, and in April 1791 he himself married Hannah Worthington, whose younger sister Frances married Representative Ames a year later. (*DHROC* 4:18n; *Ames*, p. 175)

DYER, ELIPHALET (1721–1807), a lawyer of Windham, Connecticut, represented that town as speaker of the state House of Representatives, 1784, and sat on the superior court, 1766–93, serving as chief judge beginning in 1789. He graduated from Yale in 1740, served in Congress, 1774–76, 1777–80, 1782–83, and although an Antifederalist, voted to ratify the Constitution at the state convention. (*Yale Graduates* 1:644–47; *DHROC* 3:609)

EDDINS (EDDENS), SAMUEL (d. 1803), had been the state's port inspector at York, Virginia, since 1788. During the Revolutionary War he rose from ensign of the 7th Regiment of the Virginia Line in 1776 to captain of the 1st Continental Regiment of Artillery from 1778 until war's end, when he joined the Society of the Cincinnati. (*PJM* 11:448n; *PGM* 1:448n)

EDES, BENJAMIN (1732–1803), a native of Charlestown, Massachusetts, was active in the Revolutionary movement and later in Antifederalist circles as editor and printer of the Antifederalist *Boston Gazette*, 1755–98.

EDMOND, WILLIAM (1755–1838), was a lawyer and gentleman farmer of Newtown, Connecticut, which he represented in the state House of Representatives, 1791–97. He served as a first lieutenant in the 6th Regiment of the Connecticut Line in 1775 and served two additional years in the state militia prior to graduating from Yale in 1777. (*American Conservatism*, p. 288)

EDWARDS, EDWARD (1763–1845), was a merchant of Stockbridge, Massachusetts.

EDWARDS, JONATHAN, JR. (1745–1801), was Congregational minister of New Haven, Connecticut's White Haven Church, 1768–95. He attended the College of New Jersey (Princeton), like his brothers Pierpont and Timothy, and graduated in 1765. (*Princetonians, 1748–1768,* pp. 492–96)

EDWARDS, PIERPONT (1750–1826), a 1768 College of New Jersey (Princeton) graduate, was a lawyer of New Haven, Connecticut, which he represented in the state House of Representatives, 1787–88, and served as speaker, 1788–89, before being appointed United States attorney for the state, 1789–1804. He sat in Congress, 1787–88, and at the state convention where he voted to ratify the Constitution. In the second federal election he led a campaign against Representative Sherman and was himself elected, although he resigned without taking his seat. His daughter Susanna married Samuel William Johnson, son of Senator Johnson, in 1791. Jonathan, Jr., and Timothy Edwards were his brothers. See also *DHFFC* 2:484. (*DHROC* 3:609; *Princetonians, 1748–1768,* p. 639)

EDWARDS, TIMOTHY (1738–1813), a shopkeeper and farmer of Stockbridge, Massachusetts, served with Representative Sedgwick on the commission for resolving the rival claims of Massachusetts and New York to the Genessee Tract in 1784 and subsequently earned a fortune speculating in those lands. The 1757 College of New Jersey (Princeton) graduate was a military supplier during the Revolutionary War and served on the Massachusetts Council, 1775–80. Elected to Congress in 1778, he declined to serve but sat as judge for the probate court of Berkshire County, 1778–87. Jonathan, Jr., and Pierpont Edwards were his younger brothers. (*Princetonians, 1748–1768,* pp. 182–85; *PRM* 4:497n)

EICHELBERGER, MARTIN (d. 1840), a Baltimore merchant, was weigher of the port under the state until 1789. During the Revolutionary War he served as first lieutenant in Thomas Hartley's Additional Continental Regiment, 1777–78, and in the 11th Regiment of the Pennsylvania Line, 1778–79. (*PGW* 3:107)

ELIOT, JOHN (1754–1813), Congregational pastor of Boston's New North Church from 1779 until his death, was a member of the Wednesday Night Club and several civic organizations. He graduated from Harvard in 1772 and served briefly as chaplain to the 10th Regiment of the Massachusetts Line, 1777–78, prior to his ordination. (*Harvard Graduates* 18:55–68)

ELLERY, WILLIAM (1727–1820), was a lawyer and merchant of Newport, Rhode Island, where he served as federal collector, 1790–1820, after resigning the post of continental loan commissioner he had held since 1786. The 1747 Harvard graduate sat in every Congress between 1776 and 1785 except for 1780–81 and signed the Declaration of Independence. In 1785 he was appointed the state's chief justice. See also *DHFFC* 2:540. (*Harvard Graduates* 12:134–52)

ELLICOTT, ANDREW (1754–1820), a surveyor from Ellicott City, Maryland, served as a deputy surveyor in the office of Geographer to the United States Thomas Hutchins until the latter's death in May 1789, when the office was discontinued. In July 1789 he successfully petitioned Congress for money to continue the survey of the boundary between western New York State and the Erie Triangle. In February 1791 he received instructions to survey the new federal district. See also *DHFFC* 8:191–94, 9:35–36n.

ELLSWORTH, SENATOR OLIVER, family during the First Congress: his wife Abigail Wolcott (1756–1818), whom he married in 1772 and who was a first cousin of Connecticut's longtime Lieutenant Governor Oliver Wolcott, and five children: Abigail, or "Nabby" (1774–1860); Oliver, or "Ollie" (1781–1805); Martin (1783–1857); Frances, or "Fanny" (1786–1868); and Delia (b. 23 July 1789–1840). (*DHFFC* 14:492)

ELSWORTH, DOROTHY AND VANDINE, kept a boardinghouse at 19 Maiden Lane, New York City, where House Clerk Beckley and Representatives Brown, Coles, Hartley, Hiester, Madison, Page, and White resided during the first and second sessions. Madison and Brown had boarded there during the Confederation Congress. (*LDC* 24:88, 25:97)

EMERY, SAMUEL (b. 1751), was a Boston merchant and member of the Wednesday Night Club until 1787. During the first session of Congress, he traveled as far south as Baltimore in search of a location to open a mercantile firm. He graduated from Harvard in 1774. (*Harvard Graduates* 18:419–22)

EMORY, CHARLES (ca. 1750–1811), was a planter and port surveyor of Caroline County, Maryland, which he represented in the state House of Delegates, 1788, 1789, and 1791–92. In 1795 he married Representative Seney's stepdaughter. (*Maryland Legislators* 1:306–7)

ERNEST, MATTHEW (d. 1805), was a lieutenant in the United States Artillery Regiment posted at Fort Pitt, Pennsylvania, 1789–91. See also *DHFFC* 2:522.

EVELEIGH, NICHOLAS (ca. 1748–1791), a merchant planter of Charleston, South Carolina, served as comptroller of the United States treasury from 1789 until his death in April 1791. During the Revolutionary War he rose from captain in the 2nd Regiment of the South Carolina Line in 1775 to deputy adjutant general with the rank of colonel, 1777–78. He was considered for the board of treasury in 1785, and served in the last days of the Confederation Congress in 1788. See also *DHFFC* 2:543, 9:296n.

FAIRLIE, JAMES (1757–1830), of Albany, was a clerk in the New York supreme court. (*DHSCUS* 1:650n)

FALCONER, NATHANIEL (d. 1806), a Philadelphia ship captain, served as a warden of the port, 1778–90. During the Revolutionary War he supervised a number of state- and Continental Navy-related tasks, serving in addition as superintendent of the Continental press for printing bills of credit and loan certificates, 1780–82. (*PRM* 2:48–49n; *Drinker* 3:2147)

FALLS, MOORE (1754–1834), a physician of Baltimore, was brother-in-law to George Lux by his marriage to Abigail Biddle, sister of Lux's wife Catherine, in 1785.

FEBIGER, CHRISTIAN (1749–96), a Philadelphia merchant, served as Pennsylvania's state treasurer from November 1789 until his death. A native of Denmark who settled in Boston in 1772, he was commissioned an adjutant of Samuel Gerrish's Massachusetts Regiment in 1775 and rose to lieutenant colonel of the 11th and colonel of the 3rd regiments of the Virginia Line in 1777 before retiring as a brevet brigadier general at war's end, when he became a member of the Society of the Cincinnati. (*PGW* 2:222n; *Pennsylvania Cincinnati* 1:387–90)

FELLOWS, GUSTAVUS (1736–1818), was a Boston merchant and sea captain who was involved in privateering while also serving as town selectman, 1777–83. (*PGW: Revolution* 4:162n)

FENNO, JOHN (1751–98), a failed Boston merchant, moved to New York City in January 1789 to establish the *Gazette of the United States*. Beginning in the second session Secretary of the Senate Otis awarded him several printing contracts which he retained when his office and newspaper followed Congress to Philadelphia. He married Mary Curtis of Needham, Massachusetts, in 1777. See also *DHFFC* 9:42n, 10:xxxiv–xxxviii. (*AASP* 89[1979])

FENWICK, JOSEPH (d. 1823), originally of St. Mary's County, Maryland, started a mercantile firm in Bordeaux, France, in 1786, which George Mason's son John joined as a partner in 1788. Fenwick returned to Virginia briefly in the winter of 1789–90 and was appointed United States consul at Bordeaux in June 1790. See also *DHFFC* 2:496. (*PGW* 3:53–55n)

FINNIE, WILLIAM (1739–1804), of Norfolk, Virginia, was in New York City unsuccessfully soliciting Congress and the President in the spring of 1789 and again in 1790 for a government appointment and petitioning for the settlement of his accounts as deputy quartermaster general and then quartermaster general of Virginia, 1776–80. He served as mayor of Williamsburg, Virginia, in 1786. See also *DHFFC* 7:464–69.

FISHBOURN (FISHBOURNE), BENJAMIN (1759–8 November 1790), was rejected by the Senate as collector of Savannah, Georgia, in August 1789 after holding that position under the state since 1788. During the Revolutionary War he served as paymaster of the 2nd Regiment of the Pennsylvania Line in 1776, and captain in the 4th and 1st regiments between 1777 and war's end, when he enrolled in the Society of the Cincinnati. From 1779 to 1783 he was also aide-de-camp to General Anthony Wayne, who became his political patron. He served in the state's House of Assembly, 1786–89, and as president of its Executive Council, 1788–89. See also *DHFFC* 2:491. (*PGW* 1:198–99n; *Pennsylvania Cincinnati* 1:400–405)

FISHER, JOHN, was employed as a clerk in the office of Confederation Congress Secretary Charles Thomson from at least 1776 until 1789. He seems to have been retained in some capacity by former Deputy Secretary Roger Alden after the latter became chief clerk of the state department, but left office after November 1789 in the wake of an embezzlement scandal. (*PGW* 3:297n, 4:441–48n)

FISHER, MIERS (1748–1819), a Philadelphia lawyer and Quaker antislavery activist, was a member of the city council during the First Congress. In addition to making arrangements for the federal government when it moved to Philadelphia in late 1790, he played an important behind the scenes role in many other legislative initiatives: his advice was sought on the Judiciary Act; he testified to and apparently served as secretary for the Senate committee on the Bailey Bill, which he probably drafted; he served as liaison between his fellow Quakers and the House committee on the antislavery petitions; and he penned the draft of a substitute Lighthouses Act on behalf of a committee of Philadelphia merchants. (*Philadelphia Families* 1:668–69; 1790 folder, Miers Fisher Papers, PHi; *DHFFC* 8:80, 84, 318, 334, 9:78)

FISK, JOHN (1744–97), was a merchant of Salem, Massachusetts, who served as a captain in the state navy during the Revolutionary War. (Robert Mc-Henry, ed., *Webster's American Military Biographies* [New York, 1984], p. 124)

FITCH, AUGUSTUS (1733?–1815), was a carpenter of East Windsor, Connecticut. His younger brother was the inventor and inveterate First Congress petitioner John Fitch.

FITCH, JOHN (1743–98), of Bucks County, Pennsylvania, petitioned the First Congress four times regarding patent protection for various inventions utilizing steam for inland navigation. See also *DHFFC* 8:39–41, 51–55, 60–65, 68–72.

FITCH, JONATHAN (1727–93), of Norwalk, Connecticut, was collector for Middletown, 1789–93. See also *DHFFC* 2:484.

FITZGERALD, JOHN (d. 1799), an Irish born merchant of Alexandria, Virginia, served as director of the Potowmack Company from 1785 through the First Congress. In the Revolutionary War he rose from captain in the 3rd Regiment of the Virginia Line in 1776 to lieutenant colonel and aide-de-camp to George Washington, 1776–78, simultaneously serving as major of the 9th Regiment, 1777–78. (*PGW: Revolution* 6:458)

FITZSIMONS, ANDREW, of Beaufort, South Carolina, was brother of Representative Fitzsimons.

FLEMING, GEORGE, was a merchant of Richmond, Virginia, who served as liaison between Virginia and New York Antifederalists in the summer of 1788.

FLEMING, WILLIAM (1728–95), a Scottish born physician of Staunton, Virginia, who served with George Washington during the French and Indian War, was an authority on frontier and Indian affairs. (*PGW* 3:388n)

FLINT, ABEL (1766–1825), younger brother of Royal, graduated from Yale in 1785 and served as a tutor at Rhode Island College (Brown), 1786–90. He was ordained a Congregational minister in 1791 and settled in Hartford, Connecticut. (*Yale Graduates* 4:404–7)

FLINT, ROYAL (1754–97), a 1773 Yale graduate, was a New York City merchant, bookseller, and speculator. His speculations included the 1787 purchase of three million acres in the Northwest Territory by the Scioto Land

Company, for whom he acted as agent, and the purchase of the certificates awarded under the Glaubeck Act in his capacity as attorney for the First Congress petitioner Catharine Greene. His partners in these ventures throughout the 1780s included William Constable, William Duer, and Representative Wadsworth, under whom he had served as assistant commissary general, 1778–80. In 1785 he was appointed commissioner for settling federal accounts with Massachusetts. (*Yale Graduates* 3:477–78; *DHFFC* 7:199; *LDC* 22:593n, 24:490n)

FOGG, JEREMIAH (1749–1808), represented Kensington, New Hampshire, at the state convention where he voted to ratify the Constitution. The 1768 Harvard graduate rose to the rank of captain in the 2nd Regiment of the New Hampshire Line between 1775 and 1782 when he transferred to the 1st Regiment. He was a member of the Society of the Cincinnati. (*Harvard Graduates* 17:21–24)

FOLSOM, DAVID (1750–88), originally of Newmarket, New Hampshire, settled in Harrisburg, Pennsylvania, shortly before his death. There he was involved with Senator Maclay's brother-in-law Robert Harris in erecting a nail works. (Elizabeth K. Folsom, *Genealogy of the Folsom Family, 1638–1938* [2 vols., Rutland, Vt., 1938], 1:215)

FORMAN, EZEKIEL (1736–95), served as sheriff and militia paymaster on Maryland's Eastern Shore before settling in Philadelphia upon his appointment to the Continental board of treasury in 1779. He resigned from the board four months before its dissolution in 1781 and continued as a farmer in the Philadelphia area. (*PGW* 2:43n)

FORREST, URIAH (1756–1805), was a leading merchant of Georgetown, Maryland (in present day District of Columbia), who played an active role in negotiating the transfer of land titles from his fellow proprietors to form Washington, D.C. During the Revolutionary War he served as a captain in the Maryland Battalion of the Flying Camp before being promoted to major of the 3rd Regiment of the Maryland Line in 1776 and lieutenant colonel of the 1st Regiment the next year. In 1779 he transferred to the 7th Regiment, resigning in 1781. He attended Congress in 1787. (Louise Mann-Kenney, *Rosedale* [Washington, D.C., 1989], p. 4)

FOSDICK, NATHANIEL (1760–1819), a 1779 Harvard graduate, was a merchant and federal collector of Portland, Maine, 1789–1801, having held that position under the state since 1787. See also *DHFFC* 2:503. (*PGW* 2:329)

FOSTER, WILLIAM (1746–1821), was a prominent Boston merchant whose daughter Sally married Secretary of the Senate Otis's son, Harrison Gray Otis, on 31 May 1790.

FOWLE, EBENEZER SMITH (1754–91), was commissioned a lieutenant in the artillery battalion of the federal army in June 1790. A 1776 Harvard graduate, he served as a second lieutenant in Henry Jackson's Additional Continental Regiment, 1777–78, and rejoined the United States army in 1786. See also *DHFFC* 2:503.

FOX, CHARLES JAMES (1749–1806), a member of Parliament since 1768 and longtime opponent of William Pitt the Younger's ministry, supported both the American and French revolutions, and liberal reform at home.

FRANKLIN, BENJAMIN (1706–17 April 1790), Boston born Philadelphia printer, writer, scientist, wartime minister to France, and peace commissioner to Great Britain, closed a lengthy political career in the fall of 1788 when he completed his final term as president (governor) of Pennsylvania. A delegate to the Continental Congress, 1775–76, and the Federal Convention, he signed both the Declaration of Independence and the Constitution. His last public acts involved the First Congress. In February 1790 he signed the Pennsylvania Antislavery Society's petition to Congress, and the next month he wrote a widely reprinted antislavery satire aimed at Representative Jackson. After his death, the eulogy addressed to Congress by the city of Paris entangled the legislative and executive branches in delicate questions of diplomatic protocol and the constitutional separation of powers. See also *DHFFC* 8:316, 574–75.

FRANKLIN, WILLIAM TEMPLE (1762–1823), of Philadelphia, served as private secretary to his grandfather, Benjamin Franklin, and as official secretary of the American delegation to the peace commission that signed the Treaty of Paris of 1783. In January 1790 he failed to secure an appointment as minister to France. (*PGW* 2:90–91n; Samuel Flagg Bemis, *The Diplomacy of the American Revolution* [1935; reprint, Bloomington, Ind., 1957], p. 239)

FRAUNCES, ANDREW, son of President Washington's house steward Samuel Fraunces, served as a clerk to the board of treasury, 1785–89, and principal clerk of the treasury department, 1789–93. (*PGW* 2:438)

FRAZIER, NALBRO, a native Bostonian, became a two-fifths owner in a mercantile partnership with Tench Coxe in 1784 and like him was a shareholder in the Bank of North America. The Philadelphia firm of Coxe and Frazier was dissolved in May 1790. (*Coxe,* pp. 62–63, 89n, 175n)

FREEMAN, SAMUEL (1743–1831), a selectman of Portland, Maine, beginning in 1788 and postmaster since 1776, had represented the town in the provincial congresses and Massachusetts House of Representatives, 1775–78. (*Smith and Deane,* pp. 421–25)

FROST, WILLIAM (1760–1821), was a store and tavern keeper of Sanford, Maine, where he settled in the mid 1780s. (Edwin Emery, *History of Sanford, Maine, 1661–1900* [Fall River, Mass., 1901], p. 449)

FROTHINGHAM, JOHN (b. 1750), was a lawyer and the state's excise collector of Portland, Maine, which he represented in the Massachusetts House of Representatives in 1786. (*Smith and Deane,* pp. 103–4)

FURNALD, JOHN (ca. 1742–1792), of Portsmouth, New Hampshire.

FURNIVAL, ALEXANDER (1752–1807), a Baltimore merchant, fought in the Revolutionary War as a second lieutenant in James Smith's independent company of Maryland artillery in 1776, rising to captain before retiring in 1779. He was a member of the Society of the Cincinnati. (*PGW* 2:426–27)

GAGE, GENERAL THOMAS (1721–87), was British commander in chief in America, 1763–75, and military governor of the Massachusetts colony, 1774–75.

GALE, ANNA MARIA HOLLYDAY (1756–1817), of Somerset County, Maryland, married Representative Gale sometime before 1784. Two sons and six daughters survived infancy. She was the older sister of James Hollyday. (*Maryland Legislators* 1:450)

GALE, BENJAMIN (1715–90), was a physician from Killingworth, Connecticut, whose town meeting speech during the election for the state ratification convention is the only known published attack on the Constitution by a Connecticut Antifederalist. He graduated from Yale in 1733 and represented Killingworth in the colonial legislature. (*Yale Graduates* 1:477–80; *DHROC* 3:429, 610)

GARDOQUI, DON DIEGO (JAMES) MARIA DE (1735–98), resided in New York City as Spain's *encargado de negocios,* or chief diplomatic representative to the United States, from 1785 until his return to Spain in October 1789. See also *DHFFC* 9:13n. (*PGW* 3:300)

GATES, HORATIO (1727–1806), was a major general of the Continental Army, 1775–83, and rival of George Washington during his tenure as president of the board of war, 1777–78. After the war he lived in semiretirement on his plantation "Traveller's Rest" in Berkeley County, West Virginia, until he moved permanently to New York City in September 1790 and became an advocate for veterans' rights. He was a member of the Society of the Cincinnati.

GATEWOOD, PHILEMON (ca. 1751–1824), held a state customs job in Norfolk, Virginia. (*John and Amy Gatewood and Their Descendants, 1666–1986* [Baltimore, 1987], p. 144)

GAUDIN, ELIZABETH, a Boston widow in 1789, was a schoolmistress in Reading, Massachusetts, until 1771 when she married Philip Gaudin, a mariner in the Continental Navy purportedly killed in 1777. (*PGW* 3:121–22n)

GELSTON, JOHN (1750–1831), a storekeeper in Southampton, Long Island, New York, served as collector at Sag Harbor from 1789 until his resignation in May 1790. See also *DHFFC* 2:522.

GEORGE III (1738–1820) became king of Great Britain in 1760. He suffered from porphyria. In 1783 he appointed William Pitt "the Younger" as prime minister and effectively retired from active participation in the government.

GEORGE, DANIEL (ca. 1759–1804), originally of Newburyport, Massachusetts, settled in Portland, Maine, around 1785 and became a schoolteacher, bookseller, and almanac publisher. (William Willis, *History of Portland, Maine* [reprint, Portland, 1972], p. 598)

GERRY, ANN THOMPSON (1763–1849), married Representative Gerry on 12 January 1786 and settled at their home in Cambridge, Massachusetts. During the first and second sessions of the First Congress, the family resided together in quarters at or near the home of her father, New York City merchant James Thompson. Their children at that time were Catharine (1787–1850), Thomas (b. 1788), who died in late 1789, and Elizabeth (b. July 1790). Representatives Gerry and Coles became brothers-in-law by the latter's marriage to Ann's sister Catherine on 2 January 1790.

GERRY, SAMUEL RUSSELL (1750–1807), younger brother of Representative Gerry, was appointed collector at his native Marblehead, Massachusetts, in 1790. During the Revolutionary War he served as state commissary and second lieutenant in the militia, while overseeing his absent brother's mercantile and shipping interests. See also *DHFFC* 2:504. (*PGW* 6:124n)

GIBBES, WILLIAM (1723–89), a merchant of Charleston, South Carolina, was continental loan officer for the state. (*South Carolina House* 2:275)

GIBBON (GIBBONS), JAMES (1758–1835), served as port surveyor of Petersburg, Virginia, 1789–92. In September 1789 he petitioned the First Congress unsuccessfully for commutation of half pay for his Revolutionary War service. See also *DHFFC* 2:549, 7:129–33. (*PGW* 1:290n)

GIBBONS, WILLIAM, SR. (1726–1800), was a lawyer of Savannah, Georgia, which he represented in the state House of Assembly, 1782–83, 1785–89, and 1791–93, including as speaker, 1782–83, 1786–87, and 1791–93. He also served in Congress in 1784. (*DHFFE* 2:478n)

GIBBS, HENRY (1749–94), a 1766 Harvard graduate, was a merchant of Salem, Massachusetts, and a prominent Federalist. Through his wife, Mercy Prescott, he was brother-in-law to Representative Sherman. (*Harvard Graduates* 16:358; *DHROC* 4:174)

GIBBS, WILLIAM, who served as state naval officer at Accomack, Virginia, 1787–89, was appointed federal collector at Folly Landing, Accomack County, in 1789. (*DHFFC* 2:549)

GILDER, REUBEN (1755–94), a Baltimore physician after 1783, served as a surgeon's mate to the Delaware Line, 1775–76, and a surgeon to the southern department thereafter until the close of the war, when he enrolled in the Society of the Cincinnati. In 1791 he unsuccessfully sought a federal appointment as Baltimore's health officer. (*PGW* 7:173–74n)

GILMAN, JOHN TAYLOR (1753–1828), older brother of Representative Gilman, was a shipbuilder and merchant of Exeter, New Hampshire. He served as state Representative, 1779–81, delegate to Congress, 1782–83, and state treasurer, 1783–87, and voted to ratify the Constitution at the state convention. In September 1788 he was elected a commissioner for settling accounts between the federal government and the states, but he declined reappointment in 1790 when the board was reconstituted under the Settlement of Accounts Act. See also *DHFFC* 2:515. (*PJB*, p. 181n)

GILMAN, NATHANIEL (1759–1817), of Exeter, New Hampshire, succeeded his father as continental loan officer for the state, 1783–89, but declined his appointment as commissioner of loans in 1790. He was the younger brother of John Taylor and Representative Gilman. See also *DHFFC* 2:515. (*PJB*, p. 308n)

GILPIN, GEORGE (1740–1813), a native of Cecil County, Maryland, was a wheat merchant of Alexandria, Virginia, and a director of the Potowmack Company who enjoyed a close friendship with George Washington. (*DGW* 4:141)

GLAUBECK, PETER WILLIAM JOSEPH, BARON DE (d. January 1790), was a foreign volunteer in the southern department of the Continental Army, 1777–82. His petition to Congress in May 1789 resulted in the Glaubeck Act, granting compensation for his military service as a brevet captain, 1781–82. See also *DHFFC* 7:199–201.

GLEN, HENRY (1739–1814), was a merchant of Schenectady County, New York, who served as agent of Indian affairs and deputy assistant quartermaster general for the northern department from at least 1778 until war's end. A longtime clerk of the county court, 1767–1809, he sat in the state Assembly, 1786–87, and as a Federalist Representative to Congress, 1793–1801.

GOODHUE, FRANCES "FANNY" RITCHIE (1751–1801), originally of Philadelphia, married Representative Goodhue in 1775 and resided at their home in Salem, Massachusetts. By the time of the First Congress, she had given birth to the first seven of their eight children: Frances (b. 1778), Sarah (1780–96), Mary (b. 1781), Jonathan (b. 1783), Benjamin (1785–1814), Martha (b. 1787), and Stephen (27 August 1789–31 May 1790). (*DHFFC* 14:624; Jonathan E. Goodhue, *History and Genealogy of the Goodhue Family in England and America to the Year 1890* [Rochester, N.Y., 1891], *passim*)

GOODHUE, STEPHEN (1739–1809), a merchant of Salem, Massachusetts, was the older brother of Representative Goodhue, whose business affairs he helped manage during the First Congress. In 1767 he married Martha Prescott of neighboring Danvers, through whom he was related to Representative Sherman's wife, Rebecca Prescott. (Goodhue, *History and Genealogy of the Goodhue Family,* p. 33)

GORDON, THOMASIN WHITE, of North Carolina, was the widow of Colonel John White (d. 1780) of the 4th Regiment of the Georgia Line. In August 1789 and July 1790, she and her second husband, respectively, petitioned the First Congress for the settlement of White's military claims. See also *DHFFC* 7:469–70.

GORDON, WILLIAM (1728–1807), a British born Congregational minister of Roxbury, Massachusetts, who had been active in the Revolutionary movement, returned to London in 1786 to complete his two volume *History of the Rise, Progress, and Establishment of the Independence of the United States*. The first American edition was printed in New York in 1789. (*PGW* 1:2–3n)

GORE, CHRISTOPHER (1758–1827), a Boston lawyer, was United States attorney for Massachusetts, 1789–96. His lifelong friendship with Senator King began at Harvard, from which he graduated in 1776. He voted to ratify the Constitution at the state convention and sat in the state House of Representatives from 1788 until he resigned in 1790. See also *DHFFC* 2:504. (*DHROC* 4:434–35)

GORHAM, NATHANIEL (1738–96), a merchant and land speculator of Charlestown, Massachusetts, was federal supervisor of distilled spirits for the state, 1791–96. He served in the state House of Representatives, 1778–80 and 1781–88, the Senate, 1780–81 and 1790–91, the Executive Council, 1788–90, and Congress, 1782–83, 1785–87 (1786–87 as president), and 1788–89. He attended the Federal Convention and signed the Constitution, which he voted to ratify at the state convention. In 1788 he and Oliver Phelps were principal investors in the six million acre Genessee Tract in New York, with Representative Wadsworth as a minor investor. In July 1789 he and Phelps petitioned the First Congress about the survey of the western boundary of New York, which would affect the size of the tract. See also *DHFFC* 2:504, 8:191–96. (*DHROC* 4:435)

GORHAM, STURGIS (d. 1795), of Barnstable, Massachusetts, captained a militia unit before the Revolutionary War. (*PGW* 3:155n)

GRAVES, WILLIAM (1750–99), served as the state's port inspector for Norfolk, Virginia, 1786–89. (*PGW* 3:550n)

GRAY, VINCENT, of Dumfries, Virginia, served as the state's port inspector for Quantico, 1788–89. In April 1789 he stated to George Washington his preference for an appointment as the President's steward, but accepted the post of deputy collector at Alexandria in the fall. (*PGW* 2:39–41n)

GRAY, WILLIAM, JR. (1750–1825), a merchant, represented Salem, Massachusetts, at the state convention, where he voted to ratify the Constitution.

GRAYSON, ELEANOR SMALLWOOD, wife of Senator Grayson and sister of Revolutionary War general and Maryland Governor William Smallwood, died in Dumfries, Virginia, on 22 September 1789.

GREENE, CATHARINE "KITTY" LITTLEFIELD (1755–1814), widow of General Nathanael Greene, lived at "Mulberry Grove," outside Savannah, Georgia. In the summer and part of the winter of 1789–90 she stayed in New York City with the family of Secretary of War Knox who, with her friends Representative Wadsworth and Secretary of the Treasury Hamilton, among others, helped plan her successful petition to Congress in March 1790 for the settlement of her husband's public accounts. See also *DHFFC* 7:493–592.

GREENE, NATHANAEL (1742–86), a Rhode Island forgemaster before the Revolutionary War, achieved celebrity for his services as the Continental Army's quartermaster general, 1778–80, and commander of the Army in the South from 1780 until war's end, when he joined the Society of the Cincinnati. See also *DHFFC* 9:101n.

GREENE, WILLIAM (1731–1809), was a Federalist lawyer of Providence, Rhode Island, who served as chief justice and speaker of the state's House of Deputies in 1777 and governor, 1778–86. (*PGW* 5:489–90n)

GREENLEAF, JAMES (1765–1843), a native of Boston, was a partner in the New York City mercantile firm of Greenleaf and Watson. In 1788 he married a Dutch heiress and settled as the firm's agent in Amsterdam. Through his sisters' marriages, he was brother-in-law to Nathaniel Walker Appleton, Thomas Dawes, Jr., and Noah Webster. (Allen C. Clark, *Greenleaf and Law in the Federal City* [Washington, D.C., 1901], pp. 9–10, 145)

GREENLEAF, THOMAS (1755–98), of New York City, published the *New-York Journal* from 1787 to 1793, having managed the paper since 1785. After petitioning Congress in May 1789, he received a significant portion of the First Congress's printing business. See also *DHFFC* 8:737–38. (*American Newspapers* 1:656–57; *New York*, p. 209)

GRENVILLE, WILLIAM WYNDHAM, LORD (1759–1834), Great Britain's secretary of state for the home department beginning in 1789, succeeded the Duke of Leeds as secretary of state for foreign affairs in 1791.

GRIFFIN, CYRUS (1748–1810), a lawyer of Lancaster County, Virginia, and younger brother of Representative Griffin, was appointed a federal commissioner to the Creek Nation in 1789 and United States district judge for Virginia the same year, a position he held until his death. He studied at London's Middle Temple before the war, and sat in the state House of Delegates, 1777–78 and 1786–87, and in Congress, 1778–80 and 1787–88, serving as its last president. In the intervening years he was a judge of the federal admiralty court. See also *DHFFC* 2:549–50. (*DHROC* 8:382n)

GRIFFIN, ELIZABETH BRAXTON (b. 1762), of Williamsburg, Virginia, married Representative Griffin in 1778. She was a daughter of Carter Braxton.

HABERSHAM, JOHN (1754–99), a merchant and planter of Chatham County, Georgia, was federal collector of Savannah, 1789–99. During the Revolutionary War he rose from first lieutenant in the 1st Regiment of the Georgia Line in 1776 to major in 1778, retiring at war's end when he joined the Society of the Cincinnati. He served as president of the state's Executive Council in 1784, member of the state's House of Assembly, 1785–86, and delegate to Congress in 1785. See also *DHFFC* 2:492. (*DHROC* 3:224n)

HACKER, HOYSTEED (d. 1814), a pilot for ships entering New York harbor from Long Island Sound, kept a boardinghouse at 72 Water Street. In March 1790 he signed a petition to Congress seeking additional compensation for his services as a captain in the Continental Navy. See also *DHFFC* 7:439.

HAGUE, JOHN (ca. 1758–1795), of Richmond, Virginia, served as the state's port inspector for the upper James River district, 1787–89. (*PGW* 6:412n)

HALL, AARON (1751–1814), a 1772 Yale graduate, served as pastor of the Congregational Church of Keene, New Hampshire, from 1778 until his death. He voted to ratify the Constitution at the state convention. (*Yale Graduates* 3:442–43)

HALL, GEORGE ABBOTT (d. 1791), a merchant of Charleston, South Carolina, who had served as the state's collector of that port, 1776–89, continued as federal collector from 1789 until his death. Commissioner of the state navy, 1776–80, he was appointed receiver of continental taxes in South Carolina in 1782. See also *DHFFC* 2:543. (*PGW* 1:470n)

HALL, JAMES (d. 1801), was a physician practicing in York, Pennsylvania, where he settled in 1787 after his marriage to Representative Hartley's daughter Eleanor. He was also brother-in-law to the maternal aunt of Benjamin Rush, with whom he studied in 1779 and joined in a partnership,

1784–87. (George W. Corner, ed., *Autobiography of Benjamin Rush* [Princeton, N.J., 1948], p. 86n)

HALL, JOSIAS CARVIL (1746–1814), was a physician and planter of Baltimore County, Maryland, which he represented on the state's Executive Council in 1789. During the Revolutionary War he served as colonel of the 2nd Maryland Regiment of the Flying Camp in 1776 and of the 4th Regiment of the Maryland Line thereafter until his retirement in 1781. He became a member of the Society of the Cincinnati. He married Janet Smith (1752–1812), daughter of Representative Smith (Md.), by 1775. (*PGW* 2:345)

HALL, LOTT (1757–1809), a native of Yarmouth, Massachusetts, followed in the steps of his childhood friend, Representative Thatcher, and studied law under Shearjashub Bourne in neighboring Barnstable. In 1782 he settled in Westminster, Vermont, which he represented in the state legislature. (Benjamin H. Hall, *The Halls of Eastern Vermont* [New York, 1858], pp. 658–66)

HALL, LYMAN (1724–90), was a physician, jurist, and rice planter of Burke County, Georgia. He graduated from Yale in 1747, sat in Congress, 1775–77, where he signed the Declaration of Independence, and served as governor of Georgia in 1783. (*Yale Graduates* 2:116–19)

HALL, MARY COTTON HOLT (1754–1808), of Portland, Maine, married merchant Stephen Hall in 1778. (*PGW* 2:297–98n)

HALL, STEPHEN (1743–94), was a merchant and tanner of Portland, Maine, which he represented in the Massachusetts House of Representatives, 1780–81. He was a member of the five man committee that addressed a petition to Congress in April 1789 on the subject of the proposed impost duty on molasses. He was also a leading figure behind another petition of the merchants and other inhabitants of Portland seeking changes to the Coasting Act early in the second session. He graduated from Harvard in 1765. See also *DHFFC* 8:357–59, 412–16. (*Harvard Graduates* 16:165–69)

HALL, THOMAS (1750–1814), was one of the few Charleston sea captains engaged in the foreign carrying trade in 1789. During the Revolutionary War he rose from second lieutenant in the 2nd Regiment of the South Carolina Line in 1775 to first lieutenant in 1776 shortly before he played a celebrated role in the defense of Fort Moultrie. Promoted to captain in 1779, he served as aide-de-camp to General Arthur St. Clair at Yorktown and became a member of the Society of the Cincinnati. (*DHFFC* 10:501)

HALL, WILLIAM (1759–1814), a captain in the South Carolina navy during the Revolutionary War, was appointed commander of the federal revenue cutter for the state in October 1790. (*PGW* 6:101n)

HALLAM, LEWIS (1740–1808), a London actor, co-managed (with John Henry) New York City's Old American Company, which held a regular theatrical season at the John Street Theater beginning in 1785. (*New York*, pp. 167–68)

HAMDEN, SAMUEL, represented Woolwich, Maine, in the Massachusetts House of Representatives in 1789 and 1790.

HAMILTON, ALEXANDER (1757–1804), a lawyer of New York City, served as secretary of the treasury, 1789–95. A native of the Caribbean, he was sent to school at Francis Barber's academy in Elizabethtown, New Jersey, in 1773, where he became a protégé of Representative Boudinot. After an incomplete course of studies at King's College (Columbia), he captained a provincial artillery company in 1776 and the next year joined General Washington's staff as lieutenant colonel and principal aide-de-camp. He resigned the latter position in 1781, shortly before playing a highly celebrated role in the capture of Yorktown. He was breveted a colonel at war's end, when he joined the Society of the Cincinnati. He supported strengthening the federal government in Congress, 1782–83, the Annapolis Convention, the Federal Convention, and the state ratification convention, and co-authored the *Federalist* essays. Returning to Congress in 1788, he led the fight to convene the First Congress in New York City. In state politics he was firmly allied to Senator Schuyler, whose daughter Elizabeth he had married in December 1780. He declined to be a candidate for Representative in the first federal election, but was an early and active supporter of Rufus King for Senator. (*PAH* 1:44n, 2:521, 563; *DHFFE* 3:453, 487)

HAMILTON, HENRY (d. 1796), governor of Bermuda, 1790–94, had earlier served as lieutenant governor of Canada, 1775–79, and of Quebec, 1784–85.

HAMILTON, JAMES (ca. 1752–1819), an Irish born lawyer of Carlisle, Pennsylvania, was involved in the petition of the freeholders of Cumberland County to Congress in August 1789, seeking to alter the location of the federal court. (Alfred Nevin, *Centennial Biography: Men of Mark of Cumberland Valley, Pennsylvania, 1776–1876* [Philadelphia, 1876], pp. 213–14)

HAMILTON, JOHN (1764–1822), nephew of William Cumming, was a Scottish trained lawyer of Edenton, North Carolina, who represented Chowan County in the state's House of Commons, 1789–93. He was a Federalist during the ratification of the Constitution. (*DHFFE* 4:355n)

HAMILTON, WILLIAM (1745–1813), the wealthy proprietor of Lancaster, Pennsylvania, lobbied Congress unsuccessfully on behalf of his tenants' petition for Lancaster to become the seat of government in August 1789. (*DGW* 5:160n; *DHFFC* 8:455)

HAMPTON, RICHARD (1752–92), a merchant and planter in the Camden and Orangeburg districts of South Carolina who had voted against the Constitution at the state convention in 1788, served on the state's Privy Council, 1789–90. He represented Saxe-Gotha in both the state House of Representatives, 1782–84, and Senate, 1785–91. (*South Carolina House* 3:306–7)

HANCOCK, JOHN (1737–93), a Boston merchant, was governor of Massachusetts, 1780–85, 1787–93. The 1754 Harvard graduate was an early leader in the Revolutionary movement and served in Congress, 1775–78, signing the Declaration of Independence as its president, 1775–77. Despite his well known Antifederalist leanings, as president of the state convention he introduced the compromise that ensured ratification by proposing Amendments to the Constitution. He received four electoral votes for President in the first federal election. (*DHFFE* 4:295–96)

HAND, EDWARD (1744–1802), an Irish born physician and farmer of Lancaster County, Pennsylvania, appeared on various tickets for Representative in the first federal election but won only as a Presidential Elector. He joined the Continental Army two years after resigning his commission in the British Army in 1773, rising from lieutenant colonel of the 1st Continental Regiment to colonel of the 1st Regiment of the Pennsylvania Line in 1777, adjutant general, 1781–83, and brevet major general at war's end, when he enrolled in the Society of the Cincinnati. He served in Congress, 1783–84, and in the state assembly, 1785–86. (*DHFFE* 1:364–66, 417; *LDC* 21:xxiii)

HANDLEY, GEORGE (1752–93), a planter in Augusta and Gwynn County, Georgia, served as collector at Brunswick, Georgia, 1789–93. He emigrated from England in 1775 and the next year was commissioned a first lieutenant in the 1st Regiment of the Georgia Line, rising to brevet major in 1783. He represented Brunswick in the state assembly in 1789 and voted as a Presidential Elector in the first federal election the same year. See also *DHFFC* 2:492. (*DHROC* 3:309)

HANSON, ALEXANDER CONTEE (1749–1806), a lawyer and jurist of Annapolis, Maryland, was a Presidential Elector representing the state's Western Shore in 1789. His father John Hanson was president of Congress, 1781–82. He served as George Washington's private secretary in 1776, associate justice of the state's general court from 1778 to 1789, and state chancellor from 1789 until his death. A widely read Federalist essayist, he voted for the Constitution at the state convention. (*DHFFE* 2:238)

HANSON, SAMUEL, a Maryland native, was an Alexandria, Virginia, merchant who was appointed port surveyor in 1789. As a trustee and instructor of the Alexandria Academy, he served as guardian of George Washington's two nephews, George Steptoe and Lawrance, until they were withdrawn for disciplinary reasons in April 1789. Hanson spent that April and May in New York lobbying for his revenue appointment. During the Revolutionary War he was a lieutenant colonel of the Charles County, Maryland, militia. See also *DHFFC* 2:550. (*PGW* 1:29n, 239n)

HARBAUGH, LEONARD (1749–1822), was a Baltimore contractor and inventor. He petitioned Congress for patent protection in July 1789. See also *DHFFC* 8:45.

HARDY, JOSEPH (d. ca. 1815), an accountant in the treasury office during the Confederation, went on to serve as chief clerk of the comptroller's office in the treasury department during the First Congress. In this capacity he petitioned successfully with other government clerks in January 1791 for compensation for moving to Philadelphia. He also petitioned, unsuccessfully, in March 1790 with fellow former marine and naval officers for additional compensation for his wartime services. See also *DHFFC* 7:439, 8:132. (*PAH* 7:101, 8:169)

HARMAR, JOSIAH (1753–1813), of Philadelphia, commanded the federal army on the northwest frontier as a lieutenant colonel, 1784–87, and as a brevet brigadier general until March 1791. He rose from captain of the 1st Pennsylvania Battalion in 1775, to major of the 3rd Regiment, to lieutenant colonel by 1777, serving in the 6th, 7th, 3rd, and 1st regiments of the Pennsylvania Line consecutively, before retiring as colonel in 1783. He became a member of the Society of the Cincinnati. See also *DHFFC* 2:543, 9:342n.

HARRIS, DAVID (1754–1809), whose older sister Mary married Senator Maclay in 1769, failed as a merchant at Baltimore in the late 1780s. He fought during the Revolutionary War as a lieutenant in William Thompson's Pennsylvania Rifle Regiment in 1775 and was promoted to captain of the 1st Regiment of the Pennsylvania Line the next year before retiring in 1777. See also *DHFFC* 9:75n.

HARRIS, RICHARD (1738–14 July 1790), a merchant of Marblehead, Massachusetts, and collector at that port under the state from the mid 1780s, served as federal collector from 1789 until his death. See also *DHFFC* 2:504. (*PGW* 3:192)

HARRISON, BENJAMIN (1726–91), was a planter from Charles City County, Virginia, which he represented in the colonial House of Burgesses for almost twenty years before the outbreak of the Revolutionary War. From 1774 to 1777 he sat in Congress, where he signed the Declaration of Independence and served in the state House of Delegates, 1778–81 and 1785–91, frequently as speaker. During the intervening years he served as governor. He voted against ratification of the Constitution as Charles City County representative to the state convention. (*DHROC* 8:16n)

HARRISON, GEORGE (1762–1845), a Philadelphia merchant, was a business associate of Senator Morris. (*PRM* 1:168n)

HARRISON, RICHARD (ca. 1748–1829), a New York City lawyer, served as United States attorney for New York, 1789–1801. He represented the city at the state convention where he voted to ratify the Constitution. See also *DHFFC* 2:523.

HARRISON, RICHARD HANSON (1750–1841), a native of Virginia, served as American agent in Spain, 1784–89. He returned briefly to the United States before returning to serve as consul at Cadiz, 1789–91. See also *DHFFC* 2:550.

HARRISON, ROBERT HANSON (1745–2 April 1790), of Charles County, Maryland, practiced law in Alexandria, Virginia, before joining George Washington's staff as aide-de-camp in 1775, and as his private secretary thereafter until returning to Maryland to serve as chief justice, 1781–90. He declined appointments to the Federal Convention in 1787 and the United States Supreme Court in 1789. In the first federal election Maryland split its electoral votes evenly between Harrison and George Washington. See also *DHFFC* 2:497. (*DHFFE* 4:296)

HARSIN (HARSEN), GEORGE, participated in George Washington's first inaugural procession as acting major in the 1st Regiment of New York City's militia brigade.

HART, THOMAS (1729–1808), was a merchant and nail manufacturer of Hagerstown, Maryland. An unsuccessful petition to Congress in June 1790 restated a 1784 petition seeking compensation for supplies furnished to the Southern Army in 1780. See also *DHFFC* 7:51.

HART, WILLIAM, was a "lot layer," or town surveyor, in Portsmouth, New Hampshire.

HARWOOD, BENJAMIN (1751–1826), an Annapolis merchant, was appointed receiver of continental taxes for Maryland in 1782. (*PRM* 6:374n)

HAYES, REUBEN (1766–ca. 1800), kept a school in Portsmouth, New Hampshire, 1784–88.

HAZARD, EBENEZER (1745–1817), of New York City, served as United States postmaster general from 1782 until September 1789. He married Abigail Arthur in 1783. See also *DHFFC* 9:184–85n.

HAZARD, JONATHAN (ca. 1728–1812), of South Kingston, Rhode Island, sat in Congress in 1788, led the fight against ratification of the Constitution at the state convention in 1790, and was an unsuccessful candidate for Senator in the first federal election. A frequent member of the state House of Deputies between 1773 and 1793, he served as adjutant of the 1st Regiment of the Rhode Island Line, 1777–78. (*DHFFE* 4:448)

HEDGE, TEMPERANCE "TEMPY" (d. 1845), originally of Dennis, Massachusetts, was Representative Thatcher's niece and live-in helper to his family at Biddeford, Maine, during part of the First Congress. In June 1789 she returned to Cape Cod for an extended visit, and in early 1790 she married Thatcher's protégé, Silas Lee. (Fannie Chase, *Wiscasset in Pownalborough* [Wiscasset, Me., 1941], p. 556)

HELLSTEDT, CHARLES, was Swedish consul at Philadelphia beginning in 1784.

HENDERSON, JOSEPH (d. 1794), of Boston was high sheriff of Suffolk County, Massachusetts, in 1789. He served as paymaster to the Navy Board of the eastern department, 1778–82. See also *DHFFC* 7:13–15.

HENRY, JAMES (1731–1804), was a lawyer of King and Queen County, Virginia, which he represented in the state House of Delegates in 1782, thereafter serving on the court of admiralty until his resignation to serve on the bench of the state's general court, 1788–1800. He attended Congress in 1780. (*PGW: Confederation* 1:415)

HENRY, JOHN (d. 1795), an Irish born actor, co-managed with Lewis Hallam the Old American Company, which held a regular theatrical season at New York City's John Street Theater beginning in 1785. (*New York*, pp. 167–68)

HENRY, PATRICK (1736–99), a lawyer of Prince Edward County, Virginia, who also resided at "Leatherwood" in Henry County, served as a Presidential Elector in 1789. Leader of Virginia's Antifederalists, the popular former governor declined a seat at the federal convention, voted against the Constitution at the state convention, and orchestrated the election of the state's two Antifederalist Senators as well as James Madison's near defeat in the first federal election. See also *DHFFC* 9:114–15n.

HENSHAW, SAMUEL (1744–1809), a lawyer of Northampton, Massachusetts, sat in the state House of Representatives, 1788–90. The 1773 Harvard graduate was a Presidential Elector and campaign manager for Representative Sedgwick in the first federal election. (*DHFFE* 1:751–52)

HENZEL, CHARLES (d. 1792), of Portsmouth, New Hampshire, was an unsuccessful candidate for Representative in both the first and second federal elections, and for president (governor) of the state in March 1791.

HETFIELD, MARY (1742–1801), wife of Abner Hetfield, was the younger sister of Representative and Elisha Boudinot. (*Elias Boudinot*, pp. 9, 289)

HETH, WILLIAM (1735–1808), a planter of Henrico County, Virginia, was collector at Bermuda Hundred, 1789–1802, and one of Secretary of the Treasury Hamilton's most relied-upon informants on Virginia political matters. A member of the state's Executive Council, 1787–89, in 1788 he acted as commissioner to settle Virginia's accounts with the federal government for its ceded Western lands. During the Revolutionary War he joined Daniel Morgan's rifle company as a lieutenant in 1775, transferring to the 11th Regiment of the Virginia Line in 1776 and the 3rd Regiment in 1777, retiring as its colonel at war's end when he became a member of the Society of the Cincinnati. See also *DHFFC* 2:550. (*PGW* 2:121n; *DHROC* 10:1622n)

HICHBORN, BENJAMIN (1746–1817), was a lawyer in Boston, which he represented in the Massachusetts House of Representatives in 1791. The 1768 Harvard graduate was admitted to the bar in 1771, became active in the Revolutionary movement, and served as a justice of the peace in 1783. (*Harvard Graduates* 17:36–44)

HIESTER, GABRIEL (1749–1824), of Goshenhoppen, Berks County, Pennsylvania, was younger brother of Representative Hiester.

HIESTER, JOSEPH (1752–1832), cousin of Representative Hiester, was a storekeeper in Berks County, Pennsylvania, which he represented at the state convention where he voted against ratification in 1787, in the state's General Assembly, 1789–90, and Senate, 1790–94. A noted Constitutionalist in state politics, he ran unsuccessfully as an Antifederalist candidate for Representative in the first federal election, but finally won his cousin's seat in the House in 1797. During the Revolutionary War he served in the state militia as captain, 1776–77, and lieutenant colonel, 1777–80. (*DHFFE* 1:418)

HIGGINS, JESSE (1761–1810), was the state's collector of revenues at New Castle, Delaware, 1787–89. (*PGW* 2:16–17n)

HIGGINSON, STEPHEN (1743–1828), was a Boston merchant who made a fortune as a privateer during the Revolutionary War. He served in the Massachusetts House of Representatives in 1782 and Congress in 1783, where he opposed Superintendent of Finance Robert Morris. He declined a seat at the Annapolis Convention and was nominated but not elected to a seat at the state ratification convention. In February–March 1789 he authored the anti-Hancock "Laco" essays. (*PGW* 5:240n; *PRM* 7:665n; *DHROC* 4:xxvi, 6:1770; *DHFFE* 1:451)

HILL, BAYLOR (b. ca. 1760), served as a cornet in the 1st Regiment of Continental Dragoons, 1776–77, lieutenant, 1777–80, and captain thereafter until the war's end.

HILL, JEREMIAH (1747–1820), a merchant of Biddeford, Maine, served as town clerk, 1780–88, member of the Massachusetts House of Representatives, 1787–88, and federal collector (with adjoining Pepperellborough), 1789–1809. The 1770 Harvard graduate joined James Scammon's Massachusetts Regiment as a captain in 1775, transferring to the 18th Continental Regiment in 1776 and the 1st Regiment of the Massachusetts Line the next year, when he resigned. See also *DHFFC* 2:505. (*Harvard Graduates* 17:391–96)

HILLS, JOHN (d. ca. 1818), was a surveyor and cartographer of Philadelphia, where he moved from New York City in 1786. As an officer and assistant military engineer in the British Army in America during the Revolutionary War, he drafted and collected many maps of British North America. (Peter J. Guthorn, *John Hills, Assistant Engineer* [Brielle, N.J., n.d.], pp. 7–20; *PGW* 3:507–9n)

HILLEGAS, MICHAEL (1729–1804), a former Philadelphia sugar refiner and iron manufacturer, served as treasurer of the United States, 1775–89. See also *DHFFC* 9:266n.

HILLER, JOSEPH (1748–1814), was a jeweler of Salem, Massachusetts, where he served as collector, 1789–1802, having held the post under the state since 1784. See also *DHFFC* 2:505.

HINDMAN, WILLIAM (1743–1822), was a lawyer and land speculator of Talbot County, Maryland. He served as a state senator for the Eastern Shore, 1777–85 and 1791–93, a member of Congress, 1785–86, and a member of the state's Executive Council, 1789–91. (*Maryland Legislators* 1:444–45)

HITCHCOCK, ENOS (1744–1803), was minister of the Benevolent Congregational Church of Providence, Rhode Island. In May 1790 he petitioned Congress for copyright protection. See also *DHFFC* 8:32.

HODGDON, ALEXANDER (1741–97), of Boston was Massachusetts state treasurer, 1787–92. (Oliver Roberts, *History of the Military Company of . . . Massachusetts, 1637–1888* [2 vols., Boston, 1897], 1:207)

HODGDON, SAMUEL (d. 1824), a Philadelphia merchant, served as quartermaster of the United States Army, 1791–92. He began his public career as commissary of military stores in 1777, rising to deputy commissary general the next year and commissary general, 1781–84. At the time of the First Congress he was Timothy Pickering's business partner. (*DHFFC* 2:534; *DHROC* 2:123)

HODGE, MICHAEL (1743–1816), merchant, insurance officer (1787–92), and town clerk of Newburyport, Massachusetts, served as port surveyor, 1789–92, having held that post under the state throughout the Revolutionary War and intermittently during the Confederation. See also *DHFFC* 2:505. (*PGW* 3:148–49)

HOLLINGSWORTH, LEVI (1739–1824), was a Philadelphia merchant and industrialist who held lucrative flour and beef contracts with the government under his close friend and business associate, Superintendent of Finance Robert Morris, in the last years of the Revolutionary War. During the First Congress he was active in the Rumseian Society, promoters of James Rumsey's patents for steam powered navigation. (*PRM* 2:95n; *DHFFC* 8:40)

HOLLYDAY, JAMES (1758–1807), brother-in-law of Representative Gale, was a lawyer and planter of Queen Annes County, Maryland, which he represented in the state House of Delegates in 1788, and as state Senator for the Eastern Shore, 1791–1801. He inherited the plantation "Readbourne" from his uncle James in 1786. (*Maryland Legislators* 1:452)

HOLTEN, SAMUEL (1738–1816), a former physician of Danvers, Massachusetts, ran unsuccessfully for both Senator and Representative in the first federal election. He attended Congress, 1778–80, 1783–85, and 1787, where he opposed Superintendent of Finance Robert Morris and signed the Articles of Confederation. An Antifederalist, he was forced by ill health to leave the state ratification convention before voting. He served in the state Senate, 1789–90, the Executive Council, 1789–92, and went on to serve in the Third Congress. (*DHFFE* 1:752)

HOOKER, JOHN (1761–1829), graduated from Yale in 1782 and settled in Springfield, Massachusetts, where he became a prominent lawyer and judge of the court of common pleas. By his marriage to Sarah Dwight in February 1791, he was distantly related to Representative Sedgwick. (*Yale Graduates* 4:222–23; Edward Hooker, *The Descendants of Reverend Thomas Hooker* [Rochester, N.Y., 1909], p. 121)

HOOMES, JOHN (d. 1805), a planter of Caroline County, Virginia, held a state monopoly on stagecoach travel between Alexandria and Hampton, 1787–95, served as postmaster of Bowling Green, 1790–96, and sat in the state House of Delegates, 1791–95. He had been a schoolmate of Representative Madison at Donald Robertson's school in King and Queen County, Virginia, in the 1760s. (*PGW* 6:264–65n; *PJM* 12:313n)

HOPEWELL, JAMES (d. 1817), was a planter at Town Creek in St. Mary's County, Maryland, which he represented in the state House of Delegates, 1786–87, 1789, and 1791–92. (*PGW* 3:572n; *Maryland Legislators* 1:458–59)

HOPKINS, DANIEL (1734–1814), was a minister and teacher of Salem, Massachusetts, which he represented in the colonial House of Representatives in 1775. The 1758 Yale graduate also served on the Massachusetts Council, 1776–78. (*Yale Graduates* 2:533–35)

HOPKINS, HENRY (d. 1812), was Representative Sedgwick's law student, ca. 1787. (*Sedgwick*, pp. 48, 52)

HOPKINS, JOHN, JR. (ca. 1757–1827), a merchant of Richmond, Virginia, was appointed commissioner of loans in 1789, having served as the state continental loan officer since 1780. See also *DHFFC* 2:550. (*PRM* 1:202n)

HOPKINSON, FRANCIS (1737–91), a Philadelphia lawyer, musician, poet, and essayist, served as United States district judge for Pennsylvania from 1789 until his death. He signed the Declaration of Independence as a New Jersey delegate to Congress in 1776 and played an active role in supporting the Constitution, which he voted to ratify at the state convention. See also *DHFFC* 2:534, 9:100n.

HOPKINSON, JOSEPH (1770–1842), of Philadelphia, graduated from the College of Philadelphia (University of Pennsylvania) in 1786 and was admitted to the state bar in 1791. Like his father, Francis, he was a noted musician.

HOWARD, JOHN EAGER (1752–1827), of "Belvedere" in Baltimore County, Maryland, served as governor, 1788–91. His military career began as a captain in the Flying Camp in 1776, from which he was promoted in 1777 to major of the 4th and lieutenant colonel of the 5th Regiment of the Maryland Line in 1778, retiring from the 2nd Regiment at the war's end, when he became a member of the Society of the Cincinnati. He attended Congress in 1788, and in 1791 was elected to a five year term in the state Senate. (*DHFFE* 2:157n)

HOWELL, DAVID (1747–1824), a lawyer of Providence, Rhode Island, and law professor at the College of Rhode Island (Brown), served as a state supreme court justice, 1786–87, and attorney general, 1789–90. He graduated from the College of New Jersey (Princeton) in 1766 and held various state offices before attending Congress, 1782–85, where he became an opponent of Superintendent of Finance Robert Morris's policies. An active abolitionist, he supported ratification of the Constitution. (*Princetonians, 1748–1768*, pp. 562–67)

HOWELL, JOSEPH, JR. (1750–98), of Pennsylvania served as commissioner of army accounts, 1788–92, after five years as deputy commissioner. See also *DHFFC* 9:265n.

HUBBARD, DUDLEY (1763–1816), a 1786 Harvard graduate, began the practice of law in Berwick, Maine, in 1789. (*Maine Bar*, pp. 144–45)

HUBLEY, JOHN (1747–1821), was a lawyer of Lancaster County, Pennsylvania, which he represented at the state convention, where he voted to ratify the Constitution. (*PMHB* 3[1879]:442, 11[1887]:218)

HUDSON, HENRY (ca. 1747–1823), was an insurance officer of Newburyport, Massachusetts.

HUGHES, JAMES (d. 1799), a 1780 Harvard graduate, was an attorney in Suffolk County, Massachusetts. He was known for his often salacious bon-mots and puns. (*Massachusetts Bar* 1:521)

HUME, DAVID (1711–76), was a Scottish philosopher and historian, and principal figure of the Scottish Enlightenment centered in Edinburgh.

HUMPHREYS, DAVID (1752–1818), a presidential aide, was also commissioner to negotiate with the Creeks, a secret agent in Europe, and minister to Portugal during the First Federal Congress. The 1771 Yale graduate served as captain in the 6th, 4th, and 2nd regiments of the Connecticut Line between 1777 and 1783, and as George Washington's aide-de-camp with the rank of lieutenant colonel from 1780 until the war's end, when he joined the Society of the Cincinnati. See also *DHFFC* 2:485, 9:45n. (*Yale Graduates* 3:414–20)

HUMPHREYS, JOSHUA (1751–1838), of Philadelphia, was the foremost marine architect in the United States.

HUNT, ABRAHAM (1740–1821), was a Trenton, New Jersey, merchant and postmaster. In July 1789 George Washington solicited his advice about buying horses for Mount Vernon. (*PGW* 3:245–46n)

HUNT, WILLIAM (1750–1804), was a lawyer of Watertown, Massachusetts, which he represented in the state House of Representatives, 1784–85. A 1768 Harvard graduate, he served in the department of the commissary general of the Continental Army during the Revolutionary War and as justice of the peace for Middlesex County beginning in 1783. (*Harvard Graduates* 17:46–48)

HUNTINGTON, ANNE (1740–90), of Norwich, Connecticut, married Benjamin Huntington, her second cousin, in 1765. She bore five sons and three daughters over the next sixteen years. After suffering from an illness through much of the first and second sessions, she died on 6 October 1790. See also *DHFFC* 14:503. (*The Huntington Family in America* [Hartford, Conn., 1915], pp. 150, 897–99)

HUNTINGTON, GURDON (1768–1840), of Norwich, Connecticut, was the second-eldest son of Representative Huntington. (*The Huntington Family,* pp. 899, 903)

HUNTINGTON, SAMUEL (1731–96), a lawyer of Norwich, Connecticut, and first cousin of Representative Huntington, was governor from 1786 until his death. Judge of the provincial and then state superior court, 1774–84, he also sat in Congress, 1776, 1778–81, and 1783 (as its president, 1779–81), where he signed the Declaration of Independence and Articles of Confederation. He voted in favor of the Constitution at the state convention and received two of his state's electoral votes for President in the first federal election. (*DHROC* 1:611)

HUTCHINS, THOMAS (1730–89), served as geographer to the Continental Army's southern department from 1781 until 1783 and as geographer to the United States thereafter until his death in May 1789. See also *DHFFC* 9:124n. (*JCC* 25:710)

HUTCHINSON, JAMES (1752–93), a Philadelphia physician, was professor of chemistry at the University of Pennsylvania, 1789–92. During the Revolutionary War he served as a surgeon in the Continental Army's hospital department, 1779–81, and surgeon general of Pennsylvania, 1781–83. In 1779 he married Clement Biddle's sister Lydia. (*Rush* 1:572n; *Drinker* 3:2169)

ILSLEY, ENOCH (b. 1730), was a shipowner in the West Indies trade from Portland, Maine, where he served as town selectman and treasurer. In early 1789 he sat on the five man committee of merchants and traders of Portland who petitioned Congress on the Impost Bill. (*Smith and Deane,* pp. 399–400n; *DHFFC* 8:357)

IMLAY, WILLIAM (1742–1807), was a Hartford, Connecticut, merchant who, except for a brief period in 1784 when he was commissioner for settling federal accounts with Massachusetts, served as commissioner of loans for Connecticut from 1780 until his death. See also *DHFFC* 2:485. (*PGW* 3:368; *PRM* 1:201n, 9:459–60)

INGERSOLL, JARED, JR. (1749–1822), a Philadelphia lawyer, was a member of the city's common council in 1789 and state attorney general, 1790–99. The Connecticut native graduated from Yale in 1766 and settled in Philadelphia in 1771, where he read law under Joseph Reed prior to studying at London's Middle Temple, 1774–76. Returning to America in 1778, he sat in Congress in 1780 and in the Federal Convention, where he signed the Constitution. He was married to the daughter of Charles Pettit. (*Yale Graduates* 3:184–87; *American Conservatism*, pp. 339–40)

INNES, HARRY (1752–1816), a lawyer of Danville, Kentucky, served as United States district judge from 1789 until his death. He became active in the statehood movement while Virginia's attorney for the Kentucky district, 1784–89, and opposed ratification of the Constitution. See also *DHFFC* 2:494. (*DHROC* 8:223n, 433–34)

INNES, JAMES (1754–98), younger brother of Harry, was a lawyer of Williamsburg, Virginia, which he represented in the state House of Delegates, 1781–82 and 1785–86, and at the state convention where he voted to ratify the Constitution. He enrolled at the College of William and Mary in 1771 but joined the Continental Army in 1775, serving as lieutenant colonel of the 15th Regiment of the Virginia Line, 1776–78, and briefly as judge advocate of the army in 1778 upon the resignation of Representative Laurance. He represented James City County in the House of Delegates, 1780–81, and served as attorney general of Virginia, 1786–96. (*PGW* 6:517n; *DHROC* 10:1543n)

IREDELL, JAMES (1751–99), a lawyer of Edenton, North Carolina, was an associate justice of the United States Supreme Court from 1790 until his death. Having emigrated from England to take up an appointment as a customs officer, he studied law under Senator Johnston, whose sister Hannah he married in 1773. Joining the Revolutionary cause, he served as superior court justice, 1777–79, attorney general, 1779–81, and president of the Council of State, 1788–89, and voted in favor of the Constitution at the state's first ratification convention in 1788. See also *DHFFC* 2:528. (*DHSCUS* 1:60–63)

IRVINE, WILLIAM (1741–1804), a physician of Carlisle, Pennsylvania, served as a commissioner for settling the accounts between the United States and the individual states, 1788–93. He was colonel of the 6th Regiment of the Pennsylvania Line in 1776 and of the 7th Regiment the next year, serving as brigadier general from 1779 until war's end, when he joined the Society of the Cincinnati. In the first federal election he came in second behind Senator Morris and also lost a bid as Antifederalist candidate for Representative. See also *DHFFC* 2:534–35, 9:155n. (*DHFFE* 1:418–19)

IZARD, SENATOR RALPH, family during the First Congress: his wife Alice De Lancey (1745–1832), whom he married in 1767 and who resided with him at 99 Broadway while Congress sat in New York; daughters Charlotte (1770–92), wife of Representative Smith (S.C.), and Anne (1779–1863); and sons Henry (1771–1826), who graduated from Columbia College in May 1789, George (1776–1828), and Ralph (1785–1824).

JACKSON, HENRY (1747–1809), a Boston merchant and close friend and business associate of Secretary of War Knox, served as colonel of one of the Continental Army's sixteen Additional Regiments, 1777–80, of the 9th Regiment of the Massachusetts Line, 1781–83, and of the 4th Regiment in the last year of the war, when he was breveted a brigadier general. From 1783 to 1784 he commanded the First American Regiment, the last authorized regiment of the Continental Army, and served as treasurer of the state Society of the Cincinnati from 1783 until his death. (*DHROC* 4:109n)

JACKSON, JONATHAN (1743–1810), a merchant of Newburyport, Massachusetts, was federal marshal for the state, 1789–91, and inspector of revenue for the northern district, 1791–96. The 1761 Harvard graduate served in Congress in 1782 and became a Federalist essayist during ratification. He lost his bid for Representative in the first federal election, but was elected to the state Senate in 1789. See also *DHFFC* 2:506. (*DHFFE* 1:752; *Harvard Graduates* 15:67–69)

JACKSON, WILLIAM (1759–1828), a Philadelphia lawyer and secretary to the Federal Convention, served as a presidential aide from September 1789 until 1791. During the Revolutionary War he rose from second lieutenant of the 1st Regiment of the South Carolina Line in 1776 to major in 1780, holding that rank until the end of the war when he joined the Society of the Cincinnati. He was son-in-law to Thomas Willing. See also *DHFFC* 9:235n. (*Pennsylvania Cincinnati* 1:504–7)

JACKSON, WILLIAM (1763–1836), probably a merchant, resided in Plymouth, Massachusetts.

JAMESON, DAVID, SR. (1732–93), a merchant of Yorktown, Virginia, served as member of the state council, 1777–81, lieutenant governor, 1780–81, and state Senator, 1782–83. (Lyon G. Tyler, *Encyclopedia of Virginia Biography* [5 vols., New York, 1915], 2:329)

JAQUETT, PETER (ca. 1754–1834), a farmer of New Castle County, Delaware, rose from ensign of the Delaware Line in 1776 to brevet major in 1783. He was active in the Society of the Cincinnati. (*PGW* 2:69n)

JARVIS, CHARLES (1748–1807), was a prominent physician of Boston, which he represented in the state House of Representatives, 1787–97. The 1766 Harvard graduate voted to ratify the Constitution at the state convention and was an unsuccessful candidate for Senator, Presidential Elector, and Representative in the first federal election. In 1790 he campaigned actively on behalf of Benjamin Austin, Jr., for Representative Ames's seat in the Second Federal Congress. (*DHFFE* 1:753; *Harvard Graduates* 16:376–83)

JARVIS, LEONARD, JR. (1742–1813), older brother of Charles Jarvis, was a Boston physician and then merchant, who served as state comptroller general during the First Congress. In 1790 he moved to Cambridge, Massachusetts. (*Political Parties*, p. 412; *PGW* 3:412; George A. Jarvis, *The Jarvis Family* [Hartford, Conn., 1879], pp. 200–203, 205)

JAY, JOHN (1745–1829), a New York City lawyer, was chief justice of the United States Supreme Court, 1789–95. He served in Congress, 1774–76, and as its president, 1778–79, prior to filling a number of diplomatic posts abroad during the remainder of the Revolutionary War. He returned to Congress briefly in 1784 before assuming the post of secretary for foreign affairs, 1784–89, and acting secretary of state until March 1790. In the first federal election he received nine electoral votes, the next highest after John Adams. By his marriage to Sarah Livingston in 1774 he became the son-in-law of New Jersey's Governor William Livingston. See also *DHFFC* 2:523–24, 9:79n.

JEFFERSON, THOMAS (1743–1826), an Albemarle County, Virginia, lawyer and planter, served as American minister to France, 1785–89, and secretary of state, 1789–93. He assumed the duties of the latter office on 21 March 1790 and took up residence in New York at 57 Maiden Lane on 1 May.

During the Revolutionary War he served as a delegate to Congress, 1775–76, where he wrote and signed the Declaration of Independence, as governor, 1779–81, member of the House of Delegates, 1782, and congressman again, 1783–84. See also *DHFFC* 2:550–51, 9:30n.

JENKS, JOHN (1751–1817), was a merchant of Salem, Massachusetts. Orphaned as a boy, he was raised by his guardian, Cotton Tufts. (*EIHC* 3[1861]:94–95)

JOCELIN, AMARIAH, was a sea captain and merchant of Wilmington, North Carolina. (*American Conservatism*, p. 389)

JOHNSON, ANNE BEACH (1729–96), of Stratford, Connecticut, married Senator Johnson in 1749. (*DHFFC* 14:498, 501)

JOHNSON, EDWARD (ca. 1737–1797), was a physician and planter of Baltimore County, Maryland, where he settled in 1783. He represented his native Calvert County in the state House of Delegates, 1780–81. (*Maryland Legislators* 2:492; *Political Parties*, p. 440)

JOHNSON, JOHN BARENT (1769–1803), was born and raised in Brooklyn. His diary while a student at Columbia College describes New York City weather and cultural life.

JOHNSON, JOSHUA (1742–1802), a Maryland born merchant and younger brother of Governor Thomas Johnson, served as United States consul in London, 1790–97, where he had been a partner in a mercantile firm since 1780. During the Revolutionary War he was American consul at Nantes and Maryland's agent to France. See also *DHFFC* 2:497. (*PGW* 6:184n)

JOHNSON, RINALDO (ca. 1755–1811), was a planter of Aquasco, Prince Georges County, Maryland. He married George Mason's eldest daughter, Ann, in 1789. (*DGW* 5:310n)

JOHNSON, ROBERT C. (1766–1806), graduated from Yale in 1783 and practiced law in Stratford, Connecticut, like his brother, Samuel William. He was an active Federalist. (*Yale Graduates* 4:285–87)

JOHNSON, SAMUEL WILLIAM (1761–1846), elder son of Senator Johnson, graduated from Yale in 1779 and practiced law in Stratford, Connecticut, which he represented in the state House of Representatives, 1790–97. (*Yale Graduates* 4:118)

JOHNSON, THOMAS (1732–1819), a planter and lawyer of Frederick County, Maryland, declined appointment as a federal district judge in 1789, serving instead as chief judge of the state's general court from 1790 until his appointment to the United States Supreme Court the next year, where he sat until 1793. A brigadier general of the militia throughout the Revolutionary War, delegate to Congress, 1774–76, first governor of Maryland, 1777–79, member of the state House of Delegates, 1786–88, and member of the state convention where he voted to ratify the Constitution, Johnson was also deeply involved in the development of the Potomac River. He succeeded his close friend George Washington as president of the Potowmack Company in 1789, and was appointed by him one of the three federal city commissioners in 1791. During the first federal election he received votes for both Presidential Elector and Representative. See also *DHFFC* 2:497. (*DHSCUS* 1:69–71; *DHFFE* 2:192n, 204, 206)

JOHNSTON, ZACHARIAH (1742–1800), was a planter of Augusta County, Virginia, which he represented in the state House of Delegates, 1778–92. A militia captain from 1777 until war's end, he prominently supported ratification of the Constitution at the state convention and served as a Presidential Elector in the first federal election. (*DHFFE* 2:415–16)

JOHONNOT, GABRIEL, represented Penobscot (present day Castine), Maine, in the Massachusetts House of Representatives in 1789.

JONES, DAVID (1736–1820), was a Baptist minister of New Castle County, Delaware. Ordained in 1756, he performed missionary work in the Ohio River Valley, 1772–73, before serving as a chaplain in Lambert Cadwalader's 4th Regiment of the Pennsylvania Line, 1776–83. (*PGW* 3:501n)

JONES, JOHN (ca. 1729–1793), was a planter and justice of the peace of Brunswick County, Virginia, which he represented in the state Senate, 1776–89 (as speaker, 1787–89), the House of Delegates, 1790–91, and at the state convention where he voted against ratification of the Constitution. (*DHROC* 9:574)

JONES, JOHN COATES (1754–1802), a planter of "Cedar Point," Charles County, Maryland, was appointed federal collector for the lower Potomac, at Nanjemoy, in 1789, having served as naval officer there under the state since 1786. During the Revolutionary War he rose from first lieutenant in the 7th Regiment of the Maryland Line in 1776 to captain the next year, transferring to the 4th Regiment in 1781 and to the 1st Regiment briefly before his retirement in 1783, when he joined the Society of the Cincinnati.

He represented Charles County in the state House of Delegates in 1785. (*DHFFC* 2:497)

JONES, JOHN PAUL (1747–92), a Scottish born captain and the most celebrated naval hero in the Continental Navy, left the United States in late 1787 and served in the Russian navy until 1789, when he settled in Paris.

JONES, JOSEPH (1727–1805), trained at London's Middle Temple and became a lawyer of Fredericksburg, Virginia. He represented King George County in the state House of Delegates, 1776–78, 1780–81, and 1783–85, served in Congress, 1777 and 1780–83, on the Executive Council, 1785–89, and on the bench of the state's general court, 1778–79 and 1789–1805. He was an uncle of Senator Monroe. (*DHROC* 8:526; *DHFFC* 14:877)

JONES, WALTER (1745–1815), was a planter and physician of Northumberland County, Virginia, which he represented in the state Senate, 1785–87, and at the state convention where he voted to ratify the Constitution. He declined appointment as physician general of the army's middle department during the Revolutionary War and attended the Annapolis Convention in 1786. (*DHROC* 8:xxxiv, 228n; *JCC* 8:490)

JORDAN, JEREMIAH (ca. 1733–1806), a planter of St. Marys County, Maryland, was appointed port surveyor at Lewellensburg, Maryland, in 1789. He served as county commissioner of taxes, 1782–83, 1785–86, and 1790. See also *DHFFC* 2:498. (*Maryland Legislators* 2:499–500)

JORDAN, MELITIAH (1753–1818), a lumberer and merchant of Trenton, Maine, was collector at Frenchman's Bay from 1789 until his death. See also *DHFFC* 2:507.

JUDD, WILLIAM (1743–1804), was a lawyer of Farmington, Connecticut, which he represented in the state House of Representatives, 1786–94, and at the state convention where he voted to ratify the Constitution. The 1763 Yale graduate resided in the Connecticut settlement of Wyoming Valley, Pennsylvania, during the Revolutionary War, when he served as a major in the militia in 1775 and a captain in the 3rd Regiment of the Connecticut Line, 1777–81. (*Yale Graduates* 3:25–27)

KALTESSEN (KALTEIZEN), MICHAEL (1729–1807), a native of the German state of Wurttenburg, settled in Charleston, South Carolina, by 1755, and became a wood merchant. He served in the Provincial Congress, 1775–76, the state's House of Representatives for St. Philip and St. Michael Parish,

1776–78 and 1783–90, and the ratification convention where he voted to ratify the Constitution. (*South Carolina House* 3:390–91)

KEARNEY, DYRE (d. 1791), was a lawyer of Dover, Delaware, who served in Congress, 1787–88.

KEITH, ISRAEL (1751–1819), a Boston lawyer, was a justice of the peace for Suffolk County. The 1771 Harvard graduate served as aide-de-camp to General William Heath, 1776–78. (*PGW* 3:234)

KELSO, JAMES, was a merchant of Patapsco lower ferry, near Baltimore, for a number of years before applying for the position of comptroller of customs for that city. According to Otho H. Williams, he had been a trader in convicts before the Revolutionary War, an Antifederalist activist, and a recent bankrupt. (*PGW* 2:356–57, 3:119n)

KILTY, JOHN (1756–1811), of Annapolis, Maryland, served on the state's Executive Council, 1785–91. During the Revolutionary War he rose from second lieutenant of the 4th Regiment of the Maryland Line in 1776 to captain of the 3rd Regiment of Continental Dragoons in 1778 before retiring in 1782. (*DGW* 6:103n)

KILTY, WILLIAM (1757–1821), a former physician of Prince Georges County, Maryland, emigrated from England and settled in Annapolis before the Revolutionary War, during which he served as a surgeon's mate in the 5th Regiment of the Maryland Line, 1778–80, and a surgeon, 1780–81, before transferring to the 4th Regiment, 1781–83. After the war he practiced law. (*DGW* 5:375–76n)

KING, ELIZABETH "BETSY" (1770–1817), of Scarborough, Maine, was a younger half-sister of Senator King. (*Maine Historical and Genealogical Recorder* 1[1889]:8)

KING, SENATOR RUFUS, family during the First Congress: his wife, Mary Alsop (1770–94), the only child of a wealthy New York City merchant, in whose house at 38 Smith Street they lived with their children John Alsop (b. 1788), Charles (born 16 March 1789), and Caroline (b. 1790).

KING, MILES (1747–1814), a merchant of Hampton, Virginia, represented Elizabeth City County in the state House of Delegates, 1777–79 and 1784–98, and in the state convention where he voted to ratify the Constitution. During the Revolutionary War he served as a surgeon's mate in the 1st Regiment of the Virginia Line, 1775–78. (*DHROC* 8:176; *PGW* 3:241)

KINSEY, JAMES (ca. 1731–1803), was a Quaker lawyer of Burlington, New Jersey, which he represented in the state's lower house, or General Assembly, in 1784 and in the Legislative Council in 1791. He was appointed chief justice of the state supreme court in 1789, the same year he voted as a Presidential Elector. He was also an unsuccessful candidate for Representative in the first federal election. (*DHFFE* 3:184–85)

KIRBY, EPHRAIM (1757–1804), was a lawyer of Litchfield, Connecticut, who published the first volume of his *Reports of Cases Adjudged in the Superior Court . . . of Connecticut* in 1789. (*DHSCUS* 1:658n)

KNEELAND, CHARITY, eldest daughter of Senator Johnson, was the widow of Reverend Ebenezer Kneeland, the Loyalist Anglican pastor of Stratford, Connecticut, whom she had married in 1768. (Elizabeth P. McCaughey, *From Loyalist to Founding Father: The Political Odyssey of William Samuel Johnson* [New York, 1980], pp. 136, 185, 186)

KNOX, HENRY (1750–1806), formerly a Boston bookseller, served as secretary of war, 1785–94. He helped organize the Society of the Cincinnati after a notable rise from colonel of the Continental Regiment of Artillery in 1775 to major general and commander in chief of the Continental Army upon George Washington's resignation in 1783. He was a major land speculator and developer in Massachusetts and Maine. See also *DHFFC* 2:507, 9:52n.

KNOX, LUCY FLUCKER (1757–1824), who married Henry Knox in 1774, became a principal hostess of the Republican Court at the seat of government.

KNOX, WILLIAM (1756–95), formerly a Boston merchant, was employed under his older brother Henry as a clerk in the War Department before his appointment as United States consul to Dublin, 1790–92. See also *DHFFC* 2:507.

KOLLOCK, SHEPARD, was editor of the [Elizabeth] *New Jersey Journal*, 1786–1818, which supported ratification of the Constitution. (*DHFFE* 3:51n)

KUNZE, JOHN CHRISTOPHER (1744–1807), a New York City Lutheran minister, was married to Margaretha Henrietta Muhlenberg, sister of the two Representatives, who resided in the Kunze household during the first two sessions. Senator Maclay joined them during the second session. See also *DHFFC* 9:178n.

LAFAYETTE, MARIE JOSEPH, MARQUIS DE (1757–1834), was, to his own and subsequent generations, the symbol of the bond between the two countries formed by France's participation in the Revolutionary War. The wealthy French nobleman was the highest ranking foreign volunteer in the Continental Army, serving as major general, 1777–82, in many important battles, including Brandywine, Monmouth, and Yorktown, as well as at the encampment at Valley Forge. In 1789 he headed the moderate party of liberals as vice president of the French National Assembly and commander of the National Guard.

LAMB, JOHN (1735–1800), a New York City merchant, served as collector at that port, 1789–97, having held the post under the state since 1784. He opposed ratification of the Constitution. See also *DHFFC* 2:524.

LAMBERT, DAVID (b. ca. 1754), a merchant and former alderman of Richmond, Virginia, was appointed port surveyor in 1789. See also *DHFFC* 2:551.

LAMBERT, WILLIAM, a clerk who helped prepare Virginia's accounts with the United States in early 1789, was employed as a clerk for the state department from late 1790 to 1793. (*PJM* 11:440n)

LANE, SAMUEL (1718–1806), was a farmer, shoemaker, tanner, and port surveyor of Stratham, New Hampshire, where he settled in 1741 and served as town clerk from 1774 until his death. (Charles B. Nelson, *History of Stratham, New Hampshire* [Somersworth, N.H., 1965], p. 296)

LANGDON, ELIZABETH SHERBURNE (ca. 1760–1813), sister of Samuel Sherburne, married Senator Langdon in 1777. They resided together during most of the first and third sessions, joined by their only child Elizabeth (b. 1777). See also *DHFFC* 14:650.

LANGDON, HENRY SHERBURNE (1766–1857), of Portsmouth, New Hampshire, graduated from Yale in 1785 and was admitted to the bar in 1792. He was a son of Woodbury and nephew of Senator Langdon. (*Yale Graduates* 4:422–23)

LANGDON, MARY HALL, mother of Senator Langdon, died in Portsmouth, New Hampshire, on 11 April 1789.

LANGDON, TIMOTHY (1746–1808), originally of Boston, graduated from Harvard in 1765 and settled as a lawyer in Wiscasset, Maine, in 1769. His notoriety as a drunkard led to his removal as an admiralty judge in 1785 and as a justice of the peace in 1790. (*Harvard Graduates* 16:182–85)

LANGDON, WOODBURY (1739–1805), a merchant of Portsmouth, New Hampshire, and older brother of Senator Langdon, was appointed a commissioner for settling accounts between the United States and the individual states in 1790, after declining appointment as loan commissioner for New Hampshire. He served in the state House of Representative, 1778–79, Congress, 1779, the state's Executive Council, 1781–84, Senate, 1784–85, and superior court, 1782 and 1786–91. He received votes for Representative and Presidential Elector in the first federal election. Impeached in June 1790 for neglect of duty, he resigned from the bench to accept his federal appointment before the case came to trial the following January. See also *DHFFC* 2:516. (*DHFFE* 1:810, 814–15; *PAH* 12:4–5n)

LANGHAM, ELIAS (1759–1830), served as state commissary for military stores at Point of Fork (present day Columbia), Virginia. During the Revolutionary War he rose from sergeant in the 1st Continental Artillery Regiment in 1777 to second lieutenant from 1782 until war's end, when he joined the Society of the Cincinnati. (*PJM* 12:10n)

LANSING, JEREMIAH (1754–1817), served as port surveyor at Albany, New York, 1789–90. See also *DHFFC* 2:524.

LASHER, JOHN (1724–1806), a New York City merchant, was appointed port surveyor there in 1789. See also *DHFFC* 2:524.

LAURANCE, ELIZABETH, daughter of New York City merchant Alexander McDougall, married Representative Laurance in 1772. She died after a lingering illness on 16 August 1790.

LAW, RICHARD (1733–1806), of New London, Connecticut, served as United States district judge, 1789–1806. He graduated from Yale in 1751 and sat in the provincial and state House of Representatives before attending Congress, 1777 and 1781–82. A member of the state's Council of Assistants from 1776 until his appointment as chief judge of the superior court, 1785–89, he was simultaneously mayor of New London, 1784–1806, and represented it in the state convention, where he voted to ratify the Constitution. He was defeated for Representative in the first federal election but was chosen a Presidential Elector. See also *DHFFC* 2:486. (*DHROC* 3:611; *DHFFE* 2:37, 49; *Yale Graduates* 2:257–59)

LAWRENCE, JOHN (1751–ca. 1799), nephew of Lewis and Gouverneur Morris, was a lawyer of Lancaster County, Pennsylvania. During the Revolutionary War he rose from first lieutenant in the 5th Pennsylvania Battalion in 1776 to captain of the 6th Regiment of the Pennsylvania Line, 1776–79. After the war he became a member of the Society of the Cincinnati. He married Governor Arthur St. Clair's daughter Elizabeth by 1783. (*PGW* 4:5; *Pennsylvania Cincinnati* 1:530–34)

LAWRENCE, JONATHAN (1737–1812), a New York City merchant, was forced to abandon his Long Island estate at the outbreak of the Revolutionary War and served as Senator for New York's southern district, 1777–83. (*DHFFE* 3:463n; *PGW* 3:338–39)

LEAMING, THOMAS, JR. (1748–97), unsuccessfully sought appointment as clerk to the United States district court of Pennsylvania in August 1789. He studied law under John Dickinson and began practice in Philadelphia in 1772. During the Revolutionary War he served as a captain in the Pennsylvania militia, 1776–77, and in the Philadelphia Light Horse company. (*PGW* 3:418–19)

LEAR, TOBIAS (1762–1816), as secretary to George Washington since 1786, carried messages and documents from him to the First Congress. He married Mary Long, of Lear's native Portsmouth, New Hampshire, on 18 April 1790. See also *DHFFC* 9:45n.

LEARNED, AMASA (1750–1825), was a lawyer of New London, Connecticut, which he represented in the state House of Representatives, 1779 and 1785–91. The 1772 Yale graduate voted to ratify the Constitution at the state convention and later served in the Second and Third Congresses. (*Yale Graduates* 3:449–50; *DHROC* 3:538)

LEE, ARTHUR (1740–92), younger brother of Senator Lee, was a planter of Prince William County, Virginia, which he represented in the state House of Delegates, 1781–83 and 1785. He served in Congress, 1782–84, and on the board of treasury, 1785–89. An Antifederalist essayist and longtime critic of Superintendent of Finance Robert Morris's centralist policies, he was an unsuccessful candidate against Representative Page in the first federal election and against his second cousin, Representative Lee, in the second federal election. See also *DHFFC* 9:178n. (*DHFFE* 2:312n, 364; *DHROC* 8:129n)

LEE, CHARLES (1758–1815), was a lawyer of Alexandria, Virginia, where he served as the state's naval officer for the South Potomac District, ca. 1779–1789, and as federal collector, 1789–93. The 1775 College of New Jersey (Princeton) graduate also served briefly as secretary to the board of treasury in 1780. He was an older brother of Representative Lee and son-in-law to their second cousin Senator Lee by his marriage to Anne "Nancy" Lee in February 1789. See also *DHFFC* 2:551. (*Princetonians, 1769–1775*, pp. 493–98)

LEE, FRANCIS LIGHTFOOT (1734–97), younger brother of Senator Lee and second cousin of Representative Lee, was a planter of Richmond County, Virginia. He sat in Congress, 1775–79, where he signed the Declaration of Independence, and in the state House of Delegates, 1780–81. (*DHROC* 8:224n)

LEE, HENRY "LIGHT-HORSE HARRY" (1756–1818), older brother of Representative Lee and second cousin of Senator Lee, was a planter of Westmoreland County, Virginia. The 1773 College of New Jersey (Princeton) graduate became a captain in the 1st Continental Regiment of Dragoons in 1777, major of Lee's Partisan Corps the next year, and lieutenant colonel of Lee's Legion, or the 2nd Partisan Corps, in 1780. He resigned in 1782 and joined the Society of the Cincinnati the next year. He served in Congress, 1786–88, and was a Federalist leader at the state convention, where he voted to ratify the Constitution. Committed to opening the Potomac River to navigation, he joined with Representative Madison to speculate on the development of a town at Great Falls, Virginia. In November 1791 he was elected governor of Virginia. (*Princetonians, 1769–1775*, pp. 301–8; *PGW* 1:96–97n)

LEE, JOHN (1751–1812), older brother of Silas Lee and a merchant of Penobscot, Maine, was collector of that port, 1789–1801, having served as naval officer there under the state. See also *DHFFC* 2:507.

LEE, SILAS (1760–1814), was a lawyer of Wiscasset, Maine. After graduating from Harvard in 1784 he studied law under Representative Thatcher and became his professional and political protégé, marrying his niece, Temperance Hedge, in early 1790. (*American Conservatism*, p. 261)

LEE, THEODORICK (1766–1849), a planter of Loudoun County, Virginia, was the younger brother of Representative Lee.

LEE, THOMAS (1758–1805), a lawyer of Dumfries, Virginia, was the eldest son of Senator Lee and son-in-law of George Washington's brother, John Augustine, by his marriage to Mildred Washington in 1788. (*PGW* 3:247n)

LEE, THOMAS SIM (1745–1819), was a planter of Frederick County, Maryland, which he represented in the state's House of Delegates, 1787–88. He served as wartime governor, 1779–83, a member of Congress in 1783, and a delegate to the state convention where he voted to ratify the Constitution. Like George Washington and Thomas Johnson, he was elected one of the first five directors of the Potowmack Navigation Company in 1785. (*Maryland Legislators* 2:529–30)

LEEDS, FRANCIS OSBORNE, FIFTH DUKE OF (1751–1837), also the Marquis de Carmarthen, was Great Britain's secretary of state for foreign affairs from 1783 until his resignation in April 1791.

LEFFINGWELL, CHRISTOPHER (1734–1810), was a merchant and manufacturer of Norwich, Connecticut, who was appointed the state's naval officer for that port in 1784. (*PGW* 3:209–10n)

L'ENFANT, PETER CHARLES (1754–1825), a French born architect, engineer, and city planner, renovated New York's City Hall into Federal Hall and produced the plan of Washington, D.C. He arrived in America in 1777 as a volunteer, serving as a captain in the Continental Army's Corps of Engineers from 1779 until retiring as a brevet major in 1783. He designed the insignia for the Society of the Cincinnati and the patriotic iconography for both Federal Hall and the great parade held in New York City in 1788 to celebrate the ratification of the Constitution. See also *DHFFC* 9:36n. (Kenneth R. Bowling, *Peter Charles L'Enfant: Vision, Honor, and Male Friendship in the Early Republic* [Washington, D.C., 2002])

LEVY, MOSES (1757–1826), was a prominent Philadelphia lawyer who graduated from the College of Philadelphia (University of Pennsylvania) in 1772. (*University of Pennsylvania Alumni Book*)

LEWIS, MORGAN (1754–1844), was a New York City lawyer and land speculator. He graduated from the College of New Jersey (Princeton) in 1773 and studied law briefly under John Jay before accepting a commission as deputy quartermaster general of the northern department with the rank of colonel, 1776–83. After the war he became an active member of the Society of the Cincinnati. As lieutenant colonel of the 2nd Regiment of the city's militia brigade in 1789, he led the official escort for George Washington's inaugural procession. The son of Francis Lewis, a signer of the Declaration of Independence, Lewis was also the brother-in-law of Chancellor Robert R. Livingston by his marriage to Gertrude Livingston in 1779. (*Princetonians, 1769–1775*, pp. 308–17)

LEWIS, ROBERT (1769–1829), George Washington's nephew, served as a copyist in the President's official family. See also *DHFFC* 9:136n.

LEWIS, WILLIAM (1751–1819), a Quaker lawyer of Philadelphia and a prominent abolitionist, served as United States attorney for Pennsylvania from 1789 until his appointment as federal judge for the eastern district of the state in 1791. See also *DHFFC* 2:535, 9:78n. (*DHROC* 2:729)

L'HOMMEDIEU, EZRA (1734–1811), a lawyer of Southold, Long Island, New York, was an unsuccessful candidate for Senator in the first federal election. He also lost his bid for the seat won in that election by his brother-in-law, Representative Floyd. The 1754 Yale graduate served in the state Assembly, 1777–83, Congress, 1779–83 and 1788, and the state Senate, 1784–92 and 1794–1809. (*Yale Graduates* 2:343–45; *DHFFE* 3:560)

LIBBEY, JEREMIAH (1748–1824), was postmaster of Portsmouth, New Hampshire.

LINCOLN, BENJAMIN (1733–1810), a farmer of Hingham, Massachusetts, and lieutenant governor, 1788–89, served as a treaty commissioner with the southern Indians in 1789 and collector of the ports of Boston and Charlestown, Massachusetts, 1789–1809. A major general from 1777 to the war's end, when he enrolled in the Society of the Cincinnati, he became the first secretary of war under the Articles of Confederation and received one of Georgia's electoral votes for President in the first federal election. See also *DHFFC* 2:507–8, 9:129n. (*DHFFE* 4:221)

LINDSAY, WILLIAM (1743–97), a merchant of Norfolk, Virginia, served as collector of that port and adjoining Portsmouth, 1789–97. Earlier in 1789 he had succeeded Representative Parker as the state's naval officer for the Elizabeth River district. During the Revolutionary War he rose from lieutenant of the 1st Continental Regiment of Dragoons in 1777 to captain of Lee's Legion in 1778, resigning later that year. See also *DHFFC* 2:551. (*PGW* 2:151)

LINGAN, JAMES MCCUBBIN (1751–1812), a merchant of Georgetown, Maryland (in present day District of Columbia), was appointed collector there in

1789, having served as the state's revenue officer for the upper Potomac since 1784. During the Revolutionary War he rose from 2nd lieutenant in Colonel Hugh Stephenson's Maryland and Virginia Rifle Regiment in 1776 to captain in Rawlings's Continental Regiment in 1778, retiring in 1781. See also *DHFFC* 2:498.

LINN, WILLIAM (1752–1808), minister since 1786 of the Collegiate Reformed Protestant Dutch Church, New York City's largest congregation, was elected by the House as one of Congress's two chaplains on 1 May 1789 and served until Congress moved to Philadelphia. See also *DHFFC* 9:53n. (*DHFFC* 3:254, 8:781)

LITHGOW, ARTHUR, brother of William, resided in Winslow, Lincoln County, Maine, in 1790.

LITHGOW, WILLIAM, JR. (1750–96), a lawyer of Hallowell and Georgetown (present day Bath), Maine, served as United States attorney for the Maine district, 1789–94. He was a major in the 11th Regiment of the Massachusetts Line, 1777–79, and later enrolled in the Society of the Cincinnati. See also *DHFFC* 2:508.

LITTLE, JOSIAH (ca. 1747–1830), of Newbury, Massachusetts, had business interests in shipping and real estate. (George T. Little, *The Descendants of George Little* [Auburn, Me., 1882], pp. 109–10)

LIVERMORE, EDWARD ST. LOE (1762–1832), son of Representative Livermore, studied law in Newburyport, Massachusetts, before commencing practice in Concord, New Hampshire, in 1783.

LIVINGSTON, ANNE "NANCY" HUME (ca. 1763–1841), of Rhinebeck, New York, was the daughter of Dr. William Shippen, Jr., and Senator Lee's sister, Alice. In 1781 she married Henry Beekman Livingston, brother of Chancellor Robert R. Livingston. (Ethel Ames, ed., *Nancy Shippen, Her Journal Book* [Philadelphia, 1935], p. 110)

LIVINGSTON, JOHN HENRY (1746–1825), second cousin of Chancellor Robert R. Livingston, was minister of New York City's Dutch Reformed Church. (*PGW* 4:434)

LIVINGSTON, JOHN ROBERT (1755–1851), a New York City merchant and younger brother of Chancellor Robert R. Livingston, served as secretary to the president of Congress, 1786–89. (*LDC* 25:467n)

LIVINGSTON, MUSCOE (d. 1798), was a sea captain of Norfolk, Virginia, who had received a commission as lieutenant in the Continental Navy from Benjamin Franklin in Paris in 1778. (*PGW* 3:332; *JCC* 20:769)

LIVINGSTON, ROBERT R. (1746–1813), chancellor of New York State, 1777–1801, was the head of a powerful landed family long active in New York politics. He had been the first American secretary of foreign affairs, 1781–83, was an honorary member of the Society of the Cincinnati, and as chancellor administered the inaugural oath to George Washington. See also *DHFFC* 8:728, 9:12n.

LIVINGSTON, WALTER (1740–97), a principal heir of the famous Livingston Manor of New York, served on the three man board of treasury from 1785 until it was replaced in 1789. He was deputy commissary general of the Continental Army's northern department, 1775–76, state assemblyman, 1777–79, and delegate to Congress, 1784–85. In 1767 he married Senator Schuyler's daughter Cornelia, through whom he became Alexander Hamilton's brother-in-law. New York City Mayor James Duane was another brother-in-law, and he numbered Kitty Duer and Robert R. Livingston among his legion of first cousins. Beginning in 1789 he was a partner with Kitty's husband, William Duer, in vast certificate and land speculation schemes. (George Dangerfield, *Chancellor Robert R. Livingston of New York* [New York, 1960], p. 246)

LIVINGSTON, WILLIAM (1723–90), of Elizabethtown, New Jersey, was governor of that state from 1776 until his death. His daughter Sarah married John Jay in 1774. See also *DHFFC* 9:70–71n.

LLOYD, EDWARD, IV (1744–96), a planter of Talbot County, Maryland, served in the state's Executive Council, 1777–79, House of Delegates in 1780, and Senate, 1781, 1786, and 1791. He attended Congress, 1783–84, and voted to ratify the Constitution at the state convention.

LLOYD, HENRY, II (1709–95), uncle of John Lloyd, suffered the confiscation of his New York estate during the Revolutionary War and settled in London after 1783. (New-York Historical Society *Collections* 60[1927]:884–85)

LLOYD, JOHN (1745–92), fled before the British occupation of Long Island in 1776 and settled in Hartford, Connecticut, where he became a supplier for the Continental Army. He was the nephew of Henry Lloyd II. (*PRM* 2:295n)

LLOYD, THOMAS (1756–1827), was a British born publisher and stenographer from Philadelphia. His controversial reputation as a reporter of the Pennsylvania and Maryland state ratifying conventions preceded him to New York City, where he began publishing the *Congressional Register* in May 1789. See also *DHFFC* 10:xxix–xxxiii, 12:xix–xxi.

LOCK, MERRILL (d. pre-1789), served as Maryland's revenue officer for the lower Potomac.

LOGAN, GEORGE (1753–1821), a Quaker physician and gentleman farmer of Germantown, Pennsylvania, represented Philadelphia County in the state assembly, 1785–89. He supported the Constitution during ratification but soon thereafter left the Federalist party. See also *DHFFC* 9:209n. (*DHROC* 2:729)

LOMBAERT, HERMAN JOSEPH (ca. 1756–1793), a Philadelphia merchant, was the son-in-law of Representative Wynkoop. See also *DHFFC* 9:32n.

LONG, PIERSE (1739–89), a merchant of Portsmouth, New Hampshire, represented Rockingham County in the state Senate from June 1788 until his death in April 1789. He sat in Congress, 1785–86, voted to ratify the Constitution at the state convention, and was an unsuccessful candidate for Representative in the first federal election. (*DHFFE* 1:795n)

LORING, SARAH SMITH (d. September 1790), accommodated many state legislators, including Theodore Sedgwick, at the Golden Ball Tavern on Merchant's Row in Boston after the death of her husband Benjamin Loring (1736–82). During the First Congress she opened a boardinghouse on Broadway bordering the Bowling Green, where Representatives Sedgwick and Partridge became boarders late in the first session. (*DHFFC* 14:641)

LOUIS XVI (1754–93) became king of France in 1774. His alliance with the United States during the Revolutionary War strained his treasury and hastened the economic crisis that led to the outbreak of the French Revolution in 1789, the abolition of the monarchy in 1792, and his own execution a year later.

LOVELL, JAMES (1737–1814), of Boston, was a former teacher who served as the federal naval officer for that city and nearby Charlestown, Massachusetts, 1789–1814. The 1756 Harvard graduate sat in Congress from 1777 until 1782, after which he became a receiver of continental taxes and later the state's revenue collector at Boston, 1788–89. See also *DHFFC* 2:508. His son, John Lovell, Jr. (1762–1825), married Deborah Gorham in 1786. (*Harvard Graduates* 14:31–48)

LOWELL, JOHN (1743–1802), a Boston lawyer, served as United States district judge, 1789–1801. He graduated from Harvard in 1760 and served in the state's House of Representatives, 1778, 1780–81, Congress in 1782, and the state Senate, 1784–87. From 1782 until the end of the Confederation, he sat on the bench of the court of appeals established by Congress in 1780 to try appeals from the state admiralty courts. Lowell declined to attend the Annapolis Convention and was an unsuccessful candidate for Representative against Representative Ames and for Senator in the first federal election. See also *DHFFC* 2:508. (*Harvard Graduates* 14:650–61; *DHFFE* 1:754; *DHROC* 4:xxxvi; *DHSCUS* 1:628n)

LOWES, TUBMAN (1764–1815), was a planter of Somerset County, Maryland, which he represented in the state's House of Delegates, 1789 and 1791–92. (*PGW* 3:263–64n; *Maryland Legislators* 2:552–53)

LOWTHER, TRISTRAM (d. 1790), of Bertie County, North Carolina, married a cousin of James Iredell's niece by 1782. He attended the College of New Jersey (Princeton) briefly before transferring to King's College (Columbia) in 1774. Probably a merchant, he was in New York City for several weeks in the early summer of 1789. (*Princetonians, 1776–1783,* pp. 193–94)

LOWTHER, MARGARET (b. ca. 1759–post 1824), the daughter of a New York City merchant, married Representative Page on 27 March 1790 and resided with him for the remainder of the second session. Like him, she was an accomplished poet. The first of their eight children was born at Page's plantation "Rosewell" in February 1791. (*DHFFC* 14:922–23)

LUNT, JAMES (1750–1800), was appointed port surveyor for Portland and Falmouth, Maine, in 1789. See also *DHFFC* 2:508.

LUX, GEORGE, JR. (1753–97), was a merchant and planter of "Chatsworth," his family's estate outside Baltimore. He was one of the first proponents of the federal government's exclusive jurisdiction over the seat of government. (*PGW* 6:237; *PNG* 2:368n; Kenneth R. Bowling, *The Creation of Washington, D.C.: The Idea and Location of the American Capital* [Fairfax, Va., 1991], p. 77)

LYMAN, SAMUEL (1749–1802), a lawyer of Springfield, Massachusetts, served in the state's House of Representatives, 1786–89, and Senate, 1790–

93. He was an unsuccessful candidate for Presidential Elector and for Representative in the first federal election. (*DHFFE* 1:532, 754)

LYNCH, JOHN, of Baltimore, served as the state's harbor master in 1789. During the Revolutionary War he rose from captain of the 5th Regiment of the Maryland Line in 1776 to major of the 4th Regiment by 1781, retiring at war's end when he joined the Society of the Cincinnati. (*PGW* 3:260n)

LYNN, DAVID (1758–1835), of Georgetown, Maryland (in present day District of Columbia), rose from second lieutenant of the 7th Regiment of the Maryland Line in 1776 to captain in 1779. He transferred to the 4th Regiment in 1781 and served until the war's end, when he joined the Society of the Cincinnati.

LYONS, PETER (d. 1809), emigrated from Ireland in about 1750 and became a lawyer in Hanover County, Virginia. In 1779 he was appointed judge of the state's general court, and served as judge of the state's new court of appeals from 1789 until his death.

MCALLISTER, MATTHEW (1758–1823), a lawyer of Savannah, Georgia, served as United States district attorney for Georgia, 1789–96, having served as state's attorney general since 1787. Formerly of Pennsylvania, he graduated from the College of New Jersey (Princeton) in 1779 and settled in Savannah in 1784. See also *DHFFC* 2:492.

MCCLENACHAN, BLAIR (d. 1812), was an Irish born merchant, banker, and securities speculator in Philadelphia, with close wartime business ties to Senator Morris. See also *DHFFC* 9:337n.

MCCORMICK, DANIEL, was a New York City merchant, alderman, and director of the Bank of New York.

MCGILLIVRAY, ALEXANDER (ca. 1759–1793), a leader of the Creek Nation, was named American agent to the Creeks with the rank of brigadier general under the secret articles of the Treaty of New York in August 1790. He was the first head of state received by the federal government. See also *DHFFC* 11:1191n.

MCGREGOR, COLLIN (d. 1801), emigrated from Scotland and by 1785 had settled as a merchant and land speculator in New York City. (William MacBean, *Biographical Register of Saint Andrew's Society of the State of New York* [2 vols., New York, 1922–25], pp. 211–12)

McHENRY, JAMES (1753–1816), was a retired physician of Baltimore, which he represented in the Maryland House of Delegates, 1788–89. The Irish born student of Dr. Benjamin Rush served as a surgeon to the 5th Pennsylvania Battalion, 1776–78, and thereafter as George Washington's assistant military secretary until 1780, when he became aide-de-camp to the Marquis de Lafayette, with the rank of major. He sat in the state Senate, 1781–86, Congress, 1783–85, the Federal Convention, and the state convention, where he voted to ratify the Constitution. Despite declining nomination, he received votes for Representative in the first federal election. (*DHFFE* 2:109, 181, 206; *PGW* 1:461–62)

McINTOSH, LACHLAN (1725–1806), a port surveyor and planter, served as naval officer of Savannah, Georgia, 1789–91. He served as brigadier general in the Continental Army, 1776–83, and was appointed to Congress in 1784 but did not attend. See also *DHFFC* 2:492–93. (*LDC* 26:xii)

McINTOSH, WILLIAM (1726–1801), younger brother of Lachlan and like him a Georgia planter, rose in rank from ensign in the 1st Regiment of the Georgia Line in 1776 to captain in 1777, ending the war as brevet major.

McKEAN, THOMAS (1734–1817), of Philadelphia, served as chief justice of Pennsylvania, 1777–99. He was an unsuccessful candidate for Presidential Elector in the first federal election. See also *DHFFC* 9:79n. (*DHFFE* 1:319)

McKINLY, JOHN (1721–96), an Irish born physician of Wilmington, Delaware, served as first president (governor) of the state in 1777. A political ally of Senator Read, he was appointed to Congress in 1784 but never attended. (John A. Munroe, *Federalist Delaware, 1775–1815* [New Brunswick, N.J., 1954], p. 91)

McKNIGHT, CHARLES, JR. (1750–91), was a prominent New York City physician. See also *DHFFC* 9:201–2n.

McLELLAN, JOSEPH (1733–ca. 1807), a merchant and sea captain of Portland, Maine, chaired the committee of merchants and traders of that town who petitioned Congress on the Impost Bill in May 1789. (*Smith and Deane*, p. 30n; *DHFFC* 8:357, 360)

McPHERSON, WILLIAM (1756–1813), was port surveyor of Philadelphia, 1789–92. During the Revolutionary War he served as second lieutenant in Samuel Miles's Pennsylvania Rifle Regiment, 1776–79, and brevet major thereafter until 1781 when he became aide-de-camp to General Benjamin

Lincoln for the duration of the war. He represented Philadelphia County at the state convention, where he voted to ratify the Constitution. See also *DHFFC* 2:535–36. (*PGW* 2:138)

McRoberts, Alexander (1755–1800), was a merchant and alderman of Richmond, Virginia.

Madison, Ambrose (1755–93), a planter of Orange County, Virginia, was a younger brother of Representative Madison. Like his father and brother, he speculated in lands in Kentucky. (*DHROC* 9:604; *PJM* 15:363, 378)

Madison, James, Sr. (1723–1809), father of the Representative, was a planter of Orange County, Virginia. (*PJM* 1:48n)

Madison, James, Reverend (1749–1812), a second cousin of Representative Madison, was president of the College of William and Mary in Williamsburg, Virginia, 1777–1812, and the state's first Episcopal bishop. (*PJM* 1:224n)

Madison, William (1762–1843), a younger brother of Representative Madison, represented Culpeper County, Virginia, in the state's House of Delegates in 1791. He began the study of law under Thomas Jefferson in 1782, while serving out his commission as lieutenant in a state artillery company, 1781–83. (*PJM* 10:192n)

Malcolm, William (1745–91), a New York City merchant, was commanding brigadier general of the city brigade in 1789. During the Revolutionary War he served as colonel of one of the Sixteen Additional Regiments of the Continental Army, 1777–79. (*PGW: Revolution* 5:302n)

Manigault, Gabriel (1758–1809), was a prominent planter and securities speculator of St. James Goose Creek Parish, South Carolina, which he represented in the state's House of Representatives, 1785–93, and at the state convention where he voted to ratify the Constitution. He became the son-in-law of Senator Izard and the brother-in-law of Representative Smith (S.C.) by his marriage to Margaret Izard in 1785. (*South Carolina House* 3:470–73)

Manning, James (1738–91), a native of New Jersey and 1762 graduate of the College of New Jersey (Princeton), settled two years later near Providence, Rhode Island, where he was a Baptist minister and president of the College of Rhode Island (Brown) from its founding in 1765 until his death.

He supported a stronger central government as a delegate to Congress in 1786 and during ratification of the Constitution. During the First Congress he helped draft a petition from the inhabitants of Providence seeking relief from impost and tonnage legislation in August 1789 and the next month delivered it to the seat of government where he actively lobbied on its behalf. See also *DHFFC* 8:389–91. (*Princetonians, 1748–1768,* pp. 389–93; *PGW* 3:566)

MANSFIELD, WILLIAM MURRAY, FIRST EARL OF (1705–93), was lord chief justice of Great Britain, 1756–88.

MARCHANT, HENRY (1741–96), a lawyer of Newport, Rhode Island, served as federal district judge, 1790–96. He signed the Articles of Confederation as a member of Congress, 1777–79, sat in the state House of Deputies, 1784–90, and voted for ratification of the Constitution at the state convention in 1790. He served on the committee that drafted a petition to Congress from the inhabitants of Newport seeking relief from impost and tonnage legislation in August 1789, moderated the town meeting that adopted it, and the next month delivered it to the seat of government, where he actively lobbied on its behalf. See also *DHFFC* 2:540, 8:389–90. (*DHFFE* 4:401)

MARION, FRANCIS (ca. 1732–1795), a planter of Berkeley County, South Carolina, rose from captain in the 2nd Regiment of the South Carolina Line in 1775 to colonel by war's end, when he joined the Society of the Cincinnati. He was known as the "Swamp Fox" for his guerilla maneuvers during the Revolutionary War, occasionally under Representative Sumter's command. He was elected to the state Senate in 1781, 1782, 1784, and 1791.

MARSHALL, JOHN (1755–1835), was a leading lawyer of Richmond, in Henrico County, Virginia, which he represented in the state House of Delegates, 1787–88 and 1789–91, and at the state convention, where he voted to ratify the Constitution. He declined appointment as United States attorney for Virginia in 1789. During the Revolutionary War he rose from first lieutenant of the 3rd Regiment of the Virginia Line in 1776 to captain-lieutenant of the 15th Regiment later that year to captain in 1778. He transferred to the 7th Regiment later that year and served until 1781, although he was inactive after 1779. See also *DHFFC* 2:551–52. (*DHROC* 8:527)

MARTIN, JOSEPH (1740–1808), an active promoter of the settlement of the Southwest Territory, was appointed Congress's sole agent to both the Cherokee and the Chickasaw nations in the summer of 1788, the same year he attended North Carolina's first ratifying convention. In 1777 the native Virginian became that state's agent to the Cherokees, and he was Patrick Henry's personal agent in the West. In 1785–86 he served with Senator Hawkins on the commission that negotiated the Hopewell Treaty. He returned to Virginia in 1789 and served in the state legislature, 1791–99. (*PGW* 1:384–85n; *LDC* 22:293–94, 25:191n)

MARTIN, THOMAS (ca. 1732–1805), a merchant of Portsmouth, New Hampshire, served as port surveyor, 1789–98. See also *DHFFC* 2:516.

MASON, GEORGE (1725–92), a planter of "Gunston Hall" in Fairfax County, Virginia, attended the Federal Convention but refused to sign the Constitution and subsequently voted against it as a Stafford County delegate to the state convention. He was an early leader of the Revolutionary movement and sat in the state House of Delegates, 1776–81 and 1787–88. In March 1790 the state's Executive Council named him to fill Senator Grayson's seat until the legislature could elect a permanent replacement but he declined. (*DHROC* 8:527–28; *PGM* 3:1191–92)

MASON, GEORGE, JR. (1753–96), eldest son of George Mason of "Gunston Hall," was a planter of the neighboring plantation, "Lexington," in Fairfax County, Virginia. (*PGM* 1:lxxvi–lxxvii)

MASON, JOHN (1766–1849), seventh child of George Mason, became a partner of Joseph Fenwick in a mercantile firm based in Bordeaux, France, in 1788. He returned from France in 1791 and settled in Georgetown, Maryland (in present day District of Columbia). (*PGW: Retirement* 2:2n)

MASON, WILLIAM (1757–1818), third son of George Mason, was a planter of "Mattawoman" in Charles County, Maryland. He was commissioned a captain in the Fairfax County militia in 1778 and saw brief service in the South Carolina campaign of 1780–81. (*PGM* 1:lxxviii, 2:675–76, 692–93)

MATHERS, JAMES (1750–1811), was doorkeeper of the Senate from 1789 until his death. In March 1790 he successfully petitioned Congress for compensation for extra duties. See also *DHFFC* 8:517–18, 530–31.

MATHEWS, THOMAS (1742–1812), was a merchant and planter of Norfolk, Virginia, which he represented in the state House of Delegates, 1781–82 and 1784–93 (as speaker, 1788–93), and at the state convention, where he voted to ratify the Constitution. During the Revolutionary War he served as captain of the 4th Regiment of the Virginia Line, 1776–77, and subsequently as lieutenant colonel of the state militia. He was an unsuccessful challenger to Representative Parker in the first federal election. (*DHFFE* 2:418)

MAURY, JAMES (1746–1840), was a former merchant of Fredericksburg, Virginia, who resided in Liverpool, England, in 1789 and served as United States consul there, 1789–1830. (*DHFFE* 2:406n)

MAY, JOHN, JR. (1744–20 March 1790), was a surveyor and prominent land speculator of Jefferson County, Virginia (present day Kentucky), which he represented in the state House of Delegates in 1782. He was scalped by Shawnees at the mouth of the Scioto River. (Benjamin H. Coke, *John May, Jr., of Virginia* [Baltimore, 1975], pp. 243–50)

MAY, THOMAS, represented New Castle County in Delaware's House of Assembly, 1787–88. (*DHROC* 3:49)

MEADE, GEORGE (1741–1808), a Philadelphia merchant, banker, and business associate of Senator Morris, was a member of the city's common council, 1789–91. Representative Fitzsimons married Meade's sister Catherine in 1761 and shortly thereafter became a partner in his firm, which specialized in the West Indies trade. (*PRM* 3:38n; *DHFFC* 14:778)

MEIGS, RETURN JONATHAN (1740–1823), formerly of Middletown, Connecticut, led a party of settlers in 1788 to the Muskingum River in the Northwest Territory, where he became a surveyor for the Ohio Company. During the Revolutionary War he rose from major of the 2nd Regiment of the Connecticut Line in 1775 to colonel of the 6th Regiment, 1777–81.

MELCHER, ISAAC (1749–90), of Montgomery County, Pennsylvania, saw military duty as a volunteer in Canada, 1775–76, and thereafter served as state barrackmaster until 1778, when the position was subsumed within the Continental Army. He was barrackmaster general of the army, 1779–80, joined the Society of the Cincinnati after the war, and became a gentleman farmer and speculator in lands in New York and Ohio. (*Pennsylvania Cincinnati* 2:652–56)

MELVILL, THOMAS (1751–1832), was a merchant of Boston, where he served as port surveyor, 1789–1829, having served two years as the state's naval officer there. He graduated from the College of New Jersey (Princeton) in 1769 and was a major in the Massachusetts state artillery regiment briefly in 1776. See also *DHFFC* 2:508–9. (*Princetonians, 1769–1775,* pp. 32–36)

MERCER, JOHN, of New Jersey, served as a captain in the 1st Regiment of the federal army from 1789 until his resignation the next year. Following his Revolutionary War service, he rose from lieutenant to captain in the United States infantry regiment, 1784–89. See also *DHFFC* 2:519.

MEREDITH, SAMUEL (1741–1817), a Philadelphia merchant, was appointed port surveyor in August 1789 but accepted the more lucrative appointment as United States treasurer the next month and served until 1801. He was a member of Congress from 1786 to 1788. From 1774 to 1800, he and George Clymer speculated in land in Bradford, Luzerne, Pike, Schuylkill, Sullivan, Susquehanna, Wayne, and Wyoming counties in Pennsylvania. He was extremely well connected at the seat of government, being brother-in-law to three members of the First Congress: Representative Cadwalader, by his marriage to Margaret Cadwalader in 1772; Senator Dickinson, the husband of Margaret's sister Rebecca; and Representative Clymer, who married Meredith's sister Elizabeth in 1765 and became a partner in Meredith's mercantile firm. His children were Martha, Elizabeth or "Betsey" (ca. 1775–1826), Anne (b. ca. 1776), Margaret (1781–1824), and Maria (1783–1854). See also *DHFFC* 2:536, 9:194n. (*DHFFC* 2:20, 14:673, 773–74; *Magazine of American History* 3[1879]:561)

MERSEREAU (MERCEREAU), JOSHUA (1728–1804), a lawyer and businessman of Staten Island, New York, served as deputy commissary of prisoners under Representative Boudinot during the Revolutionary War and as a member of the state legislature, 1777–86. In the summer of 1789 he was preparing to move to Tioga County, New York, where he had speculated heavily in land. (*PGW* 2:465)

MIFFLIN, THOMAS (1744–1800), a retired merchant of Philadelphia, was elected president of Pennsylvania in 1788 and served continuously (as governor after 1790) until 1799. Despite his Quaker upbringing, he joined the Continental Army as George Washington's first aide-de-camp with the rank of major in 1775, rose to quartermaster general with the rank of colonel, 1776–77, and was promoted to major general, 1777–79, enrolling in the Society of the Cincinnati at war's end. He was president of Congress, 1783–84, and a delegate to the Federal Convention, where he signed the Constitution. In the first federal election he was an unsuccessful candidate for Presidential Elector. See also *DHFFC* 9:79n. (*DHFFE* 1:319)

MILLER, JOHN, who unsuccessfully petitioned George Washington for a federal appointment in 1789, was probably the individual of that name who was appointed a judge of the Philadelphia city court in 1779 and operated a mill in Chester County, Pennsylvania, before the Revolutionary War. (*PGW* 3:70n)

MILLER, MAGNUS (d. 1807), was a Philadelphia merchant as early as 1775. (*Drinker* 3:2070–71)

MILLER, PHINEAS (1764–1803), a native of Connecticut, graduated from Yale in 1785, when he was hired by Nathanael Greene to tutor his children and transcribe his Revolutionary War papers at his estate on Cumberland Island, Camden County, Georgia. In 1796 Miller married Greene's widow Catharine, whose plantations he had helped manage since the death of her husband ten years earlier. (*Yale Graduates* 4:430–31)

MILTON, JOHN (ca. 1756–1817), formerly a planter of Burke County, was Georgia's secretary of state almost continuously from 1777 to 1799. He served as captain in the 1st Regiment of the Georgia Line, 1776–82, thereafter becoming secretary of the state Society of the Cincinnati. He represented Glynn County at the state ratification convention and was elected a Presidential Elector in the first federal election, in which he received two of Georgia's electoral votes. (*DHFFE* 2:485–86)

MINOT, GEORGE R. (1758–1802), a Boston lawyer and historian, was clerk of the Massachusetts House of Representatives, 1782–91, and secretary to the state ratification convention in 1788. After graduating from Harvard in 1778 he studied law in the office of William Tudor, where he established a lifelong friendship with his fellow student, Representative Ames. They were both members of Boston's Wednesday Night Club. Minot enjoyed some celebrity as a Federalist historian for his treatment of Shays's Rebellion in his *History of the Insurrections* (Worcester, Mass., 1788). (*DHROC* 6:1162n; *Ames*, p. 40)

MINOT, JONAS CLARK (1735–1813), older brother of George R. and like him a member of Boston's Wednesday Night Club, served as inspector of customs for the Boston district, 1789–1802. (Joseph G. Minot, *A Genealogical Record of the Minot Family in America* [Boston, 1897], p. 21)

MIRÓ, ESTEBAN (1744–95), became governor of Spanish Louisiana in 1785, with the rank of brigadier general after 1789.

MITCHELL, GEORGE R. (d. 1799), was a planter of Sussex County, Delaware, which he represented in the state House of Assembly, 1784–88. He served as speaker of the Legislative Council, 1788–92, and as a Presidential Elector in 1789. (*DHFFE* 2:97)

MITCHELL, JOHN (ca. 1713–1801), a retired surveyor and land speculator once active in the area of Belfast, Maine, probably resided in Chester, New Hampshire, in 1789. (*PGW* 4:329n)

MITCHELL, JOHN HINKLEY (1741–1816), was a Charleston, South Carolina, merchant planter. In 1790 he acted as agent to the British engraver Matthew Boulton in a failed bid for a federal minting contract. See also *DHFFC* 8:504–9.

MITCHELL, STEPHEN MIX (1743–1835), a lawyer of Wethersfield, Connecticut, was a member of the state's Council of Assistants, 1784–93, and a judge of the Hartford County court, 1789–95. He graduated from Yale in 1763 and served in the state House of Representatives, 1778–84, in Congress, 1785–88, and in the state convention, where he voted to ratify the Constitution. An unsuccessful candidate for Representative in the first federal election, he was elected to fill Senator Sherman's seat upon the latter's death in 1793. (*Yale Graduates* 3:37–39; *DHFFE* 2:55–56)

MONTESQUIEU, CHARLES LOUIS, BARON DE (1689–1755), was a French jurist, political philosopher, and author of the vastly influential *Spirit of the Laws* (1748).

MONTGOMERY, JANET (1743–1828), of Rhinebeck, New York, was the widow of the Revolutionary War hero, General Richard Montgomery, and eldest sister of Chancellor Robert R. Livingston. Before she left to visit in-laws in Ireland in the summer of 1789, she was a frequent guest at the Washingtons' home where she lobbied unsuccessfully for a federal appointment for her brother. (*PGW* 3:353–54n)

MONTMORIN DE SAINT-HEREUR, ARMAND-MARC, COMTE DE (1745–92), served as French foreign minister, 1787–91.

MOORE, CLEON (d. 1808), was a planter of Fairfax County, Virginia. During the Revolutionary War he served as captain in William Grayson's Additional Continental Regiment, 1777–78. (*PGM* 1:lxxxi, 2:700)

MOORE, JOHN SPOTSWOOD, who succeeded Corbin Braxton as the state's port inspector at West Point, Virginia, in 1788, became port surveyor there in 1789. See also *DHFFC* 2:552.

MORGAN, GEORGE (1743–1810), a merchant and land speculator of Princeton, New Jersey, launched a settlement of American colonists at New Madrid in Spanish Louisiana (present day Missouri) in 1788–89. During the Revolutionary War he was appointed an Indian agent with the rank of colonel in the Continental Army and served as deputy commissary general of the western district, 1777–79. (*PGW* 1:447–49n)

MORIARTY, JOHN (d. 1797), a native of Ireland, settled in Salem, Massachusetts, in 1777 and lost a fortune in privateering during the Revolutionary War. (*PGW: Confederation* 1:179–80)

MORRIS, GOUVERNEUR (1752–1816), was a New York City lawyer who, having traveled to Europe in 1788 as Senator Morris's business agent, served as President Washington's unofficial representative to the British government beginning in January 1790. The 1768 graduate of King's College (Columbia) represented New York in Congress, 1778–79, before moving to Philadelphia, where he served as assistant superintendent of finance, 1781–84. He resumed his residence at "Morrisania" in present day lower Bronx, New York City, shortly after the Federal Convention, where, representing Pennsylvania, he was one of the most active delegates. See also *DHFFC* 2:116, 451–67. (*DHROC* 2:730; *PGW* 4:182)

MORRIS, LEWIS, JR. (1752–1824), nephew of Gouverneur Morris, married into South Carolina's planter aristocracy in 1783 and settled permanently in Charleston. During the Revolutionary War he served as aide-de-camp to General John Sullivan, 1776–79, and to General Nathanael Greene thereafter until war's end, when he retired as a brevet lieutenant colonel and joined the Society of the Cincinnati. He represented Charleston at the state convention, where he voted to ratify the Constitution, and in the state House of Representatives, 1789–94. He was brother-in-law to Representative Huger. (*South Carolina House* 3:513–14; *PNG* 4:51n; George C. Rogers, *Evolution of a Federalist: William Loughton Smith* [Columbia, S.C., 1962], pp. 155n, 168n)

MORRIS, MARY WHITE (1749–1827), of Philadelphia, married Senator Morris in 1769. When apart, the Morrises maintained a frequent and affectionate correspondence. From May to July 1789 she joined her husband at the seat of government, where she enjoyed close relations with Martha

Washington. During the third session, the Washingtons resided at the Philadelphia home of the Morrises, who relocated next door. Mary's brother was Episcopalian Bishop William White. See also *DHFFC* 14:766–69.

MORRIS, RICHARD (1730–1810), of New York City, served as chief justice of the state supreme court from 1779 until 1790, when he retired to his country estate in Scarsdale, New York. The 1748 Yale graduate was the half-brother of Gouverneur Morris and uncle of Lewis Morris, Jr. A principal advocate of ratification of the Constitution at the state convention, he was briefly considered a candidate for both governor and United States Senator in early 1789. He was an honorary member of the Society of the Cincinnati. (*PGW* 2:443n; *PAH* 3:637n; *Yale Graduates* 2:171–72)

MORRIS, RICHARD (ca. 1746–1821), a former army supplier, was a Federalist merchant and planter of Louisa County, Virginia, which he represented in the state House of Delegates, 1788–89. He petitioned the state ratifying convention to overturn his defeat as a delegate and was technically declared the winner, although he was not seated before the convention rose. (*DHROC* 9:594–95n)

MORRIS, SENATOR ROBERT, family during the First Congress: his wife Mary White of Philadelphia; and their children Robert, Jr. (1769–ca. 1804), Esther ("Hetty"), Thomas (1771–1849), who frequently stayed with his father in New York City during the First Congress, William White (1772–98), Charles (b. 1777), Maria (1779–1852), and Henry (1784–1842). (*PRM* 3:58n, 4:247n)

MORSE, JEDIDIAH (1761–1826), a Congregational minister of Charlestown, Massachusetts, petitioned the First Congress for copyright protection of his popular *American Geography* in May 1789. A year later he helped draft the Congregational clergy's petition to Congress for a standardized edition of the Bible. See also *DHFFC* 8:xxvi, 30, 31, 33, 36, 37, 307.

MORTON, SARAH WENTWORTH (1759–1846), of Boston in 1781 married Perez Morton (1751–1837), state's attorney for Suffolk County, Massachusetts. (*PGW* 4:450; Howard Haycroft and Stanley Kunitz, *American Authors, 1600–1900* [New York, 1938], pp. 545–46)

MOSELEY, WILLIAM, was justice of the peace of Hartford County, Connecticut, 1786–91. In 1785 he became allied by marriage with the influential Wolcott family of Litchfield.

MOSS, REUBEN (1759–1809), originally of Cheshire, Connecticut, served for four years in the Continental Army before enrolling at Yale, from which he graduated in 1787. Thereafter he studied theology in New Haven under Reverend Benjamin Trumbull, 1788–91, and was ordained in 1792. (*Yale Graduates* 4:562–64)

MOULTRIE, WILLIAM (1730–1805), a planter of St. John's Berkeley, South Carolina, served in the state House of Representatives in 1783, as lieutenant governor in 1784, governor, 1785–87, and member of the state Senate, 1791. In 1788 he voted to ratify the Constitution at the state convention. The Revolutionary War hero rose from colonel of the 2nd Regiment of the state line in 1775 to brigadier general the next year to major general in 1782. He became president of the state Society of the Cincinnati.

MOUNTFORD, TIMOTHY (1732–99), was a Portsmouth, New Hampshire, sea captain.

MOUSTIER, ELEANOR-FRANÇOIS-ELIE, COMTE DE (1751–1817), resided in New York City as the French minister to the United States from January 1788 until his return to France in October 1789. See also *DHFFC* 9:13n. (*PGW* 1:37, 4:184–85n)

MUHLENBERG, CATHERINE SCHAEFER (1750–1835), married Representative F. A. Muhlenberg in 1771. They had four daughters and three sons; the youngest, John Peter David, was born in 1784. (Paul Wallace, *The Muhlenbergs of Pennsylvania* [Philadelphia, 1950], p. 265)

MUHLENBERG, GOTTHILF HENRY ERNEST (1753–1815), younger brother of the Representatives, was, like them, educated for the ministry in Halle, Germany, prior to his ordination as a Lutheran minister in 1770. After six years as pastor and an outspoken revolutionary in Philadelphia, he transferred to Lancaster, Pennsylvania, in 1780. For his notable botanical studies he was elected to the American Philosophical Society in 1785. (See Wallace, *The Muhlenbergs*)

MUIR, ADAM, served as Maryland's revenue officer for the Nanticoke River prior to 1789.

MUIR, JOHN (ca. 1750–1810), was a Scottish born merchant of Vienna, Maryland, who served as deputy naval officer under the state for several years before his appointment as collector there in 1789. (*PGW* 3:60n)

MUNSON, WILLIAM, appointed a justice of the peace of New Haven County, Connecticut, in 1787, served as revenue inspector at Middletown from 1789 until his appointment as port surveyor at New Haven in 1793. During the Revolutionary War he rose from first lieutenant in 1776 to captain in the 2nd Canadian Regiment in 1778, retiring at war's end as a brevet major. (*PGW* 2:102–5; Munson to Washington, 31 Dec. 1792, Washington Papers, DLC)

MURRAY, JOHN, was a merchant of Alexandria, Virginia. (*PGW: Confederation* 2:523)

MUSE, HUDSON (d. 1799), a merchant of Urbanna, Virginia, was appointed collector at Tappahannock in 1789, having served as the state's naval officer on the Rappahannock River, 1782–89. See also *DHFFC* 2:552. (*PJM* 11:441)

NASSON, SAMUEL (1745–1800), was a farmer and miller of Sanford, Maine, which he served as selectman, 1786–90, member of the Massachusetts House of Representatives, 1787–89, and delegate to the state convention, where he voted against ratification of the Constitution. He saw brief service during the Revolutionary War as quartermaster of James Scammon's Massachusetts Regiment in 1775 and the 7th Continental Regiment in 1776. (*DHROC* 4:436)

NATHAN, SIMON (1746–1822), a Philadelphia merchant, spent most of the 1780s in lengthy litigation with Virginia over compensation for supplying George Rogers Clark's campaign in the Northwest Territory in 1779–80. He brought the issue before Congress in a petition in July 1790. See also *DHFFC* 7:56–59. (*PJM* 3:21n)

NECKER, JACQUES (1732–1804), a Geneva born banker, served as France's minister of finance from 1776 until his dismissal in 1781. He returned to office from 1788 to 1790.

NELSON, ALEXANDER (1749–1834), formerly a partner in a Richmond based tobacco trading firm, had settled outside Staunton, in Augusta County, Virginia, by 1789. As a boy he emigrated from Ireland to Philadelphia where he was Senator Morris's protégé before moving to Virginia during the Revolutionary War. (*PJM* 6:373n)

NELSON, HENRY (1754–1805), was a farmer of Mendon, Massachusetts. During the Revolutionary War he rose from private in Joseph Read's Massachusetts Regiment in 1775 to sergeant in the 2nd Regiment of the Massachusetts Line in 1777 and lieutenant in 1782. He spent the last year of the war as paymaster to the 3rd Regiment, and retained that post in Henry Jackson's Continental Regiment until 1784. (*Memorials of the Massachusetts Society of the Cincinnati* [Boston, 1964], pp. 429–30)

NELSON, THOMAS (b. 1764), son of Virginia's Governor Thomas Nelson, Jr., who died in January 1789, served as President Washington's aide and personal secretary from October 1789 to November 1790. See also *DHFFC* 9:240n. (*DGW* 5:451)

NELSON, WILLIAM (1754–1813), was a Richmond, Virginia, lawyer when he accepted appointment as United States attorney for Virginia in December 1789. In 1791 he became judge of the state's General Court. See also *DHFFC* 2:552. (*PJM* 6:500n)

NICHOLAS, GEORGE (ca. 1749–1799), a lawyer who settled in Danville, Kentucky, in early 1789, had represented Albemarle County, Virginia, in the state House of Delegates, 1786–87, and at the state convention, where he voted to ratify the Constitution. The 1772 graduate of the College of William and Mary rose from captain of the 3rd Regiment of the Virginia Line in 1775 to major of the 10th Regiment the next year to lieutenant colonel of the 11th Regiment in 1777, when he resigned. In Kentucky he became a leader of the statehood movement and the new state's first attorney general. He was the older brother of Wilson Cary Nicholas and brother-in-law of Attorney General Edmund Randolph. (*PJM* 6:417–18n; *DHROC* 10:1258n)

NICHOLAS, JOHN, JR. (ca. 1757–1836), a planter of Albemarle County, Virginia, was an active Federalist essayist in early 1789 and the probable author of several pieces signed *Decius* that attacked Patrick Henry. During the Revolutionary War he rose from ensign of the 2nd Regiment of the Virginia Line in 1775 to first lieutenant of the 9th Regiment, 1776–77, and captain in the state militia, 1777–80. (*DHFFE* 2:392)

NICHOLAS, WILSON CARY (1761–1820), was a planter of Albemarle County, Virginia, which he represented in the state House of Delegates, 1784–86 and 1788–89, and, together with his brother George, in the state convention where he voted to ratify the Constitution. He left William and Mary College to join the Continental Army, where he rose to the command of Washington's Life Guard. (*PJM* 8:73n; *DHROC* 8:375n)

NICHOLS (NICHOLLS), FRANCIS (1737–1812), was an Irish born merchant of Pottsgrove (present day Pottstown), Pennsylvania. He joined William Thompson's Pennsylvania Rifle Battalion in 1775 as a second lieutenant, rising to major of the 9th Regiment of the state Line in 1777. After resigning in 1779 he became a Philadelphia merchant and army contractor with extensive dealings with Superintendent of Finance Robert Morris. After the war he joined the Society of the Cincinnati. (*PGW* 3:509; *PRM* 3:181n)

NICHOLSON, JAMES (1737–1804), retired "commodore" of the Continental Navy, served as assistant alderman of New York's East Ward under Representative Laurance, 1788–89, and as one of the commissioners to oversee the conversion of City Hall into Federal Hall. Senator Few married his daughter Catherine in June 1788 and they lived next door to the Nicholson residence at 91 Williams Street. Another daughter, Frances, married Representative Seney on 1 May 1790, one month after Congress received the petition signed by Nicholson and six other navy and marine officers seeking additional compensation for their wartime service. See also *DHFFC* 7:438–43, 14:542, 592.

NICKOLLS (NICHOLS), JAMES B., brother-in-law of John Swanwick, apprenticed with Representative Fitzsimons at Philadelphia and then settled as a merchant in Portsmouth, Virginia, in 1785. (*PGW* 2:143–44n)

NICOLS, JEREMIAH (1748–1806), was a planter of Kent County, Maryland, which he represented in the state House of Delegates, 1787–88, serving also as justice of the peace, 1787–89 and 1791–94. (*Maryland Legislators* 2:611)

NIXON, JOHN (1733–1808), a Philadelphia merchant and financier, served with Representative Clymer as a director of the Bank of Pennsylvania when it was founded in 1780. The next year they were asked to solicit subscribers to Senator Morris's proposed Bank of North America. He saw duty during the Revolutionary War as colonel of the independent troop known as the Pennsylvania Associators, 1775–77. (*PRM* 1:73n)

NORRIS, JOHN (1751–1808), was a merchant and distiller of Salem, Massachusetts. (*EIHC* 4:130)

NORTH, WILLIAM (1755–1836), a merchant of Duanesburg, New York, and son-in-law of New York City Mayor James Duane, served as inspector of the federal army, 1784–88. He launched his military career as second lieutenant of Henry Knox's Continental Regiment of Artillery, 1776–77, was promoted to captain in William Lee's Additional Continental Regiment in 1777, and transferred to the 16th Regiment of the Massachusetts Line in 1779. That year he began his lifelong friendship with Baron von Steuben, serving as his aide-de-camp until war's end, when he was breveted a major and joined the Society of the Cincinnati.

NOURSE, JOHN (ca. 1762–1790), was an editor of Boston's *Independent Chronicle*, 1784–89. (*Boston Printers*, pp. 390–91)

NOURSE, JOSEPH (1754–1841), served as register of the United States treasury from 1781 until 1829. See also *DHFFC* 9:266n.

O'BRIEN, MICHAEL MORGAN (d. 1804), was an Irish born Philadelphia merchant engaged in the West Indies trade. See also *DHFFC* 9:7n. (*PGW* 2:206–7n)

OGDEN, MATTHIAS (1754–91), a lawyer and land speculator of Elizabethtown, New Jersey, was a Presidential Elector in 1789. As early as mid March of that year he spearheaded the petition movement to invalidate the New Jersey federal election for Representatives in favor of his brother-in-law, Jonathan Dayton and others. He served as lieutenant colonel of the 1st Regiment of the New Jersey Line, 1776–77, becoming its colonel in 1777, and a brevet brigadier general at war's end, when he joined the Society of the Cincinnati. See also *DHFFC* 8:555–56. (*DHFFE* 3:186)

OGDEN, SAMUEL (1746–1810), owned and operated ironworks in Morris County, New Jersey. He served as a colonel of the state militia during the Revolutionary War and later speculated heavily in lands in northern New York State. In 1775 he married Euphemia Morris, sister of Gouverneur and Lewis Morris. (Lawrence Van Alstyne and Charles Burr Ogden, eds., *The Ogden Family in America: Elizabethtown Branch* [Philadelphia, 1907], pp. 104–5)

OGDEN, UZAL (1744–1822), an Episcopalian minister, became rector of Trinity Church in Newark, New Jersey, in 1788. (*PAH* 24:233n)

ORNE, AZOR (1731–96), was a merchant of Marblehead, Massachusetts, which he served as selectman, 1787–89, state Representative in 1787 and 1789, and delegate to the state convention, where he voted to ratify the Constitution. He was a candidate for Senator, Presidential Elector, and Representative in the first federal election. His lobbying of the state legislature led to its petitioning Congress on the encouragement of fisheries in 1790. See also *DHFFC* 8:141–44. (*DHFFE* 1:531, 570, 598, 755)

ORR, BENJAMIN GRAYSON (1768–1822), of Virginia, was related to two Virginia Senators: his mother was William Grayson's sister and his grandmother was James Monroe's aunt. (*PJM* 12:439n)

OSBORNE, HENRY (1751–1800), was an Irish born lawyer who filled several state offices in Pennsylvania before settling in Camden County, Georgia, in 1784. He served as a state revenue collector, 1785–91, state Assemblyman, 1786–88, chief justice, 1787–89, delegate to the state ratification convention, member of Congress for 1786–87 (which he declined to attend), and state Senator, 1789–90. He was also justice of the county inferior court briefly in 1789 before resigning to serve as chief justice of the superior court's eastern circuit, which post he held until 1791 when he was impeached and convicted of election fraud as a result of Anthony Wayne's effort to unseat Representative Jackson in the second federal election. Osborne himself, a Presidential Elector in 1789, was an unsuccessful candidate for Representative in the first federal election. In 1789 he served as a commissioner authorized to treat with the Southern Indians under an act of Congress of 26 October 1787. (*DHFFE* 2:486–87; *JCC* 33:708–11)

OSGOOD, JOSHUA BAILEY (1753–91), a 1772 Harvard graduate, was a merchant and large landowner of Fryeburg, Maine, which he represented in the Massachusetts House of Representatives in 1790. (*Harvard Graduates* 18:138–40)

OSGOOD, SAMUEL (1748–1813), was postmaster general, 1789–90. As a Massachusetts delegate to Congress, 1781–84, he opposed Superintendent of Finance Robert Morris and worked to replace him with a board of treasury, on which Osgood served from 1785–89. In 1786 he married Walter Franklin's widow, Maria Bowne (1754–1813), and settled permanently in New York City, where he became an active Antifederalist. See also *DHFFC* 2:509, 9:167n.

OSWALD, ELEAZER (1755–95), Antifederalist editor of Philadelphia's *Independent Gazetteer* from 1782 until his death, frequently attacked Robert Morris in his paper. See also *DHFFC* 9:210n.

OTIS, HARRISON GRAY (1765–1848), eldest child of Secretary of the Senate Otis, commenced legal practice in Boston in 1786, having studied law under John Lowell after graduating from Harvard in 1783. He married Sally Foster, daughter of William Foster, on 31 May 1790.

OTIS, JAMES, JR. (1725–83), was a lawyer and patriot leader of Boston from 1761 until 1769, when a saber blow to the head during a brawl with British customs officials unhinged his reason. He was declared insane in 1771 and withdrew from public life. He was the older brother of Samuel Allyne Otis, Mercy Otis Warren, and Joseph Otis.

OTIS, JOSEPH (1726–1809), was a merchant of Barnstable, Massachusetts, where he served as collector, 1789–92, having held the post under the state since 1776. He was the brother of Samuel Allyne Otis, Mercy Otis Warren, and James Otis, Jr. See also *DHFFC* 2:509. (*PGW* 5:225n)

OTIS, SAMUEL ALLYNE (1740–1814), a former merchant of Boston, was defeated by Representative Ames in the first federal election but conducted a successful campaign for the post of secretary of the Senate, which he filled from 1789 until his death. His sister was Mercy Otis Warren and his wife Mary was first cousin to Abigail Adams. See also *DHFFC* 9:5n.

OTTO, LOUIS GUILLAUME (1754–1817), French chargé d'affaires in Philadelphia from 1785, moved to New York City to become acting minister upon the Comte de Moustier's return to France in October 1789 and served until his own departure in late 1792. In April 1790 he married the daughter of St. Jean de Crèvecoeur. See also *DHFFC* 9:198n. (*PGW* 4:185n; *PTJ* 16:356)

PAGE, REPRESENTATIVE JOHN, family during the First Congress: his children Mann (b. 1766), Robert (ca. 1770–ca. 1795), Sally (b. 1771, married 1790), Alice (b. ca. 1775–post 1813), Frances (b. ca. 1777), Francis (b. ca. 1781), and Judith (b. ca. 1783), and two nephews, Mat and Nat. The family estate "Rosewell" was in Gloucester County, Virginia. (Richard Channing Moore Page, *Genealogy of the Page Family in Virginia* [New York, 1893], pp. 78–79)

PAGE, MANN, JR. (ca. 1749–1803), younger brother of Representative Page, was a lawyer and planter of "Mannsfield" in Spotsylvania County, Virginia, which he alternated representing along with Gloucester County in the state House of Delegates between 1776 and 1790. He was also a delegate to Congress in 1777. (*DHROC* 8:195n)

PAINE, ROBERT TREAT (1731–1814), a lawyer of Taunton, Massachusetts, served as state attorney general, 1777–90, and justice of the state supreme judicial court, 1790–1804. The 1749 Harvard graduate signed the Declaration of Independence as a delegate to Congress, 1774–76. (*Harvard Graduates* 12:462–82)

PALMER, JONATHAN, JR. (1747–1810), was appointed port surveyor of Stonington, Connecticut, in 1789, having served as the state's naval officer there since 1785. In addition to having served as justice of the peace and state Representative, he served eight terms as town selectman. See also *DHFFC* 2:486. (Norman F. Boas, *Stonington during the American Revolution* [Mystic, Conn., 1990], p. 90)

PARKER, COPLAND (COPELAND) (b. 1768), of Suffolk, Virginia, served under his older brother, Representative Parker, as deputy state naval officer of neighboring Portsmouth until the latter's resignation in February 1789. (*PGW* 3:103n)

PARKER, DANIEL (1754–1829), resided in Europe after 1784, when approaching bankruptcy forced him to flee the United States, despite the lucrative China trade inaugurated that year by the successful voyage of the *Empress of China*, which he co-owned with Senator Morris. Originally from Watertown, Massachusetts, he was a major subcontractor and military supplier to the French and Continental armies in association with Representative Wadsworth, William Duer, and others. (*PRM* 4:497–98)

PARKER, JAMES (1725–97), of Perth Amboy, New Jersey, was a West Indies merchant and former colonial legislator and member of the East Jersey Board of Proprietors who remained a Loyalist during the Revolutionary War. (*New Jersey Genealogical and Historical Register* 30[1899]:31–33)

PARKER, JOHN (1732–91), a shipmaster, merchant, and insurance officer of Portsmouth, served as federal marshal for New Hampshire, 1789–91, having served as sheriff of the colony, 1771–76, and sheriff of Rockingham County continually thereafter. He was a Presidential Elector in 1789. See also *DHFFC* 2:516. (*DHFFE* 1:856–57; Nathaniel Adams, *Annals of Portsmouth, New Hampshire* [Exeter, N.H., 1825], p. 300)

PARKER, JOHN, JR. (1759–1832), a lawyer of Charleston, South Carolina, represented St. James Goose Creek in the state's House of Representatives, 1785–88, attended Congress, 1786–88, and voted to ratify the Constitution at the state convention. During the Revolutionary War he was sent to study abroad with Representative Smith (S.C.) at London's Middle Temple. (*South Carolina House* 3:537; George C. Rogers, Jr., *Evolution of a Federalist: William Loughton Smith* [Columbia, S.C., 1962], pp. 88–90)

PARKER, RICHARD (1732–1813), of "Lawfield," in Westmoreland County, Virginia, served as judge of the state's general court from 1788 until his death. In the spring of 1789 he was assigned to the court circuit embracing the districts of Dumfries, Staunton, Fredericksburg, and Charlottesville. (Herbert A. Johnson, Charles T. Cullen, and Charles F. Hobson, *The Papers of John Marshall* [9+ vols., Chapel Hill, N.C., 1974–   ], 2:24n; *PJM* 12:114n)

PARSONS, SAMUEL HOLDEN (1737–89), a former treaty commissioner to the Indians of the Northwest Territory, 1785–86, and a director of the Ohio Company beginning in 1787, was appointed judge of the Northwest Territory that same year and retained the post until his death, apparently by drowning, in November 1789. The 1756 Harvard graduate was commissioned in 1775 a colonel of the 6th Regiment of the Connecticut Line, redesignated the 10th Continental Regiment in 1776, was promoted to brigadier general later that year, and held the rank of major general from 1780 until his resignation in 1782, after which he became a member of the Society of the Cincinnati. He practiced law in Middletown, Connecticut, which he represented in the state convention, where he voted to ratify the Constitution. See also *DHFFC* 2:487. (*Harvard Graduates* 14:50–73; *DHROC* 3:434, 612)

PARSONS, THEOPHILUS (1750–1813), graduated from Harvard in 1769 and practiced law in Newburyport, Massachusetts, which he represented in the state House of Representatives, 1781–91, and at the state convention where he voted to ratify the Constitution. In the first federal election he led the Essex Junto that failed to prevent the election of Senator Dalton but effectively ruined the senatorial aspirations of both Theodore Sedgwick and Rufus King, his former law student, who later moved to New York and was elected Senator there. During the First Congress John Quincy Adams also studied law under Parsons. (*Harvard Graduates* 17:190; *DHFFE* 1:512n, 521)

PARSONS, WILLIAM WALTER (1762–1801), of Middletown, Connecticut, served as high sheriff of Middlesex County in 1789. He was the eldest son of Samuel Holden Parsons. (*PGW* 6:215n)

PATERSON, EUPHEMIA WHITE (1746–1832), of New Brunswick, New Jersey, became the second wife of Senator Paterson in 1785. Their family at the time of the First Federal Congress included two surviving children from Paterson's previous marriage: Cornelia (b. 1780) and William (b. 1783). (*DHSCUS* 1:86–87n; *DHFFC* 14:679; John E. O'Connor, *William Paterson, Lawyer and Statesman* [New Brunswick, N.J., 1979], pp. 116, 117)

PATTON, ROBERT, was a Scottish immigrant and merchant of Fredericksburg, Virginia. (*DHROC* 10:1584)

PEABODY, NATHANIEL (1741–1833), a physician of Atkinson, New Hampshire, sat in the state House of Representatives, 1776–79, 1781–85, 1787–90, Senate, 1785, 1786, 1790–93, and Congress, 1779–80. A prominent Antifederalist, he was an unsuccessful candidate for Senator, Representative, and Presidential Elector in the first federal election. (*DHFFE* 1:783, 794n, 810)

PEABODY, OLIVER (1752–1831), an attorney of Exeter, New Hampshire, served as judge of probate for Rockingham County, 1790–93. After graduating from Harvard in 1773 he studied law under Nathaniel Peaslee Sargeant and Theophilus Parsons with fellow students Senator King and Christopher Gore. (*Harvard Graduates* 18:275–83)

PEACHEY, WILLIAM (1729–1802), represented Richmond County, Virginia, in the state House of Delegates in 1778, 1779, and 1780–81, and at the state convention where he voted to ratify the Constitution. He served under George Washington during the French and Indian War, and as colonel of the 5th Regiment of the Virginia Line in 1776. (*PGW* 1:477)

PEARSON, ELIPHALET (1752–1826), of Cambridge, Massachusetts, graduated from Harvard in 1773 and was appointed its professor of Hebrew and Oriental Languages in 1786. During the First Congress he served as corresponding secretary for the American Academy of Arts and Sciences. (*Harvard Graduates* 18:283–304)

PEMBERTON, JAMES (1723–1809), was a prominent Philadelphia merchant, a leader of that city's large and influential Quaker community, and chairman of the Pennsylvania Abolition Society's committee of correspondence, making him the country's foremost abolitionist organizer and activist. As such he played an important role in coordinating the national petition campaigns that resulted in the First Congress petitions on slavery and the slave trade in February 1790 and on militia duty exemptions in December 1790. See also *DHFFC* 8:220, 315–17.

PENDLETON, EDMUND (1721–1803), a lawyer of Caroline County, Virginia, was a delegate to Congress, 1774–75, and president of the state's high court of chancery, 1778–88, supreme court of appeals, 1779–1803, and the state convention where he voted to ratify the Constitution. He declined appointment as United States district judge for Virginia. See also *DHFFC* 2:553. (*DHROC* 8:528)

PENDLETON, NATHANIEL, JR. (1756–1821), nephew of Edmund Pendleton, was elected chief justice of Georgia shortly before his appointment as United States district judge for that state, 1789–96. During the Revolutionary War he fought as an ensign in the 10th Continental Regiment in 1776, was promoted to first lieutenant of the 11th Regiment of the Virginia Line later that year, and served as captain from 1777 until 1781, when he transferred to the 3rd Regiment. He was an aide-de-camp to General Nathanael Greene from 1780 until the end of the war, when he retired as a brevet major and a member of the Society of the Cincinnati. He was elected to both the Federal Convention in 1787 and the last session of the Confederation Congress, 1788–89, but attended neither. See also *DHFFC* 2:493. (*DHROC* 3:310)

PENNELL, JOSEPH, was paymaster, treasurer, and clerk of the Navy Board of the Middle Department from 1779 until the creation of an agent of marine in 1781. He retained the position of paymaster until 1783, serving thereafter as commissioner for settling the accounts of the marine department until the abolition of that office in 1786. (*PRM* 3:23n; *JCC* 30:131)

PENROSE, THOMAS (1733–1815), was a Philadelphia shipbuilder and merchant. (Josiah Granville Leach, *History of the Penrose Family of Philadelphia* [Philadelphia, 1903], pp. 38–44)

PENTECOST, DORSEY (ca. 1739–1802), was a port surveyor and farmer of Washington County, Pennsylvania. In February 1791 he petitioned Congress for preemption of a large tract of land on the Mississippi River in present day Illinois. See also *DHFFC* 8:211.

PEPOON, SILAS (1754–1817), was a storekeeper in Stockbridge, Massachusetts. He was also a brigadier general in the Massachusetts militia and one of Representative Sedgwick's political lieutenants in Berkshire County. (*Sedgwick*, p. 114; *DHSCUS* 6:182)

PERRY, PHILO (1752–98), a 1777 Yale graduate, was trained as a physician but served as rector of Trinity Episcopalian Church in Newtown, Connecticut, beginning in 1786. (*Yale Graduates* 3:699)

PETERS, RICHARD (1744–1828), a wealthy lawyer and gentleman farmer of "Belmont," his estate outside Philadelphia, was speaker of the state's General Assembly, 1789–90, and a member of the Senate, 1790–91. He served as a captain in the Pennsylvania militia, 1775–76, secretary of the board of war, 1776–81, and a member of Congress in 1783. (*DHFFC* 9:61n)

PETERSON, EDWARD, was a sea captain who resided in Newport, Rhode Island, in 1790.

PETTIT, CHARLES (1736–1806), a Philadelphia merchant and financier, was an unsuccessful Antifederalist candidate for Representative in the first federal election. One of the largest securities holders in the country, he subscribed to the Philadelphia public creditors' petitions to Congress, in August 1789 and December 1790. He was father-in-law to Jared Ingersoll. See also *DHFFC* 8:258, 264, 290, 9:137n.

PEYTON, FRANCIS (d. 1808/10), was a state legislator and justice from Loudoun County, Virginia. (*PGW* 1:286n)

PHELPS, OLIVER (1749–1809), a merchant and land speculator of Granville, Massachusetts, served in the state House of Representatives, 1778–81 and 1784–85, Senate, 1785–87, and Executive Council, 1787–88. He was an Antifederalist during the ratification debate. In 1788 he joined Nathaniel Gorham as a principal investor in the six million acre Genessee Tract in New York, with Representative Wadsworth as a minor investor. In July 1789 he and Gorham petitioned Congress about the survey of the western boundary of New York State, anticipating correctly that it would affect the size of the tract. At the time, he was in the Genessee country overseeing the development of the land. See also *DHFFC* 8:191–200, 9:20n. (*DHROC* 3:486n, 4:390n)

PHILE, FREDERICK (d. 1793), a former physician, served as federal naval officer at Philadelphia, 1789–93, having filled that office under the state since 1777 and before that as deputy naval officer since 1754. His friendship with Representative Goodhue probably dated from the latter's residence in Philadelphia as a merchant before the Revolutionary War. See also *DHFFC* 2:536, 9:103n.

PHILLIPS, GEORGE (b. 1750), was a merchant and sugar mill owner in Middletown, Connecticut, which he served as deputy to the state House of Representatives, 1787–88, and as town alderman, 1788–97. (Gaspare John Saladino, "The Economic Revolution in Late Eighteenth Century Connecticut" [Ph.D. dissertation, University of Wisconsin, 1964], p. 429)

PHILLIPS, SAMUEL, SR. (1715–90), a 1734 Harvard graduate and the father of Samuel Phillips, Jr., was a retired merchant of Andover, Massachusetts, which he represented in the colonial and state House of Representatives, 1759–78. (*Harvard Graduates* 9:431–36)

PHILLIPS, SAMUEL, JR. (1752–1802), was a gunpowder and paper manufacturer of Andover, Massachusetts, who represented Essex County in the state Senate, 1780–1800, serving as its president in 1789. The 1771 Harvard graduate was an unsuccessful candidate for Representative in the first federal election, in which he voted as a Presidential Elector. (*Harvard Graduates* 17:593–605; *DHFFE* 1:615, 756; *DGW* 5:493n)

PHIPPS, DAVID (d. 1825), of New Haven, Connecticut, served as a lieutenant in the Continental Navy, 1776–78, and commanded privateers thereafter. (*JCC* 5:697)

PICKENS, ANDREW (1739–1817), was a planter from the Ninety-Six District of the South Carolina Piedmont, which he represented in the state House of Representatives, 1782–93. He rose from captain to brigadier general in the state militia, 1775–81, acquiring fame as a partisan guerilla leader. In 1789 he served as a commissioner authorized to treat with the Southern Indians under an act of Congress of 26 October 1787. (*JCC* 33:708–11)

PICKERING, JOHN (1737–1805), was a lawyer of Portsmouth, New Hampshire, who became state president (governor) upon Senator Langdon's resignation in 1789. The 1761 Harvard graduate served as state Representative, 1783–87, attorney general, 1786–87, and delegate to the state convention, where he voted to ratify the Constitution. An unsuccessful candidate for Representative in the first federal election, he served as a Presidential Elector in 1789 and chief justice of the state supreme court, 1790–95. (*Harvard Graduates* 15:91–96; *DHFFE* 1:857)

PICKERING, TIMOTHY (1745–1829), formerly a lawyer of Salem, Massachusetts, moved to Pennsylvania after the Revolutionary War. In 1786 Pennsylvania created Luzerne County and appointed him to several offices in hopes that he, as a New Englander, could keep the peace between Pennsylvanians and the settlers who had come from Connecticut before the war. He represented the county at the state convention, where he voted to ratify the Constitution. In July 1790 his lawyer petitioned Congress for large sums due Pickering by a settlement of his accounts as quartermaster general of the Continental Army. He was appointed postmaster general in August

1791. His sister Eunice married Senator Wingate in 1765. See also *DHFFC* 8:486–93, 14:654.

PICKETT, MARTIN (1740–1804), was a planter and merchant of Fauquier County, Virginia, which he represented in the state House of Delegates, 1776–81, and at the state convention where he voted to ratify the Constitution. He also served as county sheriff, 1789–90. (*VMHB* 23[1915]:437–38; *DHROC* 9:588n)

PICKMAN, WILLIAM (1748–1815), a merchant of Salem, Massachusetts, served as naval officer for that port and neighboring Beverly, 1789–1803. Representative Goodhue knew him from childhood. See also *DHFFC* 2:510. (*PGW* 3:83)

PIERCE, JOHN (d. 1788), of Litchfield, Connecticut, served as paymaster general of the Continental Army beginning in 1781 with the additional responsibility after 1783 of settling army accounts, adjusting all army claims, and disbursing final settlement certificates. In 1787 the duties were formally combined under the office of commissioner of army accounts, which he held until his death. (*PRM* 2:83n; *DHFFC* 7:165)

PIERCE, JOSEPH (1745–1828), a Boston merchant, served in the Massachusetts Provincial Congress in 1775. He became brother-in-law to Thomas Dawes, Jr., by his marriage to Ann Dawes in 1771. (*Massachusetts Legislators*, p. 312)

PIERCE, WILLIAM (1740–89), a merchant of Savannah, Georgia, served as commissioner of pilotage for that port in 1786. He represented Chatham County in the state's House of Assembly in 1786 and was a delegate to both Congress and the Federal Convention in 1787. During the Revolutionary War he was commissioned a captain in the 1st Continental Artillery Regiment in 1776, later serving as aide-de-camp to generals John Sullivan and Nathanael Greene before retiring as a brevet major in 1783, when he became a member of the Society of the Cincinnati. (*DHROC* 3:310; *PGW* 1:88)

PIKE, NICHOLAS (1743–1819), was a teacher in Newburyport, Massachusetts, when he petitioned Congress in June 1789 for copyright protection of his *Complete System of Arithmetick*. See also *DHFFC* 8:30–31, 36–37.

PIKE, WILLIAM (1748–1804), of Newburyport, Massachusetts, began his military career as a private in the 2nd Continental Light Dragoon Regiment in 1777, shortly before seeing action at Saratoga. He rose to cornet by 1781 and served until the war's end.

PINCKNEY, CHARLES (1757–1824), a Charleston, South Carolina, lawyer and planter, declined nomination for Senator in the first federal election and served instead as governor, 1789–92. He was a delegate to Congress, 1785–87, state Representative, 1779–80, 1786–89, and a leading centralist at the Federal Convention, after which he actively promoted ratification of the Constitution. Charles Cotesworth Pinckney and Thomas Pinckney were his second cousins. (*PGW* 4:405n; *DHFFE* 1:817)

PINCKNEY, CHARLES COTESWORTH (1746–1825), a Charleston, South Carolina, lawyer and planter, was a Presidential Elector in 1789. Trained at Oxford and London's Middle Temple, he began a celebrated military career as captain in the 1st Regiment of the South Carolina Line in 1775, was promoted to colonel the next year, and retired as a brevet brigadier general at war's end, when he became a member of the Society of the Cincinnati. He was a state Representative in 1778 and 1782, president of the state Senate in 1779, and a delegate to both the Federal Convention and the state convention, where he voted to ratify the Constitution. His wife's first cousin married Senator Butler in 1771. He was also second cousin to Charles Pinckney, brother to Thomas, and brother-in-law to Edward and John Rutledge. In May 1791 he declined President Washington's offer to succeed the latter on the United States Supreme Court. (*DHSCUS* 1:669n, 725–26; *DHFFE* 1:223)

PINCKNEY, THOMAS (1750–1828), a Charleston, South Carolina, lawyer and planter, declined an appointment as United States district judge in 1789. Trained, like his brother Charles Cotesworth Pinckney, at Oxford and London's Middle Temple, he served as a captain in the 1st Regiment of the South Carolina Line, 1775–78, and as a major thereafter until the war's end, when he enrolled in the Society of the Cincinnati. He preceded his second cousin, Charles Pinckney, as governor, 1787–89, presided over the state convention where he voted to ratify the Constitution, and sat in the state House of Representatives in 1791. See also *DHFFC* 2:544.

PINTARD, JOHN MARSDEN (d. 1811), a New York City merchant, was United States consul to Madeira, 1789–99, having resided there as American agent, 1783–86. His mother, Susanna Stockton, was the younger sister of Representative Boudinot's wife. For most of the First Congress's stay in New York, Boudinot resided at Pintard's home at 12 Wall Street. Pintard returned to Madeira in mid 1790. See also *DHFFC* 2:524, 14:686. (*PGW* 3:216; *Elias Boudinot,* p. 36)

PITFIELD, BENJAMIN (d. 1793?), was a Philadelphia grocer from at least 1779. (*PGW* 2:332n)

PITT, WILLIAM "THE ELDER," LORD CHATHAM (1708–78), was active in the British government, often as prime minister, from 1746 to 1768. A moderate on colonial policy, he was a virtual icon to American Revolutionaries.

PITT, WILLIAM, "THE YOUNGER" (1759–1806), a member of the British House of Commons from 1781 until his death, served as prime minister, 1783–1801.

PLATT, RICHARD (1755–1830), a New York City businessman and one of the largest securities holders in the country, allied himself with William Duer and Secretary of the Treasury Hamilton in many financial and political ventures. A 1773 graduate of the College of New Jersey (Princeton), he rose from first lieutenant in the 1st Regiment of the New York Line in 1775 to major and aide-de-camp to General Alexander McDougall the next year, serving until the war's end, when he became a member of the Society of the Cincinnati. In 1787 he was involved in the secret merger of the Scioto Associates and the Ohio Company, of which he became treasurer. (*Princetonians, 1769–1775,* pp. 334–40)

PLEASANTS, THOMAS, JR. (ca. 1737–1804), a planter and merchant of Goochland County, Virginia, served as a commercial agent for that state in the last years of the Revolutionary War. (*PJM* 3:87n; *PRM* 2:214n)

PLUMB, WILLIAM (1749–1843), a former minister, practiced law in Middletown, Connecticut. He graduated from Yale in 1769 and served as military chaplain of the 10th Continental Regiment in 1776 and brigade chaplain, 1777–81. (*Yale Graduates* 3:355)

POLLARD, THOMAS (1742–1818), brother-in-law of Edmund Pendleton, was a former sheriff of Fairfax County, Virginia. (*PJM* 12:25n)

POOLE, JOSEPH, resided in Christiana Hundred, New Castle County, Delaware, in 1787.

POPE, EDWARD (1740–1818), a lawyer of New Bedford, Massachusetts, was appointed collector of that port in 1789, having served as its naval officer under the state. See also *DHFFC* 2:510. (*PGW* 3:301)

PORTER, AARON (ca. 1752–1837), was a physician of Biddeford, Maine, where he settled in 1773. (George Folsom, *History of Saco and Biddeford* [Saco, Me., 1830], p. 271)

PORTER, ANDREW (1743–1813), was a farmer and port surveyor of Montgomery County, Pennsylvania. Commissioned a captain of marines in 1776, he transferred to the 2nd Regiment of Continental Artillery in 1777 and again to the 4th Regiment in 1781. He was promoted to lieutenant colonel the next year and retired at war's end, when he became a member of the Society of the Cincinnati. (*PGW* 3:534; *Pennsylvania Cincinnati* 2:797–801)

PORTER, BENJAMIN JONES (1763–1847), was a physician of Falmouth, Maine. During the Revolutionary War he served as a surgeon's mate with the 11th Regiment of the Massachusetts Line, 1780–81, the 10th Regiment, 1781–83, and the 4th Regiment in 1783. In 1790 he was involved in the lumbering business with Senator King's half-brother, William King. (Bradford Whittemore, *Memorial of the Massachusetts Society of the Cincinnati* [Boston, 1964], pp. 490–91)

PORTER, ELISHA (1742–96), a 1761 Harvard graduate, was a lawyer and farmer of Hadley, Massachusetts, and served as sheriff of Hampshire County in 1789. The year before, he had voted to ratify the Constitution as a delegate to the state convention. He commanded a regiment of state militia, 1776–77, and became brigadier general of the militia in 1788. (*Harvard Graduates* 15:96–100; *DHFFE* 4:703)

POWELL, LEVEN (1737–1810), was a merchant and farmer of Loudoun County, Virginia, which he represented in the state House of Delegates, 1787–88, 1791–92, and at the state convention where he voted to ratify the Constitution. He served as a lieutenant colonel in William Grayson's Additional Continental Regiment in 1777, resigning the next year. (*DHFFE* 2:382n; *PGW* 1:286n)

POWELL, SAMUEL (1739–93), a Philadelphia merchant, served as mayor, 1789–90, and as state Senator, 1790–93. His wife Elizabeth was sister to Richard and Thomas Willing. The Powells were close friends of the Washingtons. See also *DHFFC* 9:326–27n.

POWER, ALEXANDER, was a broker and scrivener on the south side of Market Street, Philadelphia.

PRENTIS, WILLIAM (ca. 1740–ca. 1824), of Dinwiddie County, Virginia, printed the [Petersburg] *Virginia Gazette,* 1786–1800, the *Norfolk and Portsmouth Chronicle,* 1789–92, and the official debates of the state ratification convention. (*American Newspapers* 2:1469; *PJM* 4:48n)

PRICE, RICHARD (1723–91), moral philosopher and nonconformist minister, became a major champion of the American Revolution with the publication of his *Observations on the Nature of Civil Liberty* (1776) and *Additional Observations* (1777).

PROCTOR, THOMAS (1739–1806), was an Irish born Philadelphia carpenter who began a prominent military career as captain in the 1st company of the Pennsylvania artillery in 1775, rising to major the next year, and to colonel of the 4th Regiment of the Continental Artillery, 1777–81. He served as sheriff of Philadelphia County, 1783–85, and as lieutenant in the city militia from 1790. (*PGW* 3:116–17)

PROVOOST, SAMUEL (1742–1815), named Episcopal bishop of New York in 1786, was elected by the Senate as one of Congress's two chaplains on 25 April 1789 and served until Congress moved to Philadelphia. See also *DHFFC* 9:7n. (*DHFFC* 2:215, 8:781)

PURVIANCE, ROBERT (1733–1806), emigrated from England in the 1760s and settled in Baltimore, where he lost a fortune as a shipper and distiller in 1787 before his appointment as naval officer there, 1789–94. See also *DHFFC* 2:499. (*PGW* 2:332–34)

PURVIANCE, SAMUEL, JR. (d. ca. 1788), like his brother Robert, emigrated from England and became a prominent Baltimore merchant, distiller, and civic leader. In 1788, while facing imminent bankruptcy, Samuel was captured by Native Americans in the Ohio Valley and never seen again. (*DGW* 5:407–8n; *PGW* 2:332–33)

PUTNAM, BARTHOLOMEW (1738–1815), was a mariner and shipowner of Salem, Massachusetts, where he was port surveyor, 1789–1809. See also *DHFFC* 2:511.

PUTNAM, RUFUS (1738–1824), was appointed judge of the Northwest Territory, 1790–96, having served since 1788 as superintendent of the Ohio Company at Marietta, Ohio, which he helped found. He achieved prominence during the Revolutionary War as a military engineer at the siege of

Boston and at West Point. He served as lieutenant colonel of Jonathan Brewer's Massachusetts Regiment in 1775, of the 22nd Continental Regiment in 1776, and as colonel of the 5th Regiment of the Massachusetts Line thereafter until his promotion to brigadier general in 1783, when he joined the Society of the Cincinnati. See also *DHFFC* 2:511.

RAMSAY, DAVID (1749–1815), a Charleston, South Carolina, physician and historian, was an unsuccessful candidate for Representative in the first federal election. Two weeks after Congress convened he petitioned the House to overturn the election of his opponent, Representative Smith, and to grant copyright protection for his histories of the American Revolution. As chairman of Congress in 1786, he served as president pro tempore in the absence of the president. See also *DHFFC* 8:27–29, 33–35, 541–54.

RANDALL, THOMAS (ca. 1723–1797), a New York City merchant and ship pilot, chaired the Federalist committee that nominated Representative Laurance in the first federal election. (*Colonial Records of the New York Chamber of Commerce, 1768–84* [New York, 1867], pp. 157–58)

RANDOLPH, BEVERLEY (1744–97), a planter of Cumberland County, Virginia, and governor, 1788–91, served in the state House of Delegates, 1777–81, and as president of the Executive Council, 1781–88. (*DHROC* 8:11–12n)

RANDOLPH, DAVID MEADE (1760–1830), a planter of Chesterfield County, Virginia, succeeded Edward Carrington as marshal for the Virginia district in October 1791. In 1777 he captained a state militia company of dragoons. (*PGW* 3:104n)

RANDOLPH, EDMUND (1753–1813), was a lawyer of Williamsburg, Virginia, which he represented in the state House of Delegates from November 1788 until his appointment as United States attorney general, 1789–94. George Washington's aide-de-camp in the first year of the Revolutionary War, he later served as a delegate to Congress, 1779 and 1781–82, governor, 1786–88, and member of both the Annapolis and the Federal conventions. He refused to sign the Constitution but later voted for its ratification as a Henrico County delegate to the state convention. See also *DHFFC* 2:553. (*DHROC* 8:528–29, 9:592, 1004n)

RANDOLPH, JOHN, "OF ROANOKE" (1773–1833), and his older brother Theodorick Bland Randolph (1771–92), left the College of New Jersey (Princeton), where they had enrolled in the class of 1791, and attended Columbia College from 1788 until the summer of 1790. Their stepfather and legal guardian was St. George Tucker, brother of Representative Tucker and brother-in-law of Representative Bland; Attorney General Edmund Randolph was their uncle. (*Princetonians, 1791–1794,* pp. 90–92)

RANDOLPH, THOMAS MANN (1741–93), was a planter of Goochland County, Virginia, which he represented in the House of Burgesses, 1769–75. In 1779 he served as a colonel in the Virginia militia. His son Thomas, Jr., married Secretary of State Jefferson's daughter Patsy in February 1790. (*DHFFE* 2:340n)

READ, GEORGE, JR. (1765–1836), like his father, Senator Read, a lawyer of New Castle, Delaware, was appointed United States attorney for that state in 1789. See also *DHFFC* 2:490.

READ, SENATOR GEORGE, family during the First Congress: his wife Gertrude Ross Till (ca. 1730–1802), married in 1763 and residing in New Castle, Delaware; and their children George, William (1767–1846), John, and Mary or "Maria" (1770–1816).

READ, JAMES (1743–1822), younger brother of Senator Read, was a Philadelphia banker and merchant. In April 1790 he petitioned Congress for compensation as paymaster of the marine department and agent of marine in 1778 and 1783. See also *DHFFC* 7:15–18.

READ, JOHN (1769–1854), son of Senator Read and younger brother of George Read, Jr., graduated from the College of New Jersey (Princeton) in 1787 and studied law under his father before commencing practice in New Castle, Delaware, in 1791.

REED, JAMES (1723–1807), an original proprietor and large landowner of Fitzwilliam, New Hampshire, kept a tavern there before the Revolutionary War. He acquired the rank of brigadier general before retiring in late 1776 because of smallpox contracted while assigned to the northern department. His petition for invalid pension arrearages was presented to the House in August 1789. See also *DHFFC* 7:388–91.

REED, JOSEPH (1741–85), a British trained Philadelphia lawyer, served as George Washington's military secretary, 1775–76, and adjutant general of the Continental Army thereafter until resigning in 1777. He was a delegate to Congress in 1778 and president (governor) of Pennsylvania, 1778–81. (*Princetonians, 1748–1768,* pp. 200–204)

REID, JAMES R. (1750–January 1790), of Middlesex, Cumberland County, Pennsylvania, graduated from the College of New Jersey (Princeton) in 1775 and rose from first lieutenant in the 4th Regiment of the Pennsylvania Line in 1776 to captain in the 2nd Canadian Regiment ("Congress's Own") later that year to major, 1777–83. His postwar career is unknown, except that he represented Pennsylvania in Congress, 1787–89. (*Princetonians, 1769–1775*, pp. 514–17; [Pennsylvania] *Carlisle Gazette*, 3 February 1790)

REILY, WILLIAM (1751–1824), of Baltimore, rose from lieutenant in the 4th Regiment of the Maryland Line in 1776 to captain the next year, transferring to the 1st Regiment in 1781 and serving until the war's end, when he joined the Society of the Cincinnati.

REVERE, PAUL (1735–1818), was a Boston silversmith and foundry owner whose early prominence and popularity in the Revolutionary movement overcame a clouded military reputation earned as state militia officer, 1776–79, and made him an especially effective Federalist spokesman for the city's artisan class. He listed Representatives Ames and Gerry as references in his application for an office in the revenue system in February 1791. (*PGW* 7:318)

REYNOLDS, WILLIAM (d. 1802), a merchant of Yorktown, Virginia, was appointed collector there in 1794. (*PGW* 4:210n)

RICE, JAMES, served as selectman for New Haven, Connecticut, in 1785.

RICE, JOHN (ca. 1753–1803), deputy collector of Boston and Charleston, Massachusetts, under Benjamin Lincoln beginning in August 1789, had served in the same capacity under James Lovell, 1786–89. He served in the Continental Army's artillery in 1775 and as a Boston "town major" in 1779. (*PGW* 3:477n)

RICE, THOMAS (1734–1812), was a physician of Pownalborough (present day Wiscasset), Maine, which he represented in the Massachusetts Senate, 1780–83, and at the state convention, where he voted to ratify the Constitution, against the instructions of his constituents. He graduated from Harvard in 1756. (*Harvard Graduates* 14:74–77; *DHROC* 5:1012)

RICHARDSON, ARCHIBALD (1756–1804), was appointed port surveyor at Suffolk, Virginia, 1789–90. See also *DHFFC* 2:553–54.

RICHMOND, CHRISTOPHER (d. ca. 1795), agent for settling Maryland's accounts with the United States, had been state auditor since 1783. He was born in England and settled in Upper Marlborough, Maryland, by 1769. He served as lieutenant and paymaster for the 1st Regiment of the Maryland Line from 1778 until he transferred to the 2nd Regiment in 1781 and served as captain until war's end, when he joined the Society of the Cincinnati. He became a shareholder in the Potowmack Navigation Company in 1785. (*PGW* 7:523n; *DGW* 3:155)

RIGGS, CALEB (ca. 1758–1826), began the practice of law in New York City in 1793. (New-York Historical Society *Quarterly* 56[1972]:213)

RIPLEY, EZRA (1751–1841), was the Congregational minister of Concord, Massachusetts, from 1778 until his death. He became a close friend of Representative Thatcher while teaching school in Plymouth, Massachusetts, shortly after they graduated from Harvard together in 1776.

RITTENHOUSE, DAVID (1732–96), Philadelphia's other internationally known scientist and inventor (besides Benjamin Franklin), was also port surveyor, wartime munitions manufacturer, and state treasurer, 1777–89. A prominent Antifederalist, he ran unsuccessfully for the ratification convention and, in the first federal election, for Presidential Elector. (*DHFFE* 1:425–26)

RIVINGTON, JAMES (1724–1802), a New York City bookseller and stationer, was a Loyalist printer during the Revolutionary War, when he published the first American daily newspaper. Historians have recently credited him with having acted the role of a double agent for the Continental Army's secret service, beginning in 1781.

ROANE, CHRISTOPHER (1756–1828), was appointed port surveyor of Bermuda Hundred (present day Hopewell), Virginia, in 1789, having served under the state as port inspector at neighboring City Point since 1787. See also *DHFFC* 2:554. (*PGW* 3:363)

ROBERTSON, JAMES (1742–1814), was brigadier general of the Miro District of the Southern Territory from February 1791 to 1794. He represented Wake County, North Carolina, in the state's House of Commons, 1785 and 1787. See also *DHFFC* 2:530.

ROCHESTER, NATHANIEL (1752–1831), a native of Westmoreland County, Virginia, was a merchant in Hillsboro, North Carolina, from 1773 until he transfered his business activities to Hagerstown, Maryland, in the early 1780s.

RODGERS, JOHN (1727–1811), was a Presbyterian minister of New York City and runner up in the election for chaplain to the House of Representatives in May 1789. See also *DHFFC* 8:781n, 9:200n.

RODNEY, THOMAS (1744–1811), was a planter and jurist of Kent County, Delaware, which he represented in the state's House of Assembly, 1787–88. He served in Congress, 1781–82 and 1786. During ratification, he opposed the Constitution because it left too much power to the states, and wrote essays in 1788 denouncing the election of Senators Read and Bassett. He had had the latter arrested during an anti-Tory riot in June 1776. (*DHROC* 3:104n, 115; *DHFFE* 2:76–79n)

ROGERS, HEZEKIAH (1753–1811), was appointed port surveyor of New Haven, Connecticut, in 1789. He served as first lieutenant of the 5th Regiment of the Connecticut Line in 1777, transferred to the 2nd Regiment in 1781, was promoted to captain in 1782, and transferred to the 3rd Regiment the next year, when he joined the Society of the Cincinnati. He represented Norwalk in the state House of Representatives, 1786–88, and in the state convention, where he voted to ratify the Constitution. See also *DHFFC* 2:487. (*DHROC* 3:343, 437)

ROGERS, NATHANIEL (1745–1829), of Newmarket, New Hampshire, was an unsuccessful candidate for state loan commissioner in 1790, but succeeded John Parker as federal marshal the next year, at which time he was also a member of the state's Executive Council. (*PGW* 6:640n; *PJB*, p. 355n)

ROGERS, SAMUEL (ca. 1747–1804), a 1765 Harvard graduate, had been a Boston merchant before the Revolutionary War. His Loyalist sympathies led him to settle in London, where he became a banker and agent for other Loyalists' claims before Parliament. His banking business failed in 1791. (*Harvard Graduates* 16:211–12)

ROOT, JESSE (1736–1822), a lawyer of Hartford, Connecticut, and judge of the state superior court, 1789–1807, was an unsuccessful candidate for Representative in the first federal election. He graduated from the College of New Jersey (Princeton) in 1756, represented Coventry and Hartford alternately for several terms in the state House of Representatives between 1778 and 1784, attended Congress, 1778 and 1780–82, and served with Representative Wadsworth as one of Hartford's delegates to the state convention, where he voted to ratify the Constitution. Senator Ellsworth was one of his law students. (*Princetonians, 1748–1768*, pp. 163–66; *DHFFE* 2:56; *DHROC* 3:418; William R. Casto, *Oliver Ellsworth and the Creation of the Federal Republic* [New York, 1997], p. 17)

ROSS, GEORGE, JR. (1752–1832), son of a signer of the Declaration of Independence, was a lawyer of Lancaster, Pennsylvania, which he represented in the state Assembly, 1786–87. He sat on the state's Supreme Executive Council, 1787–90, simultaneously serving as vice president (lieutenant governor) of the state from November 1788 to October 1790.

ROSS, JOHN (1752–96), a physician of Burlington, New Jersey, was appointed collector there in 1789, having served as the port's naval officer under the state since 1781. See also *DHFFC* 2:520.

RUMSEY, JAMES (1743–92), was an inventor and promoter of inland steam powered navigation and a canal builder employed by the Potowmack Company. Like John Fitch, he petitioned the First Congress for a steam engine patent. At the time he was promoting his inventions in Europe, his interests were represented by members of the Rumseian Society. See also *DHFFC* 8:39–41, 48–49.

RUSH, BENJAMIN (1745–1813), was a prominent Philadelphia physician and essayist, signer of the Declaration of Independence, and political activist who maintained an extensive correspondence with the Pennsylvania congressional delegation. He was one of the committee of three that drafted the petition of the College of Physicians of Philadelphia in November 1790. See also *DHFFC* 8:312, 9:85n.

RUSH, JACOB (1747–1820), a Philadelphia lawyer who served briefly as assistant to Secretary of Congress Charles Thomson, 1776–78, a state Assemblyman, 1782–84, and an associate justice of the state supreme court, 1784–91. He was a younger brother of Benjamin Rush and close friend to David Ramsay, who graduated with him from the College of New Jersey (Princeton) in 1765. (*Princetonians, 1748–1768*, pp. 525–30)

RUSSELL, BENJAMIN (1761–1845), a former apprentice to the famous newspaper editor and Revolutionary activist Isaiah Thomas, edited Boston's *Massachusetts Centinel*, a Federalist newspaper, from 1784 to 1790, when he changed its name to the *Columbian Centinel* (16 June 1790 to 1820). He also edited the short lived French language *Courier de Boston* from April to October 1789. (*American Conservatism*, p. 261)

RUSSELL, ELEAZER (ca. 1720–1798), served as federal naval officer at Portsmouth, New Hampshire, 1789–98, after filling that office continuously under the colonial and state governments from the late 1760s. See also *DHFFC* 2:516. (*PGW* 3:225)

RUSSELL, THOMAS (1740–96), was a Boston merchant who voted to ratify the Constitution at the state convention. His interests, which included shipping, land speculation, and banking, involved him in business dealings with Superintendent of Finance Robert Morris, under whom he served as deputy agent of marine for New England. His father, James (1715–98), was a merchant of Charlestown, Massachusetts. (*PRM* 1:247n)

RUSTON, THOMAS (ca. 1740–1804), a former physician, was a prominent Philadelphia manufacturer, financier, and speculator. As chairman of the board of the Philadelphia cotton manufactory, he lobbied Congress against the cotton duty in June 1789 and petitioned a year later for further encouragement of the industry. See also *DHFFC* 8:365, 371–73, 9:91n.

RUTHERFORD, ROBERT (1728–1803), a distant relation of James Madison, was a planter in Frederick County, Virginia, and Berkeley County, West Virginia. He represented both counties in the Virginia House of Burgesses, 1766–76, and neighboring Hampshire County in the state Senate, 1776–91. (*DHROC* 9:572n; *DHFFE* 2:302n; *PJM* 12:352n)

RUTHERFURD, JOHN (1760–1840), a former New York City lawyer who had studied under Senator Paterson, was a merchant and landowner of Sussex (present day Warren) County, New Jersey, which he represented in the state's lower house, or General Assembly, 1789–90. He was an unsuccessful candidate for Representative in the first federal election, but served as a Presidential Elector in 1789 and succeeded Jonathan Elmer as Senator in 1791. (*DHFFE* 3:187)

RUTHERFURD, WALTER (1723–1804), of Paterson, Bergen County, New Jersey, was the father of John Rutherfurd. During the Revolutionary War he remained a Loyalist. (Carl E. Prince, et al., eds., *The Papers of William Livingston* [5 vols., Trenton, N.J., 1979–88], 2:569)

RUTLEDGE, EDWARD (1749–1800), a Charleston, South Carolina, lawyer, was a Presidential Elector in 1789. Educated at London's Middle Temple, he served in Congress, 1774–76, where he signed the Declaration of Independence, in the state House of Representatives, 1782, 1784, and 1786, and at the state convention where he voted to ratify the Constitution. In June 1791 he declined to succeed his brother John as an associate justice of the United States Supreme Court. His wife was the sister of Charles Cotesworth Pinckney's wife and first cousin of Senator Butler's wife Mary. (*DHFFE* 1:224; *DHSCUS* 1:727–28n)

RUTLEDGE, HENRIETTA MIDDLETON (1750–92), married Edward Rutledge in 1774. Her sister Sarah married Charles Cotesworth Pinckney the year before, and her first cousin Mary married Senator Butler in 1771.

RUTLEDGE, HENRY MIDDLETON (1775–1844), was the son of Edward Rutledge.

RUTLEDGE, JOHN, SR. (1739–1800), a lawyer and jurist of Charleston, South Carolina, served as associate justice of the United States Supreme Court from September 1789 until his resignation in March 1791. Educated at London's Middle Temple like his younger brother Edward and like him a member of Congress, 1774–75, he became the first governor of South Carolina, 1776–78 and 1779–82. With his brother-in-law, Charles Cotesworth Pinckney, he played an active role at the Federal Convention and voted to ratify the Constitution at the state convention. In the first federal election he received six of his state's electoral votes for President. (*DHSCUS* 1:15–18; *DHFFE* 1:211)

RUTLEDGE, JOHN, JR. (1766–1819), like his father John and his uncle Edward Rutledge, was a lawyer of Charleston, South Carolina. He traveled through Europe between 1787 and mid 1790. (*DHSCUS* 1:859n; *PGW: Confederation* 5:220–21n)

ST. CLAIR, ARTHUR (1734–1818), governor of the Northwest Territory, 1787–1802, was appointed major general of the federal army on the last day of the First Congress. His Revolutionary War service included colonel of the 2nd Pennsylvania Battalion in 1776, brigadier general, 1776–77, and major general from 1777 until the war's end, when he joined the Society of the Cincinnati. See also *DHFFC* 2:536, 9:6–7n. (*DHFFC* 2:131)

ST. TRYS, CHEVALIER DE, a captain of dragoons in the French army during the First Congress, first met Representative Wadsworth while accompanying Brissot de Warville on his journey through America in 1788. (*PGW* 1:91)

SAGE, COMFORT (1731–99), was a merchant of Middletown, Connecticut, where he was appointed port surveyor in 1790, having served as the state's naval officer there since 1788. See also *DHFFC* 2:487.

SARGEANT, NATHANIEL PEASLEE (1731–91), a 1751 Harvard graduate, was associate justice of the Massachusetts supreme judicial court, 1776–90, and chief justice, 1790–91. (*Harvard Graduates* 12:574–80; *Adams* 1:321–22n)

SARGENT, EPES (1748–1822), was a merchant of Gloucester, Massachusetts, where he served as collector, 1789–95. See also *DHFFC* 2:511.

SARGENT, PAUL DUDLEY (1745–1828), settled in Sullivan, Maine, about 1787, after failing as a merchant in his native Salem, Massachusetts. During the Revolutionary War he served as colonel of the 16th Continental Regiment in 1776 and in the state militia thereafter until 1781. (Emma W. Sargent, *Epes Sargent of Gloucester and His Descendants* [Boston, 1923], pp. 213–17)

SARGENT, WINTHROP (1753–1820), was secretary of the Northwest Territory, 1787–98. In December 1790 he petitioned the House for additional compensation for duties related to his office. See also *DHFFC* 2:512, 8:134–36, 148.

SARSFIELD, GUY CLAUDE, COMTE DE (1718–89), was a French military officer frequently absent from his estate at Rennes, Brittany, while socializing in Paris, London, and The Hague with eminent characters of his day. He maintained a lively correspondence with John Adams beginning in 1777. (*Adams* 2:381n)

SAUNDERS, JOHN, JR. (ca. 1724–1797), represented Salem, Massachusetts, in the state House of Representatives, 1790–94.

SAVAGE, GEORGE (d. 1824), was appointed collector at Cherry Stone, Northampton County, Virginia, 1789–90, having served as naval officer and commissioner of wrecks under the state since 1782. (*DHFFC* 2:554)

SAVAGE, JOSEPH (1756–1814), was commissioned a captain of artillery in the federal army posted at West Point in September 1789, having held that position under the Confederation's military establishment since 1786, and served until his resignation in October 1791. He began his military career as a sergeant in Richard Gridley's (subsequently Henry Knox's) Regiment of Artillery in 1775, was promoted to second lieutenant, and rose to captain-lieutenant of the 2nd Regiment in 1777 and captain in 1779, serving until 1783, when he enrolled in the Society of the Cincinnati. His sister Sarah married Representative Thatcher in 1784; Samuel Phillips Savage was their father. See also *DHFFC* 2:512.

SAVAGE, SAMUEL (1748–1831), brother of Joseph, son of Samuel Phillips Savage, and brother-in-law of Representative Thatcher, was a physician of Barnstable, Massachusetts, where he settled in 1773. The 1766 Harvard graduate sat on the court of common pleas in 1782 and served as justice of the peace in 1790. (*Harvard Graduates* 16:424–26)

SAVAGE, SAMUEL PHILLIPS (1718–97), a farmer of Weston, Massachusetts, was a retired Boston merchant who served as Middlesex County judge from 1776 until his death. In 1773 he clerked for the Boston town meeting whose impasse with the provincial authorities resulted in the Tea Party, and in 1776 he was appointed to the state's board of war. His daughter Sarah married Representative Thatcher in 1784. (*DHROC* 4:291n)

SAYWARD, JONATHAN (1713–97), a merchant of York, Maine, had been an officeholder and judge before the outbreak of the Revolutionary War, when he became a Loyalist. (*DHROC* 4:335)

SCOTT, GUSTAVUS (1753–1800), became a lawyer after studying at London's Middle Temple and settled in Cambridge, Maryland, which he represented in the state's House of Delegates, 1780–81 and 1783–85. He was elected to Congress in 1784 but never attended. He became an important promoter and investor in the Potowmack Company. (*DGW* 5:428; *PGW* 1:421n)

SCOTT, JOHN (d. 1790), was a physician of Chester, Maryland, where he was collector, 1789–90, having served as the state's naval officer there since 1787. (*DHFFC* 2:499)

SCOTT, RICHARD MARSHALL, an Alexandria, Virginia, attorney, was appointed collector at neighboring Dumfries in 1789, having served as deputy naval officer for the state's South Potomac district since 1783. See also *DHFFC* 2:554. (*PGW* 2:497–98n)

SCRIBA, GEORGE LUDWIG CHRISTIAN (1753–1836), was a New York City merchant and land speculator. William Constable was his silent partner and the driving force behind Scriba's two petitions to Congress in March 1790 to purchase up to four million acres of western lands. He participated in George Washington's first inaugural procession as lieutenant commandant of the 1st Regiment of the city's militia brigade. See also *DHFFC* 8:198–99.

SEAGROVE, JAMES (ca. 1747–1812), collector at St. Mary's, Georgia, 1789–91, represented Camden County, Georgia, at the state Assembly in 1787 and at the state ratification convention, 1787–88. Before moving from New York City in 1786, the Irish born merchant and former army supplier with close business ties to William Constable developed his own extensive mercantile network among the Spanish and Indians on the frontier, in recognition of which he was appointed agent to the Creeks in 1791. See also *DHFFC* 2:493–94. (*PGW* 3:307–8)

SEARLE, GEORGE (ca. 1751–1796), of Newburyport, Massachusetts, served as town selectman in 1787.

SEARLE, JAMES (1733–97), a Philadelphia merchant, served on the naval board, 1778, and in Congress, 1778–80, where he joined the Lee faction. He was unsuccessful as Pennsylvania's commissioner to negotiate a loan from France, 1780–82. (*PRM* 1:408–9n; *LDC* 18:588n)

SEBASTIAN, BENJAMIN (1745–1834), a clergyman and lawyer of Kentucky, participated with Representative Brown, James Wilkinson, Harry Innes, and others in a movement that may have aimed at creating an independent republic of Kentucky allied with Spain. After the "Spanish Conspiracy" collapsed in late 1789 he was offered trading privileges by Governor Miró, in exchange for promoting the settlement of Spanish Louisiana. (*PTJ* 17:124n; *Westward Expansion,* p. 232; Patricia Watlington, "John Brown and the Spanish Conspiracy," *VMHB* 75[1967]:52–68)

SEDGWICK, PAMELA DWIGHT (ca. 1753–1807), related to two important families of western Massachusetts, the Dwights and the Williamses, became the second wife of Representative Sedgwick in 1774. At the time of the first session, they had six children: Eliza Mason (1775–1827), Frances Pamela (1778–1842), Theodore, Jr. (1780–1839), Henry Dwight (1785–1831), Robert (1787–1841), and Catharine Maria (1789–1868). See also *DHFFC* 14:636, 641–42. (*Sedgwick,* p. 249n)

SEGAR, JOHN (b. 1730), of Middlesex County, Virginia.

SENTER, ISAAC (1753–99), was a physician of Newport, Rhode Island. He represented Cranston, Rhode Island, in the state House of Deputies briefly after serving as surgeon general of the state militia, 1779–81. Prior Revolutionary War service included surgeon for the 3rd Regiment of the Rhode Island Line, 1775–76, and hospital surgeon, 1776–79. (*The Journal of Isaac Senter* [Philadelphia, 1846], preface)

SEWALL, DAVID (1735–1825), a lawyer and jurist of York, Maine, served as a justice of the Massachusetts supreme judicial court from 1781 until his appointment as United States district judge, 1789–1818. The 1755 graduate of Harvard sat on the Massachusetts Council, 1776–77, and voted as a Presidential Elector in 1789. See also *DHFFC* 2:512. (*Harvard Graduates* 18:638–45; *DHFFE* 1:758)

SEWALL, DUMMER (1737–1832), a farmer and miller of Bath, Maine, was state Senator, 1788–89, 1790–91, and postmaster, 1791–1806. During the Revolutionary War he served as mustermaster for the Maine District and lieutenant colonel of the state militia. He voted to ratify the Constitution at the Massachusetts convention. (*DHROC* 7:1517n; *Massachusetts Legislators*, p. 336)

SEWALL, HENRY (1752–1845), a merchant of Hallowell, Maine, served as clerk of the United States district court for Maine, 1789–1818. Business interests kept him in New York City from July 1788 until 29 August 1789. During the Revolutionary War he rose from corporal in 1775 to major and aide-de-camp to General William Heath, 1779–83, assigned to the 18th Continental Regiment and the 12th and 2nd regiments of the Massachusetts Line. He was a member of the Society of the Cincinnati. (*PGW* 2:7–8n)

SEWALL, STEPHEN (ca. 1747–1799), served as the state's naval officer at Marblehead, Massachusetts, until his controversial replacement by Representative Gerry's brother Samuel in 1786. (Samuel Roads, Jr., *History and Traditions of Marblehead* [Boston, 1880], p. 207)

SHALLCROSS, JOSEPH, was a Quaker merchant and sometime town clerk of Wilmington, Delaware. In a letter to George Washington supporting Shallcross's application for collector of that port, he was cited as the source of important military intelligence supplied to the Continental Army during the British occupation of Philadelphia. (*PGW* 1:458n)

SHARP, JOHN (d. 1793), resided in Philadelphia in 1790. His military career began as a sergeant in the 1st Pennsylvania Battalion in 1775, from which he was promoted to second lieutenant in Moses Hazen's 2nd Canadian Regiment ("Congress's Own"), 1775–76, and in Ottendorf's Corps in 1777, to first lieutenant in Pulaski's Legion in 1778 and captain in the 1st Partisan Corps (Armand's Legion) in 1780. (*Pennsylvania Cincinnati* 2:883–85)

SHAW, BENJAMIN (1752–1815), operated a tannery in Hallowell, Maine, in 1789. The next year he moved to New Mills to run a store and sawmill.

SHAW, ELIZABETH SMITH (1750–1815), youngest sister of Abigail Adams, married Reverend John Shaw of Haverhill, Massachusetts, in 1777. (*Adams* 2:64n)

SHEAFE, JAMES (1755–1829), was a merchant of Portsmouth, New Hampshire, which he served as state Representative, 1788–90, town selectman, 1789–92, and state Senator, 1791. He came in third place behind Representative Foster in the special election to fill the seat declined by Benjamin West. The 1774 Harvard graduate overcame a reputation for wartime Loyalism sufficiently by 1786 to be appointed to the Annapolis Convention, which he did not attend. (*Harvard Graduates* 18:483–88; *DHFFE* 1:858)

SHERBURNE, SAMUEL (later changed to JOHN) (1757–1830), a lawyer of Portsmouth, New Hampshire, served as United States attorney for that state, 1789–93, while serving in the state legislature, 1790–93. He was brother-in-law to Senator Langdon by the latter's marriage to Elizabeth Sherburne in 1777. He came in second behind Representative Foster in the special election to fill the seat declined by Benjamin West. The 1776 graduate of Dartmouth served as a brigade major in the state militia during the Revolutionary War. See also *DHFFC* 2:516–17. (*DHFFE* 1:858)

SHERMAN, ISAAC (1753–1819), the third son of Representative Sherman and a 1770 Yale graduate, accompanied his brother John to Georgia in 1789 to seek greater economic opportunities. In February 1790 he petitioned Congress unsuccessfully for additional compensation for his duties as a surveyor of the Northwest Territory, to which he had been appointed by Congress in 1785. See also *DHFFC* 8:93–96. (*Yale Graduates* 3:393–95; *Sherman's Connecticut*, p. 322)

SHERMAN, JOSIAH (1729–25 November 1789), younger brother of Representative Sherman, graduated from the College of New Jersey (Princeton) in 1754 and held a number of controversial pastorates throughout Massachusetts and Connecticut before his death while awaiting installment as Congregational minister at Woodbridge, Connecticut. His wife, Martha Minot, was aunt to Representative Sherman's second wife, Rebecca Prescott. (*Princetonians, 1748–1768*, pp. 116–18)

SHERMAN, NATHANIEL (1724–97), younger brother of Representative Sherman, graduated from the College of New Jersey (Princeton) in 1753 but failed as a Congregational minister and government securities speculator. At the time of the First Congress he was living in poverty in East Windsor, Connecticut. (*Princetonians, 1748–1768*, pp. 82–83)

SHERMAN, REPRESENTATIVE ROGER, family during the First Congress: his second wife, Rebecca Prescott (ca. 1743–1793), whom he married in 1763 and who resided in New Haven, Connecticut; and his eleven children. The four children by his first wife were John (1750–1802), William, Isaac, and Chloe (1758–1840). The remaining children were Rebecca (1764–95), who married Simeon Baldwin in 1787; Elizabeth (1765–1850); Roger, Jr. (1768–1856), who graduated from Yale in 1787; Mehetabel (1774–1851); Oliver (1777–1820); Martha (1779–1806); and Sarah (1783–1866).

SHERMAN, ROGER MINOT (1773–1845), was the son of Representative Sherman's brother, Reverend Josiah Sherman.

SHERMAN, WILLIAM (1751–26 June 1789), the second son of Representative Sherman, disgraced himself as a negligent and perhaps even criminally corrupt paymaster of Seth Warner's Additional Continental Regiment, 1776–81. The 1770 Yale graduate bankrupted his father's mercantile business before the war, failed as a settler in the Susquehanna Valley after the war, and returned to New Haven, Connecticut, by 1788, where he was a store owner. Divorced and bankrupt again, he died suddenly from a cold. (*Yale Graduates* 3:395–96; *Sherman's Connecticut*, pp. 319–21)

SHIPPEN, EDWARD (1729–1806), a Philadelphia lawyer and jurist, sat on the court of common pleas and errors and appeals from 1784 until his appointment to the Pennsylvania supreme court, 1791–1805.

SHIPPEN, THOMAS LEE (1765–98), son of William Shippen, Jr., and nephew of Senator Lee, toured Europe in the late 1780s and studied law in London prior to returning to Philadelphia in late 1789. (*PGW* 2:35n)

SHIPPEN, WILLIAM, JR. (1736–1808), a prominent Philadelphia physician, married Senator Lee's sister, Alice, in 1762. He graduated from the College of New Jersey (Princeton) in 1754, studied in London and Edinburgh, 1759–62, began his lifelong career as a teacher of anatomy at the College of Philadelphia (University of Pennsylvania) in 1765, and served as director general of hospitals for the Continental Army, 1777–81. (*Princetonians, 1748–1768*, pp. 118–22)

SHORT, WILLIAM (1759–1849), was a 1779 graduate of the College of William and Mary who sat on the state's Executive Council, 1783–84, and served as secretary of the American legation in Paris under Thomas Jefferson, upon whose return to America he became chargé d'affaires, 1789–92. See also *DHFFC* 2:554.

SIDNEY (SYDNEY), ALGERNON (1622–83), British political theorist and Whig martyr, was a high official during the Commonwealth period who returned from self-imposed exile after the Restoration and was executed for treason on charges of attempting to overthrow Charles II. His *Discourses Concerning Government* (1698) had great influence in the American colonies.

SILVA, JOSE DA, was a dry goods and wine merchant of New York City in 1789.

SILVESTER (SYLVESTER), DAVID (1742–98), was a ferrymaster, selectman, and town clerk of Pownalborough (present day Wiscasset), Maine, which he represented in the Massachusetts House of Representatives, 1787–88, and at the state convention, where he voted to ratify the Constitution despite the town's instructions to the contrary. He also served as state revenue collector for Lincoln County, ca. 1786–89. (*New England Historical and Geneological Register* 86[1932]:296; *DHROC* 4:lxxviii, 5:1012; Fannie S. Chase, *Wiscasset in Pownalborough* [Wiscasset, Me., 1941], p. 495)

SILVESTER, FRANCIS (1767–1845), son of Representative Silvester, was a lawyer of Kinderhook, New York. He graduated from Columbia College in 1786 and was married to his cousin Lydia, daughter of Peter Van Schaack. (Peyton F. Miller, *A Group of Great Lawyers of Columbia County, New York* [New York, 1904], p. 56)

SILVESTER, JANE, of Kinderhook, New York, married Representative Silvester in 1764. She was the older sister of Henry and Peter Van Schaack.

SIMONDS, JONAS (d. 1816), originally of Boston, served as second lieutenant in Richard Gridley's Artillery Regiment in 1775, as first lieutenant in Henry Knox's Continental Regiment of Artillery, 1775–78, and thereafter as captain until 1781 when he transferred to the 4th Continental Regiment of Artillery, where he served until war's end. Acquitted for his leading role in the Pennsylvania Mutiny of June 1783, he became a member of the Society of the Cincinnati. He settled in Philadelphia, where he was inspector of customs by 1789. (*Pennsylvania Cincinnati* 2:887–90)

SLOCUM, HOLDER (1748–1827), was a farmer and lifelong resident of Dartmouth, Massachusetts. He served as a state Representative in 1776 and on the Executive Council, 1788–89. (*Massachusetts Legislators*, p. 340)

SMALLWOOD, WILLIAM (1732–92), lived in retirement at "Smallwood's Retreat," in Charles County, Maryland, after serving as governor, 1785–88. He was a brigadier general in the Continental Army from 1776 until his promotion to major general in 1780, retiring at war's end, when he joined the Society of the Cincinnati. His sister Eleanor was married to Senator Grayson. (*PGW* 2:41)

SMEAD, DAVID (1732–1806), was a deacon and selectman of Greenfield, Massachusetts, which he represented in the state House of Representatives, 1780–93. In 1786 he had been an active supporter of the Shaysites. (*Political Parties*, p. 417)

SMEDLEY, SAMUEL (1753–1812), of Fairfield, Connecticut, was collector of that port, 1789–92, and inspector there until his death. He became a celebrated privateer after serving as captain of marines in 1776. See also *DHFFC* 2:488. (*PGW* 3:183–84n)

SMITH, ADAM (1723–90), was a Scottish political economist whose *Inquiry into the Nature and Causes of the Wealth of Nations* (2 vols., London, 1776) presented a detailed critique of the British political and economic system in the eighteenth century.

SMITH, MARGARET "PEGGY" (1765–1842), was one of the twelve children of Representative Smith (Md.) and his wife Elizabeth Buchanan (1733–84). She married a distant cousin, Baltimore lawyer Robert Smith (1757–1842), in December 1790. In the first federal election Robert Smith served as a Presidential Elector for the state's Western Shore.

SMITH, BENJAMIN, was William Hamilton's private secretary. (*PMHB* 29:156)

SMITH, CHARLOTTE IZARD (1770–92), daughter of Senator Izard and sister-in-law of Gabriel Manigault, married Representative Smith (S.C.) in 1786. She resided with him throughout the First Congress, during which their son Thomas Loughton (February 1790–1817) was born. See also *DHFFC* 14:847.

SMITH, GEORGE W. (1762–1811), justice of the peace for Essex County, Virginia, in 1790, had been the state's port inspector at Tappahannock from May 1788 until 1789. (*PGW* 3:252)

SMITH, JAMES, was appointed manager of the Potowmack Navigation Company in 1788, having served as assistant manager since 1786. (Columbia Historical Society *Records* 15[1912]:173–74)

SMITH, NATHANIEL, of Baltimore was Maryland's inspector of salt provisions in 1789. In 1776 he served as captain of an independent company of Baltimore artillery. (*PGW* 3:176–77n)

SMITH, SAMUEL STANHOPE (1751–1819), vice president of the College of New Jersey (Princeton), 1786–95, was a prominent scientist and Presbyterian minister. (*Princetonians, 1769–1775,* pp. 42–51)

SMITH, WILLIAM (1727–1803), was an Episcopalian minister, secretary of the American Philosophical Society, and rector of the College of Philadelphia (University of Pennsylvania). See also *DHFFC* 9:177n. (*PGW* 4:64n)

SMITH, WILLIAM, a Boston merchant, served as town treasurer and secretary of the Boston Marine Society in 1789. The 1775 Harvard graduate cosigned a petition to Congress in February 1791 requesting the payment of interest on new emission bills of credit under the Funding Act. See also *DHFFC* 8:272, 302.

SMITH, WILLIAM STEPHENS (1755–1816), a gentleman farmer of Jamaica, Long Island, served as federal marshal for the New York district, 1789–1800. The 1774 College of New Jersey (Princeton) graduate rose from major and aide-de-camp to General John Sullivan in 1776 to lieutenant colonel in William Lee's and then Oliver Spencer's Additional Continental Regiments in 1777 and 1779, respectively. He served as George Washington's aide-de-camp from 1781 until the war's end, when he helped to organize the Society of the Cincinnati. He served under John Adams as legation secretary in London, 1785–88, marrying Adams's daughter Abigail in 1786. They were frequent dinner companions of both the Adamses and the Washingtons. See also *DHFFC* 2:525. (*Princetonians, 1769–1775,* pp. 425–37)

SODERSTROM, RICHARD (d. 1815), from Gothenburg, Sweden, settled in Boston in 1782 and served as Swedish consul for the Northern States beginning in 1784, while engaging in the shipping trade there and in New York. His recognition as consul by Massachusetts in 1785 caused an early confrontation between the federal government and the states over federal prerogatives. (Kenneth R. Bowling, *Peter Charles L'Enfant: Vision, Honor, and Male Friendship in the Early Republic* [Washington, D.C., 2002], pp. 42–46, 50)

SOUTHGATE, ROBERT (1741–1833), was a physician and farmer of Scarborough, Maine. (Leonard B. Chapman, *Monograph of the Southgate Family* [Portland, Me., 1907], pp. 8–10)

SOUTHWORTH, CONSTANT (1730–1813), town clerk of Mansfield, Connecticut, 1756–1805, represented that town in the state House of Representatives, 1787–92, and at the state convention where he voted against ratification of the Constitution. (*DHROC* 3:598n; Samuel G. Webber, *A Genealogy of the Southworths* [Boston, 1905], p. 205)

SPENCE, KEITH (d. 1809), a Scottish born merchant of Portsmouth, New Hampshire, and business partner to Senator Langdon's brother-in-law Henry Sherburne, received Langdon's support for appointment as commissioner of loans for New Hampshire in late 1790. He was not considered for the office following revelations of his bankruptcy at that time. (*PGW* 6:585–86n)

SPOONER, EPHRAIM (1735–1818), was a merchant and longtime town clerk of Plymouth, Massachusetts. In 1790 he was appointed justice of the court of common pleas. (Thomas Spooner, *Records of William Spooner of Plymouth, Massachusetts, and his Descendants* [Cincinnati, Oh., 1883], pp. 36–39)

SPRING, SETH, settled in Biddeford, Maine, in 1780 after Revolutionary War service. (George Folsom, *History of Saco and Biddeford* [Saco, Me., 1830], p. 287)

STADNITSKI, PIETER, a Dutch financier, was the principal broker among European investors in the American Revolutionary War public debt in the late 1780s and a major speculator in his own right. In late 1789 his banking house joined three other Dutch firms in purchasing more of the United States liquidated debt. (Mary A. Giunta and J. Dane Hartgrove, eds., *Emerging Nation* [3 vols., Washington, D.C., 1996], 3:711; *PAH* 6:337n)

STAKES, JOHN, was captain in the New York City militia brigade troop of horse in 1789.

STANIFORD, JEREMIAH (1751–1816), was jail keeper and the state's naval officer at Ipswich, Massachusetts, at the time of his appointment as surveyor of that port in 1789. See also *DHFFC* 2:513. (*PGW* 3:84n)

STEELE, JOHN (ca. 1755–1817), of Augusta County, Virginia, declined appointment as lieutenant in the federal army in June 1790, serving instead on the state's Executive Council, 1790–97. During the Revolutionary War he rose from ensign in the 9th and 1st regiments of the Virginia Line, 1777–81, to first lieutenant thereafter until the war's end. As a delegate of Nelson County, Kentucky, he voted against ratification at the state convention. (*PGW* 4:51n)

STEPHEN, ADAM (ca. 1718–1791), a planter and land speculator of Martinsburg, West Virginia, represented Berkeley County in the Virginia House of Delegates, 1780–85, and at the state convention where he voted to ratify the Constitution. His controversial Revolutionary War career began as colonel of the 4th Regiment of the Virginia Line. Promoted to brigadier general in 1776 and major general in 1777, he was court martialed for his role at the Battle of Germantown and dismissed later that year. (*DHROC* 8:244)

STERETT, SAMUEL (1756–1833), was a merchant of Baltimore, which he represented in the Maryland House of Delegates in 1789. A former clerk to the Pennsylvania Assembly, he ran unsuccessfully as an Antifederalist against Representative Smith (Md.) in the first federal election but won the seat two years later. See also *DHFFC* 9:206n. (*DHFFE* 2:243)

STEUBEN, FREDERICK WILLIAM, BARON VON (1730–94), was a Prussian military officer who settled in New York City after the Revolutionary War. His petition to Congress in September 1789, seeking additional compensation as major general and inspector general of the Continental Army, 1778–84, resulted in the Steuben Act of June 1790. See also *DHFFC* 7:201–46, 9:260–61n.

STEVENS, DANIEL (1746–1835), a Charleston, South Carolina, merchant and planter, was appointed supervisor of distilled spirits for the state on 4 March 1791 and served until 1801. He sat in the state House of Representatives, 1784–90, and Senate, 1790–91, and voted for ratification of the Constitution at the state convention. See also *DHFFC* 2:545. (*PGW* 6:101n)

STEVENS, EDWARD (1745–1820), a planter, represented the district formed by Culpeper, Orange, and Spotsylvania counties in the Virginia Senate, 1779–90. Unsuccessful as Culpeper's candidate to the state ratification convention, he served as Presidential Elector in 1789. During the Revolutionary War he was colonel of the 10th Regiment of the Virginia Line,

1776–78, resigning to serve for the duration of the war as a general in the state militia. (*DHFFE* 2:421–22; *DHROC* 9:578)

STEVENS, JOHN, SR. (1715–92), was a merchant of Hunterdon County, New Jersey, which he represented in the state's upper house, or Legislative Council, 1776–82, and at the state ratification convention, over which he presided. He attended Congress in 1784. His son, JOHN, JR. (1749–1838), of Hoboken, New Jersey, petitioned Congress in February 1790 for a patent for his improvements to the steam engine. See also *DHFFC* 8:43, 49. (*DHROC* 3:197; *DHFFE* 3:41n)

STEWART, CHARLES (1729–1800), a farmer of Hunterdon County, New Jersey, was a candidate for Representative in the first federal election. A native of Ireland, he served as commissary general of issues for the Continental Army, 1777–82, and sat in Congress, 1784–85. (*DHFFE* 3:58–59n)

STILES, EZRA (1727–95), a 1746 Yale graduate, was a Congregational minister of New Haven, Connecticut, and president of his alma mater from 1778 until his death. He petitioned Congress in December 1789 for a refund of duties paid by the college for "philosophical apparatus." See also *DHFFC* 8:362–64. (*Yale Graduates* 2:92–97)

STITH, GRIFFIN (1753–94), represented Northampton County in the Virginia House of Delegates, 1785–87. (*PJM* 12:104n)

STOCKTON, SAMUEL W. (1751–95), was a Trenton, New Jersey, lawyer and land speculator. The 1767 College of New Jersey (Princeton) graduate served as secretary of the state ratification convention and unsuccessfully solicited the post of clerk to the state supreme court in 1788. His sister Hannah married Representative Boudinot in 1762. (*Princetonians, 1748–1768*, pp. 622–25)

STODDARD, AMOS (1762–1813), of Boston, was a law student who had served as assistant clerk of the Massachusetts supreme judicial court since 1784. He fought in the Continental Army from 1779 until the war's end. (Robert McHenry, ed., *Webster's American Military Biographies* [New York, 1984], pp. 415–16)

STODDERT, BENJAMIN (1751–1813), was a merchant of Georgetown, Maryland (in present day District of Columbia), who became a major land speculator in the new federal district. During the Revolutionary War he served as captain in Thomas Hartley's Additional Continental Regiment from 1777 until his appointment as a clerk to the board of war, 1779–81.

STONE, FREDERICK (ca. 1769–1793), son of Representative Stone's deceased brother Thomas, was his uncle's ward during the First Congress. He suffered from some undisclosed illness while living with Representative Stone for at least the first two sessions.

STONE, JOHN HOSKINS (1750–1804), younger brother of Representative Stone, was a merchant of Annapolis, Maryland. During the Revolutionary War he rose from major in William Smallwood's Maryland Regiment in 1776 to lieutenant colonel in the 1st Regiment of the state Line later that same year to colonel of the regiment, 1777–79. He served on the state's Executive Council, 1779–85 and 1791–92, and represented Charles County in the state House of Delegates, 1785–87 and 1790. (*PGW* 2:499n; *Maryland Legislators* 2:784–85)

STONE, WALTER (d. 1791), a Port Tobacco, Maryland, trader and the brother of Representative Stone, served as clerk to Superintendent of Finance Robert Morris, 1781–82, and as a clerk in the office of foreign affairs in 1783. (*PRM* 2:208n)

STORER, CHARLES (1761–1829), petitioned the Senate for the honor of bringing John Adams news of his election as Vice President in April 1789. The Boston native and 1779 Harvard graduate had served as Adams's private secretary in Europe. See also *DHFFC* 8:709–10n.

STORY, JOHN (1754–91), a native of Boston trained in the mercantile line, served as commissioner for settling Pennsylvania's accounts with the United States from 1785 until the office was abolished in 1787, when he settled in New York City. Much of his time thereafter was spent unsuccessfully seeking additional compensation for his simultaneous services as deputy quartermaster general, 1778–84, and aide-de-camp to General William Alexander, 1781–83. Prior military service included paymaster of the 11th Continental Regiment, 1776–77, and quartermaster of General John Glover's brigade. (*PGW* 2:351–53n)

STOY (HOY), WILLIAM (1726–1801), was a physician to the German community of Lebanon, Pennsylvania. His petition to Congress in September 1789 sought a reward for having discovered a cure for hydrophobia. See also *DHFFC* 8:9, 11.

STRODE, JOHN (1736–1805), a planter of Culpeper County, Virginia, managed an ironworks near Fredericksburg during the Revolutionary War. In the early 1780s he established an outpost on lands he held near present day Winchester, Kentucky. (*DGW* 4:7n; *PJM* 12:248n)

STRONG, NEHEMIAH (1730–1807), of Newtown, Connecticut, practiced law in nearby Bridgeport. After graduating from Yale in 1755, he became a minister and professor of mathematics there, 1770–81. (*Yale Graduates* 2:383–88)

STUART, ARCHIBALD (1757–1832), a lawyer from Staunton, Virginia, represented Augusta County in the state House of Delegates, 1786–88, and at the state convention where he voted to ratify the Constitution. (*DHROC* 8:90n)

STUART, DAVID (1753–ca. 1814), was a physician and planter of Fairfax (present day Arlington) County, which he represented in the Virginia House of Delegates, 1785–88, and in the state convention where he voted to ratify the Constitution. He became a neighbor and confidant to the Washingtons after his marriage to the widow of Martha's son in 1783, and served as a Presidential Elector in 1789. An avid promoter of Potomac River navigation, Stuart was appointed by President Washington in January 1791 to the three man board of commissioners responsible for developing the federal city, and he served until 1794. (*DHFFE* 2:422)

STURGES, DEBORAH LEWIS (d. 1832), of Fairfield, Connecticut, married Representative Sturges in 1760. (*Yale Graduates* 2:615)

SULLIVAN, JAMES (1744–1808), younger brother of New Hampshire's Governor John Sullivan, practiced law in Biddeford, Maine, before moving to Boston in 1782. He served in the Massachusetts House of Representatives, 1775–77, 1778–79, 1783–85, on the state's supreme judicial court, 1776–82, the Executive Council, 1787–88, and the Suffolk County probate court, 1788–90, before his appointment as state attorney general, 1790–1807. A close ally of Governor John Hancock and political advisor to Representative Gerry, he supported ratification of the Constitution but strongly advocated amendments. He married John Langdon's sister Martha in 1786. (*DHROC* 4:437)

SULLIVAN, JOHN (1740–95), older brother of James Sullivan, was a lawyer of Durham, New Hampshire, who had studied law under Representative Livermore. He served as the state president (governor), 1786–88, and again as interim governor after John Langdon's resignation in 1789. That year he accepted the post of federal district judge, which he retained until his death. He presided over the state ratification convention and served as a Presidential Elector in 1789, although he lost a bid for Representative in the first federal election. See also *DHFFC* 2:517. (*DHFFE* 1:858–59)

SUMNER, JOB (1754–16 Sept. 1789), originally of Massachusetts, settled in Georgia in 1785, when the board of treasury named him commissioner of public accounts for that state. He maintained close ties to his native state, however, serving as justice of the peace for Suffolk County from 1787 until his death while en route from Savannah to New York. At the outbreak of the Revolutionary War, he left Harvard's class of 1778 and enrolled as an ensign in Thomas Gardner's Massachusetts Regiment. A first lieutenant in the 25th Continental Regiment in 1776, he rose to captain of the 3rd Regiment of the Massachusetts Line the next year, and major in 1783, retaining that rank in the federal army until 1784. He unsuccessfully challenged Jackson for Representative in the first federal election. (*DHFFE* 2:487)

SWANWICK, JOHN (1740–98), a Philadelphia merchant, was a former clerk to Superintendent of Finance Robert Morris, who appointed him cashier, or treasurer, of the office of finance in 1781. The next year Morris added the post of receiver of federal taxes in Pennsylvania, and in 1783 Swanwick became a business partner in the firm of Willing and Morris. (*PRM* 1:8)

SWIFT, JONATHAN (1667–1745), was an English author, critic, political figure, and ecclesiastic.

SYMMES, JOHN CLEVES (1742–1814), a New Jersey native, resided at North Bend (in present day Ohio) as judge of the Northwest Territory, 1789–1803, having held that position under the Confederation since 1788. See also *DHFFC* 2:521.

TALBOT, JOHN (ca. 1735–1798), originally of Bedford County, Virginia, which he represented in the colonial House of Burgesses, 1761–75, settled in Georgia in 1783 and represented Wilkes County in the state's House of Assembly, 1788–89. (*PGM* 1:xcix)

TARDIVEAU, BARTHELEMI, was a French trader from Kentucky and agent for the French settlers of the Illinois area of the Northwest Territory. (*PGW* 4:493)

TAYLOR, JOHN (ca. 1734–1794), resided in Maine during much of the Revolutionary War, but by 1780 had settled as a physician in Douglas, Massachusetts, which he represented in the state House of Representatives, 1787–88, and at the state convention in 1788. He prominently opposed ratification of the Constitution, and by the time of the first session had moved across the state line to the Antifederalist town of Smithfield, Rhode Island. (*DHROC* 4:437)

TAYLOR, JOHN, an Albany, New York, land speculator, contracted to sell Representative Madison and Senator Monroe 900 acres of land in the Mohawk Valley in 1786. Madison made the final payment in late 1790. Taylor served in the state Assembly, 1777–81 and 1786–87. (*PJM* 12:297n)

TAYLOR, RICHARD (1749–1825), of Caroline County, Virginia, was captain of the state revenue cutter *Patriot* from 1787. In October 1790 he first declined but then accepted the command of the federal revenue cutter for the southern Chesapeake. During the Revolutionary War he captained a warship of the state navy until he was disabled by grapeshot in 1781. (*PGW* 3:226n, 6:479–80n)

TELFAIR, EDWARD (ca. 1735–1807), a Scottish born merchant, represented Richmond County, Georgia, in the state's House of Assembly in 1789, when he was defeated for Representative in the first federal election but received one of his state's electoral votes for President. He signed the Articles of Confederation as a member of Congress in 1778 and 1780–82, represented Burke County in the Assembly, 1783, 1785, and 1787, and at the state ratification convention, and served as governor, 1786 and 1789–93. His wife, Sally, was the daughter of William Gibbons. (*DHROC* 3:310; *DHFFE* 4:299)

TEMPLE, SIR JOHN (1732–98), a Boston Loyalist who was denied citizenship in 1778, returned from England to serve as the British consul general in New York City from 1785 until his death. His wife was Elizabeth Bowdoin. (*PJM* 8:426n)

TEN BROECK, JOHN C. (1755–1835), was appointed port surveyor at Hudson, New York, in 1789. During the Revolutionary War he rose from second lieutenant in the 4th Regiment of the New York Line in 1775 to first lieutenant in the 1st Regiment, 1776–81, and captain thereafter until the war's end, when he joined the Society of the Cincinnati. See also *DHFFC* 2:525.

THACHER (THATCHER), JOSIAH (1733–99), a native of Lebanon, Connecticut, graduated from the College of New Jersey (Princeton) in 1760 and settled permanently in Gorham, Maine, in 1767. He resigned as its Congregational minister in 1781 and began a public service career that included state Representative, 1783–85, Senator, 1786–91, and judge of the Cumberland County court of common pleas, 1784–99. He ran a distant second to Representative Thatcher (no relation) in the first federal election. (*Princetonians, 1748–1768,* pp. 328–29; *DHFFE* 1:613, 760)

THACHER (THATCHER), OXENBRIDGE (1719–65), a leading lawyer of Boston, joined James Otis, Jr., in arguing against the writs of assistance in 1761, and went on to become a leading spokesman against the Sugar and Stamp acts. Upon his death, Samuel Adams won his seat as Boston's Representative in the Massachusetts legislature. (*Harvard Graduates* 10:322–28)

THATCHER, SARAH SAVAGE (1760–1843), of Biddeford, Maine, married Thatcher in 1784. She was the sister of Joseph Savage and the daughter of Samuel Phillips Savage, at whose home in Weston, Massachusetts, she waited to meet her husband en route home from New York City in 1789. During Thatcher's absence at the First Congress, she raised the first three of their ten children: Samuel Phillips Savage (1785–1842), Sarah (1787–1827), and George (7 Sept. 1790–1857). See also *DHFFC* 14:643, 646.

THATCHER, THOMAS (1757–1806), younger brother of Representative Thatcher, was a schoolteacher of Barnstable, Massachusetts.

THOMAS, ISAIAH (1749–1831), was editor and printer of the [Worcester] *Massachusetts Spy,* 1775–76 and 1778–1801. The paper was an influential organ of Revolutionary sentiments during the 1770s and of Federalist sentiments during the ratification debates. (*DHROC* 4:lv–lvi)

THOMAS, PHILIP (1747–1815), a physician of Frederick, Maryland, was a Presidential Elector representing the state's Western Shore in the first federal election. He represented Frederick County in the state's House of Delegates, 1777–78. In 1773 he married the daughter of John Hanson, president of Congress, 1781–82; Alexander Contee Hanson was his brother-in-law. (*DHFFE* 2:244; *Maryland Legislators* 2:811–12)

THOMPSON, GEORGE (ca. 1751–1834), was an active supporter of Representative Madison in the first federal election in Fluvanna County, which he represented in the Virginia House of Delegates, 1779–80, 1782, 1785–87, and 1790–91. During the Revolutionary War he rose to the rank of major in the state militia, 1779–81. (*DHFFE* 2:319n)

THOMPSON, THOMAS (1739–1809), was a sea captain, ship builder, and merchant of Portsmouth, New Hampshire, where he settled around 1767 after emigrating from England. In October 1776 Congress appointed him captain of the Continental Navy frigate *Raleigh*, for which Senator Langdon served as the government's agent. (*PJB*, pp. 66n, 85n)

THOMSON, CHARLES (1729–1824), a native of Ireland, settled in Philadelphia and became a teacher, merchant, and Revolutionary activist. He served as secretary of Congress, 1774–89, but was unsuccessful in obtaining an office under the Constitution. He married his second wife, Hannah Harrison (d. 1807), in 1774. See also *DHFFC* 9:10n.

THOMSON (THOMPSON), THOMAS, was an Irish born merchant who resided in the Madeiras for seventeen years before settling as a planter in Virginia in 1783. He returned to the Madeiras in 1790. Although Secretary of State Jefferson described him as "a drunkard and bankrupt," he was named consul to the Canary Islands in 1790, a post he declined. (*PTJ* 17:298, 18:143–44, 19:314, 317; *PJM* 11:203–4)

THONIGWENGHSOHARIE, CHRISTIAN, a member of the Oneida Nation of northern New York's Iroquois Confederacy, was commissioned a lieutenant in the Continental Army in 1779 but may have subsequently allied himself with the British. He was a signatory to the petition of seven Oneida and Tuscarora Indians presented to Congress in February 1791. See also *DHFFC* 7:378–80.

TILGHMAN, EDWARD (1751–1815), graduated from the College of Philadelphia (University of Pennsylvania) in 1767 and studied at London's Middle Temple from 1772 until 1774, when he settled in Philadelphia and began his career as one of the city's preeminent lawyers. He was cousin to William Tilghman and, by his marriage to Elizabeth Chew in 1774, brother-in-law to Maryland's Governor John Eager Howard.

TILGHMAN, JAMES, SR. (1716–93), was a lawyer of Kent County, Maryland, which he had represented in the colonial assembly. Like his son William, he was a Loyalist during the Revolutionary War. (*Maryland Legislators* 2:822–23; *PGW* 6:544)

TILGHMAN, RICHARD, IV (1746–1805), was a Chestertown, Maryland, planter. (James Bordley, Jr., *The Hollyday and Related Families of the Eastern Shore of Maryland* [Baltimore, 1962], pp. 271–75)

TILGHMAN, WILLIAM (1756–1827), a former Loyalist, was a lawyer from Kent County, Maryland, which he represented at the state convention, where he voted to ratify the Constitution. He also served in the state's House of Delegates, 1788–90, and the Senate, 1791–93. In the first federal election he was a Presidential Elector representing the state's Eastern Shore. (*DHFFE* 2:244–45)

TITCOMB, JONATHAN (1727–1817), a merchant of Newburyport, Massachusetts, served as its naval officer, 1789–1812, having held that position under the state during the Confederation. He sat in the state House of Representatives, 1779–83, 1784, and 1786–87, and joined Senator King as a Newburyport delegate to the state convention, where he voted to ratify the Constitution. See also *DHFFC* 2:513.

TITTLE, JOHN (ca. 1735–1800), resided in Beverly, Massachusetts, in 1790.

TOPPAN, CHRISTOPHER (1735–1818), was a merchant of Hampton, New Hampshire, which he represented at the state convention where he voted to ratify the Constitution. He was an unsuccessful candidate for both Representative and Presidential Elector in the first federal election and sat for Rockingham County in the state Senate, 1788–90. He was a cousin to Senator Wingate. (*DHFFE* 1:800n, 807–8, 810, 814–15)

TRACEY, JOHN (1753–1815), a 1771 Harvard graduate, left his native Newburyport, Massachusetts, in the winter of 1788–89 and traveled to Marietta, Northwest Territory (present day Ohio), to solicit a job under Winthrop Sargent. He accompanied Governor Arthur St. Clair back to Philadelphia in the spring of 1789. (*Harvard Graduates* 17:646–49)

TRACY, URIAH (1755–1807), a 1778 Yale graduate, was a lawyer of Litchfield, Connecticut, which he represented in the state House of Representatives, 1788–93. (*Yale Graduates* 4:63–66)

TREVETT, RICHARD (d. 1793), was appointed collector at York, Maine, 1789–93. See also *DHFFC* 2:513.

TRIST, ELIZA HOUSE, was the mistress of a boardinghouse at Fifth and Market streets in Philadelphia, where Representative Madison and other members of Congress, principally from New York and Virginia, regularly resided while in that city. (*PJM* 2:92n)

TRUMBULL, DAVID (1751–1822), son of former Governor Jonathan Trumbull and brother to Representative Trumbull and painter John Trumbull, was a merchant in his prominent family's firm based in Lebanon, Connecticut. He was associated with Representative Wadsworth as an army supplier in 1782–83. (Irma B. Jaffe, *John Trumbull* [Boston, 1975], pp. 3, 54)

TRUMBULL, JONATHAN, SR. (1710–85), of Lebanon, Connecticut, served as governor of that state, 1769–84. He was father of the Representative and of David and John Trumbull.

TUCKER, EBENEZER (1758–1845), a landowner and merchant of Little Egg Harbor, New Jersey, was appointed customs surveyor at that port in 1789. See also *DHFFC* 2:521.

TUCKER, JOHN, JR. (1753–1825), a Boston lawyer, was the first clerk of the United States Supreme Court from 1790 until his resignation in August 1791. He simultaneously served as clerk to the Massachusetts supreme judicial court, having held that post since 1783. The 1774 Harvard graduate studied law under John Lowell and was admitted to the bar in 1780. (*Harvard Graduates* 18:520–22; *DHSCUS* 1:158–60)

TUCKER, JOHN, SR. (1719–92), father of the United States Supreme Court clerk, was minister of the First Congregational Church of Newbury, Massachusetts. (*DHSCUS* 1:704n)

TUCKER, JOSEPH (1754–1812), a merchant of York, Maine, petitioned the First Congress in May 1790 with three other former agents seeking additional compensation for settling the accounts of the Massachusetts troops stationed at West Point after the Revolutionary War. See also *DHFFC* 8:98–101.

TUCKER, ST. GEORGE (1752–1827), was a Williamsburg, Virginia, lawyer, who attended the Annapolis Convention in 1786 and was appointed judge of the state's general court in 1788. In 1790 he became professor of law at his alma mater, the College of William and Mary. He was the younger brother of Representative Tucker and became the brother-in-law of Representative Bland by his marriage to Frances Bland Randolph in 1778. Upon her death in 1788 he became legal guardian to his stepsons Theodorick Bland Randolph and John Randolph of Roanoke. He was also a correspondent and confidant of Representative Page, with whom he shared some of his literary endeavors. See also *DHFFC* 14:859. (*DHROC* 8:35n)

TUCKER, SAMUEL (1747–1833), was a sea captain from Marblehead, Massachusetts, with business ties to the Goodhue brothers. George Washington commissioned him captain of the *Franklin* and later the *Hancock* in 1776; Congress followed with a captain's commission in the Continental Navy in 1777. The next year his frigate *Boston* carried John Adams to France. (*PGW: Revolution* 3:279; John F. Millar, *American Ships of the Colonial and Revolutionary Periods* [New York, 1978], p. 77)

TUDOR, WILLIAM (1750–1819), a Boston lawyer, graduated from Harvard in 1769, read law under John Adams, and supervised Ames's legal studies, 1778–81. He served as judge advocate general of the Continental Army with the rank of lieutenant colonel, 1775–78, joining the Society of the Cincinnati at war's end. See also *DHFFC* 14:615. (*Harvard Graduates* 17:252–65)

TUFTS, COTTON (1732–1815), a physician of Weymouth, Massachusetts, represented Suffolk County in the state Senate, 1781–82 and 1783–92. As Abigail Adams's uncle by marriage, he administered her family's affairs while they were in England. (*DHROC* 4:174n)

TUFTS, SAMUEL, of Gloucester, Massachusetts, had served as the state's excise officer for neighboring Newburyport until shortly before 1789. Cotton Tufts was his brother.

TURBERVILLE, GEORGE LEE (1760–98), was a planter of Richmond County, Virginia, which he represented in the state House of Delegates, 1785–89. During the Revolutionary War he rose from captain of the 15th Regiment of the Virginia Line in 1776 to major in 1778, when he retired. (*DHROC* 8:122n)

TURNBULL, ANDREW (ca. 1718–1792), a native of Scotland, traveled throughout present day Turkey before establishing a colony of Greeks at New Smyrna, on a royal grant in the British colony of East Florida in the mid 1760s. He was bankrupt by 1778 and in 1782 he resumed his occupation as a physician in Charleston, South Carolina.

TURNER, GEORGE (ca. 1750–1843), of Philadelphia, was appointed judge of the Northwest Territory in 1789. A native of England, he fought as a second lieutenant in the 1st Regiment of the South Carolina Line, 1776–77, and as a captain, 1777–83, during which time he served as deputy commissary general of prisoners and commissary of marine prisoners. He retired as a brevet major at war's end and joined the Society of the Cincinnati, for which he was assistant secretary general, 1787–91. (*PGW* 3:494–95n)

TYLER, GEORGE, a former silversmith, represented Deer Isle, Maine, in the Massachusetts House of Representatives in 1789.

TYLER, JOHN (1747–1813), a lawyer of Charles City County, Virginia, sat on the bench of the state's admiralty court, 1776, 1786–88, and General Court, 1788–1808. He served in the House of Delegates, 1778–86 (as its speaker, 1781–85), and in the state convention as its vice president, voting against ratification of the Constitution. (*DHROC* 10:1297n)

UNDERWOOD, THOMAS (1740–1815), represented Goochland County in the Virginia House of Delegates, 1777–90. (*PJM* 12:249n)

VAN BERCKEL, FRANCO PETRUS (b. 1760), succeeded his father as minister plenipotentiary to the United States from the Netherlands between 10 May 1789 and 1795. (*DHFFC* 9:46n, 14:890)

VAN BERCKEL, PIETER JOHAN (1725–1800), a former burgomaster of Rotterdam, served as minister plenipotentiary to the United States from the Netherlands from 1783 until his son replaced him in 1789, but remained in New York and New Jersey until his death. His daughter was courted by Representative Brown in 1788–89. (*DHFFC* 9:242n; *LDC* 25:346n)

VAN HORNE, DAVID (1755–1801), of New York City, was a member of the Society of the Cincinnati. During the Revolutionary War he served as captain in William Lee's Additional Continental Regiment, 1777–79. His mother, Anna French, was sister to New Jersey Governor William Livingston's wife, Susannah.

VAN SCHAACK, HENRY (1733–1823), was a former New York fur merchant whose Loyalism exiled him to Pittsfield, Massachusetts, where he became Representative Sedgwick's confidant and political lieutenant. Peter Van Schaack was his younger brother and Representative Silvester became their brother-in-law in 1764. (*DHFFC* 14:722; *DHROC* 4:64n)

VAN SCHAACK, PETER (1747–1832), a former Loyalist, practiced law in Kinderhook, New York. His older brother was Henry Van Schaack; their sister Jane married Representative Silvester, Peter's law teacher and confidant, in 1764. See also *DHFFC* 14:722. (*DHFFE* 3:502n)

VAN STAPHORST, NICHOLAS and JACOB, were brothers and partners in one of Amsterdam's most important banking firms. They belonged to the syndicate of bankers that negotiated loans with John Adams for the Confederation Congress. (*Adams* 2:445n)

VANDALSEM, WILLIAM, was a grocer at New York City's Bear Market at the corner of Greenwich and Partition streets, where he let rooms to his cousin Representative Wynkoop and Senator Maclay in 1789.

VANS, WILLIAM (ca. 1730–1820), was a merchant who represented Salem in the Massachusetts legislature. He was appointed state excise collector in March 1790. (*PGW* 5:317n)

VARICK, RICHARD (1753–1831), a New York City lawyer, served as mayor, 1789–1801, having served as city recorder since 1784, speaker of the state Assembly, 1787–88, and state attorney general, 1788–89. During the Revolutionary War he was captain of the 1st Regiment of the New York Line, 1775–76, aide-de-camp to Senator Schuyler, 1776–77, deputy commissary general of musters with the rank of lieutenant colonel, 1777–78, aide-de-camp to General Benedict Arnold, 1778–80, and George Washington's recording secretary, 1781–83. (*PGW* 6:102n)

VARNUM, JAMES MITCHELL (1748–10 January 1789), was a lawyer of East Greenwich, Rhode Island, before moving to Marietta, Ohio, as judge of the Northwest Territory from 1787 until his death. He was a director of the Ohio Company during the same period. Varnum graduated from the College of Rhode Island (Brown) in 1769 and was admitted to the bar two years later. During the Revolutionary War he rose from colonel of the Rhode Island Regiment in 1775 and 1777 and of the 9th Continental Regiment in 1776 to brigadier general of the Continental Army in 1777, retiring in 1779. He later served in Congress, 1780–81 and 1787. (*DHFFE* 4:413n)

VARNUM, JOSEPH BRADLEY (1751–1821), was a farmer of Dracut, Massachusetts, who served as state Representative, 1780–85, and Senator for Middlesex County, 1786–95. Although an Antifederalist, he voted to ratify the Constitution at the state convention. He was later defeated by Representative Gerry in the first federal election. (*DHFFE* 1:760–61)

VAUGHAN, CHARLES, one of the great landed proprietors of central Maine, resided in Hallowell, Maine, in 1790.

VAUGHAN, SAMUEL (1720–1802), was a British merchant who resided in Philadelphia from 1783 until his return to London in 1790. A prominent early American landscape architect, he designed the Pennsylvania State House yard. (*PGW* 1:92n)

VAUGHN, WILLIAM, was a merchant of Portland, Maine.

VERNON, WILLIAM (1719–1806), a merchant of Newport, Rhode Island, served on the naval board of the Eastern Department from 1777 until its dissolution in 1782. (*PRM* 1:190n)

VERPLANK, DANIEL C. (1762–1834), graduated from Columbia College in 1788 and commenced to practice law in New York City the following year. In 1785 he married Elizabeth Johnson (1763–26 February 1789), daughter of Senator Johnson.

WADSWORTH, REPRESENTATIVE JEREMIAH, family during the First Congress: his wife, Mehitable Russell (1734–1817), whom he married in 1767 and who resided in Hartford, Connecticut, and their children Harriet (1769?–1793), Daniel (1771–1848), and Catherine (1774–1841).

WADSWORTH, JAMES (1730–1817), a distant relation of Representative Wadsworth, was a lawyer of Durham, Connecticut, which he represented in the state House of Representatives, 1759–85 and 1788–89, and at the state convention where he was an Antifederalist leader and voted against ratification. The 1748 Yale graduate also served as New Haven County justice of the peace, 1788–91, and judge from 1778 until 1789 when he refused reappointment because he would not swear fidelity to the Constitution. He rose from colonel in 1775 to major general of the state militia by the time of his resignation in 1779 and attended Congress in 1784. (*Yale Graduates* 2:192–95; *DHROC* 3:613n)

WADSWORTH, PELEG (1748–1829), a merchant of Portland, Maine, served on the five man committee that addressed a petition from the merchants and traders of that town to Congress in April 1789 on the subject of the proposed impost duty on molasses. During the Revolutionary War he rose from captain in the 23rd Continental Regiment in 1776 to brigadier general in the state militia the next year, retiring in 1782. (*DHFFC* 8:357)

WAIT, THOMAS B. (1762–1830), publisher of Portland, Maine's *Cumberland Gazette*, 1785–91, served on the committee of five that addressed a petition from the merchants and traders of that town to Congress in April 1789 on the subject of the proposed impost duty on molasses. He was a confidant and correspondent of Representative Thatcher, with whom he shared a socially progressive ideology. (*New England Quarterly* 28[1955]:519–34)

WAITE, JOHN (1732–1820), was sheriff of Portland, Maine, 1776–1809. (*Maine Bar*, pp. 678–85)

WALES, SAMUEL (1747/48–94), a 1767 Yale graduate, served as professor of divinity at his alma mater, 1782–93. (*Yale Graduates* 3:257–61; Franklin B. Dexter, ed., *Literary Diary of Ezra Stiles* [New York, 1901], 3:516)

WALKER, BENJAMIN (1753–1818), a New York City merchant and securities broker, served as naval officer for that port, 1789–97, except for a leave of absence in the winter of 1790–91 when he was in Europe as an agent for the Scioto Land Company. A native of England, he was commissioned a second lieutenant of the 1st Regiment of the New York Line in 1775 and rose to captain of the 4th Regiment the next year, and aide-de-camp to Baron von Steuben, 1778–82, with the rank of major. After the war he became a close associate of Secretary of the Treasury Hamilton in administering von Steuben's financial affairs, and like them he became a member of the Society of the Cincinnati. During the Confederation he served as commissioner for settling the accounts of the hospital, marine, and clothing departments, and as the board of treasury's commissioner for investigating Senator Morris's finance office accounts. See also *DHFFC* 2:525, 8:668. (*PGW* 2:430n)

WALLACE, GUSTAVUS BROWN (1751–1802), of Stafford County, Virginia, was a member of the state House of Delegates, 1786–87. During the Revolutionary War he rose from captain of the 3rd Regiment of the Virginia Line in 1776 to lieutenant colonel of the 11th Regiment in 1778, transferring in 1781 to the 2nd Regiment and serving until the end of the war, when he became a member of the Society of the Cincinnati. (*PGW* 1:461; Lyon G. Tyler, *Encyclopedia of Virginia Biography* [5 vols., New York, 1915], 2:351)

WALLACE, JOSHUA (1752–1819), was a merchant, lawyer, and land speculator of Burlington, New Jersey, which he served as a member of the town's common council, 1788–89, and as a delegate to the state convention. He was appointed a judge of the county court of common pleas in 1784 and was elected to the state assembly in 1791. William Bradford, Jr., was his brother-in-law. (*DHFFE* 3:82n)

WALLER, BENJAMIN (1716–86), attended the College of William and Mary and became a lawyer in Williamsburg, Virginia. He served on the bench of the state's admiralty and general courts, 1776–85. (*PGM* 1:cv)

WALPOLE, SIR ROBERT (1676–1745), was Great Britain's first parliamentary leader to assume the modern role of prime minister (1721–42). During his administration, bribery and patronage were used as important tools for securing majorities in the House of Commons.

WALTON, GEORGE (ca. 1741–1804), a lawyer of Burke County, Georgia, and Presidential Elector in 1789, served as governor, 1779–80, and again from January to November 1789. A brief career as lieutenant in the 1st Regiment of the Georgia Line ended with his election to Congress in 1776, when he signed the Declaration of Independence. He attended Congress again in 1777, 1780, and 1781, and was elected to but did not attend both the Federal Convention and the state ratification convention. He served as chief justice, 1783–86, and justice of the superior court, western circuit, 1789–92. (*DHROC* 3:310; *DHFFE* 2:487–88)

WALTON, GERALD (ca. 1741–1821), of New York City, was a Loyalist during the Revolution.

WARD, GEORGE C. (1765–1801), son of the merchant Richard Ward, was state collector of revenues at Salem, Massachusetts, in 1789.

WARD, JOSEPH (1737–1812), was a Boston real estate developer and investor in government securities. Originally a schoolteacher, he was commissioned a major in the Continental Army at the outbreak of the Revolutionary War, rising to colonel and commissary general of musters from 1777 until 1780, when he declined the office of commissary general of prisoners. In February 1791 he cosigned a petition to Congress requesting the payment of interest on new emission bills of credit under the Funding Act. A Federalist, he was the patron and former teacher of *GUS* editor John Fenno. See also *DHFFC* 8:272–73, 302–3. (*LDC* 2:345, 15:40)

WARD, RICHARD (1741–1824), a Salem, Massachusetts, merchant, served in the state's House of Representatives, 1785–87. (*Political Parties*, p. 413)

WARNER, JONATHAN (1726–1814), a former colonial officeholder, was one of the largest real estate holders in Portsmouth, New Hampshire. (Gerald D. Foss, *Three Centuries of Free Masonry in New Hampshire* [n.p., 1972], pp. 506–7)

WARREN, HENRY (1764–1828), son of James and Mercy Otis Warren, was a farmer of Plymouth, Massachusetts. He served as aide-de-camp to General Benjamin Lincoln during Shays's Rebellion and was appointed clerk under him while collector of Boston. (*PGW* 3:104–5)

WARREN, JAMES (1726–1808), a merchant and gentleman farmer of Plymouth, Massachusetts, served as speaker of the state House of Representatives, 1787–88. Federalists considered him their principal Antifederalist target during the ratification debates, and in the first federal election he ran a distant second to Representative Partridge. In April 1790 he petitioned Congress for a depreciation allowance on part of his compensation as a member of the Continental Navy board for the eastern department, 1776–81. He married Mercy Otis in 1754. See also *DHFFC* 7:1–4. (*DHROC* 4:163; *DHFFE* 1:610; *Harvard Graduates* 17:655–69)

WARREN, JOHN (1753–1815), was a Boston physician and, beginning in 1783, professor of anatomy and surgery at Harvard, from which he had graduated in 1771. During the Revolutionary War he served as a surgeon for the Massachusetts militia, 1775–80, and thereafter for the Continental Army's hospital department until the war's end.

WARREN, JOSEPH, JR. (1768–April 1790), eldest son of General Joseph Warren, the martyred hero of the Battle of Bunker's Hill, graduated from Harvard in 1786 and was teaching school in Foxborough, Massachusetts, at the time of his death.

WARREN, MERCY OTIS (1728–1814), of Plymouth, Massachusetts, was a poet, playwright, historian, and prominent Antifederalist essayist. She was the sister of Samuel A. Otis and James Otis, Jr., and, after 1754, the wife of James Warren. (*DHROC* 4:438)

WARVILLE, JACQUES-PIERRE BRISSOT DE (1754–93), a French journalist and reformer, had been in America since July 1788, touring the country in preparation for writing its history. He succeeded in writing one of the most famous travelogues of America before de Tocqueville. During his travels he also served as a confidential agent for a partnership of French and American public securities investors that included William Duer and Andrew Craigie. (*PGW* 1:91n)

WASHINGTON, GEORGE (1732–99), of Fairfax County, Virginia, President of the United States, 1789–97, was a planter, provincial legislator, and prominent land speculator and advocate of Potomac River navigation. He was serving in Congress when elected commander in chief of the Continental Army in 1775. He resigned the post at war's end and became first president general of the Society of the Cincinnati. He hosted the Mount Vernon Conference of 1785, precursor of the Annapolis Convention, and later presided over the Federal Convention. See also *DHFFC* 9:4n.

WASHINGTON, MARTHA DANDRIDGE CUSTIS (1731–1802), a widow when she married George Washington in 1759, helped to establish the Republican Court shortly after her arrival at New York City on 27 May 1789. She resided with her husband throughout the First Congress. See also *DHFFC* 9:6on.

WASHINGTON, WILLIAM (1752–1810), a cousin of George Washington, became a Charleston, South Carolina, planter shortly after the Revolutionary War. He was commissioned a captain in the 3rd Regiment of the Virginia Line in 1776, served as major in the 4th Regiment of Continental Dragoons, 1777–78, and achieved celebrity as lieutenant colonel of the 3rd Regiment of Dragoons thereafter until the war's end, when he joined the Society of the Cincinnati. (*PGW: Confederation* 1:271)

WATSON, ELKANAH (1758–1842), a native of Massachusetts, was a banker and canal promoter residing in Albany, New York, in 1789. He began his career apprenticed to the Browns of Providence, Rhode Island, and operated his own mercantile firm in Nantes, France, during the Revolutionary War and briefly in the United States in the mid 1780s. (*PGW* 3:318–20)

WATSON, MARSTON (1756–1800), was a shipowner of Marblehead, Massachusetts, where he settled in 1779 following his service in the Revolutionary War as a second lieutenant in the 14th Continental Regiment and as an aide-de-camp to General Charles Lee. (An uncle of the same name also lived in Marblehead and represented that town in the state House of Representatives in 1792.) (Philip Smith, *Journals of Ashley Bowen* [2 vols., Portland, Me., 1973], p. 683)

WATSON, WILLIAM (1730–1815), a merchant of Plymouth, Massachusetts, was appointed collector of that port, 1789–1803, having served as its naval officer under the state since 1782. See also *DHFFC* 2:514.

WAYNE, ANTHONY (1745–96), originally of Pennsylvania, moved in early 1788 to his rice plantation, "Richmond," outside Savannah, which had been presented to him by the state of Georgia in recognition of his Revolutionary War record. This included service as colonel of the 4th Pennsylvania

Battalion, 1776–77, and brigadier general thereafter until war's end, when he was breveted a major general and joined the Society of the Cincinnati. Unsuccessful as a candidate for Senator in the first federal election, he defeated Representative Jackson in the second federal election, but the seat was declared vacant when questions about his legal residence and voting fraud arose. See also *DHFFC* 9:245n. (*DHFFE* 2:488–89)

WEBB, SAMUEL BLACHLEY (1753–1807), a native of Connecticut, was living in New York City by 1789 as an agent for the Boston merchant, Joseph Barrell. He began his military career as first lieutenant in the 2nd Regiment of the Connecticut Line in 1775, was promoted to lieutenant colonel and aide-de-camp to George Washington the next year, and was commanding colonel of one of the sixteen Additional Continental Regiments, 1777–81, and of the 3rd Connecticut Regiment from 1781 until his retirement as brevet brigadier general in 1783. He subsequently became a member of the Society of the Cincinnati. An outspoken Federalist during the ratification debate, he was the highest ranking military officer that Congress asked to assist in the presidential inaugural ceremony. He married Catherine Hogeboom of Claverack, New York, in late 1790 and retired to a farm there. (*DHROC* 3:605n; *DHFFC* 8:721n; *PGW* 2:276–77n)

WEBB, WILLIAM (ca. 1764–1822), served as collector of Bath, Maine, 1789–1804. See also *DHFFC* 2:514.

WEBSTER, NOAH (1758–1843), lexicographer, lecturer, teacher, and publisher of grammar textbooks, practiced law in his native Hartford, Connecticut, 1789–93. The 1778 Yale graduate resided in New York and published Federalist essays during the ratification debates. (*Yale Graduates* 4:66–79)

WEBSTER, PELATIAH (1726–95), a Congregational minister from Connecticut before becoming a Philadelphia merchant in 1755, was a political economist and Federalist essayist during the ratification debates. He graduated from Yale in 1746. (*DHROC* 13:294n; *Yale Graduates* 2:97–102)

WEEDON, GEORGE (ca. 1734–1793), a Fredericksburg, Virginia, tavern keeper and longtime friend of George Washington, commanded the 3rd Regiment of the Virginia Line from 1776 until his promotion to brigadier general, 1777–83. After the war he was active in the Society of the Cincinnati and served as mayor and city councilman. (*PGW* 1:150–51n)

WEISSENFELS, CHARLES FREDERICK, of New York City, rose from second lieutenant in the 2nd Regiment of the New York Line in 1776 to first lieutenant in 1778, and regimental quartermaster, 1779–83. He became a member of the Society of the Cincinnati.

WEISSENFELS, FREDERICK (1728–1806), was a Prussian baron who came to America with the British Army during the Seven Years War and subsequently settled as a merchant in Dutchess County, New York. He was commissioned a captain in the 1st Regiment of the New York Line at the outbreak of the Revolutionary War, and served as lieutenant colonel in the 3rd and 2nd regiments, before transferring to the 4th Regiment in 1777, from which he retired as commandant at war's end. He was a member of the Society of the Cincinnati. (John Schuyler, *Institution of the Society of the Cincinnati . . . of the State of New York* [New York, 1886], pp. 340–42)

WELCH, HEZEKIAH (1734–97), was a former merchant seaman of Boston. He was commissioned a lieutenant in the Continental Navy in 1776, commanded the *Boston* in 1778, and went on to serve as first lieutenant on the frigate *Alliance*. (*PGW* 4:120–21n)

WELLES, ARNOLD (1761–1827), was president of a Boston insurance company. (*DHFFE* 4:283n)

WELLS, JAMES, was appointed port surveyor at Smithfield, Isle of Wight County, Virginia, in 1789. (*DHFFC* 2:555)

WELLS, NATHANIEL (1740–1816), a 1760 Harvard graduate and former schoolteacher of Wells, Maine, served in the Massachusetts Senate, 1782–97, and in the state convention, where he voted to ratify the Constitution. He ran unsuccessfully for Representative in the first federal election, while serving as judge of the York County court of common pleas. (*Harvard Graduates* 14:672–73; *DHFFE* 1:761–62)

WENDELL, EDWARD (d. 1841), of Boston, graduated from Harvard in 1781 and studied law with John Lowell.

WENDELL, JOHN (1731–1808), a 1750 Harvard graduate, was a Portsmouth, New Hampshire, lawyer and land speculator. (*PRM* 1:179n; *Harvard Graduates* 12:592–97)

WEST, BENJAMIN (1746–1817), was a 1768 Harvard graduate and a prominent lawyer of Charlestown, New Hampshire. His refusal to accept his election to the First Congress forced Representative Foster's special election on 22 June. West had likewise been elected but refused to serve as a delegate to

Congress in 1781 and state attorney general in 1786, although he did attend the state convention, where he voted to ratify the Constitution. (*DHFFE* 1:841, 860; *Harvard Graduates* 17:106–12)

WEST, BENJAMIN (1738–1820), a Pennsylvania Quaker who settled permanently in London in 1763, was appointed historical painter to the king in 1772. He became acquainted with Senator Izard during the latter's European sojourn, 1771–76, and apparently stored some paintings for him, including almost certainly John Singleton Copley's masterful portrait of Izard and his wife executed in Rome in 1775. (*DHFFC* 14:830, 835–36)

WEST, ROGER (ca. 1755–1801), was justice of the peace of Fairfax County, Virginia, 1787–99, which he represented in the House of Delegates, 1788–89 and 1791–92. (*PGW* 3:571)

WEST, WILLIAM (ca. 1739–1791), was the Anglican minister of St. Paul's Parish in Baltimore beginning in 1779. (*PGW* 1:349)

WETMORE, HEZEKIAH (b. ca. 1750), a New Haven, Connecticut, merchant, was a deputy quartermaster general of the Continental Army at Newburgh, New York, during the last years of the war. He was a business partner of Representative Sherman's eldest son, John, until their mercantile firm's dissolution in 1787. That same year he played a prominent role in circulating a controversial letter among former Connecticut Loyalists that advocated a return to monarchical government under George III's second son. (*DHROC* 13:174–77n; *PRM* 7:332, 339n)

WETMORE, WILLIAM (1749–1830), a native of Middletown, Connecticut, graduated from Harvard in 1770 and was a leading lawyer in Essex County, Massachusetts, between 1774 and 1788, when he moved to Boston and invested in real estate and public securities. He became involved in land speculation and development in Maine following his 1782 marriage into the prominent Waldo family. (*Harvard Graduates* 17:447–51; *PGW* 3:219n; Robert Ernst, *Rufus King, American Federalist* [Chapel Hill, N.C., 1968], p. 31)

WEYMAN, EDWARD (ca. 1730–1793), served as port surveyor at Charleston, South Carolina, 1789–93. See also *DHFFC* 2:545.

WHARTON, SAMUEL (1732–1800), a Quaker merchant of Philadelphia and a land speculator, represented Delaware in Congress, 1782–83, and served as a judge of the court of common pleas, 1790–91. (*Drinker* 3:2229)

WHEATON, JOSEPH (1755–1828), of New York City, served as House sergeant at arms, 1789–1807. See also *DHFFC* 8:520. (*PGW* 5:328n)

WHIPPLE, JOSEPH (1738–1816), brother of William, was a merchant of
Portsmouth, New Hampshire, where he served as collector, 1789–98 and
1801–16, having held that post under the state, 1786–89. He was brother-
in-law to Joshua Brackett. See also *DHFFC* 2:517.

WHIPPLE, OLIVER, was a lawyer of Portsmouth, New Hampshire, where he
settled in 1774. He graduated from Harvard in 1766. (*Harvard Graduates*
16:430–45; *Maine Bar*, p. 48)

WHIPPLE, WILLIAM (1730–85), was a business partner of his brother Joseph
in Portsmouth, New Hampshire, from 1760. He signed the Declaration of
Independence as a member of Congress, 1776–79, saw duty as a brigadier
general of the state militia during the Revolutionary War, sat in the state assembly, 1780–84, and served as associate justice of the state superior court
from 1782 until his death.

WHITE, ANTHONY WALTON (1750–1803), moved from New Brunswick,
New Jersey, to New York City in 1788 to recover from poor business investments, in part by petitioning Congress in March 1790 for compensation
for money advanced for the use of the 1st Regiment of Dragoons, which he
commanded from 1779 until his retirement in 1782. See also *DHFFC*
7:543–44.

WHITE, JOHN (ca. 1754–20 May 1790), resided in New York City during
the first session of Congress, serving as agent in the final settlement of Maryland's accounts with the United States. His August 1789 petition seeking
compensation for additional duties as commissioner for settling the accounts of Pennsylvania, Delaware, and Maryland resulted in an enrolled
resolution in September. He was appointed postmaster of Baltimore two
months later and served until his death. See also *DHFFC* 8:123–26, 9:268n.

WHITE, WILLIAM (1748–1836), Episcopal bishop of Philadelphia since 1787
and chaplain to Congress, 1790–1800, became Senator Morris's brother-
in-law by the latter's marriage to Mary White in 1762. See also *DHFFC*
9:343n.

WHITING, ELIZABETH BURWELL, of Carter's Creek, Gloucester County,
Virginia, was the widow and executrix of Beverley Whiting (d. 1755), whose

estate was being sued in a case taken up by the Virginia legislature in late
1789, which later remitted the judgment against her. (*PGW* 3:186n)

WHITING, MATTHEW, JR. (b. ca. 1755), the son of a Prince William County,
Virginia, constituent of Representative Lee, was rumored (probably falsely)
to have been seized by Barbary pirates around 1785. For background, see
PGW 4:225–26.

WHITING, WILLIAM (1730–92), was a physician of Great Barrington, Massachusetts, which he represented in the state House of Representatives in
1776. While chief justice of the Berkshire County court of common pleas,
1781–87, he was publicly charged by Representative Sedgwick, arrested,
and convicted for seditious libel in connection with his support for the Shaysites in 1786–87. He ran unsuccessfully as an Antifederalist candidate for
Representative during the first federal election. (*DHFFE* 1:762; *DHROC*
4:385n)

WIBIRD, ANTHONY (1729–1800), was the Adamses' pastor as Congregational minister of the North Precinct of Braintree (now Quincy), Massachusetts, from 1754 until his death. He voted in favor of the Constitution
at the state's ratification convention in 1788. (*Adams* 1:16n; *DHROC* 5:940)

WIDGERY, WILLIAM (ca. 1753–1822), a native of England, was a lawyer in
New Gloucester, Maine, which he represented in the Massachusetts House
of Representatives, 1787–94, and in the state convention, where he voted
against ratification of the Constitution. He was also town selectman, 1789–
90. (*DHROC* 4:439)

WIGGIN, MARY WINGATE (1766–1840), daughter of Senator Wingate,
married Andrew Wiggin of Stratham, New Hampshire, in 1788. Their
family at the time of the First Congress consisted of daughters Harriet
(1788–1836) and Caroline (1790–1817). (Charles E. Wingate, *History of the
Wingate Family in England and America* [Exeter, N.H., 1886], pp. 153–57)

WILCOCKS, ALEXANDER (1741–1801), a Philadelphia lawyer, was city recorder in 1791. (*DHSCUS* 1:185n)

WILKINSON, JAMES (1757–1825), originally of Maryland, represented Bucks
County in the Pennsylvania General Assembly, 1781–83, before settling
permanently in Kentucky in 1784. In exchange for trading privileges along
the Mississippi, in 1787 he conspired with Louisiana's Governor Miró to

establish an independent republic of Kentucky allied to Spain. The plan, in which he may have been involved with Representative Brown, Harry Innes, Benjamin Sebastian, and others, was abandoned by late 1789. In a busy Revolutionary War career, he served in turn as aide-de-camp to Nathanael Greene, Benedict Arnold, and Horatio Gates, 1776–77, lieutenant colonel of Thomas Hartley's Additional Continental Regiment in 1777, brevet brigadier general, 1777–78, secretary to the board of war in 1778, and clothier general of the army, 1779–81. (*DHROC* 8:291n; *Westward Expansion*, pp. 232–33)

WILKINSON, NATHANIEL, represented Henrico County in the Virginia House of Delegates, 1787–88. He was the uncle of Reuben Wilkinson.

WILKINSON, REUBEN (d. 1796), the state government's collector for Savannah, Georgia, 1787–89, sat in the state's Executive Council in 1787 and the House of Assembly for Washington County in 1788. James Seagrove described him in February 1789 as a "low and illeterate" backwoodsman who was promised Senator Gunn's patronage in return for helping him get elected to Congress. (*PGW* 2:151–52; *DHFFE* 2:478)

WILLARD, JOSEPH (1738–1804), a noted scientist and astronomer, graduated from Harvard in 1765 and served as a Congregational minister in Beverly, Massachusetts, from 1773 until his appointment as president of his alma mater in 1781. (*Harvard Graduates* 16:253–65)

WILLET, MARINUS (1740–1830), a wealthy New York City merchant and landowner, ran unsuccessfully as an Antifederalist for the state ratification convention. In the spring of 1790 he undertook a mission as George Washington's private envoy to the Creek Nation, leading to the Treaty of New York of August 1790. An early leader of the Revolutionary movement in New York, he began his military career as captain in the 1st Regiment of the New York Line in 1775, rising to lieutenant colonel of the 3rd Regiment in 1776 and colonel of the 5th Regiment in 1779, retiring in 1781. He became a member of the Society of the Cincinnati and served as sheriff of New York City, 1784–88. (*DHFFE* 3:425; *PGW* 5:146–47n)

WILLIAMS, ELISHA OTHO "ELIE" (ca. 1750–1823), brother of Otho Holland Williams, was a merchant of Hagerstown, Maryland. During the Revolutionary War he served as a military contractor as well as a captain of the 7th Regiment of the Maryland Line, 1776–77. He was awarded an army contract with the federal government in September 1789. (S. W. Williams,

The Genealogy and History of the Family of Williams [Greenfield, Mass., 1847], pp. 344–45)

WILLIAMS, EPHRAIM (1760–1835), of Stockbridge, Massachusetts, was admitted to the bar in 1787, having studied under Representative Sedgwick, and subsequently became his law partner and political protégé. (*Massachusetts Bar* 2:449; *Sedgwick*, p. 160)

WILLIAMS, GEORGE (1731–97), was a sea captain and merchant of Salem, Massachusetts, which he represented in the state House of Representatives, 1776–79, 1783, and 1785. (*Massachusetts Legislators*, p. 383)

WILLIAMS, JOHN FOSTER (ca. 1744–1814), of Boston, served as commander of the federal revenue cutter for Massachusetts from 1790 until his death. During the Revolutionary War he commanded various vessels of the state navy. (*PGW* 6:520n)

WILLIAMS, JONATHAN, JR. (1750–1815), a Philadelphia merchant, authored widely reprinted Federalist essays during the ratification debate. From 1776 to 1778 he was agent at Nantes, France, for the American commissioners in Paris, who included his granduncle, Benjamin Franklin. He returned to America in 1785 and spent the next several years trying to collect debts to avoid bankruptcy. (*DHROC* 16:359–60)

WILLIAMS, OTHO HOLLAND (1749–94), was collector of Baltimore, 1789–94, having served as the state's naval officer for that port since 1783. During the Revolutionary War he commanded the 6th Regiment of the Maryland Line from 1776 until his promotion to brigadier general in 1782. He resigned the next year and enrolled in the Society of the Cincinnati. He became son-in-law to Representative Smith (Md.) by his marriage to Mary "Polly" Smith in 1785; Robert and William were their infant sons at the time of the First Congress. Williams spent most of May 1789 in New York and may have contributed to the drafting of the Collection Bill [HR-6]. "Eutaw" was his estate outside Baltimore, named for the South Carolina battlefield where he distinguished himself for bravery in 1781. Williams grew up at the junction of Conococheague Creek and the Potomac River below Hagerstown, Maryland, and platted the town of Williamsport there in 1787, which he began advocating the next year as the ideal location for the permanent seat of the federal government. See also *DHFFC* 2:499, 9:47n.

WILLIAMS, SAMUEL, represented Salem, Massachusetts, in the Provincial Congress in 1775.

WILLIAMS, WILLIAM (1731–1811), was a merchant of Lebanon, Connecticut, which he served as town clerk, 1752–96, state Representative, 1780–84, and delegate to the state convention where he voted to ratify the Constitution. The 1751 Harvard graduate sat on the bench of the Windham County court, 1775–1805, in Congress, 1775–76, where he signed the Declaration of Independence, and in the state's Council of Assistants, 1784–1803. (*Harvard Graduates* 13:163–74; *DHROC* 3:613)

WILLIAMSON, MARIA APTHORPE (ca. 1766–14 October 1790), daughter of New York City merchant Charles W. Apthorpe, married Representative Williamson on 3 January 1789 and died shortly after the death of their second child. See also *DHFFC* 14:757. (*LDC* 25:484n)

WILLING, RICHARD (1745–98), of Haverford, Pennsylvania, was the younger brother of Thomas Willing and brother-in-law of Samuel Powell.

WILLING, THOMAS (1731–1821), a prominent Philadelphia merchant, was Senator Morris's business partner from 1757 until at least 1777. He attended Congress, 1775–76, and was appointed first president of the Bank of North America in 1781, resigning in 1792 to become president of the first Bank of the United States. His sister Elizabeth was married to Samuel Powell, while William Bingham and presidential aide William Jackson were his sons-in-law. See also *DHFFC* 9:193. (*PRM* 3:121n)

WILLSON, WILLIS, represented Norfolk County, Virginia, in the state House of Delegates, 1785–87 and 1788–89. (*PGW* 3:103n)

WILSON, JAMES (1742–98), a Philadelphia lawyer and land speculator, served as an associate justice of the United States Supreme Court, 1789–98, and was one of the investors who petitioned Congress on behalf of the United Land Companies of the Illinois and Wabash in March 1790. He emigrated from Scotland in 1765, studied law under John Dickinson, and became an early theorist and pamphleteer for the Revolutionary movement. He sat in Congress, 1775–77, where he signed the Declaration of Independence, 1783, and 1785–86. He served as advocate general, or France's liaison to the Confederation government, 1781–83. A leading figure at the Federal Convention and later at the state convention, where he voted to ratify the Constitution, Wilson was also a major architect of the new state constitution of 1790. He became the first professor of law at the College of Philadelphia (University of Pennsylvania) in December 1790; that winter many congressmen attended his popular lecture series on the law. See also *DHFFC* 2:537, 8:204–7, 9:100n. (*DHSCUS* 1:44–48)

WINGATE, HANNAH VEAZIE, of Stratham, New Hampshire, was the wife of Senator Wingate's cousin Joshua. (Charles E. L. Wingate, *History of the Wingate Family in England and America* [Exeter, N.H., 1886], p. 213)

WINGATE, SENATOR PAINE, family during the First Congress: his wife Eunice (1742–1843), Timothy Pickering's sister, whom he married in 1765 and who resided in Stratham, New Hampshire; and their children Mary Wiggin; Sarah, or "Sally" (1769–1808), who married Josiah Bartlett's son, Josiah, in 1792; George (1778–1852); John (1781–1831); and Elizabeth (1783–1829). (Wingate, *Wingate Family,* pp. 153–57; *PJB,* p. 382n)

WINSLOW, SAMUEL, a 1776 Harvard graduate, was a Quaker kinsman of Secretary of War Knox's wife Lucy and, like him, a co-patentee of the Waldo Patent in Maine.

WINTHROP, JAMES (1752–1821), of Cambridge, Massachusetts, was a mathematician and former librarian of Harvard, from which he graduated in 1769. He served as judge of the Middlesex County court of common pleas, 1789–1812. An author of widely reprinted Antifederalist essays during the ratification debates, he was a candidate for delegate to the state convention and, later, for Presidential Elector and Representative of the Middlesex district in the first federal election. (*DHROC* 4:439; *DHFFE* 1:532, 654–55; *Harvard Graduates* 17:317–29)

WOLCOTT, ERASTUS (1722–93), a farmer from East Windsor, Connecticut, and older brother of Lieutenant Governor Oliver Wolcott, Sr., served in the state House of Representatives, 1768–85, the Council of Assistants, 1785–90, and on the bench of the Hartford County court, 1784–89, and the state superior court, 1789–90. He resigned as a delegate to the Federal Convention, where he was replaced by Representative Sherman, but he attended the state convention and voted to ratify the Constitution. Defeated for Representative in the first federal election, he was elected a Presidential Elector in 1789. (*DHROC* 3:614; *DHFFE* 2:59)

WOLCOTT, OLIVER, SR. (1726–97), lieutenant governor of Connecticut, 1786–96, was the father of Oliver Wolcott, Jr. He graduated from Yale in 1747 and settled in Litchfield, where he practiced medicine. He sat on the council of assistants, 1771–86, in Congress, 1776–78 and 1780–83, where he signed both the Declaration of Independence and the Articles of Confederation, and in the state convention where he voted to ratify the Constitution. In the first federal election he was a Presidential Elector. (*Yale Graduates* 2:137–39; *DHROC* 3:614; *DHFFE* 2:59–60)

WOLCOTT, OLIVER, JR. (1760–1833), a Hartford lawyer and son of Connecticut's lieutenant governor, was appointed auditor of the United States treasury, 1789–91, and comptroller thereafter until his appointment as secretary of the treasury, 1795–1800. He served as commissioner for settling the state's accounts with the United States, 1787–89, and voted for the Constitution at the state convention. See also *DHFFC* 2:488. (*DHROC* 3:359)

WOOD, AARON (1719–91), town clerk of Boxford, Massachusetts, 1789–90, was a longtime colonial and state legislator. In 1788 he voted against ratification of the Constitution and the next year was appointed special justice of Essex County. (*Massachusetts Legislators*, p. 389)

WOOD, JAMES, JR. (1741–1813), brother-in-law of Representative White, was a planter on his estate "Chelsea" in Henrico County, Virginia. He served as colonel of the 12th Regiment of the Virginia Line (later redesignated the 8th Regiment) from 1776 until war's end. Frederick County elected him to the House of Delegates in 1776 and again in 1784. Thereafter he sat on the state's Executive Council until 1796, as lieutenant governor from 1790. In the first federal election he voted as a Presidential Elector. At the time of the First Congress, he served as vice president of the state's Society of the Cincinnati. (*DHFFE* 2:423)

WOOD, LEIGHTON, JR. (1740–1805), of Hanover County, Virginia, served as the state's solicitor general from 1782 until 1791, when he became a clerk in the treasury department. (Wood to Washington, 2 Feb. 1795, Washington Papers, DLC; *PJM* 2:79n)

WOOD, MARY RUTHERFORD (d. ca. 1797), was wife of James Wood, Sr. (ca. 1707–1759), founder of Winchester, Virginia. Their eldest daughter, Elizabeth (b. 1739), married Representative White sometime between 1767 and 1775. (K. G. Greene, *Winchester, Virginia, and Its Beginnings* [Strasburg, Va., 1926])

WOODWARD, JOSEPH (ca. 1758–1838), resided in Boston, Massachusetts, in 1790.

WORMELEY, RALPH, JR. (1744–1806), was a planter of Middlesex County, Virginia, which he represented in the state House of Delegates, 1788–90, and at the state convention where he voted to ratify the Constitution. (*DHROC* 9:787n)

WRAY, JACOB (d. ca. 1797), a merchant of Hampton, Virginia, served as collector of that port, 1789–90, having held the position under the state, 1781–89. See also *DHFFC* 2:555. (*PGW* 5:277n)

WYLLY, RICHARD (1744–1801), of Savannah, was appointed commissioner of loans for Georgia in 1790. See also *DHFFC* 2:494.

WYLLYS, JOHN P. (1754–90), originally of Hartford, Connecticut, was a major in the United States infantry regiment from 1785 until his death in Harmar's defeat by the Miami Indians in October 1790. During the Revolutionary War he served for a year in the state militia before being commissioned captain in Webb's Additional Continental Regiment in 1777 and major in 1778. He transferred to the 1st Regiment of the Connecticut Line in 1781 and to the 3rd Regiment briefly before retiring in 1783. See also *DHFFC* 2:488.

WYNKOOP, REPRESENTATIVE HENRY, family during the First Congress: his third wife, Sarah Newkirk, originally of Pittsgrove, New Jersey, whom he married in 1782 and who resided at "Vredens Berg," near Bucks County, Pennsylvania; daughters Christina (1763–1841), who married Reading Beatty in 1786; Anne (1765–1815), who married James Raguet in August 1790; Margaretta (b. 1768), who married Philadelphia merchant Herman J. Lombaert in November 1789; Mary Helen, or "Maria" (1772–1809); and Susannah (1784–1849); and sons Nicholas (1770–1815), John W. (1774–93), and Jonathan (1776–1842). (*Collection of Papers Read before the Bucks County Historical Society* 3[1909]:212–15)

WYNKOOP, GERARDUS (1732–1812), of Newtown, Pennsylvania, was excise officer of Bucks County, 1784–86, which he represented in the state assembly, 1778–81 and 1786–87, and in the state's House of Representatives, 1790–92. (Richard Wynkoop, *Wynkoop Genealogy in the United States of America* [New York, 1904], p. 59; George W. Corner, ed., *Autobiography of Benjamin Rush* [Princeton, N.J., 1948], p. 178n)

WYTHE, GEORGE (1726–1806), a lawyer, jurist, and first professor of law at the College of William and Mary in Williamsburg, Virginia, served as judge of the high court of chancery from 1778 until becoming chancellor of the state in 1788. He served in Congress, 1775–76, where he signed the Declaration of Independence, and in the Federal Convention, which he left before the Constitution was signed. He represented neighboring York County at the state convention, where he voted to ratify. (*DHROC* 8:529)

YARDLEY, THOMAS (d. 1794?), of lower Makefield Township, Pennsylvania, represented Bucks County at the state convention where he voted to ratify the Constitution. He was a signatory of the petition of the citizens of New Jersey and Pennsylvania, presented to Congress in August 1789, that offered Congress a federal district spanning the Delaware River around Trenton. See also *DHFFC* 8:449–52. (*PMHB* 11[1887]:274–75)

YATES, ROBERT (1738–1801), of Albany, New York, served as associate justice of the state supreme court, 1777–90, and chief justice, 1790–98. He attended the Federal Convention but left early in protest and later voted against ratifying the Constitution at the state convention. Drafted as the Federalist candidate for governor in the spring of 1789, he narrowly failed to unseat George Clinton as governor. At the same time he was a leading candidate in the state's drawn-out election for federal Senators. He was an honorary member of the Society of the Cincinnati. (*DHFFE* 3:249n, 517, 518; John P. Kaminski, *George Clinton* [Madison, Wis., 1993], pp. 188–89)

YEATES, JASPER (1745–1817), was a lawyer of Lancaster, Pennsylvania, which he represented in the state convention where he voted to ratify the Constitution. A 1761 graduate of the College of Philadelphia (University of Pennsylvania), he served as a justice of the state supreme court, 1791–1817. (*DHROC* 2:734)

YOUNG, CHARLES, was a Philadelphia merchant and certificate speculator. (*DHFFC* 9:396n; *PRM* 3:119n)

YOUNG, JAMES, resided in Baltimore at the time he traveled to New York to petition President Washington for a job in July 1789. He was trained in the mercantile field by Thomas Mifflin. The census lists individuals of his name residing in both Charles and Queen Annes counties, Maryland, in 1790. (*PGW* 3:238–39)

No.	Short Title	Long Title	Date Introduced	Date Signed by President
		FIRST SESSION: March 4, 1789–SEPTEMBER 29, 1789		
1	OATH	A Bill to regulate the taking the oath or affirmation prescribed by the sixth article of the Constitution An Act to regulate the time and manner of administering certain oaths	Apr. 14	June 1
2	IMPOST	An Act for laying a duty on goods, wares, and merchandizes, imported into the United States	May 5	July 4
3	COLLECTION	A Bill for collecting duties on goods, wares, and merchandizes, imported into the United States	May 8	Tabled—HR See [HR–6]
4	No bill so numbered			
5	TONNAGE	An Act imposing duties on tonnage	May 25	July 20
6	COLLECTION	A Bill to regulate the collection of duties, imposed on goods, wares, and merchandizes, imported into the United States	May 27	Recommitted See [HR–11]
7	WAR DEPARTMENT	An Act to establish an Executive Department, to be denominated the Department of War	June 2	Aug. 7
8	FOREIGN AFFAIRS	An Act for establishing an Executive Department, to be denominated the Department of Foreign Affairs	June 2	July 27
9	TREASURY	A Bill to establish an Executive Department, to be denominated the Treasury Department An Act to establish the Treasury Department	June 4	Sept. 2

No.	Short Title	Long Title	Date Introduced	Date Signed by President
10	COPYRIGHT (AND PATENTS)	A Bill to promote the progress of science and useful arts, by securing to authors and inventors the exclusive right to their respective writings and discoveries	June 23	Postponed— HR
11	COLLECTION	A Bill to regulate the collection of duties imposed on goods, wares, and merchandizes, imported into the United States	June 29	July 31
		An Act to regulate the collection of the duties imposed by law on the tonnage of ships or vessels, and on goods, wares, and merchandizes, imported into the United States		
12	LIGHTHOUSES	A Bill for the Establishment and support of lighthouses, beacons, and buoys; and for authorising the several states to provide and regulate pilots	July 1	Aug. 7
		An Act for the establishment and support of Light-Houses, Beacons, and Buoys		
		An Act for the Establishment and support of Light-Houses, Beacons, Buoys, and Public Piers		
13	SETTLEMENT OF ACCOUNTS	An Act for settling the accounts between the United States and individual States	July 16	Aug. 5
14	NORTHWEST TERRITORY	An Act to provide for the government of the territory north west of the River Ohio	July 16	Aug. 7
15	COMPENSATION	An Act for allowing [making] a compensation to the President and Vice President of the United States	July 22	Sept. 24

No.	Short Title	Long Title	Date Introduced	Date Signed by President
16	COASTING	A Bill for registering and clearing vessels, ascertaining their tonnage, and for regulating the coasting trade An Act for registering and clearing Vessels, regulating the Coasting Trade, and for other purposes	July 24	Sept. 1
17	LAND OFFICE	A Bill establishing a Land Office in and for the Western Territory	July 31	Postponed—HR
18	RECORDS	A Bill to provide for the safekeeping of the acts, records, and seal of the United States; for the due publication of the acts of Congress; for the authentication of copies of records; for making out, and recording commissions, and prescribing their form, and for establishing the fees of office to be taken for making such commissions, and for copies of records and papers An Act to provide for the safekeeping of the Acts, Records, and Seal of the United States, and for other Purposes	July 31	Sept. 31
19	SALARIES-LEGISLATIVE	An Act for allowing compensation to the members of the Senate and House of Representatives of the United States, and to the officers of both Houses	Aug. 4	Sept. 22
20	INDIAN TREATIES	An Act providing for the Expenses which may attend Negotiations or Treaties with the Indian Tribes, and the Appointment of Commissioners for managing the same	Aug. 10	Aug. 20

No.	Short Title	Long Title	Date Introduced	Date Signed by President
21	SALARIES-EXECUTIVE	An Act for establishing the Salaries of the Executive Officers of Government, with their Assistants and Clerks	Aug. 24	Sept. 11
22	HOSPITALS AND HARBORS	A Bill providing for the establishment of hospitals for the relief of sick and disabled seamen, and prescribing regulations for the harbours of the United States	Aug. 27	Postponed—HR
23	COLLECTION	An Act to suspend part [obliging vessels bound up the Potomac to stop at St. Mary's or Yeocomico, to report a manifest of their cargoes] of an Act, entitled, "An Act to regulate the Collection of the Duties imposed by Law on the Tonnage of Ships or Vessels, and on Goods, Wares, and Merchandizes, imported into the United States"	Aug. 28	Sept. 16
24	TONNAGE	A Bill for suspending the operations of part of an Act, entitled "An Act imposing duties on tonnage"	Sept. 9	Not passed—S See [HR–23]
25	SEAT OF GOVERNMENT	An Act to establish the Seat of Government of the United States	Sept. 14	Postponed—S
26	COLLECTION	An Act for amending part of an Act, entitled, "An Act to regulate the Collection of the Duties imposed by Law on the Tonnage of Ships or Vessels and on Goods, Wares, and Merchandizes, imported into the United States"	Sept. 17	Not passed—S

No.	Short Title	Long Title	Date Introduced	Date Signed by President
27	TROOPS	An Act to recognize and adapt to the Constitution of the United States, the establishment of the Troops raised under the Resolves of the United States in Congress assembled, and for other Purposes therein mentioned	Sept. 17	Sept. 29
28	SALARIES-JUDICIARY	An Act for allowing certain Compensation to the Judges of the Supreme and other Courts, and to the Attorney General of the United States	Sept. 17	Sept. 23
29	INVALID PENSIONERS	An Act providing for the payment of the invalid Pensioners of the United States	Sept. 18	Sept. 29
30	SLAVE TRADE	A Bill concerning the importation of certain persons prior to the year 1808	Sept. 19	Postponed—HR
31	TIME OF MEETING	A Bill to alter the time of the annual meeting of Congress An Act to alter the Time for the next meeting of Congress	Sept. 21	Sept. 29
32	APPROPRIATIONS	An Act making appropriations for the service of the present year	Sept. 21	Sept. 29
33	COASTING	An Act to explain and amend an Act, entitled, "An Act for registering and clearing Vessels, regulating the Coasting Trade, and for other Purposes"	Sept. 23	Sept. 29

No.	Short Title	Long Title	Date Introduced	Date Signed by President

FIRST SESSION: MARCH 4, 1789–SEPTEMBER 29, 1789

No.	Short Title	Long Title	Date Introduced	Date Signed by President
1	JUDICIARY	An Act to establish the Judicial Courts of the United States	June 12	Sept. 24
2	PUNISHMENT OF CRIMES	An Act for the punishment of certain crimes against the United States	July 28	Postponed—HR
3	POST OFFICE	An Act for the temporary establishment of the Post-Office	Sept. 11	Sept. 22
4	COURTS	An Act to regulate Processes in the Courts of the United States	Sept. 17	Sept. 29
5	GLAUBECK	An Act to allow the Baron de Glaubeck the Pay of a Captain in the Army of the United States	Sept. 24	Sept. 29

INDEX

The contents of volumes 15–17 make up part of the single richest documentary archive on the history of the founding period, an archive gathered over the last half of the twentieth century for the documentary histories of the Ratification of the Constitution and of the First Federal Congress (FFC). The index that follows has been compiled with the aim of providing access to the wide variety of information to be found there. For example, the editors have indexed as broadly as possible all references to newspaper articles and their distribution, in order to trace the manner and paths by which information was reported throughout the United States in 1789. Similarly, this index reveals much about how correspondence was transmitted in the late eighteenth century. (Because there were so many instances of letters that were hand carried, this was not indexed. Readers should use the location notes to find this information.)

The correspondence of members of the FFC transcends regional or even national significance, and offers perspectives on the social, economic, cultural, and intellectual, no less than the political and constitutional, history of the period. The complexity necessarily involved in such an undertaking has been reduced by certain space- and time-saving arrangements that bear pointing out.

- Constituent relations—embracing in a most direct way citizens' expectations of their government—constitutes an especially large and challenging theme for indexing. "Constituent" is understood to include "correspondent," even when the correspondent in question is not a constituent per se. The following subentries under members' "constituent relations" specify the type of services relating to office seeking: "recommends office seekers" refers only to recommendations supplied directly to the executive branch (typically either George Washington or Tobias Lear); "supports office seeker" refers to informal expressions of support; and "as reference" refers to instances where the member appears in someone's list of references. Instances of a member discussing an application for office, or the appointment process, are indexed under the member's name as the subentry "and recommendations for office."
- Entries under First Federal Congress, House of Representatives, and Senate relate to general and organizational references to those bodies, while most references relating to their deliberations and actions on a particular topic will be found under the name of the subject.
- In recognition of the nuances of eighteenth century language and the

evolution of constitutional terms, index entries employ original wording as nearly as possible (e.g., Union, as distinct from United States).

• Because of his unique constitutional standing in the Senate, John Adams is treated as a member of Congress in all cases except constituent relations.

• The subentry "opinion on" is provided only for members. When a member's opinion is related second-hand, it is indexed as a distinct subentry (e.g., "and molasses duty").

• Individuals who later became members of the FFC, such as Hugh Williamson of North Carolina, are treated as members.

• The subentry "role" refers only to activities actually performed (e.g., political negotiations, voting, and committee service) relating to FFC business.

• Writers and recipients are specified by name under "letters to" and "letters from" only in the case of members, high level government officials (e.g., John Jay), and other non-members with copious correspondence (e.g., Tench Coxe).

• The subentry "relations with" is interpreted broadly to include friendly ties, conversations, etc. Names are specified only when the relations are between members or members and high level government officials (e.g., Thomas Jefferson).

• The entry "[*a state or section*] delegation" is used to indicate an unspecified number, or all, of a state's or section's Representatives or Senators in the FFC. There is an implied cross reference from every individual member to his respective state's delegation.

• The subentry "correspondence" under an individual's name indicates letters that are mentioned, as opposed to printed, excerpted, or calendared.

• The subentries "debate" and "role" override "opinion" under a member's name when they cover the same pages.

• Places take their present state name (e.g., Maine).

• Printed works (books, plays, and pamphlets) are indexed under their author, when known.

• Daily weather entries do not include the accounts that are printed in the heading of most days' printed correspondence.

• FFC, FFE, and NYC are used as abbreviations, when possible, for the First Federal Congress, the First Federal Elections, and New York City.

• New York City place names are indexed under New York City.

In addition to those interns and volunteers acknowledged in the introduction, the following individuals assisted with the preparation of this index: Kathleen Bartoloni, LeeAnn Chaves, Johnna Flahive, Courtney Janes, Jennifer Kenyan, Brett Levanto, Steve Rogers, and John Ragosta.

168, 283–84, 376, 775; writings of, 65. *See also* Amendments to the Constitution; *names of places*

Apothecaries, 1783, 1787

Appleton, Nathaniel: bio, 1754; letters to and from, 65, 95, 292, 506–9; office for, 65

Appleton, Nathaniel Walker, 333, 593, 916; bio, 1754

Apportionment: Amendment to the Constitution on, 725, 743, 749, 755, 775, 783, 1100, 1499; fair, 1396

Appropriations: military, limits on, 122; none expected, 1085; potential for discord over, 373–74; too high, 1427

Appropriations Act [HR-32], 1120, 1478, 1629, 1725, 1726

April Fool's Day, 183

Aquasco, Md., letter sent from, 981

Arbitrage, 1180

Archer, Abraham: bio, 1754; office for, lxxii, 987, 988, 1031, 1199, 1201; recommends office seeker, 1201

Architecture, 144; American, 34, 109; classical orders, 32, 33, 34, 35; comments on, 28, 42, 46, 48, 54, 194

Archives. *See* Congress, Confederation, papers; Congress, Continental, papers; Federal records; House, journals; Senate, journals

Aristides, 1080, 1083

Aristocracy: compared to democracy, 1063, 1592, 1593; and the Constitution, 658, 738, 812, 997–98, 1063, 1120, 1138; counter weight to king, 1653; dangers of, 641, 657–58, 1111, 1268; elective, 193; fear of President, 871; formation of, 479; hereditary favored, 1124; hereditary opposed, 701; in New York State, 82; perceptions of, 1008, 1333; President as balance to, 871; rejected, 495; and republics, 1054; Senate as, 371, 730, 792, 1063, 1080, 1268, 1654; as slavery, 657–58; strength of, 1553; suppression of, 197; tendency toward, 114, 841, 1119, 1196; threat of, 318, 436, 612; and titles, 542, 544; tools of, 1734; unlimited, 1560; in U.S., 1062, 1063, 1124; wise and virtuous, 727. *See also* Nobility

Arlington (Fairfax) Co., Va., residents, 1887

Arminianism (Jacobus Harmenson), 386, 388

Arms, right to bear: Amendment to the Constitution on, 749, 755, 989–90, 1510; defense against despotism, 1655; obviates need for standing army, 1655

Arms (heraldic) of the U.S., 22, 32, 35, 412. *See also* Seals

Armstrong, James, bio, 1754–55

Armstrong, John, Jr.: bio, 1755; letters to and from, 214–15, 480–81, 1669–70; office for, lxxv; relations with Daniel Huger, 481

Army, Continental, 368; characterized, 550, 898, 1373; civilian service in, 1114–15; commander in chief, 1900–1901; compared to British army, 79; condition, 118; disbandment, 1049; Flying Battalion, 1069; franking, xx; land bounties for, 487, 616, 807–8, 864, 933, 1776; members in, 281; military knowledge from, 1317; mutinies, 981, 1050, 1428; officers, 961, 1517, 1538; officers, foreign, 47, 498; pay, 551, 824, 1719; petition of officers and soldiers of, 477; quartermaster department, 127, 238, 839; service in. *See* Biographical Gazetteer; supplies for, 901, 1524, 1834, 1893. *See also* Public creditors, veterans; Society of the Cincinnati; Veterans

Army, federal: appointments to, lxxiv–lxxv, 1412, 1760, 1772; appropriations for, 169, 721, 1536, 1629; carried over from Confederation period, 1663; command of, 1873; conduct criticized, 1700, 1704; contracts for, 1907; courts martial, 1412; European powers and, 1317; expenses, 176; foreign born in, 1412; garrisons, 901, 1256, 1275, 1707; and Indians, southern, 747, 1467–68; interests, 1218; justice for, 1218; Kentucky and, 1524; mutinies, 1428; need for, 641, 842, 940; in Northwest Territory, 485, 945, 975, 1445; pay, 424, 864, 943, 1218, 1596; quartermaster, 1814; responsibilities, 901; service in, 1789, 1793, 1798, 1809, 1843, 1851, 1874, 1912; size of, 901, 1036, 1275, 1524, 1591, 1708; state quotas, 713; supplies for, 1059, 1231, 1337, 1383, 1546. *See also* Military Establishment; Office seeking, military

Army, standing: Amendment to the Constitution on, 1413, 1507, 1516, 1542; to enforce obedience, 1320, 1654; importance

Lear, Tobias (*cont'd*)
　from Parker, Josiah, 1496
　from Partridge, George, 1147–48
　from Stone, Michael Jenifer, 1419–20
Learned, Amasa, 399, 451; bio, 1829; letter
　from, 1429
Leather: duty, 449; importation of, 108, 292;
　manufacture of, 106
Lebanon, Conn.: letter addressed to, 395; mer-
　chants, 1893, 1909
Lebanon, Pa., physicians, 1886
Lebanon Valley, N.J., letter sent from, 237
LeCoutre, John, Indian attack on, 752
Ledyard, John, death of, 1139
Lee, Mr. (not a member), 864
Lee, Arthur, 1600, 1626; bio, 1829; on board of
　treasury, 491; letters from, 256, 343–44,
　417, 491–93, 530–31, 1093, 1165, 1235–
　37, 1422–23, 1555–56, 1600; lodgings,
　308; office for, 1165, 1497; office seekers
　and, 571, 1556, 1596; reception of Wash-
　ington, 331; regards to, 1419; and titles,
　594
Lee, Charles (1731–82), as traitor, 961
Lee, Charles (Alexandria, Va.): bio, 1830; letters
　to and from, 256, 717, 854, 1093, 1126,
　1241, 1412–13, 1558, 1687; office for,
　lxxi, 717, 926, 1126, 1146, 1220, 1241; as
　reference, 926
Lee, Francis Lightfoot: bio, 1830; letters to,
　491–93, 1422–23, 1532–33
Lee, Henry "Light-Horse Harry": articles au-
　thored by, 1701; bio, 1830; correspon-
　dence, 263; letters to and from, 46, 65,
　246, 376, 576–77, 743–45, 1490–92,
　1667–68, 1718; recommends office seeker,
　263, 577, 1147, 1201; as reliable news
　source, 1700; in Revolution, 961
Lee, John: bio, 1830; office for, lxx, 1203
Lee, Nancy, and father, 717
Lee, Richard Bland: arrival, 60, 66, 71, 77; char-
　acterized, 263, 577; and congressional pay,
　683, 693, 1210; considers resigning, 1644;
　correspondence, 146, 259, 403, 866; debate
　on Judiciary Act [S-1], 1573–74; federal-
　ism of, 147; letters in newspapers, 1107;
　papers, xvi; regards to, 164; relations with
　James Madison, 1644, 1667; return home,
　1667; seeks consulship, 1644; self charac-

terization, 951–52; social life, 699, 1060;
　travel, 3, 39, 42, 136, 263
—constituent relations
　correspondents referred to for news, 1667
　forwards *Congressional Register,* 953
　forwards newspapers, 763, 866, 1513
　inquiries about individuals, 1600
　recommends office seeker, 926, 1161–62,
　　1503
　as reference, 788
　solicited for office, 38, 263
　solicits opinion, 146
　transacts business, 146
—letters from
　to Lee, Charles, 1558
　to Lee, Theodorick, 1302, 1513–14
　to Madison, James, 1644
　to Powell, Leven, 146, 259, 403, 762–63,
　　866–67, 951–53
　to Stuart, David, 698–99
　to Temple, John, 1600
　to Washington, George, 926, 1161–62, 1503
—letters to
　from Blackburn, Thomas, 1162
　from Gilpin, George, 1452–54
　from Lee, Charles, 717
　from Lee, Henry, 576–77
—opinion on
　adjournment, 1302, 1558
　Amendments to the Constitution, 146, 763
　Judiciary Act [S-1], 699, 953
　revenue system, 259, 403, 698, 699, 763,
　　1558
　salaries, 699
　seat of government, 403, 1513–14, 1558
　titles, presidential, 951–52
—private life
　family, 1830
　law practice, 1514
　lodgings, 309, 1739, 1785
—role
　Judiciary Act [S-1], 1573
　rules, 201, 372
　Seat of Government Bill [HR-25], 1487, 1574
Lee, Richard Henry: arrival, 197, 200–201, 202,
　204–5, 206, 209, 212, 256; attendance, 1,
　67, 241; candidate for president pro tem-
　pore, 212; characterized, 422, 424, 571,
　793, 831, 1032, 1410, 1553; correspon-

dence, 928, 1027–28, 1410; election, 619;
interview with George Beckwith, 1728;
letter carried by Joe, 1687; and office seeking, 1372; papers, xv, xvi; regards from,
344; return home, 1687; in Revolution,
644; and Rhode Island delegation, 423;
and seat of government, 617; self character-
ization, 359, 644, 1321; supports office
seeker, 570; and trade discrimination, 639,
664; travel, 183, 196, 199, 206, 208, 211;
visits, 241; and the West, 639, 644–45
—constituent relations
   forwards information, 644, 1626
   forwards Judiciary Act [S-1], 928
   forwards letters, 164, 371
   franking, 1600
   recommendations for office, 1146–47
   as reference, 609, 753, 788, 971, 1053
   solicited for office, 234, 235, 299, 434, 565,
      617, 643
   supports office seekers, 299, 502, 617, 717,
      1321
   transacts business, 343, 378–79
—letters from
   to Adams, Samuel, 358–59, 501–2, 1320–21,
      1713
   to Chase, Samuel, 505
   to Henry, Patrick, 643–44, 1541–43,
      1625–26
   to Lee, Charles, 256, 717, 854, 1126, 1241,
      1412–13, 1687
   to Lee, Francis L., 1532–33
   to Lee, Henry, 376
   to Lloyd, Edward, 570
   to Lovell, James, 299–300
   to Madison, James, 557
   to Mathews, Thomas, 1634–35
   to Page, Mann, Jr., 811, 854, 1537
   to Parker, Richard, 803, 816
   to Randolph, Beverley, 634, 1635
   to Shippen, William, Jr., 1237
   to Washington, George, 208–9, 1146–47,
      1209–10
—letters to
   from Adams, Samuel, 313, 1027–28, 1386–
      87, 1418–19
   from Bourn, Silvanus, 300
   from Brown, Nicholas, 422–24
   from Bryan, George, 1179–80

from Chase, Samuel, 434, 565–66, 916–17,
   1039–40
from Galloway, David, 378–79
from Gerry, Elbridge, 235, 241–42
from Henry, Patrick, 1410
from Livingston, Anne, 617
from Lloyd, Edward, 570
from Page, Mann, Jr., 1111–12
from Parker, Richard, 967–69
from Pinckney, Charles, 164
from Sullivan, James, 249–50
from Washington, George, 1220–21
—opinion on
   adjournment, 1543
   advice and consent, nominations, 643, 717
   Amendments to the Constitution, 359, 502,
      644, 1320–21, 1413, 1532, 1541–42,
      1543, 1625, 1626, 1634–35
   appointments, 1625–26
   Creek treaty, 1542
   federalism, 359, 1320
   foreign relations, 644–45
   government, 644
   power of removal, 1069, 1321, 1625
   Punishment of Crimes Bill [S-2], 1413
   ratification of Constitution, 1626
   revenue system, 638–39, 1126, 1413
   salaries, 1626
   Seat of Government Bill [HR-25], 1413, 1533
—private life
   family, 256, 1829, 1830, 1831, 1833, 1879
   health, 66, 417, 1146, 1220–21, 1320, 1387,
      1419, 1422, 1543
   household management, 717, 1687
   legal affairs, 1492
   lodgings, xxiii, 308, 1742, 1754
—relations with
   Dalton, Tristram, 1419
   Otis, Samuel A., 234
   Sherman, Roger, 1320
   unnamed members, 423
   Washington, George, 717
—role
   advice and consent, nominations, 831
   Amendments to the Constitution, 759, 1413,
      1507
   appointments, 1220, 1237, 1321
   inauguration of President, 410
   Judiciary Act [S-1], 1543

Madison, James (*cont'd*)

on appointments, 571, 617, 1497, 1555, 1606

disagreement with, 1727

drafts and reviews addresses, 458, 584, 1241

forwards letter to, 1674

House reply to inaugural, 493

influence with, 571, 731, 1267

memorandums for, 1679–80

queried by, 532–33, 1136, 1240–41, 1497–98

receives document from, 520–26, 764

support from, 676

—role

Amendments to the Constitution, 454, 494, 501–2, 644, 676, 680, 723, 731, 740, 742, 745, 748–49, 755, 757, 759, 766, 775, 782, 819, 878, 879, 894, 923, 1101, 1105, 1213, 1289, 1310–12, 1324, 1356, 1455, 1498–99, 1526

Collection Act [HR-11], 1126

Courts Act [S-4], 1673

funding for congressional wards, 1118

Judiciary Act [S-1], 1156, 1158, 1573

power of removal, 866

revenue system, 221, 446, 492, 520, 530, 565, 879, 914, 1723, 1727

rules, 201–2

seat of government, 1475, 1487, 1526, 1574, 1619, 1665, 1668, 1672

Virginia's accounts with federal government, 324

Madison, James, Rev.: bio, 1839; letters to and from, 2, 293, 458, 1169, 1321–23; recommends office seeker, 458, 1030, 1202; regards to, 503; on surveying commission, 469

Madison, James, Sr.: bio, 1839; letter to, 953–54

Madison, William: bio, 1839; loses election, 447

Madrid, as capital, 172

Magna Carta, 724, 1329, 1330, 1368–69

Mahogany ware, manufacture of, 106

Mail: British packet, 775; contracts, 1782; delivery, 49; delivery to chambers, xxii, 845, 1244, 1408, 1416; miscarried, 98, 164, 168, 253, 1003, 1514; newspaper distribution, 356, 1361; and notification of Washington, 86; private conveyance, 768, 1183, 1451, 1551; problems posting, 1484; schedules, xxii, 48, 98, 133, 402–3, 425, 457, 694, 1339; sealing wax, 354; signifi-

cance of, 1681; size limits, 1095; speed of, 430, 547, 1325, 1410; theft, 287, 855, 1414, 1736; unreliability, xxii, 495, 499, 518, 1185, 1281; western, 1524. *See also* Frank; Post office

Maine: Antifederalists, 472, 785, 1758; counties, 399, 400; courts, state, 595, 1141, 1176, 1181; diet, 356, 358, 491; economy, 356, 357, 595, 655, 729; effect on location of seat of government, 186; egalitarianism, 989; Federalists, 472; federal office in, 102; FFE, xiii, 789; geography, 910, 1419; land investments in, 6; postal system, 566; poverty, 1293; religion, 988; revenue system, federal, lxix–lxx, 603, 622, 666, 667, 715, 716, 748, 804, 1102, 1293; revenue system, state, 715; second federal election, 65, 1262; settlement, 1293, 1904; smuggling, 910, 1277, 1301; state elections, 595; statehood, 87, 400, 667, 681, 729; Sullivan, James, influence in, 1130; and Thatcher, George, 64–65; trade, 357–58, 387, 770, 1293, 1425; weather, 44, 357, 555. *See also* Massachusetts; *names of places*

—courts, federal

joined with New Hampshire, 624, 909–10, 966, 1073, 1230

officials, lxxiii, 1182, 1302, 1546, 1609, 1617, 1787, 1833, 1877

—public opinion on

conduct of Representatives, 654

quorum, 566

revenue system, 426, 435, 530, 654, 655, 747, 1293

salaries, 842

Majorities, 54, 124, 125, 724, 1478

Malcolm, William, 367; bio, 1839; and reception of Adams, 302

Malt, duty on, 372

Manifests, cargo, 715, 716, 740, 1048

Manigault, Gabriel: bio, 1839; letters to, 718, 729

Mankind: all one blood, 466; betterment of, 631

Manliness. *See* Masculinity

Manners: cultivation of, 1055, 1166; depravity of, 793; diversity of, 1320

Manning, James, 424, 859; attends House debates, 607; bio, 1839–40; letters from, 606–7, 1430, 1504, 1514–15; and Rhode Island petitions, 606–7, 1504, 1515

Nourse, Mrs., 1374
Nourse, John: bio, 1852; letters from, 395, 562
Nourse, Joseph: attends House debates, 1463; bio, 1852; diary, 1463; office for, lxxiii, 1547, 1548
Nova Scotia, Canada: boundary, 768–69; federal army garrison near, 901; smuggling, 910; ties to U.S., 735; trade with, 490, 1345, 1365, 1437, 1520
Nullification, 567

Oath Act [HR-1]: effect of, 1661; enforcement, 850, 932; need for, 360–61; passed, 620, 644, 729, 731, 774, 782, 795–96; sent to constituents, 1092; signed by President, 720, 972
Oaths and affirmations: Antifederalists take, 1405; and citizenship, 671, 746, 1712; effect of, 1664; essay on, 513; exemptions from, 1052; false, 1437; inadequacy, 408, 769, 1326; judicial, 626, 855, 928, 930, 938, 1175; loyalty, 446, 447, 608, 672; by members, 189, 214, 243, 1397, 1661; need for, 360–61; presidential, 332, 343, 344, 375, 396, 404, 411, 414, 417; private, 1495; religious scruples about, 855, 930, 1283; and revenue system, 203, 204, 290, 291, 298, 389, 769, 1180, 1220, 1425; state officials take, 351, 1003–4, 1086, 1092, 1122, 1244, 1498, 1519, 1602, 1618, 1897
O'Brien, Michael Morgan: bio, 1852; office seeking letter from, 453; and ratification of the Constitution, 1738
Oconee River, Ga., treaty site, 1468
Office holders, federal: attitudes toward France, 1658–59; conduct, 1134; dignity of, 659, 712; entertained by President, 1219; general interest and, 720; give tone to government, 746, 782; good intentions, 705; high quality, 640–41, 1168; incorruptible, 267; insolence, 778, 1403; names sent to constituents, 1296, 1536, 1588, 1636, 1637, 1642; pay, 124, 150, 151, 1120, 1533, 1536; proliferation, 49, 530, 647, 744, 1120, 1352; promises of, 1527; public opinion on, 530, 744, 1211, 1235, 1429; recess appointments, 1267, 1725, 1726; residency requirement, 717; state interests

and, 719, 1626; and state office, 562, 610, 838. See also Revenue officers
—tenure, 893, 1268, 1282
See also Power of removal
Office holders, state: criteria for, 1427; role in ratification, 1731, 1735; should favor state over federal interests, 1626
Office holding: ambition and, 610, 844; burdensome, 1719; multiple, 151, 562, 1328; and partisanship, 1128; and private affairs, 1101, 1719; reflect principles of the government, 1156; scarcity of qualified candidates, 782; and sectionalism, 200. See also Appointments to office; Nepotism; Public service; Rotation in office; Sinecures
Office holding, qualifications for, 131, 712–13, 877; ability, 235, 574, 1007, 1130, 1139–40, 1198, 1202, 1204, 1205, 1208, 1211, 1248, 1526; age, 239, 793, 1162, 1227, 1242, 1426; American birth, 234, 241, 1227; attachment to U.S., 1160; avoid disgrace, 1243; best qualified, 5; business failure, 1147, 1163; businessman, 1426; capacity, 1202, 1205, 1319, 1552; congressional judgment, 231, 241, 1307; diligence, 1147; education, 242, 1065, 1130, 1131, 1182, 1203, 1227, 1402, 1451, 1546, 1562, 1604; expectation, 1208, 1358; experience, 230–38 passim, 242, 717, 818, 908, 909, 926, 998, 1065, 1130, 1162, 1202, 1203, 1208, 1227, 1366, 1402, 1426, 1513, 1562, 1598, 1604, 1632; familiarity with people, 1281, 1426, 1630; familiar with state government, 1426; family connections, 207, 234, 239, 242, 1007, 1607; family support, 49, 239, 1138, 1163, 1204, 1231; Federalist, 488, 844, 858, 1078, 1130, 1163, 1182, 1205, 1384, 1625–26; financial need, xviii, 235–42 passim, 389, 390, 459, 567–68, 570, 1006, 1027, 1083, 1147, 1178, 1205, 1231, 1232, 1394, 1400, 1563, 1607; fiscal responsibility, 131; fitness, 1182, 1203, 1205; friend of Washington, 1163; gentility, 1107, 1147, 1204, 1708; geographic distribution, 1242, 1274, 1303, 1324–25, 1497, 1513, 1526–27, 1600, 1637; good citizen, 1204; health and stamina, 1146, 1148, 1162, 1179, 1219, 1426, 1605, 1606; human rights advocate, 24; incum-

Piers, public. *See* Docks

Pigs, 135

Pike, Nicholas: bio, 1861; and copyrights, 621, 1360; letters to and from, 621, 753, 808, 1067–68; petition of, 808, 1861

Pike, William: bio, 1861–62; letters to and from, 1398

Pilots, ship, 524, 1043

Pinckney, Charles, Gov.: bio, 1862; in Confederation Congress, 572; letters from, 140–41, 164, 278; recommends office seeker, 1199

Pinckney, Charles Cotesworth: bio, 1862; at Federal Convention, 1285; letters to and from, 342, 832, 1685; mail forwarded to, 831; office for, 1618; oration, 961

Pinckney, Thomas: bio, 1862; office for, lxxiv, 1618

Pineapples, 1414

Pine tree, as symbol, 561

Pintard, Abigail, letter to, 256

Pintard, Eliza, member resides with, 860

Pintard, John Marsden: bio, 1862–63; characterized, 1285; members reside with, 439, 1741

Pintard, Major, 302

Piracy, 1254; trials for, 143, 571–72, 1142, 1372, 1718. *See also* Bottomry

Piscataqua River, N.H., 399

Piscataway, Md., 1412–13

Pitfield, Benjamin: bio, 1863; office seeking letter from, 598

Pitt, William "the Elder," 651, 1038, 1646; bio, 1863

Pitt, William "the Younger," 109, 110, 632, 744, 1593; bio, 1863

Pittsburgh, Pa., 135, 1021, 1453; key to the West, 1570–72; letter sent from, 964; newspaper articles printed at, 50, 1233; newspaper articles reprinted at, 773, 1368; physicians, 1761; post road, 1714

Pittsburgh Gazette, items printed in, 50, 1233

Pittsfield, Mass.: letters sent from, 964, 1143, 1300; newspaper article reprinted at, 212; public opinion, 1142–43; residents, 1895

Pittston, Me., letter sent from, 1302

Plaintain, Marcus, bugler, 1681

Planters: as members, xix, 729; revenue burden on, 597. *See also names of places*

Plato, 585, 1063, 1064

Platt, Richard: bio, 1863; letters from, 73, 153;

members reside with, 153, 1740; and Ohio Company, 41

Playing cards, duty on, 816

Plays: playwrights, 1900; political use of, 691–93, 944, 1553. *See also* Theaters

Pleasants, Thomas, Jr.: bio, 1863; letter from, 46; recommends office seeker, 1202

Plowden, Edmund, letter from, 899

Plumb, William: bio, 1863; letter from, 858

Plutarch, 626

Plymouth, Mass.: bio, 1786; collector, lxx, 753, 1147, 1198, 1901; letters sent from, 8, 289, 803, 922, 1384, 1409, 1718; residents, 1821, 1883, 1900, 1901; revenue officers, state, 922

Pocomoke River, Md., state collection district, 605–6

Poetry: on Amendments to the Constitution, 1087–89; on Federal Hall, 32; by members, 261, 614; on seat of government, 1427–29; on titles, 614–15, 1110, 1553; on Vice President, 447, 1433, 1522

Point of Fork (Columbia), Va.: fort at, 53; state revenue officer, 1204

Point of Rocks (Noland's Ferry), Md., 177

Poisoning, legitimacy of, 1411

Poland, king of, 1062

Politicians: characterized, 611, 636, 972, 1273, 1320, 1702; comments on, 128, 635; criticized, 589, 711, 722, 936, 1461, 1683

Politics: characterized, 7, 10, 39, 150, 517, 548–49, 1458; practice of, 92, 513, 514, 1553; role of surnames, 168; science of, 516, 1273. *See also* Public service

Pollard, Benjamin, office for, 1031

Pollard, Thomas: bio, 1863; office for, 85, 1202

Polluck, Isaac, boarding house, 1467, 1740

Pomfret, Conn., letters to and from, 1024, 1101

Poole, Joseph: bio, 1863; office for, 103, 434

Poor, The. *See* Social classes, poor

Pope, Alexander, quoted, 10, 868

Pope, Edward: bio, 1863; office for, lxix, 1126

"Poplar Grove," Kent Co., Del., letter sent from, 640

Poplar Run, Pa., 1570–71

Popular sovereignty. *See* Sovereignty

Population growth, 2, 165, 175, 210, 399, 436, 463, 486, 669, 918, 1117, 1475, 1478, 1584

to Mayhew, Elizabeth, 1246
to Sedgwick, Eliza, 591, 810
to Sedgwick, Pamela, 810, 821–22, 867, 922,
 958–59, 999, 1019–20, 1076, 1098–99,
 1114, 1212, 1255–56, 1313, 1361
to Van Schaack, Henry, 1017, 1146
to Van Schaack, Peter, 822, 1537, 1681
to Williams, Ephraim, 780, 817, 919
—letters to
from Ames, Fisher, 1487, 1671–73
from Benson, George, 869
from Dwight, Thomas, 813–14, 1138–39,
 1225–26, 1460–61
from Dwight, Timothy, 994
from Henshaw, Samuel, 687–88, 721, 777–
 78, 880, 1160, 1183–84, 1312, 1406,
 1447
from Lincoln, Benjamin, 850–51, 1011–12,
 1087, 1276, 1345–46
from Livingston, John R., 230–31
from Sedgwick, Pamela, 839–40, 973–74,
 991, 1013–14, 1129, 1246, 1309, 1374–
 75, 1394–95
from Van Schaack, Henry, 962–64, 1076–77,
 1093, 1142–43, 1299–1300
—opinion on
adjournment, 1099, 1232, 1396
Amendments to the Constitution, 461–62,
 1075–76, 1310, 1361
appointments, 1264
assumption of state debts, 442, 880, 911,
 1075, 1263–64, 1319
Creek Treaty, 1310
FFC, 809
judiciary, 780, 1460
power of removal, 809, 822, 919, 1255
public service, 911, 958–59
revenue system, 911, 1210–11
salaries, 911, 1075, 1114, 1142, 1255
seat of government, 1397
sectionalism, 1114
sexuality, 822
tonnage discrimination, 919
Washington, George, 999, 1098
—private life
business affairs, 1672
child rearing, 810, 1098, 1099
exercise, 1020, 1076
family, 822, 840, 880, 959, 991, 999, 1076,

1129, 1226, 1246, 1256, 1309, 1395,
 1406, 1791, 1815, 1876
finances, 919
health, 809, 810, 821, 839, 974, 999, 1020,
 1076, 1129, 1374, 1537, 1672
homesickness, 822, 1361
homestead, 1077, 1099
household management, 1098, 1114, 1395
law practice, xix, 834, 919, 1020, 1114,
 1256, 1313, 1374, 1816, 1906, 1908
lodgings, 810, 974, 1020, 1361, 1835
—relations with
Adams, John, 1267
Ames, Fisher, 777, 1673
Benson, Egbert, 1256, 1681
Burr, Aaron, 1769
Gerry, Elbridge, 777
Gore, Christopher, 1376
Hill, Jeremiah, 778
Sedgwick, Pamela, 959
Silvester, Peter, 1681
Strong, Caleb, 1587
unnamed members, 462
Washington, George, 999, 1098, 1211
—role
adjournment, 1256
appointments, 1276, 1309
congressional pay, 1075, 1255, 1406
power of removal, 1267
ratification, 461
revenue system, 919, 1000
Seat of Government Bill [HR-25], 1509,
 1671
Sedgwick, Theodore, Jr., 1076, 1098, 1114
Sedgwick Point, Me., port, 716
Sedition, threat of, 509
Seely, Ephraim, 101
Segar, John: bio, 1876; office for, 1503
Self incrimination, 1073
Senate: adjournment. See Adjournment; advice
 and consent. See Advice and consent;
 Antifederalists in, 56, 57, 60, 147, 153;
 busy, 299, 636, 689, 729, 1082, 1550,
 1636; checks and balances. See Checks and
 balances; closed doors, xi, 140, 225, 541,
 590, 642, 662, 730, 815, 854, 917, 925,
 1032, 1067, 1145, 1268, 1400; daily
 schedule, xxiii, 689, 825, 1381; dangers
 from, 829, 1268; decline of, 140, 1067,

Winchester, Va. (*cont'd*)
823, 857, 906, 1331, 1466, 1601; newspaper articles reprinted at, 16, 165, 328,
375, 667, 726, 773, 857, 1107, 1152,
1164, 1368, 1511, 1638; postal services,
1275, 1339, 1714; press, 371; public opinion, 1339, 1399–1400; residents, 1911;
visitors, 129
Winder, William, and Virginia accounts, 324
Windham, Conn., lawyers, 1791
Windsor, Conn.: letters addressed to, 146, 505;
President's tour, 1691
Windsor, Vt., newspaper articles reprinted at,
16, 714
Wines: 1783 impost on, 51; Canadian import of,
522; claret, 582; consumption, 297, 989;
discrimination among types, 409; drawback, 1036; duty, 348, 354, 441, 463, 519,
582, 795; excise, 543, 696; Madeira, 553–
54, 582, 653, 661, 691, 696; members
send home, 1313; quality, 582; smuggling,
1078; trade, 105, 409, 1180; trade statistics, 553–54
Wingate, Eunice: bio, 1910; letters to, 628–29,
1435; message relayed by, 1432
Wingate, George, letter to, 859
Wingate, Hannah Veazie: bio, 1910; letters to,
780, 1215–16, 1432
Wingate, Paine, 863; attendance, 1, 3, 1065,
1671; attends House debates, 228; characterized, 1038, 1064, 1352; in Confederation Congress, 129; and congressional
agenda, 278; correspondence, xiv, 130, 234,
278, 330, 392, 628–29, 741, 1007, 1014,
1215, 1394, 1432; influence of, 131; memorandum by, 1671; papers, xv, xvi; pay,
1671; President's New England tour, 1696;
regards to, 1121, 1366, 1497; return home,
859, 1427, 1432, 1547, 1637; self charac-
terization, 131, 187, 628–29, 1015, 1070,
1548, 1569; social life, 77, 164, 205, 649,
969, 1447; travel, 131, 1548, 1652, 1657,
1674
—constituent services
forwards legislation, 1023
forwards newspaper, 1007
as reference, 166, 323, 362, 741, 863, 1521
solicited for office, 102, 232, 234, 391,
1102
solicits information, 1006

solicits subscription, 1214
supports office seekers, 391, 990, 1070,
1206
—letters from
to Adams, John, 1447
to Belknap, Jeremy, 535–36, 969–70, 1213–
15
to Hodgdon, Samuel, 1022–23, 1129, 1407,
1547
to Lane, Samuel, 1222, 1427
to Langdon, John, 1416, 1569–70, 1609
to Parker, John, 227–28
to Peabody, Nathaniel, 620
to Pickering, John, 278, 373–75
to Pickering, Timothy, 129–31, 391–93,
1006–7, 1547–48, 1636–37
to Sargeant, Nathaniel P., 1069–70
to Toppan, Christopher, 321–22
to Wiggin, Mary W., 186–88, 1014–16
to Wingate, Eunice, 628–29, 1435
to Wingate, George, 859
to Wingate, Hannah V., 780, 1215–16, 1432
to Wingate, Sally, 250–52
—letters to
from Belknap, Jeremy, 652–53, 1064–65
from Kearney, Dyre, 417
from Lane, Samuel, 1312
from Langdon, John, 1508
from Otis, Samuel A., 234
from Pickering, John, 910
from Pickering, Timothy, 267–70
from Pickman, William, 846
from Sullivan, John, 1352
from Toppan, Christopher, 1065
from Tucker, John, Sr., 1102
—opinion on
adjournment, 780, 1569
Amendments to the Constitution, 1548
appropriations, 1070, 1427
Carroll, Charles, 536
Constitution, 373
FFC, 1214, 1548
Judiciary Act [S-1], 1006, 1069–70, 1569
life, 186–88
members, 535–36
national harmony, 373–74
office seeking, 391
power of removal, 970
President, 536, 1214
revenue system, 374, 535, 969, 1023